www.wadsworth.com

wadsworth.com is the World Wide Web site for Wadsworth and is your direct source to dozens of online resources.

At *wadsworth.com* you can find out about supplements, demonstration software, and student resources. You can also send e-mail to many of our authors and preview new publications and exciting new technologies.

wadsworth.com
Changing the way the world learns®

FROM THE WADSWORTH SERIES IN PRODUCTION

Albarran, Alan B., *Management of Electronic Media*

Alten, Stanley, *Audio in Media*, 5th Ed.

Armer, Alan, *Directing TV and Film*, 2d Ed.

Armer, Alan, *Writing the Screenplay*, 2d Ed.

Eastman, Susan Tyler, and Douglas A. Ferguson, *Broadcast/Cable Programming: Strategies and Practices*, 5th Ed.

Gross, Lynne S., and Larry W. Ward, *Electronic Moviemaking*, 4th Ed.

Hausman, Carl, Lewis B. O'Donnell, and Philip Benoit, *Announcing: Broadcast Communicating Today*, 4th Ed.

Hausman, Carl, Philip Benoit, and Lewis B. O'Donnell, *Modern Radio Production*, 5th Ed.

Hilliard, Robert L., *Writing for Television and Radio*, 7th Ed.

Mamer, Bruce, *Film Production Technique: Creating the Accomplished Image*, 2d Ed.

Meeske, Milan D., *Copywriting for the Electronic Media*, 3d Ed.

Morley, John, *Scriptwriting for High-Impact Videos: Imaginative Approaches to Delivering Factual Information*

Viera, Dave, *Lighting for Film and Electronic Cinematography*

Zettl, Herbert, *Sight Sound Motion*, 3d Ed.

Zettl, Herbert, *Television Production Handbook*, 7th Ed.

Zettl, Herbert, *Television Production Workbook*, 7th Ed.

Zettl, Herbert, *Video Basics*, 2d Ed.

Zettl, Herbert, *Video Basics Workbook*, 2d Ed.

Zettl, Herbert, *Zettl's VideoLab 2.1* CD-ROM

Television
Production
Handbook

7th Edition

Herbert Zettl

San Francisco State University

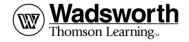

AUSTRALIA ■ CANADA ■ DENMARK ■ JAPAN ■ MEXICO

NEW ZEALAND ■ PHILIPPINES ■ PUERTO RICO ■ SINGAPORE

SOUTH AFRICA ■ SPAIN ■ UNITED KINGDOM ■ UNITED STATES

Radio, TV, and Film Editor: Karen Austin
Executive Editor: Deirdre Cavanaugh
Associate Development Editor: Ryan E. Vesely
Editorial Assistant: Dory Schaeffer
Executive Marketing Manager: Stacey Purviance
Marketing Assistant: Ken Baird
Project Editor: Cathy Linberg
Print Buyer: Barbara Britton
Permissions Editor: Susan Walters
Project Manager: Gary Palmatier, Ideas to Images
Interior and Cover Designer: Gary Palmatier
Art Director: Gary Palmatier
Copy Editor: Elizabeth von Radics
Technical Illustrator: Robaire Ream, Ideas to Images
Cover Photographers: Edward Aiona, Corbis Images, and Robert W. Ginn
Compositor: Ideas to Images
Printer: R. R. Donnelley & Sons/Willard

Printed in the United States of America

2   3   4   5   6   7   03   02   01   00

Library of Congress Cataloging-in-Publication Data

Zettl, Herbert.
   Television production handbook / Herbert Zettl. — 7th ed.
      p.   cm.
   Includes bibliographical references and index.
   ISBN 0-534-55989-1   Instructor's Edition ISBN: 0-534-55994-8
   1. Television—Production and direction Handbooks, manuals, etc.
   I. Title.
PN1992.75.Z4   1999
791.45'0232—dc21   99–25663

For more information, contact:

Wadsworth/Thomson Learning
10 Davis Drive
Belmont, CA 94002-3098
USA
www.wadsworth.com

International Headquarters
Thomson Learning
290 Harbor Drive, 2nd Floor
Stamford, CT 06902-7477
USA

UK/Europe/Middle East
Thomson Learning
Berkshire House
168-173 High Holborn
London WC1V 7AA
United Kingdom

Asia
Thomson Learning
60 Albert Street #15-01
Albert Complex
Singapore 189969

Canada
Nelson/Thomson Learning
1120 Birchmount Road
Scarborough, Ontario M1K 5G4
Canada

To Erika

Contents

CHAPTER **8** **Techniques of Television Lighting** **158**

Photo Credits

360 Systems: 10.15

Edward Aiona: 1.1, 1.2, 1.17, 1.18, 1.19, 1.20, 1.21, 1.24, 2.1, 3.17, CP4, CP20, CP21, 3.18, 3.19, 4.1, 4.5, 4.19, 4.21, 4.24, 4.29, 4.30, 5.12 (left), 6.1, 6.2, 6.3, 6.4, 6.5, 6.6, 6.7, 6.8, 6.9, 6.11, 6.14, 6.15, 6.16, 6.17, 6.18, 6.19, 6.20, 6.21, 6.22, 6.23, 6.24, 6.25, 6.28, 6.29, 6.30, 6.32, 6.33, 6.34, 6.35, 7.24, 7.36, 7.42, 7.43, 8.1, 8.2, 8.3, 8.4, 8.6, 8.8, 8.13, 8.14, 8.15, 8.16, 8.22, 9.7, 9.8, 9.11, 9.16, 9.17, 9.18, 9.19, 9.24, 9.32, 9.35, 10.1, 10.2, 10.3, 10.5, 10.9, 11.1, 11.5, 11.7, 11.8, 11.9, 11.10, 12.12, 12.19, 13.2, 13.8, 13.20, 13.21, 13.22, 13.23, 13.24, 13.25, 13.27, 13.28, 13.29, 14.1, 14.8, 14.9, 14.10, 14.11, 14.13, 14.14, 14.15, 14.16, 14.17, 14.18, 14.19, 14.20, 14.21, 14.25, 14.26, 14.28, 14.29, 14.33, 14.34, 15.9, 15.10, 15.36, 16.6

AKG Acoustics: 9.6, 9.15, 9.25, 9.34

Berkeley-Colortran, Inc.: 7.39

beyerdynamic Inc.: 9.9, 9.21, 9.22, 9.34

Chimera: 7.18, 7.19

Cinekinetic Pty Ltd., Australia: 5.14, 5.17

Cinema Products Corporation: 5.15, 5.16

Cooperative Media Group: 14.23, 14.31, 15.19

Denon Electronics: 10.14

Electro-Voice: 9.34

J. L. Fisher: 9.39

Fostex Corporation of America: 1.10, 10.10

Frezzi Energy Systems: 7.21

Fujinon Inc.: 1.5

The Grass Valley Group, Inc.: 1.13, 11.4, 11.6, 11.11, 11.14, 14.12

Lara Hartley: CP18b, CP18c, 12.18

Daniel Hubble: xxiii

Ideas to Images: 1.23, CP24 (with MetaCreations Brice 3D), CP25 (with Adobe Photoshop), 4.9 (detail), 4.10 (detail), 4.16 (detail), 7.21 (detail), 7.41 (detail), 10.11, 13.15 (with Adobe Premiere), 14.30, 15.6, 15.7, 15.12

Independent Audio LLC: 10.13

Lowel-Light Mfg., Inc.: 1.8, 7.13, 7.17, 7.22, 7.31, 7.35, 7.37

LTM Corporation of America: 7.1

Larry Mannheimer: 13.33

Mark IV Pro Audio Group: 10.7

Matthews Studio Equipment: 5.1, 5.2

Metric Halo Laboratories: 10.16

Miller Fluid Heads (USA), Inc.: 5.3, 5.8

Mole-Richardson Company: 7.3, 7.5, 7.6, 7.7, 7.8, 7.9, 7.12, 7.15, 7.16, 7.27

Neumann USA: 9.34

Nikon Inc.: 4.9, 4.10, 4.16

O'Connor Engineering Labs: 5.13

Gary Palmatier: 2.10, 2.11, 6.10, 6.12, 9.1, 13.26, 15.20

Panasonic Broadcast & Digital Systems Company: 1.6, 1.11, 3.8, 3.9, 3.10, 4.3, 12.9, 12.11, 13.3, 13.4

PhotoDisc: CP18a, CP18c (detail)

Pioneer New Media Technologies: 12.14

Professional Sound Corporation: 9.34

QTV: 16.9

Steve Renick: 4.17, 4.18, 5.11, 7.11, 7.32

Chris Rozales: 4.22, 14.22

Selco Products Company: 10.6

Sennheiser Electronic Corporation: 9.34

Shure Brothers: 1.9, 9.34, 10.17

Sony Electronics, Inc.: 3.4, 3.12, 9.34, 12.4, 12.5, 12.6, 12.7, 12.10, 13.1

Stanton Video Services, Inc.: 5.19

Telex Communications Inc.: 9.23

John Veltri: 3.13, 3.14, 4.20, 4.23, 4.27, 6.7 (lower left), 13.34

Videssence, Inc.: 7.20

Vinten Inc.: 5.4, 5.5, 5.7, 5.9, 5.10, 5.18, 5.20, 5.21, 5.22

Herb Zettl: 1.5, 1.7, 1.12, 1.14, 1.15, 1.16, 1.22, 3.6, 3.7, 3.11, CP5, CP13, CP14, CP16, CP17, CP19, CP22, CP23, 4.2, 4.12, 4.13, 4.15, 4.25, 4.26, 4.28, 5.12 (right), 6.13, 6.26, 6.27, 6.31, 7.4, 7.10, 7.14, 7.23, 7.25, 7.26, 7.28, 7.29, 7.30, 7.33, 7.34, 7.38, 7.40, 7.41, 8.5, 8.18, 9.5, 9.10, 9.12, 9.13, 9.14, 9.20, 9.29, 9.31, 9.33, 10.12, 11.12, 11.13, 12.13, 13.13, 13.14, 13.16, 13.31, 13.32, 13.35, 14.3, 14.24, 14.27, 14.32, 15.8, 15.11, 15.15, 15.18, 15.21, 15.24, 15.25, 15.26, 15.27, 15.30, 15.31, 15.35, 16.7, 16.8, 17.6, 19.1, 19.6, 20.1, 20.2, 20.3, 20.4, 20.18

The CNN logo (15.1) is courtesy of Cable News Network.

The hand-drawn storyboard (18.20) is courtesy of Nob Yamashita/Famous Frames, Inc.

The computer-generated storyboard (18.21) is courtesy of PowerProduction Software.

About the Author

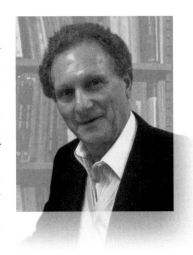

HERBERT ZETTL is a professor of Broadcast and Electronic Communication Arts at San Francisco State University, where he teaches in the areas of video production and media aesthetics. Prior to joining the SFSU faculty, he worked at KOVR (Sacramento-Stockton) and as a producer-director at KPIX, the CBS affiliate in San Francisco. While at KPIX he won an Emmy Award (shared with two colleagues from the San Francisco chapter of the National Academy of Television Arts & Sciences) for innovation in entertainment shows. Zettl has participated in a variety of CBS and NBC network television productions and is currently engaged in various experimental television productions. He was recently inducted into the prestigious Silver Circle of the National Academy of Television Arts & Sciences, Northern California chapter, for outstanding contributions to the television profession. Zettl has also been a consultant on television production and media aesthetics for universities and professional broadcasting operations here and abroad.

Zettl's other books include *Sight Sound Motion* and *Video Basics 2*, both of which, along with this book, have been translated into other languages. His numerous articles on television production and media aesthetics have appeared in major media journals in this country as well as in Europe and Asia. He has presented key papers on television production and media aesthetics at a variety of communication conventions.

His interactive multimedia CD-ROM, *Zettl's VideoLab 2.1*, published by Wadsworth Publishing Company, has won several prestigious awards, among them the Macromedia People's Choice Award, the New Media Invision Gold Medal for Higher Education, and Invision Silver Medals in the categories of Continuing Education and Use of Video.

Preface

THE SEVENTH EDITION of the *Television Production Handbook* underwent an extensive revision. The reason for such a significant change is the dramatic shift from analog to digital equipment, which has had a profound influence on production techniques. Digital technology has permeated not only such major elements as television cameras, lighting dimmer controls, audio consoles, videotape recorders, editing facilities, and various titling and graphics generators, but also such heretofore "nonelectronic" equipment as camera lenses and studio pedestals. Digital equipment has also influenced and sometimes even radically altered preproduction, production, and especially post-production procedures.

Additionally, high-definition television (HDTV) is no longer confined to the laboratories of electronic manufacturing giants; it is now being implemented by television stations and independent production companies. HDTV may well become the next medium for motion picture production and distribution as well as theater display.

To reflect these trends and prepare the student for today's and tomorrow's professional challenges, I have incorporated throughout this text the shift to digital and HDTV equipment. At the same time, I have tried not to compromise the discussion of traditional analog equipment, which will undoubtedly be in use for some time to come.

Once again the emphasis is not so much on a detailed description of the production tools, such as specific model numbers, but on *what to do with them*—the production techniques. You will find that even a basic knowledge of media aesthetics—how to use these tools to structure pictures and sound for maximum communication effectiveness—is still one of the most significant factors in learning television production. If you know how to frame an effective shot, it matters relatively little whether the camera is producing the image in analog or digital form.

Because this book is intended to serve the beginner as well as those who are more advanced in television production, each chapter is divided into two sections. Section 1 contains the basic information about a specific topic; section 2 presents more-detailed and advanced material. The two sections can, therefore, be read together or independently.

Here are some of the specific features of this edition:

Television system Regardless of whether you use the various pieces of television equipment for a field or a studio production, they operate as a system. The system shows how every production element is necessary for the proper functioning of all others and how the various production equipment, people, and processes interrelate. Once you grasp the idea of a system, you are much better prepared to see and understand how the production details interact as essential parts of a larger process. The problem is that to really understand the functioning of a specific system element, such as lighting, you need to be familiar with most of the other elements, such as cameras, lenses, position of the talent relative to set and camera, and so forth. I have therefore attempted to provide such a system overview in section 1.1: What Television Production Is All About.

Analog and digital The great emphasis on digital production equipment and its effective use requires a basic knowledge of what digital is all about. Chapter 2, Analog and Digital Television, explains the major differences between analog and digital processes and how they apply to television production. This chapter also introduces the new (and often puzzling) terminology of digital television and explains the various interlaced and progressive scanning systems.

DTV and HDTV The various scanning, sampling, and compression standards of digital television (DTV) and high-definition television are explained in several chapters. Chapter 6, Camera Operation and Picture Composition, deals extensively with framing effective shots in the horizontally stretched 16×9 HDTV aspect ratio.

Aesthetics Despite the digital television revolution, however, many traditional aesthetic factors of picture composition, lighting, and shot sequencing are relatively independent of the rapid technological development and therefore form the basis of effective television production. In fact, digital equipment is often more user-friendly than its analog counterparts and frees us to a large extent to pay more attention to aesthetic factors, such as composition, light and color, the various ways of using sound, and editing a seamless sequence of shots. The description of basic aesthetic principles is not intended to draw attention away from learning the major technical aspects of production equipment, but rather to facilitate its optimal application.

Studio and field production Because of their high level of production control and efficiency, multicamera studio shows will continue to constitute a major part of production activities. All big remotes, such as live pickups of major sporting events, operate on the multicamera studio production principle, even if the equipment is set up on location. With small, high-quality camcorders, however, and audio and lighting equipment, it is feasible to take the production to the street corner instead of simulating the street corner in the studio. To function effectively in video production, we can no longer specialize in studio or field production but must be equally proficient in both. This is why both production approaches are thoroughly integrated throughout this book.

Design Computers and the wide variety of design software have facilitated the creation and widespread use of elaborate television graphics. Even small television stations and independent producers put great emphasis on effective screen graphics. Chapter 15, Design, includes valuable information on designing for the traditional 4×3 aspect ratio as well as the stretched 16×9 HDTV screen.

Key terms As in previous editions, the key terms are listed at the beginning of each chapter. To facilitate the understanding of the text, it is intended that the student read them *before* committing to the specific chapter.

The key terms appear in ***bold italic*** in the context in which they are defined in the text and are repeated as part of the extensive glossary at the end of the book. Other glossary terms appear in *italic* type throughout the text.

Main points The main points are summarized at the end of each chapter section. These brief summaries emphasize the most important aspects of each chapter and indicate the minimal information the reader is expected to remember.

ACCOMPANYING RESOURCES: A TOTAL TEACHING AND LEARNING PACKAGE

As with previous editions, we offer a wealth of support for both students and instructors for this seventh edition of the *Television Production Handbook*.

Television Production Workbook, by Herbert Zettl

A great tool for students, this workbook enables them to apply the concepts introduced in the text to real-world production scenarios. The workbook contains tear-out worksheets in a chapter-by-chapter format that reinforce and review the chapter material.

Instructor's Manual with Answer Key to Workbook, by Herbert Zettl

This fully integrated manual is correlated chapter by chapter with the text, student workbook, and *VideoLab 2.1* CD-ROM. It features *VideoLab* exercises, a complete answer key to the questions in the student workbook, and suggested remedies for common teaching problems.

Thomson Learning Testing Tools™

This computerized testing software package for instructors is a fully integrated collection of test creation and delivery, and classroom management tools to help you create and customize tests in minutes.

Zettl's VideoLab 2.1 CD-ROM, by Herbert Zettl

This award-winning CD-ROM is the link between the *Handbook* text and the hands-on practice students need. *VideoLab 2.1* is now fully integrated into this edition of *Television Production Handbook*. As students read about specific equipment and techniques at numerous points throughout the text, they are guided to *Zettl's Video-Lab 2.1* to practice and reinforce text concepts within the CD-ROM's interactive environment. Available in cross-platform for both Macintosh and Windows use.

Communication Café

Wadsworth's Communication Café is an extensive resource center for both students and faculty of broadcasting and electronic media production, providing a wealth of online materials.

- For *instructors* it provides access to the *Faculty Resource Center,* where instructors can download supplements and find additional text information and content updates, as well as career and industry resources.

- For both *students and instructors,* it offers access to the *Student Resource Center* and all of Wadsworth's book-specific sites. Students can find out about textbook support resources, discover relevant career information, and explore links to broadcasting and electronic media sites.

http://communication.wadsworth.com

ACKNOWLEDGMENTS

As with previous editions of the *Handbook,* this seventh edition could not have been done without the generous help of a great number of people—from my students who still manage to surprise me with innovative solutions to challenging production problems, my colleagues who generously assisted me with up-to-date information, and other production experts and reviewers who prevented me from getting careless, to the "A-team" Wadsworth assembled to produce this book.

I am greatly indebted to two exceptional reviewers—Dr. Michael Korpi of Baylor University, Texas, and Professor Dan Hackel of Miami-Dade Community College, Florida, who made many valuable contributions—and to my colleague Dr. Joshua Hecht, who reviewed and helped update the audio chapters.

I would also like to thank the following reviewers of the seventh edition: Chey Acuna, California State University–Los Angeles; J. Brian Elliott, Baylor University;

John MacKerron, Towson University; April Orcutt, College of San Mateo; Chris A. Paterson, Georgia State University; Phillip Powell, Valparaiso University; and Thomas A. Sullivan, Columbia College.

Once again, Stanley Alten of Syracuse University and my colleagues at the San Francisco State University Broadcast and Electronic Communication Arts Department were always ready to help and provided valuable technical and production information. My sincere thanks go to: John Barsotti, Ron Compesi, Kim Fuscato, William Hazelwood, Jerry Higgins, Hamid Khani, Phil Kipper, Peter Maravelias, Chris Rozales, Val Sakovich, Doug Smith, Winston Tharp, Brian Weiner, and Larry Whitney.

The following people and organizations also offered generous assistance throughout the writing of this book: Phil Arnone, director of local programming, KTVU, Channel 2, Oakland–San Francisco; Larry Shenosky, director of operations, and Ken Kaplan, director of public relations, of KRON-TV, San Francisco; Robert Calo, senior producer, Dateline NBC, New York; Michael Fellner and Ben Jenkins of nmt, National Mobile Television, Torrence, California; Hal Morrison and Jay Warner of Panasonic; Frank Logan of Tektronix, Inc.; Paul Costa and Marcus Miller of Videssence; and Sony Corporation. Thanks also to the following individuals who provided product shots: Sandra Inbody-Brick, 360 Systems; Kim Mitchell, AKG Acoustics; Alesis Corporation and Stutrud Design; Alexis Kurtz, Beyerdynamic; Chimera and Burns Design Associates; Peter Bulcke, Cinema Products; David Birch-Jones, Denon Electronics; Bud Johnson, Fostex; Angela Crawford, Frezzolini Electronics, Inc.; Dave Waddell, Fujinon, Inc.; Eric Drucker, Lowel-Light Mfg., Inc.; Cathy Terwedow, Media 100, Inc.; John Clisham, Mole-Richardson; Tina Dobra, Panasonic; Bob Carr, Sachtler Corp. of America; Bruce Berenschot, Shure Brothers; Kathleen M. Duffy, Sony; Gary Stanfill, Vega; and Joanne Snider, Vinten.

I am, once again, extremely fortunate to have Wadsworth's A-team for this project, a group of professionals who were as demanding of me as of themselves: Karen Austin, radio, TV, and film editor; Cathy Linberg, project editor; Ryan Vessely, associate development editor; and Dory Schaeffer, editorial assistant—all of Wadsworth Publishing Co.; Elizabeth von Radics, copy editor; Gary Palmatier, project manager and art director, and Robaire Ream, page layout artist and illustrator, of Ideas to Images; Ed Aiona, a truly professional photographer; and Bobbie Broyer and Melanie Field, photo editors. To all A-team members: my deep gratitude and admiration!

I would also like to express my appreciation for all my colleagues and students of the Broadcast and Electronic Communication Arts Department and the professional models whose pictures helped illustrate various concepts and production processes: Tali Aiona, Ken Baird, Jerome Bakum, Rudolf Benzler, Timo Biemueller, William Carpenter, Sabrina Dorsey, Jedediah Gildersleeve, Sangyong Hong, Akiko Kajiwara, Hamid Khani, Orcun Malkoclar, Johnny Moreno, Anita Morgan, Jacqueline Murray, Richard Piscitello, Kerstin Riediger, Suzanne Saputo, and Alisa Shahonian.

To my wife, Erika, a big hug for her patience and genuine support.

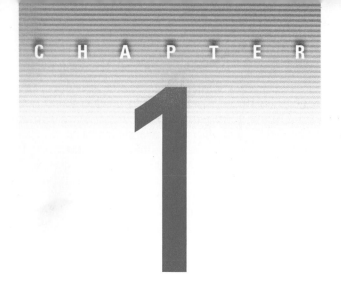

1

The Television Production Process

You may think that television production is a relatively simple task. After all, you do pretty well with your camcorder. Unlike your friends who all tell you of their problems when trying to take vacation pictures, you have never had any problem with videotaping various events and showing them on your television set. When watching a newscast from the control room at a local television station, however, you realize that television production involves much more than just operating a camcorder. Even a seemingly simple production—such as a news anchor first introducing and then showing a videotape of the mayor planting a tree in a rehabilitated neighborhood—involves a great number of intricate operations by news production personnel and the use of many sophisticated machines. A 55-second chitchat between a TV news anchor in Seattle and a skating champion in London presents a formidable challenge even for highly experienced production personnel.

When watching television, viewers are largely unaware of such production complexities. But as you could see, professional television production—regardless of whether it is done in a television station or in the field—is a complex creative process in which people and machines interact to bring a variety of messages and experiences to a large audience. Even when involved in a relatively small production, you need to know what machines and people are necessary to achieve a certain type of television communication and how to coordinate the many creative and technical elements.

Chapter 1 is designed to provide you with an overview of the various equipment and production processes. Section 1.1, What Television Production Is All About, introduces the television system and its many production elements. Section 1.2, Studios, Master Control, and Support Areas, describes the environment in which the television system operates.

K E Y   T E R M S

camcorder A portable camera with the VTR attached or built into it to form a single unit.

control room A room adjacent to the studio in which the director, the technical director, the audio engineer, and sometimes the lighting director perform their various production functions.

EFP Stands for *electronic field production.* Television production outside the studio that is usually shot for postproduction (not live). Usually called *field production.*

ENG Stands for *electronic news gathering.* The use of portable camcorders or cameras with separate portable VTRs, lights, and sound equipment for the production of daily news stories. ENG is usually not planned and is usually transmitted live or after immediate postproduction.

expanded system A television system that includes equipment and procedures that allow for selection, control, recording, playback, and transmission of television pictures and sound.

feed Signal transmission from one program source to another, such as a network feed or a remote feed.

house number The in-house system of identification for each piece of recorded program material. Called the *house number* because the code numbers differ from station to station (house to house).

intercom Short for *intercommunication system.* Used by all production and technical personnel. The most widely used system has telephone headsets to facilitate voice communication on several wired or wireless channels. Includes other systems, such as I.F.B. and cell phones.

lighting The manipulation of light to provide the camera with adequate illumination for technically acceptable pictures; to tell us what the objects on-screen actually look like; and to establish the general mood of the event.

line monitor The monitor that shows only the line-out pictures that go on the air or on videotape. Also called *master monitor* or *program monitor.*

line-out The line that carries the final video or audio output for broadcast.

log The major operational document. Issued daily, the log carries such information as program source or origin, scheduled program time, program duration, video and audio information, code identification (house number, for example), program title, program type, and additional pertinent information.

master control Nerve center for all telecasts. Controls the program input, storage, and retrieval for on-the-air telecasts. Also oversees technical quality of all program material.

monitor (1) Audio: speaker that carries the program sound independent of the line-out. (2) Video: high-quality television set used in the television studio and control rooms. Cannot receive broadcast signals.

P.L. Stands for *private line* or *phone line.* Major intercommunication device in television production.

preview (P/V) monitor (1) Any monitor that shows a video source, except for the line (master) and off-the-air monitors. (2) A color monitor that shows the director the picture to be used for the next shot.

program speaker A loudspeaker in the control room that carries the program sound. Its volume can be controlled without affecting the actual line-out program feed. Also called *audio monitor.*

studio talkback A public address loudspeaker system from the control room to the studio. Also called *S.A. (studio address)* or *P.A. (public address) system.*

system The interrelationship of various elements and processes whereby the proper functioning of each element is dependent on all others.

television system Equipment and people who operate the equipment for the production of specific programs. The basic television system consists of a television camera and a microphone that convert pictures and sound into electrical signals, and a television set and a loudspeaker that convert the signals back into pictures and sound.

1.1

What Television Production Is All About

The major problem in learning about television production is that to understand one specific production tool, such as the camera lens, you should already know the functions of many other elements, such as light levels, maximum lens apertures, or depth of field. In turn, you need to know something about how colored light behaves before you can adequately understand how a camera or color television receiver works. Because I can't cram all the necessary information into a single paragraph, and you can't learn the various production elements and operations all at once, we compromise and begin this book with a broad overview of the television production system. By viewing television production as a system, you will readily see the interconnections among the various system elements, even if they are presented piecemeal.

▶ **THE BASIC TELEVISION SYSTEM**
The equipment that converts optical images and actual sounds into electrical energy, and the people who operate it

▶ **THE EXPANDED STUDIO AND ELECTRONIC FIELD PRODUCTION SYSTEMS**
The system elements of studio and field productions, and the studio system in action

▶ **PRODUCTION ELEMENTS**
Camera, lighting, audio, videotape recording, the switcher and postproduction editing, and special effects

THE BASIC TELEVISION SYSTEM

A *system* is a collection of elements that work together to achieve a specific purpose. Each of the elements is dependent upon the proper workings of all the others, and none of the individual elements can do the job alone. The *television system* consists of equipment and people who operate that equipment for the production of specific programs. Whether the productions are simple or elaborate, or originate in the studio or in the *field*—that is, on location—the system works on the same basic principle: The television camera converts whatever it "sees" (optical images) into electrical signals that can be temporarily stored or directly reconverted by the television set into visible screen images. The microphone converts whatever it "hears" (actual sounds) into electrical signals that can be temporarily stored or directly reconverted into sounds by the *loudspeaker.* In general,

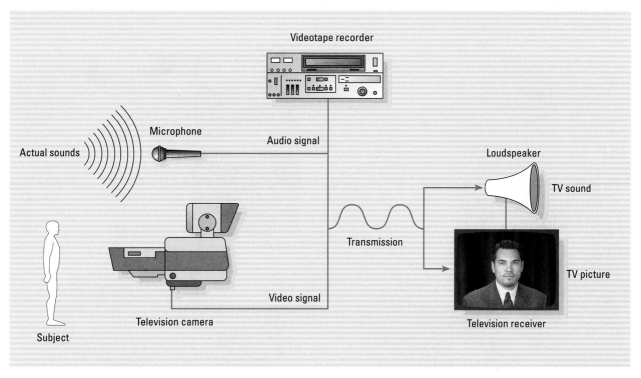

1.1 BASIC TELEVISION SYSTEM

The basic television system converts light and sounds into electrical video and audio signals that are transmitted (wireless or by cable) and reconverted by the television receiver into television pictures and sound.

the basic television system transduces (converts) one state of energy (optical image, actual sound) into another (electrical energy). **SEE 1.1**

The picture signals are called *video signals,* and the sound signals are called *audio signals.* Any small consumer *camcorder* represents such a system.

THE EXPANDED STUDIO AND ELECTRONIC FIELD PRODUCTION SYSTEMS

The basic television system is considerably expanded when doing a television production in the studio or in the field, such as a telecast of a sporting event. The *expanded system* needs equipment and procedures that allow for the selection of various pictures and sound sources; for the control and monitoring of picture and sound quality; for the recording, playback, and transmission of pictures and sound; and for the integration of additional video and audio sources and more-complex procedures.

System Elements of Studio Production

The expanded studio television system in its most elementary stage includes: (1) one or more cameras, (2) a camera control unit (CCU) or units, (3) preview monitors, (4) a switcher, (5) a line monitor, (6) one or more videotape recorders, and (7) a *line-out* that transports the video signal to the videotape recorder and/or the transmitter. **SEE 1.2** Usually integrated into the expanded video system are videotape machines for playback; character or graphic generators that produce various forms of lettering or graphic art; and an editing system.

The audio portion of the expanded system consists of (1) one or more microphones, (2) an audio console, (3) an audio monitor (speaker), and (4) a line-out that transports the sound signal to the videotape recorder and/or the transmission device (see figure 1.2).

Note that the system elements are identical, regardless of whether the individual pieces of equipment are analog or digital.

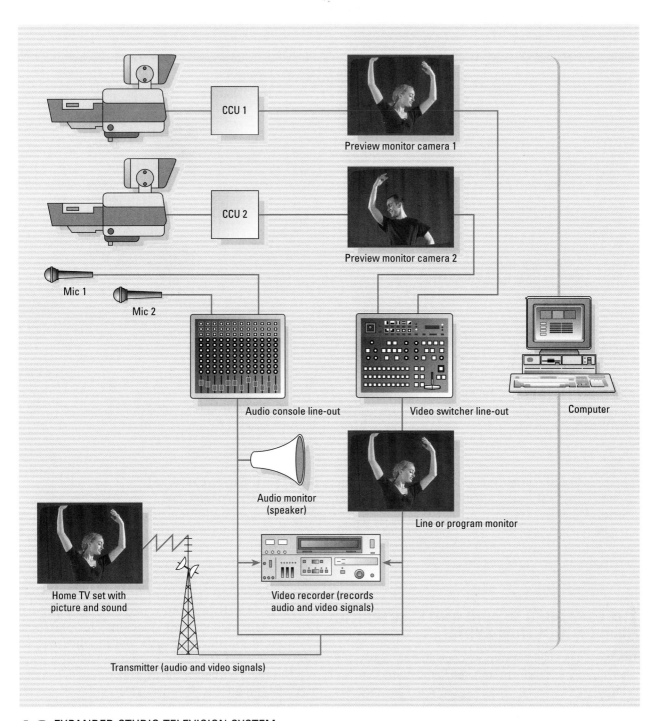

1.2 EXPANDED STUDIO TELEVISION SYSTEM

The expanded studio television system contains quality controls (CCU and audio console), selection controls (switcher and audio console), and monitors for previewing pictures and sound. All functions are computer-assisted.

The Studio System in Action

Let us now put the expanded system to work and see how the various elements interact when the news anchor in a studio introduces a videotape of the mayor planting a tree. Cameras 1 and 2 are focused on the news anchor. Camera 1 provides a close-up of the anchor, and camera 2 a slightly looser medium shot. The video signals from these cameras are fed and quality-controlled by their respective *camera control units (CCUs).* The CCUs can enhance and match certain video elements of the pictures sent by the two cameras. The video operator can, for example, lighten the dark shadow area on the anchor shown on camera 1 and reduce the glare on the anchor's forehead as seen by camera 2. Or the video operator can adjust the colors so that they look the same from camera to camera.

The quality-controlled pictures from both cameras are fed into *preview monitors,* one monitor for each camera, so you can see what they look like. A third preview monitor is necessary to show the videotape of the mayor planting the tree. These three video signals (from cameras 1 and 2 and the videotape of the mayor) are simultaneously fed into the *switcher,* which allows you to select and switch any of the three video feeds to the line-out for transmission or videotape recording. Pressing the button for camera 1 will put the close-up view of the anchor on the *line monitor,* which displays the line-out signals that go on the air or on videotape. Pressing the camera 2 button will put the slightly looser medium shot of camera 2 on the line monitor. Pressing the button for the videotape insert will put the mayor's videotape on the line monitor. Whatever appears on the line monitor will be sent to the line-out that feeds the transmission device (on-the-air or cable) and/or the "record" videotape.

The signal of the news anchor's microphone is fed into the audio console, as is the audio track of the mayor's videotape. The audio console now permits you to select between the anchor's voice and the sound track on the videotape and to control the quality of the two sound inputs. You can, for example, match the volume of the two sound sources (the anchor's and the mayor's voices), have them temporarily overlap, and even filter out some of the wind noises in the mayor's videotape.

Unaware of all the complex production maneuvers, the viewer simply sees a close-up of the personable and knowledgeable news anchor introducing the upcoming story about the mayor planting a tree and then footage of the mayor doing it.

System Elements of Field Production

ENG EFP The mayor obviously could not plant the tree in the studio, so someone had to go on location to videotape the event. Such location shooting normally falls into the *ENG (electronic news gathering)* category and is accomplished with a relatively simple field production system. All you really need is someone who operates the camcorder (and also checks the audio-recording level) and a field reporter who describes the action and tries to get some brief comments from the mayor. Once the footage is brought back to the newsroom, it is drastically cut and edited to fit the brief time segment (15 seconds or so) allotted to the tree-planting footage.

Had the tree-planting scene been a live insert, you would have had to expand the system with a portable transmitter to transport the signal from the field to the station. The ENG signal is often transmitted live to the studio. **SEE 1.3**

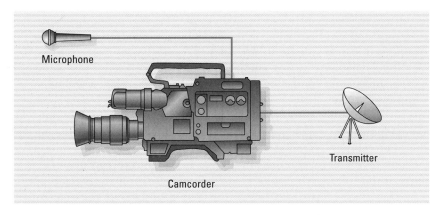

Microphone

Camcorder

Transmitter

1.3 ENG SYSTEM ELEMENTS
The ENG system consists basically of a camcorder and a microphone. The camcorder includes all video and audio quality controls as well as video- and audio-recording facilities. A portable transmitter is necessary to bring a live field report to the studio.

1.4 EFP SYSTEM
ELEMENTS
The EFP system is similar
to that for ENG, but it may
use more than one camera
to feed the output to
separate VTRs.

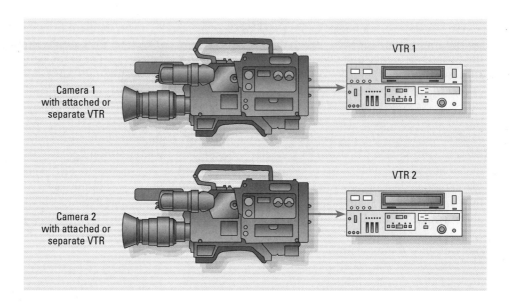

Camera 1
with attached or
separate VTR

VTR 1

Camera 2
with attached or
separate VTR

VTR 2

If the field production is more elaborate or requires two or more cameras to record the event simultaneously, you are engaged in *EFP (electronic field production)*. Sometimes field cameras that feed their output to separate *VTRs (videotape recorders)* are used. **SEE 1.4** *Big remotes* are field productions whose production system is similar to the studio's, except that cameras are placed on location and the control room is housed in a large truck trailer. For a detailed discussion of EFP and big remotes, see chapter 20.

PRODUCTION ELEMENTS

With the expanded television system in mind, we will look briefly at the basic production elements: (1) the camera, (2) lighting, (3) audio, (4) videotape recording, (5) the switcher, (6) postproduction editing, and (7) special effects. When learning about television production, always try to see each piece of equipment and its operation within the larger context of the television system, that is, in relation to all the other pieces of equipment that are used and the people who use them—the *production personnel*. It is, after all, the skilled and prudent use of the television equipment by the production team, and not simply the smooth interaction of the machines, that gives the system its value. The specific roles of the production personnel are outlined in chapter 16.

The Camera

The most obvious production element—the *camera*— comes in all sizes and configurations. Some cameras can be easily carried and operated by one person, whereas others are so heavy that they need two people to lift them comfortably onto a camera mount. The *camera mount* enables the operator to move a heavy camera/lens/ teleprompter assembly on the studio floor with relative ease. **SEE 1.5** Portable cameras are often used for ENG and EFP.

Many ENG/EFP cameras are camcorders that combine the camera and videotape recorder in one unit, much like popular consumer models. The ENG/EFP camcorders, however, are of higher quality and cost considerably more. Other ENG/EFP cameras are built so that they can "dock" with a videotape recorder unit; the VTR unit is simply plugged into the back of the camera to form a camcorder. Regardless of whether the camcorder is analog or digital, its operational features are basically identical. **SEE 1.6**

The studio television camera has three fundamental parts: the lens, the camera itself, and the viewfinder.

The lens   In all *photography* (meaning "writing with light"), the lens selects part of the visible environment and produces a small optical image of it. In still and movie cameras, the image is then projected onto film; in television cameras it is projected onto the *imaging device*, which converts the light from the optical image into an

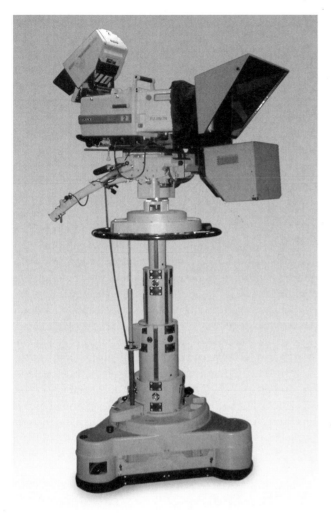

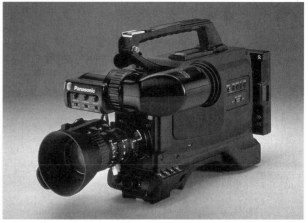

1.6 PROFESSIONAL CAMCORDER
The professional camcorder is a highly portable, self-contained camera/VTR unit. It is usually battery-powered.

1.5 STUDIO CAMERA WITH PNEUMATIC PEDESTAL
High-quality studio cameras are mounted on a studio pedestal for smooth and easy maneuverability.

electrical signal. All television cameras have a *zoom lens,* which allows you to smoothly and continuously change from a long shot (showing a wide vista) to a close-up view without moving either the camera or the object you are photographing.

The camera itself   The camera is principally designed to convert the optical image as projected by the lens into an electrical signal—the video signal. As mentioned earlier, the major conversion element is the imaging device. The imaging device is a small electronic chip called the *CCD (charge-coupled device),* which responds to light in a manner that resembles a light meter. When the CCD receives a large amount of light, it produces a strong video signal (just as the needle of a light meter goes up); when it receives faint light, it produces a weak video signal (just as the light meter needle goes down). Other optical and electronic components enable the camera to reproduce the colors and the light-and-dark variations of the actual scene as accurately as possible and to amplify the relatively weak video signal so that it can be sent to the camera control unit without getting lost on the way. For both analog or digital cameras, the basic imaging devices are the same.

The viewfinder   The *viewfinder* is a small television set mounted on the camera that shows what the camera is "seeing." Most camera viewfinders are *monochrome,* which means that the display is in black-and-white. Some consumer camcorders and high-quality studio cameras have color viewfinders, so you can see exactly the color pictures that the camera delivers.

Mounting equipment   Portable cameras and camcorders are built so that they rest more or less comfortably on your shoulder. But even the lightest camcorder seems heavy when you operate it for prolonged periods of time. In such cases a *tripod* not only relieves you of having to carry the camera, but also ensures steady pictures. The heavy studio cameras also need mounts. These range from tripods similar to those used for ENG/EFP cameras to large cranes. The most common studio camera mount is the *studio pedestal*, shown in figure 1.5, which allows you to raise and lower the camera and move it smoothly across the studio floor while it is "hot," that is, on the air.

Lighting

Like the human eye, the camera cannot see without a certain amount of light. Because it is not objects we actually see but the light reflected off them, manipulating the light falling on the objects influences the way we perceive them on the screen. Such manipulation is called *lighting*.

Lighting has three broad purposes: (1) to provide the television camera with adequate illumination for technically acceptable pictures; (2) to tell us what the objects shown on the screen actually look like, where they are in relation to one another and to their immediate environment, and when the event is taking place in terms of time of day or season; and (3) to establish the general mood of the event.

Types of illumination   All television lighting basically involves two types of illumination: directional and diffused. *Directional light* has a sharp beam and produces harsh shadows. You can aim the light beam to illuminate a precise area. A flashlight and car headlights produce directional light. *Diffused light* has a wide, indistinct beam that illuminates a relatively large area and produces soft, translucent shadows. The fluorescent lamps in a department store produce diffused lighting.

Studio lighting consists of careful control of light and shadow areas. The lighting requirements for electronic field production are usually quite different from those for studio productions. In electronic news gathering, you work mostly with available light, or occasionally with a single handheld lighting instrument that gives just enough illumination for the camera to record the event. For EFP you also use available light, especially when shooting outdoors, or highly diffused light that provides optimal visibility indoors. Some field productions, such as documentaries or dramatic scenes, require careful interior lighting that resembles studio lighting techniques. The difference is that the location lighting for EFP is done with portable lighting instruments rather than with studio lights, which are more or less permanently installed.

Lighting instruments   The lighting instruments that produce directional light are called *spotlights*, and the ones that produce diffused light are called *floodlights.* In the television studio, the various types of spotlights and floodlights are usually suspended from the ceiling. **SEE 1.7**

1.7 STUDIO LIGHTING SETUP
The typical studio lighting setup has a number of spotlights and floodlights.

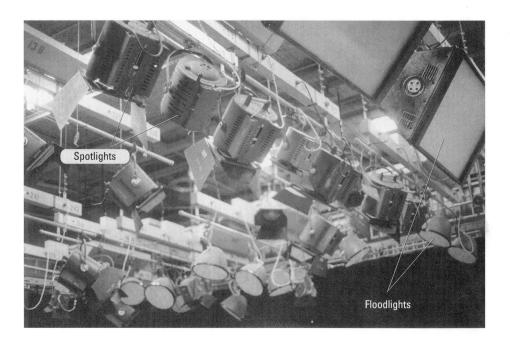

Spotlights

Floodlights

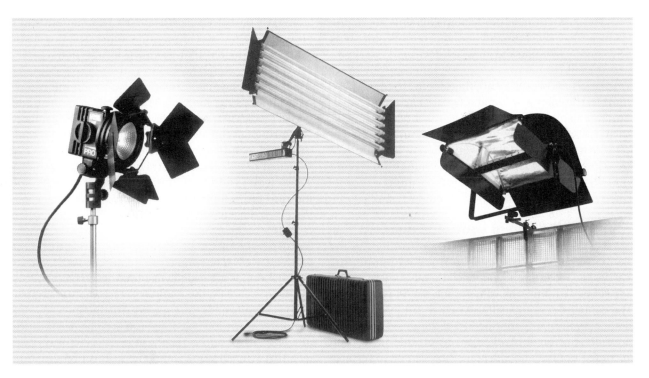

1.8 PORTABLE LIGHTING INSTRUMENTS
Portable lighting setups include highly versatile spotlights and floodlights that can be plugged into regular household outlets.

Studio lights are much too heavy and bulky to be used outside the studio, especially in field productions. Most EFPs use portable lighting packages that consist of several small, highly efficient instruments that can be plugged into ordinary electrical outlets. There are also larger fluorescent banks for large-area or virtually shadowless lighting. Most portable instruments can either be mounted on collapsible floor stands or clipped onto doors, windowsills, or furniture. These instruments generally operate as floodlights, but they can be adjusted to function as spotlights as well. **SEE 1.8**

Lighting techniques All television lighting is based on a simple principle: using some instruments (usually spotlights) to illuminate specific areas, and other instruments (usually floodlights) to control the shadows and bring the overall light on a scene to an acceptable level. In general, television lighting has less contrast between light and shadow areas than film or theater lighting. Diffused light is therefore used extensively in television lighting, especially in field productions.

Audio
Although the term *television* does not include audio, the sound portion of a television show is nevertheless one of its most important elements. Television audio not only communicates precise information, but also contributes greatly to the mood and atmosphere of a scene. If you were to turn off the audio during a newscast, even the best actors, let alone the news anchors, would have difficulty communicating news stories through facial expression, graphics, and videotape alone. The aesthetic function of sound (to make us perceive an event, or feel in a particular way) becomes obvious when you listen to the background sounds during a police show, for example. The tire-squealing sounds during a high-speed chase are real enough, but the rhythmically fast, exciting background music that accompanies the scene is definitely artificial. After all, the getaway car and the police car are hardly ever followed in real life by a third vehicle with musicians playing the background music. But we have grown so accustomed to such devices that we probably would perceive the scene as less exciting if the music were missing.

The various audio production elements are microphones, ENG/EFP and studio sound control equipment, and sound recording and playback devices.

Microphones   All microphones convert sound waves into electric energy—the audio signals. The sound signals are amplified and sent to the loudspeaker, which converts them back into audible sound. A great variety of microphones are designed to perform different tasks. To pick up a newscaster's voice, capture the sounds of a tennis match, and record a rock concert—all may require different microphones or microphone sets.

ENG/EFP sound control equipment   In ENG the audio is normally controlled by the camera operator, who wears a small earphone that carries the incoming sound. Because the camera operator is busy running the camera, the sound controls on the camcorder are usually switched to the *automatic* setting. In the more-critical EFP, the volume of incoming sounds is often controlled by a portable mixer and recorded not only on videotape but also on a portable audiotape recorder. **SEE 1.9**

Studio sound control equipment   The *audio console* is used to control the sounds of a program. At the audio console, you can (1) select a specific microphone or other sound input, (2) amplify a weak signal from a microphone or other audio source for further processing, (3) control the volume and quality of the sound, and (4) *mix* (combine) two or more incoming sound sources. **SEE 1.10**

Recall the example of the news anchor introducing a videotape of the mayor planting a tree. The first audio input is the signal that comes from the newscaster's microphone while she is introducing the videotape. Because the mayor is busy putting a tree in the ground and is not talking, the news anchor talks over the initial part of the videotape insert. To convey a sense of actuality, you mix under the anchor's narration the actual sounds on the videotape—the shovel hitting the dirt, the excited voices of the bystanders, and an occasional car horn. Then, when the mayor finally begins to speak, you increase the volume of the videotape sound track and switch off the anchor's microphone.

Sound recording and playback devices   Even when an event is recorded on videotape for postproduction, its sounds are usually recorded at the same time as the picture. In ENG the reporter's voice and the ambient sounds are picked up and recorded simultaneously with the pictures. In EFP most speech sounds, such as the interviewer's questions and the interviewee's answers, are recorded at the location simultaneously with the picture. Some sounds, such as the narrator's voice-over and musical bridges, are usually added in postproduction. But even in more-complicated studio productions such as soap operas, the background music and sound effects are often added simultaneously to the live pickup of the actors' dialogue.

In large and complex studio productions in which a single camera shoots a scene piecemeal, much in the way films are done, the audio track is subjected to many changes in postproduction. The sounds of explosions,

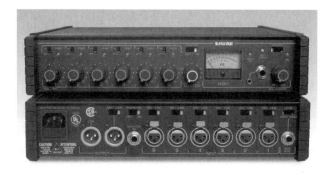

1.9 AUDIO MIXER
The portable audio mixer has a limited amount of inputs and volume controls.

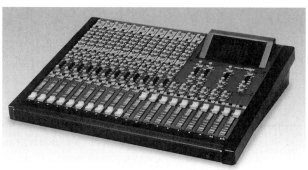

1.10 AUDIO CONSOLE
Even a relatively simple audio console has many controls to adjust the volume and quality of each incoming sound signal and to mix them in various ways.

sirens, and car crashes, for example, are normally *dubbed in* (added) during the postproduction sessions. Even parts of the original dialogue are occasionally re-created in the studio.

Prerecorded sound, such as music, is usually played back from cassettes, compact discs (CDs), and digital audiotape (DAT).

Videotape Recording

Most television shows are recorded on videotape or computer disk before they are aired. Even live football broadcasts include plenty of prerecorded material. Videotape is used for the playback of commercials, even those originally produced on film. The "instant replays" are nothing but videotape or digital videodisc replays of key moments after the fact.

One of the unique features of television is its ability to transmit a telecast *live,* which means capturing the pictures and sounds of an ongoing event and distributing them instantly to a worldwide audience. Most television programs, however, originate from videotape playback. Videotape is an indispensable element for *production* (the recording and building of a show), for *programming* (when and over which channel the show is telecast), and for distribution.

Videotape recorders   All videotape recorders, analog and digital, work on the same principle: They record video and audio signals on a single strip of plastic videotape and later convert them back into signals that can be seen as pictures and heard as sound on a television receiver. Most VTRs use various-sized videotape cassettes, similar to the ones you use in your home *VCR (video-cassette recorder)* or camcorder. Professional videotape recorders are similar to a home machine, except that they have more operational controls and more-sophisticated electronics that ensure higher quality of pictures and sound. **SEE 1.11**

Videotape recorders are classified by whether the recording is done in digital or analog form; by the electronic system used for the recording (BetacamSP, DVCAM, DVCPRO, S-VHS, Hi8, or VHS); or sometimes by the tape *format* (the width of the videotape in the video-cassette). Many VTR systems use ½-inch videocassettes (BetacamSP, digital BetacamSX, S-VHS, and VHS), but there are also systems that use small 8mm cassettes (Hi8), or even narrower digital ¼-inch (6.35mm DVCAM and DVCPRO). **SEE 1.12**

Videodiscs and hard drives   Most *videodiscs* you may use are "read-only," such as *CD-ROMs (compact disc–read-only memory)* and *DVDs (digital video discs,* also called *digital versatile discs)* that hold entire movies. *Read-only* means that you can play back the information on the disc but not record your own material onto it. Digital "read/write" discs are used in larger broadcast operations for the storage and extremely fast retrieval of single video frames, slides, or special-effects sequences.

You will see more and more the increasing use of *hard drives* that use high-capacity hard disks (in the multi-gigabyte range) for the storage, manipulation, and retrieval of video and audio information by desktop computers. Note that the read-only laser-activated discs are spelled with a *c,* and the disks used in hard drives are spelled with a *k.*

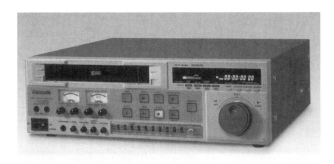

1.11 VIDEOTAPE RECORDER (VTR)
Almost all VTRs use videocassettes for recording and playback. All professional VTRs have various video and audio recording, playback, and editing controls.

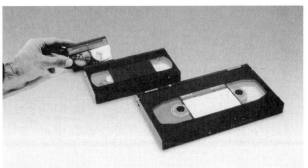

1.12 VARIOUS CASSETTE FORMATS
Videocassettes come in a variety of sizes and are manufactured for specific recording systems.

The Switcher

The *switcher* works on a principle similar to that of push buttons on a car radio, which allow you to select certain radio stations. The switcher lets you select various video sources, such as cameras, videotape, and titles or other special effects and join them through a great variety of transitions while the event is in progress. In effect, the switcher allows you to do *instantaneous editing*.

Before learning about the switcher, look for a moment at the diagram in figure 1.2 of the expanded studio television system.

Cameras 1 and 2 deliver their pictures first to the CCUs and then to the preview monitors. Preview monitor 1 shows all the pictures camera 1 is taking, and preview monitor 2 carries the pictures of camera 2. These video signals are fed into the switcher. Each camera has its own switcher input. Pressing the camera 1 button puts camera 1's signal on the line-out and shows its pictures on the line monitor. Pressing the camera 2 button puts camera 2's pictures on the line-out and line monitor. This switcher "output" is what goes on the air or is recorded on videotape.

Any switcher, simple or complex, can perform three basic functions: (1) select an appropriate video source from several inputs, (2) perform basic transitions between two video sources, and (3) create or retrieve special effects, such as split screens. Some switchers have further provisions for remote start and stop of videotape recorders. **SEE 1.13**

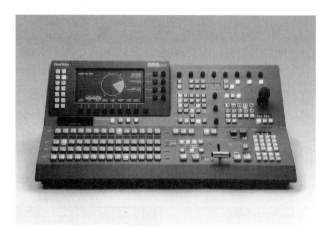

1.13 VIDEO PRODUCTION SWITCHER
The production switcher has several rows of buttons and other controls for selecting or mixing various video inputs and creating transitions and special effects. It then sends the selected video to the line-out.

Postproduction Editing

For some, postproduction editing is heaven: They feel totally in command of putting the bits and pieces of prerecorded material into a new, more telling sequence. For others it is a necessary evil. Irrespective of how you feel about postproduction, it is usually the most expensive and time-consuming production phase. In principle *postproduction editing* is relatively simple: You select from the original videotapes or digitally recorded material (which contain all the various good and bad scenes you have recorded previously) those scenes that seem most pertinent and copy them onto another videotape in a specific order. In practice, however, postproduction editing can be extremely complicated, involving such fundamentally different systems as linear and nonlinear editing as well as a great variety of editing equipment.

The *linear editing* system normally requires two *source VTRs* that contain the original material that you recorded with your camera or cameras, and the *record VTR*, which produces the final edit master tape. In *nonlinear editing* you transfer all the videotapes to a computer disk and then edit the video and audio portions pretty much as you would with a word processing program. You call up, move, cut, paste, and join the various shots much like words, sentences, and paragraphs when editing a written document. Some desktop non-linear systems will give you an accurate record only of how the material should be edited, called the *EDL (edit decision list);* others will produce even the air-quality material necessary for a finished product.

The computer plays an important part in both linear and nonlinear editing. In linear editing the computer acts as an *edit controller,* also called an *editing control unit,* which helps find a particular scene quickly and accurately, even if it is buried midtape. It starts and stops the source and record machines and tells the record VTR to perform the edit at the precise point you have designated. The more elaborate linear editing systems are computer-assisted, which means that the computer acts as an interface between the people who make the creative decisions and the machines that carry them out. The computer may, for example, ask what scene you want, exactly where you want it to start and end, and what transition you want (such as a cut or dissolve) to the next scene. Once you tell the computer, it takes over the button pushing and makes sure that the VTRs perform your editing decisions as desired. **SEE 1.14**

Nonlinear editing is done exclusively with the computer. Once the analog video and audio information

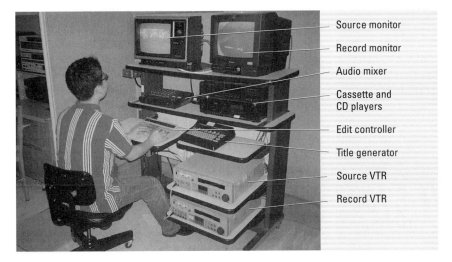

— Source monitor

— Record monitor

— Audio mixer

— Cassette and
CD players

— Edit controller

— Title generator

— Source VTR

— Record VTR

1.14 LINEAR EDIT CONTROLLER
The linear, cuts-only editing system consists of a source VTR and a record VTR,
source and record monitors, an edit controller, a title generator, cassette and
CD players, and an audio mixer.

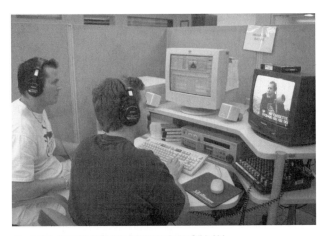

1.15 NONLINEAR EDITING DISPLAY
In nonlinear editing, all audio and video information is stored in
large-capacity hard drives. You manipulate pictures and sound
with the computer much like words and paragraphs during
word processing.

on the source tapes has been digitized and stored in the
high-capacity hard drives, you do not need VTRs in the
editing process. You can simply call up particular shots
and see whether they provide the desired sequence. The
software programs for nonlinear editing also offer a
wide choice of electronic effects and transitions. **SEE 1.15**
Once you have decided on the sequencing, transitions,
and effects, you can tell the computer to print out an EDL.

This list is necessary for editing the source tapes into the
final edit master tape. Some systems provide the EDL and
the sequenced audio and video material for the final
edited master tape without having to go back to the
original source tapes.

Keep in mind that even the most elaborate digital
editing system cannot improve the original footage or
make the creative decisions for you. The better the
original material is, the easier and more efficient your
postproduction activities will be. Thinking about postproduction even in the shooting stage makes editing
chores relatively easy and effective. Always consider
postproduction to be an extension of the creative
process, not a salvage operation.

Special Effects

Special effects can be as simple as adding a title over a
background scene, done with a *C.G.* (*character generator*),
or inserting the well-known box over the newscaster's
shoulder. **SEE 1.16** Or they can be as elaborate as the
gradual transformation of a face into a series of intensely
colored, mosaic-like screen patterns. **SEE 1.17** Modern
digital *graphics generators* and other special-effects
equipment, along with the effects capability of switchers,
allow for the creation of a great variety of effects with ease
and reliability. These effects are used frequently in
television news, music videos, and commercials. See
chapters 14 and 15.

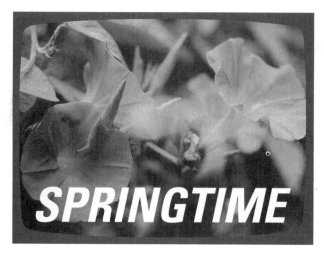

1.16 TITLE KEY

One of the most common effects is lettering *keyed* (cut into) a background scene.

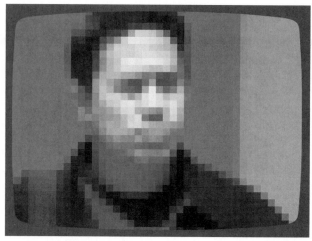

1.17 MOSAIC EFFECT

Various special-effects devices can create or alter video images without the aid of a video camera. This mosaic effect was created by digital manipulation of a video picture.

MAIN POINTS

◆ The basic television system consists of equipment and people who operate this equipment to produce specific programs. In its simplest form, the system consists of a television camera that converts what it sees into a video signal, a microphone that converts what it hears into an audio signal, and a television set and loudspeaker that reconvert the two signals into pictures and sound.

◆ The expanded studio television system adds equipment and procedures to the basic system to make possible a wider choice of sources, better quality control of pictures and sound, and the recording and/or transmission of video and audio signals.

◆ The ENG (electronic news gathering) television system consist basically of a camcorder and microphones. The EFP (electronic field production) system may include multiple camcorders or field cameras and some lighting and audio control equipment.

◆ The major production elements are the camera, lighting, audio, videotape recording, the switcher and postproduction editing, and special effects.

◆ All television cameras have three main parts: the lens; the camera itself with the camera imaging device (the CCD), which converts an optical image into an electrical signal; and the viewfinder, which reconverts the signal into visible images.

◆ Lighting is the manipulation of light and shadows that influences the way we perceive objects on the screen.

◆ The two types of illumination are directional light, produced by spotlights, and diffused light, produced by floodlights.

◆ Audio, the sound portion of a television show, is necessary to give specific information of what is said and to help set the mood of a scene.

◆ Audio production elements include microphones, sound control equipment, and sound recording and playback devices.

◆ There are a variety of analog and digital videotape recorders, which differ in terms of the electronic system used for recording as well as tape format and quality.

◆ The switcher enables us to do instantaneous editing by selecting a specific picture from several inputs and performing basic transitions between two video sources.

◆ Postproduction editing means selecting various shots from the source material and putting them in a specific sequence. In linear editing videotape is used as source material and for the final edit master tape. In nonlinear editing the digital video and audio material are stored on a computer disk and manipulated using a computer program. Some nonlinear editing systems are designed to produce an EDL (edit decision list) rather than an edited videotape. Other systems produce high-quality video and audio sequences that can be transferred directly to the edit master tape.

◆ Special effects are an important ingredient in video presentation. They range from simple lettering, produced by a character generator, to elaborate effects, produced by a graphics generator.

1.2

Studios, Master Control, and Support Areas

Telecasts can originate anywhere, indoors or outdoors, so long as there is enough light for the camera to see. With the highly portable, battery-powered cameras and recording facilities and mobile microwave transmitters, television is no longer confined to the studio. In tandem with satellite transmission, it has the whole earth as its stage. Television's ability to transmit from just about anywhere does not render the studio obsolete, however. Television studios continue to exist because, if properly designed, they can offer maximum control combined with optimal use of the television equipment. This section focuses on the three major television production centers.

▶ **THE TELEVISION STUDIO**
The origination center where television production takes place

▶ **THE STUDIO CONTROL ROOM**
Where directors, producers, and technical personnel make decisions on effective picture and sound sequences based on inputs from program, image, audio, and lighting controls

▶ **MASTER CONTROL**
The technical nerve center of a station, with program input, program storage, and program retrieval

▶ **STUDIO SUPPORT AREAS**
Space for scene and property storage and for makeup and dressing rooms

THE TELEVISION STUDIO

A well-designed studio provides for the proper environment and coordination of all major production elements—cameras, lighting, sound, scenery, and the action of performers. We look briefly here at the physical layout of a typical studio and the major studio installations.

Physical Layout

Most studios are rectangular with varying amounts of floor space. The advent of the zoom lens has drastically reduced the need for actual movement of the camera (the zoom lens can make a scene look closer or farther away without camera movement), but room size still greatly affects production complexity and flexibility.

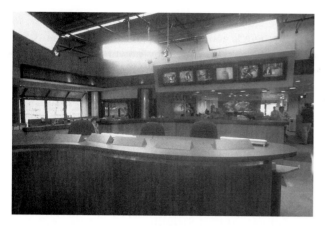

1.18 NEWS SET IN NEWSROOM
This news set is part of a working newsroom. It is supposed to project the up-to-date character of the news presentation.

Size   The larger the studio, the more complex the productions can become and the more flexible they will be. If all you do in the studio is news and an occasional interview, you may get by with amazingly little space. In fact, some news sets are placed right in the middle of the actual newsroom. **SEE 1.18**   Other news sets may take up a substantial portion of a large studio. Elaborate productions, such as musical or dance numbers, dramas, or audience participation shows, need large studios. It is always easier to produce a simple show in a large studio than a complex show in a small one. The larger the studio, however, the more difficult it is to manage. Medium-sized or even small studios are generally more efficient to run than large studios, but they are not as flexible.

Floor   The studio floor must be even and level so that cameras can travel smoothly and freely. It should also be hard enough to withstand the moving about of heavy equipment, scenery, and set properties. Most studios have concrete floors that are polished or covered with linoleum, tile, or hard plastic.

Ceiling height   Adequate ceiling height—a minimum of 12 feet—is one of the most important design factors of a television studio. If the ceiling is too low, the lights are too close to the scene for good lighting control and there is not enough room above them for the heat to dissipate. Also, the low lights and the boom microphone will encroach into the scene, as well as make it uncomfortably hot. Higher ceilings can accommodate even tall scenery. Many large studios therefore have ceilings more than 30 feet high.

Acoustic treatment   The studio ceiling and walls are usually treated with acoustic material that prevents sound from bouncing indiscriminately around the studio. This is why television studios sound "dead." When you clap your hands in an acoustically treated studio, the sound seems to go nowhere; in a more "live" studio, you hear some of the reverberations, similar to a slight echo.

Air-conditioning   Because television studios have no windows (to keep out unwanted sounds and light), air-conditioning is essential. The lights produce a great amount of heat, which has an adverse effect on performers and delicate electronic equipment. Unfortunately, many air-conditioning systems are too noisy for studio productions and must be turned off during the taping of a show—just when cool air is needed the most.

Doors   Studios need heavy, soundproof doors that are large enough to move scenery, furniture, or even vehicles in and out. There is nothing more frustrating than trying to squeeze scenery and properties through undersized studio doors or to have the doors transmit outside sounds, such as a fire truck screaming by, right in the middle of the show.

Major Installations

All studios need major installations that facilitate the production process.

Intercommunication system   The intercommunication system, or *intercom*, allows all production and engineering personnel actively engaged in the production of a show to be in constant voice contact with one another. For example, the director, who sits in the control room physically isolated from the studio, has to rely totally on the intercom system to communicate cues and instructions to every member of the production team. In most small stations, the *P.L.* (private line or phone line) system is used. Each member of the production team wears a telephone headset with an earphone and a small microphone for talkback. Larger stations use a wireless intercom system. (For a more thorough discussion of intercom systems, see chapters 19 and 20.)

Studio monitors   Studio *monitors* are high-quality television sets that display the video feed from the program switcher. A studio monitor is an important production aid for the crew and talent. The production crew can see the shots the director has selected and thus anticipate their future tasks. For example, if you see that the on-the-air camera is on a close-up rather than a long shot, you can work closer to the set without getting into camera range. Also, after seeing that one camera is on a close-up, the other camera operator can then go to a different shot to give the director a wider choice. The studio monitor is essential for the newscaster to see whether the various tape or live inserts are actually appearing as per the script. In audience participation shows, several studio monitors are usually provided so that the studio audience can see how the event looks on-screen.

Program speakers   The *program speakers* fulfill a function for audio similar to what the studio monitors do for video. Whenever necessary, they can feed into the studio the program sound or any other sound—dance music, telephone rings, or other sound effects—to be synchronized with the studio action.

Wall outlets   As insignificant as they may seem at first, the number and position of wall outlets are important factors in studio production. The outlets for camera and microphone cables, intercoms, and regular household current should be distributed along the four studio walls for easy access. If all the outlets are con-centrated on one side of the studio, you will have to string long and cumbersome cables around the various sets to get equipment into the desired positions. Outlets must be clearly marked to avoid patching cables into the wrong outlets.

Lighting dimmer and patchboard   Most studios have a dimmer control board to regulate the relative intensity of the studio lights. The lighting *patchboard,* or patchbay, connects the individual instruments to the various dimmers. Unless the patching is done by com-puter, the patchboard is usually located in the studio. The dimmer board itself is either in a corner of the studio or in the control room (discussed in detail in section 7.1).

THE STUDIO CONTROL ROOM

The *control room,* a separate room adjacent to the studio, is where all the production activities are coordinated. Here the director, associate director, technical director, and a variety of producers and production assistants make the decisions concerning maximally effective picture and sound sequences, which are to be videotaped or broad-cast live. **SEE 1.19**

1.19 STUDIO CONTROL ROOM

All control rooms have distinct controlling areas: the program control, the image control (switcher), the audio control, and sometimes the lighting and camera controls. The audio control is in an adjacent room.

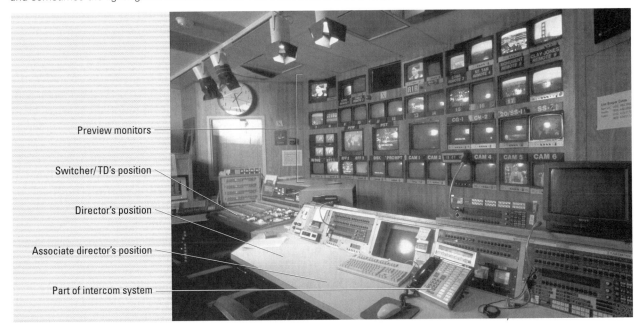

Preview monitors

Switcher/TD's position

Director's position

Associate director's position

Part of intercom system

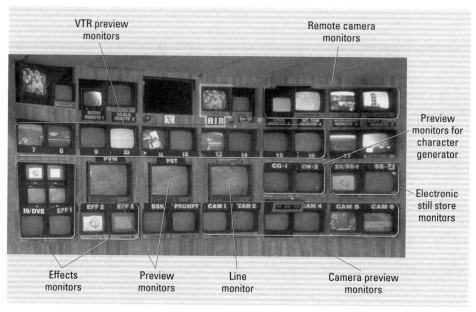

1.20 CONTROL ROOM MONITORS

Each of these monitors shows a specific video image as supplied by video sources such as studio cameras, VTRs, titles, special effects, or remote satellite feeds. The line monitor shows what the director selected to go on the air (and/or on videotape).

Program Control

Program control does not mean the critical examination, or perhaps even censoring, of program content. Rather, it refers to the equipment the director needs to select and organize the various video and audio inputs so that the end result makes sense to the viewing audience. The program control area of the control room is equipped with (1) video monitors, (2) monitor speakers for program sound, (3) intercom systems, and (4) clock and stopwatches.

Video monitors   Even a simple control room holds an amazingly large number of video monitors. There is a *preview (P/V) monitor* for each of the studio cameras and separate preview monitors for film chains, videotape recorders, and character generators or other special-effects devices. There is also a color preview monitor that shows the director and technical director the upcoming picture before it is punched up (put on the air) and the color *line monitor* (also called *master monitor* or *program monitor*) that is fed by the video *line-out*. If you do a live remote or are connected with a network, you need at least two more monitors to preview the remote and network sources. Finally, there is the off-the-air monitor, a regular television set that receives off the air what you are telecasting. It is not

uncommon to find thirty or more monitors in the control room of a medium-sized studio. **SEE 1.20**

Speakers for program sound   The production personnel in the control room, especially the director, must hear what audio is going on the air. The director has a volume control that can adjust the volume of the monitor speaker without influencing the volume of the line-out audio.

Intercommunication systems   In addition to the all-important P.L. intercom that connects the director with all other members of the production crew, there is an additional intercom system called the *P.A.* (public address system), or simply the director's studio talkback. The *studio talkback* system allows the director to talk directly to the crew or talent in the studio when the show is not in progress. With the *I.F.B.* (interruptible foldback or feedback) *system*, the director and producers can talk to the talent while the show is on the air.

Clock and stopwatches   Time is an essential organizing element in television production. Programs are aired according to a second-by-second schedule called the *log*. The two timing tools for the director are the clock and the stopwatch. The clock indicates when a certain

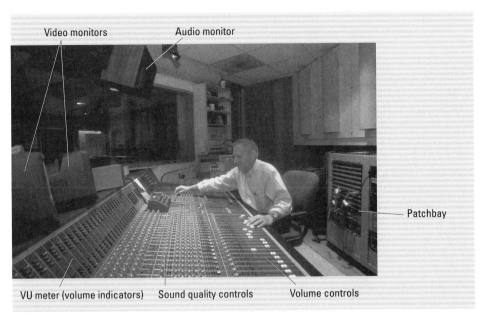

Video monitors   Audio monitor

Patchbay

VU meter (volume indicators)   Sound quality controls   Volume controls

1.21 AUDIO CONTROL
The audio control area contains the audio console, DAT (digital audiotape) machines, CDs, patchbays, various computers that display log information or assist with the audio control functions, and a monitor that shows the line-out video.

program should start or finish. All television clocks in the United States are precisely synchronized. The stopwatch is used for timing inserts, such as a 47-second videotape insert within a news program. Most control rooms have a regular clock (with hands), a digital clock (showing time in numbers), and digital stopwatches that can run forward and backward. The advantage of a clock with hands is that you can look forward in time and, for example, actually see how much time you have left until the end of a program. The digital clock simply indicates where you presently are.

Image Control

Image control refers to the selection and proper sequencing of video images as supplied by cameras or other video sources. It also includes the control of video special effects. The main piece of image control equipment is the *switcher*, which is located next to the director's position. Although the director and the person doing the switching (usually the technical director, or TD) are connected by P.L. intercom, the director often resorts to pointing and finger snapping to speed up the cues to the TD. In some stations the director does his or her own switching, but that arrangement has more disadvantages than advantages. The *C.G.* (character generator) is also located in the control room. The C.G.

operator can call up the various preprogrammed titles or create new ones even during the show.

Audio Control

The audio control booth can be considered a small radio station attached to the television control room. It usually houses the audio console and a patchbay, or patchboard; audiotape recorders and cassette machines; CD player; cue and program speakers; a clock; and a line monitor. **SEE 1.21** Because the audio engineer must be able to work undisturbed by the apparent confusion and inevitable noise in the control room, the audio control booth has visual contact with the control room through a large window but is otherwise self-contained. The audio engineer listens to the director's cues either through P.L. intercom or through a small intercom speaker.

Lighting Control

The lighting control board can be located in the control room or in a corner of the studio. The advantage of placing it in the control room is that the LD (lighting director) has close contact with other control room personnel. The lighting control operator is, as are all other production team members, connected with the director via P.L. intercom.

MASTER CONTROL

Master control is the nerve center of a television station. Every second of programming you see on your home screen has gone through the master control room of the station to which you are tuned. Master control acts as a clearinghouse for all program material. It receives program *feeds* from various sources, and telecasts them at a specific time. The major responsibility of master control is to see that the right program material (including commercials and public service announcements) is put on the air at the right time.

Master control is also responsible for the technical quality of the programs. This means that it has to check all program material being aired against technical standards set by the Federal Communications Commission (FCC) and by a critical chief engineer. **SEE 1.22** The specific activities of master control consist of program input, program storage, and program retrieval.

Program Input

Program material may come into master control directly from its own studios; from satellite or other remote feeds, such as a network show or a live telecast outside the studio; or by courier in the form of videotape. The live shows are routed immediately to the transmitter for broadcast, but the bulk of the program material (video-taped shows) must be stored before being aired.

Master control also puts together the various station breaks. A *station break* is the cluster of commercials, teasers about upcoming programs, public service announcements, and station identifications that appears between programs.

In nonbroadcast production centers, *master control* refers to a room that houses the camera control unit (CCU), high-end video-recording equipment, special-effects equipment, large-capacity computers that perform a variety of production functions, and test equipment.

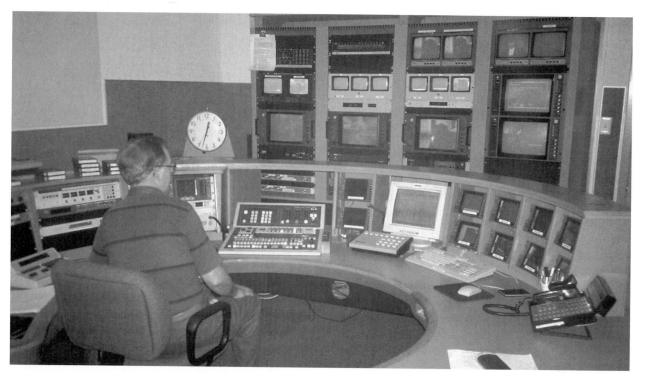

1.22 MASTER CONTROL SWITCHING AREA

Master control serves as the final video and audio clearinghouse for all program material before it is broadcast or distributed by other means (satellite, cable). Computers run all master control functions, with the master control technician overseeing the automated functions and, if necessary, taking over control manually in case of emergency.

Program Storage

All recorded program material (videotape, film, and electronically stored still images) is stored in master control itself or in a designated storage room. Each program is given a station code, or *house number*, for fast identification and retrieval. Although computer retrieval has introduced some commonality in terms, many stations have their own procedures and codes.

Program Retrieval

Program retrieval means the selection, ordering, and airing of all program material. The program retrieval is determined by the program *log*, the second-by-second listing of every program aired on a particular day. The hard-copy log contains information necessary for efficient station operation. In general, the log identifies scheduled time, length of program, program title, video and audio origin (videotape, network, live, or remote), and house numbers and other pertinent information. The program log is issued daily, usually one or two days in advance. It is normally distributed in a printed form that may be as long as sixty to seventy pages. Most stations display the log on computer screens. **SEE 1.23**

The master control switching area looks like the combined program control and switching areas of the studio control room. Master control has preview monitors for all studio cameras, videotape recorders, special effects, network and other remote feeds, plus at least one off-the-air monitor.

Although all master control switching is done by computer, all master controls have a regular switcher, which looks similar to the studio switcher. It is a fail-safe backup device. When the computer goes down, the master control operator must take over and use the manual switcher for all on-the-air program sequences. When all is going well, the computer switching will follow the sequence of events as dictated by the program log. The computer will also activate various playback operations. For example, it can start a specific VTR and switch the picture and sound on the air at the exact log time, change to a still picture and roll a digital audiotape with the prerecorded announcer's voice, switch to another brief VTR insert, and then switch to the network program. If the house number of the actual program does not match the number as specified in the log, the computer will flash a warning in time to correct the possible mistake.

HSE NUMBER	SCH TIME	PGM	LENGTH	ORIGIN VID	AUD
N 3349	10 59 40	NEWS CLOSE	015	VT4	VT4
S11	10 59 55	STATION BR	005	ESS	CART20
E 1009	11 00 00	GOING PLACES 1	030	VT5	VT5
C5590	11 00 30	FED EX	010	VT2	VT2
C 9930-0	11 00 40	HAYDEN PUBLISHING	010	VT18	VT18
C 10004	11 00 50	SPORTS HILIGHTS	005	ESS	CART21
PP 99	11 00 55	STATION PROMO SPORTS	005	VT22	VT22
E 1009	11 01 00	GOING PLACES CONT 2	1100	VT5	VT5
C 9990-34	11 12 00	HYDE PRODUCTS	030	VT34	VT34
C 774-55	11 12 30	COMPESI FISHING	010	VT35	VT35
C 993-48	11 12 40	KIPPER COMPUTERS	010	VT78	VT78
PS	11 12 50	RED CROSS	005	ESS	CART22
PP 1003	11 12 55	STATION PROMO GOOD MRNG	005	VT23	VT23
E 1009	11 13 00	GOING PLACES CONT 3	1025	VT5	VT5
C 222-99	11 23 25	WHITNEY MOTORCYCLE	020	VT33	VT33
C 00995-45	11,23 45	IDEAS TO IMAGES	010	VT91	VT91
PS	11 23 55	AIDS AWARENESS	005	ESS	CART02
E 1009	11 24 00	GOING PLACES CONT 4	100	VT5	VT5
N 01125	11 25 00	NEWSBREAK ***LIVE	010	ST1LV	ST1
C 00944-11	11 25 10	ALL SEASONS GNRL FOODS	030	VT27	VT27
N 01125	11 25 40	NEWS CONT***LIVE	200	ST1LV	ST1
C 995-89	11 27 40	BLOSSER FOR PRESIDENT	020	VT24	VT24
PP 77	11 28 00	NEXT DAY	010	VT19	VT19

1.23 COMPUTER DISPLAY OF LOG

The program log shows the schedule (start) times for each program segment, however short; program title and type; video and audio origin; the identification (house) number of the various program pieces; and other important information, such as the name of the sponsor.

STUDIO SUPPORT AREAS

No studio can function properly without a minimum of support areas. These include space for scene storage, property storage, and makeup and dressing rooms.

Scenery and Properties

Television scenery consists of the three-dimensional elements used in the studio to create a specific environment for the show or show segment. The most common scenic element is the *flat*, a wood frame covered with soft material (muslin or canvas) or hardwall (plywood or various types of fiberboard). The flat is generally used to simulate walls. Other scenic elements include columns, pedestals, platforms, doors, windows, and steps.

Furniture, curtains, hanging pictures, lamps, books, desks, and telephones are considered the properties, or *props*, and set dressings. The props used to make the set functional, such as tables and chairs, are the *set properties*. Items handled by the performers, such as the telephone, are called *hand properties*. Pictures, indoor plants, sculptures—everything used to dress up the set—constitute the *set dressings*.

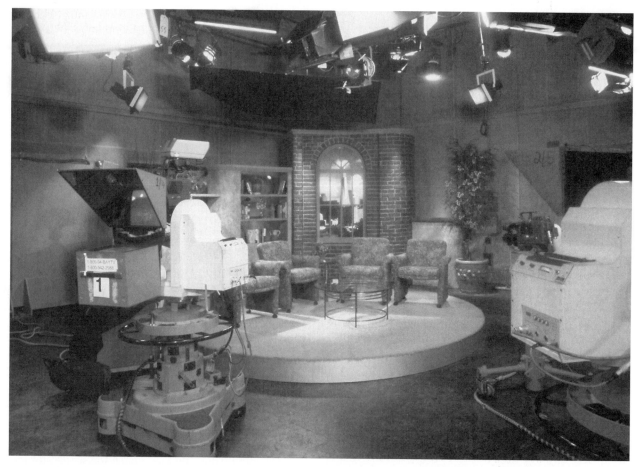

1.24 STUDIO SET

A set provides a specific environment in which the performers or actors can move about. Some sets simulate real environments such as a café or a living room; others provide suitable work space for a specific type of show. The furniture in this set is part of the set properties.

Depending on the type of show, a set will have to simulate a real environment, such as a living room, or simply provide an efficient and attractive work environment, such as an interview set. **SEE 1.24** Whatever the purpose of the set, it must allow for good lighting, favorable camera angles, optimal camera and microphone placement or movement, and smooth and logical action of the performers.

Producing a large number of vastly different television programs, from daily newscasts to complex dramas, requires large prop and scenery storage areas. Otherwise, the support areas can be fairly simple.

The most important part of any storage area is its retrieval efficiency. If you must search for hours to find the props to decorate your office set, even the most extensive prop collection is worth very little. Clearly label all storage areas, and always put the props and scenery back in the designated areas.

Makeup and Dressing Rooms

These support areas are commonplace in large production centers where soap operas or other daily series programs are produced. In smaller production centers, makeup and dressing are done wherever it's convenient.

MAIN POINTS

◆ Telecasts can originate almost anywhere, but the television studio affords maximum production control.

◆ The studio has three major production centers: the studio itself, the studio control room and master control, and the studio support areas.

◆ Important aspects of the physical layout of the studio are a smooth, level studio floor; adequate ceiling height; acoustic treatment and air-conditioning; and large, soundproof doors.

◆ Major installations include intercom systems, studio video and audio monitors, various wall outlets, and the lighting patchboard.

◆ The studio control room houses the program control with the various preview monitors, clocks, and program speakers; the image control (switcher); audio control with the audio console, patchbay, CD player, and program speakers; and sometimes the lighting control board through which the intensity of the studio lights is regulated.

◆ Master control is the nerve center of a television station. It has facilities for program input, program storage, and program retrieval. It also checks the technical quality of all the programs that are broadcast.

◆ Program retrieval is coordinated by the program log, a second-by-second listing of every program aired on a particular day.

◆ The studio support areas include space for property and scenery storage, and makeup and dressing rooms.

ZETTL'S VIDEOLAB 2.1

At this point it's time to meet the five mentors who will be sharing with you their specific production skills. They are seasoned professionals, and you would do well to heed their advice.

RUN ZVL 1 Click on the **camera** monitor and run tape 1 **Meet Sonny**. Listen to what Sonny has to say about camera operation in general.

RUN ZVL 2 Click on the **lights** monitor and run tape 1 **Meet Mary**. Mary introduces you to the art of lighting.

RUN ZVL 3 Click on the **audio** monitor and run tape 1 **Meet Phil**. Phil will later guide you through the various audio production items and their effective uses.

RUN ZVL 4 Click on the **editing** monitor and run tape 1 **Meet Veronica**. She is quite right when she tells you that editing "is where it all comes together."

RUN ZVL 5 Click on the **process** monitor and run tape 1 **Meet Herb**. As executive producer he is primarily concerned that the whole production process is done efficiently and responsibly.

2

Analog and Digital Television

The big buzzword in television, as in other branches of electronic communication, is *digital*. You have probably heard many times that digital television (DTV) will revolutionize television. In one way such claims are true; in another, they influence only minimally certain production techniques. For example, whereas the electronic characteristics of a digital camcorder differ considerably from the traditional analog one, its operation is pretty much the same. Both types of camcorders—analog or digital—require that you look through a viewfinder and point the lens in a certain direction to get the desired image. On the other hand, the switch to wide-screen DTV will require different ways of framing a shot. More so, changing from an analog (linear) editing system to a digital (nonlinear) one calls for not only different operational skills, but also a whole new concept of what editing is all about.

A good way to grasp the workings of a digital television system is to learn, first of all, some basics about general analog and digital television processes.

Section 2.1, Analog and Digital Television, explains the basics of how a color television image is created, what digital processes are all about, and how they differ from analog systems. Section 2.2, DTV Scanning Systems, introduces you to the current DTV standards and the major differences among them.

KEY TERMS

480p The lowest-resolution scanning system of DTV (digital television). The *p* stands for *progressive,* which means that each complete television frame consists of 480 lines that are scanned one after the other.

720p A progressive scanning system of DTV (digital television). It is considered an HDTV (high-definition television) system.

1080i An interlaced scanning system of HDTV (high-definition television). The *i* stands for *interlaced,* which means that a complete frame is formed from two interlaced scanning fields. Each field consists of 539.5 lines. As with the traditional NTSC analog television system, the 1080i produces 60 fields or 30 complete frames per second.

analog A signal that fluctuates exactly like the original stimulus.

aspect ratio The width-to-height proportions of the television screen and therefore of all analog television pictures: four units wide by three units high. For DTV and HDTV, sixteen by nine.

binary A number system with the base of 2.

binary digit (bit) The smallest amount of information a computer can hold and process. A charge is either present, represented by a *1,* or absent, represented by a *0.* One bit can describe two levels, such as on/off or black/white. Two bits can describe four levels (2^2 bits); three bits, eight levels (2^3 bits); four bits, sixteen (2^4 bits), and so on. A group of eight bits (2^8) is called a *byte.*

coding To change the quantized values into a binary code, represented by 0's and 1's. Also called *encoding.*

compression Reducing the amount of data to be stored or transmitted by using coding schemes that pack all original data into less space or by throwing away some of the least important data.

digital Usually to mean the binary system—the representation of data in the form of digits (on/off pulses).

DTV Stands for *digital television.* High-resolution digital television systems. Also called *ATV (advanced television).*

field (1) A location away from the studio. (2) One-half of a complete scanning cycle, with two fields necessary for one television picture frame. There are 60 fields, or 30 frames, per second.

frame A complete scanning cycle of the electron beam (two fields), which occurs every $1/30$ second.

HDTV Stands for *high-definition television.* Has at least twice the picture detail of traditional (NTSC) television. The 720p uses 720 lines that are scanned progressively each $1/30$ second. The 1080i standard uses 60 fields per second, each field consisting of 539.5 lines. A complete frame consists of two interlaced scanning fields of 539.5 lines.

interlaced scanning In this system the beam skips every other line during its first scan, reading only the odd-numbered lines. After the beam has scanned half of the last odd-numbered line, it jumps back to the top of the screen and finishes the unscanned half of the top line and continues to scan all the even-numbered lines. Each such even- or odd-numbered scan produces a *field.* Two fields produce a complete *frame.* Traditional television operates with 60 fields per second, which translates into 30 frames per second.

progressive scanning In this system the electron beam starts with line 1, then scans line 2, then line 3, and so forth, until all lines are scanned, at which point the beam jumps back to its starting position to repeat the scan of all lines.

quantizing A step in the digitization of an analog signal. It changes the sampling points into discrete values. Also called *quantization.*

refresh rate The number of complete scanning cycles per second.

RGB Red, green, and blue: the basic colors of television.

sampling Taking a great number of samples (voltages) of the analog video or audio signal at equally spaced intervals.

2.1

Analog
and
Digital
Television

Before you submerge yourself into the digital world of television, you should know how the basic television image you see on-screen is created. Many system elements and production techniques were developed to facilitate this basic technical image creation and display. Also, to really understand how various digital elements of the television system interact—such as digital cameras and nonlinear editing systems—you need to know what the basic digital processes are all about and how they differ from analog ones.

▶ **BASIC IMAGE CREATION**
The travel of the electron beam forming the television image and basic colors

▶ **BASIC COLORS OF THE VIDEO DISPLAY**
Red, green, and blue as the primary colors

▶ **WHAT DIGITAL IS ALL ABOUT**
Why digital?

▶ **BENEFITS OF DIGITAL TELEVISION**
Quality, computer compatibility and flexibility, transport, and compression

▶ **ASPECT RATIO**
The 4 × 3 and 16 × 9 aspect ratios

BASIC IMAGE CREATION

The video image is literally drawn onto the television screen by an electronic pencil—the *electron beam*. Emitted by the *electron gun,* the electron beam scans the inside surface of the television screen line by line, from left to right, much as we read. The inside of the television screen is dotted with light-sensitive picture elements, or *pixels* (round dots or tiny rectangles) that light up when hit by the beam. If the beam is powerful, the dots light up brightly. If the beam is weak, the dots light up only partially. If the beam is really tired, the dots don't light up at all. The process is similar to the large displays that use light bulbs for outdoor advertising, except that the light bulbs on the screen are extremely tiny. **SEE 2.1**

The traditional television system consists of 525 lines on the screen. It was developed by the National Television System Committee and is appropriately called the *NTSC system.* To produce an image, the electron beam scans the odd-numbered lines first. Then it jumps back to the top of the screen and scans the even-numbered lines. The complete scan of all odd-numbered or even-numbered lines, which takes ¹⁄₆₀ second, is called a *field*. A complete

2.1 INTERLACED SCANNING

A The electron beam first scans all odd-numbered lines, from left to right and from top to bottom. This first scanning cycle produces the first field.

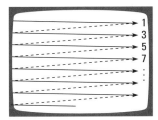

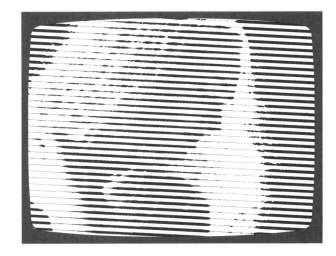

B The electron beam jumps back to the top and scans all even-numbered lines. This second scanning cycle produces the second field.

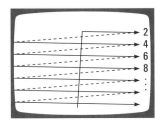

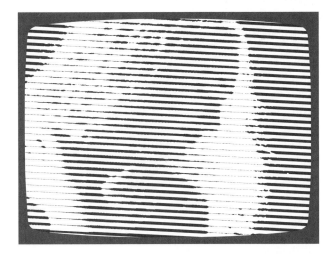

C The two fields make up a complete television picture, called a frame.

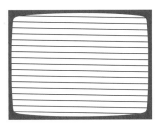

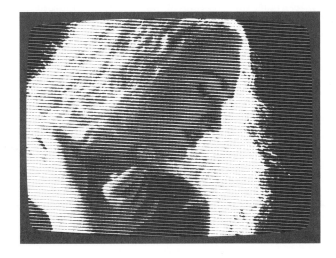

scan of all odd- *and* even-numbered lines is called a *frame*. In the traditional NTSC system, there are 30 frames per second. The beam is such a speed-reader that we perceive the various dots as a complete video image. Because the two fields scan different sets of lines, the scanning process is called *interlaced*. Section 2.2 explores the various scanning processes in more detail.

BASIC COLORS OF THE VIDEO DISPLAY

All the beautiful images you see on television—even the black-and-white pictures—are a mixture of three basic colors: red, green, and blue. Depending on how hard the pixels are hit by an electron beam, they light up in different intensities. Mixing these intensities produces all the other colors. Each line must, therefore, have groups of *RGB* (red, green, and blue) dots or rectangles. But how can a single electron beam hit each RGB group (the three dots that are grouped together) with various intensities? It can't. There must be a separate electron beam for each basic color: one for the red dots, a second for the green dots, and a third for the blue ones. **SEE COLOR PLATE 1** The three electron beams can hit each group of RGB dots with various intensities, thus producing the different color mixes. Just how these three colors create all the others is explored in chapter 3.

WHAT DIGITAL IS ALL ABOUT

All *digital* computers and digital video are based on a *binary* code that uses the either/or, on/off values of 0's and 1's to interpret the world. The *binary digit*, or *bit*, acts like a light bulb: It either carries a charge or it doesn't; it is either on or off. If it is on, it is assigned a *1*, if it is off, it is assigned a *0*.

Why Digital?

At first glance this either/or system of binary digits may seem awfully clumsy. For example, the simple decimal number 17 reads 00010001 in the binary code.[1] Nevertheless, this either/or, on/off system has great resistance

---

1. The binary system uses the base-2 numbering system. The number 17 is represented by an 8-bit binary code. All such values are mathematically represented by either 0's or 1's. An 8-bit representation of a single color pixel or sound has 2^8, or 256, discrete values. For more-detailed information on the binary system, see Andrew F. Inglis, and Arch C. Luther, *Video Engineering*, 2d ed. (New York: McGraw-Hill, 1996), pp. 47–68.

to data distortion or error. If, for example, you turn a light switch on and nothing happens, or if the light bulb flickers, there is obviously something wrong. If the light stays on when you turn the switch off, you certainly know that something went wrong again. The digital system simply ignores such aberrations and reacts only if the switch triggers the expected on/off mode of the light.

The Difference Between Analog and Digital

Before getting too technical, let's use a simple metaphor to explain the difference between analog and digital signal processing. The analog signal is very much like a ramp that leads continuously from one elevation to another. It matters little whether you use small or big steps—the ramp gradually and inevitably leads to the desired elevation. **SEE 2.2** Technically, in the digital process, the analog signal is continuously sampled. The samples are then quantized (assigned a concrete value) and grouped into 0's and 1's.

To carry on our ramp metaphor, in the *digital* domain, you would have to use steps to get to the same elevation. This is much more an either/or proposition. The elevation has now been *quantized* (divided) into a number of discrete units—the steps. You either get to the next step or you don't. There is no such thing as a half- or quarter-step. **SEE 2.3** More technically, the *analog* system processes and records a signal that fluctuates exactly like the original signal (the way you moved up or down the ramp). Digital processing, however, changes the ramp into concrete values. This process is called *digitization*.

The Process of Digitization

Digitizing an analog signal is a four-step process: (1) anti-aliasing, (2) sampling, (3) quantizing, and (4) coding. **SEE 2.4**

Anti-aliasing   In this step extreme frequencies of the analog signal that are unnecessary for its proper sampling are filtered out.

Sampling   In the *sampling* stage, the number of points along the ramp (analog signal) are selected for building the steps (digital values). The higher the sampling rate, the more steps chosen and the more they will look like the original ramp (analog signal). Obviously, a high sampling rate (many smaller steps) is preferred over a low one (several large steps).

The sampling rate of a video signal is usually expressed in megahertz (MHz). **SEE 2.5**

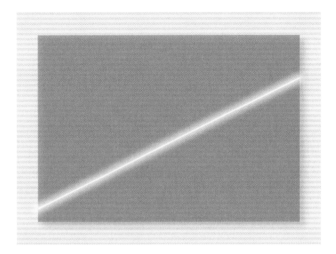

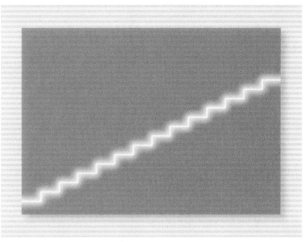

2.2 ANALOG SIGNAL

The analog signal can be represented by a ramp that leads continuously to a certain height.

2.3 DIGITAL SIGNAL

The digital signal can be represented by a staircase that leads to a certain height in discrete steps.

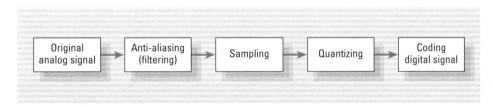

2.4 DIGITIZING DIAGRAM

The digitization of an analog signal is a four-step process: anti-aliasing, sampling, quantizing, and coding.

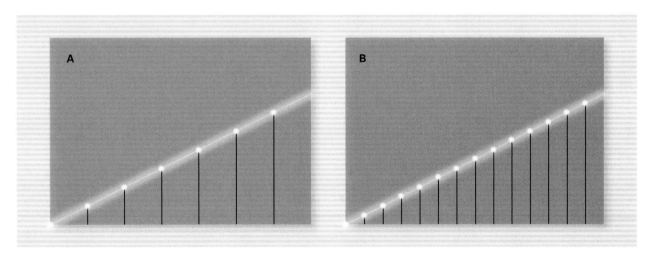

2.5 SAMPLING

A Sampling selects portions of the original analog signal. A low sampling rate transforms the ramp into a few large steps. Much of the original signal is lost.

B A high sampling rate selects more parts of the original signal. The ramp is made of more, smaller steps, making the steps look more like the original ramp. The higher the sampling rate, the higher the signal quality.

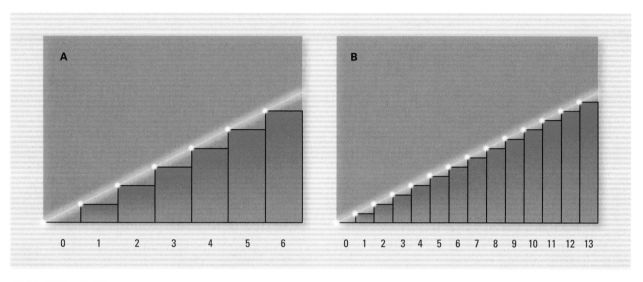

2.6 QUANTIZING

Quantizing assigns the selected signal samples a fixed position. This is the step-building stage. Each step gets a particular decimal number, indicating its height. **A** Low sampling rate: several large steps. **B** High sampling rate: many small steps.

Quantizing   At the *quantizing* digitization stage, we are actually building the steps and checking how high or low each step is relative to a scale—the *quantizing levels*. The height of each step is measured. An 8-bit quantizing has a maximum number of 256 steps (2^8). **SEE 2.6**

Coding   This process changes the quantization numbers of each step to binary numbers, consisting of 0's and 1's. **SEE 2.7**

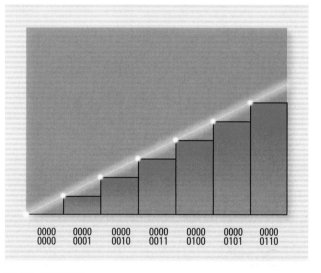

2.7 CODING

Coding assigns each step a binary number.

BENEFITS OF DIGITAL TELEVISION

Why go through all these processes? Wouldn't it be easier simply to walk up the ramp (using the analog signal) instead of climbing thousands or even millions of steps per second (digital signal)? After all, television has worked quite well before the digital revolution. Yet there are some major advantages of *DTV (digital television)* over the analog signal: (1) aspect ratio (discussed in the following section), (2) quality, (3) computer compatibility and flexibility, (4) transport, and (5) compression.

Quality

Even before the advent of advanced DTV systems, picture and sound quality have been a major concern of equipment manufacturers and production personnel. A high-end studio camera can cost up to fifty times more than a consumer camcorder, mainly because the studio camera produces higher-quality pictures. Digital television promises extremely sharp and crisp pictures that not only show a great amount of fine detail but also improved color. Such initial high-resolution picture quality is especially important for extensive postproduction.

Complex editing and the rendering of special effects require many tape generations (the number of *dubs*—copies—away from the original). Unfortunately, the greater the number of generations in analog recordings, the greater the loss of quality. This is not unlike making progressive copies of a letter by copying each previous copy. Pretty soon, the print has deteriorated so much that you can hardly read it.

But this is where digital recordings shine. There is hardly any noticeable quality loss even after dozens of generations. For all practical purposes, the twentieth generation looks as sharp as the original source tape. In fact, through some digital wizardry, you can make a copy look even better than the original recording. Another important quality factor is that the simple binary code is relatively immune to extraneous electronic signals—*noise*—that infiltrate and distort analog signals. With digital signal processing, electronic noise is held to a minimum, if not altogether eliminated.

There is a downside to these superclean signals, however, especially when dealing with sound. Sometimes digital music recordings sound so crisp and clean that they lack the warmth and texture of the original piece—or even of an analog recording. You may remember the monotone sounds of synthesized computer speech; it was missing all the complexity and subtleties (overtones) of actual speech. Higher sampling rates and more-complex digital signal combinations are trying to make up for this deficiency. High-resolution pictures require even more attention to detail, from makeup to background scenery.

Computer Compatibility and Flexibility

One of the big advantages of digital television is that its signals can be transferred directly to the computer without the need for digitization. Such compatibility is especially important for creating special effects and computer-generated images. Even a simple five-minute newscast features a dazzling display of digital effects that was all but impossible with pure analog equipment. The opening animated title, the scene that expands full-screen from the box over the newscaster's shoulder, or the graphical transition from one story to the next where one picture peels off to reveal another underneath—all show the variety and flexibility of digital effects. The multiple screens within the screen and the various lines of texts that run simultaneously on the bottom, sides, or top of the main television screen are possible only through digital effects. Computer software that allows the alteration or creation of audio and video images has become an essential digital production tool.

Signal Transport

If you have ever gotten impatient while downloading a picture or large text file from the Internet, you will appreciate the difficulty faced by **high-definition television (HDTV)** or, even more so, interactive digital television that promises the viewer/user direct communication with the originating program source. The huge amount of digital data necessary to transport a full-motion (30 frames per second), full-screen scene is enormous and needs a very wide highway *(bandwidth)* to handle the billions of digits. But how can transporting such huge amounts of digital data (called *bitstreams*) be an advantage over analog signals?

In contrast to an extremely wide, irreducible analog bandwidth, digital signals can be compressed in various ways so that they can travel on the available highway without causing gridlock and also fit into a reasonably sized storage area, such as a videotape cartridge or hard disk. But because the electronic highways are so crowded during the digital-data travel from transmitter to your home receiver, some of the digits may never make it home. Even if the digital signals are more robust than their analog counterparts, signal transmission is still a major concern of broadcasters.

Compression

Compression is the temporary rearrangement or elimination of redundant information for easier storage and signal transmission. Digital information can be compressed by regrouping the original data without throwing any of it away. Once at the destination, the data can then be restored to their original positions *(coding)* for an output that is identical to the original input. We do this frequently when "zipping" (on a Windows platform) or "stuffing" (on a Mac) large computer texts for storage and transmission and then "unzipping" them when opening the file. Or you can simply delete all data that are redundant.

Compression that results from rearranging data is called *lossless*—the regenerated image has the same number of pixels as the original. When some pixels are lost, the compression is called "lossy." Even if the lost pixels were redundant and not essential for the image creation, the regenerated image is, nevertheless, different from the original. The obvious advantage of lossless compression is that the original image is returned without any loss of quality. The disadvantage is that the lossless compression of data takes more storage space and usually takes more time to bring back from storage. Most image compression techniques are, therefore, the lossy kind.

One of the most widely used digital compression standards for still images is *JPEG* ("jay-peg"), named for the organization that developed the system—the Joint Photographic Experts Group; *motion-JPEG* is for moving computer images. Although a lossless JPEG technique exists, to save storage space most JPEG compressions are lossy. Another compression standard for high-quality video is *MPEG-2* ("em-peg two"), named and developed by the Moving Picture Experts Group. MPEG-2 is also a lossy compression technique, based on the elimination of redundant information. Image compression is explored further in chapter 12.

ASPECT RATIO

One of the most visible differences between traditional (analog) and digital television systems (DTV) is the horizontally stretched television picture. The new television *aspect ratio*—the width-to-height proportions of the screen—resembles more a small motion picture screen than the traditional television screen. Let's take a closer look at the traditional aspect ratio and the horizontally stretched DTV aspect ratio.

The 4 × 3 Aspect Ratio

The aspect ratio of the traditional television and computer screens, which date back to the earliest motion picture screens, is 4 × 3, which means that its frame is four units wide and three units high, regardless of whether the units are inches or feet. This aspect ratio is also expressed 1.33:1. For every unit in screen height, there are 1.33 units in width. **SEE 2.8**

The advantage of this classic aspect ratio is that the difference between the screen width and the screen height is not pronounced enough to unduly emphasize one dimension over the other. A close-up or extreme close-up of a face fits well in this aspect ratio, as does horizontally stretched landscape.[2] The disadvantage is that it does not accommodate wide-screen movies that have a much more horizontally stretched aspect ratio of 1.85:1.

The 16 × 9 Aspect Ratio

The horizontally stretched aspect ratio of DTV systems is 16 × 9; that is, the screen is sixteen units wide by nine units high, or 1.78:1. As you can see, this aspect ratio resembles

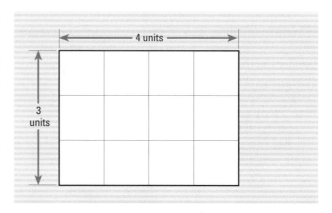

2.8 4 × 3 ASPECT RATIO

The traditional aspect ratio of the television screen is 4 × 3 (four units wide by three units high). It can also be expressed as 1.33:1 (1.33 units in width for each unit of height).

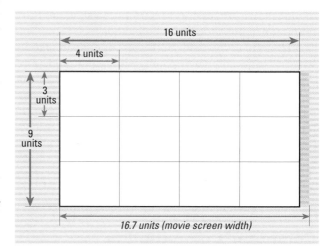

2.9 16 × 9 ASPECT RATIO

The aspect ratio of DTV is 16 × 9 (sixteen units wide by nine units high), which is a multiple of the 4 × 3 ratio ($4^2 × 3^2$). Its horizontally stretched aspect ratio of 1.78:1 resembles more that of the movie screen (1.85:1).

more that of a movie screen than the traditional television screen. **SEE 2.9**

Because this aspect ratio is so closely associated with high-definition television, it is also called the "HDTV aspect ratio." Because retaining the traditional aspect ratio would be advantageous not only in framing close-ups of people, but also in playing back the countless hours of traditional television programs that were videotaped in the 4 × 3 format, you may ask why digital television did not keep the traditional 4 × 3 ratio, much as computer screens did.

---

2. See Herbert Zettl, *Sight Sound Motion*, 3d ed. (Belmont, Calif.: Wadsworth Publishing Co., 1999), pp. 74–79.

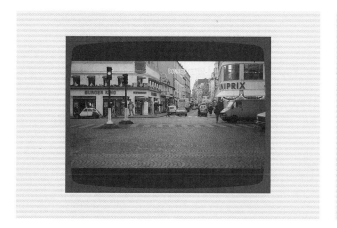

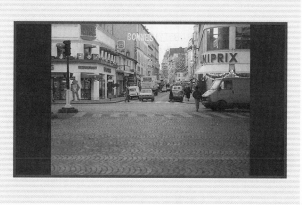

2.10 LETTER-BOX VIEW
To show wide-screen movies on a traditional (4 × 3) television screen, they must be squeezed into a "letter-box" slot, leaving black borders on the top and bottom of the screen.

2.11 WIDE-SCREEN DEAD ZONES
When programs that were produced in the traditional 4 × 3 television aspect ratio are shown on the 16 × 9 DTV screen, there are "dead zones" on both sides of the screen.

The main reason for the newer 16 × 9 aspect ratio is that it readily accommodates the wide-screen movie format. To show a wide-screen movie on traditional television, either both sides of the frame are crudely amputated, or the images are displayed in the "letter-box" that shows the movie in its full width but necessitates the black stripes at the top and bottom of the screen. **SEE 2.10** To avoid loss of picture area or the letter-box stripes, some films are subjected to the *pan-and-scan* process, whereby the more important portions of the wide-screen frame are selected to fit the 4 × 3 frame. But this process is quite costly and does not maintain the integrity of the original picture composition.

When shown on the 16 × 9 television screen, movies suffer only slight picture loss, but we are now faced with the problem of 4 × 3 television programs. We can either stretch the image to the full width of the DTV screen, thereby undoubtedly losing some of the heads and feet of the people on-screen, or we place the full 4 × 3 frame in the center of the 16 × 9 screen, leaving black stripes or some other visual information on each side. **SEE 2.11**

The 4 × 3 pictures may be stretched horizontally to some degree on the 16 × 9 screen to reduce the "dead zones" on either side, but they cannot be stretched enough to fill the screen without noticeable distortion.[3]

---

3. Such horizontal stretching is called *anamorphic distortion.* Our visual mechanism normally allows as much as a 5 percent anamorphic distortion, but any further stretching results in obvious distortion.

MAIN POINTS

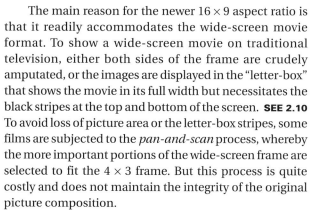

- In the basic interlaced scanning process, the electron beam reads all odd-numbered lines first (the first field), and then the even-numbered lines (the second field). The two fields constitute a single television frame. There are 60 fields, or 30 frames, per second.

- The basic colors used in television are red, green, and blue—RGB. Each of the 525 lines on the face of the display tube consists of groups of red, green, and blue dots or rectangles. These basic color dots are activated by three electron beams—one for the red dots, one for the green, and one for the blue. The varying intensities of the three beams produce the colors we see on television.

- Digital computers use the binary code, consisting of 0's and 1's. This code resists data error.

- In the digital process, the analog signal is continuously sampled. The samples are then quantized (assigned a concrete value), and coded into groups of 0's and 1's.

- Digital television produces pictures and sound of superior quality, allows many tape generations with virtually no deterioration of pictures and sound, provides great flexibility in image manipulation and creation, and permits data compression for efficient signal transport and storage.

- Compared to the traditional television aspect ratio of 4 × 3, DTV systems have an aspect ratio of 16 × 9. This horizontally stretched screen format accommodates wide-screen movies.

2.2

DTV Scanning Systems

Digital television systems produce their high-resolution pictures through either *progressive* or *interlaced* scanning systems. The progressive scanning system requires fewer scanning lines for high-quality pictures than the interlaced scanning system. This section takes a brief look at digital scanning and display systems.

▶ **PROGRESSIVE AND INTERLACED SCANNING**
The progressive scanning system and interlaced scanning system

▶ **DTV SYSTEMS**
The 480p system, the 720p system, and the 1080i system

▶ **FLAT-PANEL DISPLAYS**
Plasma displays and liquid crystal displays

PROGRESSIVE AND INTERLACED SCANNING

As mentioned in chapter 1, the television image is formed by the three RGB (red, green, and blue) electron beams that scan the light-sensitive pixels lining the inner surface of the television screen. Although color television scanning requires three electron beams, to simplify the explanation we will pretend that only a single beam is scanning the surface of the television screen.

The Progressive Scanning System

In the *progressive scanning* system, the electron beam scans each line, much like the way you read. It starts at the top left of the screen and scans the first line, then jumps back to the left at the start of the second line, scans the second line, jumps back to the third line, scans the third line, and so on. After the last line has been scanned, the beam jumps back to its original starting point at the top left of the screen. As you can see, the beam scans all lines progressively, hence the name of the system.

Retrace and blanking   The repositioning of the beam from the end of the scanned line to the starting point of the next is called *horizontal retrace*. When the beam reaches the end of the last line and jumps back to the starting point of line one, it is referred to as *vertical retrace*. To avoid any picture interference during the horizontal and vertical retraces, the beam is automatically starved so that it won't light up any pixels that might interfere with the original scan. This process is called *blanking*. Hence, *horizontal blanking* occurs during the horizontal retrace, and *vertical blanking* is during the vertical retrace. **SEE 2.12**

Flicker Because the beam in progressive scanning "reads" all the lines before it jumps back to begin reading the next page, we basically have a complete frame after each scan. To imitate the 30 frames per second of the traditional television system, we could simply have 30 complete progressive scans each second. This is a good idea, except that we are running into a problem.

This problem is known as *flicker*—noticeable periodic brightness variations. Flicker occurs when the pixels of one frame start to fade before they are activated again by the new frame scan. To avoid flicker in the progressive system, the **refresh rate** of each complete scan must be higher than in interlaced scanning. A computer screen forms its images through progressive scanning, and usually has a refresh rate of 72 or more frames per second. The refresh rate of digital television can be as low as 60 frames per second without causing noticeable flicker.

The Interlaced Scanning System

Contrary to progressive scanning, where the electron beam reads every line from top to bottom, the beam in **interlaced scanning** reads all the odd-numbered lines first, then it jumps back to the top to read all the even-numbered lines.

The 525 lines of traditional (NTSC) television are divided into two fields: 262.5 lines for the first field, and another 262.5 lines for the second field. The beam scans 60 alternate fields, or 30 complete frames, each second. This scanning speed is so fast that we perceive the two fields as a complete, relatively flicker-free picture. **SEE 2.13**

Let's apply the two scanning systems to DTV and see how they fare.

DTV SYSTEMS

After years of wrangling over the former *ATV (advanced television)* and DTV (digital television) scanning standards, the industry seems to have settled on three systems: the 480p, the 720p, and the 1080i.[4]

---

4. There are a number of digital systems that are still alive or in various stages of development: 480i (interlaced), 4 × 3 (aspect ratio); 480i, 16 × 9; 480p (progressive), 30 fps (frames per second), 4 × 3; 480p, 60 fps, 4 × 3; 480p, 30 fps, 16 × 9; 480p, 60 fps, 16 × 9; 720p, 30 fps, 16 × 9; 720p, 60 fps, 16 × 9; 720p, 24 fps, 16 × 9 (ideal for showing movies, because the frame rate of movies is also 24 fps); 1080i, 30 fps, 16 × 9; 1080p, 60 fps, 16 × 9; and 1080p, 24 fps, 16 × 9 (the ultimate format for electronically archiving and showing motion pictures, because the frame rate is the same and the resolution almost identical).

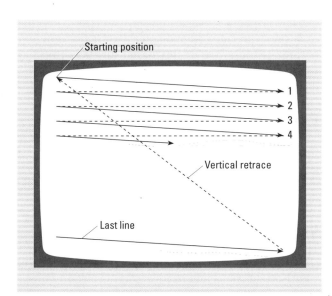

2.12 PROGRESSIVE SCANNING
In progressive scanning the beam "reads" every line from top to bottom. Each complete scan produces a television frame.

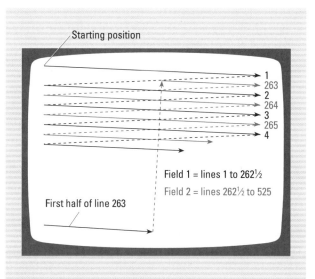

2.13 INTERLACED SCANNING
In interlaced scanning, the beam "reads" every other line from top to bottom. Each scan produces one field (odd-numbered or even-numbered lines). Two fields make up a complete frame.

The 480p System

The *480p* system uses 480 lines that are scanned progressively every ⅟₆₀ second. Although the number of lines are not much less than what you see on traditional analog television—of the 525 lines, only 486 of them actually show up on-screen—the 480p DTV system delivers dramatically sharper pictures. It also produces 60 complete frames per second—double that of traditional television (which scans half of its lines every ⅟₆₀ second, resulting in 30 frames per second). Because of its crisp pictures, the 480p system is sometimes, though erroneously, labeled HDTV.

Besides its higher-resolution pictures, the 480p system offers additional advantages:

Low number of scanning lines The lower number of scanning lines means a narrower bandwidth, which is desirable because it allows more channels to be squeezed into the available electronic air space.

No flicker Sometimes interlaced scanning causes flicker because the two fields don't mesh exactly. Progressive scanning eliminates this potential problem.

Efficient compression Images that use progressive scanning are more easily compressed and decompressed than those that use interlaced scanning.

Ease of conversion If transmitted by cable, progressively scanned images are easier and more cheaply converted at the home television set.

The 720p System

The 720 lines that are scanned progressively in the *720p* system as well as its refresh rate of 60 (all lines are scanned every ⅟₆₀ second) contribute to true high-definition television images. This means that the pictures have superior resolution and color fidelity. The advantages of the 720p system are similar to those of the 480i: a relatively low number of scanning lines, efficient compression, and ease of conversion when transmitted via cable.

The 1080i System

The *1080i* system uses interlaced scanning. Much like the standard NTSC scanning, each field of 539.5 lines is scanned every ⅟₆₀ second, producing, therefore, 30 frames per second. Proponents of the 1080i claim that it is the only system capable of delivering true HDTV pictures and that all others that have fewer scanning lines are merely

ATV systems. The high number of scanning lines of the 1080i system dramatically improves the resolution of the television picture. But in the end, as we all know, it depends on how much of the original picture quality is maintained during the entire production process and, especially, during the signal transmission.

Regardless of the relative picture quality of the three standards, they are, like any other system, finally dependent on the program content. A bad program remains bad even when received in digital form; a good program is good even if the picture quality is slightly inferior. Note, however, that picture quality becomes a real issue when using the HDTV system for instructional or training purposes, such as medical programs.

FLAT-PANEL DISPLAYS

Hand-in-hand with the development of DTV goes the search for high-definition receivers. Because there is a limit to the size of the *CRT (cathode ray tube)* of the regular television set, attention has been given to flat-panel displays, such as those on laptop computers. The advantage of flat-panel displays over regular television receivers or large-screen projection systems is that flat panels can be made very large without getting thicker. In fact, flat-panel displays resemble a large painting with a modest frame around them. The hope for flat-panel displays is that they will be hung on a wall like a painting. As always with video technology, there are two different, incompatible types of flat-panel displays that can reproduce high-definition video images: the plasma display and the liquid crystal display.

Plasma Display Panel

The *plasma display panel (PDP)* uses two transparent (usually glass) wired panels that sandwich a thin layer of gas. When the gas receives the voltages of the video signal, it activates the RGB dots that are arranged very much like those of the standard television receiver.

Liquid Crystal Display

The *liquid crystal display (LCD)* also uses two transparent sheets, but instead of gas the panels sandwich a liquid whose crystal molecules change when an electric current is applied. Rather than RGB dots, the LCD uses tiny transistors that light up according to the voltages of the video signal. Laptop computers, digital clocks, telephones, and many other consumer electronics use LCD.

The problem with both types of flat-panel displays is not that they lack the resolution or color fidelity of HDTV, but that they need to be viewed directly from the front. As you certainly have noticed, laptop displays are barely readable if you look at them from an angle. If you can sit more or less directly in front of a large flat-panel display, you perceive the video images as intended. But if you are watching it from an angle, the display is dark and lacking in definition—certainly not a good way to watch HDTV programs.

MAIN POINTS

◆ In the progressive scanning system, the electron beam scans each line, starting with line 1, then line 2, then line 3, and so on. When all lines have been scanned, the beam jumps back to its starting point to repeat the sequential scanning of all lines. Each scan of all lines results in a video frame.

◆ With interlaced scanning, the beam skips every other line during its first scan, reading only the odd-numbered lines. After the beam has scanned half of the last odd-numbered line, it jumps back to the top of the screen and finishes the unscanned half of the top line and continues to scan all the even-numbered lines. Each such even- or odd-numbered scan produces a field. Two fields produce a complete video frame.

◆ During the horizontal and vertical retraces, the beam is starved so that it will not activate the pixels and thus interfere with the clarity of the picture.

◆ The most common refresh rate of the 720p system is 60 frames per second, whereas for the 1080i system it is 30 frames per second.

◆ DTV employs three systems, the 480p (480 lines progressively scanned), the 720p, and the 1080i (1,080 lines with interlaced scanning). All have a 16×9 aspect ratio.

◆ The two flat-panel video displays are the plasma display panel (PDP), which sandwiches gas between two transparent panels, and the liquid crystal display (LCD), which sandwiches a liquid between two transparent panels. The PDP activates RGB dots; the LCD panel activates a number of tiny transistors that change according to the charge they receive.

3

The Television Camera

The television camera is the single most important piece of production equipment. Other production equipment and techniques are greatly influenced by the camera's technical and performance characteristics. Although the electronics of the television camera have become increasingly complex, its new systems make it much simpler to operate. As you probably know from operating your own camcorder, you don't have to be a skilled electronics engineer to produce an optimal image—all you need to do is press the right camera buttons. Section 3.1, How Television Cameras Work, identifies the parts, types, and characteristics of cameras and how they operate. Section 3.2, From Light to Video Image, provides more-detailed information about the function of the CCD, the nature of color, and chrominance and luminance channels.

brightness The color attribute that determines how dark or light a color appears on the monochrome television screen or how much light the color reflects. Also called *lightness.*

camcorder A portable camera with the VTR attached or built into it to form a single unit.

camera chain The television camera (head) and associated electronic equipment, including the camera control unit, sync generator, and power supply.

camera control unit (CCU) Equipment, separate from the camera head, that contains various video controls, including registration, color balance, contrast, and brightness, that enable the video operator to adjust the camera picture during a show.

camera head The actual television camera, which is at the head of a chain of essential electronic accessories. It is composed of the imaging device, lens, and viewfinder. In ENG/EFP cameras, the camera head contains all the elements of the camera chain.

charge-coupled device (CCD) The imaging device in a television camera. Usually called the *chip.*

chip A common name for the camera imaging device. Technically, it is known as the charge-coupled device (CCD). The chip consists of a great number of imaging sensing elements, called *pixels,* that translate the optical (light) image into an electronic video signal. Also called the *camera pickup device.*

chrominance channel The color (chroma) channels within the color camera. A separate chrominance channel is responsible for each of the three basic color signals: red, green, and blue.

contrast ratio The difference between the brightest and the darkest spots in the picture (often measured by reflected light in foot-candles). The optimal contrast ratio for analog cameras is normally 40:1 or slightly higher, which means that the brightest spot in the picture should not be more than forty times brighter than the darkest spot. For DTV it can exceed this ratio, depending on the quality of the camera.

ENG/EFP cameras and camcorders High-quality portable field production cameras. When the camera is docked with a VTR, or has a VTR built into it, it is called a *camcorder.*

gain Electronic amplification of the video signal.

high-definition television (HDTV) camera Studio camera that delivers pictures of superior resolution, color fidelity, and light-and-dark contrast; uses a high-quality CCD as its imaging device.

hue One of the three basic color attributes; hue is the color itself—red, green, yellow, and so on.

luminance channel A separate channel within color cameras that deals with brightness variations and allows them to produce a signal receivable on a black-and-white television. The luminance signal is usually electronically derived from the chrominance signals.

moiré effect Color vibrations that occur when narrow, contrasting stripes of a design interfere with the scanning lines of the television system.

operating light level Amount of light needed by the camera to produce a video signal.

pixel Short for *picture element.* A single imaging element (like the single dot in a newspaper picture) that can be identified by a computer. The more pixels, the higher the picture quality.

resolution The characteristic of a camera that determines the sharpness of the picture received. The lower a camera's resolution, the less fine picture detail it can show. Resolution is influenced by the imaging device, the lens, and the television set that shows the camera picture.

saturation The color attribute that describes a color's richness or strength.

signal-to-noise (S/N) ratio The relation of the strength of the desired signal to the accompanying electronic interference (the noise). A high S/N ratio is desirable (strong video or audio signal relative to weak noise).

studio camera Heavy, high-quality camera and zoom lens that cannot be maneuvered properly without the aid of a pedestal or some other type of camera mount.

sync Electronic pulses that synchronize the scanning in the various video origination sources (studio camera, remote cameras) and various recording, processing, and reproduction sources (videotape, monitors, television receivers).

sync generator Part of the camera chain; produces electronic synchronization pulses.

3.1

How Television Cameras Work

To use computer jargon, television cameras have become user-friendly, yet you still need some basic knowledge of how a camera works so that you can maximize its potential and understand how it affects the rest of a production. This section takes a close look at the camera.

▶ **PARTS OF THE CAMERA**
The lens, the camera itself, and the viewfinder

▶ **FROM LIGHT TO VIDEO SIGNAL**
The beam splitter and the imaging device

▶ **THE CAMERA CHAIN**
The camera head, camera control unit, sync generator, and power supply

▶ **TYPES OF CAMERAS**
Analog and digital cameras, studio cameras, ENG/EFP cameras and camcorders, and consumer camcorders

▶ **ELECTRONIC CHARACTERISTICS**
Aspect ratio, resolution, light sensitivity and operating light level, gain, video noise and signal-to-noise ratio, image blur and electronic shutter, smear and moiré, and contrast

▶ **OPERATIONAL CHARACTERISTICS**
Power supply, camera cable, connectors, filter wheel, viewfinder, tally light, intercom, and additional ENG/EFP elements

PARTS OF THE CAMERA

When you take vacation pictures with your camcorder, probably the last thing on your mind is what makes a video camera work. But if you were to open up a camera (not recommended) and see the myriad electronic elements and circuits, you would probably wonder how it functions at all. Despite the electronic complexity, all television cameras (including the consumer video cameras) consist of three main parts.

The first is the *lens,* which selects a certain field of view and produces a small optical image of it. The second part is the camera itself, with its *imaging,* or *pickup, device* that converts the optical image as delivered by the lens into electrical signals. The third is the *viewfinder,* which shows a small video image of what the lens is seeing. Some cameras have a small fold-out screen that does not require you to look through an eyepiece to see the camera picture. **SEE 3.1**

3.1 PARTS OF THE CAMERA

The main parts of a television (video) camera are the lens, the camera itself with the imaging device, and the viewfinder.

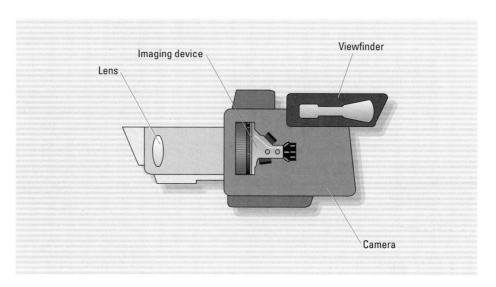

FROM LIGHT TO VIDEO SIGNAL

All television cameras, whether digital or analog, big or small, work on the same basic principle: the conversion of an optical image into electrical signals that are reconverted by a television set into visible screen images. **SEE 3.2** Specifically, the light that is reflected off an object is gathered by a lens and focused on the imaging (pickup) device. The imaging device is the principal camera element that transduces (converts) the light into electric energy—the video (picture) signal. That signal is then amplified and processed so that it can be reconverted into visible screen images.

With these basic camera functions in mind, we can examine step-by-step the elements and processes involved in the transformation of light images into color

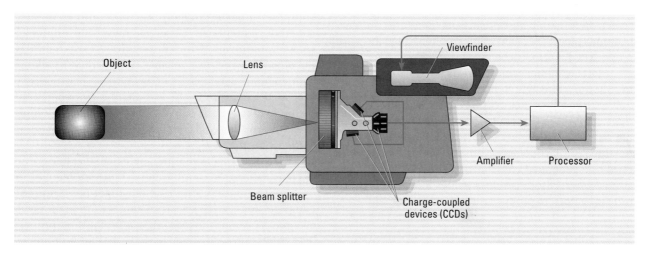

3.2 BASIC CAMERA FUNCTIONS

The light reflected off the object is gathered by the lens and focused on the beam splitter, which splits the white light of the image into red, green, and blue light beams. These beams are directed toward their respective CCDs, which transform the RGB light into electrical RGB signals; these are amplified and processed and then reconverted into video pictures by the viewfinder.

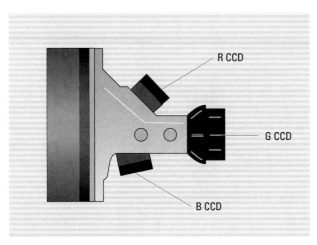

3.3 BEAM SPLITTER
The beam splitter splits the incoming white light (representing the picture as seen by the lens) into RGB (red, green, and blue) light beams and directs them to their respective CCDs.

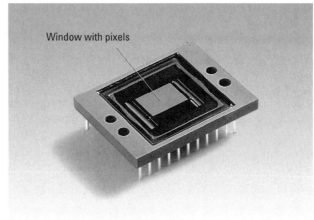

3.4 CHARGE-COUPLED DEVICE
The CCD holds many rows of thousands of pixels, each of which transforms light that enters through the little chip window into an electric charge.

television images. Specifically, we look at (1) the beam splitter and (2) the imaging device.

The Beam Splitter

The *beam splitter* consists of various prisms and/or filters that separate the white light that passes through the camera lens into the three light primaries—red, green, and blue, usually referred to as *RGB*. As discussed later in this chapter, these three primaries are then electronically "mixed" into the many colors you see on the television screen. Because all these prisms and filters are contained in a small block, the beam splitter is often called the *prism block*. **SEE 3.3 AND COLOR PLATE 2**

Most consumer camcorders do not use a prism block to split the white light into the three RGB primaries, but only a striped filter. **SEE COLOR PLATE 3** The filter, located right behind the camera lens, consists of many narrow filter stripes that separate the incoming white light into the three primary colors or into only two colors, with the third one generated electronically in the camera. Some striped filters also have clear stripes in addition to two primary colors, to produce the luminance signal.

The Imaging Device

Once the white light that enters through the lens has been divided into the three primary colors, each light beam must be translated into electrical signals. The principal

electronic component that converts light into electricity is called the *imaging device*. This imaging, or pickup, device consists of a small (about, or less than, the size of a postage stamp with a small window) solid-state device normally called a **chip** or, more technical, a **charge-coupled device (CCD)**. The CCD contains hundreds of thousands of image-sensing elements, called **pixels** (a word made up of *pix*, for picture, and *els* for elements), that are arranged in horizontal and vertical rows. **SEE 3.4**

Pixels function very much like tiles that make up a complete mosaic image. A certain amount of such concrete elements are obviously needed to produce a recognizable image. If there are relatively few mosaic tiles, the object may be recognizable, but the picture will not contain much detail. **SEE COLOR PLATE 4** The more and the smaller the tiles in the mosaic, the more detail the picture will have. The same is true for CCDs: The more pixels the imaging chip contains, the higher the resolution of the video image.

Each pixel is a discrete image element that transforms its color and brightness information into a specific electric charge. In digital cameras each pixel has a unique computer address. The electric charges from all the pixels eventually become the video signals for the three primary light colors. These RGB signals make up the *chrominance* (color) information, or the *C signal*. The black-and-white, or *luminance*, information is provided by an additional signal, the *Y signal* (see section 3.2).

THE CAMERA CHAIN

When looking at a high-quality studio camera, you can see that it is connected by cable to an electrical outlet. This cable connects the camera to a chain of equipment necessary to produce pictures. The major parts of such a *camera chain* are (1) the actual camera, called the *camera head* because it is at the head of the chain; (2) the *camera control unit*, or *CCU;* (3) the *sync generator* that provides the synchronization pulses to keep the scanning of the various pieces of television equipment in step; and (4) the power supply. **SEE 3.5**

The Camera Control Unit

Each studio camera has its own *camera control unit (CCU).* The CCU performs two main functions: setup and control. During setup each camera is adjusted for the correct color rendition, the white balance (adjusting three color signals so that they reproduce white under a variety of lighting conditions), the proper contrast range between the brightest and darkest areas of a scene, and the brightness steps within this range.

Assuming that the cameras are set up properly and have fair stability (which means that they retain their setup values), the video operator (VO) usually need control only "master black" or "pedestal" (adjusting the camera for the darkest part of the scene), and the "white level" or "iris" (adjusting the *f*-stop of the lens so that it

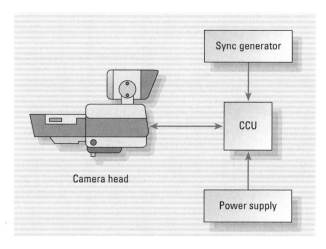

3.5 STANDARD STUDIO CAMERA CHAIN
The standard camera chain consists of the camera head (the actual camera), the camera control unit (CCU), the sync generator, and the power supply.

will permit only the desired amount of light to reach the imaging device). The VO has two primary instruments for checking the relative quality of the color signal: the *waveform monitor,* also called the *oscilloscope,* that displays the luminance (brightness) information, and the *vector scope* that shows the chrominance (color) signals. Both displays enable the VO to achieve optimal pictures. **SEE 3.6**

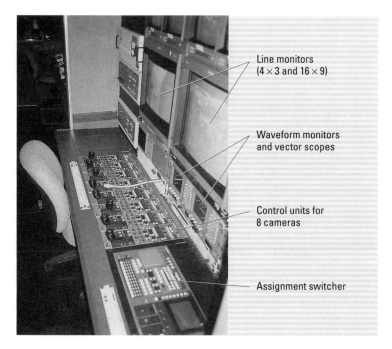

Line monitors
(4 × 3 and 16 × 9)

Waveform monitors
and vector scopes

Control units for
8 cameras

Assignment switcher

3.6 CAMERA CONTROL UNIT
The CCU adjusts the camera for optimal color and brightness and can adjust for varying lighting conditions.

Sometimes, when the actual operational controls are separated from the CCU, we speak of a *remote control unit (RCU)* or, more accurate, of an *operation control panel (OCP)*. For example, the actual CCUs may be located in master control, but the OCPs are in the studio control room. This arrangement allows the video operator to do the initial camera setup in master control and then sit in the control room with the production crew and "shade" the pictures (maintain optimal picture quality) according not only to technical standards, but also to the aesthetic requirements of the production. Now you know why the VO is also called a *shader*. The term *RCU* also refers to a small CCU that can be taken to EFP locations to make field cameras perform at optimal levels.

The Sync Generator and Power Supply

The *sync generator* produces electronic synchronization pulses—*sync*—that keep in step the scanning in the various pieces of equipment (cameras, monitors, and videotape recorders). A *genlock* provides various pieces of studio equipment with a general synchronization pulse, called *house sync*. Through the genlocking process, the scanning of video signals is perfectly synchronized, allowing you to switch among and intermix the video signals of various cameras and/or videotape recorders without the use of additional digital equipment.

The *power supply* generates the electricity (direct current) that drives the television equipment. In a studio the power supply converts AC (alternating current) to DC (direct current) power and feeds it to the cameras.

The camera cable feeds all the CCU functions to the camera and transports the video signals from the camera back to the CCU.

ENG EFP Field (ENG/EFP) cameras and all camcorders are self-contained, which means that the camera itself holds all the elements of the chain to produce and deliver acceptable video images to the VTR (videotape recorder) that is either built into the camera, attached to it, or connected to it by cable. The only part of the normal camera chain that can be detached from the field camera or camcorder is the power supply—the battery. All other controls are solidly built-in and automated. Some of the more sophisticated field cameras accept *external sync*, which means that they can be genlocked with other cameras (connected to a common sync signal).

Most cameras have built-in control equipment that can execute the CCU control functions automatically. Why, then, bother with a CCU or RCU if you can have the camera do it automatically? Because the automated controls cannot exercise aesthetic judgment; that is, they cannot adjust the camera to deliver pictures that suit the artistic rather than routine technical requirements.

TYPES OF CAMERAS

Television cameras can be classified by their electronic makeup and by how they are used. As you may have guessed, cameras grouped by their electronic makeup are either analog or digital. Cameras classified by their function are for studio or ENG/EFP use.

Analog and Digital Cameras

All cameras, analog or digital, large or small, start out with an analog video signal. The light that is transported through the lens to the beam splitter and from there to the imaging device remains analog throughout. Even after the translation of the three RGB light beams by the CCD, the resulting video signals are still analog. But from there analog and digital part company.

In the analog camera, the video signal remains analog throughout the processing inside the camera and during the recording, assuming that the VTR is also analog. In the digital camera, however, the analog RGB video signals are digitized and processed right after leaving the CCDs.

Although digital signals are much more robust than analog ones, which means that they are less prone to distortion, they are not automatically high-definition. Several brands of digital cameras on the market are, despite their superior picture quality, still operating on the traditional 525-line, 30 frames-per-second NTSC system and, therefore, not considered high-definition. Only the 720p and 1080i systems can be considered truly high-definition. In fact, purists admit only the 1080i system into that class, relegating the 720p to ATV (advanced television).

Despite the difference between analog and digital, high-end or low-end, television cameras fall into three groups: (1) studio cameras, (2) ENG/EFP cameras and camcorders, and (3) consumer camcorders. This classification is based on the primary production function of the camera, not on its electronic makeup. Regardless of whether a camera is analog or digital, it is constructed with a specific function and application in mind. Some camera types are better suited for studio use, others for the coverage of a downtown fire or the production of a documentary on pollution, and still others for taking along on vacation to record some of the more memorable sights.

Studio Cameras

The term *studio camera* is generally used to describe high-quality cameras, including *high-definition television (HDTV) cameras,* that are so heavy they cannot be maneuvered properly without the aid of a pedestal or some other type of camera mount. **SEE 3.7** Studio cameras are used for various studio productions, such as news, interviews, and panel shows, for daily serial dramas, situation comedies, or instructional shows that require high-quality video. But you can also see these cameras used in such "field" locations as concert and convention halls, football and baseball stadiums, tennis courts, or medical facilities.

The obvious difference between the standard studio camera and ENG/EFP and consumer cameras is that studio cameras can function only as part of a camera chain, whereas all other camera types can be self-contained, capable of delivering a video signal to the VTR without any other peripheral control equipment. Because the picture quality of studio cameras is determined by the VO who is operating the CCU, there are relatively few buttons on studio cameras compared with ENG/EFP cameras.

Considering that you can get pretty good pictures from a camera that fits into a briefcase, why bother with such heavy cameras and the rest of the camera chain? As indicated, the overriding criteria for the use of studio cameras are picture quality and control. But *quality* is a relative term. In many productions the extra quality and picture control achieved with studio cameras is not worth the additional time and expense necessary for operating such cameras. For example, if you are to get a picture of an approaching tornado, you are probably not thinking about optimum picture quality. Your attention is on getting the shot and then getting out of harm's way as quickly as possible. But if picture quality is paramount, such as in the production of commercials, medical shows, or dramas, you would undoubtedly choose a high-end studio camera.

The question of whether to use a 720p or a 1080i digital studio camera depends on its primary use. The 720p format will produce high-quality pictures that are more than sufficient for most local studio productions, such as news, interviews, and sports. If, however, you use studio cameras primarily for productions that depend on extremely fine detail, such as medical shows, you should

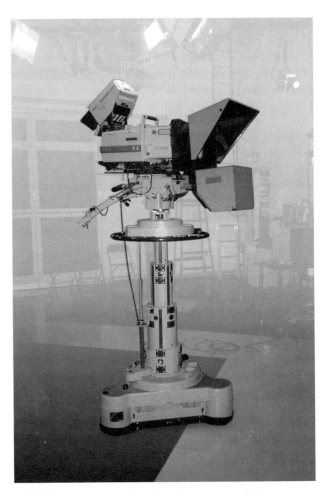

3.7 STUDIO CAMERA ON STUDIO PEDESTAL
Studio cameras have high-quality lenses and CCDs. They are quality-controlled by the CCU. Studio cameras are too heavy to be carried and are mounted on a heavy tripod or studio pedestal.

probably opt for the 1080i format. The high-quality pictures of studio cameras are also important if you anticipate a great amount of postproduction. In this case, the digital camera reigns supreme. The rule of thumb is: *The more postproduction you anticipate, the higher quality the original video should be.*

ENG/EFP Cameras and Camcorders

ENG EFP As mentioned before, the cameras for *ENG (electronic news gathering)* and *EFP (electronic field production)* are portable, which means that they are usually carried by a camera operator or put on a simple tripod. They are also self-contained and hold the whole camera chain in the small camera head. With their built-in control equipment, ***ENG/EFP cameras and camcorders*** are designed to produce high-quality pictures (video signals) that can be recorded on a separate VTR, a small VTR that is docked with the camera, or a built-in VTR. As noted, when docked with a VTR or with a built-in VTR the camera forms a ***camcorder***. **SEE 3.8**

ENG/EFP camcorders operate on the same basic principle as the small-format consumer model, except that the CCDs and video recording devices are of much higher quality. As you can see, the ENG/EFP camera has many more buttons and switches than a studio camera or a home camcorder, mainly because the video control

(CCU) functions, the VTR operation, and the audio control functions must be managed by the camera operator. Fortunately, you can switch many of these control functions to an automatic mode, much as you can when running a consumer camcorder. These automatic control features make it possible to produce acceptable pictures even in drastically changing conditions without having to readjust the camera.

You would think that high-quality digital ENG/EFP cameras and camcorders would be much larger than the high-quality analog ones. Fortunately, this is not the case. In fact, some of the high-quality digital cameras and camcorders are even smaller and lighter than their analog counterparts. **SEE 3.9**

In addition, some of the low-end digital camcorders, which nevertheless produce professional-quality video and audio, are so small that they look more like consumer camcorders than professional ENG/EFP models. **SEE 3.10**

The picture quality of the high-end ENG/EFP camera is so good that it is frequently used as a studio camera. In order to make it operationally compatible with regular studio cameras, the ENG/EFP model is placed in a specially made camera frame; a large external tally light is added; the small (1-inch) eyepiece viewfinder is replaced with a larger (5- or 7-inch) one; and zoom and focus controls are added which can be operated from the panning handles. **SEE 3.11** The most important con-

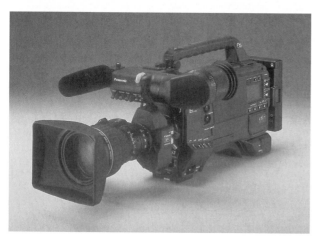

3.8 ENG/EFP CAMCORDER
This one-piece camcorder has its VTR permanently attached. Other models have a dockable VTR, which can be used independently of the camera.

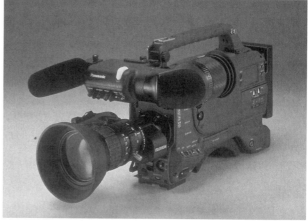

3.9 DIGITAL CAMCORDER
Although digital camcorders produce high-quality pictures, they are not larger than analog camcorders. Such high-quality camcorders are often smaller and lighter than analog models, but produce superior pictures.

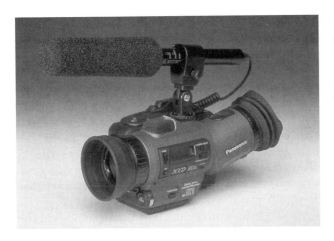

3.10 DTV CAMCORDER

This DTV (digital television) camcorder looks like a consumer model but produces amazingly good-quality video and sound.

version factor, however, is the connection of the ENG/EFP camera to a CCU so that it can be controlled just like a standard studio camera.

Consumer Camcorders

The camcorders available in department or discount electronics stores are called *consumer* camcorders. Unlike the dockable ENG/EFP camera, which you can change from a regular ENG/EFP camera to a camcorder by docking it with the VTR, the camera and VTR of the consumer camcorder are always built as a single, inseparable unit. Despite the dazzling variety advertised in the Sunday papers, most have a single-chip imaging device and more or less the same automated features, such as *auto-focus*, which focuses on what the camera believes to be your target object, and *auto-iris*, which regulates the incoming light. Some high-end consumer

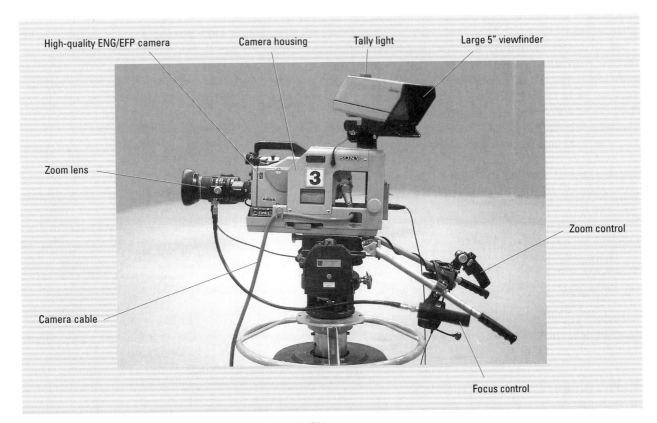

3.11 ENG/EFP CAMERA IN STUDIO CONFIGURATION

When converted for studio use, the high-quality ENG/EFP camera is mounted into a camera housing and equipped with a lens that is more suitable for studio operation, cable controls for zoom and focus, a large (5- or 7-inch) viewfinder, and an external tally light.

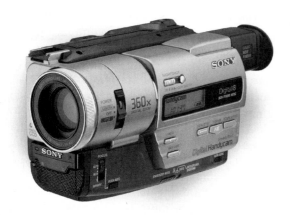

3.12 CONSUMER CAMCORDER

Small consumer camcorders have controls similar to those of professional models, with many of the functions fully automated. Most consumer camcorders have a single CCD imaging device, but some high-end models have three CCDs.

camcorders have three CCDs that deliver higher-quality pictures. **SEE 3.12**

Consumer camcorders differ most markedly, however, in the videotape section. Some of these camcorders use ½-inch videotape; others use the much smaller 8mm (a little more than ¼-inch) videotape. Because of ever-improving electronics, the size of the videotape is no longer a valid indication of picture quality. As a matter of fact, such professional digital camcorders as DVCAM or DVCPRO deliver high-quality pictures that are recorded on a ¼-inch (6.35mm) tape. In general, a three-chip (three-CCD) camcorder is better than a one-chip one, and a digital camcorder is better than an analog one. The various videotape recording methods are explored in chapter 12.

There is no better way to learn how a specific camera works than to use it for a while in a variety of production situations. You can cut this learning process short and save nerves and equipment, however, by first acquainting yourself with the major electronic and operational characteristics of various camera types.

ELECTRONIC CHARACTERISTICS

There are certain electronic characteristics common to all television cameras: (1) aspect ratio, (2) resolution, (3) light sensitivity and operating light level, (4) gain, (5) video noise and signal-to-noise ratio, (6) image blur and electronic shutter, (7) smear and moiré, and (8) contrast.

Aspect Ratio

As you recall from chapter 2, one of the most noticeable changes when moving to digital HDTV is the horizontally stretched 16×9 *aspect ratio.* This means that the traditional 4 × 3 aspect ratio for camera viewfinders and all receivers will change to 16 × 9. Because the 4 × 3 aspect ratio will be the TV standard for some time to come, and also for playing back programs that were produced in the 4 × 3 format, digital and some analog cameras will be switchable from one ratio to the other. This switchover occurs in the CCD imaging device. Regardless of whether the transition is from 16 × 9 to 4 × 3 or from 4 × 3 to 16 × 9, some CCD pixels will be lost, which inevitably affects the image resolution. Section 3.2 explores such aspect ratio changes in more detail.

Resolution

Resolution refers to the detail in the picture and is the major factor that distinguishes traditional television from ATV and HDTV pictures. **SEE 3.13 AND 3.14** Figure 3.14 has considerably more pixels per image area than figure 3.13. The latter has, therefore, the higher resolution.

The quality of a television camera is often determined by the degree of resolution of the video it produces. High-quality cameras produce high-resolution pictures; lower-quality cameras produce pictures of lower resolution. The picture resolution a camera can deliver depends on various factors, such as the quality of the lens, the number of pixels of the CCD, and the general signal processing.

A camera with a single CCD produces by necessity lower-resolution pictures than the three-chip cameras. The single CCD of low-end professional or consumer cameras has generally fewer pixel sensors than the chips in high-quality cameras. Also, the CCD in a single-chip camera must provide all the chrominance and luminance information normally done by three separate chips. The resolution of the picture finally seen on TV depends further on the videotape recording system, the transmission system, and ultimately the television set. If any one of these factors is basically low-resolution, the final outcome will be low-resolution. As you can see once again, television operates as a system in which each element is dependent on the proper functioning of all the others.

In print, resolution is often measured in *dpi,* which means *dots* (pixels) *per inch.* CCDs are usually measured by the total number of pixels. The CCDs in a good digital camera may have more than 400,000 pixels each, but a CCD in a high-definition camera may have close to

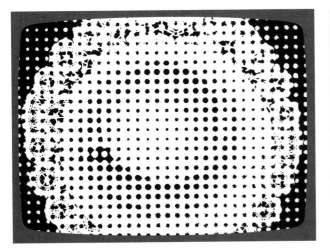

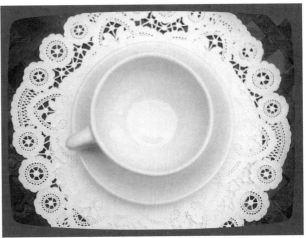

3.13 LOW-RESOLUTION IMAGE
This low-resolution picture has relatively few pixels that make up the image.

3.14 HIGH-RESOLUTION IMAGE
This high-resolution picture has a relatively high number of pixels that make up the image.

<u>2 million.</u> The resolution of television cameras and monitors is more commonly measured by the number of lines that make up the image.

You may have heard advertisements for a high-quality camera boasting of more than 700 lines of resolution. But how is this possible if the NTSC system has only 525 scanning lines? To explain this rather confusing concept, let's take another close look at figure 3.13. Note that the white dots form horizontal as well as vertical lines. Line up a piece of paper horizontally with the first row of dots: You perceive a horizontal line. To count the lines, slide the paper down toward the bottom

of the simulated screen. You may have counted the horizontal lines in figure 3.13, but on the television screen you would have counted the vertical lines. Because, in the context of resolution, you moved the paper vertically to count the number of scanning lines, they are para-doxically called *vertical lines of resolution*. In effect, resolution is measured by the way the lines are *stacked*. Standard NTSC television has a vertical stack of 525 lines. In HDTV the 1,080 scanning lines increase the vertical resolution, because the vertical stack is made up of more than twice the number of lines. **SEE 3.15** When trying to count the horizontal television lines, you need to line up

3.15 VERTICAL DETAIL
(LINES OF RESOLUTION)
To measure vertical detail, we count the vertical stack of horizontal (scanning) lines. The more lines the vertical stack contains, the higher the resolution. The number of lines is fixed by the system: The NTSC system has 525 lines, of which only 486 are visible on the screen; ATV and HDTV systems have 720 and 1,080 active (visible) lines, respectively.

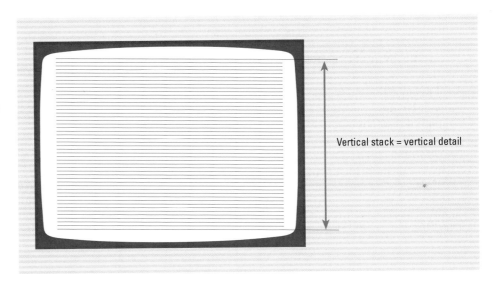

Vertical stack = vertical detail

3.16 HORIZONTAL DETAIL (LINES OF RESOLUTION)

To measure horizontal detail, we count the dots (pixels) of each horizontal line and then connect them vertically, which yields a horizontal stack of vertical lines. The more lines the horizontal stack contains (reading from left to right), the higher the resolution. This horizontal stack can contain many more lines (such as 800) than the vertical stack.

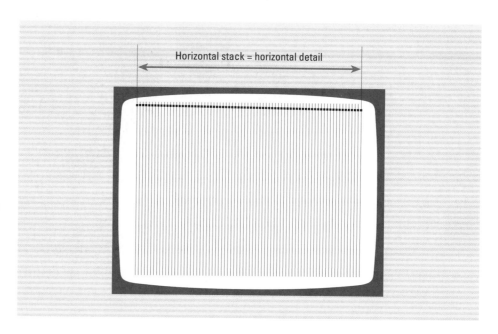

Horizontal stack = horizontal detail

the piece of paper with the vertical rows of dots at the far left and slide it horizontally to screen-right. As you can see, each dot forms the beginning of another line. Because the lines are stacked horizontally, they are called *horizontal lines of resolution.* If you count 720 dots making up the horizontal line, it is a horizontal resolution of 720 lines, which, by the way, is considered remarkably good for video. **SEE 3.16**

Because such a perceptual switch of horizontal and vertical in terms of resolution is confusing even for the engineering experts, some authors suggest calling the dots that make up the resolution in the horizontal direction *horizontal detail,* and those that make up the resolution in the vertical direction, *vertical detail.*[1] As you can clearly see, you can have many more dots horizontally than vertically; hence the horizontal resolution can have 700 or more "lines," even if the vertical detail is limited to 525 "lines."

Image enhancers are used in some cameras to boost the apparent resolution power. These electronic circuits are designed to sharpen the contour of the picture information, but they do not increase the number of pixels. You will not see more picture detail, but rather a sharper

demarcation between one picture area and the next. Human perception translates this outline into a higher resolution and hence a sharper, higher-definition picture.

Light Sensitivity and Operating Light Level

Because it is the job of the camera imaging device to *transduce* (convert) light into electricity, the camera obviously needs light to produce a video signal. But just how much light is required to produce an adequate signal? The answer depends on the light sensitivity of the imaging device and how much light the lens is able to transmit.

You may think that the single-chip (single-CCD) camera would need less light than a three-chip camera to operate effectively, because the incoming light (as transmitted by the lens) does not have to be split into RGB and directed to three CCDs. Unfortunately, the single-chip cameras in general have an inferior CCD that is not as light sensitive as the CCDs in high-quality cameras. Also, the striped filter that divides the incoming white light into RGB beams absorbs so much light that, in general, good three-chip cameras can tolerate the same or even lower operating light levels as the single-chip cameras.

The minimum **operating light level** under which cameras perform adequately is not always easy to define. It is determined by how much light the camera lens admits and how much the video signal can be boosted elec-

---

1. Andrew F. Inglis and Arch C. Luther, *Video Engineering,* 2d ed. (New York: McGraw-Hill, 1996), p. 6.

3.17 MANUAL GAIN CONTROL

The gain control compensates for low light levels. The higher the gain, the lower the light level can be. High gain causes video noise.

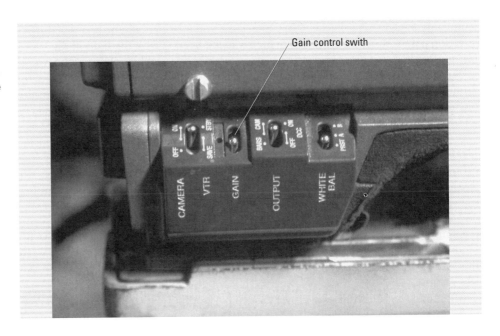

Gain control swith

Gain

A camera can produce pictures in extremely low light levels because it has the ability to boost the video signal electronically—a feature called *gain*. In effect, the electronic gain is fooling the camera into believing that it has adequate light. In studio cameras the gain is adjusted through the CCU. In ENG/EFP cameras it is controlled by a gain control switch. By flipping the switch to one of the two or four boosting positions, marked by units of *dB* (decibels), such as a +6 and +12 dB and/or a +9 and +18 dB gain, you can make the camera "see" in very dim light. **SEE 3.17** When the switch is in the high-gain position (such as +12 dB), most ENG/EFP cameras can produce pictures in light levels as low as 10 lux, or less than 1 foot-candle, which is barely enough light for you to find your way around.

The camera is not fooled that easily, however. The higher the gain, the more the picture suffers from excessive video noise (electronic interference) and color distortion—called *artifacts*. Nevertheless, because of improved low-noise CCDs, more and more ENG/EFP cameras follow the consumer camcorder's lead, giving you a choice to switch between the manual and automatic gain controls. The advantage of an automatic gain control is that you can move from bright outdoor light to a dark interior or vice versa without having to reset the

tronically—a process called *gain*—before the picture begins to deteriorate. To help us judge the relative light sensitivity of cameras, they are usually rated by a minimum operating light level (such as 2 lux, or 10 foot-candles) at which they are capable of producing acceptable pictures; *acceptable* means here that the video image is relatively free of color distortion and electronic noise, which shows up as black-and-white or colored dots in the dark picture areas.

Despite improvements, the optimal operating light level of professional cameras is still about 2,000 lux (approximately 200 foot-candles), with the lens set at an *f*-stop range of 5.6 to 8.0. These *f*-stops deliver optimally sharp pictures. Some camera viewfinders can display a zebra-striped pattern that starts pulsating when the overall levels are too high. You can then adjust the *f*-stop to limit the light transmitted by the lens (see chapters 4 and 7). Despite claims that you can use camcorders in lighting conditions as low as 1 lux (one-tenth of a foot-candle), you will find that pictures look much better with higher minimum light levels. Consumer camcorders are not normally obliged to meet broadcast standards, so you can shoot an underlighted scene even if the picture quality suffers somewhat. For more about the light standards of lux and foot-candles, and their relationship to *f*-stops, see chapters 4 and 7.

gain. Such a feature is especially welcome when you are covering a news story that involves people walking from the sunlit street to a dim hotel lobby or dark corridor. In general, digital cameras can tolerate a higher gain than analog cameras before the picture begins to show obvious artifacts. Therefore, their gain control switches go up to +30 dB.

Video Noise and Signal-to-Noise Ratio

You may have wondered what "noise" has to do with picture. The term *noise* is borrowed from the audio field and applied to unwanted interference in video. You can recognize "noisy" pictures quite readily by the amount of "snow"—white or colored vibrating spots, or artifacts, that appear throughout an image and cause it to become less distinct.

Technically, video noise works very much like audio noise. When playing regular (analog) audiotapes, you can hear the speakers hiss a little as soon as you turn on the system. But as soon as the music starts, you are no longer aware of the hiss. Only when the music is very soft are you again aware of the hiss, hum, or rumble. So long as the signal (the music) is stronger than the noise (the hiss), you won't perceive the noise. The same is true of video noise. If the picture signal is strong (mainly because the imaging device receives adequate light), it will suppress the snow. This relationship between signal and noise is appropriately enough called *signal-to-noise (S/N) ratio*. A high S/N ratio is desirable. It means that the signal is high (strong picture information) relative to the noise (picture interference) under normal operating conditions.

Image Blur and Electronic Shutter

One of the negative aspects of the CCD imaging device is that it tends to produce blur in pictures of fast-moving objects, very much like photos taken with a regular still camera at slow shutter speeds. For example, if a yellow tennis ball moves from camera-left to camera-right at high speed, the ball does not appear sharp and clear throughout its travel across the screen, but looks blurred and even leaves a trail. To avoid this blur and get a sharp image of a fast-moving object, CCD cameras are equipped with an electronic shutter.

Like the mechanical shutter on the still camera, the electronic shutter controls the amount of time that light is received by the chip. The slower the shutter speed, the longer the pixels of the CCD imaging surface are charged with the light of the traveling ball and the more the ball will blur. The higher the shutter speed, the less time the pixels are charged with the light of the moving ball, thus greatly reducing or eliminating the blur. But because the increased shutter speed reduces the light received by the CCD, the yellow ball will look considerably darker than without electronic shutter. As with a regular still camera, the faster the shutter speed, the more light the camera requires. Most professional CCD cameras (studio or ENG/EFP) have a shutter speed that ranges from $\frac{1}{60}$ to $\frac{1}{2,000}$ second. Digital camcorders can go to $\frac{1}{4,000}$ second or even higher.

Fortunately, most high-action events that require high shutter speeds occur in plenty of outdoor or indoor light.

Smear and Moiré

Both smear and moiré are specific forms of video noise. On occasion, extremely bright highlights or certain colors (especially bright reds) cause smears in the camera picture. *Smears* show up adjacent to highlights as dim bands that weave from the top of the picture to the bottom. The highly saturated color of a red dress may bleed into the background scenery, or the red lipstick color may extend beyond the mouth. Digital cameras with high-quality CCDs are practically smear-free.

Moiré interference shows up in the picture as vibrating patterns of rainbow colors. **SEE COLOR PLATE 5** You can see the *moiré effect* on a television screen when the camera shoots very narrow and highly contrasting patterns, such as the herringbone pattern on a jacket. The camera system simply cannot keep up with the rapid change from white to black and the new pattern frequency, and it goes a little crazy. Although the more expensive studio monitors have moiré compression circuits built-in, the ordinary television set does not. Therefore, even when using digital cameras, showing such moiré-producing patterns should be avoided.

Contrast

The range of contrast between the brightest and darkest picture areas that the video camera can reproduce accurately is relatively limited. That limit, called *contrast range*, is expressed as a ratio. The normal *contrast ratio* is 40:1, meaning that the brightest picture area can be only forty times brighter than the darkest one for optimal

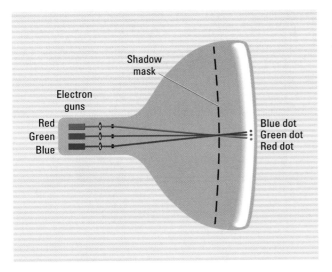

CP1 IMAGE FORMATION FOR COLOR TELEVISION

The color receiver has three electron guns, each responsible for a red, green, and blue signal. Each of the beams is assigned to its color dots.

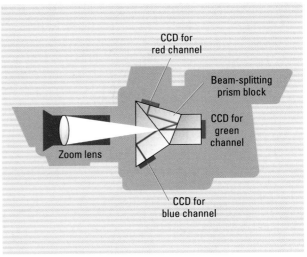

CP2 RGB BEAM SPLITTER

The prism block consists of prisms and filters that split the incoming white light into the three additive colors—red, green, and blue—and direct these into their corresponding CCDs.

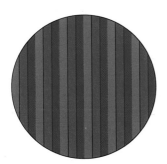

CP3 STRIPED FILTER

Most consumer camcorders have only one imaging chip, so they use a striped filter, located in front of the surface of the CCD. The filter divides the white light into RGB light beams. Each of these colors is then transduced (changed) by the single CCD into three color RGB video signals.

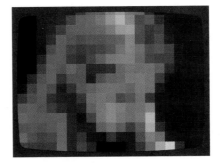

CP4 PIXELIZED SUBJECT

Pixels function very much like tiles that make up a complete mosaic image. Relatively few mosaic tiles—pixels— do not contain much detail. The more and the smaller the pixels, the sharper the picture will look.

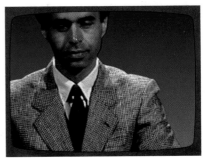

CP5 MOIRÉ PATTERN

Moiré is a visual interference pattern that occurs when the television scan lines clash with the narrow and highly contrasting pattern.

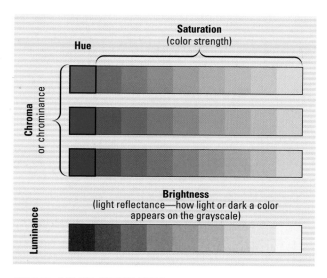

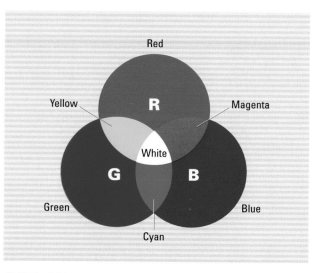

CP6 COLOR ATTRIBUTES

Hue is the term used for the base color—blue, green, yellow, and so on. *Saturation* refers to the purity and intensity of the color. *Brightness,* or *luminance,* describes the degree of reflectance—how light or dark a color appears on the grayscale.

CP7 ADDITIVE COLOR MIXING

When mixing colored light, the additive primaries are red, green, and blue. All other colors can be achieved by mixing certain quantities of red, green, and blue light. For example, the additive mixture of red and green light produces yellow.

CP8 BRIGHTNESS: INSUFFICIENT CONTRAST

Although the hue is sufficiently different for this letter to show up on the blue background of the color television set, it is barely readable on a black-and-white receiver. The brightness contrast is insufficient for good monochrome reproduction.

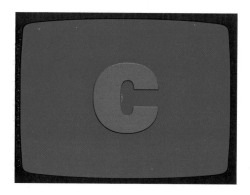

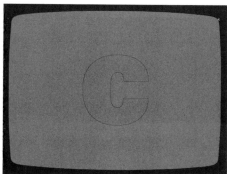

CP9 BRIGHTNESS: GOOD CONTRAST

The hues used in this picture have enough difference in brightness to show up equally well on both a color and black-and-white receiver.

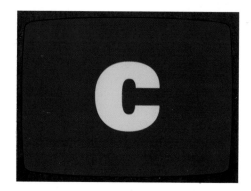

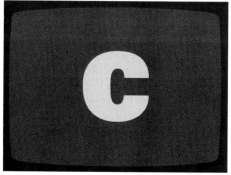

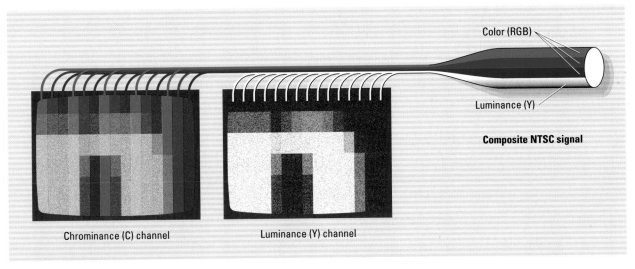

Chrominance (C) channel   Luminance (Y) channel

CP10 COMPOSITE SYSTEM

The composite system uses a video signal that combines the luminance "Y" (brightness) and color "C" information. It needs a single wire to be transported and recorded on videotape as a single signal. It is the standard NTSC system.

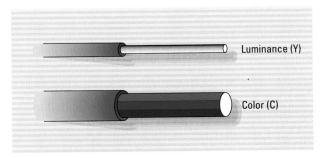

CP11 Y/C COMPONENT SYSTEM

The Y/C component system separates the Y (luminance) and C (color) information, but combines the two signals on the videotape. It needs two wires to transport the two separate signals.

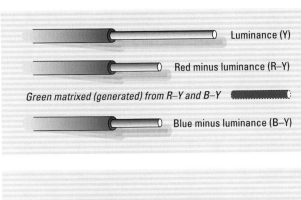

CP12 Y/COLOR DIFFERENCE COMPONENT SYSTEM

Like the RGB component system, the Y/color difference component system needs three wires to transport the three component signals: the Y (luminance) signal, the $R-Y$ (red minus luminance) signal and the $B-Y$ (blue minus luminance) signal. The green signal is then matrixed (generated) from these signals.

CP13 RBG COMPONENT SYSTEM

The RGB component system (also called the RGB system) separates the three RGB signals throughout the recording process. It needs three wires to transport the signals.

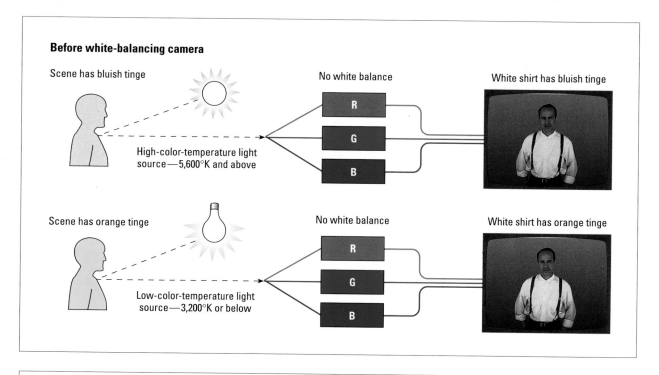

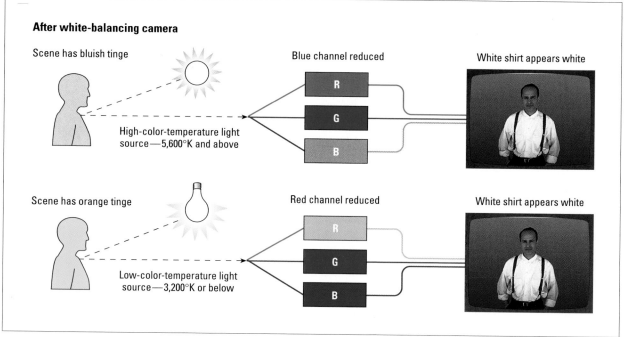

CP14 WHITE BALANCE

To counteract tinting caused by variations in color temperature, it is necessary to white-balance the camera. This adjusts the RGB channels to compensate for the unwanted color cast and make white look white.

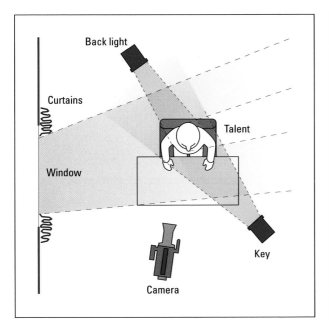

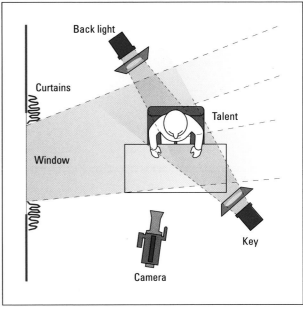

CP15 MATCHING COLOR TEMPERATURES OF DIFFERENT LIGHT SOURCES

A When illuminating an object with indoor light mixed with outdoor light coming through a window, you need to equalize the color temperatures of both light sources to ensure proper white-balancing.

B To equalize the color temperatures, you can put light-blue gels on the indoor lighting instruments to raise their 3,200°K color temperature to the 5,600°K outdoor standard.

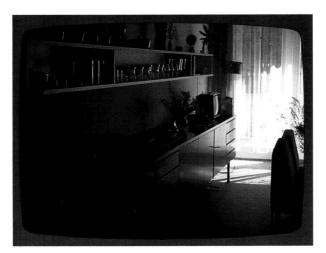

CP16 INDOOR ILLUMINATION

This indoor scene relies heavily on a back light simulating the morning sun streaming through the window. Note that the back light is coming from behind the set shining into the room. Although technically a back light, it takes on the function of a background light.

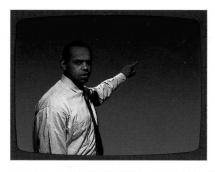
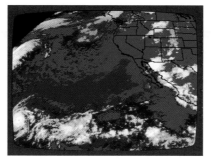
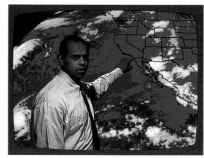

CP17 CHROMA-KEY EFFECT: WEATHERCAST

A In this chroma key, the weathercaster stands in front of a blue background.

B During the key, the blue background is replaced by this computer-enhanced satellite photo.

C The weathercaster seems to be standing in front of the satellite photo.

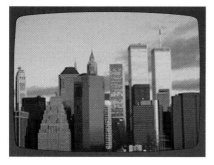
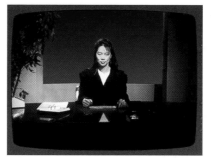
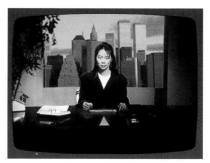

CP18 CHROMA-KEY EFFECT: WINDOW

A In this chroma key, camera 1 is on a studio card with a photo of the view.

B Camera 2 focuses on the office set in front of a blue chroma-key panel.

C Through chroma keying, there seems to be a picture window behind the executive sitting at her desk.

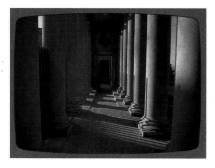
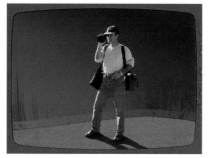
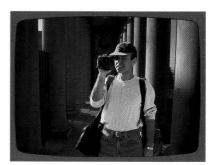

CP19 CHROMA-KEY EFFECT: SIMULATED LOCATION

A The source for the background image is a video frame of the museum exterior from the ESS system.

B The studio camera focuses on the actor playing a tourist in front of a blue chroma-key drape.

C All blue areas are replaced by the background image. The tourist appears to be in front of the museum.

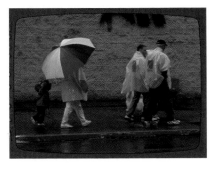
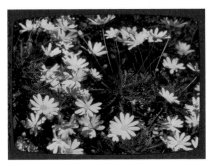
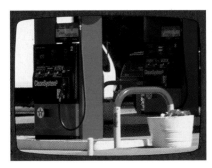

CP20 HIGH-ENERGY COLORS

The energy of a color is mainly determined by its saturation. High-energy colors are highly saturated hues, usually in the red and yellow end of the spectrum. They are especially effective when set against a low-energy background.

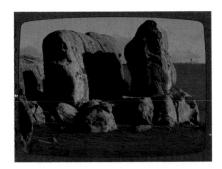
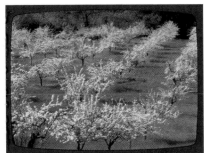
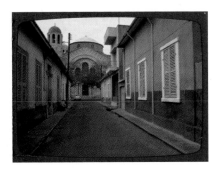

CP21 LOW-ENERGY COLORS

Low-energy colors are desaturated hues. The beige, white, and pale green colors all have a low degree of saturation.

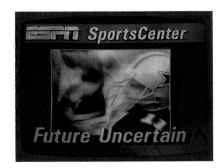
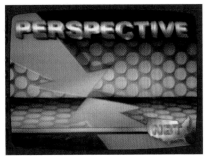
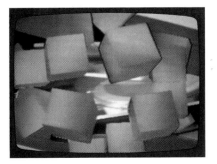

CP22 GENERATED GRAPHICS

Software specifically for graphics generators can create a variety of three-dimensional titles or moving images.

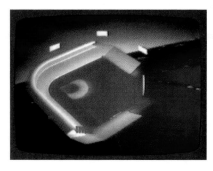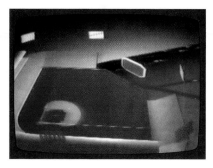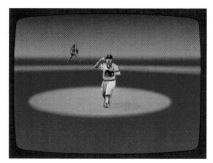

CP23 DIGITAL RENDERING
These examples show a baseball field from various points of view.

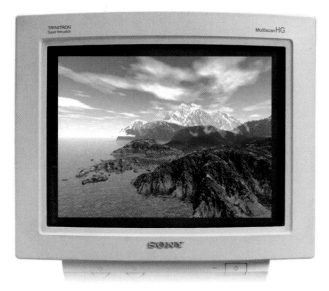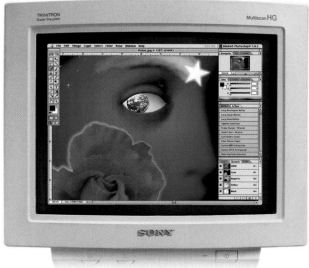

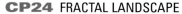

CP24 FRACTAL LANDSCAPE
Some computer programs allow you to "paint" irregular images using mathematical formulas.

CP25 GRAPHICS PROGRAM
Graphics programs offer a variety of lines and brush strokes, surface textures, and a wide choice of colors.

pictures. Digital cameras with high-quality CCDs, however, can tolerate contrast ratios as high as 100:1, which means that the brightest spot in the picture can be a hundred times brighter than the darkest one.

If a scene exceeds the camera's contrast range, either the video operator or automated circuits in the camera will adjust the picture so that it does fall within the contrast tolerances of the pickup device. This is usually done by reducing, or "pulling down," the brightest areas of the scene. Unfortunately, this pulling down of the whites renders the dark areas uniformly black, which is why you do not see much detail in the shadows of a high-contrast scene.

When shooting outdoors in sunny weather, the contrast ratio of the scene will certainly exceed 40:1—or even 100:1. There is little you can do besides adjusting the camera to the brightest areas and using reflectors to lighten dense shadows (see chapter 8). To reduce the intensity of the brightest areas, you can use *neutral density filters (NDs)*, which act like sunglasses of varying densities, reducing the amount of light that falls on the pickup device without distorting the actual colors of the scene.

In the studio try to keep the scenery, clothing, and lighting within the 40:1 ratio. This does not mean, however, that you must keep all colors to medium brightness or that you should not build contrast into the lighting. In fact, video operators like to have something white and something black on the set so that they can set the appropriate video levels. But avoid having the extremely bright and extremely dark colors right next to each other.

For example, it is difficult for the camera to reproduce true skin color if the talent is wearing a highly reflecting starched white shirt and a light-absorbing black jacket. If the camera adjusts for the white shirt by clipping the white level (bringing down the whites to acceptable limits), the talent's face will go dark. If the camera tries to bring up the black level (making the black areas in the picture light enough to distinguish shadow detail), the face will wash out. A few small, shiny items in the picture will not upset the 40:1 contrast ratio, especially when using high-quality cameras. Rhinestones on a dress, for example, make the picture come alive and give it sparkle. As mentioned, digital cameras can tolerate much higher contrasts and can usually handle a white shirt and black suit without affecting the skin colors. A moderate contrast is advisable, however, even when using digital cameras.

OPERATIONAL CHARACTERISTICS

When you compare a studio camera with an ENG/EFP camera or even a consumer camcorder, you will find that the studio camera has fewer buttons and switches than the other two types. This is because the studio camera is remote-controlled by its camera control unit. Most operational controls are on the CCU panel. The VO works all the buttons during the production for optimal picture quality.

ENG/EFP cameras and small-format camcorders, on the other hand, are self-contained; that is, they have all the switches and buttons right on the camera itself (the camera head) so you can ready the camera and keep it operational during the entire shoot. Fortunately, the automatic controls of ENG/EFP cameras and consumer camcorders make keeping the camera at optimal levels relatively easy under normal circumstances. Knowing some of the operational elements and functions of studio and field cameras will help you greatly in preparing the camera for trouble-free operation.

Operational Items and Controls: Studio Cameras

This section focuses on the major operational items and controls of studio cameras: (1) power supply, (2) camera cable, (3) connectors, (4) filter wheel, (5) viewfinder, (6) tally light, and (7) intercom. The following two sections examine the operational items and controls of ENG/EFP cameras and camcorders.

Power supply All studio cameras receive their power from a DC (direct current) power supply which is, as you have learned, part of the camera chain. The power is supplied through the camera cable.

Camera cable Camera cables differ significantly in how they carry the various electronic signals to and from the camera. When requesting cable runs, you need to know which cable the camera can accept and, especially, how long a cable run you need.

Multicore cables, which contain a great number of thin wires, have the most limited reach (up to 2,000 feet, or about 600 meters). Although this cable length is generally enough for studio work and many standard remote telecasts, it is not long enough for certain remotes, such as telecasts of ski racing or golf. Multicore cables can, however, carry a great amount of information without any adapters.

The *triaxial (triax) cables,* which have one central wire surrounded by two concentric shields, and the *fiber-optic cables,* which contain thin, flexible, glass strands instead of wires, have a much greater reach. They are also thinner and considerably lighter than the multicore cables. A triax cable allows a maximum distance of almost 5,000 feet (about 1,500 meters), and a fiber-optic cable can reach twice as far, to almost 2 miles (up to 3,000 meters).[2] Such a reach is adequate for most remote operations. Before planning a camera setup with triax or fiber-optic cables, check which cables the camera can accept and which adapters you may need.

Connectors When in the studio, the camera cable is generally left plugged into the camera and the camera wall jack (outlet). When using studio cameras in the field, however, you need to carefully check whether the cable connectors fit the jacks of the remote truck. Simple coaxial video lines all have *BNC connectors* (see figure 3.19 later in this chapter). Multicore cables come in various configurations (usually expressed in the number of pins at the cable end).

Filter wheel The *filter wheel* is located between the lens and the beam splitter. It normally holds two neutral density filters (ND-1 and ND-2) and some color-correction filters. The NDs reduce the amount of light transmitted to the imaging device without affecting the color of the scene. You use them when shooting in bright sunlight. The color-correction filters compensate for the relative bluishness of outdoor and fluorescent light and the relative reddishness of indoor and candlelight (see chapter 8). In some studio cameras, these filters can be operated from the CCU. In most others you can rotate the desired filter into position, usually with a small thumb wheel or with a switch that activates the filter wheel.

Viewfinder The *viewfinder* is a small television set that shows the picture the camera is getting. Studio cameras usually have a 5- or 7-inch viewfinder that can be swiveled and tilted so you can see what you are doing even when you're not standing directly behind the camera. **SEE 3.18** Most viewfinders are monochrome,

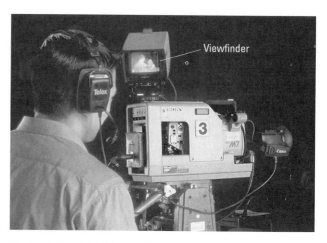

3.18 STUDIO CAMERA VIEWFINDER
The 7-inch studio camera viewfinder can be swiveled and tilted so that the screen faces the camera operator regardless of camera position.

which means you see only a black-and-white picture of the scene you are shooting. Even HDTV cameras are not always equipped with a color viewfinder. This is somewhat unfortunate, especially for HDTV, where the stretched aspect ratio and usually large projections of its pictures make color an important compositional factor.

The camera viewfinder also acts as a small information center, indicating the following items and conditions:

- *Center marker.* This shows the exact center of the screen.

- *Safe title area.* A rectangle in the viewfinder within which you should keep all essential picture information.

- *Electronic setup information.* This includes gain, insufficient-light level, or other exposure settings for optimal video levels.

- *Lens extenders.* These are magnifying devices that extend the telephoto power of a lens (see chapter 4).

- *Multiple views.* The viewfinder allows you to see the pictures other studio cameras are taking as well as special effects. Viewing the picture of another camera helps you frame your shot so that it will "cut together" with the shot of the other camera and avoid meaningless duplication of shots. When special effects are intended, the viewfinder displays the partial effect so that you can place your portion of the effect in the exact spot of the overall screen area.

---

2. If the cable length is given in meters (m) and you want to find the equivalent in feet, simply divide the meters by 3. This is close enough to give you some idea of how far the cable will reach. For greater accuracy, 1 meter = 39.37 inches, or 3.28 feet.

Tally light   The *tally light* is a big red light on top of the studio camera that signals which of the two or more cameras is "hot," that is, on the air. The light indicates that the other cameras are free to line up their next shots. It also helps the talent address, and smile at, the correct camera. There is also a small tally light inside the viewfinder hood that informs the camera operator when the camera is hot. When two cameras are used simultaneously, such as for a split-screen effect or for a superimposition (see chapter 14), the tally lights of both cameras are on. When operating a studio camera, wait until your tally light is off before repositioning your camera.

Intercom   The *intercommunication channels,* or *intercom,* are especially important for multicamera productions, because the director and technical director have to coordinate the cameras' operations. All studio cameras and several high-end field cameras have at least two channels for intercommunication—one for the production crew and the other for the technical crew. Some studio cameras have a third channel that carries the program sound. When ENG/EFP cameras are converted to the studio configuration, intercom adapters are an essential part of the conversion. As the camera operator, you can listen to the instructions of the director, producer, and technical director and talk to them as well as your fellow VOs. The various intercom functions are discussed in chapter 20.

Whereas the operational and electronic characteristics of ENG/EFP cameras and camcorders are often similar to those of studio cameras, the operational controls on the field cameras are much more elaborate and are therefore discussed separately.

Operational Items: ENG/EFP Cameras and Camcorders

ENG EFP   Although the operational items of ENG/EFP cameras are similar to those of studio cameras, they differ considerably in design and function. This section explains the operational items of field cameras and their functions: (1) power supply, (2) camera cable, (3) connectors, (4) exchangeable lenses, (5) filter wheel, and (6) viewfinder.

Power supply   Most professional camcorders are powered by a 13-volt (13.2 V) or 14-volt (14.4 V) battery that is clipped on the back of the camera. Consumer camcorders have lower-voltage batteries that are also clipped on the back of the camera-VTR unit. Substitute power supplies are household AC current and car batteries, both of which need adapters. Use a car battery only in an emergency: Car batteries are hazardous to the operator as well as to the camera.

Depending on the power consumption of the camera or camcorder, most batteries can supply continuous power for up to two hours before needing to be recharged. If your camcorder has a low power consumption, you may be able to run it for four hours with a single battery charge.

Some types of batteries used for consumer video equipment develop a "memory" if they are recharged before they have completely run down. This means that the battery signals a full charge even if it is far from being fully charged. To keep a battery from developing such a memory, run the battery until it has lost almost all of its power before recharging it, or discharge it purposely from time to time. Many battery rechargers have a discharge option, which will completely discharge a battery before recharging it.

When operating a professional camcorder, you should use a *digital battery*, which has a small chip built-in that communicates with the battery charger to receive a full charge. It also powers a "fuel gauge" that indicates just how much charge is left in the battery.

Ordinary batteries also let you know when their charge is running out; but this low-battery warning in the camera viewfinder comes often just before the battery runs down completely.

Camera cable   When using an ENG/EFP camera rather than a camcorder, you may need to connect the camera to a VTR (videotape recorder) or an RCU (remote control unit). Even a camcorder needs cables when you want to connect it to some other external equipment, such as monitor feeds, audio recorders, and so forth.

Connectors   Before going to the field location, carefully check whether the connectors on the various cables actually fit into the camera *jacks* (receptacles) and the jacks of the auxiliary equipment. There is nothing more annoying than having the whole production held up for an hour or more simply because a connector on a cable does not match the receptacle on the camera. Most professional video equipment uses *BNC* connectors for video coaxial cables, and *XLR* or *RCA phono* plugs for audio cables. Some audio equipment requires cables with *phone plugs.* Consumer equipment usually uses *RCA phono* for video cables and *mini plugs* for audio. Although there are adapters for all plugs—so, for example, you can change a BNC connector into an RCA phono plug—try to

3.19 STANDARD VIDEO AND AUDIO CONNECTORS

Most professional video cables have BNC connectors; consumer models use the RCA phono plug. All professional microphones and three-wire cables use XLR connectors; some equipment uses the two-wire phone plug; and consumer equipment uses RCA phono or mini-plug connectors.

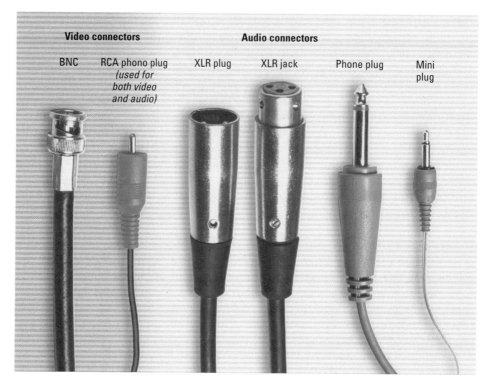

Video connectors   **Audio connectors**

BNC   RCA phono plug *(used for both video and audio)*   XLR plug   XLR jack   Phone plug   Mini plug

stay away from them. Such makeshift connections are not reliable, and each adapter introduces a potential trouble spot. **SEE 3.19**

Exchangeable lenses   When using your home camcorder, you may have had trouble getting an overall shot of a birthday party in a small living room, even if zoomed all the way out. Next time forgo your built-in zoom lens for one that has a wider angle of view. To accommodate such situations, most professional ENG/EFP cameras allow you to attach the zoom lens that gives you the optimal zoom range (see chapter 4).

Filter wheel   Much like studio cameras, field cameras and camcorders have a filter wheel that contains at least two ND and a variety of color-correction filters. You can rotate the desired filter into position by turning a small thumb wheel or by activating a filter switch on the side of the camera. The switch is sometimes labeled "color temperature."

Viewfinder   Unless converted to the studio configuration, all ENG/EFP cameras and camcorders normally have a 1½-inch high-resolution monochrome viewfinder. It is shielded from outside reflections by a flexible rubber eyepiece that you can adjust to your eye.

You can swivel the viewfinder in several directions—an important feature when the camera cannot be operated from the customary shoulder position. Some small EFP/ENG cameras and consumer camcorders have an additional thin foldout screen whose color image consists of an LCD (liquid crystal display) similar to that of a laptop computer.

Many viewfinders also act as an important communications system, showing the status of certain camera and production functions when the camera is in operation. Although the actual display modes vary from model to model, most studio and field camera viewfinders will exhibit the following "indications":

- *Tally light.* This little red light inside the viewfinder indicates whether the camera is hot (on the air). Note that ENG/EFP cameras and camcorders do not have an external tally light.

- *VTR record.* This indicates whether the videotape in the VTR (separate or docked with the camera) is rolling and recording. This indicator is usually a steady or flashing red light in the viewfinder.

- *End-of-tape warning.* The viewfinder may display a written message of how much tape time is remaining.

- *Battery status.* This indicator shows the remaining charge or a small icon, such as a crossed-out battery, that warns you immediately before the battery has lost its useful charge.

- *White balance.* This indicator shows whether the camera is adjusted to the particular tint of the light (white balance) in which you are shooting (see chapter 8).

- *Maximum and minimum light levels.* The zebra pattern can be set for a particular maximum light level. When this level is exceeded, the pattern begins to flash.

- *Gain.* In low-light conditions, the viewfinder displays when the gain is active and to what degree.

- *Optical filter positions.* The display tells you which specific filter is in place.

- *Playback.* The viewfinder can serve as a monitor when playing back from the VTR (separate or docked) the scenes you have just recorded. This playback feature provides an immediate check of whether the recording turned out all right technically as well as aesthetically. **SEE 3.20**

If all these indications are not enough for you, some camcorder viewfinders also show the date and time, the file numbers of digitally recorded material, certain titles that you may want to key into particular shots, and the exact length of the recorded material. Some viewfinders even display the audio-recording meter so that you can adjust the volume of the incoming audio. The advantage of having all this information in the viewfinder is that you can keep constant contact with the pictures the camera is taking while also checking vital operational functions.

Operational Controls: ENG/EFP Cameras and Camcorders

ENG EFP You may initially feel somewhat intimidated by all the switches and controls on professional and even consumer camcorders. Don't be. As pointed out, because the ENG/EFP camera represents not only the camera head but also the rest of the camera chain (CCU, power supply, and sync generator), it has considerably more control switches and knobs than the much more sophisticated studio cameras. As with various controls in a luxury car, you don't need to operate all of them all the time. Most of the controls are position switches, and once you have set them properly, you can forget about them for the rest of the shoot.

- The *power switch* obviously turns the camera on or off. In a camcorder it turns on the whole system, including the camera and VCR.

- The *standby switch* keeps the camera turned on at reduced power, therefore lessening the drain on the

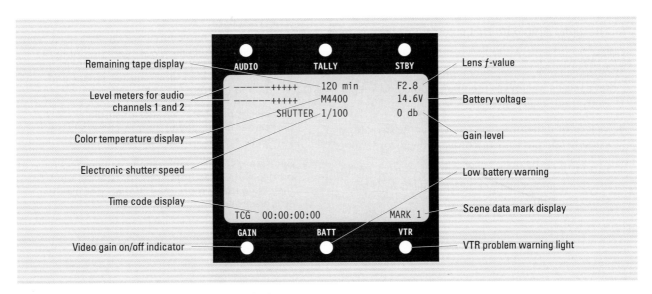

3.20 VIEWFINDER DISPLAY OF INDICATORS
The viewfinder of an ENG/EFP camera or camcorder acts also as a small control center that displays a variety of status indicators. You can see these indicators without taking your eyes off the viewfinder.

battery while keeping the camera ready to perform. It is like idling a car engine before driving off. Having a camera in the standby mode rather than continually turning it on and off is also gentler on the electronics inside the camera and prolongs its life considerably. The standby mode also keeps the viewfinder warmed up and ready to go, which is especially important for ENG/EFP cameras.

■ The *gain control* keeps the camera operational in low light levels.

■ The *white balance* adjusts the colors to the relative reddishness or bluishness of the white light in which the camera is shooting so that a white card looks white when seen on a well-adjusted monitor. Color temperature controls are part of the white-balance adjustment.

■ The *filter wheel* enables you to select the appropriate color or neutral density filter.

■ The *VTR switch* starts and stops the built-in or docked VTR, or the one connected to the camera by cable.

■ The *shutter speed control* lets you select the specific shutter speed necessary to avoid a blurred image of a moving object.

■ The *camera/bars selection switch* lets you choose between the video (pictures the camera sees) or the color bars that serve as reference for the color monitors or for the playback of the recording.

■ The *audio level control* helps you adjust the volume of the camera microphone.

■ *Sound volume and audio monitor controls* let you set a basic level for the incoming audio and keep a continuous check on it.

■ *VTR controls* help you load and eject the videotape cassette and put the camcorder in the record mode.

■ Various *jacks* enable you to connect camera, audio, intercom, and genlock cables, as well as RCU and setup equipment.

MAIN POINTS

◆ The television camera is one of the most important production elements. Other production equipment and techniques are influenced by what the camera can and cannot do.

◆ The major parts of the camera are the lens, the camera itself with the beam splitter and imaging device (CCD), and the viewfinder.

◆ The beam splitter separates the entering white light into the three additive light primaries: red, green, and blue (RGB).

◆ The imaging devices convert the light entering the camera into electric energy—the video signal. This is done by the CCD (charge-coupled device), which is a solid-state chip containing rows of a great many light-sensitive pixels.

◆ The standard camera chain consists of the camera head (the actual camera), the CCU (camera control unit), the sync generator, and the power supply.

◆ The two major types of television cameras are the standard analog and digital cameras. The analog cameras are based on the traditional 525-line, 30-frames-per-second NTSC system. The more common high-definition digital cameras operate with the 720p (progressive) or the 1080i (interlaced) scanning system.

◆ When classified by function, the three types of television cameras are the standard studio camera, the ENG/EFP camera and camcorder, and the consumer camcorder.

◆ The electronic characteristics include: aspect ratio, resolution, light sensitivity and operating light level, gain, video noise and signal-to-noise ratio, image blur and electronic shutter, smear and moiré, and contrast.

◆ The electronic characteristics of studio and ENG/EFP cameras are: power supply, camera cable, connectors, filter wheel, viewfinder, and tally light.

◆ Because ENG/EFP cameras and camcorders have a built-in CCU—and, for camcorders, a built-in VTR—they have many more operational controls than studio cameras.

3.2

From Light to Video Image

Although you don't need to be an electronics expert to operate the major television equipment, you should know at least how the light image that is captured by the lens is converted by the camera into a video picture. These basic principles will help you understand the reason for using certain pieces of television equipment, and how to use them effectively.

▶ **THE CCD PROCESS**
The solid-state imaging device that converts light into the video signal

▶ **THE NATURE OF COLOR**
Color attributes and additive and subtractive color mixing

▶ **CHROMINANCE AND LUMINANCE CHANNELS**
The three color signals, the black-and-white signal, and how they are combined

THE CCD PROCESS

As you learned in section 3.1, a CCD (charge-coupled device) is a rectangular solid-state chip that has a small window (about the size of a telephone pushbutton) that receives the light from the beam splitter. This window contains a large number of horizontal and vertical rows of light-sensing pixels. Each of the several hundred thousand pixels can collect a certain amount of light—chrominance (color) and luminance (black-and-white) information—and transduce (change) it into electric charges that make up part of the video signal. These charges are then temporarily stored in another layer of the chip so that the front window—the imaging or target area of the chip—is cleared to receive another frame of light information. The stored charges are then transferred out—"clocked out"—at a particular speed (as determined by the electronic shutter speed) and amplified to a workable signal voltage. The higher the light level a pixel receives, the stronger the signal output. **SEE 3.21**

In switchable cameras, which means that you can switch between the 4×3 and 16×9 aspect ratios, the CCDs can have a 4×3 or a 16×9 format. With 4×3 format CCDs, the top and bottom rows of pixel sensors are cut off to achieve the 16 × 9 aspect ratio. Because so many pixels are lost, the switch usually results in a lower-resolution image. With 16 × 9 format CCDs, however, the 4 × 3 scanning area is achieved by utilizing the center portion

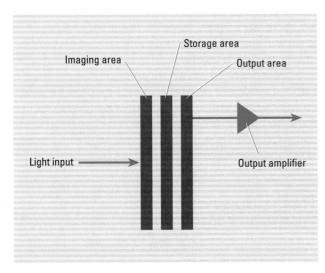

3.21 CCD PROCESS

The CCD consists of an imaging area (the window), a storage area, and an output area. The imaging area contains the pixels, the storage area stores the pixel charges, and the output area delivers them to the amplifier to form the video signal.

of the chip. Assuming that it is a high-resolution chip (many rows of pixels), its center portion should deliver basically the same resolution as the 16 × 9 format.

THE NATURE OF COLOR

When you look at a red ball, its color is not part of the ball, but simply a particular light reflected off it. The red paint of the ball acts as a color filter, absorbing all colors except the red, which it bounces back. Thus the ball is stuck with the only color it has rejected: red.

Color Attributes

When you look at colors, you can easily distinguish among three basic color sensations, called *attributes:* hue, saturation, and brightness or lightness. In television language *luminance* is still another name for brightness. **SEE COLOR PLATE 6**

Hue describes the color itself, such as a red ball, a green apple, or a blue coat. *Saturation* indicates the richness or strength of a color. The bright red paint of a sports car is highly saturated, whereas the washed-out blue of your jeans or the beige of the sand on a beach are of low saturation. **Brightness** is how dark or light a color appears on a black-and-white monitor or, roughly, how light or dark a color appears. The various brightness steps of a television image are usually shown as a *grayscale* (see chapter 15). When you see black-and-white television pictures on-screen, you see brightness variations only; the pictures have no hue or saturation. In television the hue and brightness properties of color are sometimes named *chrominance* (from *chroma*, Greek for color). The brightness properties are called *luminance* (from *lumen*, Latin for light). The chrominance, or C, channels and the luminance, or Y, channels are discussed later in this section.

Color Mixing

If you think back to your finger-painting days, you probably had three pots of paint: red, blue, and yellow. When mixing blue and yellow, you got green; when mixing red and blue, you got purple; and when smearing red and green together, you got, at best, a muddy brown. An expert finger painter could achieve almost all colors by simply mixing the primary paint colors red, blue, and yellow. Not so when mixing together colored light.

The three primary light colors are not red, blue, and yellow, but rather *red, green,* and *blue*—in television language, *RGB*.

Additive mixing   Assume that you have three individual slide projectors with a clear red slide (filter) in the first, a clear green one in the second, and a clear blue one in the third. Hook up each of the projectors to a separate dimmer. When the three dimmers are up full and you shine all three light beams together on the same spot of the screen, you get white light (assuming equal light transmission by all three slides and projector lamps). This is not surprising, because we can split white light into these three primaries. When you turn off the blue projector and leave on the red and green ones, you get yellow. If you then dim the green projector somewhat, you get orange or brown. If you turn off the green one and turn on the blue one again, you get a reddish purple, called magenta. If you then dim the red projector, the purple becomes more bluish. Because you *add* various quantities of colored light in the process, it is called *additive* color mixing. **SEE COLOR PLATE 7**   Because the color camera works with light rather than finger paint, it needs the three additive color primaries (red, green, and blue) to produce all the colors you see on the television screen. You can make all other colors by adding two or all three light beams—primaries—in various proportions, that is, in various light intensities.

Subtractive mixing   When using paint instead of colored light, your primary colors are red, blue, and yellow or, more accurately, magenta (a bluish red), cyan (a greenish blue), and yellow. In subtractive mixing, the colors filter each other out. Mixing red and green paint will not produce yellow, as it does in additive mixing, but rather a muddy brown. Blue and yellow produce green. As you can see, you are now back to your finger-painting days. Because we are using light rather than paint in the camera, the only time you come across subtractive mixing is in lighting (see chapter 8).

CHROMINANCE AND LUMINANCE CHANNELS

As stated earlier, chrominance deals with the hue and saturation attributes of a color, luminance with its brightness (black-and-white) information. The chrominance channel in a camera transports the color signals, and the luminance channel, the black-and-white signal.

Chrominance Channel

The **chrominance channel,** or *C channel,* includes all hue attributes. It consists of the three "slide projectors" that produce red, green, and blue light beams of varying intensities, except that in the television camera the "slide projectors" consist of the CCDs that produce an electrical signal of varying intensity (voltage) for each of the three primary colors. Depending on the system, the color signals can be transported by one, two, or three wires.

Luminance Channel

The *luminance channel*, or *Y channel*, is responsible for the brightness information of the color pictures. Its single luminance signal fulfills two basic functions: It translates the brightness variations of the colors in a scene into black-and-white pictures for black-and-white receivers, and it provides color pictures with the necessary crispness and definition, just like the black dots in a four-color print. Because it has such a great influence on the sharpness of the picture, the Y signal is very much favored in the digital domain. Even in high-end digital cameras, the color signals are sampled only half as often as the luminance signal or only one-fourth as often for lower-end professional and high-end consumer digital cameras.

Even if two hues differ considerably from each other, such as red and green, their brightness attributes may be so similar that they are difficult to distinguish on a monochrome (black-and-white) monitor. For example, a red letter looks quite prominent against a blue background, but it gets lost in a black-and-white rendering. The problem is that the brightness attribute or the number and the background are almost identical. Although the hues are contrasting considerably, their brightness values are the same. As a result, the letter is no longer legible in the black-and-white rendering. **SEE COLOR PLATE 8** When the brightness attributes of the two different colors are equally far apart, the letter shows up quite well in the black-and-white rendering. **SEE COLOR PLATE 9**

The Encoder

The encoder combines the three C (RGB color) signals with the Y (luminance) signal so that they can be transmitted and easily separated again by the color television receiver. This combined signal is called the *composite*, or *NTSC, signal*. If the Y (luminance) signal and the C (color) signals are kept separate, it is a *component video signal*. **SEE COLOR PLATES 10–13** We revisit the composite and component signals in chapter 12.

MAIN POINTS

◆ The solid-state charge-coupled device (CCD) consists of many horizontal and vertical rows of pixels. Each of the pixels can collect a certain amount of light and transduce it into electric charges. The charges are then stored and read out, line by line, and amplified into the video signal.

◆ Color attributes are hue, the color itself; saturation, the richness or strength of a color; and brightness, how dark or light a color appears.

◆ Color television operates on additive mixing of the three color (light) primaries—red, green, and blue.

◆ Color cameras contain a chrominance and a luminance channel. The chrominance channel processes the color signals—the C signal—and the luminance channel processes the black-and-white (brightness) signal, called the Y signal. The two types of signals are combined by the encoder.

4

Lenses

As discussed in chapter 3, the lens is one of the three major parts of the camera. In studio cameras the lens is often considerably larger than the camera itself. Lenses are used in all fields of photographic art. Their primary function is to produce a small, clear image of the viewed scene on the film or, in the case of television, in the electronic imaging device. Section 4.1, What Lenses Are, covers the basic optical characteristics of lenses and their primary operational controls. The performance characteristics of lenses, that is, how they see the world, are explored in section 4.2, What Lenses See. You can reinforce this material by running the appropriate units of Zettl's VideoLab 2.1.

aperture Iris opening of a lens, usually measured in f-stops.

auto-focus Automated feature wherein the camera focuses on what it senses to be your target object.

calibrate To preset a zoom lens to remain in focus throughout the zoom.

compression The crowding effect achieved by a narrow-angle (telephoto) lens wherein object proportions and relative distances seem shallower.

depth of field The area in which all objects, located at different distances from the camera, appear in focus. Depth of field depends upon focal length of the lens, its f-stop, and the distance between the object and the camera.

digital zoom Simulated zoom by enlarging the image pixels.

digital zoom lens A lens that can be programmed through a small built-in computer to repeat zoom positions and their corresponding focus settings.

fast lens A lens that permits a relatively great amount of light to pass through (lower minimum f-stop number). Can be used in low-light conditions.

field of view The portion of a scene visible through a particular lens; its vista. Expressed in symbols, such as *CU* for close-up.

focal length The distance from the optical center of the lens to the front surface of the camera imaging device at which the image appears in focus with the lens set at infinity. Focal lengths are measured in millimeters or inches. Short-focal-length lenses have a wide angle of view (wide vista); long-focal-length (telephoto) lenses have a narrow angle of view (close-up). In a variable-focal-length (zoom) lens, the focal length can be changed continuously from wide-angle (zoomed out) to narrow-angle (zoomed in) and vice versa. A fixed-focal-length lens has a single designated focal length.

focus A picture is in focus when it appears sharp and clear on-screen (technically, the point where the light rays refracted by the lens converge).

f-stop The calibration on the lens indicating the aperture, or iris opening (and therefore the amount of light transmitted through the lens). The larger the f-stop number, the smaller the aperture; the smaller the f-stop number, the larger the aperture.

iris Adjustable lens-opening that controls the amount of light passing through the lens. Also called *lens diaphragm*.

macro position Position on a zoom lens that allows it to be focused at very close distances from an object. Used for close-ups of small objects.

minimum object distance (MOD) How close the camera can get to the object and still focus on it.

narrow-angle lens Gives a close-up view of an event relatively far away from the camera. Also called *long-focal-length* or *telephoto lens*.

normal lens A lens or zoom lens position with a focal length that will approximate the spatial relationships of normal vision.

rack focus To change focus from one object or person closer to the camera to one farther away or vice versa.

range extender An optical attachment to the zoom lens that extends its focal length. Also called an *extender*.

selective focus Emphasizing an object in a shallow depth of field through focus, while keeping its foreground and background out of focus.

servo zoom control Zoom control that activates motor-driven mechanisms.

slow lens A lens that permits a relatively small amount of light to pass through (higher minimum f-stop number). Can be used only in well-lighted areas.

wide-angle lens A short-focal-length lens that provides a broad vista of a scene.

zoom lens Variable-focal-length lens. It can gradually change from a wide shot to a close-up and vice versa in one continuous move.

zoom range The degree to which the focal length can be changed from a wide shot to a close-up during a zoom. The zoom range is often stated as a ratio; a 15:1 zoom ratio means that the zoom lens can increase its focal length fifteen times.

4.1

What Lenses Are

The lens determines what the camera can see. One type of lens can provide a wide vista even though you may be relatively close to the scene; another type may provide a close view of an object that is quite far from the camera. Different types of lenses also determine the basic visual perspective—whether you see an object as distorted or whether you perceive more or less distance between objects than there really is. This section examines what lenses can do and how to use them.

▶ **TYPES OF ZOOM LENSES**
   Studio and field lenses, zoom range, and lens format

▶ **OPTICAL CHARACTERISTICS OF LENSES**
   Focal length; focus; light transmission, iris, and f-stop; and depth of field

▶ **OPERATIONAL CONTROLS**
   Zoom control, digital zoom lens, and focus control

TYPES OF ZOOM LENSES

When listening to production people talk about *zoom lenses*, you will most likely hear one person refer to a studio rather than a field zoom, another to a 15× lens, and still another to a zoom lens that fits a ⅔-inch image format. And all may be talking about the same zoom lens. This section looks at these classifications.

Studio and Field Lenses

As the name indicates, *studio zoom lenses* are normally used with studio cameras. *Field zooms* include large lenses mounted on high-quality cameras that are used for remote telecasts, such as sporting events, parades, and the like. They also include the zoom lenses attached to ENG/EFP cameras. The lenses of consumer camcorders are also classified as field lenses. Because you can, of course, use a field lens in the studio and vice versa, a better and more accurate way to classify the various zoom lenses is by their zoom range and lens format, that is, what camera they fit.

Zoom Range

If a zoom lens provides an overview, for example, of the whole tennis court and part of the bleachers when zoomed all the way out and (without moving the camera closer to the court) a tight close-up of the player's tense expression when zoomed all the way in, the lens has a good zoom

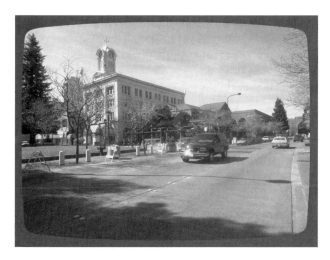
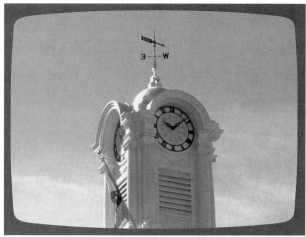

4.1 MAXIMUM ZOOM POSITIONS OF A 10× LENS
The 10× zoom lens can increase its focal length ten times. It magnifies a portion of the scene and seems to bring it closer to the camera and ultimately the viewer.

range. More precisely, the ***zoom range*** is the degree to which you can change the focal length of the lens (and thereby the angle of view, or vista) during the zoom.

The zoom range of a lens is often stated as a ratio, such as 10:1 or 40:1. A 10:1 zoom means that you can increase the focal length ten times, a 40:1, forty times. To make things easier, these ratios are usually listed as 10× (ten times) or 40× (forty times). **SEE 4.1**

You may have noticed that the zoom range on a consumer camcorder is rather limited; an optical zoom range of 15× is considered excellent. But the large (studio) cameras that are positioned in the field on top of the bleachers for sports coverage may have zoom ranges of 40× and even 70×. In the studio the cameras are well served with a 20× zoom lens. The smaller and lighter ENG/EFP camera lenses rarely exceed a 15× zoom range.

The studio, field, and ENG/EFP lenses are all detachable from the camera. Only the consumer camcorders have a built-in lens that cannot be detached from the camera. **SEE 4.2 AND 4.3**

4.2 STUDIO ZOOM LENS
High-quality studio lenses are quite heavy and often larger than the camera itself. They cannot be mounted on an ENG/EFP camera.

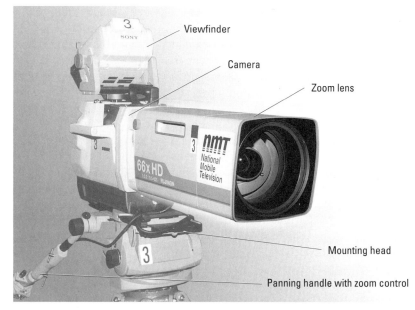

Viewfinder

Camera

Zoom lens

Mounting head

Panning handle with zoom control

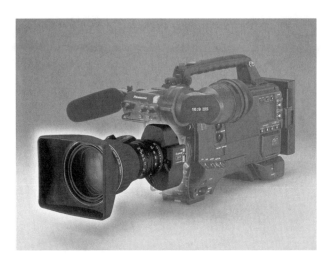

4.3 ENG/EFP ZOOM LENS
The ENG/EFP camera lens is considerably lighter and smaller than the studio zooms. Although these lenses are not as high quality as studio lenses, ENG/EFP lenses nevertheless have many of the studio zoom's features, such as servo and manual zoom controls, and servo or automatic iris control. Consumer camcorder lenses even have an automatic focus feature. This ENG/EFP lens has a converter that lets you change aspect ratios from 4 × 3 to 16 × 9.

Studio and large field lenses   Note that a 20× studio lens becomes a field lens if it is used "in the field," that is, for a production that happens outside the studio. Generally, however, field lenses have a much greater zoom range (from 40× to 70×) than studio cameras. Such a great zoom range enables the camera operator to zoom from a wide establishing shot of the football stadium to a tight close-up of the quarterback's face. Despite the great zoom range, these lenses deliver high-quality pictures even in relatively low light levels. For studio use such a zoom range would be unnecessary and often counterproductive.

ENG/EFP lenses   These lenses are much smaller, to fit the portable cameras. As mentioned, their normal zoom range extends from 13× to 17×. A 15× zoom lens would be sufficient for most ENG/EFP assignments, but sometimes you might have to get a closer view of an event that is relatively far away. You would then need to exchange the 15× zoom lens for one with much higher zoom range—such as 20× or even 36×. Such telephoto zoom lenses, however, need a much higher light level than the 15× lens to deliver usable pictures.

A more important consideration for ENG/EFP lenses is whether they have a wide enough angle of view (a very short focal length), which would allow you to shoot in highly cramped quarters, such as a car, a small room, or an airplane. Also, the wide-angle view is important for shooting in the wide-screen 16 × 9 format.

Many lenses have an *internal focus* as well as digital stabilizers that absorb at least some of the picture wiggles resulting from operating the camera in a narrow-angle (zoomed-in) position. Internal focus is explored further later in this section.

Consumer camcorder lenses   These zoom lenses generally have an optical zoom range of 10× to 18×. You may have noticed that the problem with zoom lenses on consumer camcorders is that, despite their good zoom range, the maximum wide-angle position is often not wide enough. Most camcorders have some sort of image stabilization.

Range extenders   If a zoom lens does not get you close enough to a scene from where the camera is located, you can use an additional lens element called a *range extender*, or simply an *extender*. This optical element, usually available only for lenses on professional cameras, does not actually extend the range of the zoom, but rather shifts the magnification—the telephoto power—of the lens toward the narrow-angle end of the zoom range. Most lenses have 2× extenders, which means that they double the zoom range at the narrow-angle position, but also reduce the wide-angle lens position by two times. With such a range extender, you can zoom in to a closer shot, but you cannot zoom back out as wide as you could without the extender. There are two other disadvantages to range extenders: They cut down considerably the light entering the camera, which is problematic especially in low-light conditions; and the additional lens elements cause the picture to lose some of its crispness.

Lens Format
Because camera lenses are designed to match the size of the CCD imaging device, you may hear about a *lens format* or *image format* of ⅓-inch, ½-inch, or ⅔-inch. This means that you can use only a lens that fits the corresponding CCD image format. Like film, the larger CCDs produce better pictures. The term *lens format* may also refer to whether a lens is used for standard NTSC cameras or HDTV cameras.

4.4 FOCAL LENGTH
The focal length is the distance from the optical center of the lens to the front surface of the imaging device.

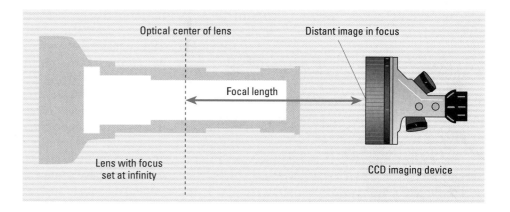

Optical center of lens · Distant image in focus

Focal length

Lens with focus set at infinity · CCD imaging device

OPTICAL CHARACTERISTICS OF LENSES

All major types of television cameras and camcorders (studio, ENG/EFP, and consumer) are equipped with zoom lenses or, as they are technically called, *variable-focal-length lenses*. This means that you do not have to put different lenses on a camera to change from a wide vista to a close-up view or from a close-up to a wider shot. Instead, a single lens can accomplish such changes in one uninterrupted zoom. Effective use of a camera depends to a great extent on your understanding of these optical characteristics: (1) focal length, (2) focus, (3) light transmission, iris, and f-stop and (4) depth of field.

Focal Length

Technically, *focal length* refers to the distance from the optical center of the lens to the point where the image the lens sees is in focus. This point is the camera's imaging device. **SEE 4.4** Operationally, the focal length determines how wide or narrow a vista a particular camera has and how much and in what ways objects appear magnified. When you zoom all the way *out,* the focal length of the lens is at the maximum wide-angle position; the camera will provide a wide vista. When you zoom all the way *in,* the focal length of the lens is at the maximum narrow-angle position; the camera will provide a narrow vista or field of view—a close-up view of the scene. **SEE 4.5** When you stop the zoom somewhere in between these extreme positions, the camera gives a view that approximates your actually looking at the scene. Because the zoom lens can assume all focal lengths from its maximum wide-angle position (zoomed all the way out) to its maximum narrow-angle position (zoomed all the way in), it is called a *variable-focal-length lens.* *READY ZVL* ❶

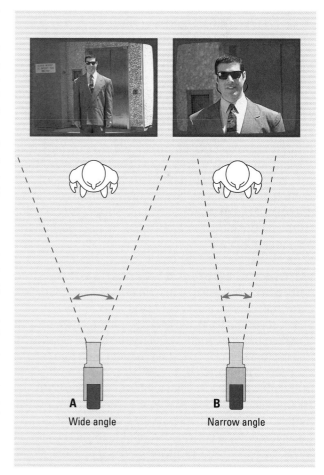

4.5 WIDE-ANGLE AND NARROW-ANGLE ZOOM POSITIONS
A The wide-angle zoom position (zoomed out) has a wider vista (field of view) than **B** the narrow-angle zoom position (zoomed in). Note that zooming in magnifies the subject.

A Wide angle · B Narrow angle

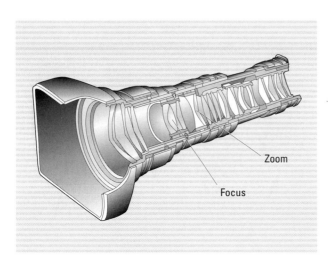

4.6 ELEMENTS OF A ZOOM LENS

A zoom lens consists of many sliding and stationary lens elements that interact to maintain focus throughout the continuous change of focal length. The front elements control the focus; the middle elements control the zoom.

On the television screen, a zoom-in appears as though the object is gradually coming toward you. A zoom-out seems to make the object move away from you. Actually, all that the moving elements within the zoom lens do is gradually magnify (zoom-in) or reduce the magnification (zoom-out) of the object while keeping it in focus. But the camera remains stationary during both operations. **SEE 4.6**

Minimum object distance and macro position   You will find that there is often a limit to how close you can move a camera (and lens) to the object to be photographed and still keep the picture in focus. This is especially problematic when trying to get a close-up of a very small object. Even when zoomed in all the way, the shot may still look too wide. Moving the camera closer to the object will make the shot tighter, but you can no longer get the picture in focus. Range extenders help little: While they provide you with a tighter close-up of the object, they force you to back off with the camera to get the shot in focus. One way to solve this problem is to zoom all the way out to a wide-angle focal length.

Contrary to normal expectations, the wide-angle zoom position often allows you to get a tighter close-up of a small object than does the extended narrow-angle zoom position (zoomed all the way in with a 2× extender). But even with the lens in the wide-angle

position, there is usually a point at which the camera will no longer focus when moved too close to the object. The point where the camera is about as close as it can get and still focus on the object is called ***minimum object distance (MOD)*** of the lens.

Although there are zoom lenses that allow you, without extenders, to get extremely close to the object while still maintaining focus over the entire zoom range, most zoom lenses have a minimum object distance of about two to three feet. High-ratio zoom lenses, such as 40× or 50×, have a much greater MOD than lenses with a rather wide-angle starting position and a relatively low zoom ratio (such as 10×). This means that you can probably get closer to an object with a wide-angle field lens that can magnify the object only ten or twelve times than with a large field lens that starts with a narrower angle but can magnify the scene fifty or more times.

Despite the relative advantage of wide-angle field lenses, many field lenses on ENG/EFP cameras have a ***macro position***, which lets you move the camera even closer to an object without losing focus. When the lens is in the macro position, you can almost touch the object with the lens and still retain focus; you can no longer zoom, however. The macro position changes the zoom lens from a variable-focal-length lens to a fixed-focal-length, or *"prime,"* lens. The fixed focal length is not a big disadvantage, because the macro position is used only in certain circumstances. For example, if you are called upon to get a screen-filling close-up of a postage stamp, you would switch the camera to the macro position. But then the camera could not be used for zooming unless you switched back to the normal zoom range.

Focus

A picture is "in focus" when the projected image is sharp and clear. The ***focus*** depends on the distance from the lens to the film (as in a still or movie camera) or from the lens to camera imaging device (beam splitter with CCDs). Simply by adjusting the distance from the lens to the film or imaging device brings a picture into focus or takes it out of focus. In television zoom lenses, this adjustment is accomplished by moving certain lens elements relative to each other through the zoom focus control (see figure 4.3).

Focus controls come in various configurations. Portable cameras have a focus ring on the lens that you turn; studio cameras have one attached to the panning handle (see figure 4.15). Most consumer camcorders have an automatic focus feature, called *auto-focus,* which is discussed in the operational controls context later in this section.

If properly preset, a zoom lens keeps in focus during the entire zoom range, assuming that neither the camera nor the object moves very much. But because you walk and even run while carrying ENG/EFP cameras, you cannot always prefocus the zoom. In such cases, you would do well by zooming all the way out to a wide-angle position, considerably reducing the need to focus. This is examined more thoroughly in the discussion on depth of field later in this section.

Presetting (calibrating) the zoom lens   There is a standard procedure for *presetting*, or **calibrating**, the zoom lens so that the camera remains in focus throughout the zoom. Zoom all the way in on the target object, such as a newscaster on a news set. Focus on the face of the newscaster (bridge of her nose or her eyes) by turning the zoom focus control. When zooming back out to a long shot, you will notice that everything remains in focus. The same is true when you zoom in again. You should now be able to maintain focus over the entire zoom range. If you move the camera, however, or if the object moves after you preset the zoom lens, you need to calibrate the zoom again.

For example, if you preset the zoom on the news anchor and then the director instructed you to move the camera a little closer and to the left so that the anchor could more easily read the teleprompter, you would not be able to maintain focus without presetting the zoom from the new position. If, after presetting the zoom on the news anchor, you were asked to zoom in on the map behind her, you would have to adjust the focus while zooming past the news anchor—not an easy task for even an experienced camera operator.

If your camera moves are predetermined and repeated from show to show, as in a daily newscast, you can use the preset features of the digital zoom lens. The lens then remembers the various zoom positions and performs them automatically with the push of a button.

Unless you have an automatic focus control, you must preset the zoom on an ENG/EFP camera even when covering a news event in the field. You may have noticed that unedited video of a disaster (such as a tornado or fire) often contains brief out-of-focus close-ups followed by quick zoom-outs. What the camera operator is doing is calibrating the zoom lens in order to stay in focus during subsequent zoom-ins.

Light Transmission: Iris and *f*-stop

Like the pupil in the human eye, all lenses have a mechanism that controls how much light is admitted through them. This mechanism is called the **iris** or *lens diaphragm*. The iris consists of a series of thin metal blades that form a fairly round hole—the **aperture**, or lens opening—of variable size. **SEE 4.7** If you "open up" the lens as wide as it will go, or, more technically, if you set the lens to its maximum aperture, it admits a maximum amount of light. **SEE 4.8A** If you "close" the lens somewhat, the metal blades of the iris form a smaller hole,

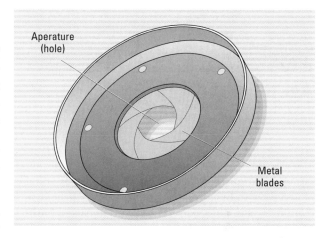

4.7 LENS IRIS

The iris, or lens diaphragm, consists of a series of thin metal blades that form, through partial overlapping, an aperture (lens opening) of variable size.

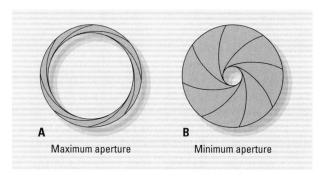

4.8 MAXIMUM AND MINIMUM APERTURE

A At the maximum aperture, the iris blades form a large opening, permitting a great amount of light to enter the lens. **B** At the minimum setting, the blades overlap to form a small hole, admitting only a small amount of light.

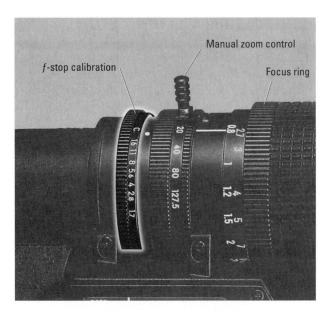

4.9 *f*-STOP SETTINGS

The *f*-stop is a calibration that indicates how large or small the aperture is.

the aperture is somewhat smaller, and less light passes through the lens. If you close the lens all the way—that is, if you set it to its minimum aperture—very little light is admitted. **SEE 4.8B** Some irises can be closed entirely, which means that no light at all goes through the lens.

***f*-stop**   The standard scale that indicates how much light goes through a lens, regardless of the lens type, is the *f-stop*. **SEE 4.9** If, for example, you have two cameras—a camcorder with a 10× zoom lens and a field camera with a large 50× lens—and both lenses are set at *f*/5.6, the imaging devices in both cameras will receive identical amounts of light.

Regardless of camera type, *f*-stops are expressed in a series of numbers, such as *f*/1.4, *f*/2, *f*/2.8, *f*/4, *f*/5.6, *f*/8, *f*/11, *f*/16, and *f*/22. The *lower f*-stop numbers indicate a relatively *large* aperture or iris opening (lens is relatively wide open). The *higher f*-stop numbers indicate a relatively *small* aperture (lens is closed down considerably). A lens that is set at *f*/2 has a much larger iris opening and, therefore, admits much more light than one that is set at *f*/16. (The reason why the low *f*-stop numbers indicate large iris openings and high *f*-stop numbers indicate relatively small iris openings, rather than the other way around, is that the *f*-stop numbers actually express a ratio. In this sense *f*/2 is actually

f/1/2—read: *f* one over two). As mentioned, most lenses produce the best pictures between *f*/5.6 and *f*/8.

Lens speed   The "speed" of a lens has nothing to do with how fast it transmits light, but with how much light it lets through. A lens that allows a relatively great amount of light to enter is called a ***fast lens***. Fast lenses go down to a small *f*-stop number (such as *f*/1.4). Most good studio zoom lenses open up to *f*/1.6, which is fast enough to make the camera work properly even in low-light conditions.

A lens that transmits relatively little light at the maximum iris opening is called a ***slow lens***. A studio lens whose lowest *f*-stop is *f*/2.8 is obviously slower than a lens that can open up to *f*/1.6. Range extenders render the zoom lens inevitably slower. A 2× extender can reduce the lens speed by as much as two "stops" (higher *f*-stop numbers), for instance, from *f*/1.7 to *f*/4 (see figure 4.9). This reduction in light transmission is not a big handicap, however, because range extenders are normally used outdoors where there is enough light.

Remote iris control   Because the amount of light that strikes the camera pickup device is so important for picture quality, the continuous adjustment of the iris is a fundamental aspect of video control. Studio cameras have a *remote iris control,* which means that the aperture can be continuously adjusted by the video operator (VO) from the CCU (camera control unit). If the set is properly lighted and the camera properly set up (electronically adjusted to the light/dark extremes of the scene), all the VO has to do to maintain good pictures is work the remote iris control—open the iris in low-light conditions and close it down when there is more light than needed.

Auto-iris switch   Most cameras, especially ENG/EFP and consumer camcorders, can be switched from the manual to the auto-iris mode. **SEE 4.10** The camera then senses the light entering the lens and automatically adjusts the iris for optimal camera performance. This auto-iris feature works well so long as the scene does not have too much contrast. There are circumstances, however, in which you may want to switch the camera over to manual iris control. For example, if you took a loose close-up shot of a woman wearing a bright white hat in sunlight, the automatic iris would adjust to the bright light of the white hat, not to the darker (shadowed) face under the hat. The auto-iris control would therefore give you a perfectly exposed hat but an underexposed

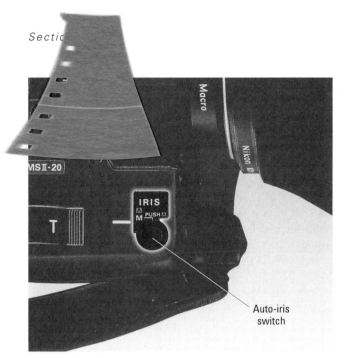

4.10 AUTO-IRIS SWITCH

The auto-iris switch lets you change the aperture control from manual to automatic. You can quickly change back to manual by simply pressing the auto-iris switch without interrupting your shoot.

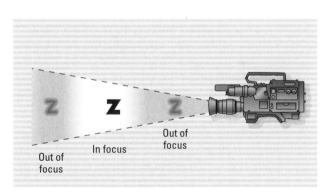

4.11 DEPTH OF FIELD

The depth of field is the area within which all objects, although located at different distances from the camera, are in focus.

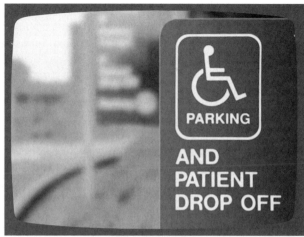

4.12 SHALLOW DEPTH OF FIELD

In a shallow depth of field, the area in which an object is in focus is rather limited.

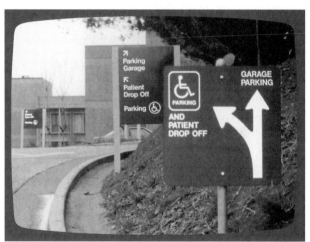

4.13 GREAT DEPTH OF FIELD

With a great depth of field, almost everything in the camera's field of view appears in focus.

face. In this case, you would switch to manual iris control, zoom in on the face to eliminate most of the white hat, and adjust the iris to the light reflecting off the face rather than the hat. *READY ZVL* ❷

Depth of Field

If you place objects at different distances from the camera, some will be in focus and some out of focus. The area in which the objects are seen in focus is called *depth of field*. The depth of field can be shallow or great, but it is always

greater behind the object than in front of it. **SEE 4.11** If you have a shallow depth of field and you focus on an object in the middleground, the foreground and background objects will be out of focus. **SEE 4.12** If the depth of field is great, all objects (foreground, middleground, and background) will be in focus, even though you focus on the middleground object only. **SEE 4.13**

If you have a great depth of field, there is a large "sharp zone" in which people or objects can move toward or away from the camera without becoming out of focus or without any need for adjusting the camera focus. If they move in a shallow depth of field, however, they can quickly become blurred unless you adjust the camera focus. A similar thing happens when you move the camera. A great depth of field makes it relatively easy to move the camera toward or away from the object, because you do not have to work any controls to keep the picture in focus. If you move the camera similarly in a shallow depth of field, however, you must adjust the focus continuously to keep the target object sharp and clear.

Operationally, the depth of field depends on the coordination of three factors: (1) the focal length of the lens, (2) the aperture (lens opening), and (3) the distance between the camera and the object.

Focal length

The focal length of the lens is the factor that most influences the depth of field. In general, wide-angle lenses and, of course, wide-angle (short-focal-length) zoom positions (zoomed out) have a great depth of field. Narrow-angle lenses and narrow-angle (long-focal-length) zoom positions (zoomed in) have a shallow depth of field. You may want to remember a simple rule of thumb:

■ *Depth of field increases as focal length decreases.*

ENG EFP When running after a fast-moving news event, should you zoom all the way in or all the way out? *All the way out.* Why? Because, first, the wide-angle position of the zoom lens will at least show the viewer what is going on. Second, and most important, the resulting great depth of field will help keep most of your shots in focus, regardless of whether you are close to or far away from the event or whether you or the event is on the move.

Aperture

Large apertures cause a shallow depth of field; small apertures cause a large depth of field. Here is another rule of thumb:

■ *Large f-stop numbers (such as f/16 or f/22) contribute to a great depth of field; small f-stop numbers (such as f/1.8 or f/2) contribute to a shallow depth of field.*

Here is an example of how everything in television production seems to influence everything else: If you have to work in low-light conditions, you need to open up the lens (increase the aperture) to get enough light for the camera. But this small f-stop reduces the depth of field. Thus, if you are to cover a news story when it is getting dark and you have no time or opportunity to use artificial lighting, the focus becomes critical—you are working in a rather shallow depth of field. This problem is compounded when zooming in to tight close-ups. On the other hand, in bright sunlight you can stop down (decrease the aperture), thereby achieving a large depth of field. Now you can run with the camera or cover people who are moving toward or away from you without too much worry about keeping in focus—provided the zoom lens is in a wide-angle position.

Camera-to-object distance   The closer the camera is to the object, the shallower the depth of field. The farther the camera is from the object, the greater the depth of field. The camera-to-object distance also influences the focal-length effect on depth of field. For example, if you have a wide-angle lens (or a zoom lens in a wide-angle position), the depth of field is great. But as soon as you move the camera close to the object, the depth of field becomes quite shallow. The same is true in reverse: If you work with the zoom lens in a narrow-angle position (zoomed in), you have a rather shallow depth of field. But if the camera is focused on an object relatively far away from the camera (such as a field camera located high in the stands to cover an automobile race), you work in a fairly great depth of field and do not have to worry too much about adjusting focus, unless you zoom in to an extreme close-up. **SEE 4.14**

■ *Generally, the depth of field is shallow when you work with close-ups and low light levels. The depth of field is great when you work with long shots and high light levels.* READY ZVL ❸

OPERATIONAL CONTROLS

You need two basic controls to operate a zoom lens: the *zoom control,* which lets you zoom out to a wide shot or zoom in to a close-up view, and the *focus control,* which slides the lens elements in front of the zoom lens back and forth until the image or a specific part of the image the zoom lens delivers is sharp. Both controls can be operated manually or through a motor-driven servo control mechanism. A third type of "control" is the use of a digital zoom lens.

4.14 DEPTH-OF-FIELD FACTORS

DEPTH OF FIELD	FOCAL LENGTH	APERTURE	ƒ-STOP	LIGHT LEVEL	SUBJECT/CAMERA DISTANCE
Great	Short (wide-angle)	Small	Large ƒ-stop number (ƒ/22)	High (bright light)	Far
Shallow	Long (narrow-angle)	Large	Small ƒ-stop number (ƒ/1.4)	Low (dim light)	Near

This chart was prepared by Michael Hopkinson of Lane Community College.

Zoom Control

Most zoom lenses are equipped with a servo mechanism whose motor activates the zoom mechanism. The automation lets you execute extremely smooth zooms. Although most servo mechanisms offer a choice of at least two zoom speeds, manual zoom controls are still used in shows where extremely fast zooms are required or where the focal length of the zoom lens must be changed with great speed. Cameras used in sports coverage are occasionally equipped with manual, rather than automatic, zoom controls. You may also find manual zoom controls used in certain television plays or game shows. Even a high-speed servo control could not deliver a zoom-in on a ringing telephone or a contestant's face fast enough to emphasize the importance of the call or the joy of the winner.

Servo zoom control   All types of cameras (studio, ENG/EFP, and consumer camcorders) have a *servo zoom control* for their lenses, usually called *servo zooms*. The servo zoom control for studio cameras is usually mounted on the right panning handle, and you zoom in and out by moving the thumb lever, similar to a rocker switch, either right or left. When pressing the right side of the lever, you zoom in; when pressing the left side, you zoom out. The farther you move the lever from its original central position, the faster the zoom will be. With the servo system, the zoom speed is automatically reduced as the zoom approaches either of the extreme zoom positions. This reduction prevents jerks and abrupt stops at the ends of the zoom range. **SEE 4.15**

ENG EFP   The servo zoom control for ENG/EFP cameras is directly attached to the lens; for consumer camcorders it is built into the camera housing. The rocker switch (similar to the thumb control of studio cameras) is mounted on top of the box that surrounds the lens. It is usually marked with a *W* (for wide) and a *T* (for tight or telephoto). To zoom in you press the *T* section of the switch; to zoom out press the *W* section. The servo control housing has a strap attached, which lets you support the shoulder-mounted or handheld camcorder while operating the zoom control. This way your left hand is free to operate the manual focus control. **SEE 4.16**

Manual zoom control   The manual zoom control on a studio camera usually consists of a small crank mounted on the right panning handle or on an extender

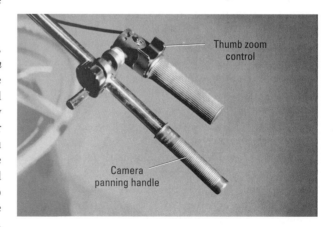

Thumb zoom control

Camera panning handle

4.15 SERVO ZOOM CONTROL FOR STUDIO CAMERA
This zoom control is attached to the camera panning handle. By moving the rocker switch with your thumb to the right or left, you zoom in or out. The more you press the switch toward the extreme rocker position, the faster the zoom will be.

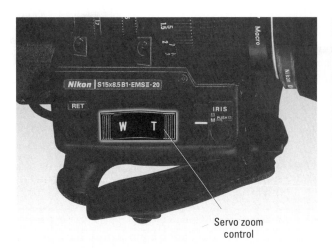

4.16 SERVO ZOOM CONTROL FOR ENG/EFP CAMERA

For ENG/EFP cameras and camcorders, the servo zoom control is part of the lens assembly.

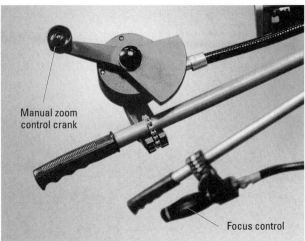

4.17 MANUAL ZOOM CONTROL FOR STUDIO CAMERA

The manual zoom control is a crank with which you can achieve extremely fast zooms. The faster you turn the crank, the faster the zoom.

at the right side of the camera. A lever next to the crank enables you to select at least two turning ratios—slow or fast. The slow ratio is for normal zooming; the fast is for exceptionally fast zooms. When you turn the crank of the zoom control, a zoom drive cable mechanically activates the zoom mechanism in the lens. Regardless of what zoom ratio you have selected, the faster you turn the crank, the faster the zoom will be. **SEE 4.17**

ENG EFP The ENG/EFP lenses have an additional manual zoom control which consists of a small lever attached to the zoom control ring on the lens barrel (see figure 4.6). By moving the lever clockwise or counterclockwise, you can achieve extremely fast zooms not possible with the servo control.

Digital Zoom Lens

The *digital zoom lens* has digital controls built-in that allow you to preset certain zooms and then trigger the operation with the push of a button. This preset device, which also remembers focus calibration, is highly accurate, provided the camera and subject are in exactly the same positions as during setup. It is most practical when using *robot cameras* (cameras whose movements are controlled by computer and not by an operator), such as during studio newscasts.

Do not confuse the digital zoom lens with a digital zoom. A *digital zoom* is not achieved with a lens, but with an electronic device that simply makes the pixels larger;

increasing the size of the pixels enlarges the image. The problem with digital zooms is that the enlarged pixels noticeably reduce the resolution of the image (recall the mosaic tiles in chapter 3). This is why professional cameras do not use digital zooms; they are used in consumer cameras only.

Focus Control

The focus control activates the focus mechanism in a zoom lens. For studio cameras the manual focus control ordinarily consists of a twist grip similar to a motorcycle throttle, usually mounted on the left panning handle. Two or three turns are sufficient to achieve focus over the full zoom range. As with the manual zoom, the focus operations are transferred by the drive cable from the panning-handle control to the lens. **SEE 4.18**

ENG EFP ENG/EFP cameras and all camcorders have a focus ring near the front of the zoom lens (see figure 4.9). You focus the lens by turning the focus ring clockwise or counterclockwise until the viewfinder shows the image to be sharp and clear. You will notice when focusing this way that the front end of the lens, including its lens shade, rotates. This rotation is not problematic unless you want to attach a special-effects filter, such as a star filter that transforms light sources into starlike light beams. When focusing with the filter attached, the effect will rotate with the lens and may end up sideways when you have the picture in focus. *Internal,* or *inner, focus (IF) lenses* do not

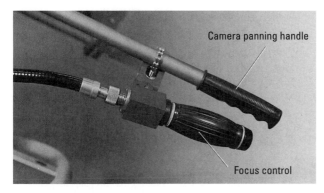

Camera panning handle

Focus control

4.18 STUDIO LENS MANUAL FOCUS CONTROL

The twist grip of the manual focus control for studio zoom lenses turns clockwise and counterclockwise for focusing.

rotate the front end when turning the focus ring. You can therefore focus IF lenses without upsetting the filter effect.

Servo focus   The servo focus control lets you preset the lens so that it keeps focus during carefully rehearsed camera and/or subject movements. Because even the smartest servo focus control will not help you stay in focus if the camera or subject movements have not been carefully rehearsed, most camera operators prefer to use the manual focus controls.

Auto-focus   The problem with *auto-focus* is that the camera does not know exactly on which object in the frame to focus. Because it cannot read your mind, it usually settles for the one that is more or less in the center of the frame and closest to the camera. If you want to focus on part of the scene that is farther in the background and off to one side, the auto-focus will not comply. Also, if you do a fast zoom, the automatic focus cannot keep up, so the picture will pop in and out of focus during the zoom. That is why experienced camera operators prefer to use the manual focus device.

MAIN POINTS

- There are various ways to classify zoom lenses: as studio and field lenses, and in terms of zoom range and lens format.

- A range extender (additional lens element) extends the telephoto power of the zoom lens (permits a closer shot) but reduces the range at the wide-angle end.

- The primary function of the lens is to produce a small, clear optical image on the front surface of the camera imaging device.

- All television cameras are equipped with zoom (variable-focal-length) lenses.

- The major optical characteristics of lenses are focal length; focus; light transmission, iris, and f-stop; and depth of field.

- The focal length of a lens determines how wide or narrow a vista the camera has and how much and in what way objects appear magnified. Zoom lenses have a variable focal length, whose major positions are wide-angle, normal, and narrow-angle (telephoto).

- A wide-angle lens (zoomed out) gives a wide vista. A narrow-angle lens (zoomed in) gives a narrow vista but magnifies the object so that it appears closer to the camera than it actually is. A normal lens (zoom position toward the wide-angle end of the zoom) approximates the angle of human vision.

- A picture is in focus when the projected image is sharp and clear. Before it is zoomed in, the lens needs to be preset (calibrated) so that focus is maintained over the zoom range. If the lens is properly focused when zoomed in, it should remain in focus when zoomed out and in again.

- The lens iris, or diaphragm, controls the amount of light passing through the lens. It consists of a series of thin metal plates that form a hole known as the aperture, or lens opening.

- The f-stop is a standard scale indicating how much light passes through the lens. Low f-stop numbers indicate large apertures; high f-stop numbers indicate small apertures.

- Studio cameras have a remote iris control, which is operated from the CCU (camera control unit). ENG/EFP cameras and consumer camcorders can be switched from manual to auto-iris mode, whereby the lens adjusts itself for optimal exposure (amount of light reaching the imaging device).

- The area in which objects at different distances from the camera are seen in focus is called depth of field. The depth of field depends on focal length of the lens, the aperture (f-stop), and distance from camera to object.

- The two basic operational controls for the zoom lens are the zoom control and the focus control. Both can be operated either manually or automatically by servo control. A third type is the use of a digital zoom lens.

4.2

What Lenses See

The performance characteristics of a lens refer to how it sees, what it can and cannot do, and how it generally behaves in common production practice. Because the camera normally processes only visual information the lens can see, knowledge of the performance characteristics—how it sees the world and how it influences the aesthetic elements of a picture—will aid you greatly in composing effective shots and in many other production tasks. Section 4.2 explores these concepts.

▶ **HOW LENSES SEE THE WORLD**
   Field of view, distortion of objects and perceived distance, movement, and depth of field of wide-angle, normal, and narrow-angle (telephoto) lenses

HOW LENSES SEE THE WORLD

Although all television cameras use zoom lenses, it might be easier for you to learn how various zoom positions influence what you see in the viewfinder by describing three zoom positions as though they were fixed-focal-length lenses (also called prime lenses). Fixed-focal-length lenses have a specific focal length that cannot be changed. They are normally classified as (1) wide-angle, or short-focal-length, lenses; (2) normal, or medium-focal-length, lenses; and (3) narrow-angle, or long-focal-length, lenses, also called *telephoto lenses*.[1]

Now let's adjust a zoom lens to correspond to the wide-angle, normal, and narrow-angle focal lengths and observe their performance characteristics. These include (1) field of view, (2) distortion of objects and perceived distance, (3) movement, and (4) depth of field.

The Wide-Angle Lens

As you recall, you need to zoom all the way out to achieve the maximum short focal length, or wide angle, of the zoom lens.

Field of view The *wide-angle lens* affords a wide vista. You can have a relatively wide *field of view*—the portion of a scene visible through the lens—with the camera rather close to the scene. When you need a wide

---

1. When HDTV cameras are used for electronic filmmaking, the director of photography sometimes uses prime lenses instead of zoom lenses to ensure maximum picture resolution.

vista (long shot) or, for example, when you need to see all five people on a panel and the studio is relatively small, a wide-angle lens (a wide-angle zoom position) is mandatory. The wide-angle lens is also well suited to provide pictures that fit the horizontally stretched 16×9 HDTV aspect ratio.

Object and distance distortion   A wide-angle lens makes objects relatively close to the camera look large and objects only a short distance away look quite small. This distortion—large foreground objects, small middle-ground, and even smaller background objects—helps increase the illusion of depth. The wide-angle lens also influences our perception of *perspective*. Because parallel lines seem to converge faster with this lens than you ordinarily perceive, it gives you a forced perspective that aids the illusion of exaggerated distance and depth. With a wide-angle lens, you can make a small room appear spacious or a hallway much longer than it really is. **SEE 4.19–4.23** Such distortions can also work against you. If you take a close-up of a face with a wide-angle lens, the nose, or whatever is closest to the lens, looks unusually large compared with the other parts of the face. **SEE 4.24**

Movement   The wide-angle lens is also a good dolly lens. Its wide field of view de-emphasizes camera wobbles and bumps during dollies, trucks, and arcs (see chapter 5). The zoom lens makes it so easy to move from a long shot to a close-up or vice versa, however, that dollying with a zoom lens has almost become a lost art. Most of the time, a zoom will be perfectly acceptable as a means to change the field of view (moving to a wider or closer shot).

You should be aware that there is a significant aesthetic difference between a zoom and a dolly. Whereas the *zoom* seems to bring the scene to the viewer, a *dolly* seems to take the viewer into the scene. Because the camera does not move during the zoom, the spatial relationship among objects remains constant. The objects appear to be glued into position—they simply get bigger (zoom-in) or smaller (zoom-out). In a dolly, however, the relationships among objects change constantly. You seem to move past them when dollying in or out.[2] Be sure to recalibrate the zoom when you have reached the end of

2. See Herbert Zettl, *Sight Sound Motion,* 3d ed. (Belmont, Calif.: Wadsworth Publishing Co., 1999), pp. 253–255.

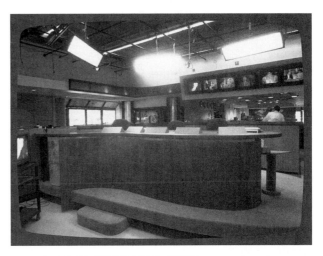

4.19 WIDE-ANGLE LONG SHOT
The wide-angle lens (zoom position) gives you a wide vista. Although the camera is relatively close to the news set, we can see the whole set.

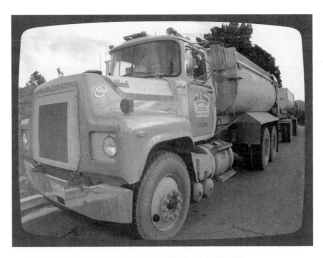

4.20 WIDE-ANGLE DISTORTION: TRUCK
The wide-angle lens intensifies the raw power of this truck. Note that the apparent size of the front grill is greatly exaggerated through the wide-angle lens.

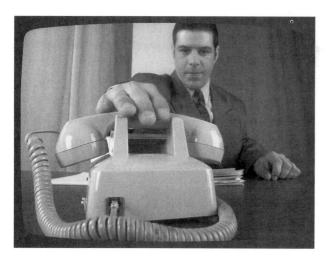

4.21 WIDE-ANGLE DISTORTION:
EMPHASIS ON FOREGROUND OBJECT
Shot with a wide-angle lens, the telephone and right hand
appear unusually large.

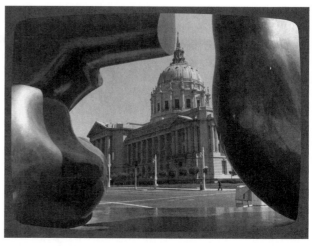

4.22 WIDE-ANGLE DISTORTION:
DEPTH ARTICULATION
Shooting through a permanent foreground piece with the wide-
angle lens creates a spatially articulated, forceful picture.

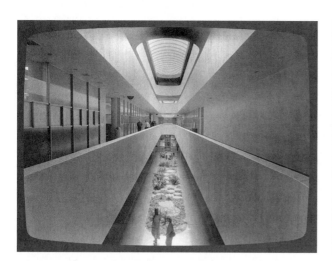

4.23 WIDE-ANGLE DISTORTION
OF LINEAR PERSPECTIVE
The length of this hallway is greatly exaggerated.

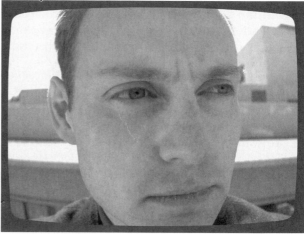

4.24 WIDE-ANGLE DISTORTION OF FACE
This face is greatly distorted because the shot was taken with
a wide-angle lens at a close distance.

the dolly so you can zoom in and out from the new position without losing focus.

When people or objects move toward or away from the camera, their speed appears greatly accelerated by the wide-angle lens. The wide-angle zoom position is often used in dance programs to emphasize the speed and distance of the dancers' leaps toward and away from the camera.

ENG EFP When covering a news event that exhibits a great deal of movement or that requires you to move rapidly, you should put the zoom lens in its extreme wide-angle position. This way you will have a much easier time keeping the event in the viewfinder and camera in focus than if you were zoomed in to a tighter focal length. The disadvantage of the extreme wide-angle lens position is that you need to be quite close to the action if you want a closer look.

Depth of field   The wide-angle lens generally has a great depth of field. When zoomed all the way out, you should have few focus problems, unless you work in low-light conditions (which requires a large aperture) or are extremely close to the object.

The Normal Lens

The zoom position for a normal focal length lies somewhere in the midrange of a zoom lens, perhaps a little more toward the wide-angle position.

Field of view   The *normal lens* offers a field of view (focal length) that approximates that of normal vision. It gives you the perspective between foreground and middle ground you actually see.

Object and distance distortion   Whereas the wide-angle lens makes objects seem farther apart and rooms seem larger than they actually are, the normal lens or the midrange zoom positions make objects and their spatial relationships appear closer to our normal vision. **SEE 4.25**

When shooting graphics such as charts that are positioned on an easel, you should put the zoom lens in the midrange position. These are the main advantages: (1) You can quickly correct the framing on the card by zooming in or out slightly or by dollying in or out without undue focus change. (2) You are far enough away from

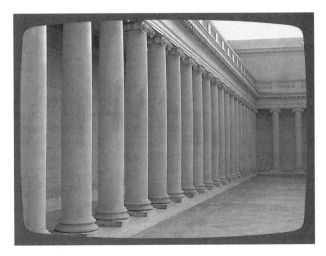

4.25 NORMAL LENS FIELD OF VIEW AND PERSPECTIVE
The normal lens gives a field of view that approximates normal vision.

the easel to avoid camera shadows, yet close enough so that the danger of someone's walking in front of the camera is minimal. (3) By placing the easel at a standard distance from the camera, a floor person can help you frame and focus on the card with minimal time and effort.

Movement   With the normal lens (midrange zoom positions), you have a much more difficult time keeping the picture in focus and avoiding camera wobbles, even if the camera is mounted on a studio pedestal. When carrying an ENG/EFP camera or camcorder, this lens position makes it hard to avoid camera wobbles even when standing still. If you need such a field of view, you should put the camera on a tripod.

Because the distance and object proportions approximate our normal vision, the dolly speed and the speed of objects moving toward or away from the camera also appear normal. But again, such movement may cause focus problems, especially when the object gets fairly close to the camera.

Depth of field   The normal lens has a considerably shallower depth of field than the wide-angle lens under similar conditions (same f-stop and object-to-camera distance). You might think that a very great depth of field would be the most desirable condition in studio opera-tions because it shows everything in focus. But a medium depth of field is often preferred in studio work and EFP, because the in-focus objects are set off against a slightly out-of-focus background. Thus, the objects are empha-sized, and a busy background or the inevitable smudges on the television scenery receive less attention. Most important, foreground, middleground, and background are better defined.[3] Of course, a large depth of field is necessary when there is considerable movement of camera and/or subjects. Also, when two objects are located at widely different distances from the camera, a great depth of field enables you to keep both in focus simultaneously. Most outdoor telecasts, such as sports remotes, require a large depth of field, the principal objective being to help the viewer see as much and as well as possible.

The Narrow-Angle, or Telephoto, Lens

When you zoom all the way in, the lens is in the maximum narrow-angle, or telephoto, position.

Field of view   The *narrow-angle lens* not only reduces the vista but also magnifies the background objects. Actually, when you zoom in, all the zoom lens does is magnify the image. You get a view as though you were looking through binoculars, which, in effect, act as telephoto lenses. **SEE 4.26**

Object and distance distortion   Because the enlarged background objects look big in comparison to the foreground objects, an illusion is created that the distance between foreground, middleground, and background has decreased. The long lens seems to compress the space between the objects, in direct contrast to the effect created by the wide-angle lens, which exaggerates object proportions and therefore seems to increase relative distance between objects. A narrow-angle lens, or telephoto zoom position, crowds objects on the screen.

This crowding effect, called aesthetic *compression*, can be positive or negative. If you want to show how crowded the freeways are during rush hour, for example,

3. Zettl, *Sight Sound Motion*, pp. 154–156.

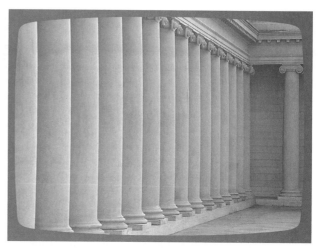

4.26 NARROW-ANGLE LENS FIELD OF VIEW AND PERSPECTIVE
The narrow-angle (telephoto) lens compresses space.

use the zoom lens in the telephoto position. The long focal length shrinks the perceived distance between the cars and makes them appear to be driving bumper-to-bumper. **SEE 4.27**

But such depth distortions by the narrow-angle lens also work to disadvantage. You are certainly familiar with the deceptive closeness of the pitcher to home plate on the television screen. Because television cameras must remain at a considerable distance from the action in most sporting events, the zoom lenses usually operate at their extreme telephoto positions or with powerful range extenders. The resulting compression effect makes it difficult for viewers to judge actual distances. **SEE 4.28**

Movement   The narrow-angle lens gives the illusion of *reduced speed* of an object moving toward or away from the camera. Because the narrow-angle lens changes the size of an object moving toward or away from the camera much more gradually than the wide-angle lens, the object seems to move more slowly than it actually does; in fact, an extreme narrow-angle lens virtually eliminates such movement. The object does not seem to change its size perceptibly even when it is traveling a considerable distance relative to the camera. Such a slowdown is especially effective if you want to emphasize the frustra-tion of someone running but not getting anywhere. Added to the compression effect (shown in figure 4.27), the

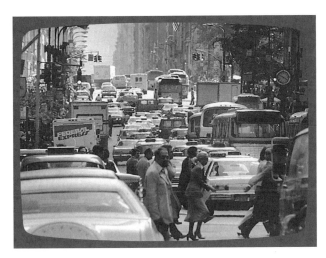

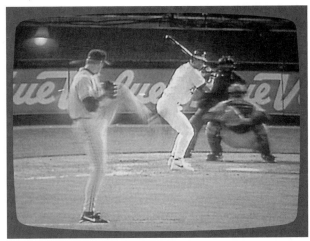

4.27 POSITIVE AESTHETIC
COMPRESSION WITH NARROW-ANGLE LENS
With a narrow-angle lens, the background is greatly enlarged
and the distance between the cars seems reduced. The
feeling of a traffic jam is heightened.

4.28 NEGATIVE AESTHETIC
COMPRESSION WITH NARROW-ANGLE LENS
This shot was taken with a zoom lens in an extreme long-
focal-length position. Note how the runner, pitcher, batter,
catcher, and umpire all seem to stand only a few feet apart
from one another. The actual distance between the pitcher
and the batter is 60½ feet.

drastic reduction of the perceived speed of traffic will certainly emphasize the congestion.

You cannot dolly with a narrow-angle lens or with a zoom lens in its telephoto position (zoomed in). Its magnifying power makes any movement of the camera impossible. If you work outdoors, even wind can become a problem. A stiff breeze may shake the camera to such a degree that the greatly magnified vibrations become clearly visible on the television screen. When you have to walk, or perhaps even run, with the portable camera for a news story or other type of electronic field production, make sure that the zoom lens is in the wide-angle position. If it is zoomed in to the telephoto position, the pictures will be rendered useless by the camera wobbles and focus problems.

In the studio the telephoto position may present another problem. The director may have you zoom in on part of an event, such as the lead guitar in a rock concert, and then, after you have zoomed in, ask you to truck (move the camera sideways) past the other members of the band. But this movement is extremely difficult to do in the telephoto zoom position. Instead, you should dolly in with a wide-angle zoom position and then truck with the lens still in the wide-angle position.

Depth of field Unless the object is far away from the camera, long lenses have a shallow depth of field. Like the compression effect, a shallow depth of field can have advantages and disadvantages. Let us assume that you are about to take a quick close-up of a medium-sized object, such as a can of dogfood. You do not have to bother putting up a background for it—all you need do is move the camera back and zoom in on the display. With the zoom lens now in a telephoto (narrow-angle) position, decreasing the depth of field to a large extent, the background is sufficiently out of focus to prevent undesirable distractions. This technique is called *selective focus*, meaning that you can focus either on the foreground, with the middleground and background out of focus; on the middleground, with the foreground and background out of focus; or on the background, with the foreground and middleground out of focus.

You can also shift emphasis easily from one object to another with the help of selective focus. For example, you can zoom in on a foreground object, thus reducing the depth of field, and focus on it, with the zoom lens in the telephoto position. Then, by refocusing on the person behind it, you can quickly shift the emphasis from the foreground object to the person (middle-

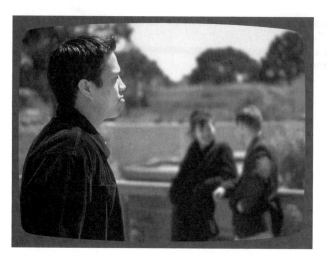

4.29 SELECTIVE FOCUS: FOREGROUND IN FOCUS
In this shot the camera-near person is in focus, drawing attention, rather than the two people farther away.

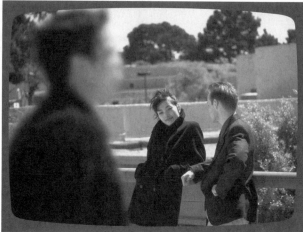

4.30 SELECTIVE FOCUS: BACKGROUND IN FOCUS
Here the focus and attention are shifted from the camera-near person (foreground) to the two people farther away.

ground). This technique is called *racking focus* or, simply, *rack focus*. SEE 4.29 AND 4.30

The advantage of a shallow depth of field also applies to unwanted foreground objects. In a baseball pickup, for example, the camera behind home plate may have to shoot through the fence. But because the camera is most likely zoomed in on the pitcher, or on other players performing at a considerable distance from the camera, you work with a relatively short depth of field. Consequently, everything fairly close to the camera, such as the fence wire, is so much out of focus that for all practical purposes it becomes invisible. The same principle works for shooting through bird cages, prison bars, or similar foreground objects.

MAIN POINTS

◆ The performance characteristics of wide-angle, normal, and narrow-angle lenses (zoom lenses adjusted to these focal lengths) include field of view, object and distance distortion, movement, and depth of field.

◆ A wide-angle lens (a zoom lens zoomed out to the wide-angle position) offers a wide vista. It gives a wide field of view with the camera relatively close to the scene.

◆ A wide-angle lens distorts objects close to the lens and exaggerates proportions. Objects relatively

close to the lens look large, and those only a short distance away look quite small. Hence, it makes objects look farther apart and makes rooms look larger than they actually are.

◆ A wide-angle lens is ideal for camera movement. It minimizes the wobbles of the camera and makes it easy to keep the picture in focus during camera movement.

◆ The normal lens gives a field of view that approximates that of normal vision. The normal lens (or midrange zoom position) does not distort objects or the perception of distance. It is used when a normal perspective is desired.

◆ When a camera is moved with the lens in the mid-range (normal lens) zoom position, camera wobbles are emphasized considerably more than with a wide-angle lens. The shallower depth of field makes it harder to keep the picture in focus.

◆ A narrow-angle lens (zoom lens in the telephoto position) has a narrow field of view and it enlarges the objects in the background. Exactly opposite of the wide-angle lens, which increases the distance between objects, the narrow-angle lens seems to compress the space between objects at different distances from the camera.

◆ The magnifying power of a narrow-angle lens prevents any camera movement while on the air. Narrow-angle lenses have a shallow depth of field, which makes keeping in focus more difficult but allows for selective focus.

Z E T T L ' S   V I D E O L A B   2 . 1

This portion of Zettl's VideoLab 2.1 lets you practice zooming and achieving optimal exposure by running through various f-stops.

RUN ZVL 1   Click on the **camera** monitor and run tape 2 **Zoom Lens**. Click on the first five modules: **Focal length, Zoom control, Normal, Wide,** and **Narrow**. Now click on the **Try it** module and watch the effects of zooming in and out.

RUN ZVL 2   Run tape 3 **Exposure Control**. Click on the first three modules: **Aperture, *f*-stop,** and **Auto iris**. Note the inverse relationship between *f*-stop number and iris aperture. Note also the liabilities when switching to auto-iris.

RUN ZVL 3   Run tape 4 **Focusing**. Click on the first six modules: **Focus ring, Depth of field, Great depth, Shallow, Rack focus,** and **Auto focus**. This tape reinforces the importance of depth of field. Again, watch the problem you may encounter when switching to auto-focus.

Always check your understanding by doing the **Try it** exercises and taking the **Quizzes**.

5

Camera Mounting Equipment

Because television cameras differ considerably in size and weight, various camera mounts are needed for ease and efficiency of operation. For example, you may find that a camera mount for the studio has to support not only a heavy camera with its large zoom lens, but also the added weight of a bulky teleprompting device. In contrast, most ENG/EFP cameras are designed to be carried on the operator's shoulder. And, as you know, some camcorders are so small that you can hold and operate them quite easily with one hand. But there are many production situations in which the ENG/EFP camera and small camcorder should be mounted on a tripod rather than carried by the operator. Section 5.1, Standard Camera Mounts and Movements, examines the basics of camera mounts, and section 5.2, Special Camera Mounts, discusses special mounting devices.

arc To move the camera in a slightly curved dolly or truck.

cam head A camera mounting head for heavy cameras that permits extremely smooth tilts and pans.

cant Tilting the shoulder-mounted or handheld camera sideways.

crab Sideways motion of the camera crane dolly base.

crane (1) Camera dolly that resembles an actual crane in both appearance and operation. The crane can lift the camera from close to the studio floor to more than 10 feet above it. (2) To move the boom of the camera crane up or down. Also called *boom*.

dolly (1) Camera support that enables the camera to move in all directions. (2) To move the camera toward (dolly in) or away from (dolly out or back) the object.

fluid head Most popular mounting head for lightweight ENG/EFP cameras. Balance is provided by springs. Because its moving parts operate in a heavy fluid, it allows very smooth pans and tilts.

high hat Cylindrical camera mount that can be bolted to a dolly or scenery to permit panning and tilting the camera without a tripod or pedestal.

jib arm Similar to a camera crane. Elevates the camera considerably higher than a studio pedestal can and permits the jib arm operator to tilt and pan the camera at the same time.

monopod A single pole onto which you can mount a camera.

pan Horizontal turning of the camera.

pedestal (1) Heavy camera dolly that permits raising and lowering the camera while on the air. (2) To move the camera up and down via a studio pedestal.

quick-release plate Mounting plate used to attach camcorders and ENG/EFP cameras to the fluid head.

robot pedestal Motor-driven studio pedestal with mounting head that is guided by a computerized system that can store and execute a great number of camera moves. Also called *robotic*.

spreader A triangular base mount that provides stability and locks the tripod tips in place to prevent the legs from spreading.

Steadicam Camera mount whose built-in springs hold the camera steady while the operator moves.

studio crane Large camera mount that supports a heavy camera as well as the camera operator.

tilt To point the camera up or down.

tongue To move the boom with the camera from left to right or right to left.

track Another name for *truck* (lateral camera movement).

tripod A three-legged camera mount, usually connected to a dolly for easy maneuverability.

truck To move the camera laterally by means of a mobile camera mount.

wedge mount Wedge-shaped plate attached to the bottom of a studio camera; used to attach the heavier cameras to the cam head.

zoom To change the lens gradually to a narrow-angle position (zoom-in) or to a wide-angle position (zoom-out) while the camera remains stationary.

5.1

Standard Camera Mounts and Movements

All ENG/EFP cameras and consumer camcorders are designed to be carried with your hands or on your shoulder, but whenever possible you should try to mount the camera on a camera support, such as a tripod. Using a camera support will reduce fatigue and prevent unnecessary and distracting camera motion. This section discusses the more common camera mounts and the basic camera movements.

▶ **BASIC CAMERA MOUNTS**
The handheld and shoulder-mounted camera, the monopod and tripod, and the studio pedestal

▶ **CAMERA MOUNTING (PAN-AND-TILT) HEADS**
Spring-loaded fluid heads, cam friction heads, and the quick-release plate and wedge mount

▶ **CAMERA MOVEMENTS**
Standard camera movements: pan, tilt, pedestal, tongue, crane or boom, dolly, truck or track, crab, arc, cant, and zoom

BASIC CAMERA MOUNTS

When using a camcorder on vacation or when running after a news story, you will probably carry your camcorder with your hands or on your shoulder. But when more precise camera work is required, you need to use a camera mount. The most common camera mounts are the tripod and the tripod dolly, and the studio pedestal. The more-elaborate camera mounts, such as jib arms, studio cranes, or special body mounts, are discussed in section 5.2.

The Handheld and Shoulder-Mounted Camera

If the camera is light enough, the most flexible camera mount is your arms or shoulder. You can lift and lower the camera, tilt it up or down, swing it around, cant it (tilt it sideways), and walk or run with it. Why then bother with tripods? First, you will be able to operate the camera much longer without getting fatigued than when carrying it. Even a small camcorder can get awfully heavy when shooting over a period of several hours. Second, and probably more important, using some kind of camera support prevents unmotivated camera motion—swinging and weaving it back and forth not unlike a firefighter using a fire hose to put out an especially nasty fire. Unless motivated, as in some commercials and MTV shows, wild and rapid camera movement draws too much attention to itself and is one of the sure signs of amateur camera handling. Third, even if you are exceptionally well coordinated, the tripod makes for smoother moves. Nevertheless, there are some techniques that professional camera operators have developed to keep the handheld or shoulder-mounted camera as steady as possible. These are explored in chapter 6.

The Monopod and Tripod

You will find that even a relatively light ENG/EFP camera can get awfully heavy during long shoots. Using a portable camera support, such as a monopod or tripod, will not only get the camera off your back, but also keep you from making unnecessary or distracting camera movements.

Monopod   The *monopod* is a single pole, or a single "pod," onto which you can mount a camera. When using a monopod, you still need to balance the camera on the single pole as you would on your shoulder, but at least you are relieved of the camera's weight. Some monopod supports have a fold-out extension with which, by stepping on it, you steady the single pole sufficiently so that you can work the camera with both hands. The advantage of such a camera support is that it is easy to carry and can be set up in less than a minute. Such monopods are by no means perfect, but they offer a welcome relief during a long shoot, not unlike finding a tree trunk or rock to sit on after a long hike.

Tripod and tripod dolly   The *tripod* is used extensively for all types of field work. Regardless of whether you use a heavy tripod for the support of a studio camera or a light one for a field camera or camcorder, all tripods work on a similar principle: They have three collapsible legs that can be individually extended so that the camera is level, even on an irregular surface such as a steep driveway, bleachers, or stairs. The tips of the legs are equipped with spikes and rubber cups that keep the tripod from slipping. Most tripods can be adjusted to a specific camera height (usually from about 16 to 60 inches) and have a built-in *spreader* that prevents the tripod legs from spreading and collapsing under a heavy load. **SEE 5.1**

     For tripods that do not have a built-in spreader, there are types of spreaders that you can place on the ground and then fasten the three tips of the tripod to each corner.

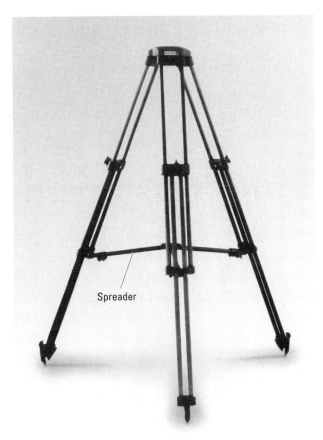

Spreader

5.1 TRIPOD WITH BUILT-IN SPREADER

The tripod is one of the most basic camera supports and is used extensively in field productions. This tripod has a built-in spreader at midlevel.

These spreaders can be adjusted to accommodate a small or large triangular base. The disadvantage of a separate spreader is that you can use it only when the ground is relatively level. **SEE 5.2**

     When setting up a tripod, you must take particular care that the tripod, and with it the camera, is level. Such a setup is especially difficult when you need to work on steps or uneven ground. **SEE 5.3** Fortunately, most high-quality tripods have provisions to accept a ball-like leveling platform, called a *leveling ball*, which allows leveling adjustments without having to adjust the length of each leg. Most pan-and-tilt heads have a built-in air bubble that indicates when the camera is level (see section 5.2).

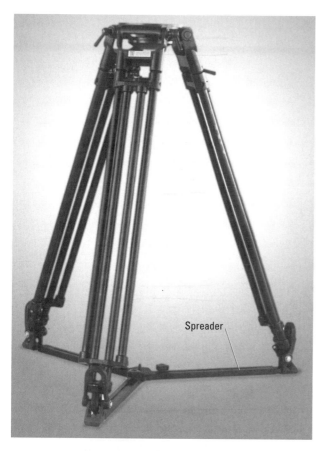

5.2 TRIPOD MOUNTED ON SPREADER

The spreader supplies additional stability for the tripod and prevents it from collapsing under a heavy load.

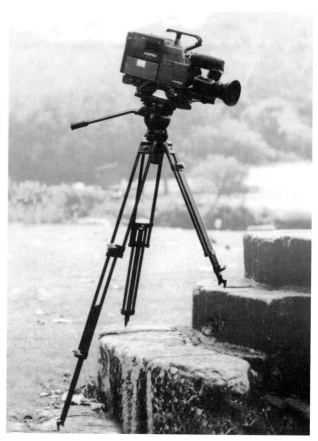

5.3 TRIPOD ON STEPS

Because each pod can be adjusted individually, the tripod can be leveled even on extremely uneven ground.

You can also place the tripod on a three-caster *dolly*, which is simply a spreader with wheels. Because the tripod and the dolly are collapsible, they are the ideal camera mount for field operations. You will find tripod dollies used even in studios equipped with studio-converted ENG/EFP cameras. The dolly base should be adjustable so that you can maneuver it through various-sized doors, and have cable guards that prevent the camera cable from getting caught under the dolly base or run over by the dolly wheels. **SEE 5.4**

The Studio Pedestal

With a studio *pedestal*, you can smoothly move a camera in all directions (assuming there is a smooth floor) and elevate and lower the camera while on the air. This up-and-down movement adds an important dimension to the art of television photography. Not only can you adjust the camera to a comfortable working height, but you can also change the eye level from which you look at an event. For example, if you are in danger of overshooting the set, you can always pedestal up (raise the camera) and look down on the scene. Or you can pedestal down (lower the camera) and look up at the scene, such as at the lead singer of a rock group. Some of the pedestals use counterweights to balance the weight of the camera in its up-and-down movement; others use pneumatic pressure, or both weights and pneumatic pressure.

Regardless of the specific balancing mechanism, all studio pedestals have similar operating features. You can steer the pedestal smoothly in any direction with a large

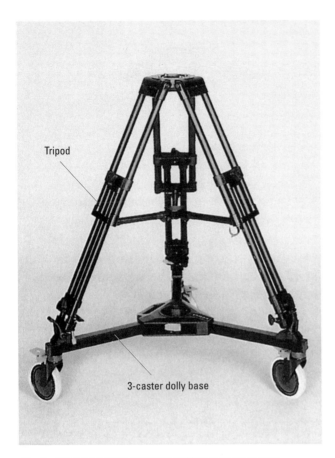

5.4 COLLAPSIBLE TRIPOD WITH DOLLY BASE
The tripod can be mounted on a dolly, which permits quick repositioning of the camera. This is called a tripod dolly.

Tripod

3-caster dolly base

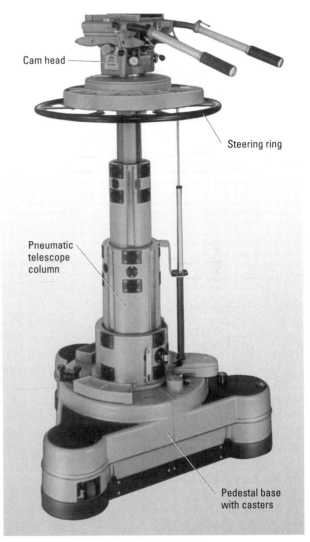

Cam head

Steering ring

Pneumatic
telescope
column

Pedestal base
with casters

5.5 STUDIO PEDESTAL
The studio pedestal permits smooth dollies and trucks and has a telescoping center column that pedestals the camera from a low of 2 feet to a maximum height of about 6 feet from the studio floor.

horizontal steering ring or steering wheel. By pulling up on the steering ring, you move the camera higher, or, as it is technically called, you *pedestal up*. By pressing down on it, you lower the camera, or *pedestal down*. Pedestals are not judged by how high they can elevate the cameras, but rather by how they move the camera relative to the floor. The more the pedestal column telescopes, the better it is. The telescoping pedestal column can be locked at any desired horizontal position.

Like tripod dollies, studio pedestals need a cable guard to prevent the heavy pedestal from running over the camera cable. Always check that the adjustable skirt of the pedestal base is low enough to push the cable out of the way, rather than roll over it. **SEE 5.5**

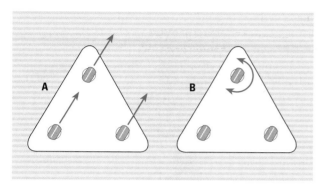

5.6 PARALLEL (CRAB) AND TRICYCLE STEERING

A In the parallel, or crab, position, all three casters point in the same direction. **B** In the tricycle position, only one wheel is steerable. A foot pedal allows a quick change from parallel to tricycle steering.

Generally, you work the pedestal in the parallel, or *crab*, steering position, which means that all three casters point in the same direction. **SEE 5.6A** If, however, you want to rotate the pedestal itself, to move it closer to a wall or piece of scenery, for example, you can switch it from the crab to the *tricycle* steering position. **SEE 5.6B**

There are also lighter pneumatic pedestals that can be adjusted to the lightweight ENG/EFP cameras. These can be taken on remote locations and used when smooth dollies, trucks, and camera elevations are required. You can disassemble such pedestals for transport and, as with tripod dollies, adjust the width of the dolly base to fit through doors. **SEE 5.7**

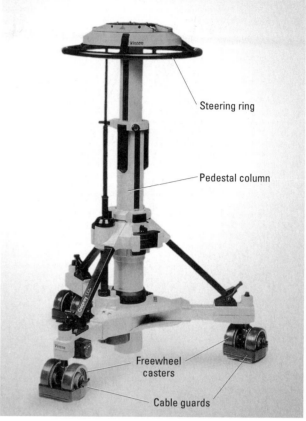

Steering ring

Pedestal column

Freewheel casters

Cable guards

5.7 PORTABLE CAMERA PEDESTAL

These pedestals are much lighter than the studio pedestals and can be disassembled and transported to various (usually indoor) field locations.

CAMERA MOUNTING (PAN-AND-TILT) HEADS

The camera mounting head connects the camera to the tripod or studio pedestal. The mounting head (not to be confused with the *camera head*, which represents the actual camera and lens) allows you to *tilt* (point the camera up and down) and *pan* (turn it horizontally) extremely smoothly. The mounting devices for the lighter tripod-supported cameras are *fluid heads;* the heavier field and studio cameras use *cam heads.*

Fluid Heads

Fluid heads are normally used for ENG/EFP cameras or consumer camcorders that weigh less than 30 pounds, although heavy-duty fluid heads can support up to 60 pounds. Such heavy-duty models are necessary for

attaching teleprompters or various pieces of transmission equipment to the ENG/EFP camcorders.

Fluid heads contain a spring-loaded counterbalancing mechanism that is encased in thick oil, which supplies the drag necessary for smooth pans and tilts. Most professional fluid heads have four controls: a tilt-and-pan drag and a tilt-and-pan lock. The drag control gives various degrees of resistance to panning and tilting to make the camera movements optimally smooth. The lock control locks the pan-and-tilt mechanism to keep the camera from moving when left unattended. **SEE 5.8** *Do not use the drag control to lock the mounting head, or the lock control to assist the drag.* Neither practice will work very well and would eventually wreck the mounting head.

The fluid head attaches to the leveling ball, which attaches to the tripod platform. As stated, the leveling ball enables you to level the camera without making adjust-

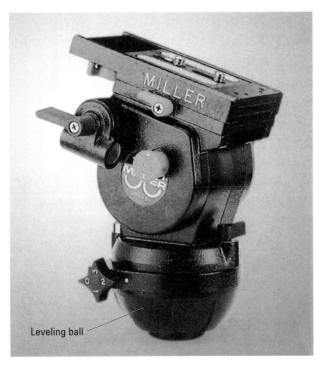

5.8 FLUID HEAD

Fluid heads are designed for mounting and operating ENG/EFP cameras and camcorders on tripods. They have a limited weight capacity.

ments to the tripod legs, assuming the tripod is relatively level already. The actual panning and tilting are done with a single panning handle or double panning handles that are attached to the mounting head. By moving the panning handle up and down, you tilt the camera; by moving it left and right, you pan the camera.

Cam Heads

Cam heads are designed to connect heavy studio or field cameras to studio or field pedestals. Like fluid heads, cam heads have separate drag and lock mechanisms. Be sure to find out exactly which knob adjusts the friction (to make your tilt-and-pan movements somewhat looser or tighter) and which one locks the camera mounting head. **SEE 5.9** As with fluid heads, *do not use the drag control to lock the cam head, or the lock control to adjust the drag.* Using the drag control to lock the camera will ruin the cam head in a very short time, and trying to use the locking device for pan-and-tilt drag control will almost always result in jerky and uneven camera movements.

Plate and Wedge Mount

How do you attach the camera to the fluid head so that the camera is fairly well balanced during tilts? This is done with an attachment mechanism called a *quick-release plate*. You attach a metal plate to the bottom of the camera

5.9 CAM HEAD

The cam head is designed for heavier cameras. It is normally used for mounting studio cameras with teleprompters onto studio pedestals.

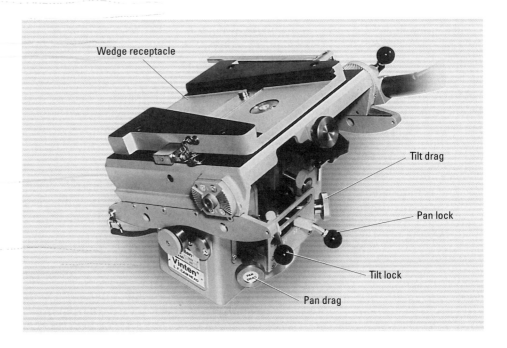

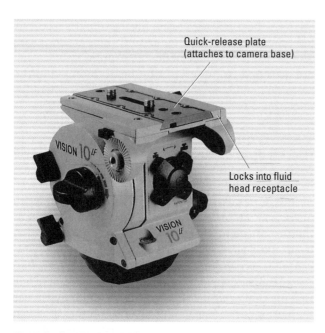

5.10 QUICK-RELEASE PLATE

The quick-release plate enables you to reattach the camera to the mounting head in a balanced position without time-consuming readjustment.

(with one or two bolts) and then simply slide the plate (with the camera attached) onto its receptacle on the fluid head. A simple lever holds the camera in the predetermined balanced position.

The problem is how far forward or backward to slide the plate so that the camera is indeed balanced. Digital technology has again come to the rescue. High-end fluid heads now have a digital readout that tells you just where to place the quick-release plate for optimal balance. Many field productions require that you take the camera off the tripod, run to a new position for a few quick shots, and then return to the tripod position. The quick-release plate makes it possible to detach the camera and put it back again in a perfectly balanced position within seconds. **SEE 5.10**

Cam heads use a similar device, called a ***wedge mount***—a wedge-shaped plate attached to the bottom of the studio camera. All you have to do is slip the camera with the wedge plate onto the cam head receptacle; the camera is then balanced and securely attached to the cam head and ready to go. **SEE 5.11**

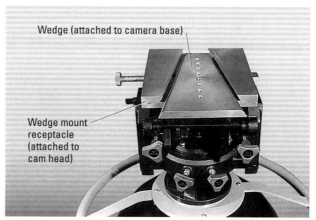

5.11 WEDGE MOUNT

The wedge mount makes it easy to connect the studio camera to the cam head in a balanced position.

CAMERA MOVEMENTS

Before learning to operate a camera, you should become familiar with the most common camera movements. *Left* and *right* always refer to the *camera's* point of view. The camera mounting equipment has been designed solely to help you move the camera smoothly and efficiently in various ways. The major camera movements are pan, tilt, pedestal, tongue, crane or boom, dolly, truck or track, crab, arc, cant, and zoom. **SEE 5.12**

- ***Pan***. Turning the camera horizontally, from left to right or from right to left. To "pan right," which means that you swivel the lens and the camera to the right (clockwise), you must push the panning handles to the left. To "pan left," which means to swivel the lens and the camera to the left (counterclockwise), you push the panning handles to the right.

- ***Tilt***. Making the camera point down or up. A "tilt up" means that the camera is made to point up gradually. A "tilt down" means that the camera is made to point down gradually.

- ***Pedestal***. Elevating or lowering the camera on a studio pedestal. To "pedestal up," you raise the pedestal; to "pedestal down," you lower the pedestal.

5.12 CAMERA MOVEMENTS

Major camera movements include pan, tilt, pedestal, tongue, crane or boom, dolly, truck or track, arc, and cant.

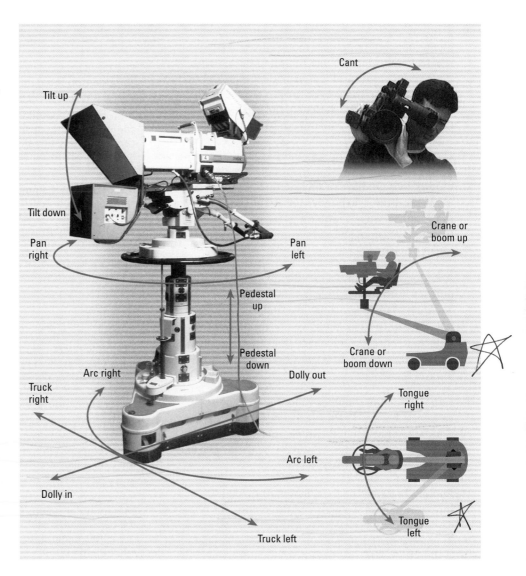

- **Tongue.** Moving the whole camera from left to right or from right to left with the boom of a camera crane. When you tongue left or right, the camera usually points in the same general direction, with only the boom moving left (counterclockwise) or right (clockwise).

- **Crane** or **boom.** Moving the whole camera up or down on a camera crane or jib arm. The effect is somewhat similar to an up or down pedestal,

except that the camera swoops over a much greater vertical distance. You either "crane, or boom, up" or "crane, or boom, down."

- **Dolly.** Moving the camera toward or away from an object in more or less a straight line by means of a mobile camera mount. When you "dolly in," you move the camera closer to the object; when you "dolly out or dolly back," you move the camera farther away from the object.

■ *Truck* or *track*. Moving the camera laterally by means of a mobile camera mount. To "truck left" means to move the camera mount to the left with the camera pointing at a right angle to the direction of the travel. To "truck right" means to move the camera mount to the right with the camera pointing at a right angle to the direction of the travel.

■ *Crab*. Any sideways motion of the crane dolly. A crab is similar to a truck, except that the camera mount does not have to stay lateral to the action the whole time; it can move toward or away from the action as well. "Crabbing" is used more in film than in television. The term is sometimes used to mean trucking.

■ *Arc*. Moving the camera in a slightly curved dolly or truck movement with a mobile camera mount. To "arc left" means to dolly in or out in a camera-left curve or to truck left in a curve around the object; to "arc right" means to dolly in or out in a camera-right curve or to truck right in a curve around the object.

■ *Cant*. Tilting the shoulder-mounted or handheld camera sideways. The result, called a *canting effect*, is a slanted horizon line, which puts the scene on a slight tilt. Through the skewed horizon line, you can achieve a highly dynamic scene.

■ *Zoom*. Changing the focal length of the lens through the use of a zoom control while the camera remains stationary. To "zoom in" means to change the lens gradually to a narrow-angle position, thereby making the scene appear to move closer to the viewer; to "zoom out" means to change the lens gradually to a wide-angle position, thereby making the scene appear to move farther away from the viewer. Although not a camera movement per se, the zoom effect looks similar to that of a moving camera and is, therefore, classified as such. *READY ZVL* ❶

MAIN POINTS

◆ The basic camera mounts are handheld and shoulder-mounted, the monopod, the tripod and tripod dolly, and the studio pedestal.

◆ Although the handheld or shoulder-mounted camera is highly flexible, it is difficult to hold the camera steady or achieve smooth camera movement, especially when the zoom lens is in the telephoto position.

◆ A monopod is a single pole upon which the camera is mounted. Tripods are used extensively for supporting ENG/EFP cameras or smaller camcorders in field productions. The tripod can be mounted on a three-caster dolly base.

◆ Studio pedestals can support heavy studio cameras and permit extremely smooth camera movements, such as dollies, trucks, and arcs. The camera can also be raised and lowered while on the air.

◆ The camera mounting head connects the camera to the camera mount and allows the camera to be smoothly tilted up and down and panned horizontally. There are two types of mounting heads: fluid heads, used for consumer camcorders or ENG/EFP cameras; and cam heads, designed for use with heavy camcorders and studio cameras.

◆ The quick-release mounting plate is used to attach camcorders and ENG/EFP cameras to the fluid head. The wedge mount attaches the heavier cameras to the cam head.

◆ The most common camera movements are *pan,* turning the camera horizontally; *tilt,* pointing the camera up or down; *pedestal,* lowering or elevating the camera on a studio pedestal; *tongue,* moving the whole camera from left to right or from right to left with the boom of a camera crane or jib arm; *crane* or *boom,* moving the whole camera up or down on a camera crane or jib arm; *dolly,* moving the camera toward or away from the object; *truck* or *track,* moving the camera laterally; *crab,* moving the whole base of a camera crane sideways; *arc,* moving the camera in a slightly curved dolly or truck movement; *cant,* tilting the camera sideways; and *zoom,* changing the focal length of the lens while the camera is stationary.

5.2

Special Camera Mounts

Special camera mounts are designed to help you operate a camera in unusual shooting conditions, such as when covering a scene in a cramped living room or field position, swooping from a view high above the event to below eye level, running up a flight of stairs, or shooting from the perspective of a speeding car. Some pedestals are designed to do without you; their movements are controlled not by the camera operator, but by a computer. This section examines such special camera mounting devices.

▶ **SPECIAL MOUNTING DEVICES**
  The high hat, the bean bag, the Steadicam, short and long jibs, and the studio crane

▶ **ROBOT PEDESTALS AND MOUNTING HEADS**
  Used for shows with rigid production formats, such as newscasts

SPECIAL MOUNTING DEVICES

Despite their flexibility, the tripod and studio pedestal cannot always facilitate the required camera movements. If during a field production, for example, the director wanted you to follow the main character from the car through the front door and down the hall with great fluidity, and then follow the character running up a flight of stairs without any distracting camera wiggles, you need a special mounting device. If the director then asked you to attach the camera to a moving car without resorting to extremely expensive equipment, how would you do it? Here are some of the more accessible mounting devices: (1) the high hat, (2) the bean bag, (3) the Steadicam, (4) the short and long jib, and (5) the studio crane.

High Hat

The *high hat* is a short (about 6 inches) cylinder-shaped or three-legged metal mount that accepts the usual fluid or cam mounting heads. You can bolt or clamp the high hat onto part of the scenery, on the bleachers of a stadium, on a fence post, or, for low-angle shots, on a piece of plywood fastened to a tripod dolly. **SEE 5.13**

Bean Bag

No kidding! The bean bag has its place as an effective camera mount. It is simply a canvas bag filled not with beans but with high-tech foam that molds itself to the shape of any ENG/EFP camera or camcorder. All you do is set the camera on the bag and then strap the bag with

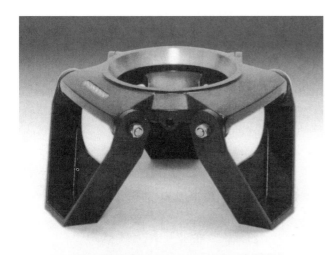

5.13 HIGH HAT
The high hat can be bolted or clamped to scenery, bleachers, or a fence post. You can use it with a fluid head or even a cam head.

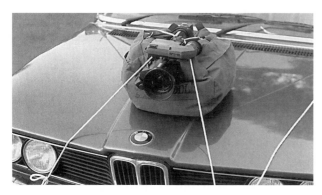

5.14 BEAN BAG

This canvas bag filled with synthetic material adjusts to any camera and any object on which the camera is mounted. Both bag and camera can be easily secured with nylon rope.

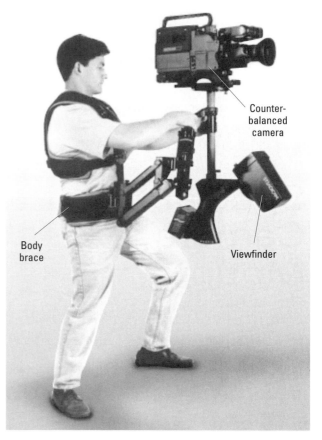

5.15 STEADICAM MOUNT

With the Steadicam mount, you can run with the camera while keeping the pictures perfectly steady. The rather heavy mechanism is connected to a body harness.

the camera to the object that acts as a camera mount. You can use this "bag mount" on cars, boats, mountain ledges, bicycles, or ladders. **SEE 5.14**

Steadicam

The *Steadicam* is a camera mount worn by the camera operator. Various springs absorb the wobbles and jitters while you run with the camera. During the take, you can watch the scene in a small viewfinder mounted below the camera. The counterbalance mechanism makes the camera so smooth that even when you run upstairs or on a mountain trail, the camera shots will come out as though you had used a large camera crane. The Steadicam harness and mount for motion picture cameras and large ENG/EFP camcorders are relatively heavy, and only experienced operators can wear them and the camera/monitor combination for an extended period. **SEE 5.15** There are, however, more-compact Steadicam mounts that support lighter (from 8 to 17 pounds) ENG/EFP cameras, or small (2- to 6-pound) digital or consumer camcorders. The camera mounts for such lightweight cameras do not need a body brace. You simply grab the whole unit with one hand and run with it, similar to carrying a small flag. **SEE 5.16**

Short and Long Jibs

The short *jib arm* is a counterbalanced camera mount designed for shooting on location. You can clamp it onto a door frame, a chair, a deck railing, or a car window and then tongue the camera sideways and boom it up and down. **SEE 5.17** That way you can not only perform smooth camera movements, but also pay full attention

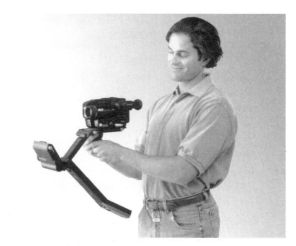

5.16 STEADICAM MOUNT
FOR LIGHTWEIGHT CAMCORDERS

The Steadicam JR mount is designed for lightweight consumer camcorders, such as the Hi8 or DTV models.

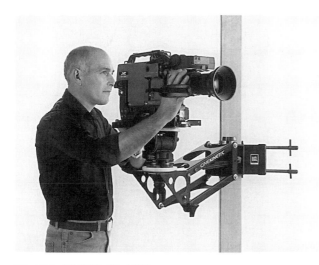

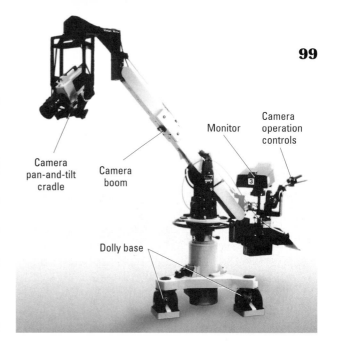

5.17 SHORT JIB ARM

This lightweight, counterbalanced jib arm can be clamped onto any suitable surface. It is especially useful when working in cramped quarters.

5.18 LONG JIB

With the long jib, the camera operator can dolly, truck, and boom the camera up or down and simultaneously pan, tilt, focus, and zoom.

to panning and zooming and the general composition of your shots.

The long jib or long jib arm is a cranelike device that lets you—by yourself—lower the camera practically to the studio floor, raise it approximately 12 feet, tongue the jib arm and swing it a full 360 degrees, dolly or truck the whole assembly, and, at the same time, tilt, pan, focus, and zoom the camera. Obviously, all these movements require practice if they are to look smooth on the air. The camera and jib arm are balanced by a monitor, the battery pack, remote camera controls, and, for good measure, actual counterweights. **SEE 5.18**

Some jib arm camera mounts are specially designed for field work. You can quickly and easily collapse the whole jib and carry it in a single 6-foot bag. Once on location you can assemble and have the 12-foot jib operational at the remote location in less than five minutes. **SEE 5.19**

Studio Crane

Although a crane is desirable for creative camera work, it is used in very few television studios. In most cases, the long jib arm is preferred over a crane, because it is lighter and can perform almost all the functions of a crane. Besides needing a great amount of operating space, a *studio crane* requires at least one dolly-and-boom operator in addition to the camera operator who sits on the boom; when the crane is motor driven, still another person is needed to drive the crane very much like a

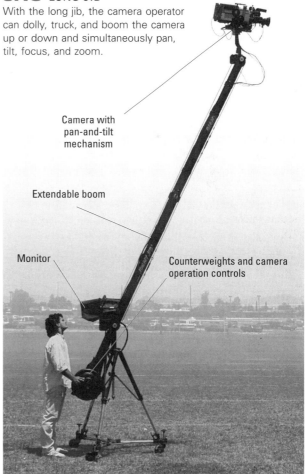

5.19 FIELD JIB

This field jib can be easily disassembled, carried in a canvas bag, and assembled again in minutes.

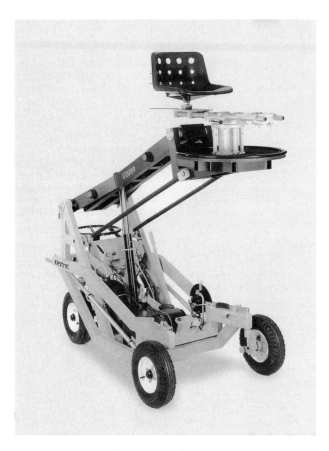

5.20 STUDIO CRANE
Studio cranes are used for elaborate productions. Besides the camera operator, cranes need one or two extra people to operate the crane itself.

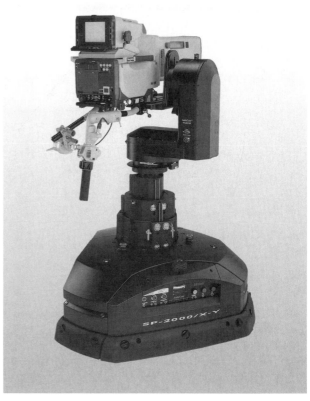

5.21 ROBOT PEDESTAL
The robot pedestal is fully automated and needs no camera operator. All necessary camera movements and functions are computer-controlled.

forklift. Some film directors still like to use the familiar crane, even when they are shooting for television. Those directors like the shot flexibility and sweeping motions the crane offers, even if it is more cumbersome to use than a jib arm. Also, some cranes allow the director to ride on the boom right next to the camera operator, which simplifies considerably the communication between director and camera operator. **SEE 5.20**

ROBOT PEDESTALS AND MOUNTING HEADS

Automated pedestals and mounting heads, sometimes called *robot pedestals* or *robotics,* are used more and more for shows with rigid production formats, such as news shows, teleconferences, and certain instructional

programs. The robot pedestal consists of a motor-driven studio pedestal and mounting head. It, as well as the remote zoom and focus controls, is guided by a computerized system that can store up to 800 camera moves. **SEE 5.21**

For example, the computer list for a portion of a news show may display and eventually activate the following scenario: While cameras 2 and 3 are still on the news anchor, camera 1 relocates to the weather area and gets ready for the opening shot by tilting up and zooming out to a long shot of the weathercaster and the map. Camera 1 is then joined by camera 2 for close-ups of the weather map. In the meantime, camera 3 trucks to the center of the news set and zooms out for a cover shot. And all this without a camera operator in sight on the studio floor. The only human beings in the studio are the news anchor, weatherperson, and sportscaster, and sometimes a lonely

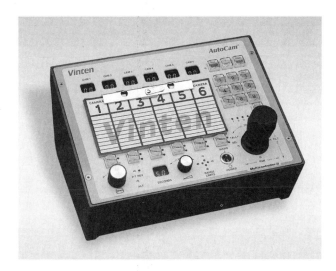

5.22 OPERATOR CONTROL PANEL
FOR ROBOT PEDESTAL
With such computer control panels, a single operator can
operate several cameras by remote control.

floor manager. Even the director no longer gives any
camera instruction, but simply checks the computer list
in the news script against the actual robotic execution of
camera shots in the preview monitors.

Because a small error in setting the pedestal wheels
on long dollies can cause the camera to end up in the
wrong place, some systems use aluminum tape on the
studio floor to guide accurate camera travel. An *operator
control panel* in the studio control room allows for remote
control of the camera movements that have not been
stored in the computer. **SEE 5.22** But what happens if the
computer fails? In such a case, you must have somebody
ready to override the automatic system, run into the
studio, grab the nearest camera, and zoom out to a long
shot of the news set.

MAIN POINTS

◆ The high hat is a short (about 6 inches) cylinder-
shaped or three-legged metal mount that accepts
the usual fluid or cam mounting heads.

◆ The bean bag is a canvas bag filled with synthetic
foam that molds itself to the shape of any ENG/EFP
camera or camcorder.

◆ The Steadicam is a spring-loaded device that keeps
the camera steady even if the operator, who wears a
harness and mount, runs with the camera. Lighter
Steadicam-like mounts are available for lightweight
camcorders; these are handheld by the operator, so
no harness is needed.

◆ The short jib arm is a camera mount that can be
attached to furniture or scenery. The long jib has a
longer arm that allows a single camera operator to
simultaneously dolly, pan and tilt, move the camera
up and down, and activate the zoom.

◆ The studio crane is larger than the jib arm and can
support a heavy camera plus the camera operator,
who sits on the crane boom. Most cranes need
additional operators to steer the crane and perform
the movements of the boom.

◆ The robot pedestal, or robotic, consists of a motor-
driven studio pedestal and mounting head. It, as
well as the remote zoom and focus controls, is
guided by a computerized system that can store
and execute a great number of camera moves.

ZETTL'S VIDEOLAB 2.1

This portion of Zettl's VideoLab 2.1 shows you the various camera moves and what they look like on the
television screen.

RUN ZVL 1 Click on the **camera** monitor and run tape 9 **Camera Moves**. Click on the first six
modules. Pay particular attention to the relationship of foreground to background
during the various moves. Click on the **Quiz** module and test yourself.

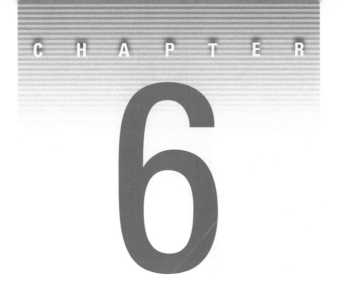

6

Camera Operation and Picture Composition

Now that you have learned the major aspects of television cameras and their lenses, you need to know how to operate a camera and compose effective pictures. Like bicycling, working a camera is something you learn by doing—there is no substitute for practice. The guidelines in this chapter are intended to enhance the learning process. Section 6.1, Working the Camera, discusses how to operate the various controls of the television camera; section 6.2, Framing Effective Shots, focuses on picture composition.

AGC Stands for *automatic gain control*. Regulates the volume of the audio or video level automatically, without using pots.

bust shot Framing of a person from the upper torso to the top of the head.

close-up (CU) Object or any part of it seen at close range and framed tightly. The close-up can be extreme (extreme or big close-up—*ECU*) or rather loose (medium close-up).

closure Short for *psychological closure*. Mentally filling in spaces of an incomplete picture.

extreme close-up (ECU) Shows the object with very tight framing.

extreme long shot (ELS) Shows the object from a great distance. Also called *establishing shot*.

follow focus Controlling the focus of the lens so that the image of an object is continuously kept sharp and clear, regardless of whether the camera and/or object move.

headroom The space left between the top of the head and the upper screen edge.

knee shot Framing of a person from approximately the knees up.

leadroom The space left in front of a person or object moving toward the edge of the screen.

long shot (LS) Object seen from far away or framed very loosely.

medium shot (MS) Object seen from a medium distance. Covers any framing between a long shot and a close-up.

noseroom The space left in front of a person looking or pointing toward the edge of the screen.

over-the-shoulder shot (O/S) Camera looks over a person's shoulder (shoulder and back of head included in shot) at another person.

shot sheet A list of every shot a particular camera has to get. It is attached to the camera to help the camera operator remember a shot sequence.

three-shot Framing of three people.

two-shot Framing of two people.

z-axis Line representing an extension of the lens from the camera to the horizon—the depth dimension.

6.1

Working the Camera

When reading about all the details of setting up and operating a camera or camcorder, you may feel overwhelmed. Don't worry. After you have studied and understood the procedures and practiced with the camera a few times, such operational details become routine, very much like driving a car. Section 6.1 helps clarify camera operation—both studio and portable—by laying out the sequential steps that you—the camera operator—need to follow before, during, and after a production. Once you are familiar with the technical details of camera operation, you will turn your attention to how to get effective, dynamic shots.

▶ **WORKING THE CAMCORDER AND EFP CAMERA**
Camera setup, operation, and care: the basic operational steps before, during, and after a field production

▶ **WORKING THE STUDIO CAMERA**
Camera setup, operation, and care: the basic operational steps before, during, and after a studio production

WORKING THE CAMCORDER AND EFP CAMERA

ENG EFP Whether you are working with a small consumer camcorder, a large professional ENG camcorder, or a high-end EFP camera with a separate VTR, you should know something about how to check and set up a camcorder before the shoot and what do with it during and after the production. Many of the operational steps are similar or identical, regardless of the type of camera, except that during EFP you normally have a few more people helping you.

When caught up in a large studio production or covering a hot news story, we tend to forget that the camera is an extremely complex piece of machinery. Although it may not be as precious or fragile as your grandmother's china, it still needs careful handling and some measure of respect. Here are some "don'ts" you should know before learning the "do's" of camera operation. These early warnings may well prevent you from damaging or losing the equipment before you ever get to use it. In this light, these don'ts represent a rather positive beginning.

Some Basic Camera "Don'ts"

▇ Do not leave the camcorder in a car—even in the trunk—for an extended period of time, unless the car is safely locked in a garage. Like people and animals, electronic equipment tends to suffer from excessive heat. More important, keeping the camera gear with you as much as possible is a fairly simple way of preventing theft.

▇ Do not leave the camcorder unprotected in the rain, hot sun, or extreme cold or, worse, exposed in your car during a hot day. When you must use the camcorder in rain, protect it with a "raincoat"—a prefabricated plastic hood—or at least a plastic sheet. A simple but effective way of keeping the rain away from the camera is a large umbrella. Some zoom lenses stick in extremely wet or cold weather. Test the lens before using it on location. Prevent the videocassettes or videodiscs from getting wet, and never use wet tapes. A wet tape may get sticky and ruin the drive motor in the VTR. You also must never introduce moisture into the electronic equipment.

▇ Do not point the lens for an extended period of time at the midday sun. Although the CCDs will not be damaged by the intensity of the sunlight, they may suffer from the heat generated by the focused sun rays. The same goes for the viewfinder: Don't leave it pointed at the sun for an extended period of time. The magnifying lens in the viewfinder can collect the sun's rays, melting its housing and electronics.

▇ Do not leave camcorder batteries in the sun or, worse, drop them. Although a battery may look rugged from the outside, it is actually quite sensitive to heat and shock.

▇ Do not lay a camcorder on its side. You run the risk of damaging the viewfinder and the clipped-on microphone on the other side. When finished shooting, cap the camera with the external lens cover and, just to make sure, by closing the aperture to the *C* (cap) position.

Given these important warnings, you can now relax and devote your full attention to learning what to do before, during, and after the shoot.

Before the Shoot

▇ Before doing anything else, count all the pieces of equipment and mark them on your checklist (see chapter 20). If you need to use auxiliary equipment, such as external microphones, camera lights, power supply, or field monitors, make sure you have the right connectors and cables. Recall that BNC is the standard connector for professional video cables, and RCA phono is the standard video connector for consumer equipment. The RCA phono connector is also used for consumer audio equipment (see figure 3.19). Take some extra adapters along, just in case you need to connect a BNC cable to an RCA phono jack.

▇ Unless you are running after hot news, first set up the tripod and make sure the camera plate fits the receptacle on the fluid head and balances the camera when locked into place. Do some panning and tilting to determine the proper pan-and-tilt drag. Check the pan-and-tilt locks. Insert the battery or connect the camcorder to its alternate power supply (AC/DC converter and transformer) and do a brief test recording with the camcorder before taking it into the field. Check that the camcorder records video as well as audio.

▇ If you are engaged in more-elaborate field productions using high-quality EFP cameras and separate VTRs, check the connecting cables and various power supplies (usually batteries). You may need a video feed from the camera (or VTR) to a battery-powered field monitor for the director. Be especially aware of connectors. In EFP a loose connector can well mean a lost production day. As with the camcorder, *hook up all the equipment you will use in the field and do a test recording before going on location.* Never assume that everything will work merely because it worked before.

▇ Check that the external microphone (usually a hand mic) and the camera mic are working properly. Most camera mics need to be switched on before they become operational. Is there sufficient cable for the external mic so that the reporter can work far enough away from the camera? If you are doing primarily news that requires an external mic for the field reporter, you may want to keep the external mic plugged in to save time and minimize costly mistakes. You can coil the mic cable and bow-tie it with a shoelace—one tug and the cable is uncoiled with the mic.

▇ Does the portable camera light work? Don't just look at the bulb. Turn on the light to verify that it works. If you have additional lights, are they all operational? Do you have enough AC extension cords to power the additional lights? Although most households have three-prong receptacles, you should still carry some three-prong to two-prong adapters to fit older household outlets.

▇ When using a separate VTR for EFP, do some test recording to ensure that the VTR is in good working order. (See chapter 12 for more details on VTR operation.)

■ Open the videocassette box and verify that it contains the cassette that fits the VTR or camcorder and that it matches the tape length indicated on the box (normally given in standard speed playing time, such as 20 minutes, 60 minutes, or 120 minutes). Check that the cassette's supply reel has enough tape to justify the indicated playing time. Even if you cannot be sure about the exact length, a 120-minute cassette should obviously have a much fuller supply reel than a 20-minute tape. Check that the safety tab is still in place. If it has been removed, you cannot record on that tape (see chapter 12).

■ Always take a few more cassettes along than you think you will need.

■ Although you are not a maintenance engineer, carry some spare fuses for the principal equipment. Some ENG/EFP cameras and professional camcorders have a spare fuse right next to the active one. Note, however, that a blown fuse indicates some malfunction in the equipment. Even if the camcorder works again with the new fuse, have the equipment checked when you return from the shoot.

■ Like carrying a medical first-aid kit, you should always have a field production kit that contains the following items: several videocassettes, an audiocassette recorder and several audiocassettes, an additional microphone and a small microphone stand, one or more portable lights and stands, additional lamps for all lighting instruments, AC cords, spares for all types of batteries, various clips or clothespins and gaffer's tape, a small reflector, a roll of aluminum foil, a small white card for white-balancing, light-diffusing material, various effects filters, a can of compressed air for cleaning lenses, and a camera raincoat. You should also carry such personal survival items as a working flashlight, an umbrella, some spare clothes, and, yes, some toilet paper. Once you have worked in the field a few times, you will know how to put together your own field production kit.

During the Shoot

After some field production experience, you will probably develop your own techniques for carrying and operating a camcorder or ENG/EFP camera. Nevertheless, there are some well-established basic steps that will help you when starting out.

Handheld camcorder operating techniques

You may think that the small, handheld camcorder is much easier to operate than its heavier cousin. This may be true if all you do with the camcorder is shoot vacation pictures. But in more-ambitious production situations, the camcorder's small size and light weight require steady hands and smooth movements.

■ To avoid jittery pictures, you must keep the camera as steady as possible. This is especially important when the zoom lens is in the telephoto position. To keep a small camcorder as steady as possible, support it in the palm of your hand and use the other hand to support the "camera arm" or the camcorder itself. **SEE 6.1** Whenever possible, press your elbows against your body, inhale, and hold your breath during the shot. Bend your knees slightly when shooting, or lean against a sturdy support to increase the stability of the camera. **SEE 6.2** Such camera handling is recommended even if an image stabilizer is built into the camera. Note that image stabilizers drain the battery relatively quickly.

■ When moving the camera, should you be zoomed in or out? Zoomed out, of course. By zooming out all the way, you put the zoom lens in the wide-angle position, which is very forgiving and does not show minor camera wobbles. Also, because of the great depth of field, you have fewer problems keeping the event in focus, even if you or the subject moves. But even with the zoom lens in the

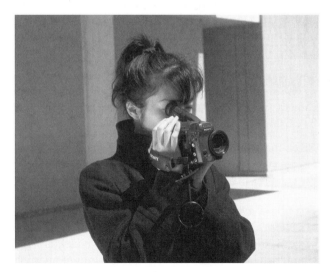

6.1 HOLDING THE SMALL CAMCORDER
Steady the camcorder with both hands, with your elbows pressed against your body.

wide-angle position, you need to move the camera as smoothly as possible.

◼ To *pan* the camera (point it sideways), move it with your whole body rather than just your arms. First, point your knees in the direction of the *end* of the pan. Then twist your body with the camera pointed toward the *beginning* of the pan. During the pan, you are like a spring that is uncoiling from the start of the action to the finish. This position is much smoother than if your knees are pointed toward the start of the action and you are forced to wind up your body during the pan. Always bend your knees slightly when shooting; as in skiing, your knees act as shock absorbers. Do not panic if you lose the subject temporarily in the viewfinder. Keep the camera steady, look up to see where the subject is, and aim the camera smoothly in the new direction. **SEE 6.3**

◼ Whenever possible, walk backward with the camera so that you can keep the event in front of you. Moving

backward also forces you to walk on the balls of your feet, which are better shock absorbers than your heels. **SEE 6.4** Watch that you do not bump into or stumble over something while walking backward. A quick check of your proposed route can prevent unexpected mishaps. With the zoom lens in the wide-angle position, you are often closer to the object than the viewfinder image indicates. Be careful not to hit something or someone with the camera, especially if you walk forward with it into a crowd of tightly spaced people.

Of course, the small camcorder is lightweight enough to be tilted, shaken, held in one hand, and moved freely through the air. Although such wild camera movement may, on occasion, fit the style of the event, it usually reflects the inexperience of the operator or disrespect for the audience. Such camera handling belongs in the special-effects category. In any case, you need to learn the standard rules of operating a camera before you can break them.

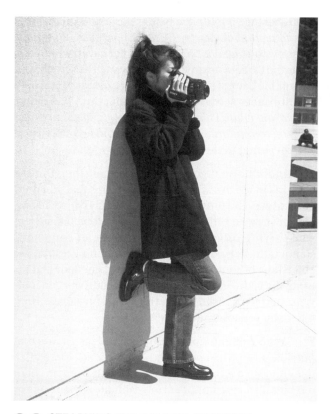

6.2 STEADYING THE CAMERA OPERATOR

Lean against a tree or wall to steady yourself and the camcorder.

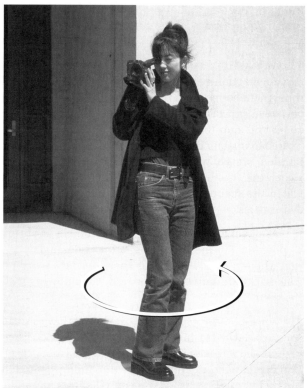

6.3 PANNING THE CAMCORDER

Before panning, point your knees in the direction of the pan, then uncoil your upper body during the pan.

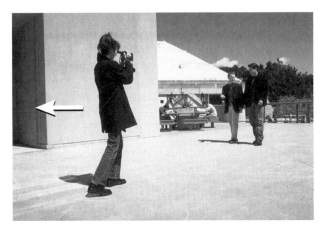

6.4 WALKING BACKWARD

When following something or somebody, walk backward rather than forward. The balls of your feet act like shock absorbers.

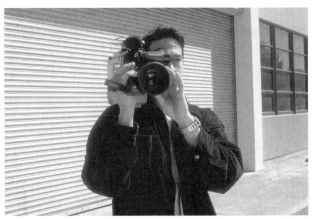

6.5 SHOULDER-MOUNTED ENG/EFP CAMERA

Carry the larger professional camcorder on your shoulder. One hand slips through the strap on the lens to steady the camcorder and to operate the zoom. Your other hand is free to operate the focus ring at the front of the zoom lens and to provide further support for the camcorder.

ENG/EFP camera or camcorder operating techniques When operating the larger, much heavier, shoulder-mounted ENG/EFP camera or camcorder, many of the rules for small camcorders still apply.

■ Assuming that you are right-handed, carry the camera on your right shoulder and slip your right hand through the support strap on the zoom lens. This will help you steady the camera while allowing you to operate the zoom and auto-focus controls. Your left hand will then be free to operate the manual focus ring. If you are left-handed, simply reverse the procedures. You can also switch the viewfinder to the other side so that you can watch the scene with your left rather than your right eye. **SEE 6.5**

■ Keep your body and, with it, the camera as steady as possible. Put the zoom lens in the wide-angle position when moving. Preset your knees during a pan, and walk backward rather than forward when moving with the event.

■ Some ENG/EFP cameras or camcorders have a small speaker attached to the side of the camera. If so, you listen to the audio with your right ear resting against the speaker. Usually, camera operators hear the audio through a molded earpiece that fits the ear. Whenever possible, check the audio level before recording.

■ Unless the camera has a fully automated white balance (as do most consumer camcorders), you must white-balance the camera before starting to shoot. *Make sure to white-balance in the same light that illuminates the scene you are shooting.* If you do not have a white card, focus the camera on anything white, such as somebody's shirt or the back of a script. Most camera utility bags have a white sheet sewn into the flap for white-balancing. *Repeat the white balance each time you encounter new lighting conditions,* such as moving from an interview at a street corner to the interior of the new restaurant.

■ Under normal conditions, put the camera in the auto-iris mode. *Normal conditions* means that you don't have to reveal picture detail in an extremely dense shadow area or struggle with extreme contrast problems, such as when trying to get a decent exposure of somebody standing in front of a brightly lit building. Despite the objections of some especially critical camera operators, using the camcorder in the auto-iris mode will generally yield better-exposed video than when trying to do it manually, especially during ENG.

■ Try to calibrate (preset) the zoom lens as much as possible, even when on the run during ENG. More often than not, such a routine will pay off with good, in-focus pictures. Just as a reminder: You calibrate a zoom lens by zooming in on the target object, such as the limousine carrying the celebrities, and then zooming back out again to the opening shot. When you then zoom in on the people getting out of the car, the camera will remain in focus even for the close-ups. Or, better yet, start with a focused close-up and then zoom back to a wider shot. In effect, what you are doing is presetting the zoom while on the air.

If you haven't calibrated the zoom lens and need to zoom in from a wide shot, you need to *follow focus* as well as you can. This means that you have to turn the focus ring to keep the picture sharp and clear while zooming in—not an easy task by any means. The focus becomes more critical when you shoot under low-light conditions. Recall that low light levels necessitate a large lens aperture (iris opening), which in turn reduces the depth of field. Unless you're shooting vacation pictures, putting a camera in the auto-focus mode is not recommended: The camera frequently gets confused about just what it is you intend to focus on, and fast zooms are frequently out of focus.

▨ Whenever the camera is running, record sound, regardless of whether somebody is talking. This sound is important to achieve continuity in postproduction editing. When working in relatively quiet surroundings, record in the _AGC_ (automatic gain control) mode. Otherwise, you need to switch to manual gain control, take a sound level, and record. (See chapters 9 and 10 for more information on ENG sound.) When the reporter is holding the external mic, do not start running away from him or her to get a better shot of the event. Either both of you run together, or you must stay put.

▨ Heed the warning signals in the viewfinder and on the VTR. It is usually the equipment, not the warning light, that is malfunctioning.

▨ In EFP you usually work with other crew members. Even with a small production team, you must assign each member specific functions. For example, you might run the camera, with somebody else taking care of all VTR functions, assuming that you work with a separate VTR. A third person can then take care of the lighting and the audio. When your ENG/EFP camera is part of a multi-camera shoot, you need a cable puller. A good cable puller will anticipate your moves and feed the cable so that you can walk or run freely to the next shooting position.

▨ Above all, *use common sense.* Always be mindful of your and other people's safety. Use sound judgment in determining whether the risk is worth the story. In ENG reliability and consistency are more important than sporadic feats, however spectacular. Do not risk your neck and the equipment to get a shot that would simply embellish a story already on tape. Leave that type of shooting to the gifted amateurs.

After the Shoot

▨ Unless you have just shot a really hot story that must air immediately, even unedited, first take care of the equipment before delivering the tape. If you are properly organized, it should take just a few minutes.

▨ Take the cassette out of the VTR and immediately replace it with a new one. Label all cassettes.

▨ Put all the switches in the *off* position, unless you are heading for another assignment. In which case, put the camera in the *standby* position.

▨ Cap the camera by closing the iris all the way and snapping on the lens cover.

▨ Roll up the mic cable and bow-tie it with the shoelace.

▨ Immediately put everything back into the designated boxes or bags. Do not wait until the next day, because you may find yourself having to cover an important news story on your way home.

▨ Have all batteries recharged as soon as you return from the assignment.

▨ If the camcorder got wet, wait until everything has dried out before putting the camera back into its case. Moisture is one of the most serious threats to ENG/EFP equipment.

▨ If you have time, check all the portable lights so they will work for the next assignment. Coil all AC extension cords—you will not have time to untangle them when rushing after your next assignment.

Working the Studio Camera

The big difference between operating an ENG/EFP camcorder and a studio camera is that the latter is always mounted on some kind of camera support—usually a studio pedestal. In one way the studio camera is easier to operate than the portable camera: All electronic adjustments are performed for you by the video operator (VO), who "shades" the camera at the CCU (camera control unit). In another way, however, you may find that operating the studio camera is more difficult, because you have to steer the pedestal (or another camera mount) and adjust the focus while composing effective pictures. Here are the important steps you need to observe before, during, and after a show or rehearsal.

Before the Show

▪ Put on your headset and check that the intercom system is functioning. You should hear at least the director, the technical director (TD), and the video operator.

▪ Unlock the pan-and-tilt mechanism on the camera mounting head and adjust the drag, if necessary. Check that the camera is balanced on the mounting head. Unlock the pedestal, and pedestal up and down. Check that the pedestal is correctly counterweighted. A properly balanced camera remains put in any given vertical position. If it drops down or moves up by itself, the pedestal is not properly counterweighted.

▪ See how much camera cable you have and whether there are any obstacles that may interfere with the cable run. Check that the pedestal skirt is low enough to move the cable out of the way, rather than roll over it.

▪ Ask the VO to uncap the camera from the CCU, and ask if you can remove the lens cap. You can then see in the viewfinder the pictures the camera actually takes. Is the viewfinder properly adjusted? Like on your home television set, the viewfinder can be adjusted for brightness and contrast. If you need framing guides, flip the switch that shows the essential area and the screen-center mark (see chapter 15).

▪ Check the zoom lens. Zoom in and out. Does the zoom lens stick, that is, does it have problems moving smoothly throughout the zoom range? What exactly is the range? Get a feel for how close you can get to the set from a certain position. If you work with a digital zoom lens, check whether the zoom lens returns to the designated position (focal length) in subsequent zooms. Preset for a few zoom positions and see whether the lens actually moves to the preset position. Is the lens clean? If it is dusty, use a fine camel-hair brush and carefully clean off the larger dust particles. With a small rubber bulb or a can of compressed air, blow off the finer dust. Do not blow on it with your mouth: You will fog up the lens and get it even dirtier.

▪ Rack through focus—that is, move the focus control from one extreme position to the other. Can you move easily and smoothly into and out of focus, especially when in a narrow-angle, zoomed-in position?

▪ Calibrate (preset) the zoom lens. Just to remind you how it is done: Zoom all the way in on the target object in the zoom range, such as the newscaster or the door on the far wall of the living room set. Focus on this far object. Now zoom all the way back to the widest-angle setting. You should now remain in focus throughout the zoom, provided neither object nor camera moves.

▪ If you have a shot sheet, this is a good time to practice the more complicated zoom and dolly or truck shots. A *shot sheet* is a list of every shot a particular camera has to get. It is attached to the camera to help the camera operator remember a shot sequence.

▪ If a teleprompter is attached to the camera, check all the connections.

▪ Lock the camera again (the pedestal and the pan-and-tilt mechanism) before leaving it. *Do not ever leave a camera unlocked, even for a short while.* Some of the newer pedestals have a parking brake. Set the brakes on the pedestal before leaving the camera.

▪ Cap the camera if you leave it for any prolonged period of time.

During the Show

▪ Put on the headset and establish contact with the director, technical director, and video operator. Unlock the camera and recheck pan-and-tilt drag and pedestal movement.

▪ Calibrate the zoom at each new camera position. See whether you can stay in focus over the entire zoom range.

▪ When checking the focus between shots, rack through focus a few times to determine at which position the picture is the sharpest. When you are focusing on a person, the hairline usually gives you enough detail to determine the sharpest focus. Or you may focus on eyes. In ECUs (extreme close-ups) focus on the nose bridge.

▪ If you anticipate a dolly with the zoom lens, set the lens at a wide-angle position. Preset the focus at the approximate midpoint of the dolly distance. With the zoom lens at the extreme wide-angle position, the depth of field should be large enough so that you need to adjust focus only when you are very close to the object or event.

■ You will find that although a camera pedestal allows you to dolly extremely smoothly, you may have some difficulty getting it to move or stopping it without jerking the camera. Start slowly to overcome the inertia, and try to slow down just before the end of the dolly or truck. If you have a difficult truck or arc to perform, have a floor person help you steer the camera. You can then concentrate on the camera operation. In a straight dolly, you can keep both hands on the panning handles. If you have to steer the camera, steer with your right hand, keeping your left hand on the focus control.

■ If you pedestal up or down, try to brake the camera before it hits the stops at the extreme pedestal positions. Generally, keep your shots at the talent's eye level unless the director instructs you to shoot from either a high (pedestal up and look down) or a low (pedestal down and look up) angle.

■ When you operate a freewheel camera dolly, always preset the wheels in the direction of the intended camera movement to prevent the dolly from starting off in the wrong direction. If the dolly has cable guards, move them down far enough to prevent your running over the camera cable or other cables on the studio floor.

■ Determine the approximate reach of the camera cable. In a long dolly, the cable may tug annoyingly at the camera. Do not try to pull the cable along with your hand. To ease the tension, loop it over your shoulder or tie it to the pedestal base, leaving enough slack so that you can freely pan, tilt, and pedestal. On complicated camera movements, have a floor person help you with the cable; otherwise, the dragging sound may be picked up by the microphone. If the cable gets twisted during a dolly, do not drag the whole mess along; have a floor person untangle it.

■ At all times during the show, be aware of all the activity around you. Where are the other cameras? The microphone boom? The floor monitor? It is your responsibility to keep out of the view of the other cameras and not hit anything (including floor personnel or talent) during your moves. Watch especially for obstacles in your dolly path, such as scenery, properties, and floor lights. Rugs are a constant hazard to camera movement. When dollying into a set that has a rug, watch the floor so that you do not suddenly dolly up onto the rug. Better yet, have a floor person warn you when you come close to the rug. Be particularly careful when dollying back. A good floor manager will help clear the way and tap you on the shoulder to prevent you from backing into something.

■ In general, keep your eyes on the viewfinder. If the format allows, look around for something interesting to shoot between shots. The director will appreciate good visuals in an ad-lib show (in which the shots have not been rehearsed). If you have a shot sheet, though, stick to it, however tempting the shot possibilities may be. Do not try to outdirect the director.

■ Watch for the tally light to go out before presetting the zoom or moving the camera into a new shooting position. This is especially important if your camera is engaged in special effects.

■ During rehearsal, inform the floor manager or the director of unusual production problems, such as if you cannot prevent a camera shadow. Mark all shot changes on your shot sheet. The director will have to decide whether to change the camera position or the lighting. The camera may be too close to the object to keep it in focus. Or the director may not give you enough time to preset the zoom again after you move into a new shooting position. Alert the director if your zoom lens is in a narrow-angle position and he or she has told you to move the camera while on the air. Sometimes it is hard for the director to tell from the preview monitor the exact zoom position of a lens.

■ If you work without shot sheets, try to remember the type and sequence of shots from the rehearsal. A good camera operator has the next shot lined up before the director calls for it. If you work from a shot sheet, go to the next shot immediately after the preceding one. Do not wait until the last minute. The director may have to "punch up" your camera (put it on the air) much sooner than you remember from rehearsal. Do not zoom in or out needlessly during shots unless you are presetting the zoom lens.

■ Mark the critical camera positions on the studio floor with masking tape. If you do not have a shot sheet, make one up on your own. Mark particularly the camera movements (dollies, trucks) so that you can set the zoom in a wide-angle position. Line up exactly on these marks during the actual show.

■ Listen carefully to what the director tells all the camera operators, not just you. That way you can co-ordinate your shots with those of the other cameras. Also, you can avoid wasteful duplication of shots by knowing approximately what the other cameras are doing.

■ Avoid unnecessary chatter on the intercom.

After the Show

■ At the end of the show, wait for the "all clear" signal before you lock the camera.

■ Ask the video engineer whether the camera may be capped.

■ Lock the camera mounting head and the pedestal, release the drag controls, and push the camera to a safe place in the studio. If so equipped, put the parking brake on. Do not leave the camera in the middle of the studio, where it can easily be damaged by a piece of scenery being moved or by other kinds of studio traffic.

■ Coil the cable again as neatly as possible in the customary figure-eight loops.

MAIN POINTS

◆ When working a camcorder or portable camera, be sure to handle it with extreme care. Do not leave it unprotected in the hot sun or uncovered in the rain.

◆ Before using the camcorder, make sure that the batteries are fully charged and that you have enough videotape or disk space for the assignment. Do an audio check with the camera mic and external mic.

◆ When shooting, pay particular attention at all times to white balance, presetting the zoom, and recording ambient sound. Except in adverse lighting conditions, switch to auto-iris control. Respond immediately to any warning signals in the viewfinder.

◆ After the production, put everything back carefully so that the equipment is ready for the next assignment.

◆ Before operating the studio camera, check the headset, camera mount (tripod dolly, pedestal, crane), and the zoom and focus mechanisms.

◆ During the show, pay particular attention to the reach and travel of the camera cable, presetting the zoom, smooth camera movements, and focus.

◆ After the show, lock the camera mounting head, cap the camera, and move it to a safe place in the studio. If possible, put the parking brake on.

6.2

Framing Effective Shots

The basic purpose of framing a shot is to show images as clearly as possible and to present them so that they convey meaning and energy. What you do essentially is clarify and intensify the event before you. When working a camcorder or ENG/EFP camera, you are the only one who sees the television pictures before they are videotaped. You therefore cannot rely on a director to tell you how to frame every picture for maximum effectiveness.

The more you know about picture composition, the more effective your clarification and intensification of the event will be. But even if you are working as a camera operator during a multicamera studio show or a large remote where the director can preview all camera pictures, you still need to know how to compose effective shots. The director might be able to correct some of your shots, but he or she will certainly not have enough time to teach you the fundamentals of good composition.

This section describes the major compositional principles and explains why and how you should frame a shot for maximum clarity and impact.

▶ **SCREEN SIZE AND FIELD OF VIEW**
  Operating with close-ups and medium shots rather than long shots and extreme long shots

▶ **FRAMING A SHOT**
  Dealing with height and width, framing close-ups, headroom, noseroom and leadroom, and closure

▶ **DEPTH**
  Creating the illusion of a third dimension in both aspect ratios: choice of lens, positioning of objects, depth of field, and lighting and color

▶ **SCREEN MOTION**
  Z-axis motion (movement toward and away from the camera) and lateral movement in both aspect ratios[1]

SCREEN SIZE AND FIELD OF VIEW

Screen size and field of view are closely related. You have probably heard film critics suggest that you see a particular film on "the big screen" even if you can rent it in a video store for home viewing.

---

1. For an extensive discussion of screen forces and how they can be used for effective picture composition, see Herbert Zettl, *Sight Sound Motion*, 3d ed. (Belmont, Calif.: Wadsworth Publishing Co., 1999), pp. 89–181.

Screen Size

Even a large television set has a relatively small screen, especially when you compare it with the average movie screen. To show objects clearly, they must be relatively large within the television screen. In other words, your field of view must generally be tighter. Your shot sequence will probably show more close-ups and medium shots than long shots and extreme long shots. Because the home viewer cannot see the whole event in its overall context, you must try to pick those details that tell an important part of the story. Shots that do not obviously relate to the event context are usually meaningless to the viewer.

When shooting for large-screen HDTV, you can use more of a film-style approach in which the story is told through long and medium shots rather than close-ups. Filmmakers do this because they know that their films will be projected on large theater screens. The close-up is reserved for especially dramatic moments.

Field of View

Field of view refers to how wide or how close the object appears relative to the camera, that is, how close it will appear to the viewer. It is basically organized into five steps: *extreme long shot (ELS)*, *long shot (LS)*, *medium shot (MS)*, *close-up (CU)*, and *extreme close-up (ECU)*. **SEE 6.6** *READY ZVL* ➊

Four other ways of designating the same shots are: *bust shot*, which frames the subject from the upper torso to the top of the head; *knee shot*, which frames the subject just above or below the knees; *two-shot*, with two people or objects in the frame; and *three-shot*, with three people or objects in the frame. **SEE 6.7** Although more a blocking arrangement than field of view, you should also know two additional shot designations. In an *over-the-shoulder shot (O/S)*, the camera looks at someone over the shoulder of the camera-near person. In a *cross-shot (X/S)*, the camera looks alternately at one or the other person, with the camera-near person completely out of the shot.

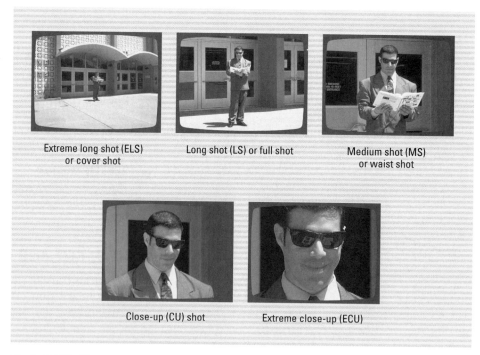

Extreme long shot (ELS)
or cover shot

Long shot (LS) or full shot

Medium shot (MS)
or waist shot

Close-up (CU) shot

Extreme close-up (ECU)

6.6 FIELD-OF-VIEW STEPS

The shot designations range from ELS (extreme long shot) to ECU (extreme close-up).

6.7 OTHER SHOT DESIGNATIONS

Other common shot designations are the bust shot, knee shot, two-shot, three-shot, over-the-shoulder shot, and cross-shot. Note that the bust shot is similar to the MS and that the knee shot is similar to the LS.

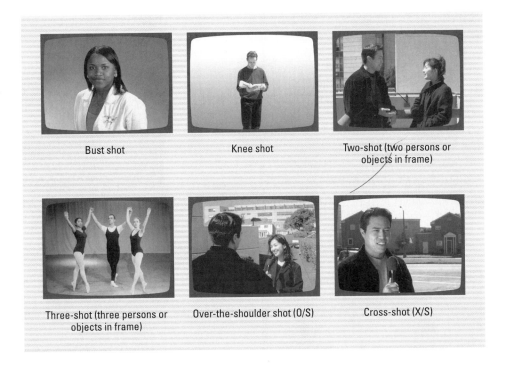

Bust shot

Knee shot

Two-shot (two persons or objects in frame)

Three-shot (three persons or objects in frame)

Over-the-shoulder shot (O/S)

Cross-shot (X/S)

Of course, exactly how to frame such shots depends not only on your sensitivity to composition, but also on the director's preference.

FRAMING A SHOT

Many high-end studio cameras, ENG/EFP cameras, and even some high-quality consumer camcorders have a switch for changing the aspect ratio from the standard 4×3 format to the DTV 16×9. Whereas the aspect ratios of traditional television (4×3) and DTV (16×9) are quite different and require significant technical changes, many of the aesthetic principles of good picture composition apply to both. Nevertheless, in framing effective shots, some aesthetic principles need to be adjusted to the specific requirements of the respective aspect ratio. This section takes a closer look at (1) dealing with height and width, (2) framing close-ups, (3) headroom, (4) noseroom and leadroom, and (5) closure.

Dealing With Height and Width

You will find that the 4×3 aspect ratio is well suited to framing a vertical scene, such as a high-rise building,

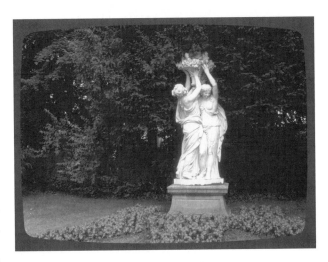

6.8 FRAMING A VERTICAL VIEW

The 4×3 aspect ratio allows you to frame a vertical scene without having to go to an extreme long shot.

as well as a horizontally oriented vista. **SEE 6.8 AND 6.9** It is also relatively easy to accommodate a scene that has both wide and high elements. **SEE 6.10**

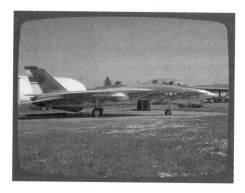

6.9 FRAMING A HORIZONTAL VIEW
The 4 × 3 aspect ratio readily accommodates a horizontal vista.

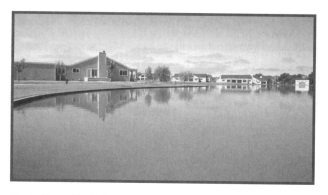

6.11 FRAMING A HORIZONTAL VIEW
The 16 × 9 aspect ratio is ideal for framing wide horizontal vistas.

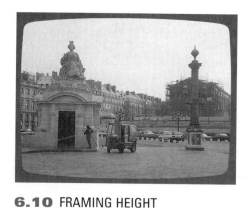

6.10 FRAMING HEIGHT
AND WIDTH IN A SINGLE SHOT
The 4 × 3 aspect ratio easily accommodates both horizontal and vertical vistas.

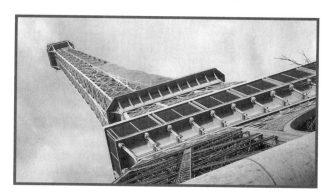

6.12 FRAMING A VERTICAL VIEW
The 16 × 9 aspect ratio makes it quite difficult to frame a vertical object. One way to frame a tall building is to shoot it from below.

Although the horizontally stretched 16 × 9 aspect ratio makes horizontal scenes look quite spectacular, it presents a formidable obstacle to framing a vertical view. **SEE 6.11 AND 6.12** You can either tilt the camera up to reveal the height of the object—shooting from below—or have other picture elements block the sides of the screen and, in effect, give you a vertical aspect ratio to frame the shot **SEE 6.13**

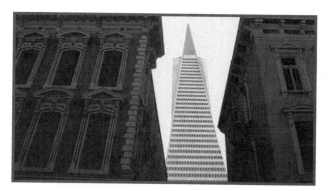

6.13 NATURAL MASKING OF THE SCREEN SIDES
You can use parts of the natural environment to block the sides of the wide 16 × 9 screen to create a vertical space to frame the vertical scene. In this shot the foreground buildings create a vertical aspect ratio for the high-rise building.

Close-ups

Close-ups (CUs) and extreme close-ups (ECUs) are common elements in the visual language of television because, compared with the large motion picture screen, normal television screens are relatively small. The 4 × 3 aspect ratio and small screen of the normal television receiver are the ideal combination for close-ups and extreme close-ups of people's heads. **SEE 6.14 AND 6.15**

As you can see, the normal close-up shows the customary headroom and part of the upper body. The ECU is somewhat trickier to frame. The top screen edge cuts across the top part of the head, and the lower edge cuts just below the top part of the shoulders. As a rough guide, you should try to place the eyes of the subject in the upper one-third of the screen. *READY ZVL* ❷

When you try to frame the same shot within the 16×9 aspect ratio, however, you are left with a great amount of leftover space on both sides of the close-up. The close-up looks somewhat lost in the wide-screen aspect ratio, and the extreme close-up looks as though it is squeezed between the top and bottom screen edges. **SEE 6.16 AND 6.17** You can solve this problem relatively easily by including some visual elements in the shot that fill the empty spaces on either side. On the other hand, the DTV aspect ratio lets you frame rather easily close-ups of two people face-to-face. Such an arrangement is quite difficult in the traditional format, because the two dialogue partners must stand uncomfortably close together.

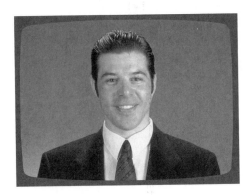

6.14 FRAMING A CLOSE-UP
The normal close-up shows the head of the person and part of the shoulders.

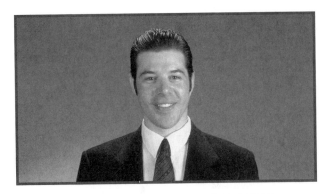

6.16 FRAMING A CLOSE-UP IN DTV FORMAT
When framing the same close-up in the 16 × 9 aspect ratio, both screen sides look conspicuously empty.

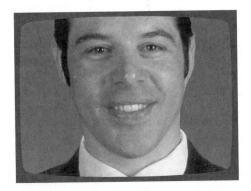

6.15 FRAMING AN EXTREME CLOSE-UP
In an extreme close-up, you should cut the top of the head, while keeping the upper part of the shoulders in the shot.

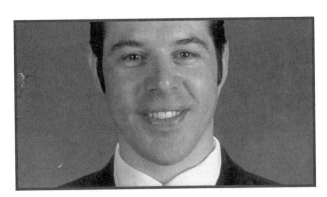

6.17 FRAMING AN EXTREME CLOSE-UP IN DTV FORMAT
In the 16 × 9 aspect ratio, the ECU of the person seems oddly squeezed between the upper and lower screen edges.

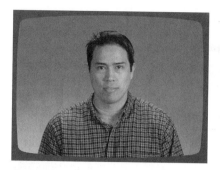

6.18 NORMAL HEADROOM

Headroom counters the magnetic pull of the upper frame. The person appears comfortably placed in the frame.

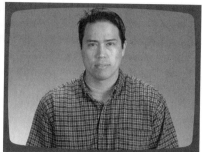

6.19 TOO LITTLE HEADROOM

With no, or too little, headroom, the person looks cramped in the frame. The head seems to be glued to the upper screen edge.

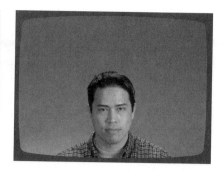

6.20 TOO MUCH HEADROOM

With too much headroom, the pull of the bottom edge makes the picture bottom-heavy and strangely unbalanced.

Headroom

Because the edges of the television frame seem to attract like magnets whatever is close to them, you should leave some space above people's heads—called *headroom*—in normal long shots, medium shots, and close-ups. **SEE 6.18** Avoid having the head "glued" to the upper edge of the frame **SEE 6.19** Because you lose a certain amount of picture space in videotaping and transmission, you need to leave a little more headroom than feels comfortable. Leaving too much headroom, however, is just as bad as too little. **SEE 6.20** You can use the frame guide in the viewfinder to see the picture area that actually appears on the television screen. The headroom rule applies to both aspect ratios. *READY ZVL* ❸

Noseroom and Leadroom

Somebody looking or pointing in a particular direction other than straight into the camera creates a screen force, called an *index vector.* You must compensate for this force by leaving some space in front of the vector. When someone looks or points screen-left or screen-right, the index vector needs to be balanced with *noseroom.*

Screen motion creates a *motion vector.* When someone or something moves in a screen-right or screen-left direction, you must leave **leadroom** to balance the force of the motion vector. In effect, you must lead the moving object with the camera rather than follow it. **SEE 6.21 AND 6.22**

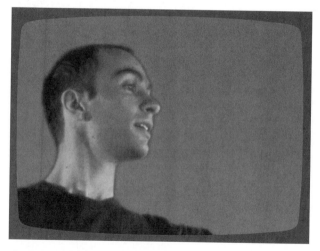

6.21 PROPER NOSEROOM

To absorb the force of the strong index vector created by the person looking toward the screen edge, you need to leave some noseroom.

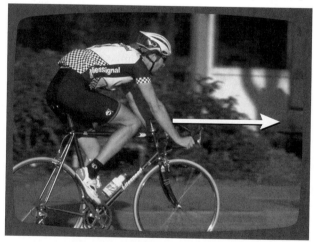

6.22 PROPER LEADROOM

Assuming that the cyclist is actually moving, his motion vector is properly neutralized by the screen space in front of him. We like to see where the person is heading, not where he has been. Note that a still picture cannot show a motion vector. What you see here is an index vector.

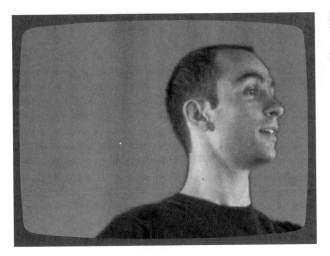

6.23 LACK OF NOSEROOM
Without noseroom, the person seems to be blocked by the
screen edge, and the picture looks unbalanced.

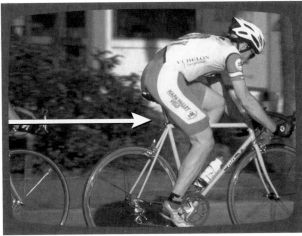

6.24 LACK OF LEADROOM
Without leadroom, the moving person or object seems to be
hindered or stopped by the screen edge.

As with the lack of headroom, a lack of noseroom
or leadroom makes the picture look oddly out of
balance; the person seems to be blocked by the screen
edge. **SEE 6.23 AND 6.24** *READY ZVL* ❹

Closure

Closure, short for *psychological closure*, is the process by
which our minds fill in information that we cannot
actually see on the screen. Take a look around you: You
see only parts of the objects that lie in your field of
vision. There is no way you can ever see an object in its
entirety unless the object moves around you or you
move around the object. Through experience, we have
learned to mentally supply the missing parts, which
allows us to perceive a whole world although we actually
see only a small part of it. Because the television screen
is relatively small, we often show objects and people in
close-ups, leaving many parts of the scene to the
viewers' imagination.

Positive closure   To facilitate closure, you should
always frame a shot in such a way that the viewer can
easily extend the figure beyond the screen edges and
perceive a sensible whole. **SEE 6.25** To organize the visual
world around us, we also like to group things together so

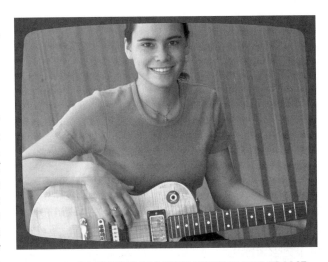

6.25 FACILITATING CLOSURE BEYOND THE FRAME
In this shot we perceive the whole figure of the person and
her guitar, although we see only part of them. This shot gives
us sufficient clues to project the figure beyond the frame and
apply psychological closure in the off-screen space.

that they form a sensible pattern. **SEE 6.26 AND 6.27** Figures 6.26 and 6.27 show obvious ways of grouping objects to form stable patterns that are easily perceived.

Negative closure   This need for closure can also work *against* good composition. For example, when framing a close-up without giving any visual clues to help viewers project the image beyond the screen edges, the head seems oddly cut off from its body. **SEE 6.28** You therefore need to provide enough visual clues to lead the viewers' eyes beyond the frame so they can

apply closure and perceive the complete person in off-screen space. **SEE 6.29**

Our desire to see screen space organized into simple patterns is so strong that it often works against reason. In the excitement of getting a good story and an interesting shot, it is easy to forget to look *behind* the object of attention; but it is often the background that unexpectedly spoils a good picture composition. Objects that seem to grow out of people's heads or a tilted horizon line are the most common compositional problems. Once you are aware of the background, it is easy to avoid illogical closure. **SEE 6.30** *READY ZVL* ⑤

6.26 TRIANGLE CLOSURE

We tend to organize things into easily recognizable patterns. This group of similar objects forms a triangle.

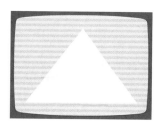

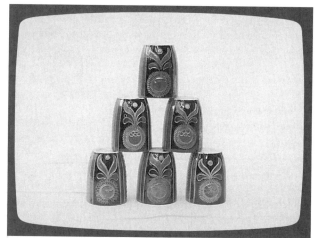

6.27 SEMICIRCLE CLOSURE

These objects organize the screen space into a semicircle.

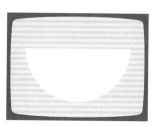

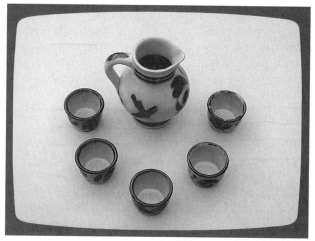

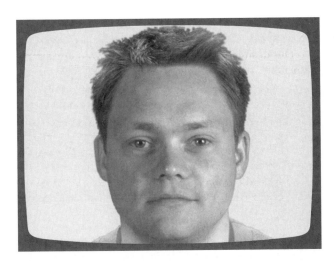

6.28 UNDESIRABLE CLOSURE WITHIN THE FRAME

This shot is badly framed, because we apply closure within the frame without projecting the rest of the person into off-screen space.

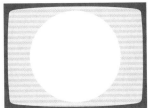

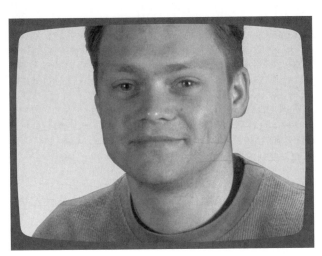

6.29 DESIRABLE CLOSURE IN OFF-SCREEN SPACE

In this ECU (extreme close-up), there are enough on-screen clues to project the rest of the person's head and body into off-screen space, thus applying closure to the total figure.

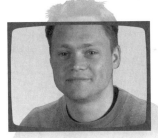

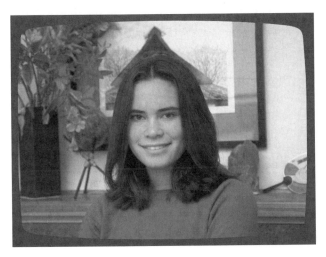

6.30 UNDESIRABLE CLOSURE

Although we know better, we perceive this person's head as pointed because of the picture in the background.

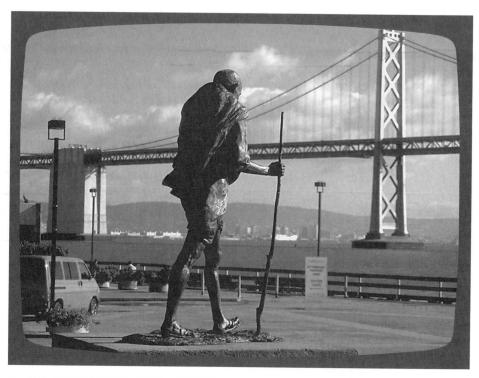

6.31 FOREGROUND, MIDDLEGROUND, AND BACKGROUND

In general, try to divide the z-axis (depth dimension) into a prominent foreground (statue), middleground (bridge), and background (hills). Such a division helps create the illusion of screen depth.

Depth

Because the television screen is a flat, two-dimensional piece of glass upon which the image appears, we must create the illusion of a third dimension. Fortunately, the principles for creating the illusion of depth on a two-dimensional surface have been amply explored and established by painters and photographers over the years. For depth staging you need to consider the following factors:

- *The choice of lens.* A wide-angle zoom position exaggerates depth. Narrow-angle positions reduce the illusion of a third dimension.

- *The positioning of objects.* The *z-axis*—the line representing an extension of the lens from the camera to the horizon—has significant bearing on depth staging. Anything positioned along the z-axis relative to the camera will create the illusion of depth.

- *The depth of field.* A shallow depth of field is usually more effective to define depth than a large depth of field, because the in-focus foreground object is more clearly set off against the out-of-focus background.

- *Lighting and color.* A brightly lighted object with strong (highly saturated) color seems closer than one that is dimly lighted and has washed-out (low-saturation) colors. On the most basic level, try to establish clear picture division into foreground, middleground, and background.
SEE 6.31 *READY ZVL* **6**

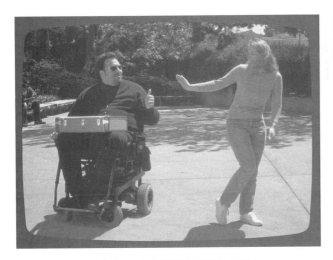

6.32 TWO PERSONS SAYING GOOD-BYE

If you have a two-shot in which the people are walking away from each other toward both screen edges, don't try to keep both of them in the shot.

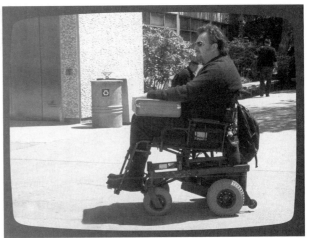

6.33 STAYING WITH ONE OF THEM

You must decide on the person you are going to keep in the frame while letting the other move off-camera.

SCREEN MOTION

Contrary to the painter or the still photographer, who deals with the organization of static images within the picture frame, the television camera operator must almost always cope with framing images in motion. Composing moving images requires quick reaction and full attention throughout the telecast. Although the study of the moving image is an important part of learning the fine art of television and film production, at this point look only at some of its most basic principles.

When framing for the traditional 4 × 3 aspect ratio and small screen, movements along the z-axis (toward or away from the camera) are stronger than any type of lateral motion (from one screen edge to the other). Fortunately, they are also the easiest to frame: You simply keep the camera as steady as possible and make sure that the moving object does not go out of focus as it approaches the camera. Remember that a wide-angle zoom lens position gives the impression of accelerated motion along the z-axis, whereas the narrow-angle position slows z-axis motion for the viewer.

When working in the 16 × 9 DTV aspect ratio, however, lateral movement takes on more prominence, so you need to be a little more deft with camera handling. Although the stretched screen width gives you a little more breathing room, you must still have proper leadroom during the entire pan. As mentioned, the viewer wants to know where the object is going, not where it has been.

If you are on a close-up and the person shifts back and forth, *do not try to follow each minor wiggle.* You might run the risk of making viewers seasick; at the very least they will not be able to concentrate on this sort of motion for very long. Keep the camera pointed at the major action area, or zoom out (or pull back) to a slightly wider shot.

When you have a two-shot and one of the persons moves out of the frame, stay with just one of them—do not try to keep both people in the frame. **SEE 6.32 AND 6.33** *READY ZVL* ❼

If even after extensive rehearsals you find that in an over-the-shoulder shot the person closer to the camera often blocks the other person, who is farther away from the camera, you can solve the problem by trucking or arcing to the right or left. **SEE 6.34 AND 6.35**

Whatever you do to organize screen motion, do it *smoothly.* Try to move the camera as little as possible, unless you need to follow a moving object or dramatize a shot through motion. Because you can move a camcorder so easily, it may be tempting for you to "animate" a basically static scene to get more life into it. Don't do it. One of the telltale signs of an amateur camera operator is excessive camera motion.

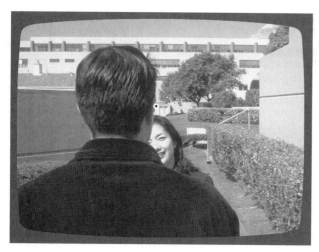

6.34 CAMERA-FAR PERSON BLOCKED

In an over-the shoulder shot, you may find that the camera-near person blocks the camera-far person.

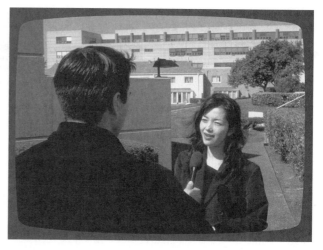

6.35 CAMERA TRUCKS TO CORRECT

To correct this over-the-shoulder shot so that the camera-far person can be seen, simply truck or arc right with the camera.

MAIN POINTS

◆ Because the television screen size is relatively small, we use more close-ups (CUs) and medium shots (MSs) than long shots (LSs). When shooting for wide-aspect-ratio, large-screen DTV, more medium shots and long shots can be used.

◆ Field of view refers to how much of a scene you show in the viewfinder, that is, how close the object appears relative to the viewer. The field of view is organized into five steps: ESL (extreme long shot), LS (long shot), MS (medium shot), CU (close-up), and ECU (extreme close-up).

◆ Alternate field-of-view designations include the bust shot, the knee shot, the two-shot, and the three-shot.

◆ In organizing the screen area for the traditional 4 × 3 and the DTV 16 × 9 aspect ratios, the major considerations are: dealing with height and width, framing close-ups, headroom, noseroom and leadroom, and closure, whereby we mentally fill in objects we cannot see.

◆ In organizing screen depth, a simple and effective way is to establish a distinct foreground, middleground, and background.

◆ In creating the illusion of a third dimension (depth staging), you need to consider choice of lens, positioning of objects, depth of field, and lighting and color.

◆ In organizing screen motion for the 4 × 3 aspect ratio, z-axis motion (movement toward or away from the camera) is stronger than lateral movement (from one side of the screen to the other). When working in the 16 × 9 aspect ratio, lateral movement becomes more prominent.

ZETTL'S VIDEOLAB 2.1

This section reinforces what you have learned about framing a shot, gives you a chance to select the most effective picture compositions, and shows you some of the motion principles.

RUN ZVL 1   Click on the **camera** monitor and run tape 6 **Composition**. Click on module 1 **Field of view**, which gives examples of the five shot divisions, ranging from ELS to ECU.

RUN ZVL 2   Now click on module 4 **Close-ups**. It will show you how effective close-ups are framed.

RUN ZVL 3   Now click on module 2 **Headroom**, which demonstrates how the magnetism of the screen edges influences how you frame a shot.

RUN ZVL 4   Now click on module 3 **Leadroom**, which shows you how to use the camera to compensate for strong lateral index and motion vectors.

RUN ZVL 5   Now click on module 6 **Closure**, which demonstrates how to frame a close-up so that the head does not seem to float in space.

RUN ZVL 6   Now run tape 7 **Picture Depth**. Click on the first three modules: **Z-axis, Lens choice**, and **Depth of field**. These modules will help you create picture depth through a limited depth of field.

RUN ZVL 7   Now run tape 8 **Screen Motion**. Click on the first three modules: **Z-axis, Lateral**, and **Close-ups**. These show you how to properly frame moving objects.

Always check yourself by taking the **Quizzes**.

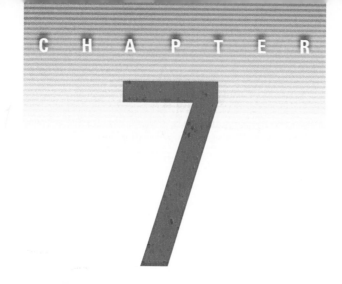

Lighting

Lighting means to control light for three principal reasons: (1) to provide the television camera with adequate illumination so that it can see well, that is, produce technically acceptable pictures; (2) to help the viewer recognize what things and people look like and where they are in relation to one another and to their immediate environment; and (3) to establish a general feeling and mood of the event.

Section 7.1, Lighting Instruments and Lighting Controls, describes the tools you need to accomplish these lighting objectives. Section 7.2, Light Intensity, Lamps, and Color Media, introduces a few more elements about light, how to control and measure it, and how to produce colored light.

barn doors Metal flaps in front of a lighting instrument that control the spread of the light beam.

baselight Even, nondirectional (diffused) light necessary for the camera to operate optimally. Normal baselight levels are 2,000 lux at $f/5.6$ (150 to 200 foot-candles). Also called *base.*

broad A floodlight with a broadside, panlike reflector.

clip light Small internal reflector bulb that is clipped to pieces of scenery or furniture with a gator clip.

color temperature Relative reddishness or bluishness of light, as measured in Kelvin degrees (K). The norm for indoor TV lighting is 3,200°K, for outdoors, 5,600°K.

cucalorus Any pattern cut out of thin metal that, when placed in front of an ellipsoidal spotlight (pattern projector), produces a shadow pattern. Also called *cookie.*

dimmer A device that controls the intensity of light by throttling the electric current flowing to the lamp.

ellipsoidal spotlight Spotlight producing a very defined beam, which can be shaped further by metal shutters.

flag A thin, rectangular sheet of metal, plastic, or cloth used to block light from falling on specific areas.

floodlight Lighting instrument that produces diffused light with a relatively undefined beam edge.

fluorescent Lamps that generate light by activating a gas-filled tube to give off ultraviolet radiation, which lights up the phosphorous coating inside the tubes.

follow spot Powerful special-effects spotlight used primarily to simulate theater stage effects. It generally follows action, such as dancers, ice skaters, or single performers moving in front of a stage curtain.

foot-candle (fc) The unit of measurement of illumination, or the amount of light that falls on an object.

Fresnel spotlight One of the most common spotlights, named after the inventor of its lens. It has steplike concentric rings.

gel Generic term for color filters put in front of spotlights or floodlights to give the light beam a specific hue. *Gel* comes from *gelatin,* the filter material used before the invention of much more heat- and moisture-resistant plastics. Also called *color media.*

HMI light Stands for *hydrargyrum medium arc-length iodide.* An extremely efficient, high-intensity light that burns at 5,600°K—the outdoor illumination norm. It needs an additional piece of equipment—a ballast—to operate properly.

incandescent The light produced by the hot tungsten filament of ordinary glass-globe or quartz-iodine light bulbs (in contrast to fluorescent light).

incident light Light that strikes the object directly from its source. An incident-light reading is the measure of light in foot-candles (or lux) from the object to the light source. The foot-candle (or lux) meter is pointed directly into the light source or toward the camera.

Kelvin degrees (K) A measure of color temperature; the relative reddishness or bluishness of white light.

lumen The light intensity power of one candle (light source radiating isotropically, i.e., in all directions).

luminaire Technical term for lighting instrument.

luminant Lamp that produces the light; the light source.

lux European standard unit for measuring light intensity. 10.75 lux = 1 fc. Usually roughly translated as 10 lux = 1 fc.

neutral density (ND) filter Filter that reduces the incoming light without distorting the color of the scene.

patchboard A device that connects various inputs with specific outputs. Also called *patchbay.*

pattern projector An ellipsoidal spotlight with a cookie (cucalorus) insert, which projects the cookie's pattern as a cast shadow.

quartz A high-intensity light whose lamp consists of a quartz or silica housing (instead of the customary glass) and a tungsten-halogen filament. Produces a very bright light of stable color temperature (3,200°K).

reflected light Light that is bounced off the illuminated object. A reflected-light reading is done with a light meter held close to the illuminated object.

scoop A scooplike television floodlight.

scrim A spun-glass material that is put in front of a lighting instrument as an additional light diffuser.

softlight Television floodlight that produces extremely diffused light. It has a panlike reflector and a light-diffusing material over its opening.

spotlight A lighting instrument that produces directional, relatively undiffused light with a relatively well-defined beam edge.

white balance The adjustments of the color circuits in the camera to produce a white color in lighting of various color temperatures (relative reddishness or bluishness of white light).

7.1

Lighting Instruments and Lighting Controls

Contrary to stage lighting or the lighting in your home, television lighting is done primarily to please the camera and, ultimately, the television viewer. It nevertheless must also fulfill certain aesthetic requirements. Studio lighting requires lighting instruments that can simulate bright sunlight, a street lantern that illuminates a lonely bus stop, the efficiency of a hospital operating room, or the horror of a medieval dungeon. It must also reflect the objectivity and credibility of a news anchor, the high energy of a game show, or the romantic mood in a soap opera scene.

When in the field, you need lighting instruments that are easy to transport and set up and flexible enough to work in a great variety of environments for a multitude of lighting tasks. This section describes the major studio and field lighting instruments and the various types of lighting controls.

▶ **STUDIO LIGHTING INSTRUMENTS**
 Spotlights and floodlights

▶ **FIELD LIGHTING INSTRUMENTS**
 Spotlights, floodlights, and handheld lights

▶ **LIGHTING CONTROL EQUIPMENT**
 Mounting devices, directional controls, and intensity controls

▶ **COLOR TEMPERATURE**
 The reddishness and bluishness of white light and how to control it

STUDIO LIGHTING INSTRUMENTS

All studio lighting is accomplished with a variety of spotlights and floodlights. These instruments, technically called *luminaires*, are designed to operate from the studio ceiling or from floor stands.

Spotlights

Spotlights produce directional, well-defined light whose beam can be adjusted from a sharp light beam like the one from a focused flashlight or car headlight to a softer beam that is still highly directional but that lights up a larger area. All spotlights have a lens that helps sharpen the beam. Most studio lighting uses two basic types of spotlights: the Fresnel spotlight and the ellipsoidal spotlight.

Fresnel spotlight Named for the early-nineteenth-century French physicist Augustin Fresnel (pronounced "fra-*nel*") who invented the lens used in it, the *Fresnel*

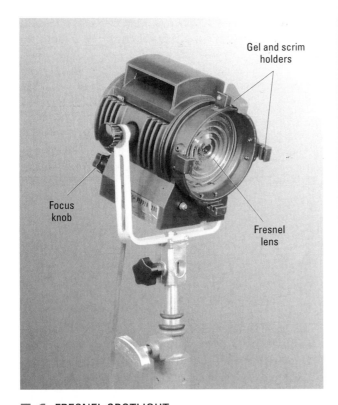

7.1 FRESNEL SPOTLIGHT

This spotlight is one of the most useful lighting instruments in the studio.

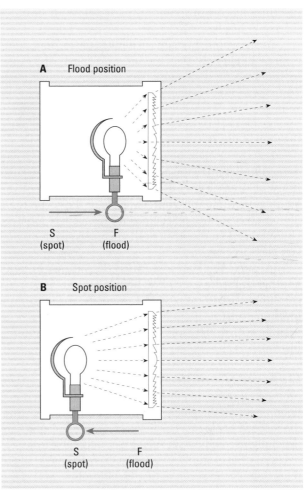

A Flood position

S (spot)   F (flood)

B Spot position

S (spot)   F (flood)

7.2 BEAM CONTROL OF FRESNEL SPOTLIGHT

A To spot (or focus) the beam, turn the focus control so that the bulb-reflector unit moves away from the lens. **B** To flood (or spread) the beam, turn the focus control so that the bulb-reflector unit moves toward the lens.

spotlight is widely used in television studio production. **SEE 7.1** It is relatively lightweight and flexible and has a high output. Its light beam can be made narrow or wide by a spot-focusing device. The spotlight can be adjusted to a "flood" beam position, which gives off a rather widespread light beam; or it can be "spotted," or focused to a sharp, clearly defined beam.

You manipulate the relative spread of the beam by changing the distance between the light bulb and the lens. Most Fresnel spotlights have a bulb-reflector unit inside the lighting instrument that slides toward or away from the lens. Some instruments have a spindle that you crank and thereby move the bulb-reflector unit toward or away from the lens; others have a ring or knob that can be turned by hand or from the studio floor with a small hook on top of a long pole. Whatever the mechanism, the result is the same. To spot, or focus, the beam, turn the control so that the bulb-reflector unit moves *away* from the lens. To flood, or spread, the beam, turn the control so that the bulb-reflector unit moves *toward* the lens. Even in the

flood position, the spotlight beam is still directional and much sharper than that of a floodlight. The flood position merely softens the beam (and with it the shadows) and simultaneously reduces somewhat the amount of light falling on the object. **SEE 7.2**

Always adjust the beam gently. You cannot adjust a light beam with the instrument turned off, but when the bulb is turned on its hot filament is highly sensitive to shock. Some Fresnel spots have external knobs that you can operate from the studio floor with a *lighting pole (a wood or plastic pole with a hook on top)*. This way you can adjust the focus, and pan and tilt the lighting instrument without climbing a ladder and doing it manually (see figure 7.1).

Fresnel spotlights come in different sizes, depending on how much light they produce. Obviously, the larger instruments produce more light than the smaller ones. The size of Fresnel spotlights is normally given in the wattage of the lamp. For example, you might be asked to rehang the 1K (1 kilowatt = 1,000 watts) Fresnel, or change the bulb in the 2K (2 kilowatts = 2,000 watts) Fresnel.

The size of lighting instrument to use depends on several factors: (1) the type of camera and the sensitivity of the imaging device, (2) the distance of the lighting instrument from the objects or the scene to be illuminated, (3) the reflectance of the scenery, objects, clothing, and studio floor, and, of course, (4) the mood you want to convey.

In most television studios, the largest Fresnel spotlights rarely exceed 5K (5,000 watts). The most commonly used Fresnels are 1K and 2K. For maximum lighting control, most lighting technicians prefer to operate with as few, yet adequately powerful, lighting instruments as possible.

Ellipsoidal spotlight   The *ellipsoidal spotlight* produces a sharp, highly defined beam. Even when in a flood position, the ellipsoidal beam is still sharper than the focused beam of a Fresnel spot. Ellipsoidal spots are generally used when specific, precise lighting tasks are necessary. For example, if you want to create pools of light reflecting off the studio floor, the ellipsoidal spot is the instrument to use.

As with the Fresnel, you can spot and flood the light beam of the ellipsoidal. Instead of sliding the lamp inside the instrument, you focus the ellipsoidal spot by moving its lens in and out. Because of the peculiarity of the ellipsoidal reflector (which has two focal points), you can even shape the light beam into a triangle or rectangle, for example, by adjusting four metal shutters that stick out of the instrument. **SEE 7.3**   Some ellipsoidal spotlights can also be used as *pattern projectors*. These instruments are equipped with a slot next to the beam-shaping shutters, which can hold a metal pattern called a *cucalorus*, or *cookie* for short. The ellipsoidal spot projects the cookie as a clear shadow pattern on any surface. Most often it is used to break up flat surfaces, such as the *cyclorama* (large cloth drape used for backing of scenery) or the studio floor. **SEE 7.4** Ellipsoidal spotlights come in sizes from 500 to 2,000 watts, but the most common is 750 watts.

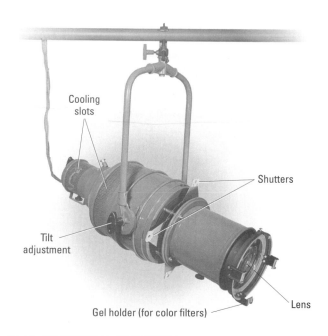

7.3 ELLIPSOIDAL SPOTLIGHT

The highly focused beam of the ellipsoidal spotlight can be further shaped by shutters. It produces the most directional beam of all spotlights.

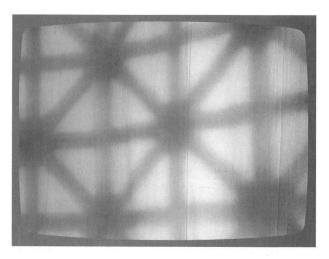

7.4 COOKIE PATTERN ON CYCLORAMA

The cookie pattern is projected by a pattern projector–equipped ellipsoidal spotlight into which you can insert a variety of metal templates. Because the spotlight can be focused, you can make the projected pattern look sharp or soft.

Follow spot   Sometimes you may find that a television show requires a *follow spot*, a powerful special-effects spotlight used primarily to simulate theater stage effects. The follow spot generally follows action, such as

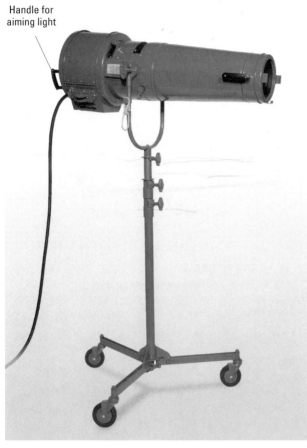

Handle for
aiming light

7.5 FOLLOW SPOT
The follow spot allows you to follow action and simultaneously adjust the light beam.

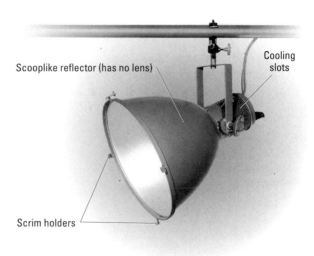

Scooplike reflector (has no lens)

Cooling slots

Scrim holders

7.6 SCOOP
The scoop is a rugged, all-purpose floodlight. Its scooplike reflector gives its beam some directionality.

bank, (4) the incandescent floodlight bank, and (5) the strip, or cyc, light.

Scoop   Named for its peculiar scooplike reflector, the *scoop* is one of the more popular floodlights. Although it has no lens, it nevertheless produces a fairly directional but diffused light beam. **SEE 7.6**

There are two types of scoops: fixed-focus and adjustable-focus. The fixed-focus scoop permits no simple adjustment of its light beam. You can increase the diffusion of the beam by attaching a *scrim*—a spun-glass material held in a metal frame—in front of the scoop. Although the light output is considerably reduced through the scrim, some lighting people put scrims on *all* scoops, not only to produce highly diffused light but also to protect the studio personnel in case the hot lamp inside the scoop shatters.

Some scoops have adjustable beams, from medium-spread positions to full flood. You may use the adjustable scoops as key lights (principal light source) and fill in the resulting shadows with other floodlights that emit a more highly diffused light. Most scoops range from 1K to 2K (1,000 to 2,000 watts), with the 1,500-watt scoop being the most popular. *READY ZVL* ❶

Softlight and broad   *Softlights* are used for even, extremely diffused lighting. They have large tubelike

dancers, ice skaters, or single performers moving in front of a stage curtain. **SEE 7.5** In smaller studios, you can use an ellipsoidal spotlight to simulate a follow spot.

Floodlights
Floodlights are designed to produce great amounts of highly diffused light. They are often used as principal sources of light (key lights) in situations where shadows are to be kept to a minimum, such as news sets and product displays, to slow down falloff (reduce contrast between light and shadow areas), and to provide base-light. With some floodlights, as with some spotlights, you can adjust the spread of the beam so that undue spill into other set areas can be minimized.

There are five basic types of floodlights: (1) the scoop, (2) the softlight and broad, (3) the fluorescent floodlight

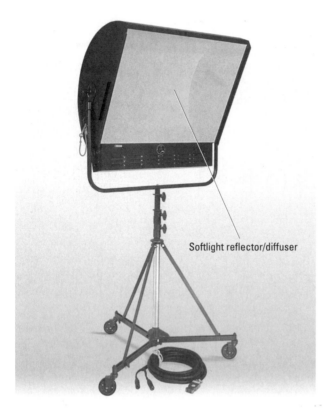

Softlight reflector/diffuser

7.7 SOFTLIGHT
The softlight produces extremely diffused light and is used for illumination with slow falloff. It renders the scene almost shadowless.

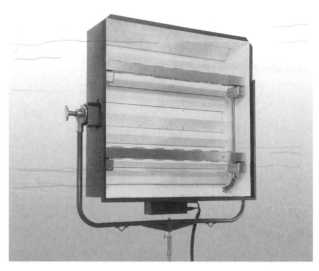

7.8 LARGE BROAD
This instrument illuminates a fairly large area with diffused light. Its light output is normally greater than that of a softlight of equal size.

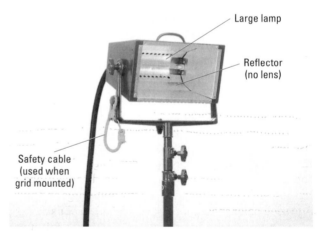

Large lamp

Reflector (no lens)

Safety cable (used when grid mounted)

7.9 SMALL BROAD
The small broad is an efficient floodlight that can be used in the studio as well as at remote locations.

lamps, a diffusing reflector in the back of the large housing, and a diffusing material covering the front opening to further diffuse the light. Softlights are often used for flat (virtually shadowless) lighting setups. You can also use softlights to increase the baselight level without affecting specific lighting where highlights and shadow areas are carefully controlled. For example, if the scene calls for a hallway with alternating bright and dark areas, you can lighten up the dark areas with softlights to provide enough baselight for the camera to "see" well even in the dark areas.

Softlights come in various sizes and act like fluorescent tubes, except that they usually burn with the indoor (3,200°K) color temperature standard. **SEE 7.7**

The ***broad*** (from *broadside*) is similar to a softlight, except that it has a higher light output that causes more distinct shadows than a softlight. Broads also have some provision for beam control. They are generally used to evenly illuminate large areas with diffused light. **SEE 7.8** Smaller broads emit a more directional light beam than

the larger types, for evenly illuminating smaller areas. **SEE 7.9** To permit some directional control over the beam, some smaller broads have *barn doors*—movable metal flaps—to block gross light spill into other set areas.

Fluorescent floodlight bank   The fluorescent floodlight bank goes back to the early days of television lighting. In those days the banks were large, heavy, and

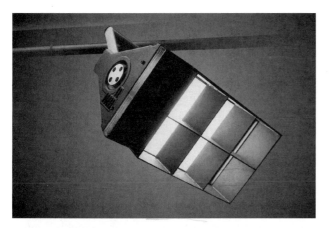

7.10 FLUORESCENT FLOODLIGHT BANK

These floodlight banks act like softlights, except that they do not get as hot as incandescent floodlights of equal output. Some floodlight banks (such as Videssence) use lamps that operate on a fluorescent-like principle called *sustained RGB lighting.*

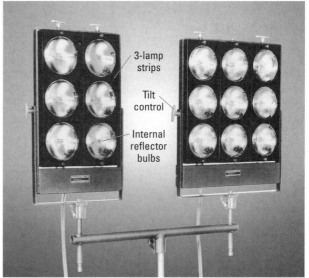

7.11 INCANDESCENT FLOODLIGHT BANK

The incandescent floodlight bank consists of rows of internal reflector lamps. These banks are useful for large-area lighting.

not very efficient. Today's fluorescent banks are relatively lightweight, much more efficient, and can burn at the standard indoor color temperature (3,200°K) or even a lower one (giving off more reddish light). By simply changing the tubes, you can achieve the standard outdoor color temperature (5,600°K), or even a much higher one (such as 7,500°K) that resembles the extremely bluish midday sunlight filtered by a hazy sky.

Another advantage of fluorescent banks is that they use less power than incandescent lamps and they burn much more coolly—a definite advantage when lighting interiors with poor ventilation. The disadvantage of fluorescent banks is that they are still quite large and bulky and their color spectrum is not even. This means that the light emitted does not reproduce all colors faithfully. Newer floodlight banks have rows of low-powered fluorescent lamps inside a housing that looks similar to a softlight. These lamps look much like the fluorescent bulbs you can now buy to replace normal incandescent bulbs. To make the light beam as soft as possible, the front of the instrument is covered with light-diffusing material. Smaller banks look more like small broads and can be used when more-precise beams are desired. **SEE 7.10**

Incandescent floodlight bank   This instrument consists of a series of high-intensity internal reflector lamps arranged in banks of six, nine, twelve, or more spots. **SEE 7.11** The floodlight bank is principally used

on big remotes, either to illuminate fairly large areas over a considerable distance or to act as a daylight booster to make the harsh shadows more transparent for the camera. Because they are large and awkward to handle, they are not often found in studios. For studio lighting, the softlight easily outperforms the floodlight bank in lighting efficiency and operational ease.

Strip, or cyc, light   This type of instrument is commonly used to achieve even illumination of large set areas, such as the *cyc (cyclorama)* or some other uninterrupted background area. Very similar to the border, or cyc, lights of the theater, television *strip lights* consist of rows of three to twelve quartz lamps mounted in long, boxlike reflectors. The more sophisticated strip lights have, like theater border lights, colored-glass frames for each of the reflector units so that the cyc can be illuminated in different colors. **SEE 7.12**

You can also use strip lights as general floodlights by suspending them from the studio ceiling, or you can place them on the studio floor to separate pillars and other set pieces from the lighted background. Strip lights are sometimes used for silhouette lighting (where the background is evenly illuminated and the foreground objects remain unlit) and special-effects chroma-key lighting (see chapter 8). *READY ZVL* ➋

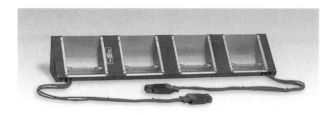

7.12 STRIP, OR CYC, LIGHT
Strip lights are used to illuminate cycloramas and other large areas needing even illumination.

FIELD LIGHTING INSTRUMENTS

ENG EFP You can use studio lighting instruments on remote locations, but you will find that most of them are too bulky to move around easily, their large three-pronged plugs or twist-lock plugs do not fit the normal household receptacles, and they draw too much power. Once in place and operating, they do not provide the amount or type of illumination you need for good field lighting. Besides, most studio lights are suspended on an overhead lighting grid. To take them down each time you have to light a remote telecast not only wastes valuable production time, but, more important, robs the studio of the lighting instruments. Unless you do big remotes where the lighting requirements rival studio lighting, you need instruments that can be easily transported and quickly set up and that give you the lighting flexibility needed in the field.

Although many portable lighting instruments fulfill dual spotlight and floodlight functions, you may still find it useful to group them, like studio lights, into those categories. Note, however, that by bouncing a spotlight beam off the ceiling or the wall, it will take on the function of a floodlight. On the other hand, you can use a small floodlight and control its beam with barn doors so that it illuminates a fairly limited area, operating as a spot.

Spotlights

Portable spotlights are designed to be lightweight, rugged, efficient (which means that the light output is great relative to the size of the instrument), easy to set up and transport, and small enough to be effectively hidden from camera view even in cramped interiors. The three most frequently used spotlights are the external reflector spot, the internal reflector spot, and the HMI Fresnel spot.

Small Fresnel spotlight If you need precise lighting for EFP, such as for a scene that takes place in an actual living room rather than a studio set, you may want to use low-powered (300- to 600-watt) Fresnel spotlights. They have all the features of the larger Fresnel spots, but they are smaller and lighter weight. You can mount them on light stands or even clip them on various braces or hangers.

External reflector spotlight Mainly because of weight consideration and light efficiency, the external reflector spot has no lens. It is therefore also called an *open-face spotlight.*

The lack of a lens makes the beam of the external reflector spotlight less precise than that of the Fresnel spot. But in most remote lighting tasks, a highly defined beam offers no particular advantage. Because you usually have to work with a minimum of lighting instruments, a fairly even illumination is often better than a dramatic yet spotty one.

Even in the field, you should try to achieve the lighting that best fits the communication purpose. For example, if you light a simple interview in a hotel room, flat lighting for optimal visibility is all you need. But if you do a documentary on big-city slums, don't light up a dark tenement as though it were a department store. Such a situation requires more-careful lighting that will retain the actual lighting conditions of the scene while still providing enough light to satisfy the requirements of the camera.

The external reflector spot can serve both of these requirements. You can spot or spread the beam of the high-efficiency quartz lamp through a focus control lever or knob on the back. **SEE 7.13** Unfortunately, the focused beam is not always even. When you place the spot close to the object, you may notice (and the camera surely will) that the rim of the beam is intense and "hot," while the center of the beam has a hole, a low-intensity dark spot. If you place the instrument too close when lighting a face, the "hot spot" of the light may cause a glowing white spot surrounded by a red area on the lighted face or, at best, a distinct color distortion. But by spreading the beam a little, pulling the instrument farther away from the person, or by placing a scrim in front of the spotlight, you can usually correct the problem.

Most external reflector spots are relatively lightweight and come in lighting kits—a suitcase containing several such instruments and light stands. They can be plugged into a regular household receptacle, and usually have a switch close to the lamp so you can easily turn the instrument on and off to extend the life of its lamp.

You may find that the relatively inexpensive 500-watt "utility lights" you can buy in any hardware store will do

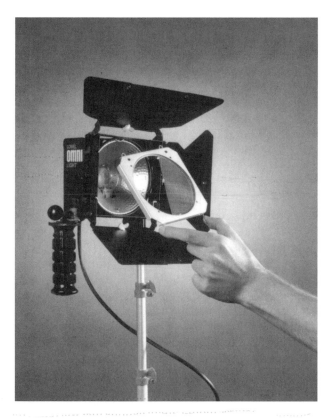

7.13 EXTERNAL REFLECTOR SPOT
The external reflector spot has no lens. Its beam spread can be adjusted to a spot or moderate flood position. It is one of the most useful lighting instruments in field production.

the same job as the more expensive instruments in lighting kits. Note, however, that the utility lights are much better suited for general-area than for specific lighting.

With any lighting instrument, always be careful not to overload the circuit; that is, do not exceed the circuit's rated amperage by plugging in more than one instrument per outlet. Extension cords also add their own resistance to that of the lamp, especially when they get warm. Ordinary household outlets can tolerate a load of up to 1,200 watts. You can therefore plug two 500-watt floodlights into the same circuit without risking a circuit overload (see chapter 8).

Internal reflector spotlight (clip light)   This spotlight looks like an overgrown, slightly squashed household bulb. You have most likely used it already in still photography or to light up your driveway. The reflector for the bulb is inside the lamp. All you need for using this kind of spot is a light socket and a clamp that fastens the bulb to a chair, door, windowsill, or small pole.

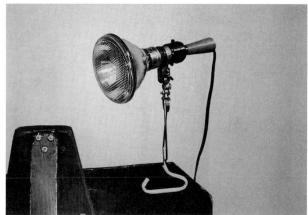

7.14 INTERNAL REFLECTOR, OR CLIP, LIGHT
The clip light consists of a normal internal reflector bulb (such as a PAR 38), a socket with an on/off switch, and a clip for fastening the lamp to a support.

Because internal reflector spots are usually clipped onto things, they are often called *clip lights*. **SEE 7.14**

You can use clip lights to light small areas and to fill in areas that cannot be illuminated with other portable instruments. The clip light is easy to use and an excellent device for providing additional subtle highlights and accents in hard-to-reach areas. Internal reflector spots come in a variety of beam spreads, from a soft, diffused beam to a hard, precisely shaped beam (often called PAR 38 lamps). For even better beam control, as well as for the protection of the internal reflector bulb, the lamp can be used in a metal housing with barn doors attached. **SEE 7.15**

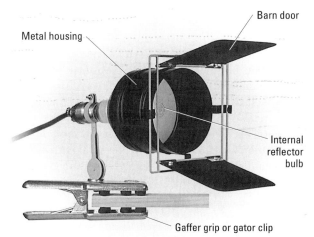

Barn door
Metal housing
Internal reflector bulb
Gaffer grip or gator clip

7.15 CLIP LIGHT WITH METAL HOUSING AND BARN DOORS
The metal housing and barn doors help control the clip light's beam.

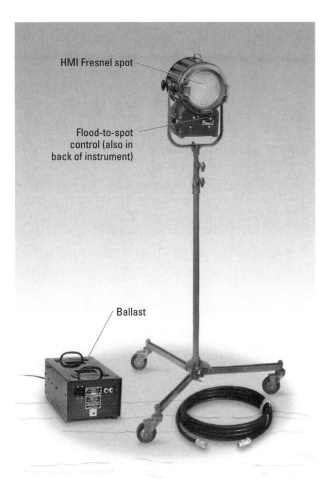

7.16 HMI FRESNEL SPOT WITH BALLAST

The HMI Fresnel spotlight burns with the daylight standard color temperature (5,600°K). It needs considerably less power than an incandescent light of equal intensity.

HMI Fresnel spot

Flood-to-spot control (also in back of instrument)

Ballast

HMI light   The *HMI light*[1] is a Fresnel spotlight that has proved highly successful in elaborate EFP, large remotes, and film productions. **SEE 7.16** It has an arc lamp that delivers from three to five times the illumination of an incandescent quartz instrument of the same wattage. This means that you can get the same level of illumination with a 500-watt HMI Fresnel as with a 2,500-watt incandescent Fresnel. The HMI lamp also generates

---

1. *HMI* stands for *hydrargyrum medium arc-length iodide.* You may want to remember the light by the simpler albeit less accurate name *halogen-metal iodide.*

considerably less heat than an incandescent lamp of the same wattage. To perform such miracles, each instrument needs its own starter and rather heavy ballast units to power the lamp. It is used primarily for simulating or supplementing outdoor light.

For normal EFP work, you may find that the 200-, 575-, and 1,200-watt instruments are the most useful. You can use them as the principal light source or to fill in shadows when shooting outdoors. Some HMI instruments have a Fresnel lens; others come as external reflector spots without a lens. The HMI lights are designed for location shooting and burn with the photographic daylight standard of 5,600°K, rather than the customary 3,200°K. The more popular instruments range from 200 to 4,000 watts. Some manufacturers provide even larger instruments (up to 18K), which are used to fill in shadows during big outdoor productions. To shoot indoors you'll need to attach a filter that lowers the 5,600°K temperature of outdoor light to the indoor standard of 3,200°K.

One of the major advantages of the superefficient HMI lights is that you can plug even the larger instruments (such as the 1,200-watt light) into an ordinary household outlet. A single plug is sufficient to power up to five 200-watt instruments without overloading the circuit, assuming that nothing else is plugged into the same circuit. Because you plug most of the lights into household outlets, you can light most interiors with a minimum of time and effort. All you actually need are plenty of extension cords and power strips. The lamp itself burns at a low thermal temperature, which keeps interiors relatively cool even when several instruments are aimed at a small action area.

Unfortunately, the HMI light is not without drawbacks. The ballast box is one. The box is relatively heavy, can get quite warm, and occasionally hums. Despite preventive circuits, HMI lights can under certain circumstances cause flicker in the video image. HMI lights take anywhere from one to three minutes to reach full illumination power from the time they are switched on. Regardless of whether the HMI lamp or ballast is warmed up at switch-off, you must wait for the power buildup each time you switch the light on again. This problem and the bulky starter-ballast unit make the HMI lights impractical for normal ENG. All HMI lights are expensive, and the high-powered HMI instruments (2K and up) are large and heavy. It is no wonder they are not used in routine electronic field productions.

Floodlights

Even the small, portable external reflector spots (see figure 7.13) operate as efficient floodlights when put in the flood position and, if possible, bounced off light-colored walls, ceilings, or a white card that acts as a diffuser. But you will find it easier to achieve flat area lighting by using portable floodlights. All portable floodlights are open-face instruments, which means they have no lens.

Most of the small floodlights can be powered by ordinary 120-volt household current, or by a 30-volt battery, provided you have the appropriate lamp for each current. The extension cables of most portable lights have an on/off switch close to the instrument, making it unnecessary to unplug the instrument every time you want to turn it off. You should keep portable lighting instruments turned off as much as possible to prolong the life of the lamp (often not more than twenty hours), to keep the performance area as cool as possible (the excessive heat radiation of the quartz instruments makes working in cramped quarters especially uncomfortable), and, finally, to conserve energy.

Although the lights are relatively small, they become extremely hot soon after being switched on, so you should not touch the instrument unless you're wearing safety gloves. Also, do not place the instruments too close to combustible materials, such as curtains, pillars, or upholstered furniture. It is always a good idea to shield such items from the heat with a strip of aluminum foil.

Incandescent floodlights   You can clamp these extremely lightweight instruments on practically anything and hide them rather easily from camera view. **SEE 7.17 AND 7.18** By combining several of them on a single stand, you can get a fairly powerful single light source. Because these floodlights give off very intense light, they are normally placed inside a collapsible softlight housing or a light-diffusing, heat-resistant umbrella.

If you need to light large interiors, you can use a number of portable lights in softlight "tents" or diffused by umbrellas. **SEE 7.19** When doing elaborate field productions, such as covering a high school basketball game, HMI floodlights prove again to be the most efficient instruments. A few 1Ks or even 575-watt instruments in the flood position are all you need to light up the gymnasium. When using HMI lights indoors, you need to white-balance the camera to the daylight

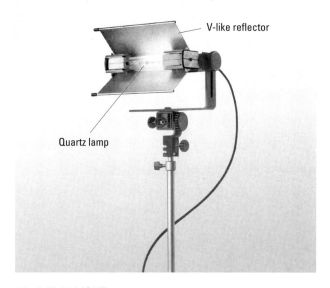

7.17 V-LIGHT
This small lighting instrument is popular in field productions because of its light weight and high output.

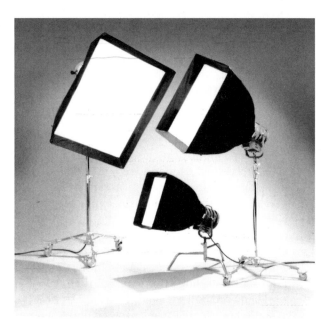

7.18 PORTABLE SOFTLIGHT
This small portable softlight resembles its bigger studio cousins in design and function, but it is smaller and operates off the normal household current.

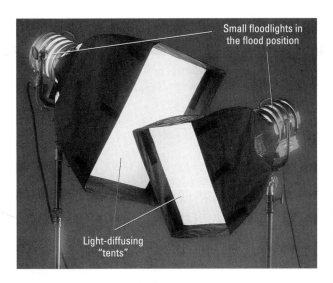

7.19 ENG/EFP LIGHTBOXES
These instruments are efficient portable softlights. The reflector "tents" can be folded up for easy transport.

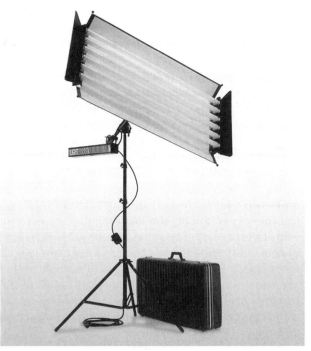

7.20 PORTABLE FLUORESCENT BANK
The portable fluorescent bank can be mounted on a light stand. It has great light and emits no heat.

color temperature (unless you use the filters on the HMI lights that lower the color temperature to the 3,200°K indoor standard). Of course, provided that you have enough room, you can also use large broads or scoops for uniform illumination even in relatively large areas.

Fluorescent floodlights Even small portable fluorescent floodlights are considerably bulkier and heavier than comparable incandescent instruments. But because fluorescent floodlights use much less power and generate practically no heat, they are frequently used for indoor EFP lighting. As mentioned, the problem with fluorescent lights is that they do not accurately reproduce all colors, even if the camera has been properly white-balanced. The most common color distortion is a greenish tint of skin color. If you run into such a color distortion problem, you can try to combat it with stage makeup or color filters. If highly accurate color reproduction is not of major concern, however, you will find the small fluorescent unit to be a valuable EFP lighting tool.

When lighting for EFP in relatively cramped quarters, you can use some of the smaller, lightweight fluorescent banks and mount them on light stands. Although somewhat heavy and bulky, they consume little power relative to light output and they keep the interior cool. **SEE 7.20**

Handheld Lights

ENG EFP Electronic news gathering requires yet another type of light, which can be mounted on top of the camera or handheld by the camera operator or assistant. These lights are relatively small, open-faced, and have a high light output. The camera-mounted lights, called *camera lights* or *eye lights,* are powered by the 12-volt battery of the camcorder or a 30-volt battery pack normally worn as a belt. **SEE 7.21 AND 7.22** Some come with interchangeable bulbs so that they can be powered by 12- or 30-volt batteries or by standard household AC current.

When using the camera light, try not to shine it directly on the scene right away. First try pointing the camera light toward the ceiling and then tilting it down gradually. This maneuver is difficult if you are alone, but if you have an assistant who takes care of the light, the procedure should become routine. The reason for this gradual illumination is that it is often annoying to a person to have a high-powered light pop into his or her eyes without at least a little warning. It also gives the auto-iris

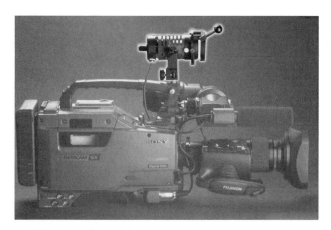

7.21 CAMERA LIGHT
This small light is mounted on the camera and powered by the camcorder battery or a battery belt. It has a high light output.

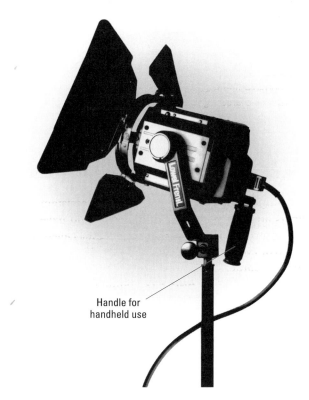

Handle for
handheld use

7.22 SMALL PORTABLE SPOTLIGHT
Small spotlights are often used in ENG/EFP. Despite their small size they have a high light output.

sufficient time to adjust to the new lighting conditions without noticeable brightness and color changes.

Generally, a good lighting instrument for ENG lets you do the following: (1) run it off a 12- or 30-volt battery; (2) change the beam from spot to flood; (3) attach barn doors for further beam control; (4) put in various reflectors and color-correction and diffusion filters; (5) either hold it or clip it on the camera or any other convenient object, such as a door or chair; and (6) use it with a light-diffusing umbrella. The ENG/EFP cameras have fortunately become so light sensitive that more often you will need handheld lights only as additional baselight or soft fill rather than as a principal source of illumination.

LIGHTING CONTROL EQUIPMENT

To understand lighting control, you need to become familiar with some specific equipment: (1) mounting devices, (2) directional controls, and (3) intensity controls.

Mounting Devices

Mounting devices let you safely support a variety of lighting instruments and aim them in the desired direction. Good mounting devices are as important as the instruments themselves. The major mounting devices specially designed and intended for studio lights are: (1) the pipe grid and counterweight battens, (2) the C-clamp, (3) the sliding rod and the pantograph, and (4) a variety of floor stands. Portable lights are mounted primarily on portable stands that are collapsible and normally part of a lighting kit. For on-location lighting, there is a variety of mounting devices available, such as small booms, cross braces, and small braces that fit over doors or furniture.

Pipe grid and counterweight battens   Studio lights are hung either from a fixed pipe grid or from counterweight battens. The *pipe grid* consists of heavy steel pipe strung either crosswise or parallel and mounted 12 to 18 feet above the studio floor. The height of the grid is determined by the height of the studio ceiling height; but even in rooms with low ceilings, the pipe should be mounted approximately 2 feet below the ceiling so that the lighting instruments or hanging devices can be easily

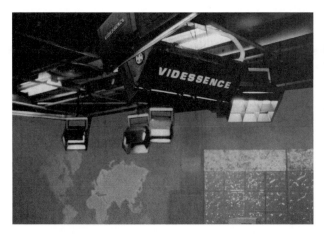

7.23 PIPE GRID
This simple pipe grid supports all the lights necessary for a news set and interview area. The instruments are Videssence RGB floodlights.

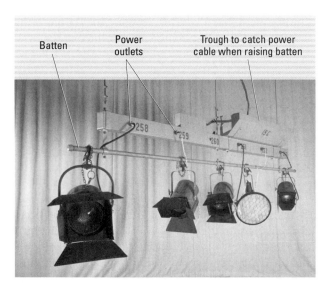

7.24 COUNTERWEIGHT BATTEN
The counterweight battens can be raised and lowered and locked at a specific operating height.

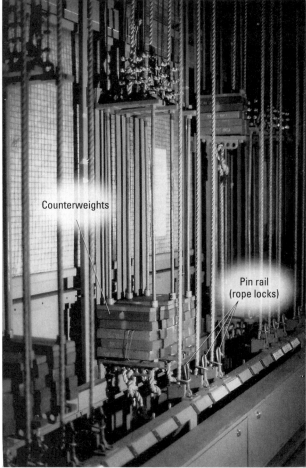

7.25 COUNTERWEIGHT SYSTEM
The battens and the lighting instruments attached to them are counterweighted by heavy steel weights and moved up and down by a rope-and-pulley system.

attached. The space above the grid is also necessary to dissipate the heat generated by the lights. **SEE 7.23**

Unlike the pipe grid, which is permanently mounted below the ceiling, the *counterweight battens* can be raised and lowered to any desired position and locked firmly in place. **SEE 7.24** The battens and the instruments are counterweighted by heavy steel weights and moved by means of a rope-and-pulley system or by individual motors. **SEE 7.25** Before unlocking a counterweight rope

to move the batten up or down, always check that the batten is properly weighted. You can do this by counting the weights and comparing them with the type and number of instruments mounted on the batten. The counterweights and the instruments should roughly balance each other. Such rope-and-pulley counterweight systems should have a sign posted that tells how many weights are necessary to balance each type of instrument, plus the weight of the empty batten.

The obvious advantage of the counterweight battens over the pipe grid system is that the instruments can be hung, adjusted, and maintained from the studio floor. You will find, however, that you cannot do entirely without a ladder. First, although you can initially adjust the

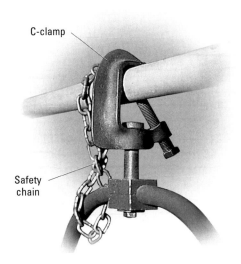

7.26 C-CLAMP

The C-clamp connects the lighting instrument to the batten. Even when the C-clamp is securely tightened in place, you can swivel the instrument clockwise or counterclockwise.

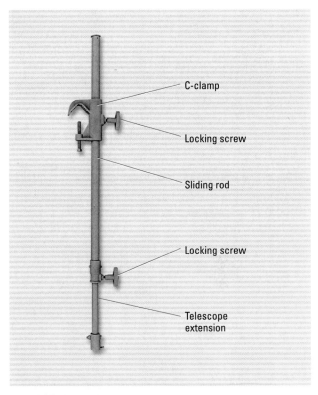

7.27 SLIDING ROD (TELESCOPE HANGER)

This sliding rod, called a telescope hanger, allows you to move the instrument up and down and lock it into position. It is primarily used on pipe grids, but also on counterweight systems when more vertical control is needed.

instruments to a rough operating position, you need to re-aim them once the battens are locked at the optimal height. Second, by the time you need to fine-tune the lights, the studio floor is generally crowded with sets, cameras, and microphones, which prevent lowering the battens to a comfortable working height. You can then squeeze the ladder into the set or use a lighting pole to do the final trimming.

C-clamp   The lighting instruments are directly attached either to the batten by a *C-clamp* or to hanging devices (discussed later). You need a wrench or key to securely fasten the C-clamp to the round metal batten. The lighting instrument is attached to this large C-clamp and can be swiveled horizontally without loosening the bolt that holds it to the batten. Although the C-clamp will support the lighting instrument and not fall off the batten even if the large bolt is loose, you should nevertheless check periodically that all C-clamps on the grid are securely tightened. As an added safety measure, all lighting instruments should be chained or secured to the batten itself by a strong steel cable loop. Similarly, the barn doors must be secured to the lighting instrument. Even if you are under severe time pressure when rehanging lights, *do not neglect to secure each instrument with the safety chain or cable.* **SEE 7.26**

Sliding rod and pantograph   If the studio has a fixed pipe grid, or if you need to raise or lower individual instruments without moving a whole lighting batten, you can use sliding rods. A *sliding rod* consists of a sturdy pipe attached to the batten by a modified C-clamp; it can be moved and locked into a specific vertical position. For additional flexibility, the more expensive sliding rods have telescope extensions. **SEE 7.27**   More-elaborate lighting systems have motor-driven sliding rods whose vertical movement can be remotely activated from the studio lighting control.

Some studios use the *pantograph*, a spring-loaded hanging device that can be adjusted from the studio floor to any vertical position within its 12-foot range. **SEE 7.28** Pantographs are often used to adjust the height of scoops or other floodlights. The advantage of a pantograph is that you can adjust it from the studio floor without climbing a ladder. The disadvantages are that it is bulky and that the

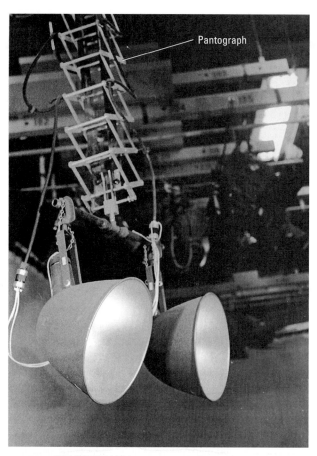

7.28 PANTOGRAPH
You can adjust this spring-loaded hanger quickly and easily by pushing it up or pulling it down with a lighting pole. The springs act as a counterweight for the lights attached to it.

7.29 FLOOR STANDS
The floor stand can support a variety of lighting instruments and can be adapted for an easel or for large reflectors.

counterbalancing springs get out of adjustment and, worse, wear out from extended use.

Floor stand   Not all studio lights are mounted on the pipe grid or battens. Some are mounted on vertical roller-caster *floor stands* that can be rolled around the studio and vertically extended. **SEE 7.29** Such stands can hold all types of instruments: scoops, broads, spots, and even strip lights. The stands usually have a switch to turn the light on and off.

Portable light stand   Because you won't find battens or grids conveniently installed when you do on-location shooting, you need to carry the lighting supports with you. A large variety of lightweight and durable mounting devices is available, and all of them consist basically of collapsible stands and extendible poles. **SEE 7.30**

You can attach to the stands and poles a wide array of portable lighting instruments and other devices, such as reflectors, scrims, and flags (see figures 7.33–7.37). In more-elaborate productions, you can use a portable boom specifically designed to hold small lighting instruments. The advantage of such a boom is that you can suspend the light over the scene out of camera range and easily relocate it as necessary. The disadvantages of a boom are that it is quite expensive, it must be handheld, and that even a small one takes up more space than is often available.

Many ingenious mounting devices are available, such as cross braces or braces that fit conveniently over doors

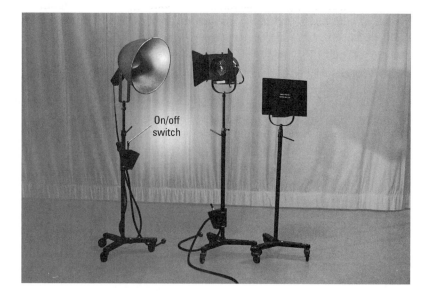

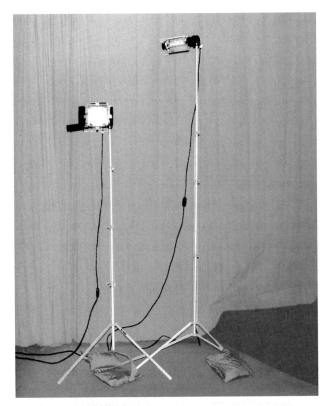

7.30 PORTABLE LIGHT STAND
These light stands are designed for relatively lightweight portable instruments and can be extended to a height of 10 feet. Because they tend to tip over when fully extended, always secure them with sandbags.

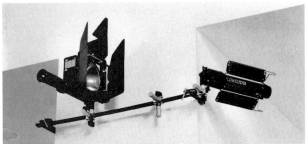

7.31 CROSS BRACE
This extendible cross brace can be clamped to scenery or furniture as a battenlike support for portable lighting instruments.

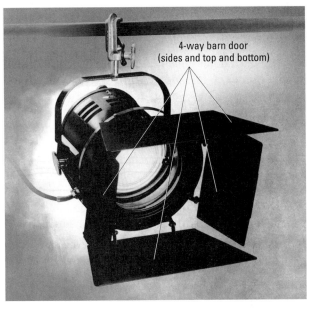

4-way barn door
(sides and top and bottom)

7.32 FOUR-WAY BARN DOOR
This four-way barn door allows you to control the beam spread on all four sides—top, bottom, left, and right.

and that let you attach small lighting instruments to scenery, desks, furniture, wastepaper baskets, or any convenient object in the remote location. **SEE 7.31** You can also make a simple lighting bridge out of 1×3 lumber that will hold one or two portable spotlights for back-lighting. Whatever mounting devices you use—including your own contraptions—see to it that the lighting instrument is securely fastened and that it is far enough away from curtains, upholstery, or other ignitable materials. *Always put a sandbag on the light stand to prevent it from tipping over.* Light stands that are fully extended tend to topple at the slightest pull on the power cable or even in a strong breeze.

Directional Controls

You are familiar with the spot and flood beam control on spotlights. Several other devices can help you control the direction of the beam, such as barn doors, flags, and diffusers.

Barn doors   This admittedly crude beam control method is extremely effective for blocking certain set areas partially or totally from illumination. *Barn doors* consist of two or four metal flaps that you can fold over the lens of the lighting instrument, thus preventing the light from falling on certain areas. For example, if you want to keep the upper part of some scenery dark without sacrificing illumination of the lower part, you simply block off the upper part of the beam with a barn door. Or if you want to eliminate a boom shadow, you can partially close a barn door. **SEE 7.32** Barn doors are also important for preventing the back light from shining into the camera lens, which can cause lens flare.

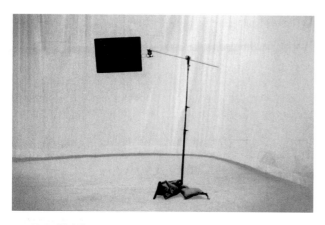

7.33 FLAG

Flags come in various sizes and densities. You use them to prevent light from hitting specific areas.

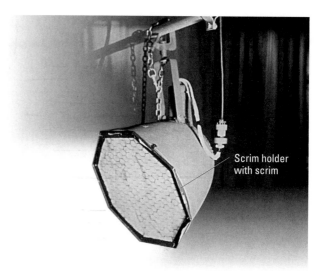

Scrim holder with scrim

7.34 SCOOP WITH SCRIM

This scrim is cut to fit a scrim holder and placed in front of a scoop to diffuse the light and reduce its intensity.

Because barn doors slide into their holders easily, they have a tendency to slide out of them just as readily. Always secure all barn doors to their instruments with the safety chain or cable. Barn doors also get very hot: Wear protective gloves while adjusting them when the instrument is turned on. *READY ZVL* ❸

Flags   Rectangular metal frames with heat-resistant cloth or thin metal sheets of various sizes, *flags* act very much like barn doors, except that you do not place them directly on the lighting instrument. They are mounted on light stands and put anywhere on the set where they can block the light from falling on a specific area without being seen by the camera. In movie lingo flags are also called gobos. To make things even more confusing, a *gobo* in television terminology refers not to a flag but to a special-effects cutout (see figure 7.4). Obviously, you can use flags only if the camera and the talent movements have been carefully blocked and rehearsed. **SEE 7.33**

Diffusers   Strictly speaking, directional controls also include the various devices that diffuse a hard light beam, such as scrims and reflectors. Because the resulting light diffusion is done more to reduce the intensity of spotlights, and thereby control falloff, than to control the direction of the light, these lighting aids are discussed in the following section on intensity controls.

Intensity Controls: Diffusers and Reflectors

The simplest way of controlling light intensity is obviously to turn on only a certain number of instruments of a specific size (wattage); move the light closer (more intensity) or farther away (less intensity) from the object to be illuminated; or focus (more intensity) or spread (less intensity) the beam of the spotlight. You can also control the beam intensity by diffusing the light through scrims, frosted gels, or wire-mesh screens in front of the lighting instrument, or by bouncing the light off reflectors.

Scrims, frosted gels, umbrellas, and wire-mesh screens   As mentioned, *scrims* are spun-glass diffusers that you can put in front of small spotlights, floodlights, or external reflector spots to achieve maximum diffusion of the light beam. **SEE 7.34** While they diffuse light, they also absorb a certain amount. This combination of diffusion and absorption functions as a dimmer. Scrims come in various thicknesses; the thinner ones absorb less light, and the thicker ones absorb more light. *Frosted gels* are white translucent sheets of plastic that have a semiopaque surface. Like scrims, they come in different densities that diffuse and therefore reduce the intensity of the light beam by varying degrees.

One of the most effective diffusion devices is the *umbrella.* The small, silvery umbrella is not to protect you from the rain, but to reflect and diffuse the light source that shines into it. You can attach the scooplike umbrella to the lighting instrument and/or the light stand and then aim the umbrella's opening in the general direction of illumination. **SEE 7.35**

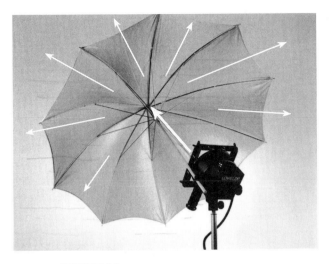

7.35 UMBRELLA

The umbrella reflector is a popular diffusion device. Note that the lighting instrument shines into, not away from, the inside of the umbrella.

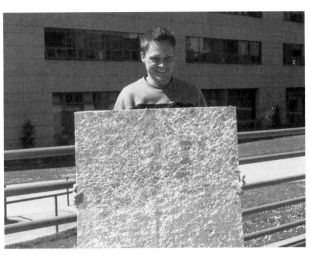

7.36 FOIL REFLECTOR

This homemade yet highly efficient reflector uses crumpled aluminum foil taped to a piece of cardboard.

You can also use a specially designed *wire-mesh screen* to diffuse and block a certain amount of light. You simply slide it directly in front of the instrument, much like scrims and frosted gels. Depending on the fineness of the mesh, the screen dims the light without influencing its color temperature. This means that the light does not take on a reddish color as it does when lamp voltage is reduced; all you do is block some of the light from falling on the object. The problem with wire-mesh screens is that the heat of the quartz lamp tends to burn up the fine metal wires within a relatively short time; the screens become brittle and eventually disintegrate.

Reflectors   Actually, reflectors are used primarily to produce highly diffused light to lighten up the dense shadows (in media aesthetic language, *to slow down falloff*) on someone's face or some object. But reflectors are also used to diffuse and lower the intensity of a light source so that it can produce even baselight. You can use anything as a reflector: somebody's white shirt or a piece of paper. Most LDs (lighting directors) prefer a large sheet of white foam core; it is lightweight, quite sturdy, simple to set up, and easily replaced if it gets scratched or broken. Any large white cardboard will do almost as well. If you need a more efficient reflector (one that reflects more light), you can crumple up some aluminum foil to get an uneven surface (for a more diffused reflection) and then tape it to a piece of cardboard. **SEE 7.36**

Commercially available reflectors are more efficient for reflecting light. You can roll or fold them for easy transport and setup. The more practical ones are large sheets of beaded white, silver, or gold cloth that can be rolled up, or large cards (similar to projection screens) that bounce back a strong light source. **SEE 7.37**   The silver reflectors obviously reflect a higher-color-temperature light than the gold-colored ones. *READY ZVL* ❹

Regardless of what instruments, mounting devices, and beam controls you use, always carry a roll of aluminum foil and several rolls of gaffer's tape. You can use foil as flags, as an efficient reflector, and to extend or make barn doors. As mentioned, it can also serve as a heat shield if you have to mount lighting instruments close to combustible materials.

Intensity Controls: Electronic Dimmers

The most precise light control is the electronic dimmer. With a *dimmer* you can easily manipulate each light, or a group of lights, to burn at a given intensity, from 0 (*off* position) to full strength.

Although dimmers are technically complex, their basic operational principle is quite simple: *By allowing more or less current to flow to the lamp, the lamp burns with a higher or lower intensity.* If you want the lighting instrument to burn at full intensity, the dimmer lets all the current flow to the lamp. If you want it to burn at a

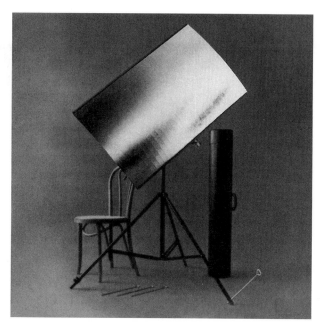

7.37 PORTABLE REFLECTOR

This Mylar reflector has a textured surface that diffuses the reflected light. It can be rolled up and carried around in a convenient case.

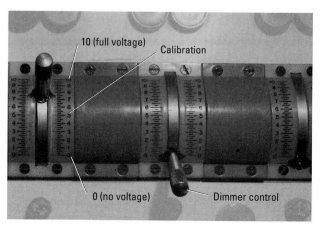

7.38 MANUAL DIMMER CALIBRATION

The higher you push the lever of this manual dimmer, the more current flows to the lamp. At the 0 setting, no current flows to the lamp; when set at 10, the lamp burns at full intensity.

lesser intensity, the dimmer reduces the voltage. To dim the light completely—called a *blackout*—the dimmer permits no current (or at least an inadequate current) to reach the lamp.

Individual dimmers   A useful dimmer system should have a fair number of individual dimmers (twenty or more), each of which has an intensity calibration. The usual calibration is normally in steps of 10, with 0 preventing any current from reaching the instrument (the light is off) and 10 allowing the full current to flow to the lamp (the lamp burns at full intensity). Although most dimmers in television studios are computer-controlled, it is easier to learn the principle of dimmers by looking at a manual system. The computer does not change the basic principle of dimming; it simply facilitates the storage and retrieval of the various dimming commands, provides a wide variety of dimming options, and activates the actual dimming process at precise moments in the production.

On manual dimmers you push the control lever to the desired setting between 0 and 10. Such calibrations are necessary not only to set the initial light intensity, but also to record the exact settings so that they can be stored and recalled with minimal effort. **SEE 7.38** Computer-

assisted dimmers have similar slide faders that can be manually or automatically controlled. A variety of controls lets you combine a great number of dimming functions, and store and recall them either automatically or by pushing a single button. It is not uncommon for a computerized dimmer to offer hundreds of individual dimming functions and storage possibilities. You can store the dimming settings on a floppy disk. Most computer dimmers keep your input in short-term memory for some time, even if you have switched them off. **SEE 7.39**

Electronic dimmers perform a variety of functions, all of which are vital to good television lighting: intensity control, illumination change, and special effects.

Intensity control   Lowering the intensity of a light is helpful not only to preserve the life of the lamp, but also to control contrast. In most lighting situations, you will find that merely turning off some lights and turning on others will not give you the control you need to achieve various degrees of *falloff*—subtle differences between light and shadow—or to make shadow areas properly transparent. With dimmers you can control falloff quite readily, without having to dim any one of the instruments so drastically that the scene takes on the reddish hue of candlelight or a sunset. This reddishness is caused by lowering the color temperature (explored in section 7.2). The 10 percent in the upper range of the light intensity is often enough to make the bright areas less "hot" (intense) or to adjust the relative density of a shadow area. Amazingly enough, dimming HMI lamps will *raise*

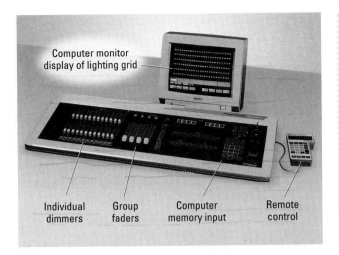

7.39 COMPUTER-ASSISTED DIMMER CONTROL

The computer-assisted dimmer can store, recall, and execute a wide variety of dimming functions. You can also switch it to limited manual control.

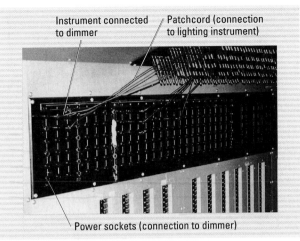

7.40 MANUAL PATCHBOARD

The patchboard enables you to establish power connections between specific lighting instruments and specific dimmers.

the color temperature, making the scene progressively more blue. *READY ZVL* ⑤

Patchboard, grouping devices, and storage and retrieval

The *patchboard*, also called *patchbay*, makes it possible to connect each lighting instrument to a specific dimmer. Let's assume that you have three lamps in your living room that you would like to connect to three dimmers in the garage. First, you must connect each dimmer to the breaker that supplies the household current to the garage. You then run wires from each dimmer to three wall outlets in the living room, numbered 1 through 3. To have the table lamp on the first dimmer, you plug the table lamp into outlet 1. You then plug the desk lamp into outlet 2, which is connected to dimmer 2. The little spotlight that illuminates your favorite painting you plug into dimmer 3. Plugging the lighting instruments into the various outlets is called *patching*. In effect, you have patched lamps 1 through 3 to dimmers 1 through 3.

You can now switch on the breakers and move dimmer 1 from position 0 to position 5; the table lamp lights up and gives off a warm, low-level light. By moving dimmer 2 to position 8, the desk lamp lights up to almost full power. To emphasize the painting with a maximum of light, you crank up dimmer 3 to position 10. If you want the table and desk lamps equally bright, you can plug both lamps into outlet 1.

The patchboard of an actual dimmer system works the same way. To patch a specific lighting instrument into a specific dimmer, you select the plug whose cable leads to that instrument and patch it into the power socket whose cable leads to the desired dimmer; you turn on the breaker that supplies the dimmer with electricity. You have made the connection between the lighting instrument and the chosen dimmer; all you have to do now is bring up the dimmer to illuminate the instrument. **SEE 7.40**

Just for practice, let's do some patching. You are asked to patch instrument 5 (a spotlight plugged into the #5 batten outlet) and instrument 27 (a scoop plugged into the #27 batten outlet at the other end of the studio) into dimmer 1. At the patchboard you look for the patchcords #5 and #27 and plug them into the receptacles for dimmer 1. When you bring up dimmer 1 at the patchboard, both instruments—spotlight 5 and scoop 27—should light up simultaneously and be dimmed at equal intensity. **SEE 7.41** If you want to control them separately, you would plug spotlight 5 into dimmer 1 and scoop 27 into dimmer 2.

The patchboard thus allows for many combinations of specific lighting instruments from different studio areas and lets you control their intensity either individually or in groups. As a safety measure, all patchboards have circuit breakers for each power connection to the dimmer. *Do not turn on the breaker before plugging the patchcord into the appropriate dimmer receptacle.* If the breaker is

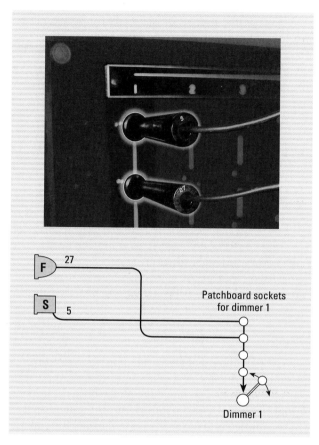

Illumination change Dimmers enable you to change quickly and easily from one type of lighting in a particular area to another. For example, you may change a bedroom set from day to night simply by dimming down one lighting setup and bringing up another. You also can light several studio areas at once, store the lighting setup in the dimmer's memory, and activate part or all of the stored information whenever necessary. Some shows may require that you go from one background color to another, such as from a red to a blue one. With the dimmer you can simply fade down all instruments that throw red light onto the background while at the same time bringing up the blue lights.

Special effects With the help of a dimmer, you can achieve a variety of special-effects lighting setups, such as various stills of flashing-light patterns, and then go back to the standard setup.

There are many types of dimmers on the market, ranging from simple rheostats to sophisticated computer-driven models. Regardless of the electronics involved, the dimmer systems used in television studios have two basic features: a series of individual dimmers that control the current flowing to the lighting instrument, and a patchboard and other grouping devices with the necessary storage and retrieval equipment.

7.41 PATCHING

As you can see, the patches for the lighting instruments (spotlight 5 and scoop 27) are both patched into dimmer 1. Consequently, both lighting instruments respond identically to any dimmer 1 setting.

on, you are "hot-patching," a practice that can damage the equipment and—especially—you.

The software program in a computer-assisted dimming system will remember your patching decisions and trigger the actual patches on command. For example, if you want to turn up all the fill lights while turning off all the spotlights or vice versa, you simply type the numbers of the various instruments and tell the computer which ones to combine for a specific group function. Then all you need to do is press the group button at the specific time, and the computer will take care of the rest. What formerly required cumbersome repatching can now be accomplished by a single computer command. The computer-assisted system, however, does not change the simple principle of patching you used with your living room lights.

COLOR TEMPERATURE

You may have noticed that a fluorescent tube gives off a different "white" light than does a candle. The fluorescent tube actually emits a bluish-green light, whereas the candle produces a reddish light. The setting sun gives off a much more reddish light than the midday sun. These color variations in light are called *color temperature*. Note that color temperature has nothing to do with physical temperature, that is, how hot the light bulb actually gets; it is strictly a measure of the relative reddishness and bluishness of white light.

This reddishness and bluishness of white light can be precisely measured and is expressed in degrees of color temperature, or *Kelvin degrees (K)*. The color temperature standard for indoor illumination is 3,200°K, which is a fairly white light with just a little reddish (warm) tinge. All studio lighting instruments and portable lights intended for indoor illumination are rated at 3,200°K, assuming they receive full voltage. Lighting instruments used to augment or simulate outdoor light have lamps that emit a 5,600°K light and they approximate more the bluish light of the outdoors.

When you dim a lamp that is rated at 3,200°K, the light becomes progressively more reddish, similar to sunlight at sunset. The color camera, when adjusted to seeing white in 3,200°K light, will faithfully show this increasing reddishness. For example, the white shirt of a performer will gradually turn orange or pink, and the skin tones will take on an unnatural red glow. Some lighting experts therefore warn against *any* dimming of lights that illuminate performers or performance areas. The skin tones are, after all, the only real standard viewers have by which to judge the accuracy of the television color scheme. If the skin colors are distorted, how can we trust the other colors to be true? So goes the argument. Practice has shown, however, that you can dim a light by 10 percent without the color change becoming too noticeable on a color monitor. Incidentally, dimming the lights by at least 10 percent will not only reduce power consumption, but just about double the life of the bulbs. *READY ZVL* ⑥

How to Control Color Temperature

How will the camera know what color you want it to reproduce, especially when a low-color-temperature light falling on the white object is slightly reddish (making the white object look reddish) or, in a higher-color-temperature lighting setup, bluish?

White balance   To guarantee that a white object looks white under reddish (low Kelvin degrees) or bluish (high Kelvin degrees) light, you need to tell the camera to compensate for the reddish or bluish light and to pretend that it is dealing with perfectly white light. This compensation by the camera is called *white balance*. When a camera engages in white-balancing, it adjusts the RGB (red, green, blue) channels in such a way that the white object looks white on the screen regardless of whether it is illuminated by reddish or bluish light. **SEE COLOR PLATE 14**

In the studio the white-balancing is usually done by the VO (video operator), who adjusts the RGB channels at the CCU (camera control unit). When operating a studio camera, you will probably be asked by the VO to zoom in on the white-balance card in the major set area and remain on it until the white balance is accomplished. For critical lighting, LDs use a color temperature meter which, when pointed at a specific light source, gives a reading of the relative temperature in Kelvin degrees.

Most consumer camcorders have fully automated white-balance controls that adjust immediately to the color temperature of the prevailing environment. The camcorder does so by "assuming" that it will see something white sometime during the take. A professional camera, however, needs a more accurate reference that will tell it precisely what is supposed to look white under a specific light.

ENG EFP   All ENG/EFP cameras have semiautomatic white-balance controls, which means that you must point the camera at something white and tell it that this is the white reference to which to adjust. This important operation of making the camera adjust to the white reference and "balance" its RGB channels until they produce white is known as *white-balancing*.

How to white-balance   You white-balance a camera by focusing on a white card, piece of foam core, or other white object that is illuminated by the lighting in which the performance will take place. Specifically, have someone hold a white card toward the camera located in the major performance area. If, for example, the show has someone sitting behind a desk, have that person or the floor manager hold the white card in front of his or her face toward the camera. Zoom in on the card until it fills the entire screen (viewfinder). Press the white-balance button (often located at the front of the camera) and wait until the viewfinder display (usually a flashing light) indicates a successful white balance.

If you don't have a white card, any white object will do, but make sure that the entire screen is filled with the object on which you perform the white-balancing. Otherwise, the camera will not know whether to white-balance on the foreground (the white object) or on the background, which may well have a different lighting setup. Most camera utility bags have a white flap that can be used for white-balancing. Will you have to white-balance again when you move from the desk area into the hallway that is illuminated by fluorescent lights? Absolutely. In fact, each time you encounter a different lighting situation, you need to white-balance again.

You may find that occasionally the camera will refuse to white-balance, although you follow exactly the procedures outlined here. This difficulty may be caused by a color temperature that is too low (light is too reddish) or too high (light is too bluish) for the automatic white balance to handle. In this case, you need to choose one of the color temperature filters on the filter wheel inside the camera (see chapter 3). Light-blue filters compensate for the reddishness of low-color-temperature light, and orange filters compensate for the bluishness of high-color-temperature light. Most professional ENG/EFP cameras remember some of these setups, so you can go back to the previous lighting environment and recall the appropriate white balance automatically. Most camerapersons prefer to white-balance from scratch, however, just to make sure that the actual colors, including white, as seen by the camera are as true as possible.

Another way to raise the color temperature of the reddish light is by putting a light-blue gel in front of the lighting instrument's lens; or you can lower the color temperature by placing a light-orange gel in front of the lens (see section 7.2).

When shooting an indoor scene that is partially illuminated by outdoor light coming through a window and by portable indoor (3,200°K) lighting instruments, you have two choices: either lower the high outdoor color temperature (bluish light) or raise the indoor color temperature (reddish light) to the high color temperature of the outdoor light streaming through the window. In elaborate field productions, the usual way is to cover the entire window with orange plastic sheets that act like gigantic filters, lowering the high outdoor color temperature to the lower indoor standard. The advantage of this method is that the whole interior is adjusted to the 3,200°K standard. Or, as just pointed out, you can put bluish filters in front of the indoor lighting instruments to raise their light to the outdoor color temperature standard. **SEE COLOR PLATE 15** *READY ZVL* ❼

In certain circumstances you can get away with mixing lights of different color temperatures so long as one or the other dominates the illumination. For example, if you are in an office that is illuminated by overhead fluorescent tubes and you need to add key and back lights (see chapter 8) to provide more sparkle and dimension to the performer, you can most likely use normal portable lighting instruments that burn at the indoor color temperature standard. Why? Because the portable instruments provide the dominant (3,200°K) light, overpowering the overhead lights that now act as rather weak fill lights. The camera will have little trouble white-balancing on the strong indoor lights while more or less ignoring the higher color temperature of the overhead fluorescent lights.

MAIN POINTS

- All studio lighting is accomplished by a variety of spotlights and floodlights.

- The most prevalent studio spotlight is the Fresnel spot. The ellipsoidal spot and the follow spot are used for special-effects lighting.

- The studio floodlights include the scoop; the softlight and broad; the fluorescent floodlight bank; the incandescent floodlight bank; and the strip, or cyc, light.

- Portable spotlights include the small Fresnel spots; the external reflector, or open-face, spot; the internal reflector spot, or clip light; and the HMI light.

- Most portable floodlights are open-faced, which means that they have no lens. Small fluorescent banks are also used as portable floodlights. Diffusers can turn a spotlight into a floodlight.

- ENG lighting is often done with small, versatile lights that are mounted on the camera or handheld.

- Lighting control equipment includes mounting devices for studio and portable lights; directional controls, such as barn doors, flags, and various focus devices; and intensity controls, such as light-diffusing scrims, frosted gels, umbrellas, wire-mesh screens, and electronic dimmers.

- With a dimmer you can easily manipulate a light, or a group of lights, to burn at a given intensity. The patchboard, or patchbay, makes it possible to connect each lighting instrument to a specific dimmer.

- Color temperature is the standard by which we measure the relative reddishness or bluishness of white light. It is measured in Kelvin degrees (K). The standard for indoor light is 3,200°K, for outdoor light, 5,600°K.

- To white-balance means to adjust the camera so that it sees a white object as white under light of various color temperatures. To do this you focus on a white object in the light that illuminates the scene you are shooting.

- Unless a camera has a fully automated white balance built-in (as most consumer camcorders do) you need to white-balance every time you change from one lighting environment to another.

7.2

Light Intensity, Lamps, and Color Media

Before learning to do actual lighting in the studio and the field, you need to study a few more elements about light, how to control and measure it, and how to produce colored light. This section adds to the technical details given in section 7.1.

▶ **LIGHT INTENSITY**
Incident and reflected light measured in lux and foot-candles

▶ **CALCULATING LIGHT INTENSITY**
The inverse square law

▶ **OPERATING LIGHT LEVEL: BASELIGHT**
Providing the optimal operating light level, or baselight

▶ **TYPES OF LAMPS**
Incandescent; quartz, or tungsten-halogen; HMI; and fluorescent

▶ **COLOR MEDIA**
Plastic sheets that change the color of light

LIGHT INTENSITY

All video cameras need a certain amount of light for optimal performance. As sensitive as our eyes are, they cannot always tell accurately just how much light a lighting instrument produces, how much light is actually on the set or on location, how much light an object actually reflects, and how much light the camera lens actually receives. If necessary, a *light meter* gives us a more accurate reading of light intensity.

Lux and Foot-candles
The standard unit of measuring light intensity is the European *lux*, or the American *foot-candle (fc)*. Because ordinary television lighting doesn't require extremely precise units of intensity, you can simply figure lux by multiplying foot-candles by a factor of ten, or you can figure foot-candles by dividing lux by ten:

✳ ■ *To find foot-candles when given lux, divide lux by ten.*

✳ ■ *To find lux when given foot-candles, multiply foot-candles by ten.*

As an example, 2,000 lux are about 200 foot-candles (2,000 × 10), and 100 foot-candles are about 1,000 lux (100 × 10). (If you want to be more accurate, use a factor of 10.75 to calculate foot-candles from lux, or lux from foot-candles.) These intensity levels, incidentally, are often used as the indoor standard for studio cameras.

Equipped with lux and foot-candles as the unit of light intensity, you can now measure either of the two types of light intensity: *incident light* and *reflected light*. The incident-light reading gives you a rough measurement of the overall, or *baselight*, levels. The reflected-light reading tells you more about how much light is reflected off the lighted object. The difference between the reflected-light readings of the lighted side and the shadow side gives you the brightness contrast.

Incident Light

The reading of ***incident light*** gives you some idea of the overall light levels in a specific set area, usually called *baselight* levels. You are actually measuring the amount of light that falls on a subject or a performance area. To measure incident light, you must stand in the lighted area or next to the subject and point the incident, or foot-candle, light meter *toward the camera lens.* The meter will give a quick reading of the overall light level (baselight) of the particular set area. If you want a more specific reading of the intensity of light coming from the particular instruments, you should point the foot-candle (or lux) meter *into the lights.* **SEE 7.42** Such a record

may come in handy, especially when you need to duplicate the illumination for a scene shot on the same set over a period of several days. For some reason, duplicating the exact lighting from one day to the next is hard to achieve, even if your computer-assisted patchboard faithfully duplicates the dimmer settings of the previous day. An incident-light check, however, guarantees identical intensities.

To discover possible "holes" in the lighting (unlighted or underlighted areas), walk around the set with the light meter pointed at the major camera positions. Watch the light meter. Whenever the needle dips way down, it is indicating a hole.

Reflected Light

The reading of ***reflected light*** gives you an idea of how much light is bounced off the various objects. It is primarily used to measure *contrast*.

To measure reflected light, you must use a reflected-light meter (most common photographic light meters measure reflected light). Point it closely at the lighted object—such as the performer's face or white blouse or the dark blue background curtain—from the direction of the camera (the back of the meter should face the principal camera position). **SEE 7.43** Do not stand between the light source and the subject when taking this reading, or you will measure your shadow instead of the light actually reflecting off the subject. To measure contrast point the meter first at the lighted side of the

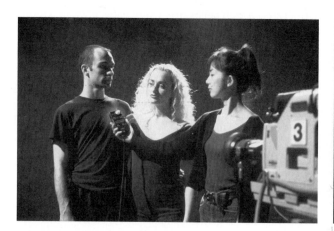

7.42 INCIDENT-LIGHT READING
To measure incident light, point the incident-light meter at the camera or into the lights while standing next to the lighted subject or performance area.

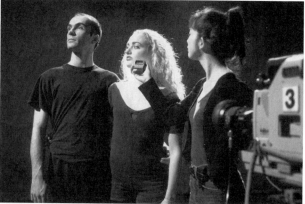

7.43 REFLECTED-LIGHT READING
To measure reflected light, point the reflected-light meter (used in normal still photography) close to the lighted subject or object.

object and then move it to the shadow side. The difference between the two readings gives you the contrast ratio. (Chapter 8 describes contrast ratio and its importance in television lighting.)

Do not be too much of a slave to all these measurements and ratios. A quick check of the baselight is all that is generally needed for most lighting situations. In especially critical situations, you may want to check the reflectance of faces or exceptionally bright objects. Some people get so involved in reading light meters and oscilloscopes that visually display the light levels against camera tolerances that they forget to look at the monitor to see whether the lighting looks the way it was intended. If you combine your knowledge of how the camera works with artistic sensitivity and, especially, common sense, you will not let the light meter tell you how to light; rather, you will use it as a guide to make your job more efficient.

CALCULATING LIGHT INTENSITY

Without getting too technical, 1 lux is the light that falls on a surface of 1 square meter (about 3 by 3 feet) generated by a single candle that burns at a distance of 1 meter (roughly 3 feet). One foot-candle is the amount of light that falls on a 1-by-1 foot surface located 1 foot away from the candle.

More technically, light intensity is subject to the *inverse square law*. This law states that if a light source radiates *isotropically* (uniformly in all directions), such as a candle or a single light bulb burning in the middle of a room, the light intensity falls off (gets weaker) as $1/d^2$, where d is the distance from the source. For example, if the intensity of a light source is 1 foot-candle (which is generally expressed as 1 *lumen*) at a distance of 1 foot from the source, its intensity at a distance of 2 feet is ¼ foot-candle. **SEE 7.44**

The inverse square law also applies to lux. In this case, the light intensity is measured off a surface of $1\,m^2$ located 1 meter from the light source of 1 lumen.

What this formula tells you is that light intensity decreases the farther away you move the lighting instrument from the object, and increases if you move the lights closer. Otherwise, the formula does little to make television lighting more accurate. As you have just learned, television lighting instruments do not radiate light isotropically. The beams of a searchlight, a flashlight, car headlights, and a Fresnel or an ellipsoidal spotlight are all *collimated* (the light rays are made to

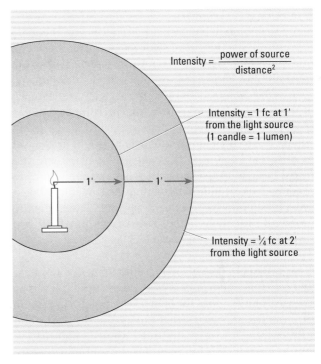

7.44 INVERSE SQUARE LAW
Note that the inverse square law applies only to light sources that radiate isotropically (uniformly in all directions). The law applies equally to lux.

run parallel as much as possible) and, therefore, do not obey the inverse square law. Even floodlights radiate their light more in the direction of the reflector opening than its back. The more collimated the light—that is, the more focused its beam—the slower its intensity decreases with distance. This is why we "focus" a spotlight when we want more light on an object and "flood" its beam when we want less light, without changing the distance between lighting instrument and object. An example of an extremely well-collimated light is a laser beam, which, as you know, maintains its intensity over a great distance. *READY ZVL* **8**

OPERATING LIGHT LEVEL: BASELIGHT

To make the camera "see well" so that the pictures are relatively free of video *noise* (artifacts in the picture, or "snow"), you must establish a minimum operating light level, called **baselight** or *base*. As you recall, baselight is the general, overall light level on a set or another event area.

Baselight Levels

Many an argument has been raised concerning adequate minimum baselight levels for various cameras. The problem is that baselight levels do not represent absolute values but are dependent on other production factors, such as the camera, lighting contrast, general reflectance of the scenery, and, of course, the aperture of the lens (ƒ-stop). When shooting outdoors on an ENG assignment, you do not have much control over baselight levels; you must accept whatever light there is. But even there you might be able to use sunlight reflectors to lighten up shadow areas, or additional lighting instruments to boost available light. Most often the problem is inadequate baselight. But there are also situations in which you struggle with controlling too much light.

Not enough baselight

Although you often hear that consumer camcorders can operate in light levels as low as 10 or even 2 lux, the light levels for optimal camera performance are much higher. Professional ENG/EFP and studio cameras normally need about 2,000 lux, or approximately 200 foot-candles, for optimal picture quality, assuming an aperture setting of (ƒ/5.6 to ƒ/8.0).

Most video cameras can work at baselight levels that are considerably lower, but they do so at the expense of picture quality. Manufacturers of some of the small-format cameras claim that they can operate properly in a baselight as low as 2 lux, which is slightly less than ¹⁄₂₀ foot-candle. By switching to the highest gain setting (which, as you recall, will electronically boost the video signal), you may indeed get an image in such low-light conditions. But such high gain will also cause increased video noise and often distorts certain colors. For home video or even ENG, video quality may be secondary to picture content, but it is of major concern for EFP and studio shows that must tolerate many copies and picture manipulations in postproduction editing. In general, digital cameras can tolerate higher gain than analog cameras without noticeable picture deterioration and, as you know, can tolerate a great number of tape generations before showing any sign of quality loss.

If you work with sets or costumes whose colors and textures absorb a great amount of light, you obviously need higher baselight levels than with a set whose brightly painted surface reflects a moderate amount of light.

Another problem with shooting in inadequate baselight is the resulting shallow depth of field. In low-light conditions, the lens iris must be fairly wide open (low ƒ-stop number) to allow as much light as possible to strike the camera pickup device. But, as you recall, a lens whose iris is set at its maximum aperture gives a fairly shallow depth of field. Consequently, focusing becomes a problem, especially when there is a great deal of object and/or camera movement. A great depth of field requires high baselight levels, because a small iris opening (high ƒ-stop number) will increase the depth of field.

Here is the rule of thumb: ***In general, a camera has less trouble producing high-quality, crisp pictures when the light level is fairly high and the contrast somewhat limited than under very low levels with high-contrast lighting.***

Too much baselight

Despite the validity of the above rule of thumb for baselight and picture quality, there will be instances when there is simply too much light for the camera to operate properly. You can cope with too much light by reducing the lens aperture, which translates into setting the ƒ-stop to a higher number, such as ƒ/22. Such small apertures do not produce optimal picture sharpness. Besides, such overlighting causes excess heat.

Another way of controlling too much light is to use a *neutral density (ND) filter*. Much like a small aperture, ND filters reduce the amount of light falling on a scene or entering the beam splitter in the camera without changing the color temperature of the light.

If, for example, you have to videotape someone who insists on having a large window in the background, you may need to reduce the amount of light coming through the window so that the person in the foreground can be lighted properly without being silhouetted against the bright background. In this case, you need to cover the entire window with large plastic sheets that act as ND filters without affecting the color temperature of the incoming light. Such ND filtering is especially important if the indoor lights operate with the outdoor color temperature standard (5,600°K). Otherwise, you need to use a plastic sheet that combines an ND filter with a slightly orange color. The ND filter will cut down the light intensity, and the orange color will lower the color temperature to the indoor 3,200°K standard. *READY ZVL* **9**

TYPES OF LAMPS

Lighting instruments are classified not only by function (spotlight or floodlight) but also by the lamp they use. When classifying instruments by the type of lamp, we no longer refer to the relative light-emitting power of an ordinary household bulb, such as a 75-watt bulb or a 100-watt bulb, but rather to a specific way of generating a light output—the *luminant*. Television lighting uses four basic types of lamps, or luminants: (1) incandescent, (2) quartz, or tungsten-halogen, (3) HMI, and (4) fluorescent.

Incandescent

These lamps resemble the ones you use in your home fixtures, except that they usually have more wattage and therefore produce higher-intensity light. The major disadvantages of *incandescent* lamps are that the higher-wattage bulbs are quite large, the color temperature becomes progressively lower (more reddish) with the age of the lamp, and they have a relatively short life.

Quartz, or Tungsten-Halogen

The *quartz* lamp is also part of an incandescent system, but its filament is encased in a quartz bulb filled with halogen gas. The advantages of a quartz lamp over regular incandescent systems are that it is smaller and maintains its color temperature over its entire life. The disadvantage is that it burns at an extremely hot temperature. *When changing quartz lights, you should not touch the lamp with your fingers.* The old lamp may still be hot enough to burn your fingers, your fingerprints will cause the new one to have a much shorter life than usual, and they may even explode. Use gloves, a paper towel, or some kind of rag when touching the lamp.

HMI

The *HMI* lamp operates on a different principle from the incandescent lamps. Instead of lighting up a filament, it lights up gas vapor inside the lamp housing. HMI lamps produce about five times more light than quartz lamps of equal wattage. Like fluorescent lights, the HMI lights produce relatively little heat. All HMI bulbs burn at the outdoor color temperature of 5,600°K. As pointed out earlier, the major disadvantage of HMI lights is that their use requires a rather clumsy ballast.

Fluorescent

Similar to HMI lamps, *fluorescent* tubes generate light by activating a gas-filled tube to give off ultraviolet radiation. This radiation, in turn, lights up the phosphorous coating inside the tubes similar to the way the electron beam lights up the television screen. Despite all claims to the contrary, fluorescent tubes have a tendency to give off a slightly greenish light or, at best, an uneven color temperature that makes it difficult to blend with other indoor or outdoor light sources.

COLOR MEDIA

You can produce a great variety of colored light simply by putting different *color media*, or *gels*, in front of the lighting instrument. Color media are sheets of highly heat-resistant plastic that act as color filters. They are used extensively to color-tint scenic backgrounds or to create color special-effects, such as in dance programs, rock concerts, or some mystery or outer-space adventure shows. (*Gel* is short for *gelatin*, which was the color medium used before the more-durable plastic was developed.)

How to Use Color Media

You can cut the color media sheets to fit the frame of the gel holders of the various lighting instruments. You then slip the gel holder with the selected gel into brackets in front of the lens of the lighting instrument. If the colored lighting does not have to be too precise, you can use wood clothespins (plastic ones melt) to hang the color sheets from the barn doors like laundry on a clothesline. The advantages of this method are that it saves you from having to cut the expensive gels and they are farther away from the heat generated by the lamp. Highly focused instruments generate so much heat that they may burn out the center of even the most heat-resistant color media. You can avoid such burns by putting the instrument into more of a flood position, thereby dissipating somewhat the heat of the beam.

Mixing Color Gels

When using color gels, the colors can mix *subtractively* or *additively*. For example, if you put a red and a green gel on top of each other, you would get no light from the instrument. This is because the gels act as subtractive filters, blocking each other's colored light.

A similar problem occurs if you shine colored lights on colored objects. We see an apple as red, because the color filters in the apple absorb all colors of white light except red, which is reflected back to our eyes. A green apple absorbs all colors except green, which is reflected back and makes the apple look green. What would happen if you shined a red light on a green apple? Would it turn yellow? No, the apple would look black. Why? Because the red light that shines on the apple contains no green. The apple, which absorbs all the red light, has nothing to reflect back. When no light is reflected from an object, we perceive it as black. Now you can see that there may be a problem using yellow objects under blue "night" illumination: The blue light contains no yellow, and the objects have, therefore, no yellow to reflect; consequently, they turn dark gray or black.

Some lighting experts prefer to give the back light that illuminates the hair a slightly bluish tone and the front lights that illuminate the face a slightly warmer color. Or they like to put a very light blue gel onto the fill light to make the shadow side slightly cooler looking and an orange gel for the key light (principal light source) to make the bright side slightly warmer looking.

Other lighting experts disagree. Here is their argument: First, the area where the colors overlap will produce a band of strange colors, sometimes even a slightly bluish gray. Second, you will run into an interesting technical problem concerning white-balancing. If you hold a white card in front of the talent in order to white-balance the camera in the performance area, on which light is the camera supposed to white-balance? On the bluish light that spills over from the back, or on the reddish one that is on the talent's face? The camera will probably opt for the reddish key light, but then the camera will think that you want to see the card white (even though it is now tinted slightly orange) and work hard to eliminate the tint. The result is color distortions throughout the scene. You could, of course, white-balance the camera in the set area first without color gels and then add the gels later. The camera would then faithfully reproduce the cool and warm colors.

To avoid such problems, most lighting experts recommend not using colored lights to illuminate talent and performance areas unless, of course, you want to achieve special effects. Recall that skin tones are the only handy reference the viewer has for adjusting the colors in the home receiver.

MAIN POINTS

- Light intensity is measured in foot-candles or lux. To find foot-candles when given lux, divide lux by ten. To find lux when given foot-candles, multiply foot-candles by ten.

- Although the general conversion factor of lux into foot-candles is 10, the more accurate conversion factor is 10.75; thus, 1 fc = 10.75 lux, and 10.75 lux = 1 fc.

- To measure incident light (baselight) levels, point the light meter from the lighted subject's position toward the camera or into the lights that are illuminating the subject.

- To measure reflected light, use a reflected (standard) light meter and point it closely at the lighted subject or object. Reflected-light readings measure primarily contrast.

- The inverse square law in illumination applies only if the light source radiates isotropically (uniformly in all directions), such as a bare light bulb or a candle. Because most television lighting instruments collimate the light (make the light rays more or less parallel), the inverse square law does not apply to the same degree. The general principle, however, still holds true: The farther away the object is from the light source, the less light will fall on it.

- Baselight is the overall light level. Cameras require a minimum baselight level for optimal operation.

- Color media, normally called gels, are plastic filters that, when put in front of the lens of a lighting instrument, give the light beam the color of the gel.

- Colored light beams mix additively, but overlaying filters mix subtractively.

Z E T T L' S   V I D E O L A B   2

You will have ample opportunity to reinforce this chapter with no less than nine lab sessions. Be sure to take the **Quizzes** *of all lab modules.*

RUN ZVL 1 Click on the **lights** monitor and run tape 6 **Instruments**. Click on the **Studio** module.

RUN ZVL 2 Run tape 8 **Design** and click on the **Silhouette** module. Note that in silhouette lighting the background is lighted, with the foreground object receiving no light.

RUN ZVL 3 Go back to tape 6 **Instruments** and click on the **Studio** module again. This time pay particular attention to the effect of the barn doors.

RUN ZVL 4 Click on the **Field** module. Notice how the umbrella is used to diffuse the light. You can now see that the light shines into the umbrella, with the umbrella reflecting the light back out to the scene.

RUN ZVL 5 Run tape 3 **Falloff**. Click on the first three modules: **Fast**, **Slow**, and **None**. Now run tape 9 **Field**. Look at the way the falloff is controlled in the **Outdoor** and **Indoor** modules.

RUN ZVL 6 Run tape 5 **Color Temperature**. Click on the **White balance** and **Light sources** modules. You will see how the color temperatures of various light sources actually change color.

RUN ZVL 7 Now click on the **Controlling** module. Note that white balance is a function of the camera to see white as white under various lighting conditions. Run tape 9 **Field** again and click on the **Mixed** module. You will revisit the problem of mixing lights of different color temperatures and see how it is solved.

RUN ZVL 8 Run tape 4 **Measurement**. The **Meters** module will show you how to use the light meter, and the **Contrast** module will give you an opportunity to measure contrast yourself.

RUN ZVL 9 Now click on the **Baselight** module and see how to measure the intensity of the overall light level.

8

Techniques of Television Lighting

The techniques of television lighting tell you what instrument to use in a particular position and how to adjust it for a desired lighting effect. In most video production situations, especially EFP, available space, time, and people are insufficient for you to accomplish motion picture–quality lighting. You may find, for instance, that the time allotted to lighting is so short that all you can do is flood the studio or location site with highly diffused light, regardless of the nature of the event to be illuminated. Although such a technique may please the camera and probably the video operator (who because of the uniform light levels has little shading to do during the production), it does not always fulfill the aesthetic requirements of the production. For example, a dramatic scene that is supposed to play at a dark street corner will not look convincing if everything is brightly and evenly illuminated by softlights. On the other hand, there is no reason to spend a great deal of time on dramatic lighting for such events as newscasts, interviews, or the corporate manager telling her employees about recent sales. Even lighting will do just fine.

The ever-present time limitation does not preclude good and creative television lighting; it simply calls for a thorough understanding of the basic lighting principles and, especially, advance planning. Section 8.1, Lighting in the Studio, covers basic and special-effects studio lighting techniques and principles; section 8.2, Lighting in the Field, addresses lighting techniques for ENG and EFP.

KEY TERMS

background light Illumination of the set, set pieces, and backdrops. Also called *set light*.

back light Illumination from behind the subject and opposite the camera.

cameo lighting Foreground figures are lighted with highly directional light, with the background remaining dark.

chroma keying Special key effect that uses color (usually blue) for the background, which is replaced by the background image during the key.

contrast ratio The difference between the brightest and the darkest spots in the picture (often measured by reflected light in foot-candles). The optimal contrast ratio for analog cameras is normally 40:1 or slightly higher, which means that the brightest spot in the picture should not be more than forty times brighter than the darkest spot. For DTV it can exceed this ratio, depending on the quality of the camera.

cross-keying The crossing of key lights for two people facing each other.

diffused light Light that illuminates a relatively large area with an indistinct light beam. Diffused light, created by floodlights, produces soft shadows.

directional light Light that illuminates a relatively small area with a distinct light beam. Directional light, produced by spotlights, creates harsh, clearly defined shadows.

falloff The speed (degree) with which a light picture portion turns into shadow area. Fast falloff means that the light areas turn abruptly into shadow areas and there is a great brightness difference between light and shadow areas. Slow falloff indicates a very gradual change from light to dark and a minimal brightness difference between light and shadow areas.

fill light Additional light on the opposite side of the camera from the key light to illuminate shadow areas and thereby reduce falloff. Usually done with floodlights.

floor plan A plan of the studio floor, showing the walls, the main doors, and the location of the control room, with the lighting grid or batten pattern superimposed over it. More common, a diagram of scenery and properties drawn onto a grid pattern.

high key Light background and ample light on the scene. Has nothing to do with the vertical positioning of the key light.

key light Principal source of illumination.

kicker light Usually directional light that is positioned low and from the side and back of the subject.

light plot A plan, similar to a floor plan, that shows the type, size (wattage), and location of the lighting instruments relative to the scene to be illuminated and the general direction of the beams.

location survey Written assessment, usually in the form of a checklist, of the production requirements for a remote.

low key Dark background and few selective light sources on the scene. Has nothing to do with the vertical positioning of the key light.

photographic lighting principle The triangular arrangement of key, back, and fill lights, with the back light opposite the camera and directly behind the object, and the key and fill lights on opposite sides of the camera and to the front and side of the object. Also called *triangle lighting*.

shading Adjusting picture contrast to the optimal contrast range; controlling the color and the white and black levels.

side light Usually directional light coming from the side of the object. Acts as additional fill light and provides contour.

silhouette lighting Unlighted objects or people in front of a brightly illuminated background.

8.1

Lighting in the Studio

Lighting means the control of light and shadows. Both are necessary to show the shape and texture of a face or object, suggest a particular environment, and, like music, create a specific mood. Regardless of whether you do lighting for dramatic or nondramatic productions, you will find that there are usually many solutions to one problem. And though there is no universal recipe that works for every possible lighting situation, there are some basic principles that you can easily adapt to a great variety of specific illumination requirements. Whenever faced with a specific lighting task, do not start with anticipated limitations. Start with how you would like the lighting to look and then adapt to the existing technical facilities and especially the available time.

Section 8.1 covers the following lighting techniques:

▶ **TYPES OF LIGHT**
Directional and diffused light

▶ **MAIN LIGHT SOURCES**
Types and functions of lighting instruments

▶ **THE PHOTOGRAPHIC PRINCIPLE, OR TRIANGLE LIGHTING**
Key light, fill light, and back light

▶ **SPECIFIC LIGHTING TECHNIQUES**
Continuous-action, large-area, cameo, silhouette, and chroma-key area lighting, and controlling eye and boom shadows

▶ **CONTRAST**
Contrast and reflectance, contrast ratio, shading, auto-iris, and measuring and limiting contrast

▶ **BALANCING INTENSITIES**
Key-to-back-light ratio and key-to-fill-light ratio

▶ **THE LIGHT PLOT**
Indicating location of instruments and their beams

▶ **OPERATION OF STUDIO LIGHTS**
Safety, preserving power and lamps, and using a studio monitor

TYPES OF LIGHT

Whatever your lighting objective, you will be working with two types of light: *directional* and *diffused*.

Directional light, produced by spotlights, illuminates a relatively small area with a distinct light beam and produces dense, well-defined shadows. The sun on a cloudless day acts like a giant spotlight, producing dense and distinct shadows.

Diffused light illuminates a relatively large area with a wide, indistinct beam. It is produced by floodlights and creates soft, transparent shadows. The sun on a cloudy or foggy day acts like an ideal floodlight, and the overcast transforms the harsh light beam of the sun into highly diffused light.

Main Light Sources

You will notice that lighting terminology is based not so much on whether the instruments are spotlights or floodlights, but rather by their functions and their position relative to the object to be lighted.

Types of Lighting Instruments

Although there are variations for the following terms, most lighting people in the photographic arts (including video) use this standard terminology.

- *Key light* is the apparent principal source of directional illumination falling upon a subject or an area; it reveals the basic shape of the object.

- *Back light* is illumination from behind the subject and opposite the camera; it distinguishes the shadow of the object from the background and emphasizes the object outline.

- *Fill light* is a generally diffused light to reduce shadow or contrast range. It can be directional if the area to be "filled in" is rather limited.

- *Background light,* or *set light,* is used specifically to illuminate the background or the set and is separate from the light provided for the performers or performance area.

- *Side light* is placed directly to the side of the subject, usually on the opposite side of the camera from the key light. Sometimes two side lights are used opposite each other for special-effects lighting of a face.

- *Kicker light* is a directional illumination from the back, off to one side of the subject, usually from a

low angle opposite the key light. Whereas the back light merely highlights the back of the head and the shoulders, the kicker light highlights and defines the entire side of the talent, separating him or her from the background.

Functions of Main Light Sources

Let's take a look at each of these instruments and see how it functions in basic lighting tasks.

Key light   As the principal source of illumination, the major function of the *key light* is to reveal the basic shape of the subject. **SEE 8.1** To achieve this, the key light must

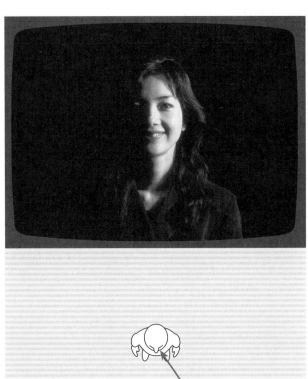

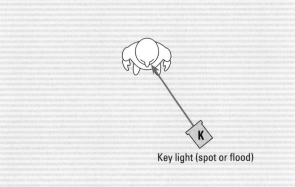

Key light (spot or flood)

8.1 KEY LIGHT
The key light represents the principal light source and reveals the basic shape of the object or person.

produce some shadows. Fresnel spotlights, medium spread, are normally used for key illumination. But you can use a scoop, a broad, or even a softlight for a key if you want softer shadows or, technically, slower *falloff*. In the absence of expensive softlights, some LDs (lighting directors) take a cue from still photographers or filmmakers and use reflectors as key and fill lights. Instead of diffusing the key and fill lights with diffusion material, such as scrims or frosted gels, you do not aim the key light (a Fresnel spot) directly at the subject, but rather bounce it off white foam core or a large white posterboard. The reflected, highly diffused light nevertheless produces distinct, yet extremely soft, slow-falloff shadows. Some LDs prefer this method over keying directly with a softlight, claiming that it gives them more gradual falloff.

Because during the day we see the principal light source—the sun—coming from above, the key light is normally placed above and to the right or left front side of the object, from the camera's point of view. Look again at figure 8.1, which shows the woman illuminated with the key light only, and notice that the falloff is very fast, blending part of her hair and shoulder with the background. To help clarify the outline and texture of the woman's right (camera-left) side, you obviously need light sources other than the single key light.

Back light   Adding illumination from behind helps separate the subject from the background. **SEE 8.2** Note how the *back light* helps distinguish between the shadow side of the woman and the dark background, emphasizing the outline—the contour—of her hair and shoulders. We have now established a clear *figure-ground* relationship, which means that we can easily perceive a figure (the woman) in front of a (dark) background. Besides providing spatial definition, the back light adds sparkle and professional polish.

In general, try to position the back light as directly behind the subject (opposite the camera) as possible; there is no inherent virtue in placing it somewhat to one side or the other. A more critical problem is controlling the vertical angle at which the back light strikes the subject. If it is positioned directly above the person, or somewhere in that neighborhood, the back light becomes an undesirable top light. Instead of revealing the contour of the person to make her stand out from the background and giving the hair sparkle, the light simply brightens the top of her head, causing dense shadows below her eyes and chin. On the other hand, if the back light is positioned too low, it shines into the camera.

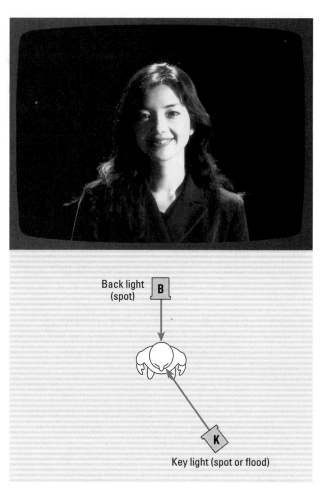

8.2 KEY AND BACK LIGHTS
The back light provides more definition to the actual shape of the subject (her hair on camera-left), separates her from the background, and gives her hair sparkle and highlights.

To get good back lighting on a set, you need a generous space between the performance areas (the areas in which the talent move) and the background scenery. Similarly, you must place "active" furniture (those properties used by the performers), such as chairs, tables, sofas, or beds, away from the walls at least 6 to 10 feet toward the center of the set. If the talent works too close to the scenery, the back lights must be tilted at very steep angles to reach over the flats, and such steep angles inevitably cause undesirable top light.

Fill light   Now take another look at figure 8.2. The difference between the light and the shadow sides of the face are extreme, and the light side of the face changes to

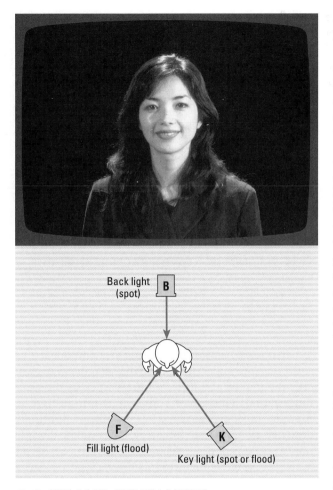

8.3 KEY, BACK, AND FILL LIGHTS
The fill light makes the shadow side (camera-left) more transparent and reveals details without erasing the form-revealing shadows altogether.

eliminated. This gives the subject a flat look—shadows no longer help define shape and texture.

When doing critical lighting in a specific area and you don't want the fill light to spill over too much into the other set areas, you can use a Fresnel spotlight as fill by spreading the beam as much as possible or by putting a scrim in front of the lens. You can then use the barn doors to further control the spill.

With the three main light sources in the triangle position, you have established the basic photographic principle of television lighting. But you are not done just yet. You must now fine-tune the lighting arrangement. Take a good hard look at the lighted object or, if possible, the studio monitor to see whether the scene (in our case, the close-up of the woman) needs some further adjustment for optimal lighting. Are there any undesirable shadows, or shadows that distort rather than reveal the object? How is the light balance? Does the fill light wash out all the necessary shadows? Or are the shadows still too dense? Is the key/fill combination too strong for the back light?

Background, or set, light   You use the *background light*, or, as it is frequently called, the *set light*, to illuminate the background (walls, cyclorama) of the set or portions of the set that are not a direct part of the principal performance area. In order to keep the shadows of the background on the same side as those of the person or object in front of it, the background light must strike the background from the same direction as the key light. **SEE 8.4**   As you can see in the figure, the key light is placed on the camera-right side, causing the shadows on the subject to fall on the camera-left side. Consequently, the background light is also placed on camera-right to make the shadows on camera-left correspond with those of the foreground. If you place the background light on the opposite side from the key, the viewer may assume that there are two separate light sources illuminating the scene or, worse, that there are two suns in our solar system. *READY ZVL* ❶

Background light frequently goes beyond its mere supporting role to become a major production element. Besides accentuating an otherwise dull, monotonous background with a slice of light or an interesting cookie, the background light can be a major indicator of the show's locale, time of day, and mood. **SEE COLOR PLATE 16** A cookie projection of prison bars on the cyc, in connection with the clanging of cell doors, immediately places the event in a prison. **SEE 8.5**

a dense shadow abruptly. This change is called falloff. *Falloff* means the speed (degree) to which a light picture portion turns into shadow area. If the change is sudden, as in figure 8.2, it is *fast falloff*. With fast falloff, the shadow side of the subject's face is also very dense; the camera sees no shadow detail. To slow down the falloff, that is, to make the shadow less prominent and more transparent, you need some *fill light*. **SEE 8.3**   Not surprisingly, you place the fill light on the opposite side of the camera from the key light. A highly diffused floodlight or reflected light is generally used as fill. The more fill light you use, the slower the falloff becomes. When the intensity of the fill light approaches or even matches that of the key light, the shadows, and with them the falloff, are virtually

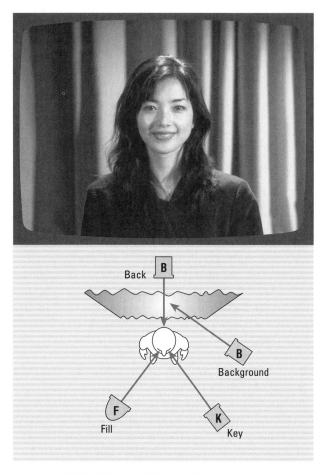

8.4 BACKGROUND LIGHT ADDED
The background light illuminates the background area. It must be on the same side of the camera as the key light in order to keep the background shadows (curtain) on the same side as the foreground shadows (woman).

A long slice of light or long shadows falling across the back wall of an interior set suggests, in connection with other congruent production clues, late afternoon or evening. Dark backgrounds and distinct shadows generally suggest a *low-key* scene (dark background with selective fast-falloff lighting) and a dramatic or mysterious mood. A light background and a generally high baselight level are usually regarded as a *high-key* scene with an upbeat, happy mood. That is why comedies are much more brightly lighted (higher baselight level and less contrast) than mystery dramas (lower baselight level and more contrast). Do not confuse *high-key* and *low-key* with high and low vertical hanging positions of the key light or with the intensity with which it burns. *READY ZVL* ❷

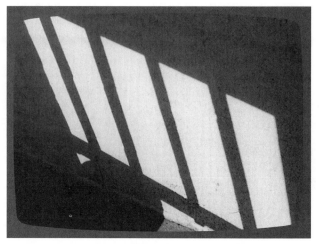

8.5 SETTING LOCALE WITH BACKGROUND LIGHT
Background lighting can place an event in a specific locale or environment. Here the background light produces barlike shadows, suggesting that the scene takes place in a prison.

In normal background lighting of an interior setting, try to keep the upper portions of the set rather dark, with only the middle and lower portions (such as the walls) illuminated. The reasons for this common lighting practice are obvious. First, most indoor lighting is designed to illuminate low work areas rather than the upper portions of walls. Second, the performer's head is more pleasingly contrasted against a slightly darker background. Too much light at that height might cause a *silhouette* effect, rendering the face unusually dark. On the other hand, furniture and medium- and dark-colored clothing are nicely set off by the lighter lower portions of the set. Third, the dark upper portions suggest a ceiling. You can darken the upper portions of the set easily by using barn doors to block off any spotlight (including the background lights) that would hit those areas.

Side light   Usually placed directly to the side of the subject, the *side light* can function as key or fill light. When used as a key, it produces fast falloff, leaving half of the face in dense shadow. When used as a fill, it lightens up the whole shadow side of the face. When used as key and fill on opposite sides, the sides of the face are bright, with the front of the face remaining shadowed. If properly done, such an effect can be quite dramatic. **SEE 8.6**   The side light becomes an essential light source if the camera's shooting arc is exceptionally wide. If, for instance, the camera moves around the

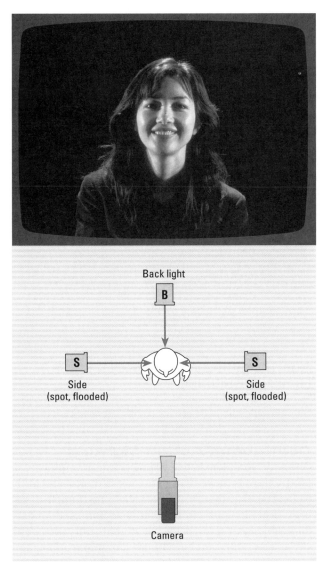

8.6 SIDE LIGHT

The side light strikes the subject from the side. It can act as key and/or fill light. In this case, two opposing side lights are used as key and fill.

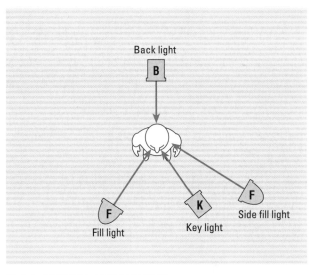

8.7 SIDE FILL-LIGHT SETUP

The side fill light provides soft illumination, with the key (spot) adding sparkle. When the key is turned off, the side fill takes over the function of the key light.

subject from a 6 o'clock to a 10 o'clock position, the side light takes on the function of the key light and provides essential modeling (lighting for three-dimensional effect). Although Fresnel spots in a wide-beam adjustment are generally used for side lighting, using broads as side lights can produce interesting lighting effects.

For extrabrilliant high-key lighting, you can support the key light with side fill light. The fill light gives the key side of the subject basic illumination, with the key light providing the necessary sparkle and accent. **SEE 8.7**

Kicker light   Generally a sharply focused Fresnel spot, the *kicker light* strikes the subject from behind and on the opposite side of the camera from the key light (that is, the fill-light side). Its main purpose is to highlight the contour of the subject at a place where key-light falloff is the densest and where the dense shadow of the subject opposite the key-lighted side tends to merge with the dark background. The function of the kicker is similar to that of the back light, except that the kicker "rims" the subject not at the top-back, but at the lower side-back. It usually strikes the subject from below eye level. **SEE 8.8**   Kicker lights are especially useful for creating the illusion of moonlight.

THE PHOTOGRAPHIC PRINCIPLE, OR TRIANGLE LIGHTING

As one of the photographic arts, television is subject to lighting principles. The most basic *photographic lighting principle*—or, as it is frequently called, basic *triangle lighting*—consists of three main light sources: key light, back light, and fill light. Each source is positioned so that it can optimally fulfill its assigned function: the back light

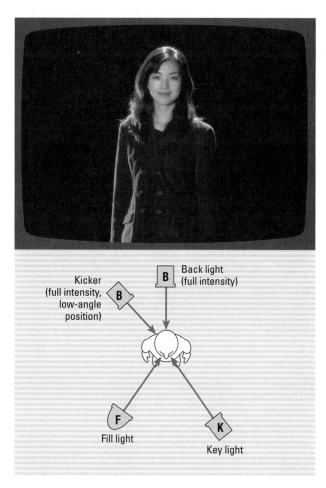

8.8 KICKER LIGHT

The kicker light rims the subject opposite the key, emphasizing contour. Like the back light, the kicker helps separate the foreground subject from the background.

opposite the camera and directly behind the subject, and the key and fill lights on opposite sides of the camera and to the front and side of the subject. This arrangement is the lighting triangle. **SEE 8.9**   *READY ZVL* ❸

SPECIFIC LIGHTING TECHNIQUES

Once you are familiar with how to apply the photographic principle in a variety of lighting situations, you can move on to a few specific lighting techniques. These include: (1) continuous-action lighting, (2) large-area lighting, (3) cameo lighting, (4) silhouette lighting, (5) chroma-key area lighting, and (6) controlling eye and boom shadows.

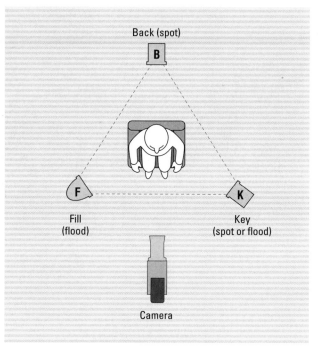

8.9 THE PHOTOGRAPHIC PRINCIPLE, OR TRIANGLE LIGHTING

The three principal lights—key, back, and fill—form a triangle, with the back light at its apex, opposite the camera.

Continuous-Action Lighting

One added problem in television lighting for multicamera productions is movement of the performer(s) and of the camera(s). Fortunately, the basic lighting triangle of key, back, and fill lights can be multiplied and used for each performance or set area. Even if there are only two people sitting at a table, you have to use a multiple application of the basic lighting triangle. **SEE 8.10**

To compensate for the movement of the performers, you should illuminate all adjacent performance areas so that the basic triangle-lighted areas overlap. The purpose of overlapping is to give the performers continuous lighting as they move from one area to another. It is all too easy to concentrate only on the major performance areas and to neglect the small, seemingly insignificant areas in between. You may not even notice the unevenness of such lighting until the performers move across the set. All of a sudden they seem to be playing a "now you see me, now you don't" game, popping alternately from a well-lighted area into dense shadow. In such situations a light meter comes in handy to pinpoint the "black holes."

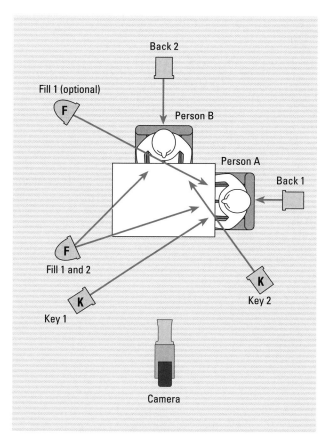

8.10 MULTIPLE TRIANGLE APPLICATION

In this lighting setup, a separate lighting triangle with its own key, back, and fill light is used for each of the two persons (performance areas). If floodlights are used for the keys, you can probably dispense with the fill lights.

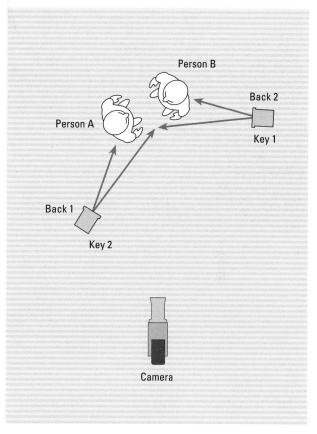

8.11 CROSS-KEYING

In this lighting setup, the key light for person A (the camera-near person) also functions as back light for person B (the camera-far person), and the back light for person A is the key for person B.

When lighting several set areas at once for continuous action, you may not have enough instruments to apply the overlapping triangle lighting. You may need to place the lighting instruments so that each can serve two or more functions.

In reverse-angle shooting, for instance, the key light for one performer may become the back light for the other and vice versa. This technique is generally called *cross-keying*. **SEE 8.11** Or you may have to use a key light to serve also as directional fill in another area. Because fill lights have a diffused beam, you can use a single fill light to lighten up dense shadows in more than one area.

Of course, the application of lighting instruments for multiple functions requires exact positioning of set pieces such as tables and chairs, clearly defined performance areas, and *blocking* (movements of performers). Directors who decide to change blocking or move set pieces after the set has been precisely lighted are not very popular with the lighting crew.

Accurate lighting is always done with basic camera positions and points of view in mind. It therefore helps immensely to know at least the basic camera positions and the range of all major camera viewpoints before starting with the lighting (see figure 8.20). For example, an object that appears perfectly well lighted from a 6 o'clock camera position may look woefully unlit from a 10 o'clock position. Sometimes, as in variety shows or rock concerts, "unlighted" shots from shooting angles that lie outside the lighted parameters may look quite dramatic; in most other shows of less flexible lighting formats, such as daytime serials or instructional programs, these shots simply look bad.

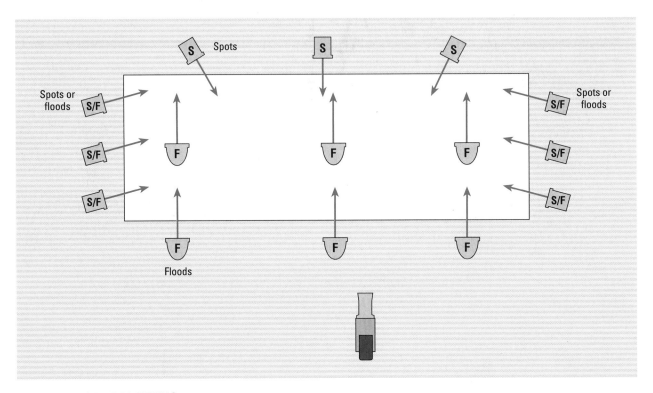

8.12 LARGE-AREA KEYING

In this lighting setup, the Fresnel spots at the left and right sides function as keys and directional fill lights. Fresnel spots are also strung out as regular back lights behind the main action area. If necessary, scoops provide additional fill light from the front.

Large-Area Lighting

For lighting a large area, such as an audience or orchestra, the basic photographic principle still holds. All you do is partially overlap one triangle on another until you have adequately covered the entire area. Instead of key-lighting from just one side of the camera and fill-lighting from the other, however, key-light from both sides of the camera with the beam of the instruments in the flood position. The key lights from one side act as fill for the other side. Because the key-light beams cross each other, this method also (however inaccurately) is called cross-keying, but try to stay away from such double meanings; all they do is confuse the LD and crew.

The back lights are strung out in a row or a semicircle opposite the main camera position. The fill lights (broads or scoops) usually come directly from the front. If the cameras move to the side, some of the key lights also function as back lights. You can also use broads or fluorescent banks instead of Fresnel spots for this type of area lighting. **SEE 8.12**

Cameo Lighting

Certain television shows, especially those of a dramatic nature, are staged in the middle of an empty studio against an unlighted background. This technique, where the performers are highlighted against a dark background, is commonly known as *cameo lighting* (from the cameo art form in which a light relief figure is set against a darker background). **SEE 8.13** Like the close-up, cameo lighting concentrates on the talent and not the environment.

All cameo lighting is highly directional and is achieved most effectively with barn-doored spotlights. In small studios the background areas are carefully shielded from any kind of distracting spill light with black, light-absorbing draperies. The problems with cameo lighting are that it often exceeds the 40:1 ratio between the darkest and brightest spot in the picture, which leads to noisy pictures and some color distortion in the dark areas. Also, because the lighting is highly directional, the talent must meticulously adhere to the rehearsed blocking. A slight deviation means that the talent steps out of the light and,

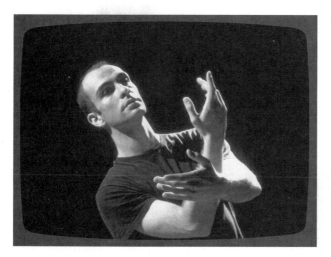

8.13 CAMEO LIGHTING
In cameo lighting, the background is kept dark, with only the foreground person illuminated by highly directional spotlights.

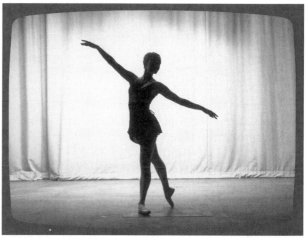

8.14 SILHOUETTE LIGHTING
In silhouette lighting, only the background is lighted, with the figure in front remaining unlighted. It emphasizes contour.

for all practical purposes, disappears from the screen. Finally, if a microphone boom is used for sound pickup, its distinct shadows present a constant hazard.

Silhouette Lighting

The lighting for a silhouette effect is exactly opposite of cameo lighting. In *silhouette lighting* you light the background but leave the figures in front unlighted. This way you see only the contour of objects and people, but not their volume and texture. Obviously, you light in silhouette only those scenes that gain by emphasizing contour. **SEE 8.14** You can also use silhouette lighting to conceal the identity of a person appearing on-camera. *READY ZVL* ❹

To achieve silhouette lighting, use highly diffused light (usually from softlights or scoops with scrims) to evenly illuminate the background.

Chroma-Key Area Lighting

The chroma-key set area consists normally of a blue (and occasionally a green) background. It is used to provide a variety of backgrounds that are electronically generated, replacing the blue or green areas during the key. This process is called *chroma keying*. A popular use of the chroma key is a weather report. Although the weathercaster seems to be standing in front of a large weather map, he or she is in fact standing in front of an empty, evenly lighted blue backdrop. Even during the chroma keying, when the blue areas are electronically

replaced by the weather map, the weathercaster sees only the empty blue area and must look into a monitor to see the map. **SEE COLOR PLATE 17** (Chapter 14 further explains the chroma-key process.)

The most important aspect of lighting the chroma-key set area is even background illumination, which means that the blue background must be lighted with highly diffused instruments, such as softlights or floodlight banks. If there are unusually dark areas or hot spots (undesirable concentrations of light in one spot), the electronically supplied background image looks discolored or, worse, has a tendency to break up. When lighting the foreground, such as for the weathercaster, prevent any of the lights used for the foreground area from hitting the chroma-key area. Such a spill would upset the evenness of the chroma-key background illumination and lead to keying problems.

You may have noticed that the outline of a weathercaster sometimes vibrates with a variety of colors or that the contour is not sharp during a chroma key. One of the major reasons for such vibrating outlines is that especially dark colors or shadows at the contour line take on a blue tinge, caused by a reflection from the blue background. During the chroma-key process, these blue spots become transparent and let the background picture show through. To counteract the bluishness of the shadows, try putting yellow or light-orange gels on all back lights or kicker lights. The back lights then not only separate the foreground subject from the background picture through contour illumination, but also neutralize the blue shadows through the complementary yellow color. As a result, the outline of the weathercaster will remain sharp even during the chroma key. Be careful, however, not to let any of the yellow light hit the face, arms, or hands of the person standing in the chroma-key area.

Because the blue reflections from the sky are so hard to control outdoors, green is generally used in EFP as the background color for chroma keying.

Controlling Eye and Boom Shadows

Two fairly persistent problems in studio lighting are the shadows of eyeglasses and microphone booms. Depending on the specific lighting setup, such unwanted shadows can present a formidable challenge to the lighting crew. Most often, however, you will be able to correct such shadow problems rather quickly.

Key light and eye shadows   The key light striking the subject from a steep angle will cause large dark shadows in any indentation and under any protrusion, such as in the eye sockets and under the nose and chin. If the subject wears glasses, the shadow of the upper rim of the frames may fall directly across the eyes, thus preventing the camera (and the viewer) from seeing them clearly. **SEE 8.15**

There are several ways of reducing these undesirable shadows. First, try to lower the vertical position of the light itself or use a key light farther away from the subject. When you lower it (with a movable batten or a rod), notice that the eye shadows seem to move farther up the face, or at least get smaller, the lower the key light moves and the nearer it approaches the subject's eye level. As soon as the shadows are hidden behind the upper rim of the glasses, lock the key light in position. Such a technique works well so long as the subject does not move around too much. **SEE 8.16**   Second, you can try to reduce eye shadows by illuminating the person from both sides with similar instruments. Third, you can reposition the fill light so that it strikes the subject directly from the front and from a lower angle, thus placing the shadows upward, away from the eyes.

Boom shadows   Although you may not normally use a large microphone boom in the studio except for some dramatic productions, the principles of dealing with boom shadows also apply to handheld microphone booms, such as fishpoles or even handheld shotgun mics.

When you move a boom microphone in front of a lighted scene—in this case, a single person—and move the boom around a little, you may notice shadows on the background or on the actor whenever the microphone or boom passes through a spotlight beam. (You can easily

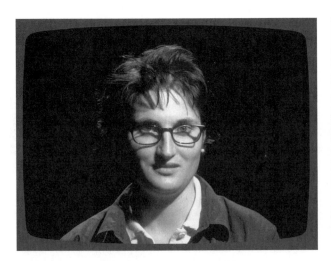

8.15 SHADOW CAUSED BY GLASSES
The angle of the key light causes the shadow of the woman's glasses to fall right across her eyes.

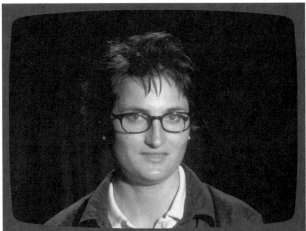

8.16 KEY LIGHT LOWERED
By lowering the key light, the shadow moves up and is hidden behind the glasses.

8.17 LOCATING THE SHADOW-CAUSING LIGHT

The instrument that causes the undesirable boom shadow lies at the extension of a line drawn from the shadow to the microphone causing it.

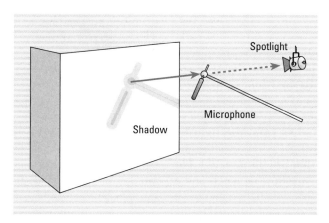

substitute a broomstick or the lighting pole for the boom to check for shadows.) Such shadows are especially distracting when they move in and out during a highly dramatic scene, or show up clearly on the wall or drape in back of the company president's office. You can deal with boom shadows in two ways: move the lights and/or mic boom so that the shadow falls out of camera range, or use such highly diffused lighting that the shadow becomes all but invisible.

First of all, you need to find the light that is causing the boom shadow. As simple as this may seem, it is not always so easy to spot the troublemaking instrument, especially if several spotlights are illuminating various adjacent areas on the set. The easiest way to locate the light is to move your head directly in front of the boom shadow and look at the microphone suspended from the boom. The shadow-causing light will now inevitably shine into your eyes. More technically, the instrument lies at the extension of a line drawn from the shadow to the microphone causing it. **SEE 8.17**

The first thing to try is simply turning off the offending instrument. You may be pleasantly surprised to find that you have eliminated the shadow without impeding the overall lighting. If such a drastic step seriously weakens the lighting setup, try to position the boom so that it does not have to travel through the key light. If you use a handheld fishpole boom, walk around the set while pointing the mic toward the sound source. Watch the shadow move on the background wall until it is out of camera range. If the microphone is still in a position for optimal sound pickup, you have solved the problem. You may locate such a shadow-safe spot more readily when holding or placing the boom parallel to the key-light beam, rather than when crossing it. Some LDs use the key and fill lights close to side-light positions to provide a "corridor" in which to operate the boom.

Another simple way to avoid boom shadows is to light more "steeply" than usual. You do this by moving the key light closer to the set area. The closer the lights are to the performance area, the steeper they will have to be angled to hit the target. The boom will now cast its shadow onto the studio floor rather than on the talent's face or background scenery and thus be out of camera range. The downside to this technique is that the steep key lights produce unusually long and noticeable shadows under the eyes and chin.

You can also try to use barn doors to block off part of the key light that causes the boom shadow. Such a technique is especially useful when the shadow appears in the upper part of the background scenery.

Because the diffused light of broads and softlights casts soft, less defined shadows, one obvious solution to the problem is to light everything with diffused light so that the shadows are barely noticeable. Such flat lighting is rarely used in scenes that employ a microphone boom for audio pickup, however. Some lighting people try to "wash out" the boom shadow with additional background light on any area that shows the shadow. The problem with this technique is that you end up with an excessive amount of background light that may cause undesirable silhouette effects whenever somebody walks in front of it.

Contrast

In chapter 3 you learned that the color camera can tolerate a relatively limited contrast between the lightest and darkest spots in a scene if it is to show subtle brightness differences in the dark picture areas, the middle ranges, and the light picture areas. *Contrast* does not depend so much on how much light comes from the lighting instruments as on how much light is reflected by the colors and various surfaces that are illuminated. For example, a white refrigerator, a yellow raincoat, and a polished brass plate reflect much more light than does a dark-blue velvet cloth, even if they are illuminated by the very same source. If you place the brass plate on the velvet cloth, there may be too much contrast for the television camera to handle properly—and you have not even begun with the lighting.

What you have to consider when dealing with contrast is a constant relationship among various factors, such as how much light falls on the subject, how much light is reflected, and how much difference there is between the foreground and background, or the lightest and the darkest spots in the same picture. Because we deal with relationships rather than absolute values, we express the camera's contrast limit as a ratio.

Contrast Ratio

The difference there is between the brightest and the darkest spots in a picture (often measured by reflected light in foot-candles) is the **contrast ratio**. Most video cameras have a contrast ratio of 40:1, which means that the brightest area should be only forty times lighter than the darkest picture area. If this brightness spread is greater than 40:1, the camera cannot reproduce the subtle brightness differentiations in the light as well as in the dark picture areas. Digital cameras tolerate a higher contrast, but you can, of course, apply the 40:1 ratio for those cameras as well.

The brightest spot, that is, the area reflecting the greatest amount of light, is called the *reference white* and it determines the "white level." The area reflecting the least amount of light is the *reference black*, which determines the "black level." With a contrast limit of 40:1 or 50:1, the reference white should not reflect more than forty or fifty times the light of the reference black. Remember that the contrast is determined not necessarily by the amount of light generated by the lamps but by how much light the objects reflect back into the camera lens.

Shading

By watching a *waveform monitor*, which graphically displays the white and black levels of a picture, the video operator (VO) adjusts the picture to the optimal contrast range, an activity generally called *shading*. **SEE 8.18** To adjust a less-than-ideal picture, the VO tries to "pull down" the excessively bright values to make them match the established white level (which represents a 100 percent video signal strength). But then, because the darkest value cannot get any blacker and move down with the bright areas, the darker picture areas are "crushed" into a uniformly muddy, noisy dark color. If you insist on seeing detail in the dark picture areas, the video operator can

8.18 WAVEFORM MONITOR WITH WHITE AND BLACK LEVELS

The waveform monitor shows a graph of the video signals with its white and black levels.

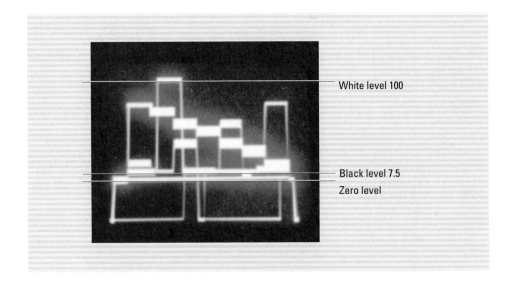

White level 100

Black level 7.5

Zero level

"stretch the blacks" toward the white end. But that causes the bright areas to lose their differentiation and take on a uniformly white and strangely flat and washed-out color. In effect, the pictures look as though the contrast control in the television receiver is set much too high and the brightness much too low, or as though the contrast is set much too low with the brightness turned much too high. Slowing down excessive falloff through fill light and staying away from highly contrasting clothing (starched white shirt and black coat) or set colors (white columns in front of a black or dark purple curtain) will greatly reduce or eliminate this contrast problem.

Auto-Iris

Although setting the camera on *auto-iris* (whereby the camera adjusts the aperture automatically for optimal exposure) is often quite effective, especially in ENG, it does not work well with high-contrast scenes. The auto-iris faithfully responds to the brightest picture area—no matter how bright—and reduces it to the peak signal level (100 percent signal strength), moving the rest of the brightness values down toward the black end of the scale. The farther the brightest spot has to be pulled down to meet the acceptable white level, the more the dark colors are "crushed into the mud." That means if the camera adjusts for an overly bright spot in the picture, all the other picture areas will become proportionally darker.

Fortunately, most professional ENG/EFP cameras have an electronic contrast compression device that helps the camera maintain the brightness differentiation in the dark areas (stretching the blacks) without overexposing the whites too much. This is why much ENG and even some EFP is done with the camera on auto-iris. Still, the best assurance for high-quality pictures is to try to limit the contrast ratio in the scene to 40:1.

Measuring Contrast

You measure contrast with a reflected-light reading: by first pointing the light meter close to the object that serves as the reference white (often a small white card on the set) and then to the object that serves as the reference black (the darkest spot in the scene or a black card on the set). Even if you don't have a light meter or waveform monitor for checking the contrast ratio, you can tell by looking at the monitor: The white areas, such as the white table cloth in your restaurant set, are extremely bright relative to the faces of the people sitting at the table. If they wear something dark, such as a purple dress or a blue coat, everything will look uniformly dark—there are no shadow details. *READY ZVL* ⑤

Limiting Contrast

To keep the contrast ratio within the tolerable limits of the camera (normally 40:1), follow these three guidelines:

- Be aware of the general reflectance of the objects. A highly reflecting object obviously needs less illumination than a highly light-absorbing one.

- Avoid extreme brightness contrasts in the same shot. For example, if you need to show a new line of white china, do not put it on a dark purple tablecloth, but on a lighter, more light-reflecting cloth. This way you can limit the amount of light falling on the porcelain without making the tablecloth appear too dark and muddy.

- Lighten the shadow areas through a generous amount of fill light. This will show some of the detail otherwise hidden in the shadow and at the same time reduce contrast.

All three contrast-limiting techniques are especially important when lighting people. If, for example, a performer is doing a commercial in a light-colored, highly reflecting kitchen set, you may find that despite normal illumination of the performer, his face appears quite dark against the light background. Pouring more light on his face will not remedy this situation, because it just causes more light to spill onto the already bright background. Instead, you should reduce the amount of illumination on the reflecting background. Against the somewhat darker background, his face will look properly illuminated.

Even the best video operator has trouble maintaining skin color if the talent wears a starched white shirt and a black suit. If the VO (or the auto-iris camera) adjusts for the extreme bright areas, the face will go dark and the black suit will look uniformly black. But when the VO tries to shade for the dark areas to reveal some detail in the suit, the face will take on the washed-out look of an overexposed picture. Ask talent to wear clothes that do not contrast too much with the skin tones.

BALANCING INTENSITIES

Even if you have carefully adjusted the position and beam of the key, back, and fill lights, you still need to balance their relative intensities. For example, it is not only the direction of the lights that orients the viewer in time, but also their relative intensities. For example, a strong back light and low-intensity key and fill lights can suggest moonlight.[1]

There is some argument about whether to first balance the key and back lights, or the key and fill lights. Actually, it matters little which you do first, so long as the end effect is a well-balanced picture. How to balance the three lights of the lighting triangle depends on what you intend the lighting to tell the viewer. You can't, therefore, use precise intensity ratios among key, back, and fill lights as an absolute guide for effective lighting. Nevertheless, there are some ratios that have proved beneficial for a number of routine lighting assignments. You can always start with these ratios and then adjust them to the specific lighting task.

Key-to-Back-Light Ratio

In normal conditions back lights have approximately the same intensity as key lights. An unusually intense back light tends to glamorize people; a back light with an intensity much lower than that of the key tends to get lost on the monitor. A television performer with blond hair and a light-colored suit will need considerably less back light than a dark-haired performer in a dark suit. The 1:1 key-to-back-light ratio (key and back lights have equal intensities) can go as high as 1:1.5 (the back light has one and a half times the intensity of the key) if you need a fair amount of sparkle or if the talent has dark, light-absorbing textured hair.

Key-to-Fill-Light Ratio

The fill-light intensity depends on how fast a falloff you want. If you want fast falloff for dramatic effect, little fill is needed. If you want very slow falloff, higher-intensity fill is needed. It is therefore futile to state a standard key-to-fill-light ratio. But for starters, you may want to try a fill-light intensity that is half that of the key light and go from there. Remember that the more fill light you use, the less modeling the key light is doing but the smoother the texture (such as of a person's face) becomes. If you use almost no fill light, the dense shadows reveal no picture detail, and you run the risk of some color distortion in the shadow areas. If, for example, a detective refers to a

---

1. See Herbert Zettl, *Sight Sound Motion*, 3d ed. (Belmont, Calif.: Wadsworth Publishing Co., 1999), p. 34.

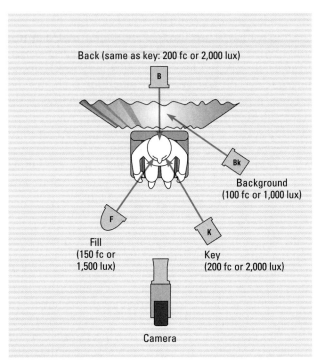

Back (same as key: 200 fc or 2,000 lux)

Background (100 fc or 1,000 lux)

Fill (150 fc or 1,500 lux)

Key (200 fc or 2,000 lux)

Camera

8.19 LIGHTING RATIOS

Lighting ratios differ, depending on the specific lighting task. These ratios are a good starting point.

small scar on the left side of a woman's face and a close-up of her face shows nothing but a dense shadow where the scar should be, or when the shadow hides an important switch in a product demonstration, the key-to-fill-light ratio is obviously wrong.

If you are asked to light for a high-baselight, low-contrast scene (high-key lighting), you may want to use floodlights for both the key and the fill, with the fill burning at almost the same intensity as the key. As you know by now, *high key* has nothing to do with the actual positioning of the key light, but rather the intensity of the overall light level. The back light should probably burn with a higher intensity than the key or the fill light to provide the necessary sparkle. In a low-key scene, the back light is often considerably brighter than the key and fill lights. **SEE 8.19**

Again, as helpful as light meters are in establishing rough lighting ratios, do not rely solely on them. Your final criterion is how the picture looks on the well-adjusted monitor.

THE LIGHT PLOT

The *light plot* shows (1) the location of the lighting instruments relative to the set and illuminated objects and areas, (2) the principal directions of the beams, and, ideally, (3) the type and size of the instruments used.

In drawing a successful light plot, you need an accurate *floor plan* that shows the scenery and the stage props, the principal talent positions, and the major camera positions and shooting angles. Because all this information is generally not available for routine shows, they are lighted without the use of a light plot. If you have to light an atypical show, however, such as an interview of the university president with members of the board of trustees, a light plot makes the lighting less arbitrary and saves the crew considerable time and energy. You can also use it again later for similar setups.

An easy way to make a light plot is to put a transparency over a copy of the floor plan and draw the lighting information on the transparency. Use different icons for spotlights and floodlights, drawing arrows to indicate the main directions of the beams. **SEE 8.20 AND 8.21** Try to work with the set designer (usually the art director) or the floor manager (who is responsible for putting up the set) as much as possible to have them place the set in the studio where you won't have to move any, or only a few, instruments to achieve the desired lighting. Moving the lights to suit the location of the set is much more difficult and time-consuming than moving the set to suit the available lighting positions.

Successful studio lighting is when you get it done on time. Don't fuss over a single dense shadow somewhere on the background while neglecting to light the rest of the set. If you are really pressed for time, turn on some floodlights and back lights that hang in approximate positions and hope for the best. More often than not, the lighting will look quite acceptable.

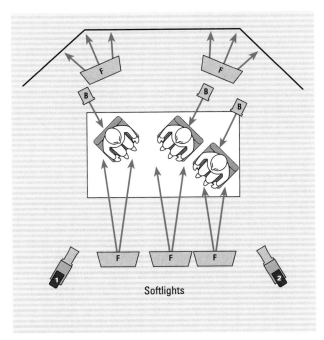

Softlights

8.20 LIGHT PLOT FOR
FLAT LIGHTING OF INTERVIEW

This light plot shows the slow-falloff (flat) lighting setup for a simple interview. Ordinarily, such a simple setup would not require a light plot. Note that the sketch is not to scale.

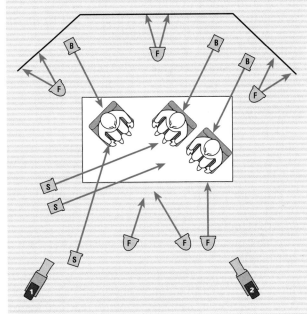

8.21 LIGHT PLOT FOR INTERVIEW,
USING FLOODS AND SPOTS

This interview is lighted for faster falloff. It uses spots for key and back lights, and scoops for fill lights and background lights.

OPERATION OF STUDIO LIGHTS

When initially hanging the lights, divide the studio into major performance areas and hang the appropriate instruments (spotlights and floodlights) in the triangular arrangements of the basic photographic principle. Try to position the instruments so that they can serve multiple functions, that is, light more than one person or several parts of the set. This will help you illuminate all major performance areas adequately with minimum effort and instruments.

Safety

In the actual operation of lighting instruments and the associated control equipment, you should heed the rule for all production activities: *Safety first.* As mentioned in chapter 7, always secure the lighting instruments to the battens, and the barn doors and scrims to the lighting instruments, with safety chains or cables. Check all C-clamps periodically, especially the bolts that connect the lighting instruments to the hanging device. Be careful when plugging in lights and when moving active (switched-on) instruments. Because the hot lamps are especially vulnerable to physical shock, try not to jolt the instrument; move it gently.

Always wear gloves when working with active lighting instruments. The gloves will protect you from burns when touching the extremely hot quartz lamps and will give you some protection from electric shock.

When replacing lamps, wait until the instrument has cooled somewhat. Always turn off the instrument before reaching in to remove a burned-out lamp. As a double protection, unplug the light at the batten. *Do not touch the new quartz lamp with your fingers.* Fingerprints, or any other stuff clinging to the quartz housing of the lamp, cause the lamp to overheat and burn out. Wear gloves or, if you have nothing else, use a tissue or even your shirttail when handling the lamp.

When moving ladders for fine trimming (fine beam adjustment), watch for obstacles above and below. Do not take any chances by leaning way out to reach an instrument. Position the ladder so that you can work from behind, rather than in front of, the instrument. When adjusting a light, try not to look directly into it; look

instead at the object to be lighted and see how the beam strikes it. If you must look into the light, wear dark glasses and do so only briefly.

When patching lights at the patchboard, have all dimmers in the *off* position. Do not "hot-patch" by connecting the power cord of the instrument to the power outlet at the light batten. Hot-patching can burn your hand and also pit the patches so that they no longer make the proper connection.

Preserving Lamps and Power

Try to warm up large instruments through reduced power by keeping the dimmer low for a short while before supplying full power. This will prolong the lamp life and the Fresnel lenses, which tend to crack when warmed up too fast. This warm-up period (about one to three minutes) is essential for getting HMI lights up to full operation. Do not overload a circuit: It may hold during rehearsal but then go out just at the wrong time during the actual show. If extension cords start to get hot, unplug and replace them immediately with lower-gauge (thicker wire, such as 16- or 14-gauge) cables.

Do not waste energy. Try to bring the lights down as close as possible to the object or scene to be illuminated. As you know, light intensity drops off considerably the farther the light moves from the object. Bring the lights up full only when necessary. Dry runs (without cameras) can be done just as efficiently when illuminated by work lights as by full studio lighting.

Using a Studio Monitor

If you intend to use a (well-adjusted) color monitor as a guide for lighting, you must be ready for some compromise. As noted, the lighting is correct if the studio monitor shows what you want the viewer to perceive. To get to this point, you should use the *monitor* as a guide to lighting, rather than the less-direct light meter. But you may run into difficulties. The video operator may tell you that she cannot set up the cameras (adjust them for an optimal video signal) before you have finished the lighting. And your argument probably is (and should be) that you cannot finish the lighting without checking it on the monitor.

Approach this argument with a readiness for compromise, because both parties have a valid point. You can do the basic lighting without the camera. An incident (foot-candle or lux) light reading can help you detect gross inadequacies, such as insufficient baselight levels or extremely uneven illumination. With some experience you can also tell whether a shadow is too dense for adequate reproduction of color and detail. But for the fine trimming, you need at least one camera. Ask the VO to work with you; after all, it is also the VO's responsibility to deliver technically acceptable pictures. The single camera can be roughly set up to the existing illumination and pointed into the set. With the direct feedback of the picture on the studio monitor, you can proceed to correct glaring discrepancies or simply touch up some of the lighting as to beam direction and intensity. After this fine trimming, all cameras can be set up and balanced for optimal performance.

MAIN POINTS

◆ All lighting uses directional and/or diffused light.

◆ The key light is the principal source of illumination and reveals the basic shape of the object.

◆ The back light distinguishes the shadow of the object from the background and emphasizes the object outline. It gives the object sparkle.

◆ The fill light reduces falloff and makes the shadows less dense.

◆ The background, or set, light illuminates the background of the scene and the set. The side light acts as additional fill. The kicker light is used to outline the contour of an object that would otherwise blend in with the background.

◆ Most television lighting setups use the basic photographic principle, or triangle lighting, of key, back, and fill light.

◆ Specific lighting techniques include continuous-action lighting, large-area lighting, cameo lighting, silhouette lighting, chroma-key area lighting, and controlling eye and boom shadows.

◆ Falloff indicates how fast the lighted side of a subject changes to a shadow, and how dense the shadows are. Fast falloff means that the light and shadow areas are clearly marked and that the shadows are dense. Slow falloff means that the transition from light to shadow is more gradual and that the shadows are transparent.

◆ A low-key scene has a dark background with selective fast-falloff lighting and a dramatic or mysterious mood. A high-key scene has a light background, a generally high baselight level, and usually an upbeat, happy mood.

◆ Contrast is the difference between the lightest and darkest areas in a picture.

◆ The contrast ratio is the contrast as measured by reflected light. The normal optimal contrast ratio is 40:1. For digital cameras, it can be higher, which means that it can tolerate a higher contrast.

◆ Balancing intensities of the various lights depends largely on the desired effect.

◆ The light plot indicates the location of the lighting instruments, the principal direction of the light beams, and sometimes the type and size of the instruments used.

◆ Exercise caution during all lighting operations. Do not look directly into the instruments, and wear gloves when handling the hot lights.

8.2

Lighting in the Field

ENG EFP Remember that when lighting field productions, you are not working in the studio, where all the lighting equipment is in place and ready to go. Every piece of equipment, however large or small, must be hauled to the remote location and set up in places that always seem either too small or too large for good television lighting. Also, you never seem to get enough time to experiment with various lighting setups to find the most effective one. You must therefore get the job done with a maximum of planning and a minimum of equipment. Whatever the remote lighting task, you need to be especially efficient in the choice of instruments and their use. This section explains the particular techniques of field lighting and describes some of its essential requirements.

▶ **ENG LIGHTING**

Shooting in outdoor light, at night, and in indoor light; and working with daylight, fluorescents, and baselight

▶ **EFP LIGHTING**

Safety, power supply, location survey, and lighting setup

ENG LIGHTING

ENG EFP Although there is no clear-cut division between lighting for ENG and EFP, there is enough difference between the two techniques to warrant a separate discussion. When engaged in electronic news gathering, you generally shoot in whatever light there is. But when doing EFP, you may be expected to make the office of a corporate president look like the best Hollywood can produce or to illuminate the hearing room of the board of supervisors so that it rivals a courtroom scene in the latest blockbuster movie—all without adequate time or equipment.

When engaged in ENG, you will find yourself confronted with both outdoor and indoor lighting problems. Most of the time, you have to work with available light—the illumination already present at the scene. But on some occasions you have to supplement ambient light, and on others you must provide all the light for a scene. In any case, you have to work quickly and efficiently to obtain not only adequate lighting, but also the most effective lighting possible under the circumstances.

Shooting in Outdoor Light

ENG EFP The ideal light for outdoor shooting is an overcast day. The clouds or fog act as diffusers for the hard sunlight, providing an even illumination similar to that of softlights. Do not be surprised if you have to use an ND and/or color-correction filter when white-balancing the camera on an overcast day. The light of a cloudy day is often surprisingly bright and has a high color temperature.

Because the diffused light of an overcast day creates rather soft shadows, and therefore low-contrast lighting, you can usually put the camera on auto-iris. But even in diffused lighting, try not to position a person in front of a white or otherwise light background. The auto-iris will read and adjust to the light background rather than to the person, who will then look underexposed. If you have to shoot against a light background, switch to manual iris control, zoom in on the person (thereby avoiding as much of the bright background as possible), and adjust the iris to meet the light requirements of the person rather than the background.

Most lighting problems occur when you shoot in bright sunlight. Here are some hints:

▪ Whenever possible, place the on-camera person in the shadow area. The shadow area produces even, slow-falloff lighting similar to that of an overcast day. Be careful, however, not to shoot against a bright, sunlit background. A bright background would immediately show the subject in silhouette. If you tried to adjust the aperture to the light in the shadow area (opening the iris by lowering the *f*-stop), the background would be grossly overexposed.

▪ If you can't avoid the bright sun, try to shoot *with* the sun, not against it, always avoiding bright backgrounds. Do not use the camera in the auto-iris mode. Bright backgrounds or unimportant picture detail may under-expose the important parts of the scene. If you have no time to do anything but aim and shoot, however, switching the camera to auto-iris is still better than having to worry constantly about exposure.

If you cannot avoid placing a subject against the sun, try to get as close a shot as possible and use a reflector to bounce as much light on the person as you can. **SEE 8.22**

Bright sunlight inevitably produces dense shadows. Watch where the shadows are and consider them when

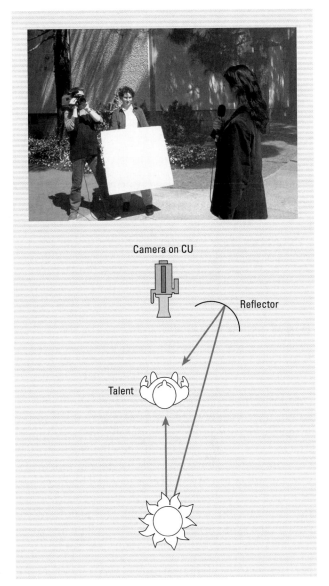

8.22 SHOOTING AGAINST THE SUN

When shooting against the sun, reflect as much sun as possible back to the talent with a simple reflector (in this case, a white card).

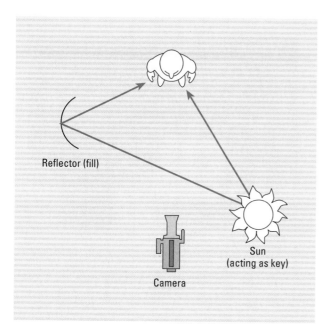

8.23 USE OF REFLECTOR
When shooting in bright sunlight, the dark shadows can be easily lightened with a reflector.

composing shots. There is little you can do about shadows when you rush after a breaking news story. But if you set up an on-location interview, and if you are lucky enough to have an assistant, you can lighten the shadows (slow down the falloff) somewhat by asking the assistant to hold a white card or a simple reflector so that it bounces back some of the sunlight and renders the dense shadows more transparent. **SEE 8.23** Reflectors will also help you contain the extremes between bright sunlight and dense shadow within the 40:1 contrast ratio. *READY ZVL* **6**

■ Here is a typical contrast problem you may encounter in ENG: You are to cover a brief interview with the winner of a women's golf tournament. During the interview the dark-haired woman insists on wearing a white sun-visor that has become her good-luck charm. What can you do?

One of the quickest solutions is to cut out the visor by zooming in to an extreme close-up (ECU) and setting the aperture according to the light on her face. The use of a reflector would help little, because its reflected light would spill beyond the face to the visor, making matters worse. You could also go to a medium or long shot, in which case the white visor would be small enough in the picture not to dominate the total exposure.

Shooting at Night

ENG EFP When covering a nighttime event, you sometimes have enough illumination from car headlights, a blazing fire, or the lights of an emergency vehicle to get pictures that at least reflect the atmosphere and excitement of the event. More often, however, you need to get a shot of the police chief or the fire marshal or the reporter describing the event. In this case, you need more light to produce acceptable pictures. Here are some points to consider:

■ Assuming that you have only one camera light and no assistant, clip the light on top of the camera and aim it straight at the field reporter. The closer the reporter is to the camera (which is also the light source), the stronger the illumination. You can change the light intensity by moving just one or two steps toward or away from the reporter.

■ If you have an assistant, he or she can hold the light somewhat above camera level (to avoid shining the light directly into the reporter's eyes) and a little to the side of the camera so that the single camera light acts as a key light. Try to use any additional light source, such as a lighted store window or a street lamp, as fill by positioning the subject appropriately. **SEE 8.24** Don't worry about mixing color temperatures; we readily accept color distortions when seeing events shot at night. You could also use the store window as a key light and have your assistant hold a reflector on the opposite side to generate some fill. **SEE 8.25** Once again, avoid shooting against a brightly lighted background.

■ If you are to cover a brief feature report outside the county hospital, for example, and if you are not under great time pressure, use a portable light mounted on a light stand as a key. If you have a second light, use it for fill. Because the fill light should have less intensity than the key, put a scrim in front of the lens, put the fill light in the flood position, or move it farther away. **SEE 8.26** Whenever possible, plug the lights into regular household outlets rather than using batteries as a power source.

■ If the reporter needs a remote teleprompter, check that the light in the teleprompter is working. Otherwise, you have to illuminate the copy with an external light.

■ Whenever you go on a night assignment, carry a flashlight. It helps locate equipment in the car, exchange batteries and videotape on location, and perhaps may even help you and the reporter find your way back to the car.

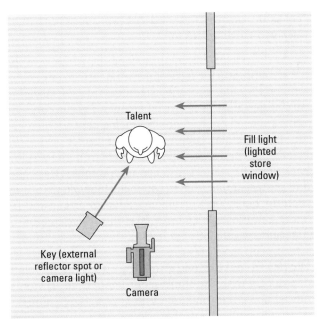

8.24 AVAILABLE FILL LIGHT

A lighted store window can provide much-needed fill light when shooting at night. The camera probably white-balances on the brighter key.

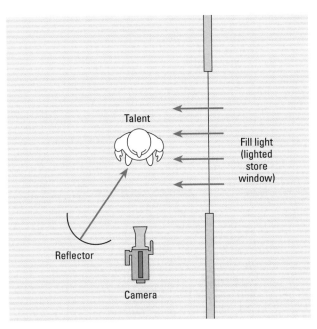

8.25 AVAILABLE KEY LIGHT

Here the window serves as key light and, through the use of a reflector, also as fill light.

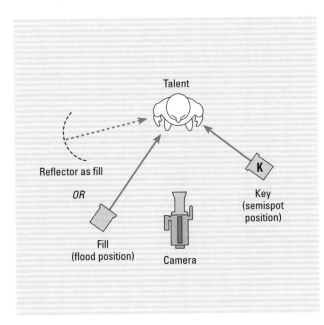

8.26 PORTABLE LIGHT AS KEY

A portable spotlight can serve as key, with another spot, or a reflector, serving as fill light. You should put the fill light in the flood position and move it farther away from the subject to reduce its intensity.

Shooting in Indoor Light

ENG EFP You encounter various amounts and types of light when shooting indoors. Some interiors are illuminated by the daylight that comes through large windows, others by fluorescent banks that make up a light ceiling. Still others have desk and floor lamps augmenting the little daylight that manages to penetrate draped windows. The major problem here is not so much how to supply additional light, but how to match the various color temperatures.

Working with daylight The typical problem is having to shoot against a large window. Often a company official wants to make his or her statement from behind a desk, and the desk may be located in front of a large picture window. The lighting problem is identical with that of a person standing in front of a bright background: If you set the iris according to the background brightness, the person in front tends to appear in silhouette. If you adjust the iris for the person in front, the background is overexposed. Here are some possible solutions:

■ Draw the drapes or the blinds and light the person with portable instruments. Or go to a tight close-up and

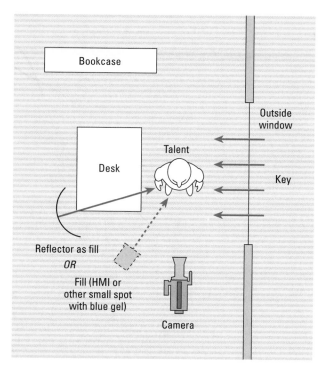

8.27 WINDOW LIGHT AS KEY

The daylight shining through a window can serve as the key, and a reflector as the fill light. If you use a portable light as fill and/or as back light, you need to bring its color temperature up to the 5,600°K daylight standard.

cut out as much background as possible. Unfortunately, many windows do not have drapes or blinds, and not all company officials look good on an ECU.

■ Move the camera to the side of the desk and have the person face the camera. You can then shoot parallel to the window. **SEE 8.27** You can use the light from the window as key, and fill with an additional light on a stand. If you use an HMI light, you do not need to worry about mixing different color temperatures. As you recall, HMIs burn at the daylight standard of 5,600°K. But if you use an external reflector spot for fill light, you need to boost the color temperature by inserting either a dichroic daylight filter or a light-blue gel. Put the instrument into the flood position to avoid harsh shadows or, better yet, diffuse its beam with a scrim. To make the picture look really professional, place another HMI spot or external reflector

spot (with a dichroic filter and in the spot position) behind the person to add back light.

■ If the person insists on having the window in the background, you must cover the window with large color temperature filters and/or ND filters (plastic sheets) of varying densities. In case of emergency, you can cover the windows neatly with ordinary tracing paper, which has an ND filter effect. Unless you use a reflector next to the camera that bounces some of the light from the window back onto the subject, you can use portable HMI lights and portable quartz lights with light-blue filters (raising them to the 5,600°K daylight standard) as key and fill lights. But these procedures take up a great amount of time and are generally left to EFP.

Working with fluorescents   The basic problem of working with the fluorescent lights used in stores, offices, and public buildings is their color temperature. It is usually higher than the 3,200°K indoor standard of incandescent lights. Even if some fluorescent tubes burn at the warmer indoor color temperature, they have a strange greenish blue tint. So if you turn on the camera light for additional illumination, you are confronted with two color temperatures. Some lighting people advise turning the fluorescents off altogether when working with quartz lights (3,200°K), but this is unrealistic. If you need to get a fast-breaking story and you shoot in a hallway that is illuminated by fluorescent lights, you certainly do not have time to locate and persuade the building manager to turn off the lights and then to relight the scene before starting to shoot.

If the fluorescent lights give enough illumination, simply use the appropriate color temperature filter (to bring down the high color temperature of the fluorescents) and white-balance the camera with the available light. If you have to use a camera light for additional illumination, either boost the color temperature of the camera light (by inserting a dichroic filter), or white-balance the camera with the illumination provided by the camera light (3,200°K). As mentioned in chapter 7, the portable incandescent lights—including the camera light—are strong enough to wash out the fluorescent baselight. Assuming that you have plenty of time for the shoot, you can use the portable fluorescent banks for additional light sources on the subject.

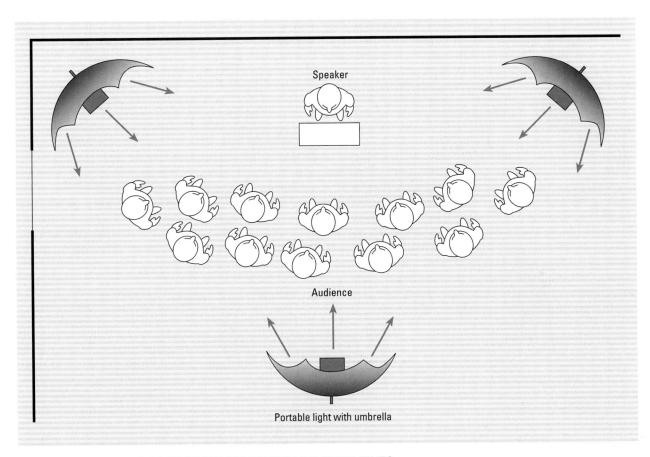

8.28 ESTABLISHING BASELIGHT WITH PORTABLE INSTRUMENTS
To establish an adequate baselight level, you need highly diffused light. Here three portable quartz lights and reflecting umbrellas provide maximally diffused baselight for the entire area.

Working with baselight Sometimes you have to deal with groups of people who are gathered in locations with inadequate illumination. Typical examples are convention meetings in small rooms, gatherings in hotel lobbies, or people in hallways. Most of the time, a camera light provides enough illumination to cover the speaker and individual audience members. If you are to do rather extensive coverage of such an event, however, you need additional illumination. The quickest and most efficient way to light such a location is to establish a general, nondirectional baselight level. Simply use two or three external reflector spots in the flood position and bounce them off the ceiling or walls. If that is not possible, direct the lights on the group, but diffuse the light beam with scrims. The most efficient method is to use two or three portable, high-intensity lights and diffuse their beams with light diffusion umbrellas. **SEE 8.28**

EFP LIGHTING

ENG EFP An electronic field production can range from a simple interview in someone's office to complex scenes shot on location. One of the advantages of lighting for EFP is that you generally have more planning and setup time than in ENG. But you will soon find out that in

EFP, as in ENG, time is at a premium. You must therefore plan within the realistic context of available time and equipment. Be prepared to compromise, and strive for optimal lighting relative to the other production requirements. Major points to consider in EFP include safety, power supply, location survey, and lighting setup.

Safety

ENG EFP As in all types of television production, you must be safety conscious at all times. No production, however exciting or difficult, excuses you from abandoning safety for expediency or effect. Be especially careful with electric power when on location. A charge of 110 volts can be deadly. Secure cables so that people do not trip over them. String them above doorways, or tape them to the floor and cover them with a rubber mat or flattened cardboard at points of heavy foot traffic. A loose cable can not only trip somebody, but also topple a lighting instrument and start a fire. See that all light stands are secured with sandbags. As discussed in chapter 7, lighting instruments must be as far away as possible from combustible material, such as drapes, books, tablecloths, wood ceilings, and walls. It pays to double-check. If they must be close to walls and other combustible material, insulate them with aluminum foil.

Power Supply

ENG EFP In EFP you have to work with three types of power for lighting instruments: (1) household current (usually from 110 to 120 volts), (2) generators, and (3) 12- or 30-volt batteries.

The most frequently used power supply is household current. When using regular wall outlets, be aware of the power rating of the circuits, which is usually 15 or 20 amps (amperes) per circuit. This rating means that you can theoretically plug in a 1,500-watt (or 2,000-watt) instrument, or any combination of lights that does not exceed 1,500 (or 2,000) watts, without overloading the circuit, provided nothing else is on the same circuit. But that is not always wise to do. Recall the discussion about extension cords that build up additional resistance, especially when warm. Just to be on the safe side, *do not load up a single circuit to full capacity*. Otherwise, you may find that the lights go out just at the most important part of the shoot.

A simple way to figure the total wattage per circuit is to multiply the number of amps of the circuit by 100 (assuming the household current rates between 110 and 120 volts). This gives you an upper limit: 15 amps (100

volts = 1,500 total wattage) or 20 amps (100 volts = 2,000). But don't press your luck. Try to use lower-wattage instruments per circuit just to make sure that the lights will work properly during the entire production.

If you need to power more lights than a single circuit can handle, plug them into different circuits.

Determining the circuits   Normally, several double wall outlets are connected to the same circuit. You can determine which outlets are on the same circuit by plugging one low-powered lamp into a particular outlet. Find the specific circuit breaker that turns off the lamp. Now plug the light into the next convenient outlet and switch off the same circuit breaker or fuse. If the light goes out, the plugs are on the same circuit. If the light stays on, it's a different circuit.

Safe power extensions   Obviously, you need enough extension cords to get from the outlets to the light. You can minimize cable runs by using power strips (multiple-outlet boxes), especially if you use low-wattage lights. The larger the wires in the extension cords (lower gauge ratings), the more wattage they can handle without getting unduly hot. Have enough and various kinds of adapters available so that lights can be plugged into the existing household outlets.

Whenever there is doubt about the availability or reliability of power, use a generator, the responsibility of which falls to the engineering crew. The circuit ratings and allowable combined wattage of the lights per circuit still apply.

For relatively simple on-location productions, you may power the lights with batteries. First, check whether the lamps in the portable lights are appropriate for the voltage of the battery. Obviously, you cannot use a 12-volt lamp with a 30-volt battery. Second, check that the batteries are properly charged and that there are enough spares to last for the entire production. Turning off the lights whenever possible saves battery power and extends the life of the lamps.

Location Survey

ENG EFP One of the most important aspects of lighting for EFP is a thorough *location survey* of the remote site. **SEE 8.29** The survey checklists in figure 8.29 are intended for relatively simple productions, as are all other discussions of EFP. The lighting for large and complex electronic field productions is more closely related to motion picture techniques and is not included here.

8.29 EFP LOCATION SURVEY

INDOORS	OUTDOORS
AVAILABLE LIGHT	
Is the available light sufficient? If not, what additional lights do you need? What type of available light do you have? Incandescent? Fluorescent? Daylight coming through windows?	Do you need any additional lights? Where is the sun in relation to the planned action? Is there enough room to place the necessary reflectors?
PRINCIPAL BACKGROUND	
Is there any action planned against a white wall? Are there windows in the background? If so, do they have curtains, drapes, or venetian blinds that can be drawn? If you want to use the daylight from the window, do you have lights that match the color temperature of the daylight (5,600°K)? If the window is too bright, or if you have to reduce the color temperature coming through the window, do you have the appropriate ND or color filters to attach to the window? You will certainly need some reflectors or other type of fill-light illumination.	How bright is the background? Even if the sun is not hitting the background at the time of the survey, will it be there when the actual production takes place? When shooting at the beach, does the director plan to have people perform with the ocean as background? You will need reflectors and/or additional lights (HMIs) to prevent the people from turning into silhouettes, unless the director plans on ECUs most of the time.
CONTRAST	
If there are dense shadows or if the action moves through high-contrast areas (light to dark), you need extra fill light to reduce the contrast.	Does the production take place in bright sunlight? You must then provide for a generous amount of fill light (reflectors and/or HMI spotlights) to render the shadows transparent. Are people moving from the sunlight into dense shadow areas and back into sunlight? Make provisions to reduce the contrast (reflectors that light the people in the shadow areas).

8.29 EFP LOCATION SURVEY *(continued)*

INDOORS	OUTDOORS
LIGHT POSITIONS	
Can you place the lights out of camera range? What lighting supports do you need (light stands, gaffer grip, clamps)? Do you need special mounting devices, such as battens or cross braces? Are the lighting instruments far enough away from combustible materials? Are the lights positioned so that they do not interfere with the event? People who are not used to television complain mostly about the brightness of the lights.	If you need reflectors or additional lights on stands, is the ground level enough so that the stands can be securely placed? Will you need to take extra precautions because of wind? (Take plenty of sandbags along, or even some tent pegs and rope, so that you can secure the light stands in case of wind.)
POWER REQUIREMENTS	
Do you know exactly where the outlets are, what the rating of the circuits is, and which outlets are on the same circuit? Make a rough sketch of all outlets and indicate the distance to the corresponding light or lights. What adapters do you need to plug lights into the available outlets? If the electrical circuits on location are protected by fuses, are there appropriate spare fuses? Do you have the necessary cables, extension cords, and spider boxes so that you can get by with a minimum of cable runs? In the projected cable runs, have you applied all possible safety precautions?	You do not need to use lighting instruments very often when shooting outdoors, unless you shoot at night or need to fill in particularly dense shadows that cannot be reached with a simple reflector. Your main concern will be power and how to get it to the lighting instruments. Do you have the necessary power available nearby? Do you need a generator? If you can tap available power, make sure you can tell the engineer in charge the approximate power requirement for all lights. (Simply add up the wattage of all the lights you plan to use, plus another 10 percent to ensure enough power.) Do you have enough extension cords to reach all the lighting instruments?

Lighting Setup

ENG EFP To achieve good lighting with as few instruments as possible, it is important to acquaint yourself with the planned production. Find out from the director what type of shooting is intended (short scenes with time to relight for each new camera position or shot, or long uninterrupted scenes that stress the continuity of action). Ask the director for the principal camera positions and shots (extreme angles, camera movement, field of view). After some field experience, you will notice that, as in studio productions, EFP lighting situations repeat themselves and you can do a good lighting job within a limited time frame and with little wasted effort. Here are some typical EFP situations:

Baselight illumination   If you are pressed for time, and if the action within the room is not specified, you can use floodlights to produce a general illumination (see figure 8.28). Although this technique is anything but imaginative, it gets the job done and is certainly better than highly specific lighting that happens to be in the wrong places.

Available light   In general, compared with studio shows, scenes that are shot in available light look strangely lifeless, mainly because they lack back light. Try to set up a back light whenever possible. You may have to place the light stands to the side to keep them out of camera range, or suspend the back lights from a

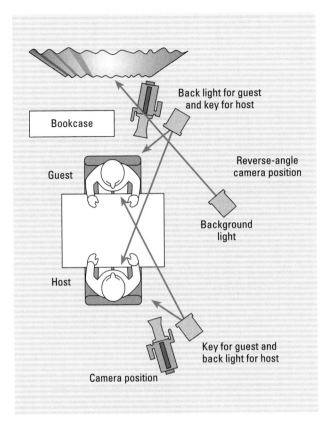

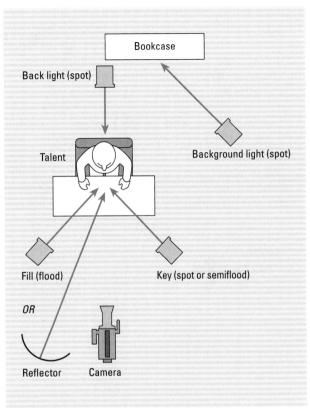

8.30 INTERVIEW LIGHTING WITH MINIMAL INSTRUMENTS

The two portable lights serve multiple functions: key and back lights for the host and guest. If you have a third light, use it as a background light.

8.31 TRIANGLE LIGHTING IN EFP

Here the photographic principle is applied in an EFP scene. The fill light is in the flood position and/or has a scrim to diffuse and reduce the intensity of the beam. You can also use a reflector in place of the fill light.

cross brace or a homemade lighting bridge. If you have a limited amount of lighting instruments, sacrifice the fill light for the back light. You can always use a reflector to substitute for the fill.

The office interview   You can light the typical office interview with two or three lights. **SEE 8.30** Two external reflector spots, placed so that they shine over the shoulder of the participants sitting opposite each other, serve as multiple-function key and back lights. You can use the third instrument as a background light. This lighting can also be set up for an interview in a hotel room, hallway, living room, or any other such location. (See figure 8.27 for how to deal with office windows.)

The company official's announcement   This situation usually has the official standing next to a chart or sitting behind a desk, on a desk, or in a comfortable chair. In all of these cases, you can apply the basic photographic principle of key, fill, and back lights. If you have a fourth light, you can use it as a background light or to light the chart. If you do not have enough baselight, diffuse the fill light as much as possible so that it spills throughout the area. **SEE 8.31** If you are working with only three lights, substitute a reflector for the fill and use the third instrument as a background light or to illuminate the object the official may want to demonstrate. The lights must be high enough to not throw distracting shadows on the desk or behind the official. The more diffused the light, the less the person's wrinkles will show but the flatter the picture will look. Always keep the back light in the spot position. If the office is ordinarily illuminated by fluorescent lights, leave them on to provide the necessary baselight. The quartz lights on the official will dictate the proper color temperature.

Large interiors and large groups   To illuminate large interiors, you can use a few floodlights (such as Omni lights with umbrellas) or, if time and equipment permit, several floodlight banks that serve as multiple key and fill lights. If you have some idea of shooting angles and the action, try to set up a few back lights to give the scene the necessary sparkle. It is usually safer to provide an adequate amount of even light than to light selectively, especially if the action is not specifically blocked. *READY ZVL* ❼

MAIN POINTS

- ◆ The best outdoor shooting light is an overcast day. If the weather is sunny, try to place the talent in the shadow rather than the sun.

- ◆ Avoid bright backgrounds. Reflectors are a great help in filling in shadows when shooting outdoors.

- ◆ When shooting at night for ENG, use the camera light as the principal light source if no other light is available. Use any other available light for fill.

- ◆ When shooting against a large picture window, filter the intensity and lower the color temperature of the light to match that of the key and fill lights used on the person in front of the window.

- ◆ Never disregard safety for expediency or effect.

- ◆ When powering portable lights with household current, check the capacity of the circuits. Do not overload the circuits.

- ◆ Before any EFP lighting, do a location survey.

ZETTL'S VIDEOLAB 2.1

*Once again some of the lab modules let you do some actual lighting. Note the lighting effect of the various instruments of the triangle setup. The **Try it** modules offer further hands-on sessions. Again, be sure to take all the **Quizzes**.*

RUN ZVL 1 Click on the **lights** monitor and run tape 7 **Triangle Lighting**. Click on the **Key**, **Back**, and **Fill** modules and observe their specific lighting functions. Note how they all contribute to the basic (triangle) photographic principle. Do the lighting exercises in the **Try it** module.

RUN ZVL 2 Run tape 8 **Design** and click on the **High key**, **Dramatic**, and **Horror** modules. Think about how you would duplicate these lab exercises in the studio. Do the **Try it** exercises.

RUN ZVL 3 Just for good measure, run tape 7 **Triangle Lighting** again and practice some of the **Try it** exercises.

RUN ZVL 4 Go back to tape 8 **Design** and click on the **Silhouette** module. Recall that cameo is the direct opposite lighting effect from silhouette. Try to achieve cameo and silhouette effects when practicing lighting in the **Try it** module.

RUN ZVL 5 Run tape 4 **Measurement**. Do some more measurement exercises with the **Contrast** module.

RUN ZVL 6 Run tape 9 **Field** and click on the **Outdoor** module. See how a reflector can help you get good pictures in bright sunlight. Don't forget that shooting in the shade is easier than using all sorts of reflectors in bright sunlight.

RUN ZVL 7 Just for good measure, now click on the **Indoor** module and watch how you can use umbrellas to quickly produce a sufficient amount of baselight.

9

Audio: Sound Pickup

We are usually so engrossed in the barrage of colorful pictures when watching television that we are often totally unaware of sound—unless there is an audio problem. All of a sudden we realize that without sound we have a hard time following what is going on. But so long as we can hear the sound track, we can turn away from the TV and still know pretty much what's happening on-screen. But isn't a picture worth a thousand words? Apparently not in television. Because so much information is transmitted by someone talking, the infamous "talking head" is not such a bad production technique after all, provided the person talking has something worthwhile to say.

Sound is important for establishing mood or the intensification of action as well. A good chase sequence invariably has a barrage of sounds, including agitated music and the squealing of tires. The sound track also helps us connect the visual fragments of the relatively small, low-definition television image to form a meaningful whole.

If sound is, indeed, such an important production element, why do we fail to have better sound on television? Even when you produce a short scene as an exercise in the studio, you will probably notice that although the pictures may look acceptable, it is usually the sound portion that could stand some improvement. It is often assumed, unfortunately, that by sticking a microphone into a scene at the last minute, the audio requirements have been satisfied. Don't believe it. Good television audio needs at least as much preparation and attention as the video portion. And, like any other production element, television audio should not simply be added—it should be *integrated* into the production planning from the very beginning.

Section 9.1, How Microphones Hear, covers the sound pickup portion of **_audio_** (from the Latin verb *audire*, to hear), including the electronic and operational characteristics of microphones. In Section 9.2, How Microphones Work, you learn about the more technical aspects of sound-generating elements the microphone uses in ENG/EFP. *READY ZVL* ❶

KEY TERMS

audio The sound portion of television and its production. Technically, the electronic reproduction of audible sound.

cardioid Heart-shaped pickup pattern of a unidirectional microphone.

condenser microphone A microphone whose diaphragm consists of a condenser plate that vibrates with the sound pressure against another fixed condenser plate, called the backplate. Also called *electret* or *capacitor microphone*.

direct insertion Recording technique wherein sound signals of electric instruments are fed directly to the mixing console without the use of speaker and microphone. Also called *direct input*.

dynamic microphone A microphone whose sound pickup device consists of a diaphragm that is attached to a movable coil. As the diaphragm vibrates with the air pressure from the sound, the coil moves within a magnetic field, generating an electric current. Also called *moving-coil microphone*.

fishpole A suspension device for a microphone; the mic is attached to a pole and held over the scene for brief periods.

flat response Measure of a microphone's ability to hear equally well over the entire frequency range.

foldback The return of the total or partial audio mix to the talent through headsets or I.F.B. channels. Also called *cue-send*.

frequency response Measure of the range of frequencies a microphone can hear and reproduce.

impedance Type of resistance to the signal flow. Important especially in matching high- or low-impedance microphones with high- or low-impedance recorders. A high-impedance mic works properly only with a relatively short cable, whereas a low-impedance mic can take up to several hundred feet of cable. Impedance is also expressed in terms of high-Z or low-Z.

lavaliere microphone A small microphone that can be clipped onto clothing.

omnidirectional Pickup pattern in which the microphone can pick up sounds equally well from all directions.

pickup pattern The territory around the microphone within which the microphone can "hear well," that is, has optimal sound pickup.

polar pattern The two-dimensional representation of a microphone pickup pattern.

ribbon microphone A microphone whose sound pickup device consists of a ribbon that vibrates with the sound pressures within a magnetic field. Also called *velocity mic*.

shotgun microphone A highly directional microphone for picking up sounds over a great distance.

system microphone Microphone consisting of a base upon which several heads can be attached that change its sound pickup characteristic.

unidirectional Pickup pattern in which the microphone can pick up sounds better from the front than from the sides or back.

wireless microphone A system that transmits audio signals over the air, rather than through microphone cables. The mic is attached to a small transmitter, and the signals are received by a small receiver connected to the audio console or recording device.

S E C T I O N

9.1

How Microphones Hear

The *pickup* of live sounds is done through a variety of microphones. How good or bad a particular microphone is depends not only on how it is built, but especially on how it is used. Section 9.1 focuses specifically on the specific make and use of microphones.

▶ **ELECTRONIC CHARACTERISTICS OF MICROPHONES**
Sound-generating elements (dynamic, condenser, and ribbon), pickup patterns (omnidirectional and unidirectional), polar patterns, pop filter, windscreen, and system microphones

▶ **OPERATIONAL CHARACTERISTICS OF MICROPHONES**
Mobile microphones (lavaliere, hand, boom, headset, and wireless) and stationary microphones (desk, stand, hanging, hidden, and long-distance)

ELECTRONIC CHARACTERISTICS OF MICROPHONES

Choosing the most appropriate *microphone*, or *mic* (pronounced "mike"), and operating it for optimal sound pickup requires that you know about three basic electronic characteristics: (1) sound-generating element, (2) pickup patterns, and (3) special microphone features.

Sound-Generating Element

All microphones *transduce* (convert) sound waves into electric energy, which is amplified and reconverted into sound waves by the loudspeaker.

The initial conversion is accomplished by the *generating element* of the microphone. There are three major types of sound-converting systems, which are used to classify microphones: *dynamic, condenser,* and *ribbon.* Section 9.2 explores how the various types of microphones transduce sound into electrical signals.

Dynamic microphones These are the most rugged. *Dynamic microphones* can tolerate reasonably well the rough handling that television microphones frequently (though unintentionally) receive. They can be worked close to the sound source and still withstand high sound levels without damage to the microphone or excessive input overload (distortion of extremely high-volume sounds). They can also withstand fairly extreme temperatures. As you can probably guess, they are an ideal outdoor mic.

192

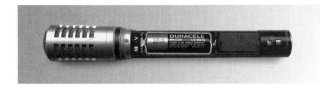

9.1 POWER SUPPLY BATTERY FOR CONDENSER MICROPHONE

Most condenser microphones are powered by a battery rather than from the console (phantom power); be sure to observe the + and − poles as indicated in the battery housing.

Condenser microphones   Compared to dynamic mics, *condenser microphones* are much more sensitive to physical shock, temperature change, and input overload, but they usually produce higher-quality sound when used at greater distances from the sound source. Some of the newer mics that are used primarily for recording songs have reverted back to electronic tubes, which, when used as preamplifiers, give the sound an exceptionally warm quality. Unlike dynamic mics, the condenser microphone (or, more precisely, the *electret condenser*) needs a small battery (AA or the rectangular 9-volt) to power its built-in preamplifier. Although these batteries last for about 1,000 hours, you should always keep spares on hand, especially if you are using condenser mics for ENG or EFP. Many times condenser mic failures can be traced to a dead or wrongly inserted battery. **SEE 9.1**

Ribbon microphone   Similar in sensitivity and quality to the condenser mics, *ribbon microphones* produce a "warmer" sound, frequently preferred by singers. Unlike condenser mics, which you may use outdoors under certain circumstances, ribbon mics are strictly indoor mics. *READY ZVL* ❷

Pickup Patterns

Whereas some microphones hear, like our ears, sounds from all directions equally well, others hear sounds better when they come from a specific direction.

The territory within which a microphone can hear well is called its *pickup pattern*; its two-dimensional representation is called the *polar pattern*, as shown in figures 9.2 through 9.4.

In television production you need to use both omnidirectional and unidirectional microphones, depending on what and how you want to hear. The *omnidirectional* microphone hears sounds from all (*omnis* in Latin) directions equally well. **SEE 9.2**   The *unidirectional* microphone hears better in one (*unus* in Latin) direction—the front of the microphone—than from its sides or back. Because the polar patterns of unidirectional microphones are roughly heart-shaped, they are called *cardioid*. **SEE 9.3**

The *supercardioid, hypercardioid,* and *ultracardioid* microphones have progressively narrower pickup patterns, which means that their hearing is more and more

9.2 OMNIDIRECTIONAL PICKUP AND POLAR PATTERNS

The omnidirectional pickup pattern is just like a small rubber ball with the mic in its center. All sounds that originate within its pickup pattern are heard by the mic without marked difference.

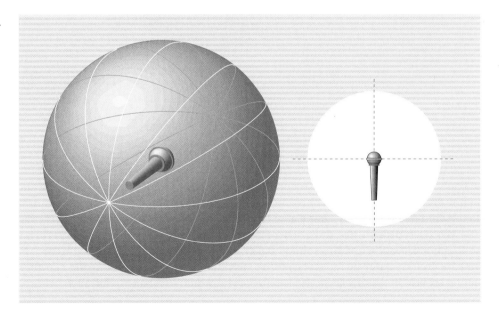

9.3 CARDIOID PICKUP AND POLAR PATTERNS

The heart-shaped pickup pattern makes the mic hear better from the front than from the sides. Sounds to its rear are virtually eliminated.

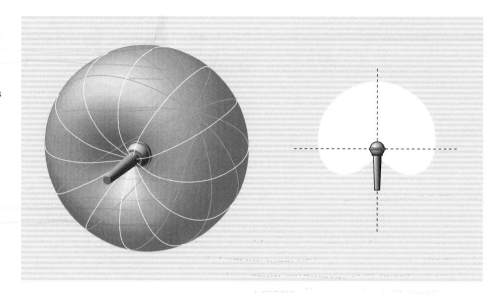

9.4 HYPERCARDIOID PICKUP AND POLAR PATTERNS

The supercardioid or hypercardioid pickup patterns narrow the sound pickup. They have a long but narrow reach in front and eliminate most sounds coming from the sides. They also hear sounds coming from the back.

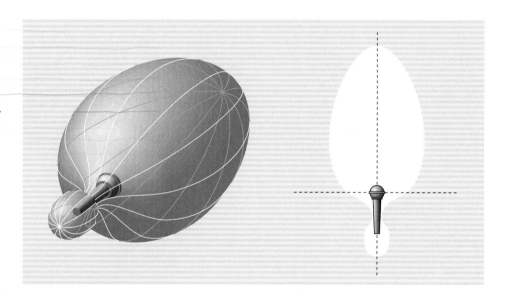

concentrated in the front. Their claim to fame is that they can hear sounds from far away and make them appear to be relatively close. These mics also hear sounds that are in back of them, but because they concentrate on hearing in one direction (a narrow path in front), they still belong to the unidirectional group. **SEE 9.4**

Which type you use depends primarily on the production situation and the sound quality required. If you are doing a stand-up report (standing in front of the actual scene) on conditions at the local zoo, you would want a rugged, omnidirectional mic that not only favors speech but also includes some of the animal sounds for authenticity. If, on the other hand, you are videotaping a singer in the studio, you should probably choose a higher-quality mic with a more directional cardioid pickup pattern. To record an intimate conversation between two soap opera characters, a hypercardioid shotgun mic is probably your best bet. Unlike the omnidirectional mic, the shotgun mic can pick up their conversation from relatively far away without losing sound presence (the closeness of the sound), while ignoring to a large extent many of the other studio noises, such as people and cameras moving about, the humming of lights, or the rumble of air conditioning. A table of the most common microphones and their characteristics is included in section 9.2 (see figure 9.34). *READY ZVL* ❸

Special Microphone Features

Microphones that are held close to the mouth have a built-in *pop filter,* which eliminates the sudden breath pops that might occur when someone speaks directly into the mic. **SEE 9.5** When used outside, all types of microphones are susceptible to wind, which they reproduce as low rumbling noises. To reduce wind noise, put a *windscreen* made of acoustic foam rubber over the microphone. **SEE 9.6** Some windscreens are made from synthetic material that resembles more a shag rug remnant than a sophisticated audio device. Whatever you use, bear in mind that the rumble of wind noise cannot be eliminated totally. The only way to have no wind noise on the videotape is to shoot when there is no wind.

To eliminate the need for several microphones with various pickup patterns, a **system microphone** has been developed, consisting of a base upon which several "heads" can be attached. These heads change the pickup pattern from omnidirectional to hypercardioid. You will find, however, that most audio engineers favor the individual mics built for specific applications.

OPERATIONAL CHARACTERISTICS OF MICROPHONES

Some microphones are designed and used primarily for sound sources that are moving, whereas others are used more for stationary sound sources. When grouped according to their actual operation, there are "mobile" and "stationary" microphones (see figure 9.34). Of course, any of the mobile mics can be used in a stationary position, and the stationary mics can be moved about if the production situation so requires.

The mobile microphones include (1) lavaliere, (2) hand, (3) boom, (4) headset, and (5) wireless, or RF mics. The stationary microphones include (1) desk, (2) stand, (3) hanging, (4) hidden, and (5) long-distance mics. Once put into place and properly aimed at the sound source, they are not moved during the show or show segment.

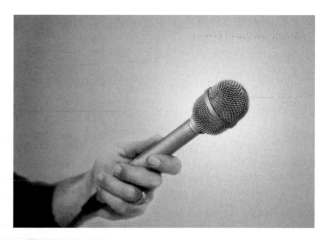

9.5 POP FILTER
The built-in pop filter eliminates breath pops.

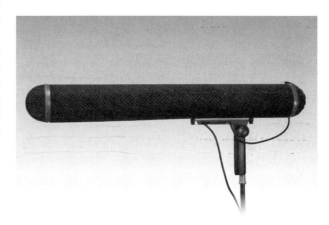

9.6 WINDSCREEN
The windscreen, normally made of acoustic foam rubber, covers the whole microphone to reduce or eliminate the low rumble of wind noise.

Lavaliere Microphones

The first of the mobile type, the **lavaliere microphone**, usually referred to as a *lav,* is probably the most frequently used on-camera microphone in television. The high-quality lavalieres range in size from a thimble to a fingernail and can be fastened to clothing with a small clip. Because of their size, they are unobtrusive and look more like jewelry than a technical device. **SEE 9.7**

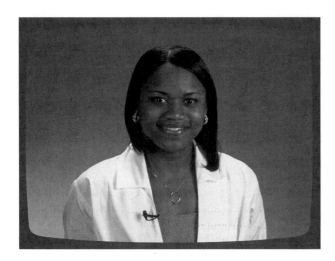

9.7 LAVALIERE MICROPHONE
This lavaliere mic is properly attached for optimal sound pickup.

The omnidirectional lavaliere microphone, with a dynamic or condenser sound-generating element, is designed primarily for voice pickup. The quality of even the smallest one is amazingly high. Once the lavaliere microphone is properly attached to the performer (approximately 6 to 8 inches below the chin, on top of the clothes and away from anything that could rub or bang against it), the sound pickup is no longer a worry. The audio engineer too has less difficulty "riding the gain" (adjusting the volume) of the lavaliere than the boom or the hand mic. Because the distance between the mic and the sound source does not change during the performance, an even sound level can be achieved more easily than with other mobile microphones.

The use of lavaliere microphones frees the lighting people from "lighting around the boom" to avoid shadows. They can concentrate more on the aesthetic subtleties of lighting as required by the scene.

Although the action radius of performers is still limited by the lavaliere cable, the cable is so light and flexible that they can move quickly and relatively unrestricted in a limited studio area without having to hold a microphone or worry about being properly followed by a boom mic. For greater mobility you can plug the lavaliere into a small transmitter and use it as a wireless mic (see figure 9.23). Despite their small size and high-quality sound pickup characteristics, lavs are durable and relatively immune to physical shock. Because lavs are so small and lightweight, some production people

unfortunately show much less concern when dropping a lav than other, larger mics. If you happen to drop a mic, check it immediately to see if it is still operational.

When to use lavaliere microphones   Here are some typical productions that use lavs as the primary microphone:

News   The lavaliere is the most efficacious sound pickup device for all types of news shows. You can also use it outdoors with a small windscreen attached for ENG/EFP.

Interviews   So long as the interview takes place in one location, the wearing of lavaliere mics by the interviewer and each guest ensures good, consistent voice pickup.

Panel shows   Rather than use desk mics, which are apt to pick up the unavoidable banging on the table, you can achieve good audio with individual lavaliere mics.

Instructional shows   In shows with a principal performer or television teacher, the lavaliere works fine so long as the instructor moves within a limited performance area (from a desk to an easel with charts, for example).

Dramas   More and more dramatic productions, especially when shot with multiple cameras in the studio, use wireless lavalieres for audio pickup. In such productions the lavs are hidden from camera view. If properly attached to the talent's clothing so that the voices do not sound muffled, a lavaliere mic seems the ideal solution to a traditionally difficult sound pickup problem. Once the levels are set, the audio engineer need do very little to keep the voices balanced. More important, the lighting director (LD) can design the lighting without worrying about boom or camera shadows.

The main problem with using lavalieres for drama is not operational, but aesthetic: Because the lavaliere mic is always at the same distance from its sound source, long shots sound exactly the same as close-ups. The unchanging mic presence does not contribute to a credible sound perspective (see chapter 10). Wireless mics are discussed in more detail later in this chapter.

ENG/EFP   The lav is often used for field reports, in which case you need to attach the windscreen. Wireless lavs are used when the field reporter needs a great deal of mobility. For example, it you talk with a farmer about the drought while walking with him in the parched field, two wireless lavs will solve the audio problem. Wireless lavs can also save you many headaches when you're asked to do the audio pickup during a tour through the newly completed community center led by the proud mayor.

Music   The lavaliere mic has been successfully used for singers (even when accompanying themselves on a guitar, for example) and for the pickup of certain instruments, such as a string bass, where it is taped below the fingerboard. In the realm of music, there is still room for experimentation; do not be too limited by convention. If the lavaliere sounds as good as or better than a larger, more expensive mic, stick to the lavaliere.

There are also some disadvantages to the lavaliere:

- The wearer cannot move the mic any closer to his mouth; consequently, if there is extraneous noise, it is easily picked up by this omnidirectional mic.

- The lavaliere can be used for only one sound source at a time—that of the particular wearer. Even for a simple interview, each participant must wear his or her own microphone. For a small discussion group, you need several.

- Although the lavaliere mic allows considerable mobility, it limits the performer's activity to some extent. When two or more performers are "wired," their movements are even more restricted. When greater mobility is desired, the lav must be connected to a wireless system.

- Because it is attached to clothing, the lavaliere tends to pick up occasional rubbing noises, especially if the performer moves around a great deal. This noise is emphasized when the microphone is concealed underneath a blouse or jacket.

- If the performer's clothes generate static electricity, the discharge may be picked up by the mic as loud, sharp pops.

- If two lavalieres are at a certain distance from each other, they may cancel out some frequencies and make the voices sound strangely "thin" (see figure 9.28).

How to use lavaliere microphones   Lavalieres are easy to use, but there are some points you need to consider.

■ Make sure to put it on. You would not be the first performer to be discovered sitting on, rather than wearing, the microphone by airtime.

■ To put on the microphone, bring it up underneath the blouse or jacket and then attach it on the outside. Clip it firmly to the clothing so that it does not rub against anything. Do not wear jewelry in proximity to the mic. If you get rubbing noises, put a piece of foam rubber between the mic and the clothing.

■ Thread the cable underneath the clothing and fasten it so that it cannot pull the microphone sideways.

■ If you must conceal the mic, do not bury it under layers of clothing; keep it as close to the surface as possible.

■ If you encounter electrostatic pops, try to treat the clothes with antistatic laundry spray, available in supermarkets. Some experts claim that by putting an actual (but loose) knot in the mic cable just below the mic, you can eliminate most of the rubbing and popping noises.

■ If you use the *dual-redundancy* microphone system (which uses two identical microphones for the sound pickup in case one fails), fasten both mics securely and use a clip designed to hold two lavalieres so that they do not touch each other.

■ Avoid hitting the microphone with any object you may be demonstrating on-camera.

■ If the lavaliere is a condenser mic, check that the battery is in good condition and installed correctly.

■ Double-check that the little transmitter is turned on (there are normally two switches—one for power and the other for the mic) and that it is turned off when leaving the set.

■ After the show, turn off the transmitter, take the microphone off, and remove the cable from under the clothing before leaving the set. Put the mic down gently.

ENG EFP When using a lavaliere outdoors, attach the windscreen. You can also make a windscreen by taping a small piece of acoustic foam or cheesecloth over the mic. Experienced EFP people claim that by covering the mic, wrapped in cheesecloth, with the tip of a child's woolen glove, the wind noise is virtually eliminated.

Hand Microphones

As the name implies, the *hand microphone* is handled by the performer. It is used in all production situations in which it is most practical, if not imperative, that the performer exercise some control over the sound pickup. Hand microphones are used extensively in ENG, where the reporter often works in the midst of much commotion and noise. In the studio or onstage, hand mics are used by singers and by performers who do audience participation shows. With the hand mic, the performer can walk up and talk at random to anyone in the audience. For singers, the hand mic is part of the act. They switch the mic from one hand to the other to visually support a transition in the song, or they caress and cuddle it during an especially tender passage.

Most important, however, the hand mic enables singers to exercise sound control. First, they can choose a hand mic whose sound reproduction suits their voice quality and style of singing. Second, they can "work" the mic during a song, holding it close to the mouth to increase the feeling of intimacy during soft passages or farther away during louder, more external ones. Third, the hand mic gives them freedom of movement, especially if it is wireless.

The wide variety of uses makes heavy demands on the performance characteristics of a hand mic. Because it is handled so much, it must be rugged and capable of withstanding physical shock. Because it is often used extremely close to the sound source, it must be insensitive to plosive breath pops and input overload distortion (see section 9.2). When used outdoors on remote locations, it must withstand rain, snow, humidity, heat, and extreme temperature changes and yet be sensitive enough to pick up the full range and subtle tone qualities of a singer's voice. Finally, it must be small enough to be handled comfortably by the performer.

Of course, no single mic can fulfill all these requirements equally, which is why some hand mics are built for outdoor use, whereas others work best in the controlled

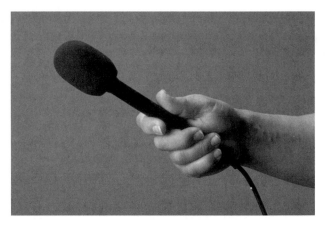

9.8 DYNAMIC HAND MICROPHONE FOR OUTDOOR USE

The hand microphone is rugged, has a built-in windscreen, and is cushioned to prevent rubbing sounds from the talent's hands.

studio environment. Normally, you should use *dynamic* mics for outdoor productions. Their built-in pop filter and sometimes even built-in windscreen produce acceptable audio even in bad weather conditions. **SEE 9.8** *Condenser* or *ribbon* mics would not fare as well outdoors but are excellent for more-demanding sound pickup, such as of singers. **SEE 9.9**

The major disadvantage of the hand microphone is what we just listed as one of its advantages: the sound control by the performer. If a performer is inexperienced

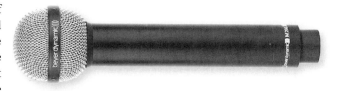

9.9 RIBBON MICROPHONE FOR QUALITY SOUND PICKUP

This ribbon microphone (Beyer 500) has a built-in pop filter and an excellent frequency response. Because of its warm tone, it is a favorite with singers. *(Note: Beyerdynamic is a trade name—not the type of microphone. The mic pictured here is a ribbon microphone.)*

in using a hand mic, he or she might produce more pops and bangs than intelligible sounds, or may, much to the dismay of the camera operator, cover the mouth or part of the face with the mic. Another disadvantage of most hand mics is that their cables can restrict movement somewhat, especially in ENG, when a field reporter is tied to the camcorder. Although wireless hand mics are successfully used in the studio, stay away from them when working outdoors. A cable is still the most reliable connection between the mic and the audio mixer or VTR.

How to use hand microphones   Working the hand mic requires dexterity and foresight. Here are some hints:

◾   Although the hand mic is fairly rugged, treat it gently. If you need both hands during a performance, do not just drop the mic; put it down gently or wedge it under your arm. If you want to impress on the performer the sensitivity of a microphone, especially that of the hand mic, turn it on to a high volume level and feed the clanks and bangs back out into the studio for the performer to hear. Even a gentle handling of the microphone produces awesome noises.

◾   Before the telecast check your action radius to see if the mic cable is long enough for your actions and laid out for maximum mic mobility. The action radius is especially important in audience participation shows, where the talent has to carry the mic into the audience, or in ENG, where the reporter is closely tied to the camcorder.

◾   Always test the microphone before the show or news report by speaking into it or lightly scratching the pop filter or windscreen. Do not blow into it.

◾   When using a directional hand mic, hold it close to your mouth at approximately a 45-degree angle to achieve optimal sound pickup. Unlike the reporter, who speaks *across* the omnidirectional hand mic, the singer sings *into* the mic. **SEE 9.10 AND 9.11**

◾   If the mic cable gets tangled, do not yank on it. Stop and try to get the attention of the floor manager.

◾   When walking a considerable distance, do not pull the cable with the mic. Tug the cable gently with one hand while holding the microphone with the other.

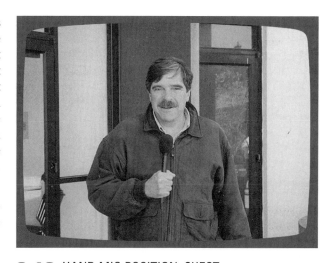

9.10 HAND MIC POSITION: CHEST
When used in a fairly quiet environment, the hand mic should be held chest high, parallel to the body.

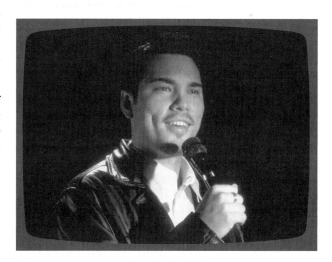

9.11 POSITION OF DIRECTIONAL HAND MIC DURING SONG
For optimal sound pickup, the singer holds the microphone close to his mouth, at approximately a 45-degree angle.

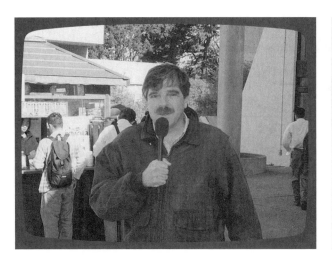

9.12 HAND MIC POSITION: MOUTH

In a noisy environment, the hand mic must be held closer to the mouth. Note that the talent is still speaking across, rather than into, the mic.

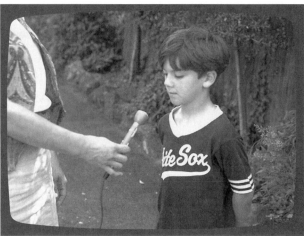

9.13 WRONG USE OF HAND MIC WITH CHILD

This is the wrong way to hold a hand mic when interviewing a child. With the interviewer standing, the camera cannot get a good two-shot.

ENG EFP When in the field, always test the microphone before the show or news report by having the camcorder operator record some of your opening remarks and then play them back for an audio check. Insist on a mic check, especially if the crew tells you not to worry because they've "done it a thousand times before"!

■ When doing a stand-up news report in the field under normal conditions (no excessively loud environment, no strong wind), hold the microphone at chest level. Speak toward the camera, across the microphone rather than into it. If the background noise is high, raise the mic closer to your mouth while still speaking across it. **SEE 9.12**

■ When interviewing someone, hold the microphone to your mouth whenever you speak and to the guest's whenever he or she answers. This obvious procedure is often unfortunately reversed by many novice performers.

■ Do not remain standing when interviewing a child. **SEE 9.13** Crouch down so that you are at the child's eye level; you can then keep the microphone close to the child in a natural way. You become a psychological equal to the child and also help the camera operator frame an acceptable picture. **SEE 9.14**

■ Always coil the mic cables immediately after use to protect the cables and have them ready for the next project.

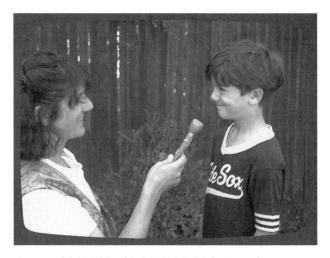

9.14 CORRECT USE OF HAND MIC WITH CHILD

This is the correct way to interview a child. The child is more at ease, and the camera operator is able to frame a better shot.

Boom Microphones

When a production, such as a dramatic scene, requires that you keep the microphone out of camera range, you need a microphone that can pick up sound over a fairly great distance while making it seem to come from close up (called *presence*) and which keeps out most of the extraneous noises surrounding the scene. The *shotgun*

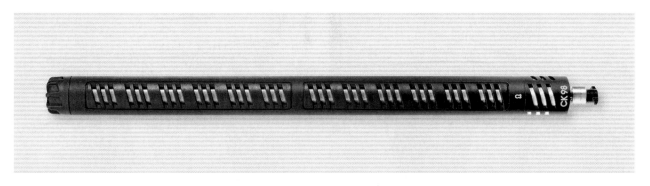

9.15 SHOTGUN MIC

The shotgun mic has a highly directional (super- or hypercardioid) pickup pattern and a far reach, permitting the pickup of sounds that are relatively far away.

microphone fills that bill. It is highly directional (supercardioid or hypercardioid) and has a far reach with little or no loss of presence. **SEE 9.15** Because it is usually suspended from some kind of boom, or is handheld with your arms acting as a "boom," we call it a *boom microphone.*

This section examines the following boom operations: (1) the handheld shotgun, (2) the fishpole boom, and (3) the giraffe, or tripod, boom. The large perambulator boom is discussed in section 9.2.

Handheld shotgun   The most common ways of using the shotgun mic in EFP or small studio productions are to hold it by hand or to suspend it from a *fishpole* boom. Both methods work fairly well for short scenes, where the microphone is to be kept out of camera range. The advantages of holding it or suspending it from a fishpole boom are: (1) The microphone is extremely flexible—you can carry it into the scene and aim it in any direction without any extraneous equipment; (2) by holding the shotgun, or by working the fishpole, you take up very little production space; and (3) you can easily work around the existing lighting setup to keep the mic shadows outside camera range.

The disadvantages are: (1) You can cover only relatively short scenes without getting tired; (2) you have to be close to the scene to get good sound pickup, which is often difficult, especially if the set is crowded; (3) if the scene is shot with multiple cameras (as in a studio production), you are often in danger of getting in the wide-shot camera view; and (4) when you are holding it, the microphone is apt to pick up some handling noises, even if you carry it by the shock mount.

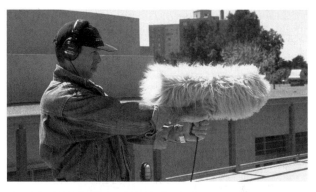

9.16 HANDHELD SHOTGUN MIC

Always hold the shotgun mic by its shock mount. When outdoors, a windscreen is mandatory. This mic has an additional "windjammer" attached.

ENG EFP **How to use shotgun microphones**   When holding the shotgun mic during a production, pay particular attention to the following points. **SEE 9.16**

▨   Always carry the shotgun mic by the shock mount. Do not carry it directly; otherwise, you end up with more handling noises than actors' dialogue.

▨   Do not cover the *ports* (openings) at the sides of the shotgun with anything but the windscreen. These ports must be able to receive sounds to keep the pickup pattern directional. Holding the mic by the shock mount minimizes the danger of covering the ports.

▨   Watch that you do not hit anything with the mic and that you do not drop it.

▨   Aim it as much as possible toward whoever is speaking, especially if you are close to the sound source.

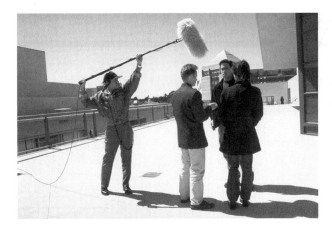

9.17 FROM-ABOVE MIC POSITION
The short fishpole is usually held as high as possible and
dipped into the scene from above.

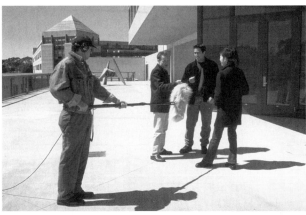

9.18 FROM-BELOW MIC POSITION
The fishpole can also be held low with the mic aimed at the
sound source from below.

▓ Always wear earphones so that you can hear what the
mic is actually picking up. Listen not only to the sound
quality of the dialogue, but also for unwanted noise. If you
hear sounds that are not supposed to be there, tell the
director about the interference immediately after the take
(from start to stop of the show segment being videotaped).

▓ Watch for unwanted mic shadows.

ENG EFP **Fishpole boom**   An extendible metal pole that
lets you mount a shotgun mic, a *fishpole* is used
mostly outdoors for EFP and ENG, but can, of course, be
used for brief scenes in the studio in place of the big
perambulator boom. You will find that a short fishpole is
relatively easy to handle, whereas working a long or fully
extended fishpole can be quite tiring, especially during
long uninterrupted takes.

ENG EFP **How to use fishpole microphones**   When
using the fishpole, many of the foregoing points
apply. Here are some more:

▓ Check that the mic is properly shock-mounted so that
it does not touch the pole or the mic cable.

▓ Fasten the mic cable properly to the pole. Some
commercially available fishpoles run the cable inside the
pole rather than outside.

▓ Hold the fishpole from either above or below the
sound source. **SEE 9.17 AND 9.18** If you are recording
two people talking to each other, point the mic at whoever
is speaking.

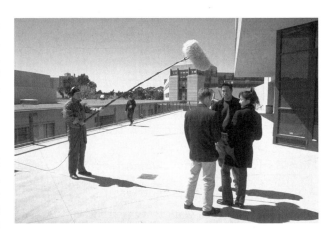

9.19 HANDLING THE LARGE FISHPOLE BOOM
The long fishpole can be anchored in the belt and raised and
lowered similar to an actual fishing pole.

▓ If the actors speak while walking, walk with them at
exactly the same speed, holding the mic in front of them
during the entire take.

▓ Watch for obstacles that may block your way, such
as cables, lights, cameras, pieces of scenery, or tree
stumps. Because you usually walk backward while
watching the actors, rehearse your walk a few times.

▓ Before each take check that you have enough mic
cable for the entire walk.

▓ If you have a long fishpole, anchor it in your belt and
lower it into the scene as though you were "fishing" for
the appropriate sound. **SEE 9.19**

9.20 GIRAFFE, OR TRIPOD, BOOM

The small giraffe boom can be repositioned through its tripod dolly. The boom can be tilted up and down and panned horizontally. The mic can be rotated to the exact pickup position.

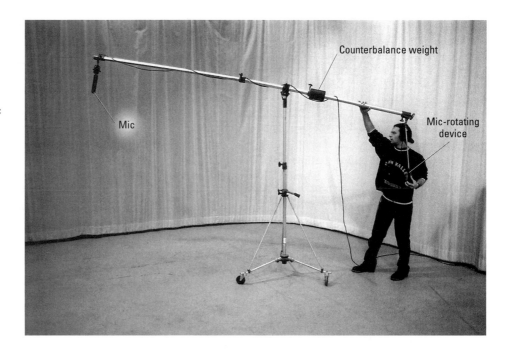

Counterbalance weight

Mic

Mic-rotating device

Giraffe, or tripod, boom Many studios use a small boom, called a *giraffe*, or *tripod, boom*. The giraffe consists of an extendible horizontal boom arm that is mounted on a tripod dolly. **SEE 9.20**

You can tilt the boom up and down and simultaneously rotate the mic in the desired direction. And you can reposition the entire boom assembly by simply pushing it. The advantages of the giraffe boom for studio work are: (1) Unlike the fishpole, you do not have to hold the boom assembly with the mic. (2) The giraffe takes up relatively little studio space. (3) Because of its low height and narrow wheelbase, you can move it easily from one studio to another through narrow doorways or hallways. (4) It can be disassembled quickly and taken to remote locations if necessary.

Unfortunately, even the giraffe is not without serious operational disadvantages: (1) The lighting must be carefully adjusted so that the boom shadows fall outside of camera view (see chapter 8). (2) Because of the considerable weight of a good shotgun mic, the extension of the relatively light giraffe boom is limited. It requires that the boom operator stand closer to the sound source, a position that tends to increase the general noise level. (3) Because the boom has to remain relatively low during operation, the risk of getting the boom or the mic in the picture is increased considerably. (4) Because of its light

weight, the boom is subject to shock and vibrations, which, despite its shock mounts, are often transferred to the microphone.

How to use boom microphones The following tips on operating the small giraffe boom also apply to the big perambulator boom. (See section 9.2 for more information on the big boom.)

▪ Try to keep the mic in front of the sound source and as low as possible without getting it in the picture. Do not ride the mic directly above the talent's head—the performer speaks from the mouth, not the top of the head.

▪ Watch the studio line monitor (which shows the picture that goes on the air or is videotaped). Try to ascertain during rehearsal how far you can dip the microphone toward the sound source without getting it or the boom in the picture. The closer the mic, the better the sound. (In boom-mic operation, you never get close enough to violate the minimum distance required of cardioid mics to avoid breath pops or similar sound distortions.) *The optimum distance for boom mics is when the talent can almost touch the mic by reaching up at about a 45-degree angle.*

▪ If the boom gets in the picture, it is better to pull it back than to raise it. By retracting, you pull the microphone out of the camera's view and at the same time keep the mic in front of, rather than above, the sound source.

◾ Watch for shadows. Even the best LD cannot avoid shadows, but can only redirect them. If the boom positions are known before the show, work with the LD to light around the major boom positions. You may sometimes have to sacrifice audio quality to avoid boom shadows.

   If you discover a boom shadow when the camera is already on the air, do not suddenly move the microphone—everyone will be sure to see the shadow travel across the screen. Rather, try to sneak it out of the picture very slowly or, better, just keep the mic and the shadow as steady as possible until a relief shot permits you to move the mic into a more advantageous position.

◾ Anticipate the movements of performers so that you can lead them with the mic rather than frantically follow them. Unless the show is very well rehearsed, do not lock the pan-and-tilt devices on the boom. If the performers rise unexpectedly, they may bump their heads on the locked microphone.

◾ Listen for good audio balance. If you have to cover two people who are fairly close together and stationary, you may achieve good audio balance by simply placing the mic between the two and keeping it there until someone moves. Favor the weaker voice by pointing the mic more toward it. More often, however, you will find that you must rotate the unidirectional mic toward whomever is talking. In fully scripted shows, the audio engineer in the booth may follow the scripted dialogue and signal the boom operator whenever the mic needs to be rotated from one actor to the other. *READY ZVL* ❹

Headset Microphones

ENG EFP The *headset microphone* consists of a small but good-quality omni- or unidirectional mic attached to earphones. One of the earphones carries the program sound (whatever sounds the headset mic picks up or is fed from the station), and the other carries the cues and instructions of the director or producer. Headset mics are used in certain EFP situations, such as sports reporting, or in ENG from a helicopter or convention floor. The headset mic isolates you sufficiently from the outside world so that you can concentrate on your specific reporting job in the midst of much noise and commotion, while at the same time keeping your hands free to shuffle

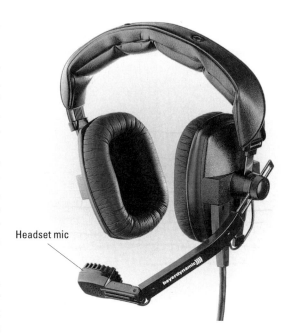

Headset mic

9.21 HEADSET MICROPHONE

The headset mic is similar to an ordinary telephone headset, except that it has a higher-quality microphone.

papers, grab people for an interview, pilot a helicopter, or even run a camera. **SEE 9.21**

Wireless Microphones

ENG EFP In production situations in which complete and unrestricted mobility of the sound source is required, *wireless microphones* are used. If, for example, you are recording a group of singers who are also dancing, or if you are asked to pick up a skier's groans, breathing, and the clatter of the skis on a downhill course, the wireless mic is the obvious choice. Wireless mics are also used extensively for newscasts, EFP, and occasionally for multicamera studio productions of dramatic shows.

   Wireless mics actually *broadcast* their signals. They are therefore also called *RF (radio frequency) mics* or *radio mics*. Wireless microphones come as either hand or lavaliere mics. The battery-powered transmitter of the wireless hand mic is built into the microphone itself. Some models have a short antenna protruding from the bottom of the mic, but most have the antenna incorporated into the microphone housing. **SEE 9.22**

   The wireless lavaliere mic is connected to a small battery-powered transmitter that is either worn in the hip

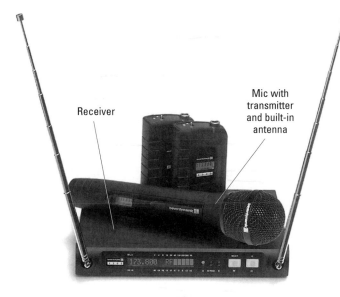

9.22 WIRELESS HAND MIC AND RECEIVER
The wireless hand mic normally has the transmitter built into the housing. The antenna is either built into the mic or sticks out at the bottom. Lavaliere mics have a separate transmitter that is worn by the talent. The receiver picks up the signal and sends it via ordinary mic cable to the audio console. The receiver is tuned to the frequency of the hand mic's transmitter.

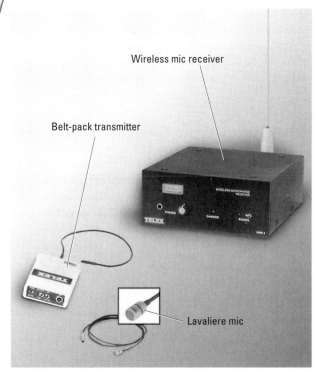

9.23 WIRELESS LAVALIERE MIC AND RECEIVER
Wireless lavaliere mic has a separate transmitter that is worn by the talent. The receiver picks up the mic's signal and routes it via ordinary mic cable to the audio mixer or console.

pocket or taped to the body. The antenna is strung inside the clothing and/or around the waist.

The other important element of the wireless microphone system is the receiver. **SEE 9.23** The receiver tunes into the frequency of the wireless transmitter and can receive the signal from as far as 1,000 feet (approximately 330 meters) under favorable conditions. When conditions are more adverse, the range may shrink to about 100 feet (about 33 meters). To ensure optimal signal reception, you can set up several receiving stations in the studio as well as in the field. When tuned to the same frequency, one receiver can take over when the signal from the other gets weak. This is called *diversity reception*.

The wireless mic works best in the controlled environment of a studio or stage, where you can determine the precise range of the performer's movements and find the optimal position for the receiver(s). More and more singers prefer working with the wireless hand mic because it affords them unrestricted movement. It is also useful in audience participation shows, where the performer walks into the audience for brief unplanned interviews. The wireless lavaliere mic has been used

successfully for musicals and dramatic shows and, of course, in many ENG/EFP situations.

Despite the obvious advantages of using wireless mics, there are also some major disadvantages:

■ The signal pickup can be quite uneven, especially if the sound source moves over a fairly great distance and through hilly terrain—a skier, for example. If you do not have line of sight between the transmitter (on the performer) and the receiver, you may encounter fades and even occasional dropouts. Diversity reception, which uses multiple receivers, is a must in such situations.

■ The perspiration of the person wearing the transmitter can reduce signal strength, as does, of course, the increasing distance from transmitter to receiver.

■ Large metal objects, high-voltage lines and transformers, X-ray machines, microwave transmissions, and cellular phones can all interfere with the proper reception of the wireless-mic signal.

▓ Although most wireless equipment offers several frequency channels, there is still some danger of picking up extraneous signals, especially if the receiver is not tuned accurately or if it operates in the proximity of other strong radio signals. Interference is evident by pops, thumps, signal dropouts, and even the pickup of police emergency calls.

▓ Even if you use several wireless mics, they need to be fed into a mixer for audio control.

How to use wireless microphones   The basic operational techniques of the wireless mic are identical to those of the wired lavaliere and hand microphones, but here are some additional points to consider:

▓ Always install new batteries before each shoot—and carry plenty of spares. With a weak battery, the upper frequencies of a tone start to sound thin.

▓ The transmitter antenna must always be fully extended. You can tie one end of a rubber band to the tip of the antenna and tape the other end to the clothing of the performer. That will keep the antenna fully extended while preventing it from being snapped off its connector when the wearer moves. Try to keep the antenna from touching the skin, because excessive moisture can interfere with the signal.

▓ If you must tape the transmitter to the body, avoid attaching the tape directly to the skin, unless you use "ouchless" tape. You can also use an elastic bandage to keep the transmitter in place.

▓ Position the receiver(s) so that there are no blind spots (ideally in line of sight with the transmitter at all times).

▓ Always test the sound pickup over the entire range of the sound source. Watch for possible interfering signals or objects.

Desk Microphones

As the name implies, *desk microphones* are usually put on tables or desks. These stationary mics are widely used in panel shows, public hearings, speeches, press conferences, and all other programs where the performer is speaking from behind a desk, table, or lectern. These mics are used for voice pickup only. Because the performer behind the desk is usually doing something—shuffling papers, putting things on the desk, accidentally bumping the desk with feet or knees—desk microphones must be

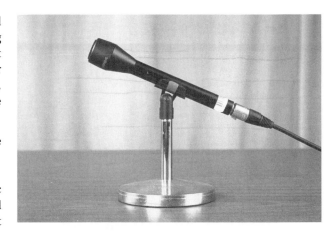

9.24 DESK MICROPHONE ON DESK STAND
In television production, desk mics are usually hand mics clipped to a desk stand.

rugged and able to withstand physical shock. Dynamic, omnidirectional microphones are generally used. If a high separation of sound sources is desired, however, unidirectional mics are used as well. Generally, most hand mics double as desk mics—all you do is place them in a desk stand or mount them on a gooseneck floor stand and position them for optimal sound pickup. **SEE 9.24**

Boundary microphone   One type of desk mic is the *boundary microphone* or, as it is commonly called, the *pressure zone microphone (PZM).*[1] These mics look quite different from ordinary microphones and operate on a different principle. **SEE 9.25**

The boundary microphone is mounted or positioned close to a reflecting surface, such as a table or a plastic plate accessory. **SEE 9.26** When placed into this sound "pressure zone," the microphone receives both the direct and the reflected sounds concurrently. Under optimal conditions the PZM produces a clearer sound than ordinary microphones. Its chief advantage, however, is that it can be used for the simultaneous voice pickup of several people with equal fidelity. Boundary mics have a wide, hemispheric pickup pattern and are therefore well suited for large group discussions and audience reactions. You can, for example, simply place the PZM on a table and achieve a remarkably good pickup of the people sitting around it. Unfortunately, when used as a table mic, the PZM also picks up paper rustling, finger tapping, and the thumps of people knocking against the table.

---

1. PZM is a trademark of Crown International, Inc.

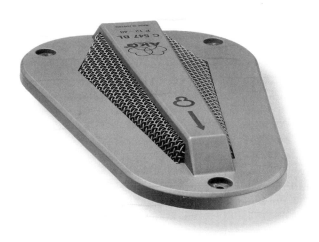

9.25 BOUNDARY, OR
PRESSURE ZONE, MICROPHONE
This mic must be mounted or put on a reflecting surface to
build up the "pressure zone" at which all sound waves reach
the mic at the same time.

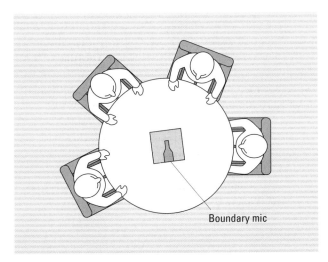

9.26 BOUNDARY MICROPHONE
USED FOR MULTIPLE PICKUP
With the boundary microphone in the middle of the table, the
sound pickup is equal for all people sitting around the table.

How to use desk microphones　Desk mics, like
peanuts, seem to be irresistible—not that performers
want to eat them, but when sitting or standing behind a
desk mic, they feel compelled to grab it and pull it toward
them, no matter how carefully you might have positioned

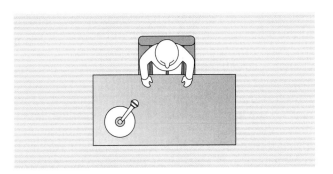

9.27 DESK MICROPHONE
PLACEMENT FOR SINGLE PERFORMER
The desk mic should be placed to the side of the talent and
aimed at the talent's collarbone so that he or she speaks
across, rather than into, it. If the talent uses a monitor, put
the mic on the monitor side.

it. Polite or not-so-polite requests not to touch the mic
seem futile. Sooner or later the talent will move the mic.
To counter this habit, consider taping the mic stand to
the table, or at least tape the microphone cable securely
and unobtrusively so that the mic can be moved only a
short distance.

As with the hand mic, no attempt is made to conceal
the desk mic from the viewer. Nevertheless, when placing
it on a desktop or lectern, you should consider the camera
picture as well as optimal sound pickup. Performers
certainly appreciate it if the camera shows more of them
than the microphone. If the camera shoots from straight
on, place the mic somewhat to the side of the performer
and point it at his or her collarbone rather than mouth,
giving a reasonably good sound pickup while allowing
the camera a clear shot of the performer's face. **SEE 9.27**

When integrating the mic most unobtrusively in the
picture, do not forget about the mic cable. Even if the
director assures you that the mic cable on the floor will
never be seen, don't bet on it. Try to string the cable as
neatly and unobtrusively as possible and use gaffer's or
black masking tape to secure it to the desk and floor. The
viewer inevitably interprets a shot that shows cable
"spaghetti" as inefficiency and sloppiness, regardless of
the overall quality of the show.

Here are a few more tips on using a desk mic:

■　When using two desk mics for the same speaker as a
dual-redundancy precaution, use identical mics and place
them as close together as possible. As noted, *dual-
redundancy* is the rather clumsy term for using two mics

for a single sound source so that you can switch from one to the other in case one fails. Do not activate them at the same time unless you are feeding separate audio channels. If both mics are on at the same time, you may experience *multiple-microphone interference*. When two mics are close to each other yet far enough apart that they pick up the identical sound source at slightly different times, they can cancel out certain sound frequencies, giving the sound a strangely thin quality. If you must activate both mics at the same time, place them as close to each other as possible so that they receive the sound simultaneously.

■ When using desk mics for a panel discussion, do not give each member a separate mic unless they sit far apart. Using one mic for two panel members not only saves mics and setup time, but also minimizes multiple-microphone interference. *Place the mics so that they are at least three times as far apart as any mic is from its user.* **SEE 9.28**

■ Position the microphones to achieve optimal sound pickup from all participants. Finalize the mic positions only after having seen the total panel setup and the interaction of the members. Participants will not only respond to the moderator, but also talk among themselves, turning in opposite directions. Place the mics so that one mic will pick up a panel member addressing a person on the left, and the other mic for addressing a person on the right.

■ Although almost a lost cause, remind the panel members—or anyone working with a desk mic—not to reposition it once it is set and to avoid banging on the table or kicking the lectern, even if the discussion gets lively. Tell participants not to lean into the mics when speaking.

■ When two people sit opposite each other, give each one a mic.

ENG EFP When on an ENG assignment, always carry a small desk stand along. You can then use the hand mic, or even the shotgun mic, usually clipped to the camera, as a desk mic. A clamp-on mic holder with a gooseneck is very handy, especially when adding your mic to a cluster of other mics on a speaker's lectern during a news conference.

Stand Microphones

Stand microphones are used whenever the sound source is fixed and the type of programming permits them to be seen. For example, there is no need to conceal the microphones of a rock group; on the contrary, they are an important show element. You are certainly familiar with the great many ways rock performers handle the stand mic. Some tilt it, lift it, lean against it, hold themselves up by it, and, when the music rocks with especially high intensity, even swing it through the air like a sword (not recommended, by the way).

9.28 MULTIPLE-MICROPHONE SETUP
When using a multiple-microphone setup, keep the individual mics at least three times as far apart as the distance any mic is from its user.

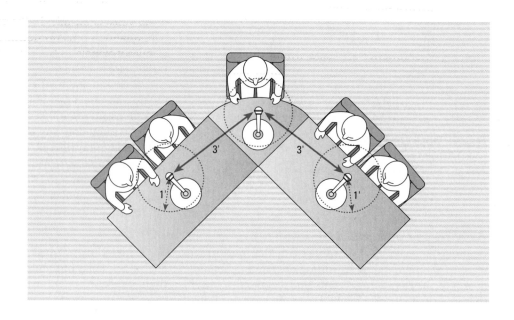

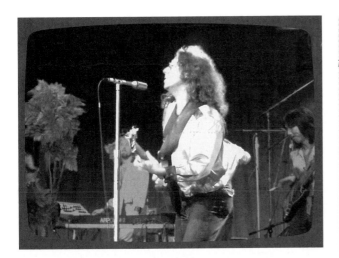

9.29 STAND MIC FOR SINGER
The singer stands in front of the stand mic and sings directly into it.

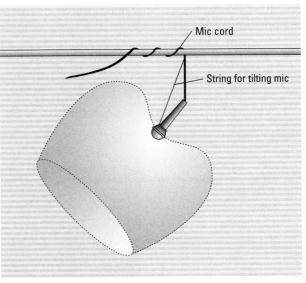

Mic cord

String for tilting mic

9.30 HANGING-MICROPHONE AUDIO POOL
Hanging microphones are high-quality unidirectional mics that are normally suspended from the lighting grid. The talent must remain in its "audio pool" to be properly heard.

The quality of stand mics ranges from dynamic hand mics clipped to a stand to highly sensitive condenser mics used exclusively for music recording sessions.

How to use stand microphones　Stand mics are usually placed in front of the sound source, regardless of whether the source is a singer or an amplifier of an electric guitar. **SEE 9.29**　In some cases, such as for the pickup of a singer using an acoustic guitar, you may attach two microphones to a single stand.

Hanging Microphones

Hanging microphones are used whenever any other concealed-microphone method (boom or fishpole) is impractical. You can hang the mics (high-quality cardioid, but also lavalieres) by their cables over any fairly stationary sound source. Most often, hanging mics are used in dramatic presentations where the action is fully blocked so that the actors are in a precise location for each delivery of lines. A favorite spot for hanging mics is the upstage door (at the back of the set), from which the actors deliver their hellos and good-byes when entering or leaving the major performance area. The boom can generally not reach that far to adequately pick up the actors' voices. The actors have to take care to speak only within the "audio pool" of the hanging microphone. Similar to the spotlight pool, where the actors are visible only as long as they move within the limited circle of light,

they are heard only when they are within the limited range of the audio pool. **SEE 9.30**

The sound quality from hanging mics is not necessarily the best. The sound source is always relatively far away from the microphone, and if the performer is not precisely within the audio pool (the pickup pattern), his or her voice is off-mic. In the case of the upstage door, such quality loss is no detriment but rather an asset, because it signals a physical and psychological distance of the person departing. Unfortunately, hanging mics have the annoying tendency to pick up the shuffling of feet and the rumbling of moving camera pedestals almost as well as the voices. A further disadvantage is that the light cables may cause a hum in the audio pickup.

Hanging mics are nevertheless popular in dramas, studio productions, and audience participation shows. They are easy to set up and take down and, when in the right positions, produce acceptable sound.

You may find that a single suspended boundary mic (PZM) will meet the audio requirements better than several regular hanging mics. Mount it on a sound-reflecting board (such as 3- by 4-foot Plexiglas or plywood), suspend it above and in front of the general sound-generating area (such as an audience area), and

9.31 PZM USED AS HANGING MIC

When using a PZM (boundary mic) as a hanging microphone, mount it on an additional sound-reflecting board and angle it toward the sound source for optimal pickup. The shotgun mics are for the host and guests' audio pickup.

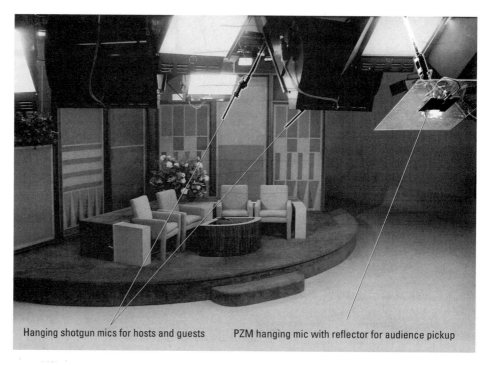

Hanging shotgun mics for hosts and guests   PZM hanging mic with reflector for audience pickup

angle the reflecting board for optimal pickup. **SEE 9.31** Regardless of whether the sound source is near the PZM or farther away, the sounds still have good presence. This positive aspect turns negative in dramatic productions, where sound *perspective* (close-ups sound closer and long shots sound farther away) is an important factor. This is one of the reasons why in complex productions the boom is still preferred over the PZM.

How to use hanging microphones Although no particular skill is required for hanging a mic, here are some tips:

■ Hang the mic as low as possible to get reasonably good presence. Use tape or fishing line to tilt the mic somewhat toward speakers or musicians (see figure 9.30).

■ If necessary, mark the studio floor for the actor at the spot of the best sound pickup.

■ Secure the mic cable sufficiently so that the mic does not come crashing down. A small piece of gaffer's tape will do the trick.

■ Separate the mic cables as much as possible from the light, or any other power, cables. If that is not possible,

cross the mic and power cables at right angles to minimize electronic interference.

■ Do not place the mic next to a hot lighting instrument.

■ Be especially careful when striking (taking down) hanging microphones. Do not drop the mic or the cable connectors onto the studio floor or, worse, somebody's head.

■ Do not inadvertently hit hanging mics against ladders, lighting poles, or lighting instruments.

Hidden Microphones

You may sometimes find that you need to hide a small lavaliere microphone in a bouquet of flowers, behind a centerpiece, or in a car, to pick up a conversation during studio productions or in EFP where microphones should be out of camera range. **SEE 9.32**

Realize that it is quite time-consuming to place a hidden mic so that it yields a satisfactory pickup. Often you get a marvelous pickup of various noises caused by people hitting the table or moving their chairs, but only a poor pickup of their conversation. Worse, if hidden mics are too close to hardwall scenery, the set may act as an echo chamber and produce considerable sound distortion.

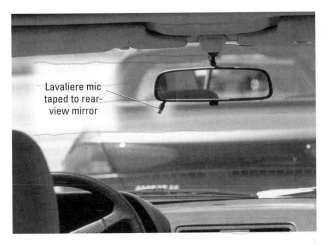

9.32 LAVALIERE AS HIDDEN MIC

This "hidden" lavaliere microphone is attached to the rear-view mirror to pick up the conversation inside the car. Note that the mic is not covered, to ensure optimal sound pickup.

Again, the PZM can serve as an efficient "hidden" mic, especially because it looks nothing like an ordinary mic. You may get away with not hiding it at all; simply place it on a table among other eclectic objects.

How to use hidden microphones   Hiding mics seems to present unexpected problems. These tips may minimize or eliminate some of them:

▓   Try to shock-mount the lavaliere so that it does not transfer unintentional hanging noises. Use the lavaliere clip or put some foam rubber between the mic and the object to which it is attached.

▓   Do not try to conceal the mic completely, unless there is an extreme close-up of the object to which it is attached.

▓   Realize that you must hide not only the microphone, but the cable as well.

▓   Secure the microphone and cable with tape so that they do not come loose. The setup must withstand the rigors of the rehearsals and the videotaping sessions.

▓   If cables are a problem, you can use a wireless lavaliere and hide the transmitter in some appropriate place.

▓   Do not hide a mic in such enclosed spaces as empty drawers or boxes. The highly reflecting enclosure will act as a small reverberation chamber and make the voices sound as though the actors themselves were trapped in the drawer.

Long-distance Microphones

You may hear of long-distance microphones, especially in relation to sports coverage. We have finally realized that it is often the sounds more than the pictures that carry and communicate the energy of a sport. The simplest way to pick up the sound at a sporting event, such as a tennis match or a hockey game, is to place normal shotgun (hypercardioid) mics at strategic positions and aim them at the main action.

Coverage of a single tennis match may involve six or more microphones to pick up the sounds of the players, the judges, and the crowd. Place a fairly dense windscreen on every long-distance mic to eliminate wind noises as much as possible. An old-fashioned but successful means of picking up sounds over fairly long distances is the *parabolic reflector microphone,* which consists of a small parabolic dish (similar to a satellite dish) that has an omnidirectional microphone facing inward at its focal point. All incoming sounds are reflected toward and concentrated at the mic. **SEE 9.33**

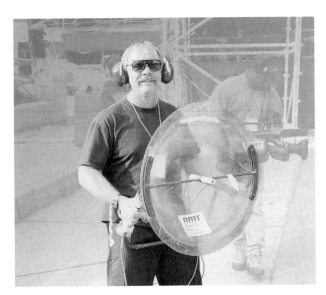

9.33 PARABOLIC REFLECTOR MICROPHONE

The parabolic reflector mic is used primarily for sound pickup over long distances, such as crowd noises in a stadium.

The parabolic reflector mic is often used to pick up voices over long distances, such as the signals of the quarterback during a football game or the enthusiastic chanting of a group of home-team fans. Because the parabolic reflector directs the higher sound frequencies to the mic better than the lower ones, the sounds take on a slight telephonic tone. We tend to ignore this impaired sound quality, however, when the mic is used primarily for ambient (surrounding) sounds that communicate the feel of an event (such as a football game), rather than precise information.

MAIN POINTS

◆ Audio is the sound portion of a television show. It transmits specific information (such as a news story), helps establish the specific time and locale of the action, contributes to the mood, and provides continuity for the various picture portions.

◆ The three major types of microphones are dynamic, condenser, and ribbon. Each type has a different sound-generating element that converts sound waves into electric energy—the audio signal.

◆ Some microphones can hear sounds equally well from all directions; others hear better from a specific direction.

◆ Microphones are classified according to their operation and are either mobile or stationary. The mobile types include lavaliere, hand, boom, headset, and wireless microphones. The stationary types are desk, stand, hanging, hidden, and long-distance microphones.

◆ The lavaliere microphone, or lav for short, is the most common in small studio operations. It is usually clipped to clothing. Although it is extremely small, it provides high-quality sound reproduction.

◆ Hand microphones are used when the performer needs to exercise some control over the sound pickup.

◆ When the microphone must be kept out of camera range, it is usually mounted on and operated from a fishpole or microphone boom. All boom mics are highly directional.

◆ The headset microphone is used when the talent needs both hands free to take notes or work with scripts. Sports announcers usually use headset microphones. They are practical for sportscasting or for ENG from a helicopter or convention floor.

◆ When unrestricted mobility of the sound source is required, a wireless, or RF (radio frequency), microphone is used. Wireless mics need a transmitter and receiver.

◆ Desk microphones are simply hand mics clipped to a desk stand. They are often used for panel discussions.

◆ Stand microphones are employed whenever the sound source is fixed and the type of programming permits the mics to be seen by the camera, such as in rock music concerts.

◆ Hanging microphones are popular in some studio productions because the mics are kept out of camera range without using booms.

◆ Hidden microphones are small lavaliere mics concealed behind or within set dressings.

◆ Long-distance mics are shotgun or parabolic reflector mics that pick up sound over relatively great distances.

9.2

How Microphones Work

Section 9.1 examined sound pickup and the electronic and operational characteristics of microphones. This section takes a closer look at how sound-generating elements work, as well as at mic and line inputs and what connectors to use. It also explores further considerations of microphone use in ENG/EFP and in the studio.

▶ **SOUND-GENERATING ELEMENTS**
The diaphragm and the sound-generating element within dynamic, condenser, and ribbon microphones

▶ **SPECIFIC MICROPHONE FEATURES**
High and low impedance, frequency response, flat response, balanced and unbalanced mics and cables, and audio connectors

▶ **MIC SETUPS FOR MUSIC PICKUP**
Possible setups for various musical events

▶ **MICROPHONE USE SPECIFIC TO ENG/EFP**
Ambient sounds and line-out tie-in

▶ **MICROPHONE USE SPECIFIC TO THE STUDIO**
The big, or perambulator, boom

SOUND-GENERATING ELEMENTS

Simply speaking, microphones convert one type of energy to another—sound waves to electric energy. But the particular process each mic uses to accomplish this conversion determines its quality and use. All microphones have a diaphragm, which vibrates with the sound pressures, and a sound-generating element, which transduces (changes) the physical vibrations of the diaphragm into electric energy.

Dynamic Microphones

In the *dynamic* microphone, the diaphragm is attached to a coil—the *voice coil.* When someone speaks into the mic, the diaphragm vibrates with the air pressure from the sound and makes the voice coil move back and forth within a magnetic field. This action produces a fluctuating electric current which, when amplified, transmits the vibrations to the cone of a speaker, making the sound audible again. Because of this physical process, dynamic mics are sometimes called *moving-coil microphones.*

Because the diaphragm-voice coil element is physically rugged, the microphone can withstand and accurately translate high sound levels or other air blasts close to the microphone.

Condenser Microphones

In the *condenser* microphone, also called *electret* or *capacitor* microphone, the movable diaphragm constitutes one of the two plates necessary for a condenser to function. The other, called the backplate, is fixed. Because the diaphragm moves with the air vibrations against the fixed backplate, the capacitance of this condenser is continuously changed, thus modulating the electric current. The major advantage of the condenser microphone over other types is its extremely wide *frequency response* and pickup sensitivity. But this sensitivity is also one of its disadvantages. If placed close to high-intensity sound sources, such as the high-output speakers of a rock band, it overloads and distorts the incoming sound—a condition known as *input overload distortion.* The condenser is a superior recording mic, however, especially when used under the highly controlled conditions of studio recording. You will find that some high-quality lavalieres are condenser rather than dynamic microphones.

Ribbon Microphones

In the *ribbon* or *velocity* microphone, a very thin metal ribbon vibrates within a magnetic field, serving the function of the diaphragm-voice coil element. The ribbon is so fragile, however, that even moderate physical shocks to the microphone, or sharp air blasts close to it, can damage and even destroy the instrument. When it is used outdoors, even the wind moves the ribbon and thus produces a great amount of noise. You should not use this kind of mic outdoors or in production situations that require its frequent movement. A good ribbon mic is nevertheless an excellent recording mic, even in television productions. Although it has a low tolerance of high sound levels, the delicate ribbon responds well to a wide frequency range and reproduces with great fidelity the subtle nuances of tone color, especially in the bass range.

Sound Quality

Semiprofessional mics do not have as wide a frequency response as high-quality microphones, which means that high-quality mics can hear higher and lower sounds than the less expensive models. (Frequency response is discussed in depth later in this section.) Other, less definable quality factors are whether a microphone produces especially "warm" or "crisp" sounds. For example, many singers prefer working with a ribbon mic because it produces such a warm sound. Do not be misled by specifications, "professional" and "semiprofessional" labels, or the personal preferences of singers or sound engineers. Listen carefully and use whatever microphone gives you the sound you want.

The type of mic to use depends on such a variety of factors that specific suggestions would probably be more confusing than helpful at this stage.[2] For example, studio acoustics, the type and combination of instruments used, and the aesthetic quality of the desired sound all play important parts in the choice and placement of microphones. In general, rugged dynamic—omnidirectional or cardioid—mics are used for high-volume sound sources such as drums, electric guitars, and some singers; whereas condenser or ribbon mics are used for the more-gentle sound sources, such as strings and acoustic guitars. Figures 9.36 through 9.38 give some common mic setups. The microphone table shows some of the more popular mics and their most common use. **SEE 9.34**

SPECIAL MICROPHONE FEATURES

When working with audio equipment, you will probably hear some terms that are not self-explanatory: *high-* and *low-impedance* mics, *flat response,* and *balanced* and *unbalanced* mics and cables. Although these features are quite technical in nature, you need to know at least their operational requirements.

Impedance

When working with sound equipment, you have to watch that the impedance of the microphone and the recorder match. **Impedance** is a type of resistance to the signal flow. You can have high-impedance (sometimes abbreviated *high-Z*) and low-impedance *(low-Z)* microphones. A high-impedance microphone (usually the less expensive and lower-quality mics) works only with a relatively short cable (a longer cable has too much resistance), whereas a low-impedance mic (all high-quality professional mics) can take up to several hundred feet of cable. If you must feed a low-impedance recorder with a high-impedance mic or vice versa, you need an *impedance transformer.* Many electric instruments, such as an electric guitar, have a high-impedance output. In order for them to match up with low-impedance equipment, they have to be routed through a "direct box"—a box that contains the transformer-like electronics that adjust the high-impedance signal to a low-impedance one.

---

2. See Stanley Alten, *Audio in Media,* 5th ed. (Belmont, Calif.: Wadsworth Publishing Co., 1994), pp. 368–428.

9.34 TABLE OF MICROPHONES

MICROPHONE	ELEMENT TYPE *PICKUP PATTERN*	CHARACTERISTICS	USE
S H O T G U N M I C — L O N G			
Sennheiser MKH 70	Condenser *Supercardioid*	Excellent reach and presence, there-fore excellent distance mic. Extremely directional. Quite heavy when held on extended fishpole.	Boom, fishpole, handheld. Best for EFP and sports remotes to capture sounds over considerable distances.
S H O T G U N M I C S — S H O R T			
Sennheiser MKH 60	Condenser *Supercardioid*	Good reach and wider pickup pattern than long shotguns. Less presence over long distances, but requires less precise aiming at sound source. Lighter and easier to handle than long shotgun mics.	Boom, fishpole, handheld. Especially good for EFP indoor use.
Neumann KMR 81 i	Condenser *Supercardioid*	Slightly less reach than the MKH 60, but has warmer sound.	Boom, fishpole, handheld. Especially good for EFP indoor use. Excellent dialogue mic.
Sony ECM 672	Condenser *Supercardioid*	Highly focused, but slightly less presence than long shotguns.	Boom, fishpole, handheld. Especially good for EFP indoor use.

9.34 TABLE OF MICROPHONES *(continued)*

MICROPHONE	ELEMENT TYPE / PICKUP PATTERN	CHARACTERISTICS	USE
HAND, DESK, AND STAND MICS			
Electro-Voice 635N/D	Dynamic / *Omnidirectional*	An improved version of the classic 635A. Has good voice pickup that seems to know how to differentiate between voice and ambience. Extremely rugged. Can tolerate rough handling and extreme outdoor conditions.	Excellent mic (and therefore standard) for all-weather ENG and EFP reporting assignments.
Electro-Voice RE50	Dynamic / *Omnidirectional*	Similar to the E-V 635N/D. Rugged. Internal shock mount and blast filter.	Good, reliable desk and stand mic. Good for music pickup, such as vocals, guitar, and drums.
Beyerdynamic M58	Dynamic / *Omnidirectional*	Smooth frequency response, bright sound. Rugged. Internal shock mount. Low handling noise.	Good ENG/EFP mic. Especially designed as an easy-to-use hand mic.
Shure SM57	Dynamic / *Cardioid*	Good-quality frequency response. Can stand fairly high input volume.	Good for music, vocals, electric guitars, keyboard instruments, and even drums.
Beyerdynamic M160	Ribbon / *Hypercardioid*	Sensitive mic with excellent frequency response. Can tolerate fairly high input volume.	Especially good for all sorts of music pickup, such as strings, brass, and piano. Also works well as a stand mic for voice pickup.
Beyerdynamic M600	Dynamic / *Hypercardioid*	Similar in smoothness to the classic Beyer 500 ribbon mic, but a little more rugged. Highly directional.	Good vocal mic. Very good for a variety of music and voice recordings. Especially good for all stand mic functions.
AKG D112	Dynamic / *Cardioid*	Rugged. Specially built for high-energy percussive sound.	For close miking of kick drum.

9.34 TABLE OF MICROPHONES *(continued)*

MICROPHONE	ELEMENT TYPE *PICKUP PATTERN*	CHARACTERISTICS	USE
LAVALIERE MICS			
Sony ECM 55	Condenser *Omnidirectional*	Excellent presence. Produces close-up sounds. But, because of this excellent presence, does not mix well with boom mics, which are normally farther away from the sound source.	Excellent for voice pickup in a controlled environment (studio interviews, studio news, and presentations).
Sennheiser MKE 102	Condenser *Omnidirectional*	Mixes well with boom mics. Excellent, smooth overall sound pickup. However, it is very sensitive to clothes noise and even rubbing of cable. Must be securely fastened to avoid rubbing noises.	Excellent for most lavaliere uses. Works well as concealed mic.
Sony ECM 77	Condenser *Omnidirectional*	Highly directional. Isolates most ambient noise when used for speech pickup in noisy surroundings. High directionality can be a problem when mic shifts from original point. Blends well with boom mic. Mic and cable are quite sensitive to rubbing on clothes. Must be securely fastened.	Excellent pickup of all sounds. Good for concealed mic use and even for the pickup of some musical instruments.
Professional Sound PSC MilliMic	Condenser *Omnidirectional*	Extremely small, yet has excellent pickup quality. Blends well with boom mics. Well shielded against electro-magnetic interference.	Excellent as concealed mic for interviews, dramas, and documen-taries. Works well outdoors.

Frequency Response

The ability of a microphone to hear extremely high and low sounds is known as the *frequency response*. A good microphone hears better than most humans and has a frequency range of 20 to 20,000 Hz (hertz, which measures cycles per second). Many high-quality mics are built to hear equally well over the entire frequency range, a feature called *flat response*. High-quality mics generally have a high frequency range and a flat response.

Balanced and Unbalanced Mics and Cables, and Audio Connectors

All professional microphones have a *balanced* output that is connected by three-wire microphone cables to a balanced input at recorders and mixers. Two of the wires carry essentially the same audio signal (but out of phase), and the third wire is a shield that acts as a ground. The balanced line rejects hum and other electronic interference. All balanced (three-wire) microphones and mic cables use three-pronged connectors, called *XLR connectors*.

When working with semiprofessional equipment, you may come across *unbalanced* mics and cables that use only two wires to carry the signals: one for the audio signal and the other for the ground. These unbalanced lines use a variety of two-wire connectors: the *phone plug*, the *RCA phono plug*, and the *mini plug*. **SEE 9.35** *READY ZVL* ⑤

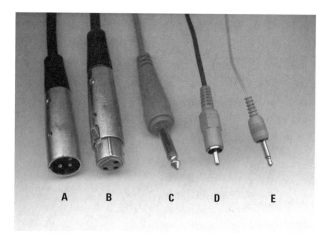

9.35 AUDIO CONNECTORS
Balanced audio cables use XLR connectors (**A** and **B**); unbalanced cables use the phone plug (**C**), RCA phono plug (**D**), and the mini plug (**E**).

The problem with unbalanced (two-wire) mics and lines is that they are much more susceptible to hum and other electronic noise than the balanced mics and lines. There are adapters that enable you to connect an XLR to the unbalanced connectors or vice versa. Note, however, that *every adapter is a potential trouble spot*. If at all possible, try to find a mic cable with the appropriate connector already attached.

Mic Setups for Music Pickup

The following suggestions of how to mike musical events should be taken with a grain of salt. Any two audio experts would rarely agree on just how a musical event should be miked and what mics to use. Nevertheless, the suggested setups will help you get started.

The sound pickup of an instrumental group, such as a rock band, is normally accomplished with several stand microphones. These are placed in front of each speaker that emits the amplified sound of a particular instrument or in front of unamplified sound sources, such as singers and drums. The microphone to use depends on such factors as studio acoustics, the type and combination of instruments, and the aesthetic quality of the desired sound.[3]

Generally, the rugged dynamic, omnidirectional, or cardioid mics are used for high-volume sound sources, such as drums, electric guitar speakers, and some singers, whereas ribbon or condenser mics are used for the "more gentle" sound sources, such as strings and acoustic guitars. Although many factors influence the type of microphone used and its placement, the figures in this section give some idea of how three different yet typical musical numbers may be miked. Again, the final criterion is not what everybody tells you, but whether the playback loudspeakers reflect what you had in mind.

Microphone Setup for Singer and Acoustic Guitar

For a singer accompanying himself or herself on an acoustic guitar, you may try to attach two microphones on a single mic stand, such as a Beyer M160 for the singer, pointing just below the mouth, and another pointing at the guitar. **SEE 9.36** Of course, you can also use two stands, but they usually get in the way of good shots.

---

3. See Alten, *Audio in Media*, pp. 379–405.

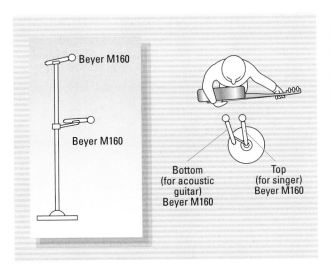

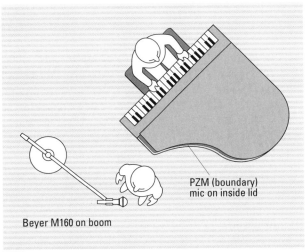

9.36 MIC SETUP FOR
SINGER AND ACOUSTIC GUITAR

The mic setup for a singer accompanying himself or herself
on an acoustic guitar is to have one mic for the voice and
another lower on the same mic stand for the guitar.

9.37 MICROPHONE SETUP FOR SINGER AND PIANO

If the singer's mic is to be out of camera view, it should
be suspended from a boom. The piano is miked separately.
For an on-camera mic, the singer can use a hand mic.

Microphone Setup for Singer and Piano

If the concert is rather formal, with the vocalist singing
classical songs, you should keep the mics out of the
pictures. You may want to try a Beyer M160 mic
suspended from a small giraffe boom. For the piano tape
a boundary mic (such as an Audio Technica AT-854R or
a Shure 819) on the lid in the low-peg position or directly
on the sound board. **SEE 9.37**

If the recital consists of popular songs, such as light
rock, a hand mic, such as a Beyer M500 or a Shure SM58,
may be the more appropriate choice for the singer. The
miking of the piano does not change.

Microphone Setup for Small Rock Group and Direct Insertion

When setting up for a rock group, you need microphones
for the singers, drums, and other direct sound-emitting
instruments, such as saxophones and pianos, as well as
for the speakers that carry the sound of amplified
instruments, such as electric guitars or keyboards. The
sound signals of electric instruments, such as the bass,
are often fed directly to the mixing console without the
use of a speaker and microphone. This technique is called
direct insertion or *direct input*. Because, as you recall,
most electric instruments are high impedance and all
other professional sound equipment is low impedance,
you need to match impedances through the direct box.
You simply plug the high-impedance instrument into the
direct box and connect the output of the direct box to the
input on the mixing console.

When setting up mics and speakers, watch out for
multiple feedback or microphone interference. For the
band members to hear themselves, you must supply the
foldback sound mix either through earphones or speakers.
Foldback, also called *cue-send,* is the return of the total
or partial audio mix from the mixing console to the
musicians. **SEE 9.38**

MICROPHONE USE SPECIFIC TO ENG/EFP

**ENG
EFP** The sound pickup requirements in ENG/EFP do not
differ significantly from those in studio operation.
In the field as in the studio, your ultimate objective is
optimal sound. You will find, however, that sound pickup
in the field is much more challenging than in the studio.
When outdoors there is the ever-present problem of wind

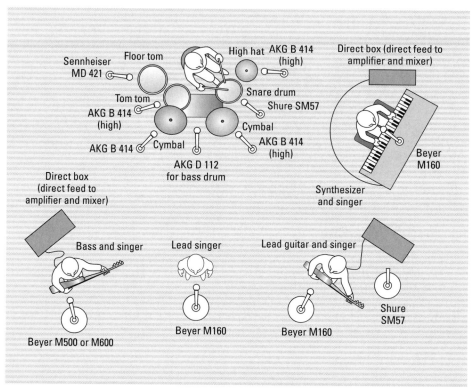

9.38 MICROPHONE SETUP FOR SMALL ROCK BAND
The types and placement of microphones in this illustration are merely a suggestion for how you may start with the mic setup. The final criterion for a successful setup is when the sounds coming out of the control room speakers are satisfactory.

noise and other unwanted sounds, such as airplanes or trucks passing by during a critical scene. The best way to combat wind noise is to use a highly directional mic, cover it with an effective windscreen, and hold it as close to the sound source as possible. But contrary to most studio shows, *ambient* (environmental) sounds are often needed to support the video.

When on an ENG assignment, always have a microphone open to record the ambient sounds, even when shooting "silent" footage. In fact, when using the hand mic for a stand-up report (with the reporter telling about a news event while standing in a particular location), you should also turn on the shotgun mic, which is clipped to the camera, for the ambient sounds. If possible, feed each mic into a separate VTR audio track. Such ambient sounds are essential for sound continuity in postproduction editing. The split tracks allow the video editor to control the mix between the reporter's voice and the ambient sounds.

If you have only one microphone which you must use for voice pickup, record the ambient sounds on a small, portable audiocassette recorder or on videotape after finishing the voice work. Again, the editor will appreciate some authentic sounds with which to bridge the edits.

You may find that a seemingly simple audio pickup, such as a speech in a large conference room, can turn into a formidable audio problem, especially if you cannot get close enough in the crowded and noisy room for a clean voice pickup. In this case it may be easier to ask the engineer in charge (usually the audiovisual manager of the hotel or conference room) to assist you with a *line-out tie-in*. In such a setup, you do not need a microphone to pick up the speaker's sound, but simply a direct feed from the audio control board of the in-house audio system to the audio input of your camcorder. In effect, you "tie in" to the audio feed from the audio system of the conference room.

MICROPHONE USE SPECIFIC TO THE STUDIO

When working with large, multicamera studio productions, such as situation comedies or soap operas, you will find that despite the presence of lavaliere mics, the big perambulator boom is very much alive and well. In the controlled environment of the studio, the big boom is still one of the most effective ways of getting a high-quality mic close to the talent while keeping it out of camera view. **SEE 9.39**

There are several reasons why the big boom has not achieved great popularity in routine studio productions:

- Using the big boom requires two operators: the boom operator, who works the microphone boom, and the boom dolly operator, who helps reposition the whole assembly whenever necessary.

- The floor space that the boom takes up may, in a small studio, cut down considerably the maneuverability of the cameras.

- Like the giraffe boom, the big boom requires a manipulation of the lighting so that its shadow falls outside of camera range. Even in larger studios, the lighting problems often preclude the use of a boom, available personnel and space notwithstanding.

- The boom is difficult to operate, especially when the actors are moving about.

The big boom nevertheless has several advantages, especially when used for multicamera shows that are done live-on-tape or contain fairly long uninterrupted takes:

- It allows smooth and rapid movement of the microphone above and in front of the sound sources and from one spot to another anywhere in the studio within its extended range. You can extend or retract the microphone with the boom, simultaneously pan the boom horizontally, move it up and down vertically, and rotate the mic to allow for directional sound pickup. During all these operations, the whole assembly can be moved to various locations, in case the boom cannot reach the sound source when fully extended.

- It can ride high enough to keep the boom and its mic out of camera view.

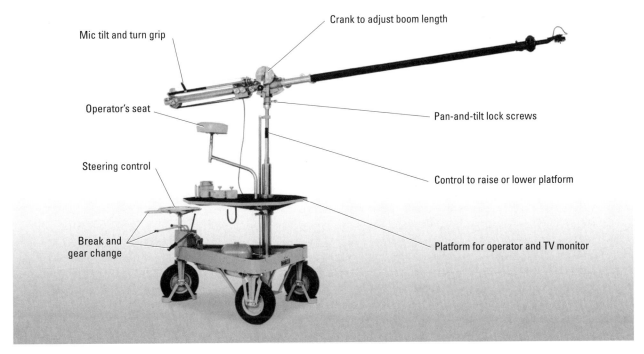

9.39 BIG OR PERAMBULATOR BOOM

The big, or perambulator, boom can extend to a 20-foot reach, pan 360 degrees, and tilt up and down. The microphone itself can be rotated by about 300 degrees—almost a full circle.

■ It permits the mounting of high-quality shotgun mics.

■ It can reach into performance areas without having the whole boom assembly move too close to the scene.

The operation of the big boom is similar to that of the giraffe (see figure 9.20). The major operational difference between the giraffe and the big boom is that the latter allows better sound pickup. With the big boom, you can move the microphone much more quickly and smoothly and can reach with the mic much farther into the scene than with the giraffe.

MAIN POINTS

◆ All microphones have a diaphragm, which vibrates with sound pressure, and a generating element, which transduces the physical vibrations of the diaphragm into electric energy. In the dynamic mic, the diaphragm is attached to the voice coil. The air pressure makes the voice coil move back and forth within a magnetic field. This type of generating element is quite rugged.

◆ In the ribbon, or velocity, mic, a thin, metal ribbon vibrates within a magnetic field. Because the ribbon is fragile, the mics are generally used indoors under controlled conditions.

◆ The condenser mic has a condenser-like generating element. The movable diaphragm constitutes one of the two condenser plates; a fixed backplate is the other. The varying air pressure of the incoming sounds moves the diaphragm plate against the fixed backplate, thus continuously changing the

capacitance of the condenser and modulating the current of the audio signal. Condenser mics have a wide frequency response.

◆ Impedance, usually expressed as high-Z or low-Z, is a type of resistance to the signal flow. The impedances of mics and electric instruments must be matched with that of the other electronic audio equipment. When using the direct-insertion (direct input) method, whereby the output of electric instruments is patched directly into the mixing console, the high-Z instruments must first be routed through a direct box, which changes the signal to a low-Z impedance.

◆ High-quality microphones pick up sounds equally well over a wide frequency range. They can hear higher and lower sounds without distortion—called a flat response—than can low-quality mics.

◆ Microphones can be balanced or unbalanced. Most professional mics have a balanced output. Balanced microphone cables have two wires for the audio signal and a third wire as a ground shield. The balanced audio cable prevents external signals from causing a hum in the audio track. Unbalanced cables have only a single wire for the audio signal and a second wire as a ground. They are less immune to unwanted signal interference, such as a hum or buzz.

◆ All professional microphones and audio equipment use the three-pronged XLR connectors. Unbalanced plugs include the phone plug, the RCA phono plug, and the mini plug.

◆ Foldback is the return of the total or partial audio mix from the mixing console to the musicians.

◆ In complex multicamera shows, such as soap operas, the microphones are suspended from one or two big booms.

ZETTL'S VIDEOLAB 2.1

The audio section of the lab shows you the various microphones and their uses and lets you actually hear the mic types and their pickup patterns. It also demonstrates how to use the different mics and how to avoid common pitfalls of audio pickup.

RUN ZVL 1 Click on the **audio** monitor and run tape 1 **Meet Phil**. Even as a review, his brief introduction to audio is full of surprises.

RUN ZVL 2 Run tape 3 **Microphones** and click on the **Mic choice** and **Transducer** modules. Note that *transducer* is synonymous with *generating element*. Both mean to translate sound waves into electric energy—the sound signal.

RUN ZVL 3 Click on the **Pickup patterns** module. It lets you select a particular pattern and listen to how each one influences the sound pickup. You may want to listen to each of the pickup patterns a few times to make sure you hear the obvious as well as the more-subtle differences.

RUN ZVL 4 Click on the **Mic types** module. Again, you can choose a particular mic type (hand mic, lavaliere, and so forth) and learn how to handle the various mics for optimal results.

RUN ZVL 5 Run tape 4 **Connectors** and take the **Quiz**.

10

Audio: Sound Control

The previous chapter dealt mostly with sound pickup—the various types of microphones and their uses. This chapter explores controlling and designing sound in television production. The field of sound control and sound design involves highly sophisticated equipment, intricate processes, and trained ears. Section 10.1, Sound Controls and How to Use Them, identifies this equipment and describes its use. Section 10.2, Mixing and Sound Aesthetics, familiarizes you with basic information on analog and digital audio mixing and aesthetic factors. To keep things manageable, this chapter is limited to the major equipment and basic techniques of television production.

AGC Stands for *automatic gain control*. Regulates the volume of the audio or video level automatically, without using pots.

audio control booth Houses the audio, or mixing, console; digital cart, cassette, CD, DVD, and DAT machines; a reel-to-reel audiotape recorder and a turntable; a patchbay; computer(s); speakers; intercom systems; a clock; and a line monitor.

audio production room For postproduction activities such as sweetening, composing music tracks, adding sound effects or laugh tracks, and assembling music bridges and announcements.

automatic dialog replacement (ADR) The synchronization of speech with the lip movements of the speaker in postproduction. Not always automatic.

calibrate To make all VU meters (usually of the audio console and the record VTR) respond in the same way to a specific audio signal.

cassette A video- or audiotape recording or playback device that uses tape cassettes. A cassette is a plastic case containing two reels—a supply reel and a takeup reel.

compact disc (CD) A small, shiny disc that contains information (usually sound signals) in digital form. A CD player reads the encoded digital information using a laser beam.

DAT Stands for *digital audiotape*. The sound signals are encoded on audiotape in digital form. Includes digital recorders as well as digital recording processes.

digital cart system A digital audio system that uses built-in hard drives, removable high-capacity disks (such as the Iomega zip format), or read/write optical discs to store and access almost instantaneously a great amount of audio information. It is normally used for the playback of brief announcements and music bridges.

DVD Stands for *digital videodisc*. The standard DVD can store 4.7 gigabytes of information. Also called *digital versatile disc* to accommodate audio use.

environment General ambience of a setting.

equalization Controlling the audio signal by emphasizing certain frequencies and eliminating others.

figure-ground Emphasizing the most important sound source over the general background sounds.

MIDI Stands for *musical instrument digital interface*. A standardization device that allows the interfacing of various digital audio equipment and computers.

mini disc (MD) Optical 2½-inch-wide disc that can store one hour of CD-quality audio.

mixing Combining two or more sounds in specific proportions (volume variations) as determined by the event (show) context.

mix-minus Type of multiple audio feed missing the part that is being recorded, such as an orchestra feed with the solo instrument being recorded.

peak program meter (PPM) Meter in audio console that measures loudness. Especially sensitive to volume peaks, it indicates overmodulation.

sound perspective Distant sound must go with a long shot, close sound with a close-up.

surround sound Sound that produces a soundfield in front of, to the sides of, and behind the listener by positioning loudspeakers either to the front and rear, or to the front, sides, and rear of the listener.

sweetening Variety of quality adjustments of recorded sound in postproduction.

VU meter Stands for *volume-unit meter*. Measures volume units, the relative loudness of amplified sound.

10.1

Sound Controls and How to Use Them

When watching a television program, we are generally not aware of sound as a separate medium. Somehow it seems to belong to the pictures, and we become aware of the audio portion only when it is unexpectedly interrupted. But in your own videotapes, you probably notice that there are always some minor or even major audio problems that tend to draw attention away from your beautiful shots. Although audio is often treated casually, you quickly realize that the sound portion is, indeed, a critical production element that requires your full attention.

▶ **AUDIO CONTROL AREAS: STUDIO**
The audio control booth and the audio production room

▶ **AUDIO PRODUCTION EQUIPMENT: STUDIO**
The audio console, the patchbay, audio recording systems, and various uses of the computer

▶ **AUDIO PRODUCTION EQUIPMENT: FIELD**
The mixer and field recording equipment

AUDIO CONTROL AREAS: STUDIO

When using a camcorder on vacation, you are probably fully occupied with the proper framing of shots and with zooming in and out, relying on the built-in microphone and automatic volume control to take care of the audio. During ENG the audio requirements are still relatively minor; the camera mic normally picks up the ambient sounds, and the hand mic or lavaliere picks up the reporter's or interviewee's comments. When watching a more complicated field production, you will see considerably more audio equipment used: mic cables, field mixers, small loudspeakers, several lavaliere or fishpole mics covered with windscreens, and a variety of recording equipment. But when walking into the audio control booth of a television control room, or the audio production room of a television station, the variety and complexity of equipment will quickly impress on you the importance of studio sound control.

Audio Control Booth

The *audio control booth* houses the audio, or mixing, console; digital cart, cassette, compact disc (CD), digital videodisc (DVD), and digital audiotape (DAT) machines; a reel-to-reel analog and/or digital audio-

10.1 AUDIO CONTROL BOOTH

The television audio control booth contains a variety of audio control equipment, such as the control console with computer display, patchbay, CD and DVD players, DAT machines, loudspeakers, intercom systems, and a video line monitor.

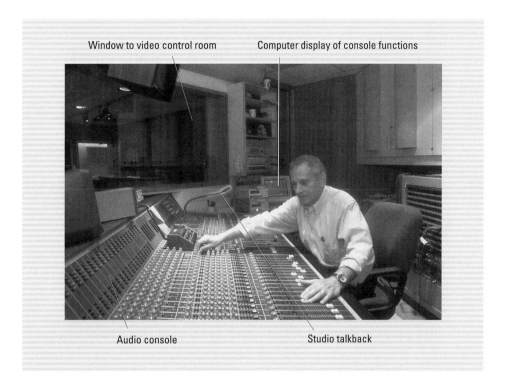

Window to video control room   Computer display of console functions

Audio console   Studio talkback

tape recorder; and, largely for nostalgic reasons, a turntable. There is also physical patchbay despite the presence of computer patching, and one or more desktop computers fulfilling various functions. You will also find cue and program speakers, intercom systems, a clock, and a line monitor. One audio engineer (or audio technician or audio operator) operates the audio controls during a show. **SEE 10.1**

Recall from chapter 1 that most audio booths are separate from the program control section yet in close proximity to it. Some provide visual access to the studio or, at least, to the program control room.

Audio Production Room

Because of the many and various audio demands in post-production, larger stations and independent production houses have still another *audio production room*. This facility, which resembles a small control room of a recording studio, is not used for the sound control of studio shows. Rather, it is for such postproduction activities as making some sounds more prominent while eliminating unwanted ones—an activity called

sweetening—composing music tracks, adding sound effects to the audio track of a play or a laugh track to a situation comedy, or assembling various music bridges and announcements for the next day's programming.

The audio production room usually contains a fairly elaborate audio console, two or more multitrack audio-tape recorders (ATRs) and DAT machines, digital cart and cassette machines, CD and DVD players, keyboards (synthesizers) and samplers, and at least one *digital audio workstation (DAW)*—a computer system for editing, signal processing, mixing, and synchronizing video and audio. Despite the computer-activated patching and routing, many audio production rooms also contain a physical patchbay to route audio signals. The room also contains several high-fidelity monitor speakers. **SEE 10.2**

As you can see, the sound production facilities resemble those for sound recording or mixing sessions more than those for controlling the audio during a television production. Because our concern at this point is with the proper handling of sound during a television studio production, EFP, or big remote, we will concentrate on the basic equipment in the television audio booth.

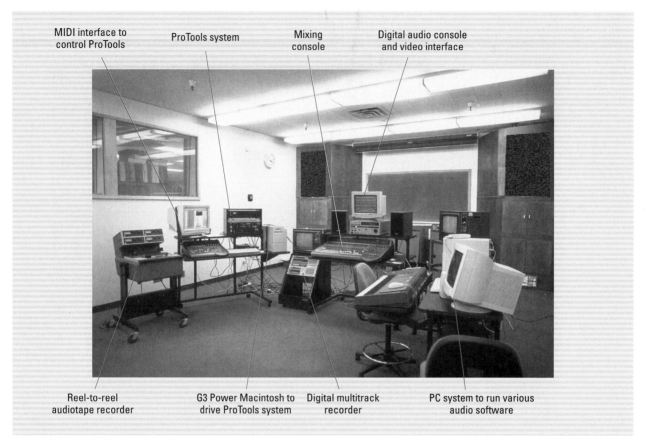

MIDI interface to control ProTools — ProTools system — Mixing console — Digital audio console and video interface

Reel-to-reel audiotape recorder — G3 Power Macintosh to drive ProTools system — Digital multitrack recorder — PC system to run various audio software

10.2 AUDIO PRODUCTION ROOM

The audio production room is equipped to handle most postproduction tasks. It typically contains an audio console, a patchbay, a digital audio workstation (DAW), reel-to-reel audiotape recorders, digital cart players, MIDI interface, and DAT recorders.

AUDIO PRODUCTION EQUIPMENT: STUDIO

Let's take a closer look at the following major components of audio equipment: audio console, patching, audio recording systems, and various uses of the computer.

Audio Console

Regardless of individual designs—analog or digital—all *audio consoles,* or audio control boards, are built to perform five major functions:

- *Input:* to preamplify and control the volume of the various incoming signals

- *Mix:* to combine and balance two or more incoming signals

- *Quality control:* to manipulate the sound characteristics

- *Output:* to route the combined signals to a specific output

- *Monitor:* to listen to the sounds before their signals are actually recorded or broadcast. **SEE 10.3**

Input   Studio consoles have multiple inputs in order to accept a variety of sound sources. Even small studio consoles may have as many as sixteen or more inputs. Although that many inputs are rarely used in the average in-house production or broadcast day, they nevertheless need to be available for the program you may have to do the next day.

Let us now take a closer look at the input section of an audio console. Each input module requires that you select either the *mic* or the *line* input. All microphones deliver a relatively low-level (weak) incoming signal that

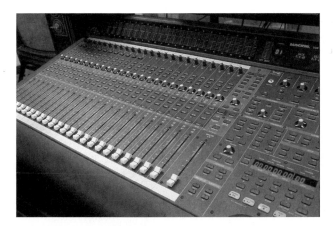

10.3 AUDIO CONSOLE

Each module of this audio console contains a volume control (slide fader), various quality controls, and assignment switches. It can route several mixes to various destinations.

must be boosted by a preamplifier, or *preamp*, to reach the line level. All incoming audio signals must reach line-level strength before being sent on to the various input controls. These signals are sent to the mic input.

If the incoming signal already has line-level strength, such as signals coming from CD players, DVD players, or DAT recorders, they need no preamplification. You therefore route these signals to the line input.

Because not all input levels of microphones or line signals are the same, they run the risk of becoming overamplified. To prevent this from occurring, you can adjust the signals individually with the *trim control*.

Regardless of input, the audio signals are then routed to the volume control, a variety of quality controls, switches (mute or solo switch) that silence all the other inputs when you want to listen to a specific one, and assignment switches that route the signal to certain parts of the audio console and to signal outputs. **SEE 10.4** *READY ZVL* ❶

Volume control   All sounds fluctuate in *volume* (loudness). Some sounds are relatively weak, so you have to increase their volume to make them perceptible. Other sounds come in so loud that they overload the audio system and become distorted, or outweigh the weaker ones so much that there is no longer proper balance between the two. The volume control that helps you adjust the incoming sound signals to their proper level is usually called a *pot* (short for *potentiometer*) or a *fader* (also called *attenuator* and *gain control*).

To increase the volume, which makes the sound louder, push the fader up, away from you. To decrease the

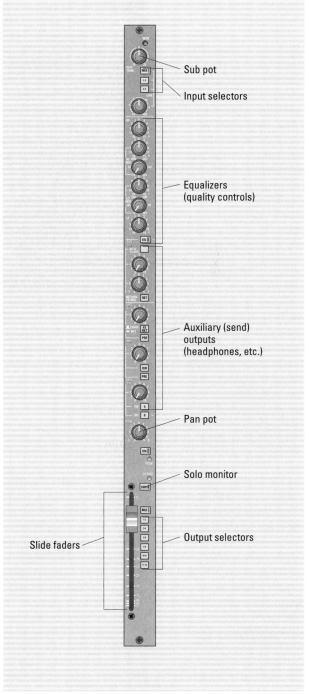

10.4 AUDIO CONSOLE MODULE

The major controls on this module are slide fader volume control, equalizers, assignment switches, mute switch (silences this input), pan pot (moves the sound horizontally from one stereo speaker to the next), and various other quality controls.

10.5 SLIDE FADERS
Pushing the fader up
increases the volume;
pulling it down decreases
the volume.

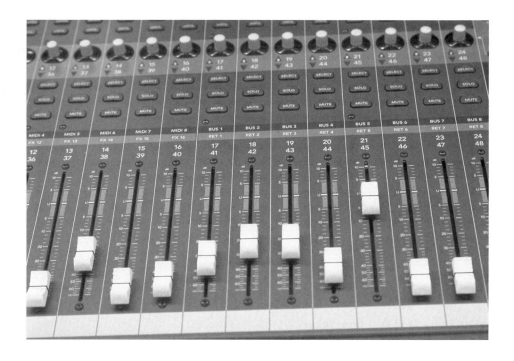

volume, turn the knob counterclockwise or pull the fader down, toward you. **SEE 10.5**

Mix   The audio console lets you combine, or *mix,* the signals from various inputs, such as two lavaliere mics, background music, and the sound effect of a phone ring. The *mix bus* combines—mixes—these various audio signals with the specific volume assigned by you. Without the mixing capability of the board, you could control only one input at a time. The completed mix is then fed to the line-out.

A mix bus is like a large intersection at which the cars (signals) from several streets (inputs) come together (are mixed) and then move out again as a unit (mixed sound signal) along a wide, single street (output, or line-out). *READY ZVL* ❷

Quality control   All audio consoles have various controls that let you shape the character of a sound (see figure 10.4). Among the most important are equalization, filters, and reverberation (reverb) controls.

The process of controlling the audio signal by emphasizing certain frequencies and eliminating others is called *equalization*. It can be accomplished manually or automatically through an *equalizer,* which works very much like the tone control on a home stereo receiver. It can boost or reduce selected frequencies and thereby

influence the character of the sound. For example, you can make a sound more brilliant by boosting the high frequencies or more solid by boosting the lows, or you can eliminate a low-frequency hum or a high-frequency hiss. Filters eliminate automatically all frequencies above or below a certain point. The *reverb* controls can add an increasing amount of reverberation to each of the selected inputs.

Among the additional quality controls on large consoles are switches that allow you to accommodate the relative strengths of incoming sound signals or that prevent input overloads, and others that let you "pan" the stereo sound to a particular spot between the two stereo speakers.

Output   The mixed and quality-processed signal is then routed to the output, sometimes called *line-out.* Just to make sure that the mixed signals stay within the acceptable volume limits, they are regulated by final volume controls—the master pots—and metered by volume indicators, the most common of which is the *VU (volume unit) meter*. As the volume varies, the needle of the VU meter oscillates back and forth along a calibrated scale. **SEE 10.6** If the volume is so low that the needle barely moves from the extreme left, you are "riding the gain" (or volume) "in the mud." If the needle oscillates around the middle of the scale and peaks at, or occasionally over, the

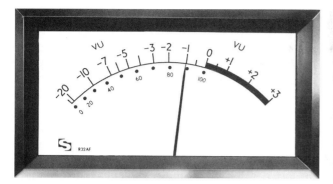

10.6 ANALOG VU METER

The VU meter indicates the relative loudness of a sound. The upper figures ranging from –20 to +3 are the volume units (decibels). The lower figures represent a percentage scale, ranging from 0 to 100 percent signal modulation (signal amplification). Overmodulation (too much signal amplification) is indicated by the red line on the right (0 to +3 VU).

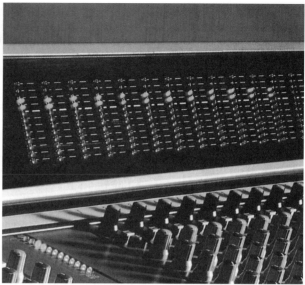

10.7 LED VU METER

The LED (light-emitting diode) VU meters indicate overmodulation (too much signal amplification) by lighting up in a different color (usually red).

red line on the right, you are riding correct gain. If the needle swings almost exclusively in the red on the right side of the scale, and even occasionally hits the right edge of the meter, the volume is too high—you are "bending the needle," "spilling over," or "riding in the red."

Much like the amplifier in a home stereo system, the VU meter in some audio consoles consists of light-emitting diodes (LEDs), which show up as thin, colored light columns that fluctuate up and down a scale. When you ride the gain too high, the column shoots up on the scale and even changes its color.

Some audio consoles have an additional *peak program meter (PPM),* which measures loudness. A PPM reacts more quickly to the volume "peaks" than the needle of the VU meter and clearly shows when you are over-modulating (riding the gain too high). **SEE 10.7**

Output channels   We often classify audio consoles by the number of output channels. Older television consoles had several inputs but only one output channel, because television sound was monophonic. Today, however, even small television consoles have at least two output channels to handle stereophonic sound or to feed two sources (such as headphones and a videotape recorder) simultaneously with two independent mixes. With HDTV the sound requirements also change. Very much like motion pictures, large-screen TV displays will require *surround sound,* which involves multiple discrete output channels and a variety of speakers that are strategically placed in front, to the sides, and in back of

the display screen. This increasing demand for high-quality audio has led to greater use of multichannel (output) consoles in television in the audio control booth and especially in the audio production room.

To identify how many inputs and outputs a specific console has, they are labeled with the number of input and output channels, such as an 8 × 1 or a 32 × 4 console. This means that the small 8 × 1 console has eight inputs and one output; the larger 32 × 4 console has 32 inputs and four outputs. With a single output channel, the 8 × 1 board obviously is monophonic.

Most larger television audio consoles have eight or more output channels (with eight master pots and eight VU meters), each of which can carry a discrete sound signal or mix. The advantage of multiple outputs is that you can feed the individual signals onto a multitrack audiotape recorder for postproduction mixing.

If, for example, there are twenty-four inputs but only two outputs, you need to mix the various input signals down to two, which you can then feed to the left and right channels of a stereo recorder. But if you want to keep the various sounds separated to exercise more control in the final postproduction mix, or if you want to feed separate surround-sound speakers, you need more outputs. Even when covering a simple rock concert, for example, you may have to provide one mix for the musicians, another for the audience, one for the videotape recorder, and yet another for the multitrack ATR. You will be surprised at how fast you run out of available inputs and outputs even on a rather big console.

In-line consoles   Some of the more elaborate consoles, called *in-line consoles,* have input/output, or *I/O,* modules, which means that each input has its own output. If, for example, there are twenty-four inputs and each one receives a different sound signal, you could send each of them directly to the separate tracks of a twenty-four-track recorder without feeding them through any of the mix buses. That way you use the console to control the volume of each input, but the console does not function as a mixing or quality-control device. In fact, the sound is sent to the tape recorder in its raw state. The mixing and quality control of the various sounds are all done in the postproduction and mixdown sessions. The I/O circuits let you try out and listen to all sorts of mixes and sound manipulations without affecting the original signal sent to the recorder.

Phantom power   Don't let the name scare you: The "phantom" in supplying power is more like "virtual." All it means is that the audio console, rather than a battery, supplies the preamplification power to some condenser mics.

Monitor and cue   All consoles have a monitor system, which lets you hear the final sound mix or allows you to listen to and adjust the mix before switching it to the line-out. A separate audition or cue return system lets you hear a particular sound source without routing it to the mix bus. This system is especially important when you want to cue a DAT or cassette, or check the beginning sounds of a CD or DVD track while on the air with the rest of the sound sources.

Computer-assisted consoles   Many newer consoles contain a computer through which you can preset, store, recall, and activate many of the audio control functions. For example, you can try out a particular mix with specific volume, equalization, and reverberation values for each of the individual sounds, store it all in the computer's memory, try something else, and then recall the original setup with the press of a button.

Digital consoles   These consoles look like their analog cousins except that they have centralized controls that trigger various sound control and routing functions for each input module. These controls are not unlike the delegation controls of a video switcher.

Patchbay

The primary function of the *patchbay,* or patch panel, is connecting and routing audio signals to and from various pieces of equipment. You can accomplish this by using actual wires that establish specific connections, or with a computer that treats the signals as files and simply rearranges them according to your instructions. Whatever method you use, the principle of patching is the same. Here we use wires, called *patchcords,* to explain a simple patching procedure.

Assume that you want to have two microphones, a remote feed from a field reporter, and a CD operating during a newscast. Mics 1 and 2 are the newscasters' lavalieres. The remote feed comes from the field reporter with a live story. The CD contains the opening and closing theme music for the newscast.

Just as the individual lighting instruments can be patched into any of the dimmers, any one of these audio sources can be patched to individual volume controls (pots or faders) in any desired order. For instance, suppose you want to operate the volume controls in the following order, from left to right: CD, lavaliere 1, lavaliere 2, remote feed. You can easily patch these inputs to the audio console in that order. If you want the inputs in a different order, you do not need to unplug the equipment. All you do is pull the patchcords and repatch the inputs in the different order. **SEE 10.8**

Wired patchbay   All wired patch panels contain rows of holes, called *jacks,* which represent the various outputs (from microphones, cartridges, turntables, or tape recorders) and inputs (to different pots or channels of the audio console). The upper rows of jacks are normally the outputs (which carry the signals from mics, CDs, and so forth). The rows of jacks immediately below the output jacks are the input jacks that are connected to the audio console. The connection between output and input is made through the patchcord.

Patchbays are usually wired so that the various input jacks are directly below the output jacks. To accomplish a

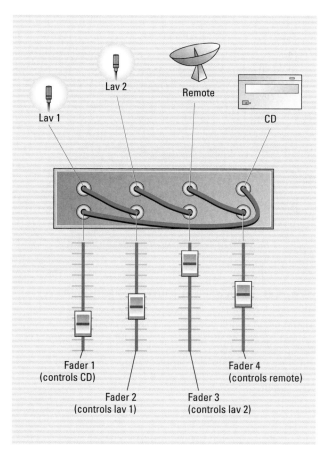

10.8 PATCHING

This patching shows that the signal outputs (audio sources) of two microphones, a remote feed, and a CD are grouped in the following order of fader inputs: CD, lavaliere 1, lavaliere 2, remote feed.

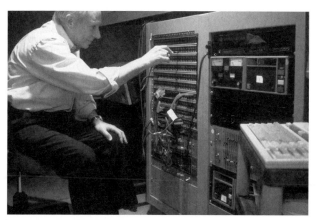

10.9 PATCHBAY WITH PATCHES

All patchbays connect the signal outputs (mics, CDs, VTRs) to specific input modules of the audio console. The patching is accomplished by connecting the audio outputs (top row) to the inputs (bottom row) with a patchcord.

proper patch, you must plug the patchcord from one of the upper output jacks into one of the lower input jacks. **SEE 10.9** Patching output to output (upper-row jack to another upper-row jack) or input to input (lower-row jack to lower-row jack) will give you nothing but severe headaches.

To reduce the number of patchcords, certain frequently used connections between outputs (a specific mic, DAT machine, or CD) and inputs (specific volume controls assigned to them) are directly wired, or *normaled*, to one another. This means that the output and input of a circuit are connected without a patchcord. By inserting a

patchcord into one of the jacks of a normaled circuit, you break, rather than establish, the connection.

Although patching helps make the routing of an audio signal more flexible, it can also cause some problems: Patching takes time; patch cords and jacks get worn out after frequent use, which can cause a hum or an intermittent connection; and many patchcords crisscrossing each other are confusing and look more like spaghetti than orderly connections, making individual patches difficult to trace. Also, when patching with a corresponding fader still set at a reasonably high volume, the pop caused by plugging or unplugging the patchcord can cause even the most robust speaker to blow. Once again, although physical connections are certainly possible, the computer performs many of the patching functions.

Computer-assisted patching In computer-assisted patching, the sound signals from the various sources, such as mics, direct boxes, CDs, DVDs, or videotapes, are routed to the patch panel programmer, which assigns the multiple signals to specific fader modules of the audio console for further processing. To route lavaliere 1 to pot 2, and the CD to pot 1, for example, you don't need any physical patches; you simply enter the routing information into the computer (patch panel programmer), which tells the electronic patch panel to connect the inputs to the desired faders on the console, show the information on the display screen, and store your patching commands on a floppy disk for future use.

Audio Recording Systems

The sound of routine television productions is usually recorded simultaneously with the pictures on one of the audio tracks of the videotape recorder. There are occasions, however, when you need to back up your sound recording with a separate audio recording, or record the audio on a separate system for high-end postproduction. Even if you may not want to be an audio expert, you need to know what systems are available to you.

In general, audio recording systems can record audio signals in analog or digital form. As explained in chapter 2, *analog* means that the signal fluctuates exactly like the original stimulus; *digital* means that the signal is translated into many discrete digits (on/off pulses). Although much audio recording is done digitally, analog recordings are still prevalent in television production.

On analog videotape the audio is still analog, as is the sound recorded on normal audiocassettes and reel-to-reel audiotape recorders. In digital television, such as all ATV (advanced television) and HDTV (high-definition television), all audio is digital, so you obviously need the appropriate playback systems that reproduce digital video as well as digital audio. Digital recording devices include digital audiotape recorders, hard drives, digital cart systems, and read/write optical discs. We discuss CDs in this context, although the manufacturing is normally done by a CD production company.

Recall that analog and digital recordings are not compatible. For example, you cannot play back a digitally recorded sound track on a regular VTR.

Analog Recording Systems

The two most common analog recording systems are the open-reel audiotape recorder and the cassette tape system. The audio cartridge recorder has been replaced almost entirely by digital equipment.

Open-reel audio recorder   The *open-reel,* formerly called reel-to-reel, *audiotape recorder (ATR)* is generally used for multitrack recording or for playing back longer pieces of audio material. For example, the background music and the sound effects, such as traffic noise, are

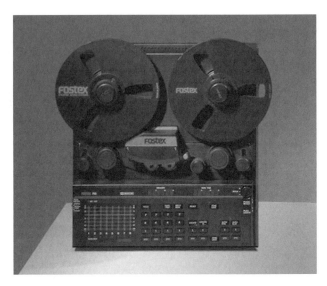

10.10 OPEN-REEL AUDIOTAPE RECORDER

This open-reel ATR can record up to eight separate audio tracks on a ¼-inch audiotape and can locate automatically certain cue points. It can interface with the SMPTE time code for audio/video synchronization. All the controls, including the standard operational controls of *play, fast forward, stop, rewind,* and *record* are on a panel that can be detached and used from a remote location.

generally premixed (prerecorded) on audiotape and then played back and mixed again with the dialogue during an actual production. The ATR is also used to record material for archival purposes. Although a great variety of ATRs are used in television production, they all operate on similar principles and with similar controls.

All professional ATRs, analog as well as digital, have five control buttons that regulate the tape motion, in addition to the switch for the various recording speeds: (1) *play,* which moves the tape at the designated recording speed; (2) *fast forward,* which advances the tape at high speed; (3) *stop,* which brakes the reels to a stop; (4) *rewind,* which rewinds the tape at high speed; and (5) *record,* which activates both the erase and record heads. **SEE 10.10** Many tape recorders have a cue control, which enables you to hear the sound on a tape even when running at fast-forward or rewind speeds.

The tape moves from a *supply reel* to a *takeup reel* over at least three heads: the erase head, the record head, and the playback head. **SEE 10.11** This head assembly arrangement is standard for all analog tape recorders.

10.11 ANALOG AUDIOTAPE HEAD ASSEMBLY
The head assembly of an analog reel-to-reel ATR consists of an erase head, a record head, and a playback head.

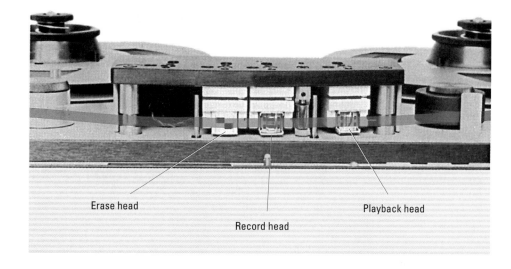

Erase head   Record head   Playback head

When the ATR is being used for recording, the erase head clears the portions of the tape that receive the recording (tracks) of all audio material that might have been left on the tape from a previous recording; the record head then puts the new audio material on the tape. When the tape is played back, the playback head reproduces the audio material previously recorded. The erase and record heads are not activated during playback.

Some audio production rooms in large stations have multitrack recorders that use wider formats than the standard ¼-inch, such as ½-, 1-, or 2-inch, to accommodate the multiple (up to thirty-two) tracks. High-quality four-track machines use ½- or 1-inch tape. The 2-inch tape is used for sixteen or more tracks.

Cassette tape system   Professional *cassette* systems are similar to the one you have at home or carry around, except that they have more-sophisticated electronics to reduce noise, and more-durable tape transports that allow faster forward and rewind speeds.

As you know from experience, cassettes are easy to store and handle and can play up to 180 minutes of audio material. Despite the narrow tape, cassettes produce good sound, especially if they are the newer, metal-particle-coated variety. Despite the digital revolution, analog cassettes are still popular in television productions. But if you want superior audio quality from cassettes, you should use a DAT recorder.

Analog cart system   The analog cart machines used a single reel that formed an endless loop that rewinded itself as it played and then cued itself automatically. They have largely been replaced by *digital cart systems*, which are described in the following section.

Digital Recording Systems
The major digital recording systems include: (1) the digital audiotape recorder, (2) MDM recorders, (3) the DTRS recorder, (4) computer disks (hard disks and high-capacity floppies), (5) mini discs, and (6) CDs and DVDs.

Digital audiotape recorder   *Digital audiotape—DAT—recorders* can be open-reel or cassette recorders. The open-reel DAT machines look and operate much like the analog open-reel recorders; they have a supply and a takeup reel, and the tape passes by a stationary head assembly.

In television production you will most likely work with a DAT cassette recorder. These machines operate more like videocassette recorders than audiocassette recorders. The major difference is that the audio signals are recorded by rotating heads onto the entire width of the cassette tape. The DAT cassettes are smaller than analog cassettes but can record at their slowest speed up to four hours of high-quality audio. As with videotape, however, the slower tape speeds produce lower-quality recordings. **SEE 10.12**

10.12 ANALOG AND DAT CASSETTES

The DAT cassette is considerably smaller than the regular analog audiocassette.

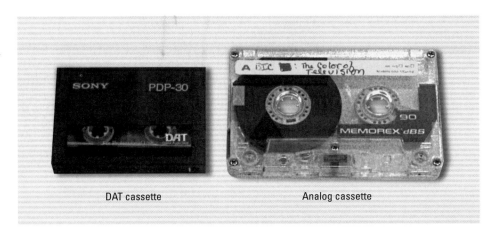

DAT cassette

Analog cassette

Besides recording sound with the customary digital, virtually noise-free high fidelity, the DAT recorder has, among others, the following features that are especially important for video production:

- High-speed search and extremely accurate cuing

- Permits slating (identifying a scene or take) through a built-in microphone

- Can record simultaneously with the audio material a time code for cuing and for matching sound and pictures in postproduction

- Shows the time remaining on the tape

- Synchronizes, if desired, its internal time code with an external time code (such as the one supplied by or to the cameras)

- Records and shows the current date and time
  SEE 10.13

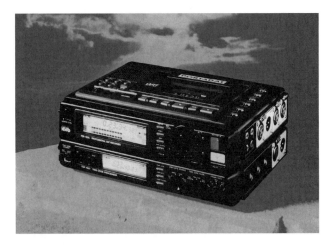

10.13 PORTABLE DAT RECORDER

This small DAT recorder weighs less than 5 pounds, including the 2-hour battery. It has two stereo inputs and allows off-tape monitoring, which means you can listen to what is being recorded on the cassette.

MDM recorders   *MDM* stands for *modular digital multitrack recorders* and borrows not only the rotating-heads system of the videotape recorder, but also the videotape itself. One of the MDM systems, *ADAT* (Alesis digital audiotape recorder) uses the S-VHS videotape recording system and the S-VHS tape cassette. Using a regular 120 S-VHS tape, you can record about 100 minutes of high-quality, eight-track audio.

DTRS   Short for *digital tape recording system, DTRS* uses Hi8 videotape for its multitrack recordings. By synchronizing two DTRS machines, you can get a 16-track recording.

Computer disks   Assuming your desktop computer has the necessary audio processing capability, you can, of course, record digital audio on any other digital storage device, such as a hard disk in your computer, or any other removable large-capacity storage disks, such as the Iomega Jaz or Zip cartridges. The removable cartridges are a convenient way to store and/or exchange audio files without digital recorders.

There are a variety of optical digital storage devices, such as the MD (mini disc), the CD (compact disc), the DVD (digital versatile disc when used for audio), and the digital cart system.

10.14 PROFESSIONAL CD PLAYER

Professional CD players allow random access to various tracks. The play sequence can be stored and displayed on playback.

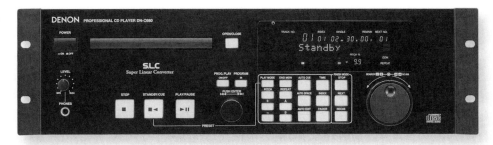

Mini disc   The *mini disc (MD)* is a small (about 2½ inch) read-only or read/write optical disc that can store an hour of high-quality digital stereo audio. Its small size, large storage capacity, and easy cuing make it a useful playback device for television productions.

CD and DVD   The professional *compact disc (CD)* players are a frequently used medium in television (and radio) stations for playing back commercially produced music and other audio material. Similar to the ones used in the home, they are built more solidly and have more-sophisticated and reliable controls, including remote controls. **SEE 10.14** Professional CD players permit random access of a specific track; let you enter, store, and activate various play sequences; and display, among other things, the menu of the play list, what the disc is playing, and how much of the segment is remaining.

Most CDs are "read-only" discs, which means that you cannot record on them, but use them for playback only. The decoding (playback) is accomplished by a tiny laser beam that scans the rotating CD from the inside out. Although they can withstand a theoretically unlimited amount of playbacks without any signs of deterioration, they are, nevertheless, quite vulnerable. If you scratch the shiny side or even the label side, the disc will refuse to play past the scratch. And if there are too many fingerprints on a CD, the laser may try to read the fingerprints instead of the imprinted digits. So when handling CDs, try to keep your hands off the surface, and always put down the disc on its *label side* and not on its shiny side.

You can also use "read/write" discs that allow you to record as well as play back audio material and, if it is a read/write CD-ROM, also video material.

A *DVD*, which stands for *digital video disc* or *digital versatile disc*, is similar to the familiar CD-ROM. Compared with the CD-ROM, which holds 650 megabytes of information, a standard DVD can store 4.7 gigabytes of high-quality video and audio information—more than two hours of broadcast-quality audio and video. Some experimental DVDs can hold up to 18 gigabytes. If you use the DVD for audio information only, you can obviously squeeze a great amount of high-quality digital audio on even the DVD standard format.

Digital cart system   The digital recorder/players that constitute a *digital cart system* use mostly read/write optical CDs or mini discs for recording and playback. Sometimes digital cart machines use regular high-capacity removable computer disks. These digital systems operate very much like a home CD player. You can select a particular cut and start the audio track instantly. You can also interface the digital cart with a desktop computer that lets you assemble a play list and automatically cues and starts various audio segments. **SEE 10.15**

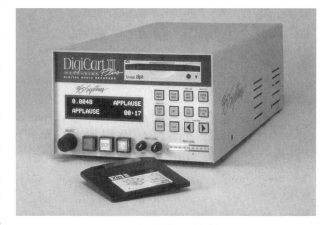

10.15 DIGITAL CART RECORDER/PLAYER

This digital cart machine uses a removable high-density computer disk and allows random and instant cuing and playback via remote control.

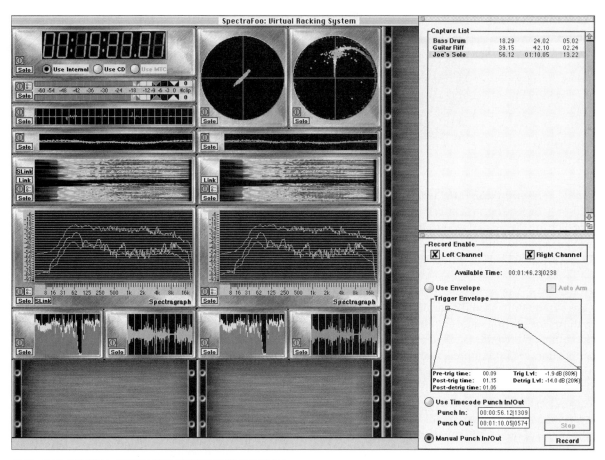

10.16 DIGITAL AUDIO WORKSTATION DISPLAY

There are several computer programs that facilitate audio editing, audio quality control, audio effects, and audio/video synchronization.

Audio/Video Postproduction

If you want to replace an existing sound track, insert some audio material, or provide a new sound track that fits the video exactly (such as the sound of starting a car or a dog barking), you need to synchronize the video and audio tracks. When using analog video- and audiotape, you need a machine called a *synchronizer*. But you will find that most audio/video matching is done digitally, using a computer program.

Analog audio synchronizer

Most audio synchronizers uses the *SMPTE time code,* which divides the audiotape into imaginary "frames." These frames correspond with those of the videotape and provide a mutual "time address" as specified by hours, minutes,

seconds, and frames (30 frames make up 1 second). In effect, you are dealing with matching video and sound files rather than video and audio tracks. (For more information on time code, see chapter 13.)

Digital audio workstation

The *digital audio workstation (DAW)* is designed for editing the various sound tracks and synchronizing them with the video tracks. For more information about the function of digital workstations, see chapter 12. **SEE 10.16**

Basically, the DAW lets you enlarge the audio display so that you can manipulate the existing audio track at will. With the **MIDI** (musical digital interface) standardization device, you can input a variety of other audio sources for additional manipulation of the audio track.

Lip-sync   When using *lip-sync,* the singers do not actually sing, but simply synchronize their lip and body movements to the sound of the complete recording. This technique has caused quite a furor among rock fans who learned that the singers in some famous bands were not actually singing but were merely mouthing the words to a recording during "live" concerts. In video lip-synching is more readily accepted. The technique requires that the singer can clearly hear the playback. If there are slight synchronization problems for some reason, stay away from close-ups.

Automatic dialogue replacement   The *automatic dialogue replacement (ADR)* in television is borrowed directly from motion pictures. Many sounds, including dialogue, recorded simultaneously with pictures do not always live up to the expected sound quality. They are therefore replaced by sounds re-created in the studio. Most of the time, the ADR is anything but automatic and requires painstaking re-creations and mixing of dialogue, sound effects, and ambient (environmental) sounds.

Elaborate ADR has the actors repeat their lines while watching themselves on a large-screen projection. Recording sound effects is usually done with the *Foley stage,* in which a variety of equipment is set up in a recording studio to produce common sound effects, such as footsteps, opening and closing doors, and so forth. The Foley stage uses equipment much like that of traditional radio and film productions, which includes different types of floor sections, little doors with various locks and squeaks, and boxes with different types of gravel. The Foley artists step on the various surfaces to produce the desired sound effects of someone walking in a hallway or on a driveway. Foley offers this equipment in efficiently packaged boxes so that it can be transported by truck, sound-effect artists included.

AUDIO PRODUCTION EQUIPMENT: FIELD

ENG EFP   Unless you are engaged in a big remote (see chapter 20), your audio equipment in the field is much less elaborate than its studio counterparts. This is not because you don't need to produce optimal audio in the field, but simply that in ENG the audio requirements are more modest. Similarly, in EFP most of the quality control is

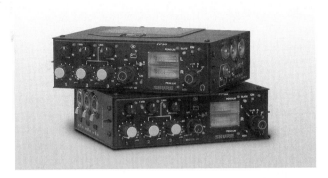

10.17 PORTABLE MIXER
This portable mixer has three inputs and one output. The volume controls are rotary knobs.

done in postproduction in the studio. But don't be fooled into thinking that field audio is somehow easier than studio audio. On the contrary—sound pickup and recording in the field are actually more difficult. In the field you have to worry about wind noise, barking dogs, traffic sounds, airplanes overhead, chattering onlookers, or rooms that produce the dreaded inside-a-barrel sounds. The key to good field audio is keeping the primary sounds as separate from the environmental sounds as possible.

For example, although you always try to record the field reporter's mic on one track and the ambient sounds on another, there will nevertheless be circumstances in which you need to balance the primary (field reporter) and secondary (ambient) sounds in the field. This is where the field mixer comes in.

Mixer

ENG EFP   If you have only one or two mics in the field, you can use the two audio inputs on the VTR for controlling the volume, so no mixer is necessary. But if you want to control the volume of more than two sources, such as four people with lavaliere mics discussing a new bridge in the midst of traffic sounds, and mix them down to a single output for videotaping, you need a portable mixer. An audio mixer differs from a console in that it normally serves only the input (volume control) and the *mixing* (combining two or more signals) functions. **SEE 10.17**

Most portable mixers have only four or, at best, eight inputs and one or two output channels. Even then the mixers have separate mic and line inputs. Make sure that you plug the equipment into the right inputs. Plug low-level signal sources into the mic input, and high-level input sources into the line-level input. If you are not sure whether a particular piece of audio equipment produces a mic-level or a line-level signal, do a brief test recording.

Mixers normally have no sound quality controls. They mix and output sounds the way they came in—that is, possibly with hisses and hums. Even though some digital mixers have more inputs as well as equalizers for each input, elaborate mixing in the field is not recommended, unless you do a live telecast, as discussed in section 10.2. And though you probably don't aim for a stereo audio pickup in the field, the two output channels are important for keeping the primary audio (such as the field reporter) and the secondary audio (ambient sounds) separate as much as possible for more effective postproduction mixing.

MAIN POINTS

♦ The audio area of a television studio includes the basic audio control booth, which is used for the sound control of daily broadcasts and, in larger operations, the audio production room, which is used for audio postproduction. Unless they have their own studio, independent production houses have only an audio production room.

♦ The major audio equipment includes an audio console; a patchbay; audio recording systems, including the analog audiotape recorder (ATR), the digital audiotape recorder (DAT), cassette and digital cart systems, compact disc (CD) and digital video disc (DVD) players; and, of course, various computers that control the equipment and synchronize video and audio in postproduction.

♦ Audio consoles perform five major functions: input—select, preamplify, and control the volume of the various incoming signals; mix—combine and balance two or more incoming signals; quality control—manipulate the sound characteristics; output—route the combined signal to a specific output; and monitor—route the output or specific sounds to a speaker or headphones so that they can be heard independent of the line-out signal.

♦ Audio/video synchronization matches each video frame with the corresponding audio. It also includes lip-sync and automatic dialogue replacement (ADR). Most audio/video synchronization is done with a digital audio workstation (DAW) that treats sound as computer files, much like a word processor operates with text files.

10.2

Mixing and Sound Aesthetics

Even the most sophisticated digital audio equipment will help you little if you don't have a "good ear," that is, aesthetic sensitivity and judgment when dealing with sound. This section explores the major areas of sound control and audio aesthetics.

▶ **BASIC AUDIO OPERATION**
Volume control, including calibration with VTR, riding gain, and automatic gain control

▶ **LIVE AND POSTPRODUCTION MIXING**
Live studio mixing, live mixing in ENG/EFP, postproduction mixing, and controlling sound quality

▶ **AESTHETIC FACTORS**
Environment, figure-ground, perspective, continuity, energy, and surround sound

BASIC AUDIO OPERATION

The description of basic audio elements in section 10.1 should give you a pretty good idea about what is available for producing a good television audio track. Now you must learn to operate all this equipment. You simply need practice. Fortunately, in most studio productions the audio tasks consist mostly of making sure that the voices of the news anchors or panel guests have acceptable volume levels and are relatively free of extraneous noise, and that the sound appears with the pictures when videotapes are played. In field productions you need to ensure that the microphone input is actually recorded on the designated videotape and, occasionally, also on audiotape tracks. Most likely, you will not be asked to do intricate sound manipulations during complex recording sessions—at least not right away. Consequently, the focus here is on the basic audio control factors: volume control, including sound calibration, riding gain, and working with automatic gain; field and studio mixing; and, finally, what a "good ear" means—the various aesthetic factors of sound control.

Volume Control

Before you can do proper volume control so that the incoming sounds are adjusted for optimal reproduction on videotape, you need to adjust the volume of the line-out sound—the sound that leaves the audio console or mixer—and the input volume of the videotape recorder. Then you need to learn the finer points of adjusting the volume of the incoming sound sources and of using the *AGC*—the automatic gain control.

Audio system calibration Before doing any serious volume adjustment or mixing, you need to make sure that the audio console and the VTR on which you are recording the audio "hear" in the same way—that the VTR input volume (recording level) matches the console output (line-out signal). This process is called audio system calibration, or simply *calibration*. To **calibrate** a system is to make all the VU meters (usually of the audio console and the record VTR) respond in the same way to a specific audio signal. (Note that audio calibration has nothing to do with the zoom lens calibration, whereby you adjust the zoom lens so that it stays in focus during the entire zoom range.)

Here are the major steps of audio calibration:

1. With all faders on the console or mixer turned all the way down, activate the calibration tone, which is either a continuous tone or an intermittent beep. Most professional audio consoles and mixers have such a tone generator built-in.

2. Bring the master (line-out) fader on the console or mixer up to the 0 VU mark.

3. Bring the fader that controls the calibration tone up until the master (line-out) VU meter reads 0 VU. While bringing up the fader, you should hear the sound becoming progressively louder until it has reached the 0 VU level.

4. Now turn up the incoming volume control on the VTR until its VU meter also reads 0 VU. When both the master VU meter of the console or mixer and the VU meter of the VTR read the same 0 VU level, the system has been calibrated.

From this point on throughout the recording, the VTR operator should not touch the audio input level, even if the VU meter indicates low volume levels. It is up to you— the console operator—to maintain proper audio levels.

Because the VTR is now receiving exactly what you send from the console or mixer, you can confidently engage in some serious volume control. **SEE 10.18**

Taking a level   Except when literally running after a story on an ENG assignment, you should always "take a level" before starting the videotape recording. *Taking a level* means to adjust the fader so that the talent's speech falls more or less within the tolerable volume range (not

10.18 AUDIO SYSTEM CALIBRATION

An audio system is calibrated when all VU meters respond in the same way to a specific audio signal. Here the line-out of the audio mixer is calibrated with the input (record level) of the VTR. Both VU meters show the same value.

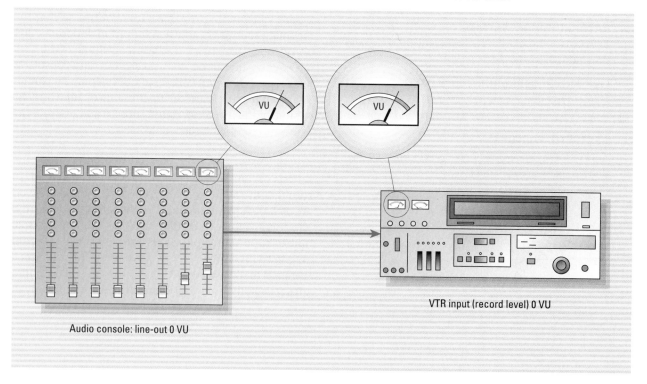

VTR input (record level) 0 VU

Audio console: line-out 0 VU

riding in the mud and not bending the needle). Ask the talent to talk long enough for you to see where the lower and upper limits of the speech volume are and place the fader somewhat in the middle between these two extremes. An experienced performer will stay within this volume range even in subsequent takes.

Unfortunately, when asked to give a level most performers consider it an intrusion on their concentration and simply count rapidly to three or four; then, when they are on the air, their voices rise to the occasion—and also in volume. Always be prepared for this sudden volume increase. Experienced performers give a few of the opening sentences in about as loud a voice as they will use when on the air.

When overmodulating speech (riding the gain consistently at too high a level), you end up not with a recording that is slightly too loud, but with distorted sound. Although it is relatively easy to boost sound that was recorded at a slightly lower than normal level (even at the risk of amplifying some of the noise with the low-level sounds), it is very difficult and often impossible to fix overmodulated, distorted sound in postproduction.

ENG EFP **Using the automatic gain control in ENG/EFP** Be especially conscious of this problem when on ENG or EFP assignments, when you may have little time to watch the sound levels. If you are on an ENG assignment and cannot watch the VU meter on the camcorder or VTR, switch on the *AGC* (automatic gain control). The AGC boosts low sounds and reduces high-volume sounds so that they conform to the tolerable volume range. The AGC does not discriminate between wanted and unwanted sounds, however. It faithfully boosts the noise of the passing truck, the coughing crew member, or even the noise of the pauses when the field reporter is thinking of something clever to say, as much as it boosts the faint but important utterances of a tired eyewitness. Whenever possible, and especially when in noisy surroundings, switch off the AGC, take a level, and hope for the best. When using DAT, turn down the pot (volume control) a bit from where you had it while taking a level. This way you can be pretty sure not to over-modulate once you are on the air.

LIVE AND POSTPRODUCTION MIXING

Although the basic principles of sound mixing are the same regardless of where and when you do it and what equipment you use, there are some important differences between live and postproduction mixing, and mixing in the field and in the studio.

Live mixing means that you combine and balance sounds while the production is in progress. *Postproduction mixing* means that you create the final videotape sound track in the audio production room after the production of the videotape segments.

Live Studio Mixing

Your studio mixing may range from the relatively simple task of riding gain for the newscaster's lavaliere mic or balancing the voices of several panel members during a discussion, to the more complicated job of switching among various audio sources during a newscast, or recording a rock band or even a dramatic scene for an interactive multimedia program on how to recognize potential shoplifters.

As with the setup of mics for a complex production, there is no formula for how an optimal mix is achieved. When riding gain for the single mic of the news anchor, simply keep his or her level within the tolerable audio range and make sure that the anchor is clearly heard. When controlling the audio of the panel, riding gain will be easiest if every member wears a lavaliere. Once the levels are set, you will probably have little to do except bring down the fader somewhat if one of the members gets excited and starts talking much louder than normal.

When using desk mics, the most important audio job is before the show even starts—the mics setup. Remember to place the mics at least three times as far apart as the distance of any mic to the panel members (as described in chapter 9). Such placement will eliminate any possible multiple-microphone interference. After taking preliminary levels, adjust the mics for optimal positions and tape them down. Take another level, adjust the faders for all mics, and hope that the banging and kicking of the table by the panel members will be kept to a minimum.

The multisource newscast is more challenging. For example, you may need to switch quickly from the anchor's introduction to *SOT (sound on tape)*, and from there to the co-anchor, to the guest in London (remote source), back to the co-anchor, to another VTR, back to the anchor, to a commercial, and so forth. You will find that labeling each audio input will greatly facilitate your audio control: Simply put a strip of masking tape below the faders and mark them with a grease pencil. As for volume control, you have to watch the remote sources and the SOT segments more than the mics of the anchors and weathercaster (whose voice levels you have set before the newscast).

The mixing for the rock band or dramatic scene for the multimedia project can be quite complicated and is best left to an audio expert. Again, the initial choice of mics and their proper placement are more challenging than the mixing itself. You may also have to patch the mics for various audio feeds, such as foldback, mix-minus, audience feed, or videotape feed. A ***mix-minus*** feed is a type of foldback in which you send into the studio a complete mix (usually the band or orchestra) minus the sound generated in the studio (such as the singer's voice). Regardless of the complexity of the setup, there are some basic steps to follow:

1. Label each input.

2. Calibrate the audio system.

3. Check the mics individually by having an assistant lightly scratch the surface of each mic. Having someone talk in the vicinity of the mic is not as accurate—you may well think you are testing one mic while actually receiving sound from another.

4. If foldback is required, check the foldback levels in the studio.

5. Do a brief test recording and listen to the mix on playback.

6. Adjust the necessary quality controls until the singer's voice sounds the way you like it to sound.

7. As in field production, try to record major sound sources (voice and instruments, dialogue and sound effects, guitar, bass, keyboard) on separate tracks. Such separation makes postproduction mixing much easier than if you mix everything live on a single track.

8. Anticipate the director's cues. For example, be prepared to open (activate) the talent's mic so that you can react immediately to the director's cue.

9. Do not panic and lose your temper if you hear some accidental noise, such as a door slamming shut or something being dropped. Although such noise may sound to you like irreparable damage at the time, most viewers will not even be aware of it. Don't take this friendly advice as an invitation to sloppy sound control, but rather as an appeal to common sense. If, however, you are doing a recording meant for postproduction, alert the director of such incidents and let him or her make the decision whether or not to do a retake.

Live Mixing in ENG/EFP

ENG EFP You usually do not need a mixer when doing ENG. You can plug the external mic into one of the camcorder audio inputs, and the camera shotgun mic into the other audio input.

In EFP mixing, however, there are always assignments for which you have to control more audio sources than the two microphones. Even a simple assignment such as covering the opening of the local elementary school's new multipurpose room will most likely require that you mix at least four microphones: the field reporter's mic, the lectern mic for the speeches, the audience mic, and a mic to pick up the school chorus.

Despite the number of mics, the mixing itself is fairly simple. Once you have set the level for each input, you probably need to ride gain only for the reporter's mic during interviews and for the various speakers at the lectern. You may also want to bring up (increase the gain of) the audience mic to emphasize the applause for the various community members honored by the school superintendent. Although in an emergency you could probably pick up most of these sounds by pointing a shotgun mic to the various areas, the multiple-mic setup and the portable mixer afford you the necessary control.

Here are a few guidelines for basic live ENG/EFP mixing:

▣ Even if you have only a few inputs, label each one with what it controls, such as field reporter's mic, audience mic, and so forth. You would be surprised at how quickly you forget whose mic corresponds to which fader. In case you have to turn over the audio control to someone else, he or she can take over without long explanations.

▣ Calibrate the console with the VTR(s). Record the 0 VU control tone on the videotape for at least ten seconds.

▣ Double-check all inputs from wireless mic systems. For some reason, they have a tendency to malfunction just before the start of the event.

▣ If recording for postproduction, try to put distinctly different sound sources on separate audio tracks of the videotape, such as the reporter's and guests' voices on one track and the speaker's lectern mic, the audience mic, and the chorus on the other. That way it will be easier in the sweetening session to balance the reporter's voice with the other sounds.

▣ It is usually easier to do complicated and subtle mixing in postproduction rather than live in the field. This does not mean that you should forgo filtering out as much unwanted sound as possible during the on-location pickup, assuming that the mixer has some basic quality controls available. But if it doesn't, don't worry. Save the more subtle mixing and quality control until you are back in the audio production room, where you have good speakers, all the necessary quality controls, and, most important, the time and quiet necessary for good mixing.

▣ If you do a complicated mix in the field, protect yourself by feeding it not only to the camcorder and VTR, but also to a separate audiotape recorder for probable remixing in postproduction.

Postproduction Mixing

Postproduction mixing is normally done in the audio production room. In television, audio postproduction involves not only the proper mixing and quality control of the sound track, but also, if not especially, the synchronization of the sound track with the video portion. As mentioned, computerized DAWs play a major role in audio mixing, various phases of audio control, and especially in audio/video synchronization. But do not assume that the computer will do the job for you. Even relatively simple audio postproduction tasks, such as editing a sound track of a conversation or doing some audio sweetening—filtering out an annoying hum or supplying narration and background music to a documentary—can become formidable and time-consuming tasks. Even experienced audio production people labor long hours over what may seem a relatively simple sweetening job. But don't worry—nobody will ask you to do complicated audio postproduction unless you have had a great deal of experience in audio, and audio for video production.

Mixdowns, during which a multitude of discrete audio tracks are combined and reduced to stereo or *surround-sound* tracks, are even more complicated and should definitely be left to the audio expert. Mixing surround sound is especially complicated, because you must deal not only with complicated aural mixes, but with complex spatial relationships as well.

Controlling Sound Quality

The control of sound quality is probably the most difficult aspect of audio control. You need to be thoroughly familiar with the various types of signal processing equipment (such as equalizers, reverberation controls, and filters) and you also need a trained ear. As with the volume control in mixing, you must be careful how you use these quality controls. If there is an obvious hum or hiss that you can filter out, by all means do so, but do not try to adjust the quality of each input before you have done at least a preliminary mix.

For example, you may decide that the sound effect of a police siren sounds much too thin; but when mixed with the traffic sounds, the thin and piercing siren may be perfect for communicating mounting tension. Before making any final quality judgments, listen to the audio track in relation to the video. An audio mix that sounds warm and rich by itself may lose those qualities when juxtaposed with a cool, tense video scene. As in all other aspects of television production, the communication goal and your aesthetic sensitivity, not the availability and production capacity of the equipment, should determine what you want the audience to hear. No volume meter in the world can substitute for aesthetic judgment.

Finally, remember that the key to good television audio lies in an optimal original sound pickup and your sensitive ears, and that all types of audio design in postproduction mixing take time.

AESTHETIC FACTORS

As reiterated throughout this chapter, the bewildering array of audio equipment is of little use if you cannot exercise some aesthetic judgment—make some decisions about how to work with television sound artistically, rather than just technically. Yet aesthetic judgment is not arbitrary or totally personal; there are some common aesthetic elements to which we all react similarly.

When dealing with television sound, you should pay attention to five basic aesthetic factors: environment, figure-ground principle, perspective, continuity, and energy.

Environment

Whereas in most studio recordings we try to eliminate as much ambient sound as possible, in the field these sounds, when heard in the background of the main sound source, are often important indicators of where the event takes place or even how it feels. Such sounds help establish the general *environment* of the event.

For example, when covering a downtown fire, the sirens, the crackling of the fire, the noise of the fire engines and the pumps, and the tense voices of the firefighters and onlookers are important in communicating some of the excitement and apprehension to the television viewers. Consider the recording of a small orchestra: In a studio recording, the coughing of a crew member or musician would, during an especially soft passage, certainly prompt a retake. Not so in a live concert. We have learned to identify occasional coughing and other such environmental sounds as important indicators of the immediacy of the event.

ENG EFP Environmental sounds are especially important in ENG. As mentioned, try to use one mic and one audio track of the videotape for the recording of the main sound source, such as the reporter or the guest, and the other mic (usually the camera mic) and the second audio track for the recording of the ambient sounds. Separating the sounds facilitates mixing them in the proper proportions in postproduction. *READY ZVL* ❸

Figure-ground

One important perceptual factor is the *figure-ground* principle, whereby we tend to organize our environment into a relatively mobile figure (a person, a car) and a relatively stable background (a wall, houses, mountains). If we expand this principle a little, we can say that we can single out an event that is important to us and make it the foreground while relegating all other events to the background—the environment.

For example, if you are looking for someone and finally discover her in a crowd of people, that person immediately becomes the focus of your attention—the foreground—while the rest of the people become the background. The same happens in the field of sound. We have the ability to perceive, within limits, the sounds we want or need to hear (the "figure") while ignoring to a large extent all other sounds (the "ground"), even if they are relatively louder.

As you recall, when showing close-ups of someone in a noisy environment, we usually make the figure (CU of person talking) louder and the background sounds softer. In long-shots we increase the volume of the environmental sounds so that the figure-ground relationship is more equal. When emphasizing the foreground, the sounds must not only be louder, but also have more *presence* (sound closer).

You can now see why it is so important to separate sounds as much as possible during the recording. If you record background and foreground all on one track, you have to live with whatever the mic picked up; manipulating the individual sounds would be very difficult, if possible at all. With the figure sounds on one track and the background sounds on the other, the manipulation is relatively easy.

Perspective

Sound perspective means that close-up pictures are matched with relatively nearby sounds, and long shots correspond with sounds that seem to come from farther away. Close sounds have more presence than distant sounds—a sound quality that makes us feel in proximity to the sound source. Generally, background sounds have less presence and close-ups have more presence.

Such a desirable variation of sound presence is virtually eliminated when using lavaliere mics in a drama. Because the distance between mic and mouth is about the same for each actor, their voices exhibit the same presence regardless of whether they are seen in a close-up or a long shot. The necessary presence must then be achieved in time-consuming and costly postproduction sessions. This is why boom mics are still preferred in many multicamera productions of television plays, such as soap operas. The boom mic can be moved close to an actor during a close-up and somewhat farther away during a long shot—a simple solution to a big problem.

Continuity

Sound *continuity* is especially important in postproduction. You may have noticed the sound quality of a reporter's voice change depending on whether he or she was speaking on- or off-camera. When on-camera the reporter used one type of microphone and was speaking from a remote location. Then the reporter returned to the acoustically treated studio to narrate the off-camera segments of the videotaped story, using a high-quality mic. The change in microphones and locales gave the speech a distinctly different quality. This difference may not be too noticeable during the actual recordings, but it becomes obvious when edited together in the final show.

How do you avoid such continuity problems? First, use identical mics for the on- and off-camera narration. Second, if you have time for a sweetening session, try to match the on-camera sound quality through equalization and reverberation. Third, if you recorded some ambience of the on-camera location, mix it with the off-camera narration. When producing this mix, feed the ambient sounds to the reporter through earphones while he or she is doing the voice-over narration; this will help the reporter re-create the on-site energy.

Sometimes you may hear the ambience punctured by brief silences at the edit points. The effect is as startling as when an airplane engine changes its pitch unexpectedly. The easiest way to restore the background continuity is to cover up these silences with prerecorded ambience. Always record a few minutes of "silence" (room ambience or background sound) before and after videotaping or whenever the ambience changes decisively (such as a concert hall with and without an audience).

Sound is also a chief element in establishing visual continuity. A rhythmically precise piece of music can help a disparate series of pictures seem continuous. Music and sound are often the important connecting link among abruptly changing shots and scenes. *READY ZVL* ❹

Energy

Unless you want to achieve a special effect through contradiction, you should match the general energy of the pictures with a similar sound intensity. *Energy* refers to all the factors in a scene that communicate a certain degree of aesthetic force and power. Obviously, high-energy scenes, such as a series of close-ups of a rock band in action, can stand higher-energy sounds than a more tranquil scene, such as lovers walking through a field of flowers. Good television audio depends a great deal on your ability to sense the general energy of the pictures or sequences and to adjust the volume accordingly.

Surround Sound

Surround sound is a technology that produces a sound-field in front of, to the sides of, and behind the listener, enabling you to hear sounds from the front, sides, and back. Developed originally for film reproduction, it is now used for HDTV. The most prevalent system is Dolby 5.1, which positions three speakers in front and two in the back for sound reproduction. **SEE 10.19**

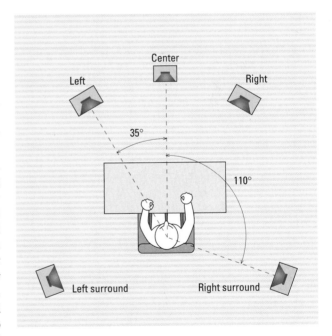

10.19 SURROUND SOUND
The 5.1 Dolby surround-sound system uses five speakers—three in front, and two in back.

Obviously, you need the proper speaker placement to benefit from surround sound. Good surround-sound mixing generally restricts on-screen dialogue to the middle front speaker and laterally spreads action to all three front speakers. But if you are surrounded by a sound environment—such as when amid downtown traffic, when playing in an orchestra, or when participating in a sporting event—all five speakers are active.

MAIN POINTS

◆ Audio system calibration means to adjust the VTR input (recording level) to match the volume of the console output (line-out signal). All VU meters in the system must respond in the same way to a specific audio signal (control tone).

◆ Before videotaping or going on the air, you need to take a level—to adjust the volume control (fader) so that the incoming sound (talent's remarks, musical instrument) falls within the acceptable levels as indicated by the VU meter.

◆ Live EFP mixing normally involves a small mixer. Try to record the principal audio (such as the talent's voice) separate from the background sounds (audience) as much as possible to facilitate postproduction mixing. Unless you do a live feed, avoid mixing in the field.

◆ When there are a variety of audio inputs, mark each input so that you can quickly activate and control each one as necessary.

◆ When recording an event on several sound tracks, you need a mixdown to combine the various tracks to a single audio track, or stereo or surround-sound tracks.

◆ The five major aesthetic factors in sound control are: environment—sharpening an event through ambient sounds; figure-ground—emphasizing the most important sound source over the general background sounds; perspective—matching close-up pictures with nearby sounds, and long shots with distant sounds; continuity—maintaining the quality of sound (such as a reporter's voice) when combining various takes; and energy—matching the force and power of the pictures with a similar degree of sound.

◆ Surround sound is a technology that produces a soundfield in front of, to the sides of, and behind the listener, enabling you to hear sounds from the front, sides, and back.

ZETTL'S VIDEOLAB 2.1

This section of the lab covers some of the important aesthetic factors of sound.

RUN ZVL 1   Click on the **audio** monitor and run tape 5 **Mixers**. Click on the **Calibration** module. Pay particular attention to the sequence in which you calibrate the output of the audio board or the field mixer with the VTR audio input. You can do a hands-on calibration when taking the **Quiz**.

RUN ZVL 2   Run tape 2 **Systems** and take the **Quiz**. Now run tape 5 **Mixers** again. Observe carefully the various parts of mixers (**Parts** module), how the signals flow through the audio console or mixer (**Signals** module), and how to exercise sound control through the mixer (**Control** module).

RUN ZVL 3   Run tape 6 **Aesthetics** and click on the **Environment** module. Note how the sound contributes to establish a specific environment.

RUN ZVL 4   Now click on the **Continuity** module. You can clearly hear how sound can help or hinder visual continuity.

11

Switching, or Instantaneous Editing

When watching a television director during a multicamera live show, such as a pickup of a basketball game, you might be surprised to find that the major activity of the director is not to tell the camerapersons what to do, but to select the most effective shots from the variety of video sources displayed on a row of preview monitors. In fact, the director is engaged in a sort of editing, except that the director does the selection of shots—the editing—during rather than after the production. Cutting from one video source to another or joining sources by other transitions (dissolves, wipes, and fades) while a show is in progress is known as **switching** or *instantaneous editing*.

Unlike postproduction editing, in which you have the time to deliberate exactly which shots and transitions to use, switching demands instantaneous decisions. The aesthetic principles of switching are identical to those used in postproduction; however, the technology involved is quite different. Instead of off-line or on-line editing systems, the major editing tool is the video *switcher* or a computer that performs the switcher functions.

Section 11.1, How Switchers Work, acquaints you with the basic functions, layout, and operation of a production switcher in a television control room. Section 11.2, What Switchers Do, looks at some specific switching systems and features.

KEY TERMS

auto transition An electronic device that functions like the fader bar.

bus A row of buttons on the switcher. A pair of buses is called a *bank*.

delegation controls Controls on a switcher that assign specific functions to a bus.

downstream keyer (DSK) A control that allows a title to be keyed (cut-in) over the picture (line-out signal) as it leaves the switcher.

effects bus Rows of buttons that can generate a number of electronic effects, such as keys, wipes, and mattes.

fader bar A lever on the switcher that activates preset transitions, such as dissolves, fades, and wipes of different speeds. It is also used to create superimpositions.

key bus A row of buttons used to select the video source to be inserted into a background image.

key level control Adjusts the keyed signal so that the title to be keyed appears sharp and clear. Also called *clip control* or *clipper*.

M/E bus Short for *mix/effects bus*. A row of buttons that can serve a mix or an effects function.

mix bus Rows of buttons that permit the mixing of video sources, as in a dissolve and a super.

preview/preset bus Rows of buttons used to select the upcoming video (preset function) and to route it to the preview monitor (preview function) independent of the line-out video. Also called *preset background*.

program bus The bus on a switcher whose inputs are directly switched to the line-out. Also called *direct bus* or *program background*.

switching A change from one video source to another during a show or show segment with the aid of a switcher. Also called *instantaneous editing*.

11.1

How Switchers Work

When you look at a large production switcher with all the different-colored rows of buttons and various levers, you may feel as intimidated as when looking into the cockpit of an airliner. But once you understand the basic principles and functions of a simple switcher, you can operate a relatively complex one. Even the most complex, computer-assisted video-switching system performs the same basic functions as a simple production switcher, except that large switchers have more video inputs and can perform more visual tricks.

This section explores what a production switcher does and how it basically works.

▶ **BASIC SWITCHER FUNCTIONS**
Selecting video sources, performing transitions between them, and creating special effects

▶ **SIMPLE SWITCHER LAYOUT**
Program bus, mix buses, preview bus, effects buses, and multifunction switchers and additional switcher controls

▶ **BASIC SWITCHER OPERATION**
Cut or take, dissolve, super, fade, and additional special-effects controls

BASIC SWITCHER FUNCTIONS

The basic functions of a production switcher are (1) to select an appropriate video source from several inputs, (2) to perform basic transitions between two video sources, and (3) to create or access special effects. Some switchers can automatically switch the program audio with the video.

As introduced in chapter 1, each video input on a switcher has a corresponding button. If you have only two cameras and all you want to do is cut from one to the other, two buttons (one for camera 1 and the other for camera 2) are sufficient. By pressing the camera 1 button, you put camera 1 "on the air," that is, route its video to the line-out, which carries it to the transmitter or the video recorder. Pressing the camera 2 button will put camera 2 on the air. If you had three cameras, you would need three buttons, each dedicated to a camera input. What if you wanted to expand your switching to include a VTR, a character generator (C.G.), and a remote feed? You would need three additional buttons—one for the VTR, one for the C.G., and one for the remote feed. When you want the screen to "go to black," you need an additional *blk* (black) button. The row of buttons, called a *bus*, has increased to six. Production switchers have not only many more buttons on each bus, but several buses as well. Let's find out why.

SIMPLE SWITCHER LAYOUT

It may be easier to understand the various parts of a switcher by constructing one that fulfills the basic switcher functions: cuts, dissolves, supers, and fades. It should also let you see the selected video inputs or effects before you punch them up on the air. While building a switcher, you will realize that even a simple switcher can get quite complicated and that we need to combine several of the functions to keep it manageable.

Program Bus

If all you wanted to do is *cut* (switch instantaneously) from one video source to another without previewing them, you could do with a single row of buttons, each one representing a different video input. **SEE 11.1** This row of buttons, which sends everything you punch up directly to the line-out (and from there to the transmitter or video recorder), is called the ***program bus***. The program bus represents, in effect, a selector switch for the line-out. It

is a direct input/output link and, therefore, is also called the *direct bus*. Note that there is an additional button at the beginning of the program bus, labeled *blk* or *black*. Instead of calling up a specific picture, the *blk* button puts the screen to black.

Mix Buses

If you want the switcher to do *dissolves* (during which one image is gradually overlapping and replacing the other), *supers* (overlapping, or mixing, of two images), and *fades* (gradual appearance of an image from black or disappearance to black) in addition to simple cuts, you need two more buses—the ***mix buses***—and a lever, called the ***fader bar***, that controls the speed of the mix (dissolves and fades) and the nature of the super. **SEE 11.2**

When moving the fader bar to the full extent of travel, the picture of one bus is faded in while the picture of the other bus is faded out. The actual dissolve happens when the video images of the two buses temporarily overlap. When you stop the fader bar somewhat in the middle, you arrest the dissolve and create a *superimposition* of the two video sources.

How does the program bus get this "mix" to the line-out? You must add still another button to the program bus that can transfer to the line-out the video generated by

11.1 PROGRAM BUS

Whatever source is punched up on the program bus goes directly to the line-out.

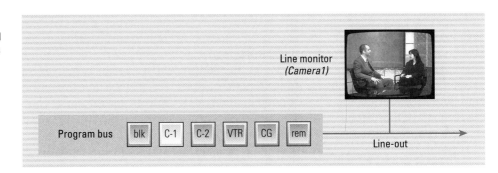

11.2 PROGRAM BUS WITH MIX BUSES AND FADER BAR

The mix buses A and B enable the mixing of two video sources.

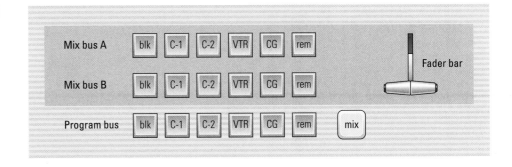

mix buses. This *mix* button is at the far right of the program bus.

Preview Bus

The *preview bus* is identical to the program bus in the number, type, and arrangement of buttons. Their functions are also similar, except that the "line-out" of the preview bus does not go on the air or to a recording device, but simply to a *preview (P/V) monitor*. If, for example, you press the camera 1 button on the preview bus, camera 1's picture appears on the preview monitor without affecting the output of the program bus, such as the C.G. text. If you don't like camera 1's picture and want to switch to camera 2, you simply press the camera 2 button on the preview bus. The program bus will still display the C.G. text on the line monitor. The preview bus is also called *preset bus* if it also functions as a monitor that shows various preset effects. The preview/preset bus is explored further later in this chapter.

Like the two-screen computer display on a post-production editor, the preview and line monitors are usually side by side to show whether two succeeding shots will cut together well, that is, preserve vector continuity and mental map positions.

As you can see, our simple switcher has grown to 26 buttons, arranged in four buses, and has a fader bar added. **SEE 11.3**

Effects Buses

If you now wanted your switcher to perform some special effects, such as a variety of wipes (one image framed in a geometrical shape gradually replacing the other), title keys (lettering inserted into a background picture), and other image manipulations (shape and/or color transformations), the basic design would have to include at least two or more *effects buses* and one additional fader

bar. You would probably then want to expand the other video inputs to accommodate several more cameras, two or three VTRs, *electronic still store (ESS) systems*, a graphics generator, and remote feeds. In no time your switcher would have so many buttons and levers that controlling them all would be a formidable task, especially during a multicamera, live or live-on-tape production.

Multifunction Switchers

To keep switchers manageable, manufacturers have designed buses that perform multiple functions. Rather than have separate program, mix, effects, and preview buses, you can assign a minimum of buses various *mix/effects (M/E)* functions. When you switch two *M/E buses* (A and B) to the mix mode, you can dissolve (mix) from A to B, or even do a super (by stopping the dissolve midway). By switching to the effects mode, you can achieve special effects, such as a variety of wipes from A to B. You can even assign the program and preview buses various M/E functions while still preserving their original functions. The buttons with which you delegate what a bus is to do are, logically enough, called **delegation controls**. The following discussion identifies the various buses and how they interact on a simple multifunction switcher. **SEE 11.4**

Major buses   As you can see, the switcher in figure 11.4 has only three buses: a preview/preset bus (lower row of buttons), a program bus (middle row), and a key bus (upper row). It also has a number of button groups that let you create certain effects.

The program bus always directs its output to the line-out. If, for example, you press the *C-1* button on the program bus, camera 1 is on the air. If you then press the *VTR* button, you cut from camera 1 to the VTR video. If you don't need to preview the upcoming pictures and your

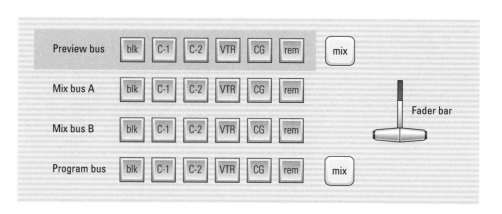

11.3 BASIC PRODUCTION SWITCHER WITH PREVIEW BUS

This basic production switcher has a program bus, two mix buses, and a preview bus. Note that the preview bus is identical to the program bus, except that its output is routed to the preview monitor and not to the line-out.

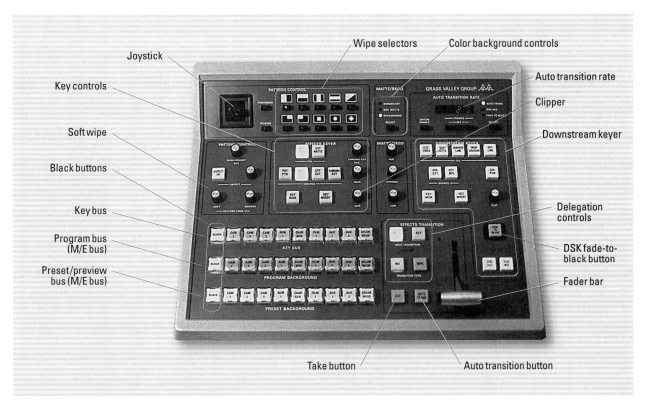

Joystick

Key controls

Soft wipe

Black buttons

Key bus

Program bus
(M/E bus)

Preset/preview
bus (M/E bus)

Wipe selectors   Color background controls

Auto transition rate

Clipper

Downstream keyer

Delegation
controls

DSK fade-to-
black button

Fader bar

Take button   Auto transition button

11.4 MULTIFUNCTION SWITCHER

This multifunction switcher (Grass Valley 100) has only three buses: a preview/preset bus, a program bus, and a key bus. You can delegate the program and preview/preset buses' M/E functions.

switching is "cuts-only," you can do it all on the program bus. When assigned a mix or effects function, it becomes M/E bus A. **SEE 11.5**

The *preview/preset bus* lets you preview the video source that you selected as your next shot. Whatever you press on this preset bus will automatically appear on the

preview/preset monitor. As soon as you activate a certain transition (cut, dissolve, wipe), this preview picture will replace the on-the-air picture as shown on the line monitor. As you can see, this preview/preset bus now functions as M/E bus B. You can now understand why this is called a preview/preset bus. It is a preview

11.5 SWITCHING ON THE PROGRAM BUS

When switching on the program bus, the transitions will be cuts-only. With camera 1 on the air, you can cut to camera 2 by pressing the *C-2* button.

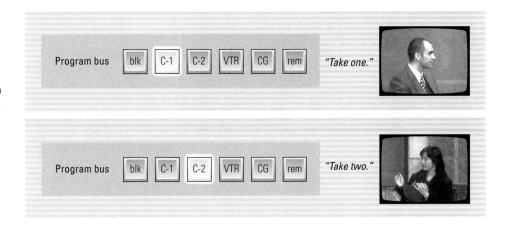

Program bus | blk | C-1 | C-2 | VTR | CG | rem | *"Take one."*

Program bus | blk | C-1 | C-2 | VTR | CG | rem | *"Take two."*

bus because it lets you preview the upcoming source. It is a preset bus because it lets you preset the upcoming shot. Despite its dual function, this bus is generally known as the preview bus.

Complicating the terminology a little more, both the program and preview/preset buses are sometimes called "background" buses, because they can serve as background for various effects. Let's assume that you have camera 1 punched up on the program bus (M/E bus A), showing a CU (close-up) of the latest computer model. When you insert the name of the computer over this shot, the program bus supplies the background image (the CU of the computer) for this title key.

The third (top) row of buttons is the **key bus**. It lets you select the video sources, such as lettering supplied by the C.G., to be inserted into the background image, supplied by the program bus.

Delegation controls These controls let you choose a transition or effect. **SEE 11.6** On this multifunction switcher they are located right next to the fader bar.

By pressing the background button *(bkgd)*, you put the program and preview/preset (A and B) buses in mix mode. Whatever you punch up on the program bus (A) will go on the air and, therefore, show up on the line monitor. Whatever you press on the preview/preset bus (B) will show up on the preview monitor, ready to replace—through a cut—the picture from bus A presently on the air.

By additionally pressing the red *mix* button in the delegation section of the switcher, you have expanded the transitions from cuts-only to include dissolves as well. You can now cut from one video source to another or dissolve between them. When you press the red *wipe* button instead of the *mix* button, the transition will be a wipe instead of a dissolve (see chapter 14).

By pressing the *key* button, you activate the top (key) bus. On this bus you can select a proper key source, such as the C.G., that is to be inserted into the background picture presently activated on the program bus (A), and, therefore, on the air. Going back to our computer example, the *C-1* button on the program bus (A) would provide the background image of the computer, and the *CG* button on the key bus, the name of the computer.

The advantage of a multifunction switcher is that you can achieve all these effects with only three buses. If you had continued the architecture—the electronic design logic—of the switcher you were building, you would have needed at least five buses, two fader bars, and several additional buttons to achieve the same key effect.

Before going on to some other major switcher controls, let's put some of the theory into practice and do some simple switching.

BASIC SWITCHER OPERATION

Although you are now working with a specific switcher (Grass Valley 100) whose controls are arranged in a particular way, most multifunction switchers operate on a similar M/E principle, called *switcher architecture*. Once you know how to operate a specific production switcher, you can transfer those skills to another.

Look again at the switcher in figure 11.4. How would you achieve a cut, a dissolve, a super, a fade from black, and a fade to black?

Cut or Take

As you recall, the program bus (A) lets you cut from one source to another by simply pressing the corresponding button. If you want camera 1 on the air, press the *C-1* button; to cut to camera 2, press the *C-2* button. The problem with such direct switching is that the next shot will not appear on the preview monitor. Unless you have a preview monitor for each video input in the control room, you would see the new picture only when it is on the air. To see whether the upcoming shot (camera 2) is,

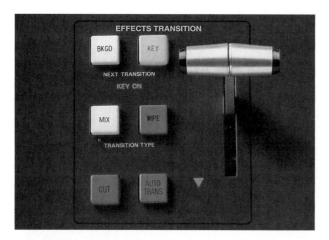

11.6 DELEGATION CONTROLS
The delegation controls assign the function of the buses and the specific transition mode.

indeed, the one you want or whether the new shot will cut together well (provide visual continuity) with the one already on the air (camera 1), you should see it on the preview monitor before putting it on the air. To do this you punch up camera 2 on the preset bus and then cut from the preset bus to the program bus.

But wait! You first need to tell the program and preview buses that they are supposed to interact as a pair of M/E buses. Pressing the *bkgd* (background) delegation button will accomplish this assignment. M/E bus A (also the program bus) is now feeding camera 1's picture to the line monitor (and to the line-out), and M/E bus B (also the preset bus) is feeding camera 2's picture to the preview monitor, ready to replace camera 1's picture. **SEE 11.7**

To perform the actual cut from camera 1 to camera 2, you press the *cut* button. The picture on the line monitor will instantly switch from camera 1 to camera 2, and the picture on the preview monitor from camera 2

to camera 1. The light of the *C-1* button on the program bus (indicating that its video source is on the air) will dim, and the *C-2* button will light (indicating that camera 2 is now on the air). The opposite will happen on the preset bus: The *C-2* button will dim (indicating that its source is no longer previewed), and the *C-1* button will light (indicating that its source is now fed to the preview monitor). By pressing the *cut* button, you have, in effect, transferred the output of the preview bus to the program bus, and the former output of the program bus back to the preview bus. This maneuver is also called *flip-flop switching.* **SEE 11.8**

What if you were to press the *cut* button again? Would you get the same flip-flop effect between the preview bus (which now shows camera 1) and program bus (which has camera 2 on the air)? Yes. This flip-flop feature of the *cut* button is helpful whenever you have to switch quickly and repeatedly between the same two

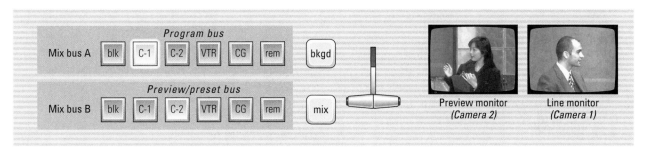

11.7 DUAL FUNCTION OF PROGRAM AND PRESET BUSES

When delegated a background and mix function, the program bus becomes M/E bus A, and the preview/preset bus becomes M/E bus B. Here camera 1 is punched up on bus A and is on the air. Camera 2 is preset to replace camera 1 as soon as you press the *cut* button.

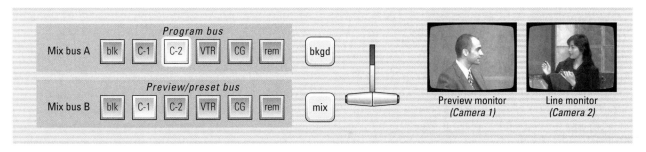

11.8 IMAGE CHANGE AFTER CUT

When the cut is completed, the program bus shows camera 2 on the air, while the preview/preset bus switches automatically to camera 1.

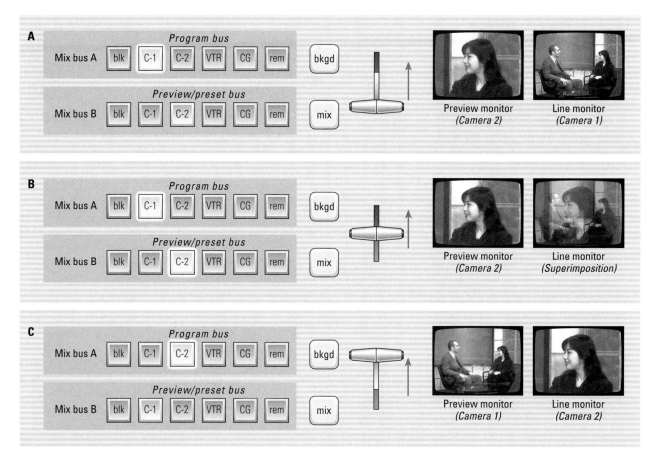

11.9 DISSOLVE

Once assigned the mix function through the mix delegation control, you can dissolve from camera 1 to camera 2. Assuming that camera 1 is on the air on bus A, you need to preset camera 2 on bus B. By moving the fader bar to the full extent of travel, you activate the dissolve from camera 1 to camera 2. Once the dissolve is completed, camera 2 will replace camera 1 on the program bus. Note that you can move the fader bar either up or down for the dissolve.

video sources. For example, in switching an interview, the single *cut* button lets you react quickly to what is being said and perform with great accuracy repeated cuts between the close-ups of the host and guest.

Dissolve

To achieve a dissolve, you must also press the *mix* button to delegate the mix function to both buses. If, for some reason, the *bkgd* button has been turned off, you need to also press this button again. When both the *bkgd* and *mix* buttons are lighted, the switcher is in the correct mix mode.

To dissolve from camera 1 to camera 2, you need to first punch up camera 1 on the program bus (A) to put camera 1 on the air. Now punch up camera 2 on the preview bus (B). As soon as you press the *C-2* button on the preset bus, it will light up dimly and route camera 2's video to the preview monitor. But instead of pressing the *cut* button as you would during a take, you move the fader bar all the way up (away from you) or down (toward you) to the full extent of travel. The speed of the dissolve depends on how fast you move the fader bar. When you have reached the limit of travel with the fader bar, the dissolve is complete and camera 2's picture will have replaced camera 1's picture. **SEE 11.9**

You can watch the dissolve on the line monitor, which displays camera 1's picture at the start of the dissolve and camera 2's picture at the end of it. Although you had both buses act temporarily as M/E buses A and B, they quickly snap back to their program and preview functions.

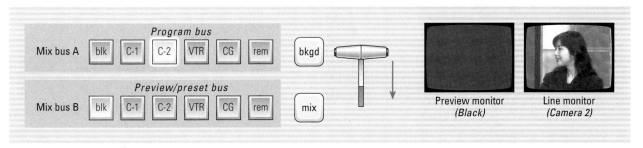

11.10 FADE

When fading to black from camera 2, you need to punch up the *blk* button on bus B (preview/preset) and then dissolve into it by moving the fader bar to the full extent of travel.

Because the program bus has command over what picture is on the air, the preset bus transfers camera 2's video input to the program bus and camera 1's picture to its own bus just in case you want to dissolve back to camera 1 at the end of the dissolve.

You can also use the ***auto transition*** device to execute the dissolve. Instead of moving the fader bar up or down, you can press the *auto trans* button, which then takes over the fader bar function. The rate of the dissolve is determined by the number of frames you input. Because our television system operates with 30 frames per second, a frame rate of 60 would give you a 2-second dissolve.

Super

If you were to stop the dissolve halfway between the program (A) and preset (B) buses, you would have a superimposition (see figure 11.9b). Both buses will be activated, each delivering a picture with exactly one-half video (signal strength). If you want to favor the picture from bus A (make the "old" video source stronger), simply stop the travel of the fader bar before it reaches midpoint. To favor the source from bus B (the "new" image), move the fader bar past the midpoint.

Fade

A *fade-in* is a dissolve from black to a picture; to "fade to black" or "go to black" is a dissolve from the on-the-air picture to black. Using our switcher, how would you fade in camera 2 from black? Here is the switching sequence:

1. Press the *blk* button on the program bus. Because the program bus delivers its picture to the line-out, the line monitor shows black video.

2. Press both *bkgd* and *mix* buttons. As you recall, these delegation controls will assign the program and preset buses' mix/effects functions.

3. Press the *C-2* button on the preset bus.

4. Move the fader bar to the opposite position. The speed of the fade-in is determined by how fast you move the fader bar.

To fade to black from camera 2 (which has been transferred to the program bus and is, therefore, on the air) you press the *blk* button on the preset bus and move the fader bar to the opposite limit of travel. **SEE 11.10** Because you literally dissolve from an image to black, you can also use the auto transition control for the fade to black.

Additional Special-Effects Controls

Because you have become so proficient in performing simple switcher operations, you can work with a few more controls to create a variety of special effects. These include: (1) wipe controls and wipe patterns, (2) key and clip controls, (3) the downstream keyer, and (4) color background controls. At this point don't worry about exactly how these controls are operated. Although each professional production switcher has most or all of these additional controls, they often require different means of operation. To become efficient in using a particular switcher, you need to study its operations manual and, above all, practice switching as you would when learning to play a musical instrument.

Realize that these controls do not by themselves create the effect; rather, it is the *special-effects generators (SEGs)* that perform this task (see chapter 14). On most production switchers, the SEG and other electronic special-effects equipment are built-in. When doing complicated postproduction editing, you will find that the standard switcher SEG will not give you enough variety. Postproduction switchers are often connected to

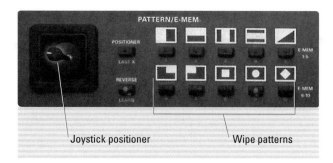

Joystick positioner   Wipe patterns

11.11 WIPE MODE SELECTORS

The wipe mode selectors offer a choice of geometrical wipe patterns. The configurations can be placed in a specific screen position using the joystick.

additional digital effects equipment that can produce a great amount of complex special effects.

Wipe controls and wipe patterns When pressing the *wipe* button in the delegation control section in addition to the *bkgd* button, all transitions will be wipes. Recall that during a wipe, the source video is gradually replaced by the second video that is framed in some geometrical shape. You can select the specific pattern in the group of buttons called *wipe mode selectors*. Common wipe patterns are expanding diamonds or circles. **SEE 11.11** On large switchers these controls can be extended to nearly 100 different patterns by inputting a code into the switcher. You can also control the direction of the wipe (whether a horizontal wipe, for example, starts from screen-left or screen-right during the transition). The joystick positioner lets you move some patterns anywhere on the screen. Other controls give the wipes a soft or hard edge and give letters different borders and shadows.

Key and clip controls *Keying* lets you insert lettering or another picture into the existing, or background, scene. The most common use of keys are to put lettering over people or scenes, or the famous box above the newscaster's shoulder. The key bus lets you select the particular video source to insert into the background scene, such as the titles from the C.G. The **key level control**, or *clip control*, adjusts the key signal so that the

letters appear sharp and clear during the key. On our (GV 100) switcher you would use the following steps to achieve a key:

1. On the preset bus, select the background into which you want to insert a key.

2. On the key bus, select the video source to be keyed (normally the C.G.).

3. In the delegation control section (effects/transition group), press the *key* and *mix* buttons.

4. In the effects keyer group, press the *key bus* button, which will make the key source appear on the preview monitor.

5. Adjust the clipper and gain controls (turn clockwise or counterclockwise) until the key looks sharp. If the key does not appear as indicated in step 4, adjust the clipper until it does.

6. Press the *cut* button to activate the key. The background image and the key should both appear on the line monitor.

For more information about how a key works, as well as an additional form of keying called the chroma key, see chapter 14.

Downstream keyer The "downstream" in *downstream keyer (DSK)* refers to the manipulation of the signal at the line-out (downstream), rather than at the M/E (upstream) stage. With a downstream keyer, you can insert (key) a title or other graphic over the signal as it leaves the switcher. This last-minute maneuver, which is totally independent of any of the controls on the buses, is done to keep as many M/E buses as possible available for the other switching and effects functions. Most switchers with a DSK have a *master fader* (additional fader bar or, more common, a fade-to-black auto transition) with which you can fade-to-black the base picture together with the downstream key effect (see figure 11.4).

You may ask why this fade-to-black control is necessary when, as just demonstrated, you can fade to black by simply dissolving to black on the program bus. The reason for the extra fade control is that the effect produced by the DSK is totally independent of the rest of the (upstream) switcher controls. The *blk* button on the program bus will eliminate the background but not the key itself. Only the *blk* button in the downstream keyer section (to the right of the fader bar) will fade the entire screen to black.

As an example, let's set up a simple DSK effect at the end of your product demonstration of the latest computer model and then fade to black. Your last scene shows a CU of the computer as the background, with the name of the computer inserted by the DSK. Recall that one way to fade to black is to press the *blk* button on the preset bus and then dissolve into it by moving the fader bar or pressing the *auto trans* button. But when you look at the line monitor, the background image (CU of computer) has been replaced by black as it should, but the name of the computer remains on-screen. You now know why. The downstream keyer is unaffected by what you do in the upstream part of the switcher—such as going to black on the M/E bus. Totally independent of the rest of the switcher controls, the DSK obeys only those controls in its own (downstream) territory, hence the need for its own black controls.

Color background controls Most switchers have controls with which you can provide color backgrounds to keys and even give the lettering of titles and other written information various colors or colored outlines. Color generators built into the switcher consist of dials that you can use to adjust hue (the color itself), saturation (the color strength), and brightness or luminance (the relative darkness and lightness of the color) (see figure 11.4). On large production switchers, these color controls are repeated on each M/E bus.

MAIN POINTS

◆ Instantaneous editing is the switching from one video source to another, or the combining of two or more sources while the show, or show segment, is in progress.

◆ All switchers, simple or complex, perform the same basic functions: selecting an appropriate video source from several inputs, performing basic transitions between two video sources, and creating or accessing special effects.

◆ The switcher has a separate button for each video input. There is a button for each camera, VTR, C.G., and other video sources, such as a remote input. The buttons are arranged in rows, called buses.

◆ The basic multifunction switcher has a preset bus for selecting and previewing the upcoming shot; a program bus that sends its video input to the line-out; a key bus for selecting the video to be inserted over a background picture; a fader bar to activate mix effects; and various special-effects controls.

◆ The program bus is a direct input/output (I/O) link and is therefore also called the direct bus. Whatever is punched up on the program bus goes directly to the line-out. It can also serve as a mix/effects (M/E) bus.

◆ The preview/preset bus is used to select the upcoming video (preset function) and route it to the preview monitor (preview function).

◆ The M/E bus can serve a mix (dissolve, super, fade) or an effects function.

◆ The key bus is used to select the video source to be inserted (keyed) into a background image.

◆ Delegation controls are used to assign the buses specific functions.

◆ The actual transition is activated by moving the fader bar from one limit of travel to the other, or by an auto transition control that takes on the functions of the fader bar.

◆ Most switchers offer additional effects, such as a variety of wipe patterns, borders, and background colors.

11.2

What Switchers Do

This section gives a brief overview of types of analog and digital switchers and switching software. Virtually all new switchers are digital in design and partially or fully computer-driven. With the predominance of component video recorders, the electronic design of switchers has changed accordingly.

▶ **SWITCHER TYPES AND FUNCTIONS**
Production and postproduction switchers, master control switchers, and routing switchers

▶ **ELECTRONIC DESIGNS**
Component and composite, analog and digital, and audio-follow-video switchers

SWITCHER TYPES AND FUNCTIONS

When looking more carefully at switchers, and especially when you begin to operate them, you will notice that they are designed to fulfill specific production functions. The major types of switchers are: (1) production switchers, (2) postproduction switchers, (3) master control switchers, and (4) routing switchers.

Production Switchers

Production switchers are used in multicamera studio or field productions. You will find them in studio control rooms and remote trucks. Their primary purpose is to select specific video sources to go on the air; to connect the selected video through cuts, dissolves, or wipes; and to create and apply keys and other effects. Production switchers must let you perform these tasks reliably and with relative ease. When switching a live football game, there is no room for error.

Production switchers must offer enough inputs to accommodate the various video sources available. Even a moderate studio production may require inputs from three cameras, a C.G., two or three VTRs, an ESS (electronic still store) system, and two or three remote feeds (such as a mobile ENG truck, network program, or satellite hookup). Because each button on a switcher can handle only a single input, this production would require a bus with a minimum of ten buttons, counting the *blk* button as a black video input. Despite the fact that large production switchers have thirty or more inputs, there are occasions when a TD (technical director) feels strapped for more, especially during live coverage of international news or large sporting events. You may then have to press into service an additional switcher that can take over a specific assignment, such as all the instant replays.

Although the primary function of production switchers is to facilitate instantaneous editing—selecting various video sources and sequencing them through transitions—they are expected to perform more and more complex effects that rival those of postproduction editing. Are such effects necessary or even appropriate when switching a live or live-on-tape show? Isn't the primary task of live switching to select shots and sequence them properly through a variety of transitions? Yes. But because audiences have become so accustomed to the visual razzle-dazzle of postproduction effects, live shows (such as news and sports) cannot afford to look any less exciting. At least so goes the argument.

A more persuasive argument is that expensive switchers cannot be limited to the few live or live-on-tape productions done in most television stations; they must be able to perform the more-complex postproduction tasks as well. Fortunately, all production switchers have a considerable number of digital effects built-in, and they can easily be hooked up to complex digital effects equipment to be used as postproduction switchers. Because switchers are basically computer-driven, they allow you to store a great number of preproduced special effects and recall them instantly by pressing a single button, without having to climb all over the panel to reach the necessary buttons and levers.

Postproduction Switchers

The switcher in postproduction is not used for instantaneous editing, but for creating transitions and special effects. The *postproduction switcher* is simply one of the elements of the postproduction system. A good postproduction switcher is not necessarily the one with the most video inputs, but rather the one that offers the greatest number of key effects and other multilevel equipment that can build, step by step, a highly complex effect. In postproduction the preview monitor, which, when using a production switcher, displays the shot you are about to put on the air, is called the *look-ahead preview,* because you can scrutinize each effects step before adding it to the other layers.

Because all sophisticated postproduction switchers use digital technology, they can be interfaced smoothly with other computer-assisted equipment, such as edit controllers, a variety of linear and nonlinear video storage devices, DVE (digital video effects) units, and

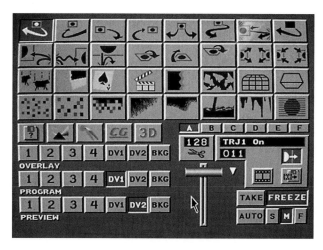

11.12 COMPUTER SWITCHER DISPLAY
This software program displays and activates all basic switcher functions.

even audio equipment. Postproduction switchers are basically menu-driven, which means that you activate the major switcher functions, not by pressing buttons on the switcher panel, but y choosing options on pull-down menus in a software program. The computer responds to the software commands, activating the switcher buttons and, if everything goes right, delivering the specified effect or transition.

Because such switchers are computer-driven, couldn't we do away with the actual switcher and simply use computer software to execute the various transitions of cut, mix, and wipe? Yes. There are software programs for both the Windows and Apple Macintosh platforms that function as basic switchers. Instead of pressing a button, you click a mouse. **SEE 11.12**

Computer technology notwithstanding, the switcher as you know it will have its place for some time. Even the most sophisticated computer switchers are simply not as flexible and functional as the actual switcher panel with its buttons and levers. A TD pressing buttons on a switcher panel is still the most effective means of instantaneous editing, provided the TD presses the right buttons at the right time.

Master Control Switchers

Computer-assisted switching is especially helpful in master control. In fact, the computer is so important in master control operation that often the engineer assists the computer, rather than the other way around. The

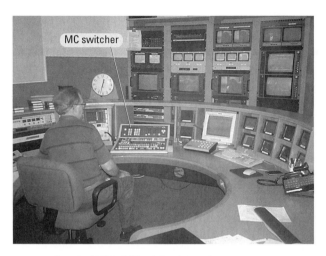

11.13 MASTER CONTROL SWITCHER

The computerized master control switcher switches specific video and audio sources automatically.

computerized *master control switcher* not only remembers and activates transition sequences, but also cues, rolls, and stops VTRs and video cart machines and calls up any number of still shots from the ESS system. **SEE 11.13**

Routing Switchers

Routing switchers route video signals to specific destinations. For example, you should use a routing switcher to feed various monitors with the line-out video, then switch to the preview video, and then to the satellite video. Or you may assign the line-out signal to be recorded by VTR 5 instead of VTR 2, because VTR 2 is involved in editing. The buttons on a routing switcher are usually arranged in rows that look very much like the program bus on a production switcher or part of a computer-controlled system.

ELECTRONIC DESIGNS

Although the ability to operate a switcher does not hinge on an intimate knowledge of its electronic design, you should have some idea of the major electronic characteristics: composite and component, analog and digital, and audio-follow-video switchers.

Composite and Component Switchers

Like a composite VTR, the *composite switcher* is built to transport and process the NTSC video signal that combines the luminance (Y) and color (C) signals into a single one. Composite switchers need only a single wire to transport the video signal. If you use the switcher strictly for multicamera live switching, such as a studio show or a sports remote, the composite switcher is perfectly adequate, because you deal only with NTSC signals. For high-quality postproduction, however, you need a switcher that allows Y/C component, color difference (Y/R–Y, B–Y), or RGB signal processing (see chapter 12). **SEE COLOR PLATES 10–13**

Component switchers process the video signal in either the Y/C or the color difference configuration. In the Y/C component switcher, the luminance and color information are processed separately and transported via two wires. In the color difference component switcher, three signals (a luminance and two color signals or RGB) are transported separately by three wires throughout the switcher and processed separately. If you use a component video recorder in postproduction editing, you cannot interface a composite switcher—it would not know what to do with the separate video signals.

Newer switchers are built to adapt to either composite or component signals, or to accept either configuration.

Analog and Digital Switchers

Although most *analog switchers* have a digital device for DVE or the storage of such effects, they basically process the analog video signals as supplied by cameras or VTRs in their original analog form. *Digital switchers,* on the other hand, process all incoming video signals digitally. Most digital switchers are component systems, but some let you change from component to composite configuration.

One advantage of digital switchers is that you can use as the video source signals that come directly from digital equipment, such as digital cameras, digital editing systems, computer hard drives, read/write optical discs, and any number of digital storage devices. Another advantage is that digital signals are less prone to interference by video noise than are analog signals.

Fortunately, digital switchers have maintained the architecture—the switching logic—of their analog counterparts. What this means to you is that the digital

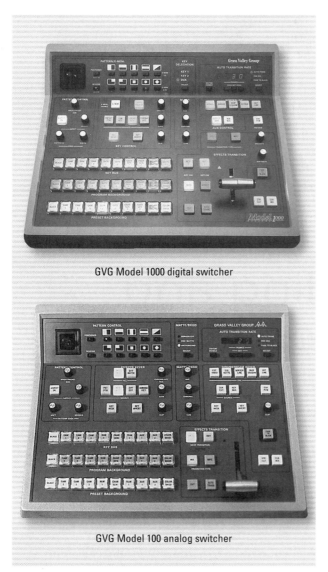

GVG Model 1000 digital switcher

GVG Model 100 analog switcher

11.14 DIGITAL SWITCHER
The appearance and operational functions of the digital switcher are very similar to those of its analog cousin.

switcher panel still has M/E, program, preview/preset, and key buses and fader bars much like an analog switcher. In fact, the appearance of a switcher alone will not tell you whether it is analog or digital. **SEE 11.14** More important, there is much similarity in the operation of the two types.

Audio-Follow-Video Switchers
Audio-follow-video switchers switch the audio with the pictures that go with it. For example, when switching a scene in which two people are talking on the phone, a telephone-quality audio filter cuts in every time you switch to the person on the far end of the conversation. When switching back to the "close" person, the switcher cuts out the audio filter and you hear the regular audio.

Master control switchers are audio-follow-video switchers, which means that they automatically change the accompanying audio along with the video source.

MAIN POINTS

◆ Production switchers are used to facilitate instantaneous editing during multicamera productions. They must have enough video inputs to accommodate the number of video sources used during the production.

◆ Postproduction switchers are used for creating transitions and special effects, rather than for instantaneous editing.

◆ Master control switchers are computer-driven. They not only switch from one program source to the next, but also roll VTRs and video cart machines and call up DVE (digital video effects) or ESS (electronic still store) video.

◆ Routing switchers simply direct a video signal to a specific destination.

◆ Composite switchers are built to transport and process NTSC video signals.

◆ Component switchers are built to handle Y/C component, color difference, or RGB video signals. There are switchers that can handle both composite and component signals.

◆ Analog switchers process analog video inputs throughout the switching operation. They often treat special effects digitally, however.

◆ Digital switchers are mainly component switchers, processing the video inputs exclusively in digital form. They normally maintain the switcher architecture (switching logic and the arrangement and functions of buses) in a similar way to analog switchers.

◆ Audio-follow-video switchers switch the audio with the pictures that go with it.

12

Video-Recording and Storage Systems

Although one of television's great assets is its capability to transmit an event "live," that is, while the event is in progress, most programs have been prerecorded on some kind of video-recording device. Even live newscasts contain a preponderance of recorded material. In corporate video or in independent production houses, almost all program material originates from some kind of video storage system.

Because of the importance of video recording, manufacturers are constantly striving to compress more and more video and audio material onto ever smaller storage devices, while making the retrieval of program material as quick and simple as possible. Section 12.1, How Video Recording Works, acquaints you with the major tape- and disk-based video-recording and storage systems. A tape-based system uses videotape as the storage medium for analog or digital video and audio signals. Disk-based systems store only digital video and audio signals on computer hard disks or read/write optical discs. Section 12.2, How Video Recording Is Done, introduces you to some of the operational uses of video recording and the major studio and ENG/EFP recording procedures.

analog recording systems Record the continually fluctuating video and audio signals generated by the video and/or audio source.

component system A process in which the luminance (Y) signals and color (C) signals, or all three color signals (RGB), are kept separate throughout the recording and storage process. Comprises the Y/C component, Y/color difference component, and RGB component systems.

composite system A process in which the luminance (Y, or black-and-white) signal and chrominance (C, or red, green, and blue) signal as well as sync information are encoded into a single video signal and transported on a single wire. Also called *NTSC signal*.

compression Reducing the amount of data to be stored or transmitted by using coding schemes that pack all original data into less space or by throwing away some of the least important data. Can be *lossy* or *lossless*.

control track The area of the videotape used for recording the synchronization information (sync pulse). Provides reference for the running speed of the VTR, for the placing and reading of the video tracks, and for counting the number of frames.

digital recording systems Sample the analog signals and convert them into discrete on/off pulses (bits).

disk-based video recorder All digital video recorders that record or store information on a hard disk or read/write optical disc.

electronic still store (ESS) system An electronic device that can grab a single frame from any video source and store it in digital form on a disk. It can retrieve the frame randomly in a fraction of a second.

field log A record of each take during the videotaping.

framestore synchronizer Image stabilization and synchronization system that stores and reads out one complete video frame.

isolated (iso) camera Feeds into the switcher and has its own separate video recorder. Or one that feeds directly into its own video recorder.

JPEG A video compression method mostly for still pictures, developed by the Joint Photographic Experts Group.

MPEG A compression technique for moving pictures, developed by the Moving Pictures Experts Group.

RGB component system Analog video-recording system wherein the red, green, and blue signals are kept separate throughout the entire recording and storage process and are transported on three separate wires.

tape-based video recorder All video recorders (analog and digital) that record or store information on videotape.

time base corrector (TBC) Electronic accessory to a video recorder that helps make playbacks or transfers electronically stable.

video leader Visual material and a control tone recorded ahead of the program material. Serves as a technical guide for playback.

videotape recorder (VTR) Electronic recording device that records video and audio signals on videotape for later playback or postproduction editing.

videotape tracks Most videotape systems have a video track, two or more audio tracks, a control track, and sometimes a separate time code track.

Y/C component system Analog video-recording system wherein the luminance (Y) and chrominance (C) signals are kept separate during signal encoding and transport, but are combined and occupy the same track when actually laid down on videotape. The Y/C component signal is transported by two wires.

Y/color difference component system Analog video-recording system in which three signals—the luminance (Y) signal, the red signal minus its luminance (R–Y) signal, and the blue signal minus its luminance (B–Y)—are kept separate throughout the recording and storage process.

12.1

How Video Recording Works

If you were to follow all the latest developments of video-recording and storage devices, you would probably be very confused. Some television stations swear that the old-fashioned analog videotape recording systems are still the best; others consider them obsolete, opting to work exclusively with digital videotape or disk recording systems. Instead of video and audio signals, cable companies are providing "data streams" and high-capacity data storage systems that can feed highly compressed video and audio "data" to 500 or more channels simultaneously. When walking around a postproduction facility, you'll probably find a great many disk-based editing systems.

The advantage of disk-based storage over tape is that it allows random access—an important feature in editing. Section 12.1 should help you make sense out of these various recording and storage devices.

▶ **TAPE- AND DISK-BASED RECORDING SYSTEMS**
Analog and digital systems, linear and nonlinear systems, composite and component systems, sampling, and compression

▶ **TAPED-BASED RECORDING AND STORAGE SYSTEMS**
How videotape recording works, operational VTR controls and electronic features, and major analog and digital systems

▶ **DISK-BASED RECORDING AND STORAGE SYSTEMS**
Hard disk systems, read/write optical discs, and data transfer

TAPE- AND DISK-BASED RECORDING SYSTEMS

A *tape-based video recorder* uses videotape for the recording, storage, and playback of video and audio information. A *disk-based video recorder* uses either large-capacity computer hard disks or read/write optical discs. Note that the hard disks of computers are spelled with a *k*, whereas all optical discs, including audio CDs, audio/video CD-ROMs, and DVDs, are spelled with a *c*. This section examines this recording technology in terms of (1) analog and digital systems, (2) linear and nonlinear systems, (3) composite and component systems, and (4) compression.

Analog and Digital Systems
As you recall from chapter 2, *analog recording systems* record the continually fluctuating video and audio signal

as created and processed by a video source (such as the analog camera) and an audio source (such as the microphone) on videotape and retrieve the recorded information as an identical continually fluctuating signal from the videotape.

Digital recording systems convert the analog video signals by *sampling* (selecting part of) the scanned image and translating it into digital code. The actual digital recording stores not video and audio signals, but data. When stored on a hard disk, the individual on/off pulses look the same, regardless of whether they represent an unforgettable musical performance or your monthly telephone bill.

Analog videotape recording Analog video-taping is similar to the analog audiotape-recording process. The electronic impulses of television pictures (video signal) and sound (audio signal) are recorded and stored on the plastic videotape by magnetizing its iron-oxide coating. During playback the stored information is converted again into video and audio signals and translated by the television set into television pictures and sound. The amount of electronic information is many times greater for video than for audio recording.

Not surprisingly, there are many different systems of treating and recording the video signals. Some are designed primarily for operational ease (as, for instance, in small consumer camcorders); others are designed for high-quality recordings whose pictures will deteriorate relatively little in a limited amount of dubs during postproduction.

Digital videotape recording In digital videotape recording, the VTRs (videotape recorders) store a staggering amount of digital information. Like digital audiotape recording, digital videotape recording requires a specific kind of tape. As mentioned in previous chapters, the advantage of digital recording is that it does not deteriorate in quality even after numerous dubs.

Linear and Nonlinear Systems

Although the terms *linear* and *nonlinear* apply more to the way the recorded information is retrieved rather than stored, you may also hear tape-based systems described as linear recording devices, and disk-based systems as nonlinear ones.

Linear systems All tape-based systems are linear. Linear systems record their information serially, which means that during retrieval you need to roll through shots 1 and 2 before reaching shot 3. Even if a tape-based system records the information digitally rather than in analog, it does not allow random access.

Nonlinear systems All disk-based systems are nonlinear, which means that you can randomly access (call up in any order) any shot without having to roll through previous material. For example, you can access shot 3 directly, without having to first roll through shots 1 and 2. Random access is especially important when editing, because it lets you call up instantaneously any video frame or audio "file" (information), regardless of where it is stored on the disk. The difference between linear and nonlinear systems is discussed further in the context of postproduction editing in chapter 13.

Composite and Component Systems

The division of video recorders into *composite* and *component* systems is important because the two are not compatible and they differ in production application. Analog and digital recording systems can treat their signals in one of four basic ways: (1) composite, (2) Y/C component, (3) Y/color difference component, and (4) RGB component.

Composite system The analog *composite system* combines the color (C, or chrominance) and brightness (Y, or luminance) information in a single (composite) signal. Only one wire is necessary to transport the composite signal. **SEE COLOR PLATE 10** Because this electronic combination was standardized some time ago by the National Television System Committee (NTSC), the composite signal is also called the *NTSC signal* or, simply, *NTSC.* The NTSC system is in contrast to other composite worldwide systems (such as the European PAL) that force a standard conversion every time they don't match. Most such standard conversions are taken care of in the satellite that distributes the signals.

The major disadvantage of the composite signal is that the slight interference between chrominance and luminance information is worsened and, therefore, more noticeable with each videotape generation.

Y/C component system In the analog *Y/C component system*, the luminance (Y) and chrominance (C) signals are kept separate during the encoding ("write") and the decoding ("read") processes. The signals are then combined and occupy the same track when stored, that is, actually laid down on the videotape. The Y/C configuration requires two wires to transport the Y/C component signal. **SEE COLOR PLATE 11**

To maintain the advantages of Y/C component recording, other equipment used in the process, such as monitors, must also keep the Y and C signals separate. This means that you cannot play a Y/C component videotape on a regular VHS recorder, or any other such NTSC system. The advantage of the Y/C component system is that it produces higher-quality pictures that will suffer less in subsequent tape generations than do NTSC tapes.

Y/color difference component system

In the analog *Y/color difference component system*, the luminance signal, the red signal minus luminance (R–Y), and the blue signal minus luminance (B–Y) are transported and stored as three separate signals. The green signal is generated again (matrixed) from these three signals. This system needs three wires to transport the three separate signals. **SEE COLOR PLATE 12**

RGB component system

In the analog *RGB component system*, the red, green, and blue signals are kept separate and treated as separate components throughout the recording and storage process. Each of the three signals remains separate even when laid down on the videotape. Because the RGB system needs three wires to transport the component signal, all other associated equipment, such as switchers, editors, and monitors, must also be capable of processing the three separate RGB signal components. This means that they all must have "three wires" to handle the video signal, instead of the single wire of the normal NTSC system—all in all a rather expensive requirement. **SEE COLOR PLATE 13**

The big advantage of the three-signal analog component system is that even its analog recordings maintain much of their original quality even through many tape generations. Such a feature is especially important if a production requires many special effects, such as animation scenes, that need to be built up through several recordings.

Obviously, the Y/C, Y/color difference, and RGB component systems eventually must combine the separate parts of their video signals into a single NTSC composite signal for traditional analog broadcast or tape distribution.

Sampling   You will undoubtedly hear people talk about the relative benefits of 4:2:2 over 4:1:1 sampling ratios in all forms of video recording. All this means is that in the digitizing process, the C (color) signals are sampled at one-fourth for 4:1:1 and one-half for 4:2:2 the sampling frequency of the Y (luminance) signal. The luminance signal receives such privileged treatment because it is a major contributor to the sharpness of the picture. The color signals produce good color for most normal production requirements. If, however, you require high-quality color that can stand up to a variety of special effects, such as various blue-screen or chroma-key effects (see chapter 14), you need equipment that uses a higher sampling ratio. The preferred sampling frequency for high-end production is, therefore, the 4:2:2 ratio, which means that the two color signals are sampled at half of the luminance frequency.

Confused? Don't worry. The most important things to remember about these systems is that, in comparison, the video signal of the NTSC composite system is of lower quality than that of the Y/C component system, which is somewhat inferior to the Y/color difference component system or the RGB component system. A 4:2:2 sampling ratio produces better pictures than a 4:1:1 frequency, although the latter certainly produces good pictures, too. In fact, you would probably notice the difference between the two sampling ratios only when building complex effects or when recording under extreme lighting conditions.

Other important points to remember are that some of these systems are incompatible with the others, and all need their own recording and playback equipment. Also, digital recordings are of superior quality to analog recordings, especially when you need to make many dubs during editing or for rendering special effects in postproduction.

Compression

As you recall from chapter 2, *compression* means the rearrangement or elimination of redundant picture information for easier storage and signal transport. *Lossless compression* means that we simply rearrange the data so that it takes up less space. This technique is similar to repacking a suitcase to make all the stuff fit into it. In *lossy compression* we throw away some of the unnecessary items and, therefore, can use a much smaller suitcase.

Digital picture storage takes a great amount of time for transport and a great amount of hard disk space. Because it is much easier to store and travel with a smaller digital "suitcase," most compression systems are the lossy kind—they throw away redundant data that will not harm the noticeable quality of the picture. The following discussion elaborates on the two compression standards—JPEG and MPEG2—introduced in chapter 2. If necessary, please review the earlier discussion before continuing.

JPEG   The *JPEG* system is generally used for compressing still images. Most still photos in your computer are compressed by JPEG. Because JPEG treats each frame as a still image, when applied to moving images such compression is inefficient and requires a relatively large digital "suitcase" for storage and transport. Therefore, for moving images the MPEG system is used.

MPEG-2   The *MPEG* standard was developed for moving television and film images. Rather than compress each frame independent of all others, the MPEG-2 system predicts how the next frame will change and then keeps only the pixels that make up the change. The problem with this system is not that the predictions may prove wrong and that the bicycler you have followed with your camera all of a sudden goes in the opposite direction, but rather with editing. Because some of the predictable frames are very lossy, they can't be used as the starting or end point of an edit. The system therefore sends a full frame periodically (say, every fifth or tenth frame) that is independent and not the result of a comparison with the previous one. The editor can then go to the full frame to do the actual cut. Being restricted to every fifth or tenth frame for a cut does not please an editor who may need to match each frame of lip movement with the corresponding sound, but in most cases a five-frame cutting restriction is not too much of a handicap. This is why systems designed for editing include these reference frames as often as feasible. Some systems recalculate a complete frame anywhere in the compressed video.

Interframe and intraframe compression   If the elimination of redundant pixels (lossy compression) stretches over several frames, as it does in MPEG-2, it is called *interframe compression*. If the rearrangement (lossless compression) or elimination of redundant pixels (lossy compression) occurs within each single frame, it is called *intraframe compression*. As you will see later in this chapter, the DV-based recording system uses intraframe compression, which means that an edit can be made at each frame.

Despite the relative efficiency of the various compression techniques, you can still use the old compression/quality formula: The less compression, the better the image quality.

TAPE-BASED RECORDING AND STORAGE SYSTEMS

This section explores (1) how videotape recording works, (2) what the operational VTR controls are, their electronic features, and how they function, and (3) the major analog and digital VTRs presently in use.

How Videotape Recording Works

Generally speaking, a *videotape recorder (VTR)* is any electronic recording device that records video and audio signals on videotape for later playback or postproduction editing. During video recording, the videotape moves past a rotating *head assembly* that "writes" the video and audio signals on the tape during the recording process and "reads" the magnetically stored information off the tape during playback. Some VTRs use two or four heads for the record/play (or write/read) functions. Some digital VTRs have even more read/write heads for various video, audio, and control tracks. In the play mode, some recorders use the same heads used for recording to read the information off the tracks and convert it back into video signals. Others use different heads for the record and play functions. For a simple explanation of how video recording works, the following discussion uses an analog VTR with only two record/playback heads.

Record/playback heads   The two heads are mounted opposite each other either on a rapidly spinning head drum or on a bar that spins inside a stationary head drum, in which case they make contact with the tape through a slot in the drum. To gain as much tape space for the large amount of video information without undue tape or drum speed, the tape is wound around the head drum in a slanted, spiral-like configuration. Based on the Greek word for spiral—*helix*—we call this tape wrap, and

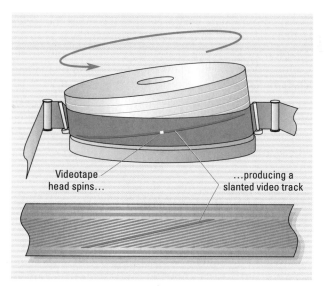

12.1 HELICAL SCAN, OR SLANT-TRACK, SYSTEM

The video track is slanted to gain a sufficient amount of area on a narrow tape.

often the whole video-recording system, the *helical scan,* or *slant-track,* system. **SEE 12.1**

Videotape tracks   Most videotape recorders put at least four separate *videotape tracks* on the tape: the *video track* containing the picture information, two *audio tracks* containing all sound information, and a *control track* that controls the videotape and rotation speed of the VTR heads. **SEE 12.2** (Some recording systems, such as Hi8, discussed later in this chapter, do not use a control track.) This section takes a closer look at these tracks and their major characteristics.

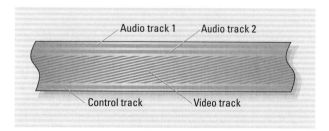

12.2 BASIC VIDEOTAPE TRACK SYSTEM

The basic videotape track system consists of a slanted video track, two or more audio tracks, and a control track.

Video track   When you record the video signal in the normal NTSC composite configuration, one pass of the head records a complete field of video information (Y + C). The next pass of the head—or, with a two-head machine, the second head—lays down the second field right next to it, thus completing a single video frame. Because two fields make up a single frame, the two heads must write 60 tracks (30 frames) for each second of NTSC video.

In Y/C component VTRs, the separate luminance and chrominance signals are combined and laid down on a single track with each pass of the record head. In the RGB and Y/color difference component systems, three passes are required to lay the three signals next to each other.

Audio tracks   The audio information is recorded on longitudinal tracks near the edge of the tape. Audio can also be recorded by the rotating "flying" heads that lay down the video tracks. Because of the demand for stereo audio and for keeping certain sounds separate even in monophonic sound, all VTR systems provide at least two audio tracks.

Control track   The control track contains evenly spaced blips or spikes, called the *sync pulse,* which mark each complete television frame. These pulses synchronize the tape speed (the speed with which the tape passes from the supply reel to the takeup reel in the cassette) and the rotation speed of the record heads so that a tape made on a similar machine can be played back without picture breakups. As explained in chapter 13, the control track is also essential for precise videotape editing. Some VTRs have a *sync track* (reserving the control track for editing purposes) and still another track for additional data, such as the *SMPTE time code.* Because space is so scarce in small-format videotape, some systems squeeze the time code and other data between the video and audio portion of a single track.

Digital systems   As mentioned, digital recording systems translate the video signal into digital form and record it as digital information. What you actually record is no longer a video signal, but on/off pulses that are usually coded as 0's and 1's. Just as there are analog VTRs, there are digital videotape recorders that process the video as NTSC composite, Y/C component, or RGB or Y/color difference component signals. Some digital systems, such as the *DVCPRO* or the *DVCAM* system, use very small (¼-inch) cassette tapes for their high-quality recording.

12.3 DVCPRO
TRACK PATTERN
The digital DVCPRO system
writes ten tracks to record a
single video frame.

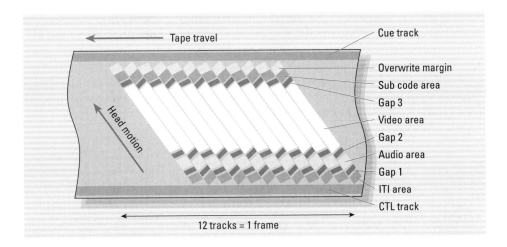

High tape and record head speeds make up for the lack of tape width. Instead of using just two tracks for recording a full frame of video, these systems use as many as ten or more tracks to record a single frame of video. **SEE 12.3**

There are also tape-based digital data recorders, which have as their origin computer systems that store a massive amount of data on tape. When adapted for video, they look and work for all practical purposes exactly like digital VTRs, except that they do not record digital video and audio signals, but simply digital data that can be reconfigured into picture and sound on retrieval. Fortunately, as a production person, you don't have to worry too much about exactly how the machine stores digital data, so long as you know its specific production function.

Operational Controls and Electronic Features

Fortunately, the basic operational controls and features of videotape recorders are similar, regardless of whether they record analog or digital information. When you look at a typical VTR, you will probably see the same controls as you have on your home VCR, except that the professional models have a few additional shuttle and edit controls. Each of these buttons or knobs lets you control a specific VTR function. **SEE 12.4**

12.4 BASIC
VTR CONTROLS
Standard VTR controls are
similar to those on a home
videocassette recorder.

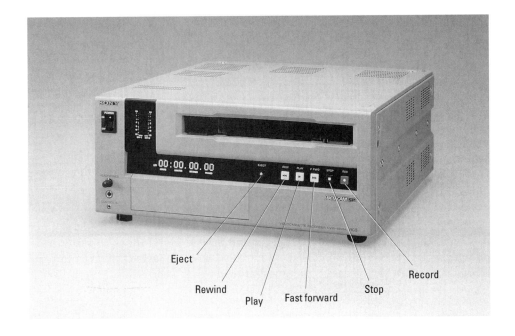

Operational controls   The most basic controls on any VTR—regardless of type or sophistication, analog or digital—are the *play, stop, record, fast-forward, rewind,* and *eject* buttons and audio volume controls. The more sophisticated VTRs have these additional functions: (1) standby, (2) pause or still, (3) search or shuttle, (4) tracking, (5) audio monitor for volume control, and (6) audio dub. All VTRs have a variety of input and output jacks.

The play, stop, record, fast-forward, rewind, and eject controls function exactly like those on a VCR at home. The latter controls and their functions warrant brief explanations.

Standby   This control threads the tape and rotates the video heads, but the tape is still stationary.

Pause or still   This control will stop the tape with the heads still moving. The rotating heads will continuously scan the adjacent video fields and produce a still—or freeze—frame on the video monitor in the camera viewfinder. But do not keep the machine in pause too long—the heads are apt to scrape the iron-oxide coating off the tape and leave nothing but clogged heads and video noise on the monitor.

A home VCR will probably kick out of pause mode if the tape has had enough abuse. Some professional recorders, however, will not do this automatically, to avoid interfering with the creative process. Regardless, don't leave the tape too long in pause mode, especially if you want to use it for editing.

Search or shuttle   This control lets you advance or reverse the tape at variable speeds that may be much higher or lower than the normal record/play speed. The *shuttle* feature is especially important when searching for a particular shot or scene on the videotape. You can advance the video frame by frame or rattle through a whole scene until you find the right picture. You can also slow down the shuttle enough to get a jogging effect, which shows a frame-by-frame advancement of the videotape.

Some elaborate recorders have separate shuttle and jog controls. You should note that in the search or shuttle mode, the heads are still engaged and in contact with the tape. If you have a rough idea of where a particular scene is located, use the fast-forward or rewind controls instead of search. The fast-forward and rewind modes disengage the heads, thus preventing excessive tape and head wear.

Tracking control   *Tracking* adjusts the speed of the head drum motor slightly to align the playback head with the videotape tracks. Tracking errors usually show up as a jittery picture. To fix tracking errors, simply manipulate the tracking control until you see a stable picture. High-end recorders usually track well and rarely need manual adjustment.

Audio controls   These controls include the track selection that is to receive or play back a specific sound feed, the volume control, and VU monitoring for each audio channel. Some recorders have separate volume controls for sound recording and playback. The *audio dub* control lets you record sound information without erasing the pictures already recorded on the video track.

Input and output jacks   The most important jacks (receptacles) are the video input (camera or any other video feed, such as the signal from a television set) and video output (to other VTRs for editing and to monitors or television sets). Most consumer VTRs have an *RF (radio frequency)* output, which lets you use a regular television set as a monitor. You simply connect the coaxial cable from the RF output of the VTR to the antenna input of the television set and switch the set to a particular channel (usually channel 3 or 4). The RF signal also carries the audio.

Besides the RF connection, the VTR also has separate video and audio output jacks that operate independently of the RF. They are designed for RCA phono plugs and are normally color-coded white and yellow, or red and yellow. Good television receivers have similar video and audio input jacks. If you do not use a coaxial cable for the RF connection, you can connect the VCR to the television set by plugging in an RCA phono cable into the video-out at the VCR and the video-in at the TV set. Then you connect the audio-out at the VCR to the audio-in at the TV set in the same way.

On professional VTRs you might have a choice of selecting regular (analog) and hi-fi (digital) audio. Depending on how the sound on the videotape was recorded, you may have to switch to or from hi-fi audio. If the audio doesn't play back properly, try the other mode.

Time base corrector and framestore synchronizers   All videotape systems need some device that stabilizes the picture and eliminates jitter during playback. Two of the most common are the *time base corrector (TBC)* and the more versatile digital framestore

12.5 BETACAM SX DIGITAL STUDIO VTR

This high-quality digital Betacam VTR has all the controls of a standard VCR, plus additional shuttle and editing controls. The major operations are displayed in a function window.

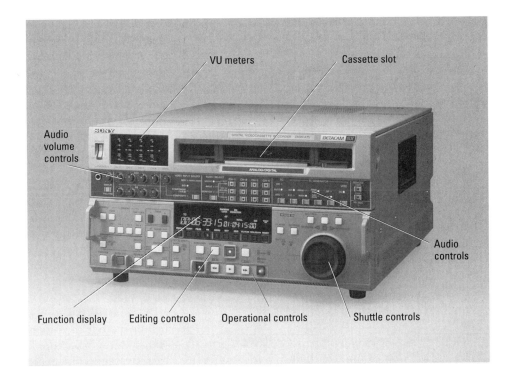

VU meters · Cassette slot · Audio volume controls · Audio controls · Function display · Editing controls · Operational controls · Shuttle controls

synchronizer. Both electronic devices adjust the scanning of the source signal to that of the playback device in order to keep both synchronization "clocks" in step. The digital *framestore synchronizer* grabs each frame of the video signal and stores it momentarily until its scanning has adjusted to that of another video source. This system is so efficient that you can switch among various independent video sources that have their own sync. Normally, you need to provide the same synchronization information—called *house sync*—to all video sources if you expect to switch among them without any temporary picture breakup. Most high-end VTRs have a built-in TBC; others need to be connected to one for jitter-free pictures.

Major Analog Videotape Recorders

Professional VTR models are as varied and change as rapidly as consumer models do. Rather than concentrate on various makes and models, this overview looks at the quality differences and specific functions of tape-based recording systems.

You can accomplish many production tasks with less-than-top-of-the-line VTRs. Even home VCRs are sufficient if all you want to do is look for a particular shot or scene. The more popular tape-based analog VTRs found in many large and small television stations and production centers include Betacam SP, S-VHS, Hi8, and VHS.

Betacam SP   The *SP* of this system stands, quite accurately, for *superior performance*. It is the improved version of the original Betacam recording process. Betacam SP is used extensively in broadcast stations, independent production companies, and demanding corporate video operations. This system keeps the Y (luminance) signal and the Y/color difference signals (R–Y and B–Y) separate throughout the recording process and is, therefore, a Y/color difference component system. Two of its four audio tracks produce high-fidelity sound. The digital Betacam SX, which produces the same high-quality picture and sound, suffers virtually no quality loss in subsequent dubs. **SEE 12.5**. Portable Betacam recorders can be docked with ENG/EFP cameras to form a camcorder. **SEE 12.6**

The Betacam SP system normally uses 30-minute cassettes, but it can also accommodate large cassettes that provide, despite the relatively high tape speed, up to 90

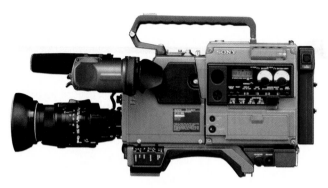

12.6 BETACAM SP VTR DOCKED WITH CAMERA

Most professional cameras can be docked with a high-quality VTR, such as this portable Betacam SP.

minutes of recording time. As with all other high-end professional equipment, the Betacam systems do not come cheaply.

S-VHS The S-VHS videotape recorder is a greatly improved version of the well-known consumer VHS recorders, which most of us use at home. You can find S-VHS recorders in television newsrooms, in editing suites of corporate production houses, and especially in schools that teach video production or that produce programs for a local cable station. **SEE 12.7** A small S-VHS recorder

can be docked with most professional ENG/EFP cameras, and many good camcorders have an S-VHS VTR built-in.

The S-VHS system records video information as Y/C component signals. This Y/C separation allows the original video quality to be maintained through several tape generations. High-end models have a built-in TBC that ensures picture stability during playback and editing. The S-VHS recorders provide four sound tracks (two of which are for high-fidelity sound) and a separate control track.

Because the S-VHS VTRs operate with separate Y/C video signals, they are only downward compatible with regular VHS recorders, which means that you can play the lower-quality VHS tapes on an S-VHS machine but cannot play an S-VHS tape on a home VHS machine. Because S-VHS is a Y/C component system, you need S-VHS monitors for playback and postproduction editing.

Hi8 The Hi8 system got its name from the 8mm width (a little more than ¼-inch) of its cassette tape. The small Hi8 cassette, which looks like a slightly fatter audio-cassette, can record up to 120 minutes of video and audio material. The tape has two digital audio tracks for stereo audio and a third high-fidelity monophonic track. Although Hi8 recorders use a Y/C component recording system, the Hi8 has in/out connectors for both composite NTSC video and Y/C component signals.

12.7 S-VHS STUDIO VTR

This high-quality ½-inch VTR records the video signal in the Y/C component configuration with hi-fi sound.

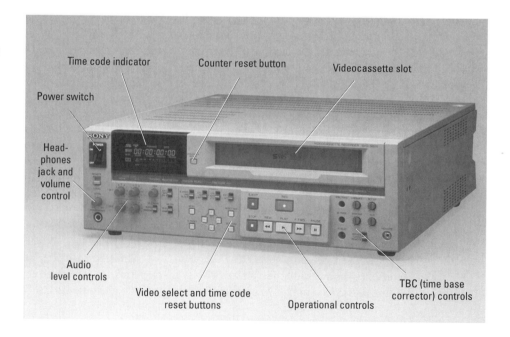

Time code indicator

Counter reset button

Videocassette slot

Power switch

Head-phones jack and volume control

Audio level controls

Video select and time code reset buttons

Operational controls

TBC (time base corrector) controls

12.8 ANALOG VTR TABLE

TYPE	RECORDING FORMAT	CASSETTE	PRODUCTION CHARACTERISTICS
Betacam SP	Y/C component Y/color difference	½-inch	High quality. Standard high-end analog recording system in studio VTRs and camcorders.
S-VHS	Y/C component, but actually recorded as a composite signal	½-inch	Good quality. Downward compatible with VHS.
Hi8	Y/C component	8mm (somewhat more than ¼-inch; slightly thicker than an audiocassette)	Amazingly good first-generation recording quality. Must be dubbed up to a higher-quality format for extensive postproduction editing.
VHS	NTSC composite	½-inch	Quality not good enough for broadcast applications or extensive postproduction. Used extensively in off-line work.
STILL IN USE			
1-inch VTR	NTSC composite	1-inch reel-to-reel tape	Old format, but still used because of excellent quality and initial expense.

The one-piece Hi8 camcorder, which is as small and handy as any other 8mm model, delivers amazingly high quality pictures and sound. Hi8 recordings do not tolerate multiple generations, however, and they erode relatively fast. Even multiple playbacks from the source tape cause some deterioration of the original video quality. If you intend to do postproduction, you should transfer, or "bump up," the original Hi8 source tapes to S-VHS or, better yet, to Betacam SP before doing any postproduction editing.

VHS   The VHS system, which you most likely have in your home, records the signals in the composite NTSC format and therefore produces pictures that are noticeably inferior in color fidelity and resolution to those of the Y/C component S-VHS system. Nevertheless, the VHS system serves important production functions. You can use the inexpensive machines for basic program screening, previewing and logging of scenes shot for postproduction editing, documenting shows for tape archives, and even for off-line editing. Logging and editing procedures are explored in chapter 13.

Some of the old-fashioned but excellent 1-inch reel-to-reel machines are still in use. Because they are easier to cue than analog cassette machines, they are mostly used for instant replays in sports. **SEE 12.8**

Major Digital Videotape Recorders

At this point you may wonder why we bother with digital recording systems when the analog VTRs described produce perfectly acceptable pictures and sound. The major advantage of digital videotape recorders is that they produce high-quality pictures and sound that maintain their quality through repeated dubs. There are other advantages as well:

■ They need not be converted (unlike analog recordings) for computer storage on a hard disk for nonlinear editing.

■ They can be easily computer-manipulated.

■ They are less susceptible to deterioration than analog tapes when stored over a long period of time.

Here are some of the more popular models in production and postproduction facilities: D-1, D-2, D-3, D-5, Digital Betacam, Digital-S, DVCPRO (D7), and DVCAM. It was no oversight that "D-4" is missing. Like "unlucky 13" in western culture, the number 4 has negative connotations in Japanese society and was—so goes the rumor—purposely skipped by the VTR manufacturer.

D-1 system   This VTR is especially useful for extensive postproduction involving many tape generations and extensive special effects, which is why you still see D-1 systems in some postproduction houses. Because the component color difference or component RGB signals are kept separate throughout the recording process, the image quality remains basically unaffected by even the most complex manipulation. This system is not compatible with any other, however, and requires RGB component monitors and switchers. It has a high sampling ratio (4:2:2 for color difference and 4:4:4 for RGB).

D-2 system   The D-2 VTR processes the video signal in its composite NTSC configuration, which means you can use it instead of analog VTRs and in tandem with regular switchers and monitors. It uses 19mm (about ¾-inch) cassettes and has a 4:2:2 sampling ratio and no compression.

D-3 system   Like the D-2 machine, the D-3 VTR is composite NTSC, which means that it can be integrated with other standard video equipment, such as monitors and switchers, without an additional interface. The D-3 VTR has a 4:2:2 sampling ratio and no compression. The major difference between D-2 and D-3 VTRs is that the D-3 machine uses the smaller ½-inch cassette. The smaller cassette makes the D-3 VTRs small enough to be used as camcorder VTRs. The digital audio has CD quality. Whereas most digital cassettes hold up to ninety minutes of programming, some of the ½-inch digital VTRs (such as the recording system developed by Panasonic) can record up to four hours on a single cassette and produce viewable pictures and intelligible sound at 100 times the normal shuttle speed. **SEE 12.9**

D-5 system   Like the D-1 system, the D-5 VTR is RGB component and has a 4:2:2 sampling ratio and no compression. All four audio tracks are high-fidelity and reproduce CD-quality sound. Besides being a superior postproduction machine, the D-5 VTR can be docked with an ENG/EFP camera to form a camcorder.

12.9 D-3 STUDIO VTR

This D-3 digital VTR can record up to four hours of programming on a single ½-inch cassette. It has standard VTR controls, but shows its operational functions (VU levels, tape remaining, time code) in a display window.

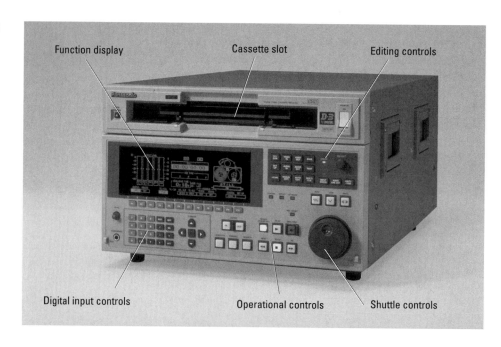

Function display   Cassette slot   Editing controls

Digital input controls   Operational controls   Shuttle controls

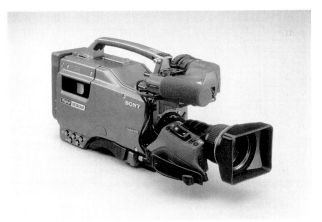

12.10 DIGITAL BETACAM CAMCORDER

This digital Betacam recorder is docked with a high-quality camera, a combination called a *digital camcorder.*

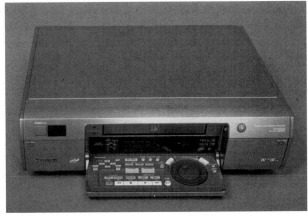

12.11 DVCPRO VTR

Although the digital DVCPRO VTR is smaller than its analog cousins, it has pretty much the same operational features.

D-6 system This system was specifically developed for high-end HDTV (high-definition television) recording. It uses the customary 4:2:2 sampling ratio but no compression. It also squeezes ten hi-fi digital audio tracks onto its 19mm (almost ¾-inch) tape. Without compression it is strictly a recording and postproduction tool, impractical for broadcast.

Digital Betacam There are several digital Betacam formats. One of them is the Digital Betacam, which is very similar to the Betacam SP except that it records in digital form. It is color difference component and has a 4:2:2 sampling ratio. It uses ½-inch tape that can record continuously for about three hours. In its studio configuration, the digital Betacam has superior recording quality and is used for complex postproduction tasks requiring many tape generations. As a portable VTR, it can be docked with ENG/EFP cameras. The analog and digital Betacam VTRs are still widely used in professional television and video production. **SEE 12.10** As with all other component systems, the digital Betacam needs its own associated equipment, such as component monitors.

Digital-S or D-9 This system, developed by JVC, uses ½-inch cassettes that can record more than 100 minutes of programming. It accepts composite, Y/C component, and RGB component and Y/color difference signals. The unique feature of the Digital-S VTR is that it is compatible with any digital system and downward compatible with analog S-VHS: You can play back S-VHS tapes on the Digital-S recorder (but you cannot play a Digital-S cassette on an analog S-VHS machine).

DVCPRO or D-7 system This Panasonic system is an improved version of the consumer *DV (digital video)* format. The main difference is that the DVCPRO and the high-end DVCPRO 50 have additional control and cue tracks, a better sampling ratio (4:2:2 for DVCPRO 50), and a considerably higher tape speed. The DVCPRO uses a very small cassette whose ¼-inch (6.35mm) metal-particle tape can record about two hours of programming. The Y/color difference component signals are sampled in a 4:1:1 or 4:2:2 ratio and compressed in an efficient intraframe system. Despite its relatively compact size and small cassette, the DVCPRO's video and audio quality rivals, if not excels, Betacam SP standards. **SEE 12.11** DVCPRO camcorders and recorders are highly portable; a complete DVCPRO editing system is about the size of a briefcase—source and record display screens included.

DVCAM Sony's DVCAM VTR has a 4:1:1 sampling ratio when recording Y/color difference component signals. Like the DVCPRO, it uses intraframe compression and the ¼-inch (6.35mm) cassette. The cassettes contain various tape lengths, capable of recording up to three hours of programming. Besides the DVCAM's small size and excellent audio and video quality, the recordings suffer virtually no deterioration during postproduction because they stay compressed through the entire editing process.

DV system   This VTR is the forerunner of the DVCPRO system. It was originally designed for the consumer market, but quickly found its way into newsrooms because of the astonishingly good quality and small size of the camcorder and VTR. The mini-tape cassette can record up to one hour of continuous programming. Its tapes can be played and edited on the DVCPRO system, provided you use a specific cassette adapter.

Digital video cart machines   Video cart machines record, manage, and automatically play back a great variety of videocassettes. The digital machines come in numerous tape formats and systems, but basically do the same thing—record and play back short program segments, such as commercials, station promotions, and announcements, during station breaks. The computer displays a menu of the 500 to 1,000 cassettes available, selects the appropriate tape, plays it at the scheduled time, puts it back, and keeps a log of its actions. These gigantic cart machines are still used only in larger television stations. They have, however, been largely replaced by video servers—large-capacity computer systems. **SEE 12.12**

DISK-BASED RECORDING AND STORAGE SYSTEMS

The basis for nonlinear postproduction editing is the development of large-capacity hard disks or read/write optical discs with fast access times. All nontape digital video-recording systems operate on the same principle: to store digital data in specific files that can be identified by the computer and randomly retrieved. If that sounds familiar, it's because disk-based systems are, indeed, specialized computers. This is why you can use or modify a desktop computer rather easily for video and audio storage. This overview looks at (1) hard disk systems, (2) read/write optical discs, and (3) methods of data transfer.

Hard Disk Systems
These systems include: (1) large-capacity hard disks, (2) portable hard disks, and (3) electronic still store systems.

Large-capacity hard disks   The simplest way of storing and retrieving digital video and audio information for postproduction editing is with large-capacity hard

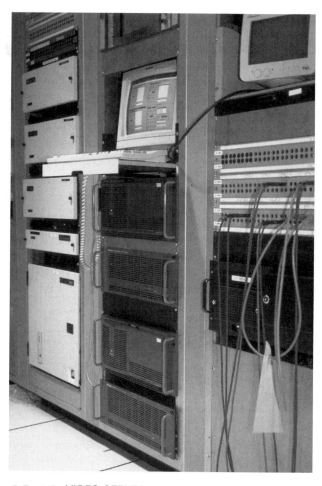

12.12 VIDEO SERVER
The video server consists of large-capacity computer disks that can store a great number of brief program segments, such as commercials and promotional announcements.

disks. The storage capacity of these hard disks has been expanded exponentially, and their access time (the time it takes to find and retrieve specific data) has decreased so much that they are now used extensively for digital postproduction. Some hard disk systems distribute the data over several smaller-capacity hard disks, called *disk arrays,* which were developed to cut down on access time and increase data transfer rates.

Portable hard disks   These small hard disks, called *field packs,* are designed to be docked with ENG/EFP cameras. The field pack is about the size of a dockable VTR yet can hold enough digital video and audio information for a 20-minute recording. The portable hard

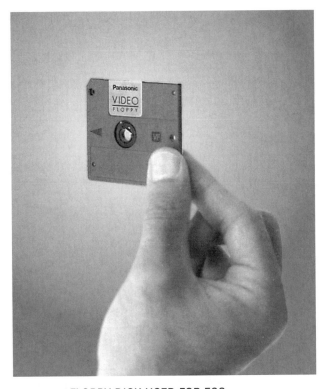

12.13 FLOPPY DISK USED FOR ESS
This tiny floppy disk, a little larger than a postage stamp, stores up to 200 still pictures (video frames), which can be randomly accessed by the ESS system.

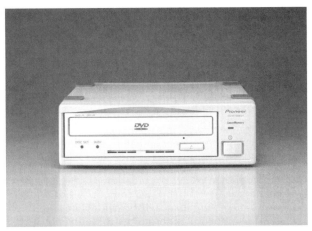

12.14 READ/WRITE OPTICAL VIDEODISC
This read/write optical videodisc operates with a laser beam, similar to a CD. Unlike the CD, however, it not only can play, it can also record information.

disk allows you to do some rough editing in the field—a big advantage in ENG. When docked with an Ikegami camera, the portable hard disk is called a *CamCutter*.

Electronic still store system   In effect a large slide collection that allows you to access any slide in about a tenth of a second, the *electronic still store (ESS) system* can grab any frame from various video sources (camera, videotape, computer) and store it in digital form on a hard disk. It is not unusual to find ESS systems that hold several thousand images. Each still has its own filename (address) and can therefore be accessed randomly and almost instantaneously during the production or in postproduction editing. Large-capacity graphics generators work similarly with titles and a limited amount of stills, such as the vital statistics of sports figures or people in the news. Some of the smaller ESS systems use regular-sized (3½-inch) floppies. Even a tiny 2-inch floppy can hold up to 200 frames. **SEE 12.13**

Read/Write Optical Discs

Like audio CDs and CD-ROMs, the *read/write optical disc*, or *optical videodisc*, uses a laser beam to encode (write) and decode (read) the digital information. But unlike CDs and most CD-ROMs, which are read-only, the optical videodisc lets you play back (read) and also record (write) new video and audio material. It functions similarly to videotape or hard disks. The great advantage of the read/write optical disc is its extremely fast access time; you can precisely locate, cue, and play a certain scene in a fraction of a second. This retrieval speed makes it a convenient device for the quick and accurate playback of relatively brief scenes. **SEE 12.14**

Data Transfer

Even if you don't have to digitize the video and audio information from an analog videotape for digital storage, you still need to transfer the data recorded by the digital camcorder to a temporary digital storage device, such as the editing computer's hard disk, for postproduction editing. Fortunately, there are cables called *FireWire* (Apple) or i-link (Sony) that can do this for you. (The more formal name for this transfer standard is IEEE 1394.) Assuming that the plugs fit both the camcorder and the computer port, these cables let you transfer all your camcorder footage directly to the editing computer. Obviously, such a transfer is much faster than digitizing analog tape footage before storing it on the hard disk of the editing computer.

MAIN POINTS

◆ There are both tape-based and disk-based video-recording systems. Some disk-based systems (such as a home VCR) record and store the information in analog form; others record and store it in digital form.

◆ All tape-based systems are linear. Disk-based systems are nonlinear and allow random access.

◆ Video recorders are also classified by how they transport and record the video signal. Recorders that operate with the NTSC composite system combine the luminance (black-and-white, or Y) information and the chrominance (red, green, and blue, or C) information in a single signal. Y/C component recorders transport the Y and C separately, but combine the two signals on the videotape. The Y/color difference component system consists of Y, R–Y, and B–Y signals, which are kept separate throughout the recording process. In the RGB component system, the red, green, and blue signals are kept separate throughout the transport as well as on the videotape. None of these systems is compatible with the others, and all need their own recording and playback equipment.

◆ Component systems deliver better-quality video than composite systems.

◆ All tape-based systems use the helical scan, or slant-track, recording method. One or more heads rotate with, or through, the head drum to put the video tracks on the tape that moves past the rotating heads. The audio is recorded simultaneously on an audio track(s). The control track marks each frame and also synchronizes tape speed and head rotation speed. Some recorders use still another track for the time code or other control information.

◆ Digital tape-based systems translate the analog audio and video signals into digital on/off pulses and put the digital information on videotape similar to the analog system.

◆ The advantage of digital recording is that the image quality does not deteriorate during subsequent dubbing.

◆ The basic operational controls of all VTR models are play, stop, record, fast forward, rewind, eject, and an audio volume control.

◆ The TBC (time base corrector) and framestore synchronizers are electronic devices that help stabilize the playback of video recorders.

◆ Disk-based recording systems use high-capacity hard disks and read/write optical discs. All disk-based systems are nonlinear, permitting random access.

◆ Hard disk systems include high-capacity hard disks, portable hard disks, and the ESS (electronic still store) system.

◆ Read/write optical discs operate similarly to audio CDs or multimedia CD-ROMs, except that they can be used for recording as well as playback. They offer extremely fast and accurate retrieval of program segments.

12.2

How Video Recording Is Done

Now that you have read all about the various video-recording systems, you need to know what to do with them. This section introduces you to the major operational uses of video recording and the video-recording procedures in studio production and ENG/EFP.

▶ **USES OF VIDEO RECORDING AND STORAGE**
  Show building, time delay, program duplication and distribution, and record protection and reference

▶ **OPERATIONAL VIDEO-RECORDING SYSTEMS**
  Quality choice, single and multiple videotape recorders (VTRs), and iso VTRs

▶ **VIDEO-RECORDING PRODUCTION FACTORS**
  Preproduction (schedule, equipment, preparation for postproduction editing), and production (video leader, time code and recording checks, record-keeping, and specific aspects of disk-based video recording)

USES OF VIDEO RECORDING AND STORAGE

Video recording is primarily used for (1) building a show, (2) time delay, (3) program duplication and distribution, and (4) the creation of a protection copy of a video recording for reference and study.

Building a Show

One of the major uses of videotape is to build a television show from previously recorded tape segments. This building process is done through *postproduction editing.* The building process may include assembling multiple segments shot at different times and locations, or may simply be the condensing of a news story by cutting out the nonessential parts. It also includes the stringing together of longer multicamera scenes that were switched (instantaneously edited) and recorded on videotape. A good example of this technique is the recording of the relatively long and uninterrupted scenes of soap operas.

Time Delay

Through video recording, an event can be stored and played back immediately, or hours, days, or even years after its occurrence. In sports many key plays are recorded and shown immediately after they occur. Because the playback of the recording happens so quickly after the actual event, they are called *instant replays.* Network shows that you can watch at the same schedule time in each time zone are time delayed through videotape. For example, through video recording you can delay the broadcast time so that the same network newscast at 6 P.M. in New York is seen at 6 P.M. in San Francisco.

Program Duplication and Distribution

Video recordings can be easily duplicated and distributed to a variety of television outlets by mail, courier, cable, coax or fiber-optic cable, or satellite. Through satellite, a single video recording can be distributed simultaneously to multiple destinations with minimal effort.

Record Protection and Reference

To record important events, such as key school board meetings, panel discussions of the company management, or local baseball games, you should not rely on a single VTR: Record the video and audio signals to a separate VTR or similar video-recording device. If one recorder malfunctions, you still have the other for backup. You will also end up with two master tapes, which may come in handy when making copies of the show or doing postproduction editing.

Videotape is excellent for preserving a television event for reference or study, especially one-time happenings such as sporting events, political gatherings, a difficult medical operation, and examples of supreme human achievement or failure. Such videotaped records can be stored, retrieved, and distributed via television with relative ease. Digital signals on videotape have a longer shelf life than analog recordings; but for all practical purposes, both types of recording will keep a long time if properly stored—reasonable room temperature, low moisture, and especially away from strong magnetic fields. Computers can keep records of tape archives and facilitate access to specific programs.

OPERATIONAL VIDEO-RECORDING SYSTEMS

Your preproduction facilities request involves not only cameras, lights, and microphones, but video-recording equipment as well. Think of the recording equipment as part of an operational system. There is no need to request two or three high-quality digital VTRs to cover a simple interview with the college president for a weekly campus show; a single camcorder is sufficient. On the other hand, if you are asked by a medical school to record an especially complicated operation, you may want to use at least one other high-quality recorder for backup.

Quality Choice

The quality of the recorder is determined by your intentions for the recorded material. If you use it for immediate and one-time playback, such as showing somebody what's wrong with her golf swing, a simple VHS recorder will certainly do. But if you need high-quality video for educational purposes, or if the recorded material is to undergo extensive postproduction, you need high-quality recording systems. For example, if the aforementioned operation, which depends on seeing minute detail and color differences, is to be edited and distributed to other medical facilities as educational material, you need the best recording equipment you can get.

If you are asked to do a commercial that contains many special effects, you need, again, the best available recording system. As a matter of fact, a digital Betacam, DVCAM, or DVCPRO system would probably be the appropriate choice, because the video will not deteriorate during the many generations needed in building the special effects.

Operational Video Recorder Systems

The basic operational systems include the use of a single videotape recorder, multiple recorders, and iso recorders.

Single VTR   One of the simplest ways to record is to use a single VTR for the output from a single camera, such as a camcorder. Most ENG/EFP uses a single camera, even if the material is slated for extensive postproduction. When using multiple cameras, the switcher output is

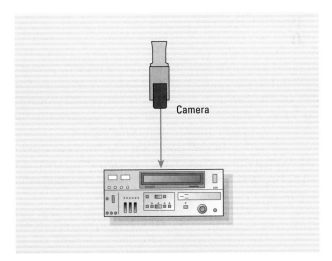

12.15 SINGLE CAMERA AND SINGLE VTR
The simplest VTR system is to have each camera feed its own recorder.

generally fed to a high-quality VTR located in the VTR room or in the VTR section of a remote truck. **SEE 12.15**

Multiple VTRs Multiple VTRs are used either for protection of the switcher line-out material or for recording the program material provided by the *isolated (iso) camera,* a separate camera that feeds directly into its own VTR.

Iso camera/VTR setups are used in the multicamera coverage of planned events, such as political conventions and especially sports. The iso camera is normally used *in addition to* the multicamera/single-VTR setup, usually in an isolated strategic position from where it can cover key elements of the event. It feeds its output continuously into a second, separate iso VTR for instant replays, but also into the switcher so that it can be used as an additional camera during the on-the-air switching. **SEE 12.16**

You can use the iso setup in all situations where you may need some additional material when editing the live-on-tape event for later distribution. For example, if you do a live-on-tape coverage of a local band and then discover that the cameras show the clarinets when they were supposed to be on the trumpets, you can easily fix this problem by cutting back to the conductor, provided you had an iso camera on the conductor during the original videotaping.

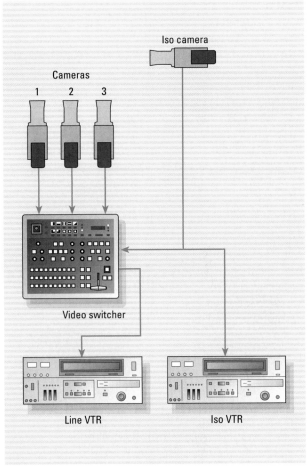

12.16 ISO CAMERA AND VTR
An iso camera, which feeds its own VTR, is used in addition to the regular multicamera/single-VTR setup. The iso camera can also be used as part of the regular multicamera setup. Note that the iso VTR feeds back into the switcher for instant replays.

When you see a key play repeated from various angles during instant replays, two or more iso cameras were used. In large sports remotes, such as network coverage of big games, all the cameras feed not only into a switcher, but also into their designated VTRs. The cameras serve double duty—as part of the live multicamera feed and as iso cameras for instant replay. **SEE 12.17** Obviously, such an extravaganza is expensive and certainly not necessary for the average multicamera production.

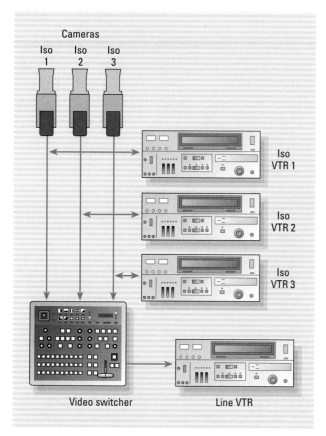

12.17 DUAL-FUNCTION ISO CAMERAS

In this setup all cameras feed into the switcher as well as their own iso VTRs. The iso VTRs feed back into the switcher for instant replays.

VIDEO-RECORDING PRODUCTION FACTORS

There are certain operational steps in video recording that are necessary for effective preproduction, production, and postproduction activities. Because postproduction is explored extensively in chapter 13, this discussion is limited to the major preproduction and production factors of video recording. Preproduction steps include: (1) preparing the schedule, (2) making an equipment checklist, and (3) edit preparation. The production section focuses on (1) the video leader, (2) recording checks, (3) time code, (4) recordkeeping, and (5) specific aspects of disk-based video recording.

Preproduction

Production efficiency is determined to a large extent by how well prepared you are. This production preparation is called *preproduction.* Unless you are working in news, where the equipment and people are scheduled to respond immediately to unexpected situations, you need to follow some procedures that will guarantee you the availability of the equipment and time needed to get your video-recording project done. But even the most careful scheduling will not help if the camcorder battery is not charged or you forget to bring the right connecting cable for the iso VTR during a field production.

Schedule Is the videotaping equipment actually available for the studio production or remote shoot? Most likely, your operation will have more than one type of video recorder available. Which VTR do you need? Be reasonable in your request. You will find that VTRs or camcorders are usually available for the actual studio or field production, but not always for your playback demands.

If you need a VTR simply for reviewing the scenes shot on location, or for timing purposes, do not request digital "on-line" VTRs. Have the material dubbed down to a regular ½-inch VHS format and watch it on your home VCR. That way you free the high-quality machines for more-important tasks and you are not tied to a precise schedule when reviewing your tapes.

Unless you use the camcorder as the source VTR when doing the dubbing-up, you must schedule not only the record VTR (the high-quality format you want to use for editing), but also the source machine that plays the source tapes (such as a DVCPRO format).

In all of your time and equipment requests, be sensitive to the other production people who need to work with the same machines you do.

Equipment checklist Like a pilot who goes through a checklist before every flight, you should have your own equipment checklist every time you do a production. Such a list is especially important in field productions. This brief checklist is limited to video recording and uses the generic term *VTR* throughout, referring to tape-based as well as disk-based systems.

■ *VTR status.* Does the VTR actually work? If at all possible, do a brief test recording to ensure that it functions properly.

■ *Power supply.* If you use a VTR in the field, or if you use a camcorder, do you have enough batteries for the entire shoot? Are they fully charged? When using household current for the power supply, you need the appropriate AC-to-DC adapter. Before leaving for the field location, check that the connecting cable from the power supply fits the jack on the VTR or camcorder. Do not try to make a connector fit if it is not designed for that jack. You may blow more than a fuse if you do.

■ *Correct tape.* Do you have the correct tape, that is, the cassette format that fits the camcorder or VTR? Although the difference between a ½-inch and a ¼-inch DVCPRO tape is obvious, you may not see the difference between the normal ½-inch VHS and the S-VHS cassettes, or a Hi8 and a DVCPRO tape. Videotapes can look similar and even identical when you're in a hurry. Also check that the various boxes contain the correct tapes. For example, the Sony DVCAM VTRs and Panasonic DV camcorders require metal evaporated tape, but Panasonic DVCPRO systems use metal-particle tape. Do not rely solely on the label. Because cassettes can be loaded with various lengths of tape, also look at the supply reel to see if it contains the amount of tape indicated on the label. If, for example, the box says that it contains a 120-minute tape but your check shows only a very thin layer of tape on the supply reel, the box is obviously mislabeled.

■ *Enough tape.* Do you have enough tape for the proposed production? This is especially important when recording a live event in its entirety for playback at a later time or for live-on-tape productions. If the largest cassette does not hold enough tape for the entire event, you need to schedule two machines or you will lose a few minutes during the tape change. Especially when doing multiple recordings for instant replay, you need three or four times the normal tape supply. Tape does not take up much room and is relatively inexpensive. Always take more along than you think you'll need.

■ *Record protection.* If a VTR refuses to record despite a careful check of the connecting cables, pull the cassette out again and see whether it is in the recording mode. All cassettes have a device to protect the videotape from accidental erasure. VHS and S-VHS ½-inch cassettes have a small tab on the back edge at the lower left. When this tab is broken off, the cassette is record-protected. **SEE 12.18** Is the cassette now permanently disabled for future recordings? Not at all: To restore its recording

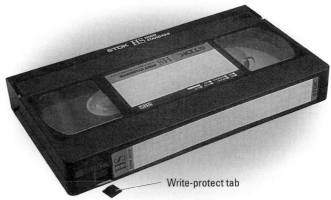

12.18 VHS CASSETTE TAB REMOVED

To protect VHS and S-VHS cassettes from erasure, you need to break off the tab. To reuse the cassette for recording, put a small piece of masking tape over the hole.

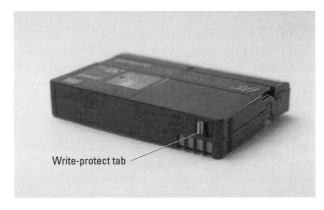

12.19 DIGITAL VIDEOCASSETTE IN RECORD-INHIBIT POSITION

Like a computer floppy disk, DV cassettes have a movable tab that prevents accidental erasure. To record on the cassette, the tab must be in the closed position.

capability, simply put a small piece of masking tape over the tab opening.

Similar to computer floppy disks, other cassettes have a tab that you can move into or out of a record-protect position. **SEE 12.19** Routinely check the record-protect tab before using a cassette for recording. Although you cannot record on a record-protected tape, any cassette will play back with or without a record-protect device in place.

Edit preparation   Before starting your postproduction activities, you may need to prepare your videotapes ahead of time for certain types of editing. If, for example, the record (edit) VTR uses a **control track** for recording the synchronization information (sync pulse) and gives you a choice between insert and assemble edit, you need to record a continuous control track on the *edit master tape* (the tape onto which you copy the selected portions of the source tapes), before you can do any insert editing.

The easiest way to lay down the control track is to "record black," that is, a black video signal. This "blacking" of an edit master tape takes time. Laying a 60-minute control track takes 60 minutes. Note, however, that you need to blacken a tape only if you intend to use it as an edit master and then only if you intend to do insert editing. If you edit in the assemble mode, or if the VTR does not need a control track (such as the Hi8), such previous blacking of videotape is unnecessary.

If you intend to do nonlinear editing, all videotapes—regardless of whether they store analog or digital information—must be transferred to the hard disk of the nonlinear editing system. Transferring analog tape to digital disks is always a time-consuming affair. If, for example, your news footage is recorded with a normal analog camcorder, a nonlinear digital editing unit may not be the right choice. In the time it takes to digitize your tape for proper storage on the computer's hard disk, you could have assembled your footage on a conventional analog cuts-only editing unit. If you are in a hurry, stay away from nonlinear editing, unless you use a digital camcorder and a FireWire cable for transferring the digital information from tape to the hard disk. The biggest advantage of nonlinear over linear editing is that you can view and save multiple versions of a scene.

When using tape for editing or on-the-air playback, preview a minute or so of each tape to verify that the label on the box matches the one on the tape and that the tape label matches its content. You may consider such procedures redundant and a waste of time. They are not. By having a triple-checking routine, you will not only prevent costly production errors, but also save time, energy, and, ultimately, nerves.

Production

If you have followed the basic preproduction steps, you should have little trouble during the actual recording, although there are still some things that need attention: (1) video leader, (2) recording checks, (3) time code, (4) recordkeeping, and (5) specific aspects of disk-based video recording.

Video leader   When playing back a properly executed video recording, you will notice some front matter at the head of the recording: color bars, a steady tone, an identification slate, perhaps some numbers flashing by, with accompanying audio beeps for each number. These items, collectively called the **video leader**, help adjust the playback machine to the audio and video values of the record machine. **SEE 12.20**   Let us look at them one by one.

Because *color bars* help the videotape operator match the colors of the playback machine with those of the record machine, it is important that you record the color bars (fed by color-bar generators located in master control or built into ENG/EFP cameras) for a minimum of thirty seconds each time you use a new videotape or begin a new taping session. Some VOs (video operators) prefer to have the color bars run for a full minute or more so that they do not have to rerun the bars if the equipment requires more adjustment than normal.

Most audio consoles can generate a *test tone* that you need in calibrating the console line-out level with the input (record) level of the VTR (see chapter 10). You should record this 0 VU test tone along with the color bars. Obviously, these test signals should be recorded with the equipment that you use for the subsequent videotaping. Otherwise, the playback will be referenced to color bars and test tone but not to the videotaped material. The director refers to these test signals as "bars and tone." When doing a studio show, you will hear the director call for bars and tone right after the videotape roll. In EFP the VTR operator will, hopefully, take care of this reference recording. *READY ZVL* **1**

The *slate* gives important production information along with some technical details. Normally, the slate indicates the following identification data:

- Show title

- Name of series (if any)

- Scene number (corresponding to that in the script)

- Take number (how often you record the same thing)

- Recording date

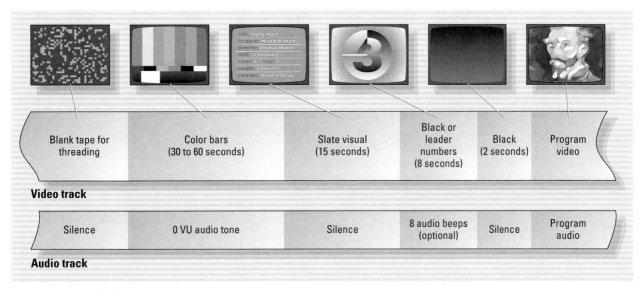

Video track

| Blank tape for threading | Color bars (30 to 60 seconds) | Slate visual (15 seconds) | Black or leader numbers (8 seconds) | Black (2 seconds) | Program video |

Audio track

| Silence | 0 VU audio tone | Silence | 8 audio beeps (optional) | Silence | Program audio |

12.20 VIDEO LEADER
The video leader helps adjust the playback machine to the audio and video values of the record machine.

Some slates also list the director, the location (especially for EFP), the possible playback date, and additional in-house information, such as reel numbers, editing instructions, name of producer, and so on.

In the studio the slate is usually generated by the C.G. (character generator) and recorded right after the color bars. **SEE 12.21** In the absence of a C.G., you can use a small whiteboard with a 4 × 3 aspect ratio (four units wide by three units high). Because the information on the slate changes from take to take, the slate surface should be easily cleaned (chalk or dry-erase markers work well). The slate identifies the scene as well as the take, so you must use it every time you record a new take, regardless of how short or how complete the take may be. *READY ZVL* ❷

Assume that you are the director of the weekly "President's Chat" production. You have just recorded about ten seconds of the first take when the college president stumbles over the name of the new dean. You stop the tape, keep calm, roll the tape again, and wait for the "in-record" confirmation from the VTR operator. Before repeating the president's introduction, you need to record the slate again. It reads: scene 1, take 1. But shouldn't the slate read: scene 1, take *2?* Yes—the C.G. operator obviously forgot to change the slate. Should you

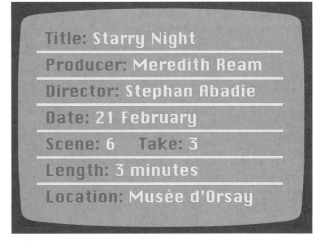

Title: Starry Night
Producer: Meredith Ream
Director: Stephan Abadie
Date: 21 February
Scene: 6   Take: 3
Length: 3 minutes
Location: Musée d'Orsay

12.21 CHARACTER-GENERATED SLATE
The slate gives pertinent information about the production. It is recorded at the beginning of each major take.

go on, or stop the tape again to correct the slate? In this case, you might as well keep going. The VTR operator can note the false 10-second start and record the second take as take 1. If, however, you are breaking up the president's "chat" into several short takes to be assembled in post-production, the slate numbers must be accurate.

Leader numbers and *beeps* are used for the accurate cuing of the videotape during playback. The leader numbers flash at 1-second intervals from 10 to 3 or from 5 to 3 and are usually synchronized with short audio beeps or a continuous tone. The last two seconds are kept in black and silent so that they do not appear accidentally on the air if the videotape is punched up early. The first frame of recorded program material should appear at the zero countdown. When cuing a videotape for playback, you can stop the tape at a particular leader number, say "2," or advance the tape right to the first video frame. When you stop the tape at the last leader number, 2, you must preroll the tape exactly two seconds before the program material is to appear on the air.

Recording checks   As the VTR operator, you are responsible for seeing that the pictures and sound are actually recorded on the videotape. Here are some checkpoints that greatly reduce recording problems:

■   Always do a brief test recording, then play the tape back to ensure that the whole system works properly. Just because you see a picture on the VTR monitor during the recording does not mean that the signal is actually recorded on the videotape. You can also use these tests to record some of the ambient sounds.

■   Reset the tape counter on the VTR before starting the actual program recording. If you use time code for the videotaping, make sure it is recorded with the picture.

■   Wait until the VTR has reached operating speed and has stabilized before starting to record. This *lockup time* may take anywhere from one-half to four seconds. The VTR has a control light that flashes during the lockup period and remains steady once the system is locked, that is, sufficiently stabilized for recording.

■   Watch the audio and video levels during the recording. If you do not have a separate audio setup, but instead feed the mic directly into the VTR, pay particular attention to the audio portion. You may find that a director becomes so captivated by the beautiful camera shots that he or she does not even hear, for example, the talent giving an African country the wrong name, an airplane noise interrupting the medieval scene shot on location, or the wireless mic cutting out briefly during an especially tender moment of a song.

■   When recording for postproduction, record enough of each segment so that the action overlaps the preceding and following scenes. At the end of each take, record a few seconds of black before stopping the tape. This "run-out" signal acts as a pad or cushion, and greatly facilitates editing.

   Ask the director whether you should videotape the camera rehearsals. Sometimes you get a better performance during rehearsal than during the actual take. The camera rehearsals (which are run like a full dress rehearsal) can then be edited into the rest of the production.

■   Again, be sure to slate every take you have on tape, rehearsal or not. When you are in a hurry or out in the field, *audio-slate* each take by having the audio operator use the console mic, or the floor manager a studio lavaliere or shotgun mic, to read the brief slate information into it: "President's Chat, take 12." Some directors like an additional brief verbal countdown, such as "five, four, three" with the last two seconds silent before the cue to the talent. Many field productions are slated more extensively only at the beginning of the video recording, with subsequent takes being only verbally slated.

■   Do not waste time between takes. If you are properly prepared, you can keep the intervals to a minimum. Although the playback of each take may occasionally improve the subsequent performance by cast and crew, it often does not justify the time it takes away from the actual production. If you pay close attention during the videotaping, you do not need to review each take.

   Long interruptions not only waste time, but also lower the energy level of the production team and talent. On the other hand, do not rush through taping sessions at a frenetic pace. If you feel that another take is necessary, do it right then and there. It is far less expensive to repeat a take immediately than to re-create a whole scene later simply because one of your single takes turned out to be unusable. As one wise production expert says: "There is never enough time to do it right, but always enough time to do it over."

Time code   The *time,* or *address, code* is an electronic mark on each frame. If you need to record time code simultaneously with each take, make sure that the time code is recorded on its designated address track or, if necessary, on a free audio track. Unless the camera or VTR has a built-in time code generator, you need a separate time code generator for the address system. Time code can also be laid down later in postproduction, as explained in chapter 13.

Recordkeeping   Keeping accurate records of what you videotape and the proper labeling of videotapes may seem insignificant while in the middle of a pro-duction, but they are critical if you want to locate a particular scene or a specific tape among the various boxes. You will be surprised at how quickly you can forget the "unforgettable" scene and especially the number and sequence of takes.

Keeping accurate records during the taping saves much time in postproduction editing. Although you will most likely log the various takes and scenes when reviewing the videotape after the production, you are still greatly aided by a rough record kept *during* the production, called a ***field log***. As a VTR operator, you should keep a field log even when recording in the studio. A field log is especially useful in more-complex field productions (hence its name) that involve a number of locations. Mark the good takes (usually with a circle) and identify especially those takes that are unusable. Label each videotape and box, and mark the field log with the corresponding information. **SEE 12.22**

12.22 FIELD LOG

The field log is kept by the VTR operator during the taping. It normally indicates the tape or reel number, scene and take numbers, approximately where the take is located on the tape, and other information useful in postproduction editing.

	Production Title: Traffic Safety				Producer/Director: Elan Frank	
	Taping Date: 4/15			Location: Intersection of Bonita & Crest Roads		
Tape	Scene	Take	OK or No Good	Counter #	Event	
5	1	①	OK	0082	Car running stop sign	
		2	NG	0094	VTR problem	
		③	OK	0251	Z-axis shot	
		④	OK	0463	Camera pans past stop sign	
	2	1	NG	0513	Pedestrian too far from car	
		②	OK	0766	Good Z-axis shot	
	6	1	NG	0992	Ball too soon in street	
		2	NG	1332	Ball too late	
		③	OK	1371	Ball ____ ____ ___ of car	

Specific aspects of disk-based video recording   The preproduction and production elements discussed here apply equally, regardless of whether you record with an analog or digital VTR. You will find that most of the VTR recording techniques are still valid, even when working with a disk-based system. There are, of course, different production requirements when you use the disk-based system for editing, which is the subject of chapter 13.

MAIN POINTS

◆ Video recording is primarily used for: building a whole show by assembling parts that have been recorded at different times and/or locations; time delay; duplication and distribution of programs; and records for protection, reference, and study.

◆ The production purpose should determine the type of video recorder used. Simple material destined for home consumption does not need top-of-the-line videotape recorders (VTRs). High-quality VTRs are necessary for productions that require a great amount of color fidelity and resolution, and for material requiring extensive postproduction.

◆ Video recording is done with single or multiple video recorders. Camcorders feed their attached VTRs or hard disk packs. Other single VTRs are normally used for the recording of the switcher output. Multiple VTRs are used for protection of the line-out material or for iso cameras.

◆ The important preproduction steps for video recording include scheduling, equipment checklists, and specific edit preparations. Take along enough tape and be sure that it fits the specific camcorder or VTR. Check that all cassettes have the protection tab in place.

◆ The major production factors in video recording are the video leader (color bars, test tone, slate information, and leader numbers and beeps), recording checks, time code, accurate record keeping, and specific aspects of disk-based operations. Slate all takes.

◆ The field log is kept during the actual studio or field production. It lists all tape numbers, scenes, takes, and comments about shots and audio.

ZETTL'S   VIDEOLAB   2.1

You will have more opportunity to learn from Veronica, our ace editor, and do some editing yourself in the chapter 13 lab. For now you can reinforce some of the information on video leaders and slating.

RUN ZVL 1   Click on the **editing** monitor and run tape 3 **Tape Basics**. Click on the **Leader** module for some additional information about the video leader.

RUN ZVL 2   Now run tape 8 **Pre-edit Procedures** and click on the **Preparations** module. It reiterates the importance of slating each take and of keeping accurate field logs.

13

Postproduction Editing

Almost all programs you see on television have been edited in some way, either during or after the actual production (the shooting and recording of the event). When editing is done after (*post* in Latin), it is known as *postproduction editing*. Its processes and principles differ considerably from *switching,* the instantaneous editing done during production.

Today more and more postproduction editing is done with disk-based nonlinear systems rather than tape-based linear equipment. This development has a profound influence on how we edit. *Nonlinear editing* resembles more the cut-and-paste approach of word processing; in *linear editing* you select portions from one tape and copy them onto another. Despite the dramatic evolution of editing equipment and techniques, however, you, as the editor, remain unquestionably in charge of aesthetic decisions. *READY ZVL* ❶

Section 13.1, How Postproduction Editing Works, acquaints you with basic editing functions and major editing systems. Section 13.2, Making Editing Decisions, helps you sharpen your aesthetic judgment about why and how to assemble shots. Despite the predominance of nonlinear editing, linear editing is discussed first, because knowing how linear editing works will help you understand nonlinear editing and how to apply it with maximum efficiency.

AB-roll editing Creating an edit master tape from two source VTRs, one containing the A-roll, and the other the B-roll. The editing is initiated by the edit controller rather than through switching.

AB rolling The simultaneous and synchronized feed from two source VTRs (one supplying the A-roll, the other the B-roll) to the switcher for instantaneous editing as though they were live sources.

assemble editing Adding shots on videotape in a consecutive order without first recording a control track on the edit master tape.

complexity editing The juxtaposition of shots that primarily, though not exclusively, helps intensify the screen event. Editing conventions as advocated in continuity editing are often purposely violated.

continuity editing The preserving of visual continuity from shot to shot.

control track (pulse-count) system Counting system used to identify exact locations on the videotape. It counts the control track pulses and translates this count into elapsed time and frame numbers. It is not frame-accurate.

cutaway A shot of an object or event that is peripherally connected with the overall event and that is often neutral as to its screen direction (such as straight-on shots). Used to intercut between shots to facilitate continuity.

edit controller Machine that assists in various editing functions, such as marking edit-in and edit-out points, rolling source and record VTRs, and integrating effects. Often a desktop computer with a specific software program. Also called *editing control unit.*

edit decision list (EDL) Consists of edit-in and edit-out points, expressed in time code numbers, and the nature of transitions between shots.

edit master tape The videotape on which the selected portions of the source tapes are edited. Used for the record VTR.

field log A record of each take during the videotaping.

insert editing Inserting shots in an already existing recording, without affecting the shots on either side of the insert. Produces highly stable edits. Requires the prior laying of a control track on the edit master tape.

linear editing Nonrandom editing that uses videotape as source. Uses tape-based systems.

mental map Tells viewer where things are or are supposed to be on- and off-screen.

nonlinear editing Allows instant random access to and easy rearrangements of shots. The video and audio information is stored in digital form on computer hard disks or read/write optical discs. Uses disk-based systems.

off-line editing Produces an EDL or a videotape not intended for broadcast.

on-line editing Produces the final high-quality edit master tape for broadcast or program duplication.

record VTR The videotape recorder that edits the program segments as supplied by the source VTR(s) into the final edit master tape. Also called *edit VTR.*

slate (1) Visual and/or verbal identification of each videotaped segment. (2) A small blackboard or whiteboard upon which essential production information is written. It is recorded at the beginning of each take.

source videotape The tape with original footage in an editing operation.

source VTR The videotape recorder that supplies the program segments to be assembled by the record VTR. Also called the *play VTR.*

time code Electronic signal that provides a specific and unique address for each electronic frame.

time code system Gives each television frame a specific address (number that shows hours, minutes, seconds, and frames of elapsed tape). It is frame-accurate.

vector Refers to a force with a direction. *Graphic vectors* suggest a direction through lines or a series of objects that form a line. *Index vectors* point unquestionably in a specific direction, such as an arrow. *Motion vectors* are created by an object or screen image in motion.

VTR log A list of all takes on the source videotapes compiled during the screening (logging) of the source material. It lists all takes—both good (acceptable) and no good (unacceptable)—in consecutive order by time code address. Often done with computerized logging programs.

window dub A "bumped-down" copy of all source tapes that has the time code keyed over each frame.

13.1

How Postproduction Editing Works

Although editing equipment and techniques change almost from day to day, the basic editing functions remain the same—to combine, trim, correct, and build. How you do this depends a great deal on just what the editing job involves and how much postproduction time is available. If, for example, you need to edit an MTV segment that consists of many complex effects that have to match the music track exactly, you cannot use a simple, tape-based cuts-only editor, no matter how hard you try. On the other hand, a high-end disk-based system would be equally out of place for paring down a 20-minute speech to a few significant sound bites to fit the 10-second slot in the evening newscast. By the time you had transferred the analog tape to digital disk storage, you could have easily finished the editing with the cuts-only editor. Even if you had covered the speech with a digital camcorder and then transferred the digital tape to the hard disk of a high-end digital editing system, you would probably not have gained any time advantage. The most expensive equipment is not always the best choice.

Section 13.1 explores the major editing procedures and systems and what they do best. Although editing, like bicycling, is difficult to learn from a book, this section will at least make you comfortable when you are finally called upon to do it.

▶ **EDIT MODES: OFF- AND ON-LINE**
Defined by quality and by editing intent

▶ **BASIC EDITING SYSTEMS**
Basic linear and nonlinear systems and how their uses differ

▶ **LINEAR EDITING SYSTEMS**
Source and record VTRs, edit controller, and single-source, expanded single-source, and multiple-source systems

▶ **LINEAR EDITING FEATURES AND TECHNIQUES**
Assemble and insert editing, control track (pulse-count) editing, and SMPTE/EBU time code editing

▶ **CONTROL TRACK AND TIME CODE EDITING**
Using the control track (pulse count) and time code systems

▶ **AB ROLLING AND AB-ROLL EDITING**
Creating an edit master tape from two source VTRs

▶ **NONLINEAR EDITING SYSTEMS**
Basic desktop systems and extended high-capacity systems

▶ **NONLINEAR EDITING FEATURES AND TECHNIQUES**
Digitizing, compressing, and storing information, and shot selection and juxtaposition

▶ **PREEDITING PHASES**
The shooting, review, decision-making, and operational phases

EDITING MODES: OFF- AND ON-LINE

There are two basic editing modes, off-line and on-line. In the *off-line* mode, you put the shots together to get a rough idea of what the edited program will look like. This initial edited "sketch" is often called the *rough-cut*. In the *on-line* mode, the tape is assembled in the final version.

You may get confused by what *on-line* and *off-line* really mean, because these terms are often used for different things and processes. For example, some people may use *on-line* to refer to the quality of the equipment used: "Off-line is not as good as on-line." Others may mean the quality of the final edited product: "On-line is worthy of broadcast or other forms of broadcastlike distribution; off-line is not." Still others may distinguish between the two modes by their editing intent: If the edited tape or digital arrangement is done for the sole purpose of serving as a guide for the final editing (much like the rough-cut in film editing), the editing is considered off-line. But when the same type of editing is intended from the beginning as the final version for broadcast (or other form of presentation), its editing has become on-line.

It seems that editing intent is the most accurate criterion for the on-line/off-line distinction. For example, if you edit a news story that is to go on the air in a few minutes, you are engaged in **on-line editing**, even if you use a simple cuts-only editor. On the other hand, if all you get from your high-quality nonlinear editing system is an *edit decision list (EDL)* rather than an edit master tape, you are definitely involved in **off-line editing**. Quality and intent, however, often go together.

Because the off-line videotape is not shown on the air, picture quality is of much less concern than are the logic and the aesthetic impact of the intended shot sequence. Therefore, linear (videotape) off-line editing is usually done with relatively low-quality and inexpensive equipment. High-quality video, on the other hand, needs high-quality tape-based systems. Low-end nonlinear systems cannot produce air-quality images and are used strictly to create an EDL or lower-quality videotape. They are, obviously, off-line. But the high-end nonlinear systems that are capable of generating high-quality video are generally called on-line, even if they are used to do only a rough-cut.

BASIC EDITING SYSTEMS

As explained in chapter 12, all taped-based recording systems are linear, and all disk-based systems are nonlinear. Similarly, all editing systems using videotape are linear, regardless of whether the information recorded on the tape is analog or digital. All editing systems that are disk-based are nonlinear. What exactly does this mean from a production point of view? Let's look at how recorded information is retrieved.

Linear Systems
When you want to locate a shot that is in the middle of the tape, for example, you need to roll through shots 1 and 2 before reaching shot 3. From there you need to roll through shots 4, 5, 6, and so forth until you reach shot 25. You cannot simply jump from shot 3 to shot 25, ignoring shots 4 through 24. Because tape-based systems do not allow random access of shots or frames, all tape-based editing systems are linear, regardless of whether the tapes contain analog or digital signals.

Nonlinear Systems
When information is stored on a disk-based editing system, you can jump to shot 3 directly, without having to roll through shots 1 and 2. You can call up shot 25 without rolling through the preceding ones. Being able to jump to a specific shot or frame in such a nonlinear way gives you random access to the information. In effect, the nonlinear editing system operates like a large ESS (electronic still store) system that allows you to identify and access each frame, or frame sequence (which then composes a shot), in a fraction of a second. Because the

13.1 NONLINEAR DISPLAY OF SHOTS TO BE EDITED

A nonlinear editing system can display a number of still frames, a choice of transitions and effects, and displays of various audio tracks. It allows you to run shot sequences with or without sound and preview various transitions and effects.

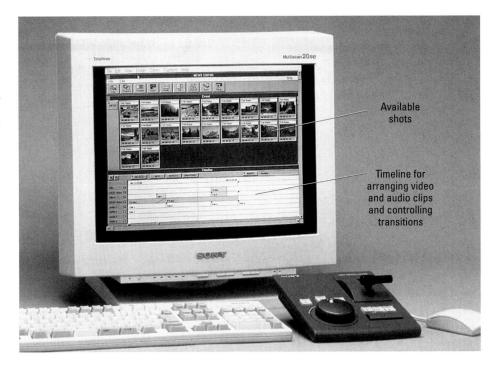

Available shots

Timeline for arranging video and audio clips and controlling transitions

system is nonlinear, it can display any two or more frames side by side on a single computer screen so you can see how well the shots will edit together. **SEE 13.1**

Editing Principle

This big operational difference between the two systems has changed the fundamental concept of how editing works. *Linear editing* is basically selecting shots from one tape and copying them in a specific order onto another tape. *The operational principle of linear editing is copying.*

Nonlinear editing allows you to select and rearrange various frames and shots. Rather than copy certain images (linear editing), you sort through the image files and put them in a specific order. *The operational principle of nonlinear editing is rearranging video and audio data files.*

LINEAR EDITING SYSTEMS

Regardless of how complex tape-based linear editing systems may be, they all work on the basic principle: One or several VTRs play back portions of the tape with the original footage, and another VTR records on its own tape the selected material from the original tape. The different tape-based systems fall into three categories: (1) the single-source system, (2) the expanded single-source system, and (3) multiple-source systems.

Single-Source System

A basic system that has only one VTR supplying the material to be edited is called a *single-source,* or *cuts-only, editing system.* The machine that plays back the tape with the original footage is called the **source VTR** or the *play VTR.* The machine that copies the selected material is called the **record VTR** or the *edit VTR.* In the same manner, the tape with the original footage is the **source videotape,** and the one onto which the selected portions are recorded in a specific editing sequence is the **edit master tape.** To see what is on both the source and edit master tapes, you need monitors for both VTRs. **SEE 13.2**

When doing the actual editing, you use the source VTR to find the exact in- and out-points of the footage you want to copy to the edit master tape. The record VTR does the actual copying of the material supplied by the source VTR and joins the frames at predetermined points—the *edit points.* You have to tell the record VTR when to start recording (copying) the source material and when to stop recording. An "in" or "entrance" cue tells the record VTR when to start recording the source material; an "out" or "exit" cue tells it when to stop recording. Assisting you in this task is a piece of equipment called the **edit controller** or *editing control unit.*

Edit controller   This machine automates editing to a certain extent. It memorizes some of your commands

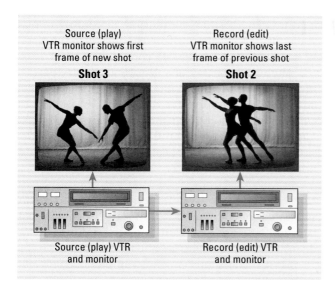

Source (play)
VTR monitor shows first
frame of new shot
Shot 3

Record (edit)
VTR monitor shows last
frame of previous shot
Shot 2

Source (play) VTR
and monitor

Record (edit) VTR
and monitor

13.2 BASIC TAPE-BASED SINGLE-SOURCE SYSTEM
The source VTR supplies specific sections of the source
tape (displayed on the source VTR monitor). The record
VTR copies in a specific sequence and adds each new shot
to the previously recorded shot (displayed on the record
VTR monitor).

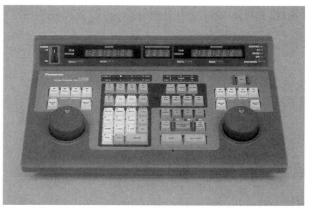

13.3 EDIT CONTROLLER
The edit controller is an interface between the source and
record VTRs. It displays elapsed tape time and frames,
controls VTR rolls, stores edit-in and edit-out points and tells
the VTRs to locate them on the tape, and offers previewing
before the edit and reviewing after the edit.

and executes them with precision and reliability.
SEE 13.3 Most edit controllers perform the following
basic functions:

- Control VTR search modes (variable forward and
  reverse speeds) separately for the source and record
  VTRs to locate scenes.

- Read and display elapsed time and frame numbers,
  or time code (frame address) for accurate cuing of
  the source and edit master tapes.

- Mark and remember precise edit-in and -out
  points (cues).

- Back up, or "backspace," both VTRs exactly to the
  same preroll point. On some edit controllers, a
  switch gives you several preroll choices, such as a
  2-second or 5-second preroll. *Preroll* helps the VTRs
  achieve optimal speed for jitter-free recording.

- Simultaneously start both machines and
  synchronize their tape speeds.

- Make the record VTR perform in either the
  assemble or the insert edit mode (discussed later
  in this section).

Most single-system edit controllers can also do
additional editing tasks, such as letting you do a trial run
before performing the actual edit, performing separate
edits for video and audio tracks without one affecting the
other, or producing intelligible sounds at various speeds.

Computer-assisted edit controller With the
regular control unit, you need to operate various control
buttons and dials to initiate the search functions, the
selection of edit-in and -out points for the source and
record VTRs, and the VTR prerolls. A computer-assisted
edit controller facilitates all these functions, stores your
editing commands, and then triggers the various functions. The compact laptop digital editing systems contain
source and record VTRs that can record up to two hours
of programming material; source and record LCD (liquid
crystal display) video monitors; audio speakers; and an
edit controller that can remember a hundred editing
decisions. **SEE 13.4**

Expanded Single-Source System
You will notice that the basic single-source editing
system may not always give you enough flexibility. For
example, in a documentary on rush-hour traffic, you
may want to add more traffic sounds to intensify the
shots of a downtown gridlock, or you may want to mix
in music under some wedding scenes. Such manipulation between the source tape audio and the desired

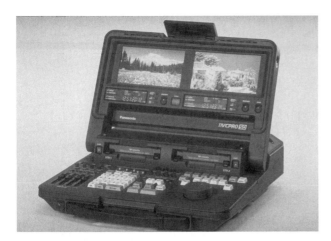

13.4 LAPTOP EDITOR
This briefcase-sized laptop editor by Panasonic contains source and record VTRs, video displays for the two VTRs, audio speakers, and an edit controller that can remember a hundred editing decisions.

audio track on the videotape requires interfacing an audio *mixer.* If you also want to add titles to the documentary, you need a *C.G. (character generator)* and a *switcher* that can mix the titles with the scene from the source tape, without the edit master tape undergoing

another generation. Note that the line-outs from the audio mixer and video switcher go directly to the record VTR and not through the edit controller.

There is a variety of software available that can transform a desktop computer into a sophisticated edit controller or nonlinear editing system. As an edit controller, the computer interfaces with the source and record VTRs, the audio mixer, and the video switcher and offers a variety of special effects and transitions. **SEE 13.5** *READY ZVL* ❷

Preread function   Because the single-source editing system has only a single source VTR, edits are normally cuts-only, that is, you cannot do transitions such as dissolves or wipes. Right? Yes and no.

Most single-source systems can produce only cuts and are, therefore, called "cuts-only" systems; but because some record VTRs have a *preread function* built-in, you can have the VTR read (play) a particular scene while simultaneously recording new material on the same videotape. (The videotape is pulling itself up by its own bootstraps.) This means that you can create a dissolve, or any other available transition, between two shots that are supplied by only one source VTR. Although such a feat is commonplace with nonlinear editing systems, linear single-source systems normally use two or more source

13.5 EXPANDED
SINGLE-SOURCE SYSTEM
The expanded single-source system integrates special effects, a video switcher, and an audio mixer.

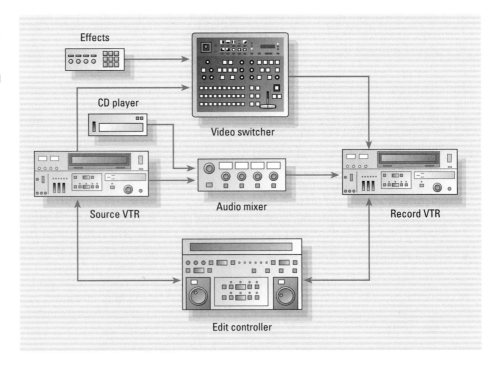

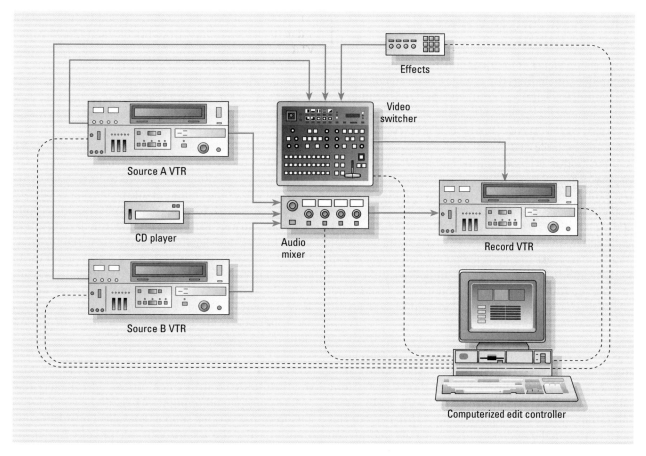

13.6 MULTIPLE-SOURCE EDITING SYSTEM

The multiple-source editing system has two or more source VTRs (A and B) and interfaces special effects, audio, and switcher equipment or functions.

VTRs for transitions other than cuts. You will find this preread function especially useful when inserting titles—without having to make yet another dub.

Multiple-Source Systems

The tape-based *multiple-source editing system* consists of two or more source VTRs (generally labeled with letters, *A, B, C,* etc.), a single record VTR, and a computer-assisted edit controller. Like the expanded single-source system, the multisource systems can, and usually do, include an audio mixer, a switcher, and special-effects equipment. The computerized edit controller directs the functions of the source A and B VTRs, the C.G. or effects generator (unless part of the software

program), the audio mixer, and, finally, the edit and record functions of the record VTR. **SEE 13.6**

The multiple-source editing systems allow you to run synchronously two or more source VTRs and combine the shots from any of them quickly and effectively through a variety of transitions or other special effects. The big advantage of this system is that it can facilitate a great variety of transitions, such as cuts, dissolves, and wipes. Another advantage is that you can arrange all even-numbered shots on the A-roll (the tape used for the source A VTR) and all odd-numbered shots on the B-roll (the videotape for the source B VTR). By switching from A-roll to B-roll during the editing, you can quickly assemble the "preedited" shots, as explained later in this chapter.

LINEAR EDITING FEATURES AND TECHNIQUES

This section focuses on various linear editing features and techniques, including (1) assemble and insert editing and (2) control track (pulse-count) and time code editing.

Assemble and Insert Editing

Most professional VTRs let you switch between two major editing modes: *assemble* editing and *insert* editing.

Assemble editing   When in the assemble mode, the record VTR erases everything on its tape (video, audio, control, and address tracks) just ahead of copying the material supplied by the source VTR. When you use a tape that has last year's vacation pictures on it to chronicle your new vacation adventures, the camcorder will, in effect, use ***assemble editing*** every time you shoot a new scene: It will simply erase what was there before and replace it with the new video and audio.

The same happens in a more sophisticated editing system. Even if the edit master tape has a previous recording on it, the assemble mode will clear the portion of the tape that is needed for the first shot. When editing shot 2 onto shot 1, the record VTR will, again, erase everything on the tape following shot 1 to make room for all the video, audio, address, and control track information contained in shot 2. The same happens when you assemble the subsequent shots. **SEE 13.7**

The problem with assemble editing is that control track that is assembled from the bits and pieces copied over from the various source tape segments is not always smooth and evenly spaced on the record VTR. For example, the record VTR is expected to make a perfectly continuous control track out of the fragments from shots 1, 7, and 11 of tape A and shots 15 and 17 of tape B—not an easy job by any means. Unfortunately, even the best VTRs do not always succeed in this. A slight mismatch of sync pulses will cause some edits to "tear," causing a *sync roll*, which means that the picture will break up or roll momentarily at the edit point during playback. **SEE 13.8**

The primary advantage of assemble editing is that it is fast. You do not have to first lay down on the edit master tape a black video signal with its continuous control track before you begin editing. In fact, you can use any tape for the edit master, regardless of whether it contains previous video material (not recommended for use as an edit master in any case) or has a control track already recorded on it. Because of its speed, some "hot news" editing is done in the assemble mode.

Insert editing   Wouldn't it be sensible to lay down a continuous control track on the edit master tape before copying and trying to match all the control track bits from the various source tape selections? You could then instruct the record VTR not to copy under any circumstances the control tracks from the source tapes, but to yield to the one on the edit master. This is indeed

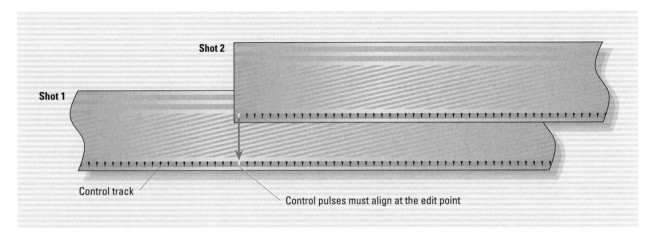

Shot 2

Shot 1

Control track

Control pulses must align at the edit point

13.7 ASSEMBLE EDITING

In the assemble mode, the control track from each selected source segment is copied by the edit master tape. Here shot 2 replaces all recorded information at the tail end of shot 1, including shot 1's control track.

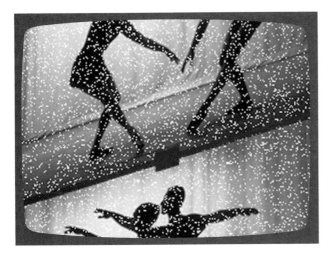

13.8 SYNC ROLL
Even a slight misalignment of the control tracks from shots 1 and 2 will cause a sync roll—a momentary breakup of the picture at the edit point.

possible and it is called *insert editing*. To prepare the edit master tape for insert editing, you need to record a continuous control track on it. The simplest way to do this is to record "black," with the video and audio inputs in the *off* position. As though it were recording an important event, the VTR faithfully lays down a control track in the process. The "blackened" tape has now become an edit master, ready to receive the unforgettable scenes from your source tapes.

The recording of black (and thereby laying a control track) happens in *real time*, which means that you cannot speed up the process, but must wait 30 minutes for laying a 30-minute control track. Though this may seem like wasteful time, it has the following advantages:

- All edits are equally roll-free and tear-free.

- You can easily insert new video and/or audio material anywhere in the tape without affecting anything preceding or following the insert.

- You can edit the video without affecting the sound track, or the audio without affecting the pictures. This is especially important when you want to insert some shots without disturbing the continuity of the original sound track. In fact, the most efficient way of editing news, documentaries, or music programs is to lay down the audio track first and then insert-edit the video to fit the audio track. **SEE 13.9**

CONTROL TRACK AND TIME CODE EDITING

All linear editing systems are guided by the *control track* or a specific address code. Besides its electronic synchronization function, the control track can locate and mark approximate edit-in and -out points, roll both VTRs at the

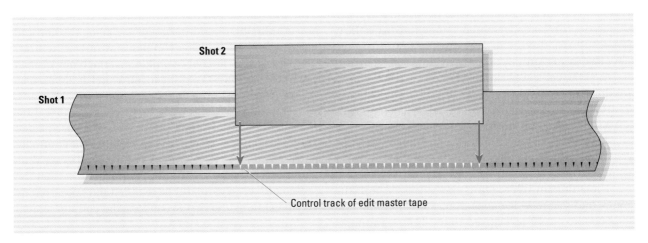

Shot 2

Shot 1

Control track of edit master tape

13.9 INSERT EDITING
In the insert editing mode, the source material is transferred without its control track and placed according to the prerecorded control track of the edit master tape.

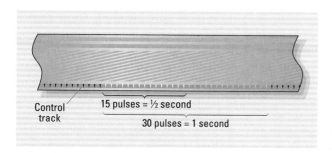

13.10 CONTROL TRACK PULSES

The control track, or pulse-count, system counts the control track pulses to mark a specific spot on the videotape. Every thirty pulses mark one second of elapsed tape time.

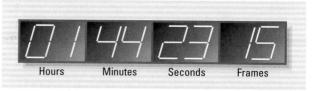

13.11 PULSE-COUNT OR ADDRESS CODE DISPLAY

This display shows elapsed hours, minutes, seconds, and frames. The frames roll over (to seconds) after 29, the seconds to minutes, and the minutes to hours after 59; the hours are reset to 0 after 29.

appropriate time, have the record VTR start copying the new material at approximately the dedicated edit-in point, and stop it at approximately the designated edit-out point. The *control track (pulse-count) system* of editing is used to identify fairly exact locations on the videotape. It counts the control track pulses and translates this count into elapsed time and frame numbers. This system is not frame-accurate, however.

The more sophisticated and more accurate linear systems use the time code to accomplish these tasks. The *time code system* gives each television frame a unique address—a number that shows hours, minutes, seconds, and frames of elapsed tape. The time code system is frame-accurate.[1]

Control Track, or Pulse-Count, Editing

As you now know, the control track on a videotape marks each frame of recorded material. It therefore takes thirty control track "spikes" to mark each second of tape play. **SEE 13.10** Any one of the individual spikes, or *sync pulses,* of the control track can become an actual edit-in or edit-out point (frame). By counting the number of control track pulses, you can, for example, locate specific edit-in and -out points with greater accuracy than simply by looking at the video pictures. *Control track editing* is also called *pulse-count editing* because the edit controller counts the number of control track pulses.

The edit controller counts the pulses of both the source and record videotapes from the beginning and displays the count as elapsed time—hours, minutes,

seconds, and number of frames. Because there are 30 frames per second, the seconds are advanced by one digit after 29 frames (with the thirtieth frame making up the next second). The seconds and minutes roll over to the next after 59.[2] **SEE 13.11**

Finding the right address   The major problem with the pulse-count system is that, although it can identify a specific frame with a pulse-count number, it is not frame-accurate. This means that you may get different frames when advancing repeatedly to the same pulse count number.

Imagine that you need to find a specific address in an extremely long row of identical houses—but there are no house numbers on any of them. If you are told to find the tenth house on the left, you should have no trouble. You simply start at the beginning of the row and count the houses until you reach the tenth house. The task gets more difficult when you have to find house number 110. And what if you have to find house number 1,010? You are sure to miscount somewhere along the line and get to the wrong address. What if you were to start counting somewhere in the middle of the block instead of at the beginning? Counting to ten would definitely take you to a different house than the one originally intended.

The pulse-count system experiences similar difficulties. The control track pulses do not have specific addresses but are simply counted by the edit controller and, as you have seen, translated into temporary time and frame addresses. Assuming that you have reset the pulse counter to zero and have rolled the tape from its very beginning, the first second on the counter should

---

1. Even with the so-called frame-accurate editing system, there will be times when you are one or two frames ahead or behind the cut as marked.

2. In countries that use a 25-frame-per-second system (such as the European PAL system), the rollover occurs, of course, after the twenty-fourth frame (instead of the twenty-ninth as in the NTSC system).

show the number 30 in the second column of the tape counter. If you rewind the tape to 0 and run it again to the first-second mark, you will most likely get the same frame number (30) displayed. But just as with counting houses, the edit controller has a tendency to get off-track when counting thousands of pulses repeatedly and often at high speed.

Realize that when you advance the tape by only two minutes, the edit controller must count 3,600 pulses. So if you were to back up the tape to the beginning and run it again for two minutes, you would probably end up with a different frame, even if you started the tape at 0 as displayed by the edit controller and stopped it when it indicated exactly two minutes. Why? Because during high-speed shuttles or repeated threading and unthreading, the tape may stretch or slip, or the unit may simply skip some pulses when counting thousands of them. Fortunately, many editing jobs, such as news, do not have to be frame-accurate, and a slight frame discrepancy does not present a serious handicap.

Finding the right starting point
Another potential problem of the control track system is that it begins counting from whatever starting point you assign. If, for example, you forget to reset the counter to 0 at the beginning of the tape, or if you have not rewound the tape completely when resetting the counter to 0, the count will be off. Because the addresses given to frames by the pulse-count system are temporary and, in effect, arbitrary, the pulse-count system is not an address code.

When editing in the pulse-count mode, always be sure to reset the counter to 0 at the beginning of the tape and not somewhere in the middle of it. *READY ZVL* ❸

Time Code Editing
When more-precise editing is required, such as when editing video to the beat of music or in synchronizing dialogue or specific sound effects to the video track, you need to edit with a system that uses a precise address system. The *time code* is an electronic signal that provides a specific and unique address for each electronic frame. The address is recorded on either an audio track, an address code track of the videotape, or integrated into, or recorded alongside, the video signal. From there it can be visually displayed, as in the pulse-count system, in elapsed time and frame number (see figure 13.11). With time code, each of the houses in our example now has its own house number affixed, so you no longer have to count the houses to find a specific one; you can simply look for

its address and, for example, drive to house number 1,010 without worrying about all the previous numbers.

Because each frame has its own address, you can locate a specific frame relatively quickly and reliably, even if buried in hours of recorded program material or despite an occasional tape slippage during repeated high-speed shuttles. Once the edit controller is told which frame to use as an edit point, it will find it again no matter how many times you shuttle the tape back and forth and will not initiate an edit until the right address is located.

There are several time code systems available. Even a Hi8 consumer camcorder, for example, can generate its own time code. Most professional editing equipment is built to read the *SMPTE/EBU time code. SMPTE* (pronounced "sempty") stands for Society of Motion Picture and Television Engineers. *EBU* is short for European Broadcasting Union.

Time code read/write mechanisms
To get the time code on the videotape, you need a time code generator, and to retrieve it, a time code reader. The time code generator writes (records) the time code on either the cue track, address code track, or an audio track of the videotape.

Many studio VTRs, portable professional VTRs, and camcorders have a built-in time code generator or plug-in provisions for it. Most others have jacks for attaching a time code generator.

Time code recording
In larger studio productions, the time code is routinely recorded with the program. High-quality camcorders produce their own time code and lay it on a designated track when you are videotaping. In smaller productions or when using a camcorder that does not have a built-in time code generator, the time code is often added after the program has already been recorded on videotape. For example, when you dub down (make a smaller-format copy) for a *workprint*, or "bump up" (make a larger-format copy) for the actual editing copy, you can lay down the time code simultaneously on the source tape and the copy.

You can set the code to correspond with the actual time of day or simply to start from 0 regardless of time of day. Unless you need to pinpoint the exact time of the event when editing, the 0 start method is more practical. A common practice is to use the hour number to indicate the tape (reel) number. For example, you would mark the first tape with 01/00/00/00, the second tape with 02, and continue with the time code that was recorded at the end of tape 01, and so forth. The third tape would show 03 in the hour column. Actually, you can start anywhere with the time code, so long as it continues within the source tape and from tape to tape.

Audio/video synchronizing   The time code lets you run not only several VTRs in sync, but also video- and audiotape recorders. Because the synchronization is frame-accurate, you can match video and audio tracks frame by frame. You can, for example, strip low-quality speech sounds and other sound effects off the videotape and replace them frame by frame with new dialogue and sound effects from an audiotape. As explained in chapter 10, this process is called *ADR (automatic dialogue replacement)*. *READY ZVL* ➍

AB ROLLING AND AB-ROLL EDITING

Although both of these techniques are relatively crude and mostly rendered obsolete by nonlinear editing, they have their place in television production nonetheless. These methods are useful not for their accuracy, but for their

speed. Both techniques resemble instantaneous editing (switching) more than postproduction editing.

AB rolling is similar to cutting between two cameras in a live production, except that the video sources feeding into the switcher are not cameras but two source VTRs—one containing the A-roll videotape, the other the B-roll. *AB-roll editing* is similar to AB rolling, except that the editing decisions are executed by the edit controller rather than the switcher.

AB Rolling

Because two separate sources supply visual material simultaneously in AB rolling, you can switch at any given point from the material on the A-roll (source A VTR) to the B-roll (source B VTR) and vice versa, and combine them with any transition device available in the switcher. **SEE 13.12**

The advantages of AB rolling are that it can greatly speed up the editing process and it allows you to redo the editing a number of times until you are satisfied with your shot sequence. If you don't like the editing you have just done, you can rewind the source VTRs and recut the production again. Even the most experienced post-

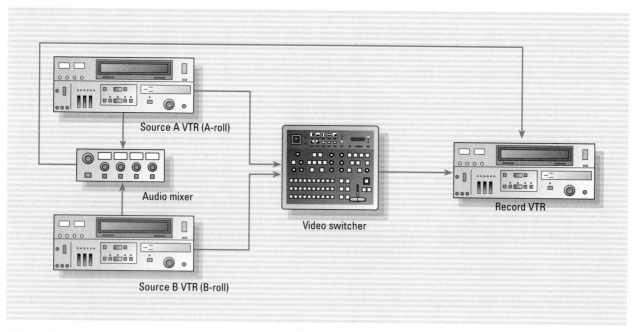

Source A VTR (A-roll)

Audio mixer

Source B VTR (B-roll)

Video switcher

Record VTR

13.12 AB ROLLING

In AB rolling, the source A VTR supplies the A-roll, and the source B VTR supplies the B-roll. Both machines are synchronized and feed their video material into the switcher. Because they represent two simultaneous video feeds, they can be switched (instantaneously edited) as if they were two live sources.

13.13 AB ROLLING TO COMMON SOUND TRACK

In this AB-roll editing example, the A-roll consists of long and medium shots of the band; the B-roll contains CUs of the individual members. Because both source VTRs are synchronized, you can use the A-roll sound track to insert the B-roll video.

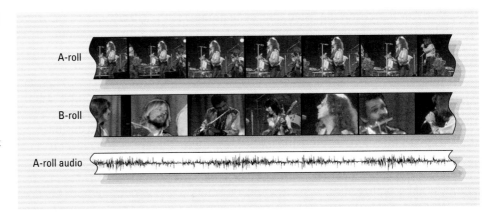

production editors using conventional linear editing equipment can't match the speed of AB rolling. But what you gain in speed, you lose in accuracy. AB rolling works best when the edit points between the A and B rolls do not have to be too precise.

Here is an example of an editing assignment that lends itself well to AB rolling: Assume that one of the source tapes—the A-roll—contains primarily long and medium shots of a rock band. The second source tape—the B-roll—has various close-ups of the band members. Assuming that the source tapes have a common time code, or, in this case, a common audio track (the band playing), you can roll both tapes (A and B) simultaneously and keep them in sync; feed them into the switcher as two separate video sources; cut, dissolve, or wipe between the long shots on the A-roll and the close-ups on the B-roll as though they were live sources; and record the switcher's line-out signal on the record VTR. Because the two source tapes are synchronized by the time code, you can feed the sound track from only one source tape to the record VTR and still maintain lip-sync for the A-roll and B-roll video. **SEE 13.13**

AB-Roll Editing

If you now substitute the edit controller for the switcher, you are engaged in AB-roll editing. Let's edit the rock video once again, but this time with the edit controller. Again, the A-roll has the long and medium shots of the group, and the B-roll the close-ups. You can first lay down (record) the entire sound track on the edit master tape while recording black. The recording of the sound track and black video will also establish the control track necessary for insert editing.

Now you can use the sound track as a guide and insert-edit into the long shots of the A-roll the various

close-ups on the B-roll with a variety of transitions. By running the two source VTRs in sync, you do not have to engage in time-consuming shuttles to search for the appropriate close-up—you can simply choose between the A- and B-roll shots at any given moment. Although this method is considerably slower than AB rolling, it is much more precise. For example, if you want a close-up of the lead guitarist at the exact moment when he begins his solo, the edit controller can locate the starting frame with precision and ease. To attempt a similarly precise cut during AB rolling would probably require several retakes.

In a nutshell, the difference between AB rolling and AB-roll editing is that in AB rolling you switch (do instantaneous editing via the switcher) between the two source VTRs as though they were live video sources; in AB-roll editing, you use the edit controller to set up the transitions between the source A VTR and the source B VTR.

The advantage of AB-roll editing is that you can access the source material from two sources rather than just one, which makes the linear system a bit more flexible. The A and B rolls do not have to run in sync from beginning to end, and you can advance either tape to a specific edit-in point and copy the material over to the record VTR without having to change videotapes on the source machine. AB-roll editing also facilitates special-effects transitions, keying titles, and mixing A- and B-roll audio tracks.

In AB-roll editing, the edit controller has its hands full: It must respond to edit-in and -out points for the source A VTR, source B VTR, and record VTR; initiate prerolls for all three machines; and tell the record VTR when to start recording and the switcher what transition to perform. Fortunately, the computer can handle these various control functions with ease and efficiency. Once you have entered your *EDL (edit decision list)* into the computer, it will seek out the listed time code numbers specifying the edit-in and -out points and faithfully initiate the various transitions as stipulated by the EDL—assuming that everything works right.

NONLINEAR EDITING SYSTEMS

All nonlinear editing systems are basically computers that store digital video and audio information on high-capacity hard disks or read/write optical discs. Recall that the fundamental difference between linear and nonlinear editing systems is that linear systems copy information from one videotape to another, whereas nonlinear systems create and arrange picture and sound data files in a particular order. Instead of editing one shot next to another, you are basically engaged in *file management*.

Depending on the sophistication of the computer, the new arrangement of data can be retrieved either as an off-line EDL or as on-line video and audio signals that you can watch on a regular monitor and speaker and transfer to the final edit master tape using the record VTR. Some disk-based camcorders have a simple editing system built into the hard disk and can deliver edited footage right from the recorder.

Because of improved hardware, software, and compression methods, combined with high-capacity hard disks and optical discs, even desktop software can produce high-quality video and CD-quality audio in the editing process. High-end nonlinear editing systems can process high-quality video and audio without quality loss. **SEE 13.14**

High-end on-line systems have all these features and more. Their hard disks can store more than a hundred hours of Betacam SP–quality video with relatively low compression. Thanks to efficient sampling and compression methods (such as 4:2:2 sampling and MPEG-2 compression), these systems deliver high-quality video and DAT-quality audio. High-end systems can display and mix twenty-four or more audio tracks.

The controls for nonlinear systems come in various configurations. Some use the standard computer keyboard and mouse; others simulate film controls in an attempt to lure hard-core film editors to the world of nonlinear editing. Giving you even more options (and headaches), most nonlinear systems can be linked as networks for sharing video and audio data files, for audio sweetening, or to send rough-cuts (off-line edited programs) to a client for final approval.

13.14 BASIC NON-LINEAR EDITING SYSTEM

The basic nonlinear editing system consists of a computer with large-capacity storage devices and editing/effects software. The output of this editing system is an EDL as well as high-quality on-line video and audio material.

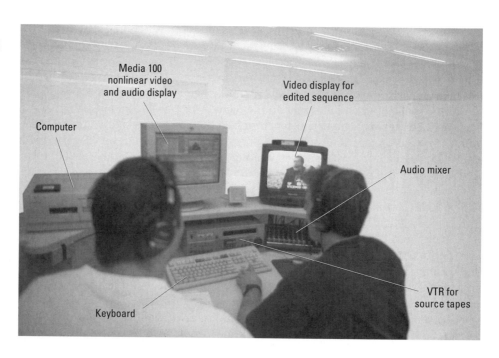

Computer

Media 100 nonlinear video and audio display

Video display for edited sequence

Audio mixer

Keyboard

VTR for source tapes

Nonlinear Editing Features and Techniques

Nonlinear editing systems are as varied as desktop computers. Not surprisingly, their features, software programs, and techniques are quite varied and more complicated than word processing programs. You will need the operating manual close by, even if you have some experience in nonlinear editing. Despite the different models, there are features and techniques common to all nonlinear systems: (1) digitizing, compressing, and storing information; and (2) juxtaposing and rearranging the video and audio files.

Digitizing Information

You may be surprised to hear that one of the real bottlenecks in nonlinear editing is transferring analog videotaped information to digital and storing the information in the computer's memory. If you have ever backed up material from a hard disk, you know that it can try your patience. Transferring analog videotapes to digital storage devices of the editing systems takes even longer. Even if your footage was recorded on a digital camcorder or VTR, transferring it from tape to hard disk takes time. Keep in mind that the computer is moving millions of bytes every second and is putting them into the right files so you can quickly find them again. This transfer and storage job increases dramatically if you want to digitize and store full-screen, full-motion (30 frames per second) video and DAT-quality audio.

Whenever transferring your source tapes to the hard disk of the editing system, *do a backup at the same time*.

Fortunately, most nonlinear systems work with some kind of compression.

Compression

Recall from chapter 2 the detailed discussion of compression: Compression is like trying to put your entire wardrobe into a carry-on suitcase. Sometimes you succeed by refolding your clothes and by using all the available space. This is the *lossless* kind of compression. Most compressions are of the *lossy* kind, which means that you need to leave some clothing behind. Do you really need three sweaters or can you get along with one? Obviously, the less you leave behind, the more complete your wardrobe will be. In compression terms, the less compression there is, the higher quality the video and sound will be.

The more important problem for you as a postproduction editor is that the generally accepted MPEG-2 interframe compression standard makes it difficult to do precise frame-accurate editing. As you remember, to save "suitcase space," not all frames contain the complete video information. For frame-accurate editing, you need MPEG-2 systems that use frequent reference frames or that can calculate the full frame wherever you want to cut. Only the intraframe technique, in which each frame undergoes its own compression, allows you to use any given frame as an edit-in or -out point without additional decoding software.

Storing Information

The greatest library in the world is useless if the books are not cataloged so that you can easily find them. The same is true of video material, regardless of whether it is stored on videotape or a hard disk. You already know about the SMPTE time code that gives a unique address to each frame—but the "house number" does not tell you what the house *looks* like. Similarly, the time code reveals nothing about the nature of the shot it is identifying. What is necessary, therefore, is a list that tells you what is actually stored. Computerized logging systems that create file "menus" or shot lists are available that transfer to a data file the SMPTE time code addresses of the scenes you want. There are also software systems that help you create a file list of what is stored. Such lists show the in- and out-numbers for each shot and such information as name of shot, content, and so forth. A shot list, or rather a file menu, is similar to a regular VTR log.

Juxtaposing and Rearranging Video and Audio Files

Now you are finally ready to do some editing, or, rather, juxtapose images and rearrange video and audio files. Because you have equally fast and easy access to each of the stored frames, you have the ultimate multiple-source editing system at your disposal. To duplicate the same feat with a taped-based system, you would need a separate source VTR for each single frame recorded on the source tapes. As pointed out before, nonlinear editing is comparable to rearranging letters, words, sentences, and paragraphs through word processing.

Because the stored information allows random access, you can call up any frame, or video and audio sequence, in a fraction of a second and have it displayed as a series of still images on the computer screen. Such

13.15 VIDEO SOFTWARE DISPLAY

This shot display shows the last frame of the previous shot and the first frames of the new shot. Also note the visualized audio tracks.

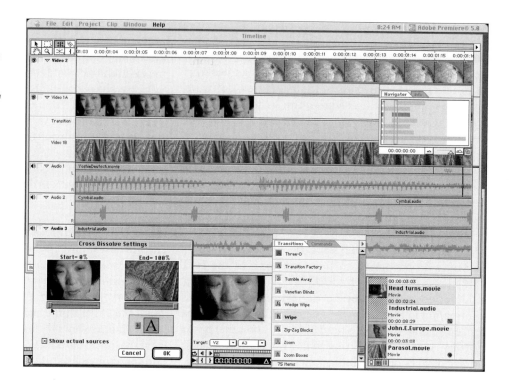

access speed comes as great relief to videotape editors who were used to waiting anxiously for a particular shot that was buried somewhere toward the end of the source tape. Now you simply click the mouse or press a button, and the next series of frames appears on-screen.

Besides having almost instant access to any frame of the stored video and audio data, you can juxtapose two frames or a series of frames to see how well they cut together. The side-by-side display consists, in effect, of the last frame of the previous shot and the first frame of the following shot. **SEE 13.15**

By running the newly "edited" sequence, you can see whether it fulfills your story continuity and aesthetic requirements. If it does not, you can call up another frame or sequence instantaneously and try out a new arrangement. You can also test a number of fancy transitions. Once you are satisfied, the computer will record and remember the in- and out-numbers for each of the selected sequences before putting the material back into storage. The complete list of such in- and out-numbers constitutes the final *edit decision list (EDL).*

When working with an off-line system, the EDL becomes the instructions for the edit controller in the on-line tape-based system. The edit controller can then cue the source tapes to the proper shot sequences and tell the record VTR what to copy. In an on-line nonlinear system, you can record the video and audio outputs of the computer directly on the edit master tape.

PREEDITING PHASES

While shooting video and recording audio during the production, experienced production people are already thinking of postproduction editing. The actual editing will also be greatly facilitated if you spend some time looking over and keeping accurate records of what you have shot. Finally, you have to select the most effective shots and decide how to put them together to give the video program clarity and impact. The preediting phases include: (1) the shooting phase, (2) the review phase, (3) the decision-making phase, and (4) the operational phase.

Shooting Phase

Much of the editing is predetermined by the way the material is shot. Some novice directors or camera operators stop one shot or scene and begin the next without any *pads* (overlapping action) or consideration for continuity. Others have the ability and foresight to visualize transitions between shots and scenes and to provide images that cut together well in postproduction. The key here is to visualize not just individual shots, but a shot *sequence*. Imagining a shot sequence will help you compose shots that can be joined together to form seamless (or jerky) transitions. Here are some suggestions:

▦ When videotape recording, do not stop exactly at the end of a scene—record a few more seconds before stopping the tape. For example, if the field reporter has just ended the introduction to a story, have him or her remain silent and in place for a few more seconds. This pause will give you a video pad in case the end of the actual report and the beginning of the following scene do not provide proper video or audio continuity. For the same reason, roll the tape for several seconds before beginning an action that will be used in the edited version. A change in the angle and field of view (moving the camera closer or farther away from the event) between shots will also help make the cuts look organic and smooth.

▦ Always get some cutaway shots. A *cutaway* is a brief shot that establishes continuity between two shots; provides the necessary video pad when editing according to sound bites (portion of videotaped interview in which we see and hear the person talk); and, in more-ambitious productions, helps bridge jumps in time and/or location. The cutaway may or may not be part of the principal action, but it must somehow be related to the actual event. Good cutaways are relatively static and neutral as to screen direction. Examples are straight-on shots of onlookers, signage, buildings that show the location, house numbers, or objects that are part of the story (such as the book the guest has written).

ENG EFP When on an ENG assignment, try to get some cutaway shots that identify the location of the event. For example, after covering the downtown fire, get a shot of the street signs of the nearest intersection, the traffic that has backed up because of the fire, and some close-ups of onlookers and exhausted firefighters. For good measure, also get several wide shots of the event location. You will then have cutaways that not only facilitate transitions, but also show exactly where the fire took place. Always record the ambient sound with the cutaways. The sound is often as important as the pictures for smooth transitions. Also, the continuity of ambient (background) sound can help immensely in preserving shot continuity, even if the visuals do not cut together too well.

▦ Always record a minute or two of "room tone" or any other kind of ambient sound, even if the camera has nothing to look at.

ENG EFP Whenever possible during ENG, *slate* (identify) the various takes verbally. This can be done simply by calling out the name of the event and the take number, such as: "Market Street police station, take 2." You can do the slating on the camera mic or the portable (reporter's) mic. After saying the take number, count backward from five or three to zero. This counting is similar to the beeper after the slate in studio productions. It helps locate the take and cue it up during the editing process, especially if no address code is used. *READY ZVL* ❺

Review Phase

Unless you deal with news footage that must be edited immediately for playback during the upcoming newscast, you need to make copies of all the source tapes. This way you can preserve the original source tapes for the actual editing while reviewing the tape copies. After transferring the analog or digital source tapes to the hard disk of the editing system, back up the hard disk immediately. You may think that backing up is overkill and basically a waste of time. This is true until your superdependable computer crashes.

Reviewing   Now you are finally ready to look at all the material recorded on the source tapes and log the various shots and scenes. Before you can make any decisions about what to include and what to cut, you need to know what is there. Regardless of whether you are editing a brief news story or a play that was shot film-style, you must look at everything on the source tape or, more likely, on the stack of videotapes that contain the bits and pieces of the source material, to get an overall impression of what you have to work with. Repeated screening of the source tapes will reveal new things every time you play them and will suggest optimal ways of sequencing.

Even if you have not taken part in the actual production, this preview should give you (the editor) an idea of what the story is all about. When you work in corporate television, where many of the productions have specific instructional objectives, you need to know what these objectives are. If you cannot deduce story or objectives from the first preview, ask someone who knows. After all, the story and communication objective will greatly influence your selection of shots or scenes and their sequencing. Read the script and discuss the communication objectives with the writer or producer/director. Discussions about overall story, mood, and style are especially important when editing plays or documentaries.

When editing someone else's ENG footage, however, you rarely get a chance to learn enough about the total event. Worse, you have to keep to a rigid time frame ("Be sure to keep this story to twenty seconds!") and work with limited footage ("Sorry, I just couldn't get close enough to get good shots"). Also, you have precious little time to get the job done ("Aren't you finished yet? We go on the air in forty-five minutes!"). Very much like a reporter, an ENG camera operator, or an emergency-room doctor, the ENG editor has to work quickly yet accurately and with little preparation.

Get as much information as you can about the story before you start editing. Ask the reporter, the camera operator, or the producer to fill you in. After some practice you will be able to sense the story contained on the tape and edit it accordingly. You will also find that you often get a better idea about the story by listening to the sound track than by looking at the pictures.

Time code and window dub   All critical editing requires a time code. Unless you recorded the time code during the videotaping, you need to add it to all the source tapes. Like "blackening" the edit master tape for insert editing, laying the time code takes place in real time—adding thirty minutes of time code takes thirty minutes of recording time.

But while you are laying the time code, you can simultaneously make a window dub. A *window dub* is a "bumped-down" (lower-quality, such as VHS) copy of all source tapes that has the time code keyed in a window over each frame. **SEE 13.16** *READY ZVL* ⑥

When working with tape-based systems, a window dub is necessary for creating an accurate VTR log during the preview phase. It will also help you compile a preliminary EDL without having to touch the original source tapes. As pointed out before, never use the original source tapes for previewing or logging unless you are working with news footage. Each pass will impair the quality of the source tapes; and each time you play the source tapes, you run the risk of damaging them.

Logging   With the exception of editing for news or other such events that go on the air right after they occur, you should make a list of every take on the source tapes, regardless of whether it is usable or properly slated. This list, called the *VTR log*, represents a much more precise record of what is on the source tapes than the *field log* kept by the VTR operator during the production. Nevertheless, you will find that a well-documented field log will speed up your VTR logging as much as a badly kept one will slow you down. For example, a field log whose tape numbers match only the numbers on the tape boxes but not those given to the actual tapes is certain to raise your blood pressure.

The purpose of the VTR log is to help you locate specific shots on the source tapes without having to

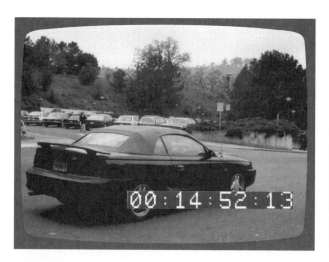
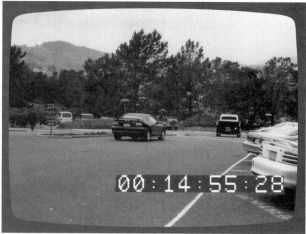

13.16 TIME CODE DISPLAY IN WINDOW DUB
The window dub shows the unique time code number keyed over each frame.

13.17 VTR LOG

The VTR log contains all the necessary information about the video and audio recorded on the source tapes. Notice the notations in the *Vectors* column: *g, i,* and *m* refer to graphic, index, and motion vectors. The arrows show the principal direction of the index and motion vectors. Z-axis index and motion vectors are labeled with ⊙ (toward the camera) or ● (away from the camera).

Tape No.	Scene/ Shot	Take No.	In	Out	OK/ NG	Sound	Remarks	Vectors
4	2	1	01 44 21 14	01 44 23 12	NG		mic problem	m ←
		②	01 44 42 06	01 47 41 29	ok	car sound	car A moving through stop sign	m ←
		③	01 48 01 29	01 50 49 17	OK	brakes	car B putting on brakes (toward camera)	⊙ m
		④	01 51 02 13	01 51 42 08	ok	reaction	pedestrian reaction	→, i
	5	1	02 03 49 18	02 04 02 07	NG	car brakes ped. yelling	ball not in front of car	⊙m ←m ball
		2	02 05 02 29	02 06 51 11	NG	"	Again, ball problem	⊙m ←m ball
		③	02 07 40 02	02 09 12 13	OK	car brakes ped. yelling	car swerves to avoid ball	⊙↘m ←m ball
	6	①	02 12 03 28	02 14 12 01	ok	ped. yelling	kid running into street	→i ←m child
		②	02 17 08 16	02 21 11 19	ok	car	cutaways car moving	⊙↓m ↘↙
		3	02 22 15 03	02 26 28 00	NG	street	lines of sidewalk	↔ g

preview them over and over again, or to help manage the video and audio data files in a disk-based system.

The following is the major information a VTR log should contain. **SEE 13.17**

▓ *Tape (or reel) numbers.* These refer to the number the VTR operator has given the tape during production. He or she should have labeled not only the box but also the cassette with a number and title of what the tape contains. Write the title in the *Remarks* column. If you use time code in the field, the *Hour* column on the field log usually indicates the tape number.

▓ *Scene and take numbers.* Use these only if they are useful in locating the material on the source tape. If you have properly slated the various scenes and takes, copy the numbers from the slates. Otherwise, simply list all shots as they appear on the source tape in ascending order.

▓ *Time code.* Enter the time code number of the first frame of the shot in the *In* column and the last frame of the shot in the *Out* column, regardless of whether the shot is OK or no good.

▓ *OK or no good.* Mark the acceptable shots by circling the shot number or by writing *OK* or *NG* (no good) in the appropriate column. If you kept a field log during production, you can now see if you agree with previous determinations of whether a take was OK or no good.

When evaluating shots look for obvious mistakes, but also for whether the shot is suitable in the context of the defined communication purpose and/or overall story. An out-of-focus shot may be unusable in one context but quite appropriate if you try to demonstrate impaired vision. Look behind the principal action: Is the background appropriate? Too busy or cluttered? It is often the background rather than the foreground that provides the necessary visual continuity. Will the backgrounds facilitate continuity when the shots are edited together?

▓ *Sound.* Here you note in- and out-cues for dialogue and sound effects that need attention during editing. Listen carefully not only to the foreground sounds but also to the background sounds. Is there too much ambience? Not enough? Note any obvious sound problems, such as trucks going by, somebody hitting the microphone or kicking the table, intercom chatter of the crew, or talent flubs in an otherwise good take. Write down the nature of the sound problem and its time code address.

■ *Remarks.* Use this column to indicate what the shot is all about, such as "CU of watch," and to record the audio cues (unless you have a designated audio column).

■ *Vectors.* *Vectors* indicate the major directions of lines or motions within a shot. Noting such directional vectors will help you locate specific shots that continue or purposely oppose a principal direction.

There are three types of vectors: graphic, index, and motion. A *graphic vector* is created by stationary elements that guide our eyes in a specific direction, such as a line or the edge of a book. An *index vector* is created by something that points unquestionably to a specific direction, such as an arrow or a person's gaze. A *motion vector* is brought about by something moving. Take another look at the *Vectors* column in figure 13.17. The g, i, and m refer to the vector type; the arrows indicate the principal direction. The circled-dot symbol indicates movement or pointing toward the camera; the dot alone indicates movement or pointing away from the camera.

There are several good computerized logging programs available. Because the computer can display each frame with its time code address, you don't need window dubs for logging. The program also lets you identify the various shots, providing space for noting the name of the scene or shot and for identifying certain audio segments. Note, however, that the computer will not do the logging all by itself. It cannot tell how you want to name a particular shot, for example, or whether you consider a take acceptable or unacceptable.

For the actual logging, you can take the window dubs home and view them on your home VCR. Although the VCR will not show the high-quality pictures of the source tapes, it is certainly sufficient for giving you an idea of what video and audio material you have. It also lets you freeze the starting and ending frames of each shot so you can read and log the respective time code numbers.

If you shot the material yourself, you are probably familiar with most takes. You can therefore get by with a rather sketchy VTR log that indicates reel and take numbers and some identification of the shots. But if you are given material that was shot by someone else, you should log as much about it as possible so that you will not have to go back to the source tapes to look for

appropriate shots. The more careful and accurate you are with the logging, the more time, money, and nerves you will save during the actual editing. *READY ZVL* ❼

Decision-Making Phase

The decision-making phase involves the selection and sequencing of shots within the context of the total story and communication purpose.

ENG/EFP editing   In ENG editing you need to select those shots that tell the story most accurately and forcefully. It is not uncommon to cut a story to about seven seconds of visuals, although the ENG camera/reporter team may have spent a whole day risking their lives to get the visual material.

Editing electronic field productions is often done in a similar way. The editing time in both ENG and EFP is usually restricted and does not allow you to ponder over a shot sequence or try out several different ways before settling on the most appropriate one. Nevertheless, both ENG and EFP require that you look at the source material repeatedly to see what you have to work with. After a few such screenings, the story will pretty much reveal itself. In ENG you don't have time to make a *workprint* (window dub or lower-quality dub). All the previewing and editing is done with the actual source tapes. When doing EFP, lower-quality window dubs of the source tapes are essential. The window dub allows you repeated viewing without affecting the source tapes.

Postproduction editing   Although all editing takes place *post*—after—the shooting phase, we refer to postproduction editing here as more-deliberate editing than when dealing with ENG and routine EFP. When you edit a fully scripted EFP or studio show, the script pretty much determines the shot sequence. Your main concern is picking the shots that most effectively fulfill the story and selecting appropriate and effective transitions (see chapter 14). When working with a linear system, you can save a great amount of actual editing time by simply watching the window dubs and making a list of the edit-in and -out points for each selected shot. This list will be your preliminary EDL. Because this list is usually written by hand, this decision-making activity is called *paper-and-pencil editing.* **SEE 13.18** *READY ZVL* ❽

When using a computer-assisted logging system, the computer will store your decisions and print out the preliminary EDL. Once you decide on the final shot

13.18 HANDWRITTEN EDIT DECISION LIST
Paper-and-pencil off-line editing normally produces a handwritten EDL containing information similar to that generated by a computer system.

| Production Title: Traffic Safety | | | Production No: 114 | | | Off-line Date: 07/15 | | |
| Producer: Hamid Khani | | | Director: Elan Frank | | | On-line Date: 07/21 | | |

Tape No.	Scene/Shot	Take No.	In	Out	Transition	Approx. length	Sound
5	2	2	01 46 13 14	01 46 15 02	CUT	2 sec.	car
		3	01 51 10 29	01 51 11 21	CUT	1 sec.	car
	3	4	02 05 55 17	02 05 56 02	CUT	.5 sec.	ped. yelling—brakes
		5	02 07 43 17	02 08 46 01	CUT	2+ sec.	brakes
		6	02 51 40 02	02 51 41 07	CUT	1 sec.	ped. yelling—brakes

sequencing, you can print out the final EDL that eventually triggers all the commands of the edit controller during on-line editing. **SEE 13.19**

Similarly, off-line nonlinear systems will produce an EDL rather than a high-quality videotape. This EDL will control the sequencing during the playback of the stored material. Note, however, that this playback is strictly "off-line," meaning that the edited sequence is not yet recorded on video and that it does not have the quality of the final edit master tape. What you see during this playback is simply video and audio data files arranged in a particular way. And, if after seeing this rough-cut, your producer or client asks for a minor or even major change, you don't have to reedit the whole show. All you do is rearrange some computer files and generate a new EDL—a process that takes considerably less time than reediting tape. Nonlinear on-line systems can also translate your editing decisions into high-quality digital video and audio or NTSC signals and transfer them to the final edit master tape.

Operational Phase

Now you have to sit down and practice. You cannot learn editing simply by reading a book—even this one. Also, there are so many linear and nonlinear editing systems on the market that it would be impossible to list them all.

The variety of editing equipment places more and more importance on the aesthetic principles—how to achieve a shot sequence that looks seamless or that purposely jolts the viewer out of his perceptual complacency. Such principles are the focus of section 13.2. Nevertheless, here are some basic operational steps for editing on either tape-based or disk-based systems:

■ If you share editing facilities, double-check on their availability. Have you requested additional equipment you may need to interface, such as a C.G., switcher, audio equipment, or DVE (digital video effects)?

■ If working with a tape-based system, check the tapes that you intend to use for edit masters. Use only new tapes for the record VTR. When doing insert editing, the edit master tapes must have black recorded on them. (Remember that the recording of black will give you the continuous control track needed for the inserting editing). To minimize tracking problems, many editors like to lay the control track with the VTR that is actually used as a record VTR during the editing process.

■ Stack the source tapes in the order in which they are logged. Protect the tapes against accidental erasure by removing the tab or by sliding the record lock. Unless you are editing news, make a backup copy of all source tapes before starting the actual editing.

13.19 COMPUTER-GENERATED EDL

The computer-generated EDL is similar to the handwritten one. It contains in- and out-numbers for both the source VTR and the record VTR, and the nature of the transitions.

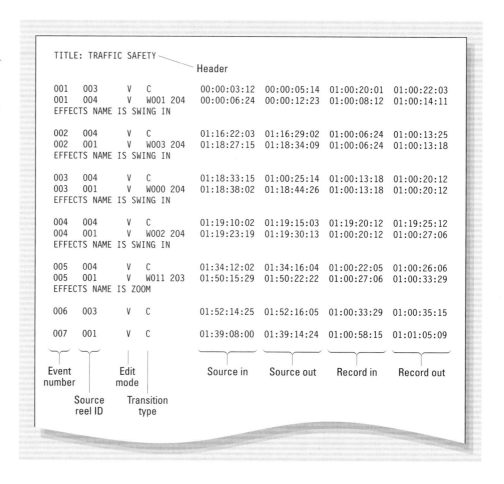

TITLE: TRAFFIC SAFETY — Header

Event number	Source reel ID	Edit mode	Transition type	Source in	Source out	Record in	Record out
001	003	V	C	00:00:03:12	00:00:05:14	01:00:20:01	01:00:22:03
001	004	V	W001 204	00:00:06:24	00:00:12:23	01:00:08:12	01:00:14:11

EFFECTS NAME IS SWING IN

002	004	V	C	01:16:22:03	01:16:29:02	01:00:06:24	01:00:13:25
002	001	V	W003 204	01:18:27:15	01:18:34:09	01:00:06:24	01:00:13:18

EFFECTS NAME IS SWING IN

003	004	V	C	01:18:33:15	01:00:25:14	01:00:13:18	01:00:20:12
003	001	V	W000 204	01:18:38:02	01:18:44:26	01:00:13:18	01:00:20:12

EFFECTS NAME IS SWING IN

004	004	V	C	01:19:10:02	01:19:15:03	01:19:20:12	01:19:25:12
004	001	V	W002 204	01:19:23:19	01:19:30:13	01:00:20:12	01:00:27:06

EFFECTS NAME IS SWING IN

005	004	V	C	01:34:12:02	01:34:16:04	01:00:22:05	01:00:26:06
005	001	V	W011 203	01:50:15:29	01:50:22:22	01:00:27:06	01:00:33:29

EFFECTS NAME IS ZOOM

006	003	V	C	01:52:14:25	01:52:16:05	01:00:33:29	01:00:35:15
007	001	V	C	01:39:08:00	01:39:14:24	01:00:58:15	01:01:05:09

■ In a tape-based system, set up both source and record VTRs. The record VTR must be in the assemble or insert mode. Calibrate the audio levels of the source and record VTRs (see section 10.2).

■ When finished editing, rewind the edit master tape and play it without interruption. You may discover some discrepancies between the video and audio tracks or problems with continuity that you did not notice when you worked edit by edit. Nonlinear editing lets you rearrange the video and audio data files to smoothen the transitions. Audio *sweetening* is a little more cumbersome with linear systems. Complex audio sweetening requires that you strip the audio track off the videotape for the necessary manipulation and then dub the audio track back onto the videotape again. In order to be frame-accurate, you need to have SMPTE code synchronization equipment.

■ When working with a disk-based system, allow plenty of time for digitizing and transferring the source tapes to the hard disk of the editing system. Back up the stored material, even if it is time-consuming. Backing up video and audio files is much less time consuming than trying to redigitize source tapes or even transfer digital VTR information in case the hard disk crashes.

■ Put the various tapes of a specific scene in one file (also called a "bin") and those of the next scene in another. This storage method will make it easier for you to visualize where things are and to call up the various shots.

MAIN POINTS

◆ There are two basic editing modes, off-line and on-line. Editing intent is the most accurate criterion for the on-line/off-line distinction.

◆ Off-line and on-line editing is also determined by the quality of the editing equipment used. High-quality systems are on-line, lower-quality systems are off-line. More precise, it is the designated use of the edit master tape that determines what is on- and off-line. If the editing is done to produce a tape or edit decision list (EDL) that serves as a guide for the final edit master tape, the editing is off-line. If the edited tape is used on the air, the editing process is on-line.

◆ Linear systems are all tape-based and do not allow random access of information. Nonlinear systems are all disk-based and allow random access.

◆ Linear editing is performed with single-source, expanded single-source, and multiple-source systems. Single-source systems have a source (or play) VTR and a record (or edit) VTR, which are normally governed by an edit controller. Expanded single-source systems are computer-assisted and may contain an audio mixer, switcher, and C.G. (character generator). Multiple-source systems have two or more source VTRs and permit a great variety of transitions.

◆ In assemble editing, all video, audio, control, and address tracks are erased on the edit master tape to make room for the shot to be copied over from the source tape (containing its own video, audio, control track, and address code information). The various control tracks of the copied shots are, ideally, aligned so that they form a continuous control track. There are occasional video breakups at the edit points.

◆ In insert editing, the control track of the source tape is replaced by the continuous control track of the edit master tape. It prevents breakups at the edit points and allows separate video and audio editing.

◆ The control track, or pulse-count, editing system uses pulses of the control track for locating specific edit-in and -out points, automatic prerolling of the source and record VTRs, previewing and executing the edit at a specific point on the edit master tape, and reviewing the edit. The control track system does not supply a specific frame address, however, and it is not frame-accurate.

◆ Time code editing uses a specific code (number) that gives each frame a unique address. It fulfills the same functions as the control track system but is frame-accurate. The most popular time code is the SMPTE/EBU time code.

◆ In AB rolling, two VTRs (A-roll and B-roll) feed their material simultaneously into two separate video inputs of the switcher. The editing is done by switching between the A-roll and B-roll tapes.

◆ In AB-roll editing, the switcher is replaced by the edit controller that helps to select the various shots from the source A VTR and the source B VTR.

◆ Nonlinear editing requires digitizing all analog source tapes before storing them on the hard disk or optical disc storage systems. Digital source tapes must still be transferred to the hard disk of the editing system. Most storage systems use some kind of compression to store a maximum amount of video and audio data. Off-line nonlinear editing produces an EDL. The actual on-line editing must be done with a tape-based system. On-line systems produce high-quality video and audio sequences that can be transferred directly to the NTSC edit master tape.

◆ The preediting process occurs in four phases: shooting, review, decision-making, and operational. Many of the more obvious transitions from shot to shot are already considered in the shooting phase. In the review phase, the recorded material is checked for quality and suitability relative to the intended show. All takes are logged and identified. Except for ENG and some EFP, the decision-making phase is to produce an EDL, either through paper-and-pencil or off-line editing. The operational phase involves the actual copying of shots onto the edit master tape for taped-based systems, and the arrangement of video and audio data files for disk-based systems.

13.2

Making Editing Decisions

Good editors must be able to tell a story efficiently while maximizing viewer interest. This requires that they operate an editing system, visualize a smooth shot sequence while looking at a number of single shots, and select the appropriate transitions for such a sequence. Good editors can also detect continuity problems, such as the talent holding the coffee cup in his left hand in the medium shot and in his right hand in the following close-up. Once you have mastered the various buttons and dials of an editing system, you will realize that the real art of editing is in applying aesthetic principles of sequencing of shots and storytelling. This section demonstrates some of the major ones.[3]

▶ **EDITING FUNCTIONS**
Combining, trimming, correcting, and building

▶ **BASIC TRANSITION DEVICES**
The cut, the dissolve, the wipe, and the fade

▶ **MAJOR EDITING PRINCIPLES**
Continuity editing—subject identification, the mental map, vectors, movement, color, and sound; and complexity editing—context and ethics

EDITING FUNCTIONS

Editing is done for different reasons. Sometimes you need to arrange shots so they tell a story. Another time you may have to cut out all extraneous material to make a story fit a given time slot, or you may want to cut out the shot where the talent stumbled over a word, or substitute a close-up for an uninteresting medium shot. These different reasons are all examples of the four basic editing functions: (1) combine, (2) trim, (3) correct, and (4) build.

Combine

The simplest editing is when you combine program portions by simply hooking the various video-recorded pieces together in the proper sequence. The more care that was taken during the production, the less work you have to do in postproduction. For example, most soap operas are shot in long, complete scenes or in even longer sequences with a multicamera studio setup; the

---

3. For a more detailed treatment of aesthetic principles, see Herbert Zettl, *Sight Sound Motion*, 3d ed. Belmont, Calif.: Wadsworth Publishing Co., 1999.

sequences are then simply combined in postproduction. Or, you may select various shots taken at a friend's wedding and simply combine them in the order in which they occurred. *READY ZVL* **9**

Trim

Many editing assignments involve trimming the available material to make the final videotape fit a given time slot or to eliminate extraneous material. As an ENG editor, you will find that you often have to tell a complete story in an unreasonably short amount of time and that you have to trim the available material to its bare minimum. For example, the producer may give you only twenty seconds to tell the story of a downtown fire, although the ENG team had proudly returned with ten minutes of exciting footage.

Paradoxically, when editing ENG footage, you will discover that although you have an abundance of similar footage, you may lack certain shots to tell the story coherently. For example, when screening the fire footage, you may find that there are many beautiful shots of flames shooting out of windows and firefighters on ladders, pouring water into the building, but no pictures of the wall collapsing, which injured a firefighter. The trimming here refers to the pruning down of material, which involves getting rid of some of the shooting-flame shots, as spectacular as they may be. But the word *trim* is also used differently in editing. The *trim* control on an edit control unit allows you to add or subtract frames from a designated edit point. *READY ZVL* **10**

Correct

Much editing is done to correct mistakes, either by eliminating unacceptable portions of the scene or by replacing them with better ones. This type of editing can be simple—merely cutting out the few seconds during which the talent made a mistake. But it can also be challenging, especially if the retakes do not quite match the rest of the recording. You may find, for example, that some of the corrected scenes differ noticeably from the others in color temperature, sound quality, or field of view (shot too close or too loose in relation to the rest of the footage). In such cases the relatively simple editing job becomes a formidable postproduction challenge.

Build

The most difficult, but also the most satisfying, editing assignments are when you can build a show from a great many takes. Postproduction is no longer ancillary to production, but constitutes the major production phase. For example, when you use a single camcorder during a field production, you need to select the best shots and put them in the proper sequence in postproduction editing. Or, if you use a single high-quality camcorder or studio camera to shoot a more ambitious production "film-style," you adopt motion picture techniques and repeat a brief scene, such as someone getting out of a car, several times: once in a long shot (called the "master scene"), again from a different angle such as a medium shot, and then perhaps two or three more times to get various close-ups. Then you shoot a similar sequence, except that the person is now getting *into* the car. The last part of the shooting day may include a long-shot, medium-shot, and close-up sequence of filling the car with gas.

In postproduction you cannot simply select some shots and combine them in the sequence in which they were taken; you have to pick the most effective shot and transition method and establish the desired *story* sequence—regardless of the original shot sequence. All the transitions are created in postproduction. Then the sound effects are added: traffic, off-camera voices, car door opening and closing, gas pump, and so on. The show is literally *built* shot by shot. *READY ZVL* **11**

BASIC TRANSITION DEVICES

Whenever you put two shots together, you need a transition between them, a device that implies that the two shots are related. There are four basic transition devices: (1) the cut, (2) the dissolve, (3) the wipe, and (4) the fade. Although all four have the same basic purpose—to provide an acceptable link from shot to shot—they differ somewhat in function, that is, how we are to perceive the transition in a shot sequence.

The Cut

The *cut* is an instantaneous change from one image (shot) to another. It is the most common and least obtrusive transition device, assuming that the preceding and following shots show some continuity. The cut itself is not visible; all you see are the preceding and following shots. It resembles most closely the changing field of the human eye. Try to look from one object to another located some distance away. Notice that you do not look at things in between, as you would in a camera pan, but that your eyes jump from one place to the other, as in a cut.

The cut, like all other transition devices, is basically used for the clarification and intensification of an event. *Clarification* means that you show the viewer the event as clearly as possible. For example, in an interview show, the guest holds up the book she has written. To help the viewer identify the title of the book, you cut to a close-up of it.

Intensification means that you sharpen the impact of the screen event. In an extreme long shot, for example, a football tackle might look quite tame; when seen as a tight close-up, however, the action reveals its brute force. By cutting to the close-up, the action has been intensified.

The Dissolve

The *dissolve,* or *lap dissolve,* is a gradual transition from shot to shot, the two images temporarily overlapping. Whereas the cut itself cannot be seen on-screen, the dissolve is a clearly visible transition. Dissolves are often used to provide a smooth bridge for action. Depending on the overall rhythm of an event, you can use slow or fast dissolves. A very fast one functions almost like a cut and is, therefore, called a *soft cut.* For an interesting and smooth transition from a wide shot of a dancer to a close-up, for instance, simply dissolve from one camera to the other. When you hold the dissolve in the middle, you will create a *superimposition,* or *super.*

Matched dissolves are used for decorative effects or to indicate an especially strong relationship between two objects. For instance, a decorative use would be a sequence of two fashion models hiding behind sun umbrellas. Model one closes her sequence by hiding behind an umbrella; model two starts his sequence by appearing from behind the umbrella. You can match-dissolve from camera 1 to camera 2.

Because dissolves are so readily available in multi-camera switching, you may be tempted to use them more often than necessary or even desirable. If overused, your presentation will lack precision and accent and will bore the viewer.

The Wipe

There are great variety of *wipes* available. One of the simplest wipes is one picture seeming to push the other off the screen. Other wipes look as though the top picture is peeled off a stack of others, or diamonds expanding from the center of the top picture, gradually showing the one underneath. The wipe is such an unabashed transition device that it is normally classified as a special effect. Studio switchers and editing software programs are often rated by how many different wipes they can perform.

The wipe tells the viewers that they are definitely going to see something else, or it injects some interest or fun into the shot sequence. Wipes and other such effects will be especially magnified on the large HDTV 16 × 9 screen. Like with any other special effect, you should be extra careful using the wipe; overused or inappropriate wipes easily upstage the shots they are connecting. (The various wipes and special-effects transitions are discussed in chapter 14.)

The Fade

In a *fade* the picture either goes gradually to black (fade-out) or appears gradually on the screen from black (fade-in). You use the fade to signal a definite beginning (fade-in) or end (fade-out) of a scene. Like the curtain in a theater, it defines the beginning and end of a portion of a screen event.

As such, the fade is technically not a true transition. Some directors and editors use the term *cross-fade* for a quick fade to black followed immediately by a fade-in to the next image. Here the fade acts as a transition device, decisively separating the preceding and following images from each other. The cross-fade is also called a "dip to black."

Do not go to black too often—the program continuity will be interrupted too many times by fades that all suggest final endings. The other extreme is the never-go-to-black craze: Some directors do not dare go to black for fear of giving the viewer a chance to switch to another channel. If a constant dribble of program material is the only way to keep a viewer glued to the set, the program content, rather than the presentation techniques, should be examined. *READY ZVL* ⑫

MAJOR EDITING PRINCIPLES

To give your editing direction and make your sequencing choices less arbitrary, you need to know the specific event context. **SEE 13.20** Take a look at these five frames, representing the beginnings of brief shots recorded on the source tape. How would you arrange them so that they cut together well while effectively telling the story. But what story? The event context is getting into a car to drive home after work.

Without peeking ahead, number the shots in the order you would sequence them. Now look at the three edited versions. **SEE 13.21–13.23** Identify the one you think is the best combination of shots.

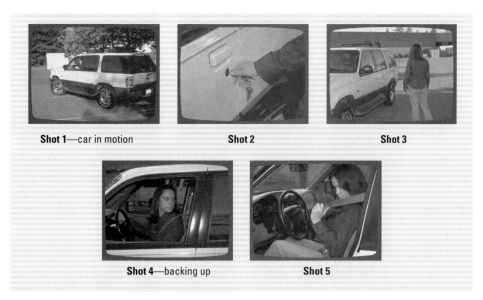

Shot 1—car in motion   Shot 2   Shot 3

Shot 4—backing up   Shot 5

13.20 SOURCE TAPE SHOT SEQUENCE
The event context for these shots is somebody getting into the car to drive home after work.
This sequence is as it appears on the source tape.

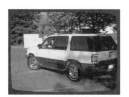 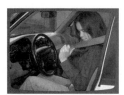 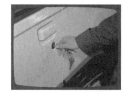 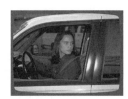 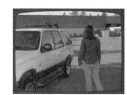

13.21 EDITING SEQUENCE 1
Evaluate this sequence to determine whether the shots are ordered logically.

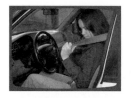 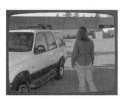 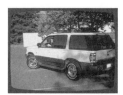 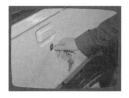 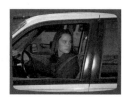

13.22 EDITING SEQUENCE 2
Evaluate this sequence to determine whether the shots are ordered logically.

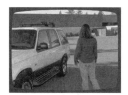 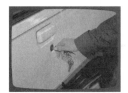 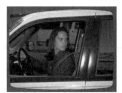 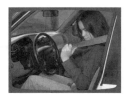 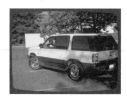

13.23 EDITING SEQUENCE 3
Evaluate this sequence to determine whether the shots are ordered logically.

If you selected sequence 3, you made the right choice. Here is why: Obviously, the driver needs to walk to the car (shot 3) and unlock the door (shot 2) before fastening the seatbelt (shot 5). The next action is to back the car out (shot 4). Finally, we see the car driving off (shot 1).

Nonlinear editing is not unlike the preceding exercise: to supply structure to a number of shots, initially represented as individual stills, which you then run as sequences. You probably noticed that this is the exact opposite of linear editing, where you start out with running sequences and then freeze particular frames that mark the edit-in and -out points.

This shot selection was based primarily on story continuity. An equally important aspect of editing concerns three major aesthetic principles: (1) continuity editing, (2) complexity editing, and (3) context. You should realize that all editing principles—including aesthetic ones—are conventions and not absolutes. They work well under most circumstances and are a basic part of the visual literacy of most television viewers and television production personnel. Depending on the event context and communication aim, however, some of the "do's" of editing may easily become the "don'ts," and vice versa.

Continuity Editing

Continuity editing means to achieve story continuity despite the fact that great chunks of the story are actually missing, and to assemble the shots in such a way that viewers are mostly unaware of the edits. Specifically, you need to observe these aesthetic factors: (1) subject identification, (2) the mental map, (3) vectors, (4) movement, (5) color, and (6) sound.

Subject identification   The viewer should be able to recognize a subject or an object from one shot to the next. Therefore, avoid editing between shots of extreme changes in distance. **SEE 13.24** If you cannot maintain visual continuity for identification, bridge the gap by telling the viewer that the shot is, indeed, the same person or thing.

Despite what was just noted, trying to edit together shots that are too similar can lead to even worse trouble— the *jump cut*. It occurs when you edit shots that are identical in subject yet slightly different in screen location. When edited together, the subject seems to jump from one screen location to another for no apparent reason. **SEE 13.25** To avoid a jump cut, try to find a succeeding

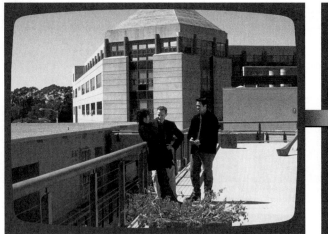 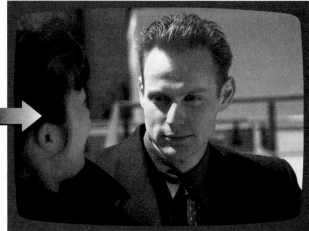

13.24 EXTREME CHANGES IN DISTANCE
When you cut from an extreme long shot to a tight close-up, viewers may not recognize exactly whose close-up it is.

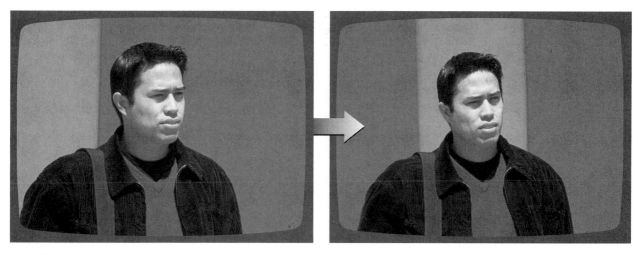

13.25 JUMP CUT

If the size, screen position, or shooting angle of an object is only slightly different in two succeeding shots, the object seems to jump within the screen.

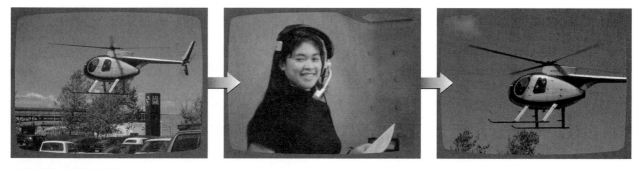

13.26 CUTAWAY

You can avoid a jump cut by changing image size and/or angle of view, or separating the two shots with a cutaway, as shown here.

shot that shows the object from a different angle or field of view, or insert a cutaway shot. **SEE 13.26**

Mental map Because television has a relatively small screen, you normally see little of a total scene in the on-screen space. Rather, the many close-ups suggest, or should suggest, that the event continues in the off-screen space. What you show in the on-screen space defines the off-screen space. For example, if you show person A looking screen-right in a close-up obviously talking to an off-screen person (B), you would expect person B to look screen-right on a subsequent close-up. **SEE 13.27 AND 13.28** What you have done—quite unconsciously—is to help the viewer construct

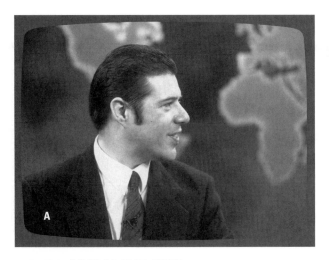

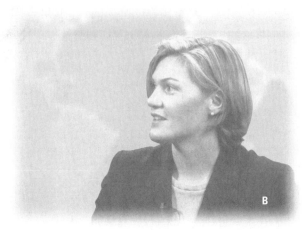

13.27 MENTAL MAP SHOT 1

Here person A's screen-right gaze (his index vector) suggests that person B must be located in the off-screen space to the right.

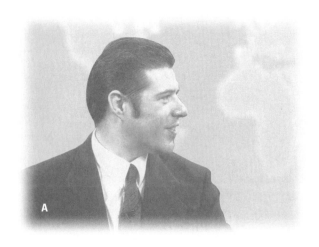

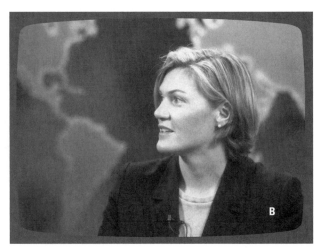

13.28 MENTAL MAP SHOT 2

When we now see person B in a close-up looking screen-left, we assume person A to be in the left off-screen space.

a *mental map* that puts people and things in a logical place, regardless of whether they are in on- or off-screen space. Once in place, you expect the subsequent screen positions to adhere to your map.

The mental map is so strong that if the subsequent shot showed person B also looking screen-right, the viewers would think that both persons A and B are talking to a third party.

To help you facilitate and maintain a mental map, you need to know something more about vectors.

Vectors   Continuity editing is little more than using graphic, index, and motion vectors in the source material to establish or maintain the viewer's mental on- and off-screen map. If you were to apply the vectors to the example of on-screen person A talking to off-screen

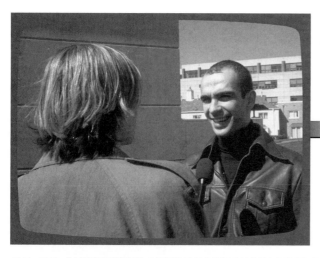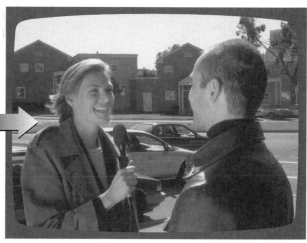

13.29 MAINTAINING SCREEN POSITIONS IN REVERSE-ANGLE SHOOTING
In this over-the-shoulder reverse-angle shot sequence, the interviewer and interviewee maintain their basic screen positions.

person B, the screen-right index vector of A needs to be edited to the screen-left index vector of B. The index vectors that are converging in the two shots indicate that A and B are talking with each other, rather than away from each other.

Maintaining screen positions is especially important in over-the-shoulder shots. If, for example, you show a reporter interviewing somebody in an over-the-shoulder two-shot, the viewer's mental map expects the two people to remain in their relative screen positions and not switch places during a reverse-angle cut. **SEE 13.29**

One important aid in maintaining the viewer's mental map and keeping the subjects in the expected screen space in reverse-angle shooting is the vector line. The *vector line* (also called *the line*, the *line of conversation and action,* or the *hundredeighty*) is an extension of converging index vectors or of a motion vector in the direction of object travel. **SEE 13.30**

When doing reverse-angle switching from camera 1 to camera 2, you need to position the cameras on the same side of the vector line. **SEE 13.31** Crossing the line with a camera will inevitably switch the subjects' screen positions and make them appear to be playing musical chairs, thus upsetting the mental map. **SEE 13.32**

Crossing the motion vector line with cameras (placing cameras on opposite sides of a moving object) will reverse the direction of object motion every time you cut. In order to continue a screen-left or screen-right

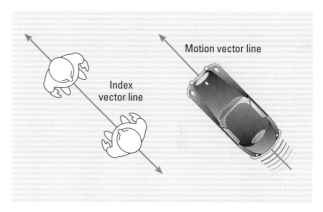

13.30 VECTOR LINE
The vector line is formed by extending converging index vectors or a motion vector.

object motion, you must keep both cameras on the same side of the vector line. **SEE 13.33**

Movement   When editing, or cutting an action with a switcher, try to continue the action as much as possible from shot to shot. The following covers some of the major points to keep in mind.

▧   To preserve motion continuity, cut during the motion of the object or subject, not before or after it. For example,

13.31 VECTOR LINE AND PROPER CAMERA POSITIONS

To maintain the screen positions of persons A and B in over-the-shoulder shooting, the cameras must be on the same side of the vector line.

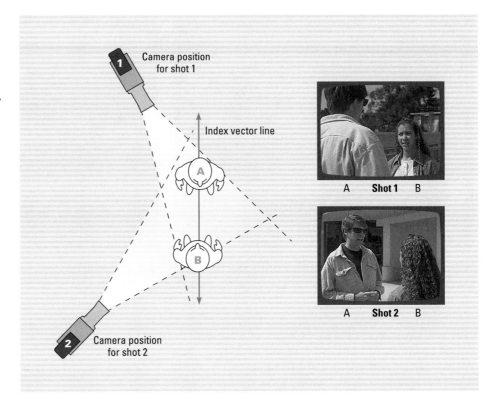

13.32 CROSSING THE VECTOR LINE

When one of the cameras crosses the vector line, persons A and B will switch positions every time you cut between the two cameras.

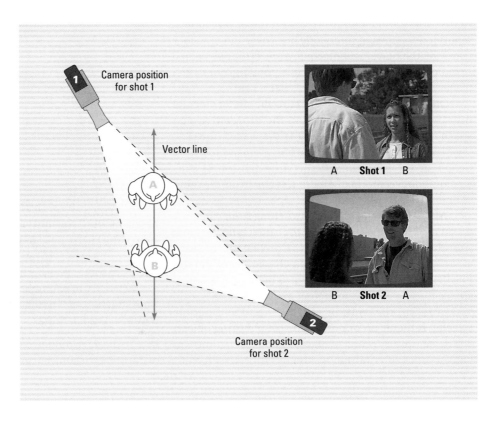

13.33 CROSSING THE MOTION VECTOR LINE
When crossing the motion vector line with cameras, the object motion will be reversed in each shot.

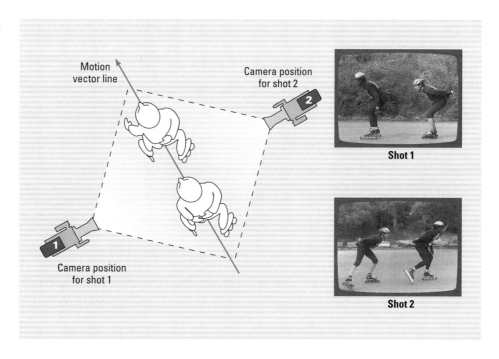

if you have a close-up of a man preparing to rise from a chair, cut to a wider shot just after he has started to rise but before he finishes the movement. Or, if you have the choice, you can let him almost finish the action on the close-up (even if he goes out of the frame temporarily) before cutting to the wider shot. But do not wait until he has finished getting up before going to the wider shot.

■   If one shot contains a moving object, do not follow it with a shot that shows the object stationary. Similarly, if you follow a moving object in one shot with a camera pan,

do not cut to a stationary camera in the next shot. Equally jarring would be a cut from a stationary object to a moving one. You need to have the subject or camera move in both the preceding and the subsequent shots.

■   When working with footage in which the action has been shot from both sides of the motion vector line (resulting in a reversal of screen directions), you must separate the two shots by a cutaway or a head-on shot so that the reversed screen directions can be perceived as continuing. **SEE 13.34**

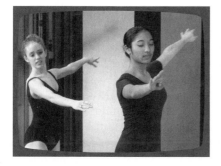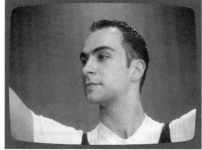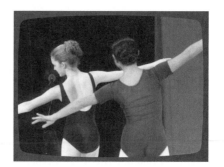

13.34 CUTAWAY
If you want to suggest continuing motion of two shots that show the objects converging, you need to insert a cutaway that has a neutral direction.

Color   One of the most serious continuity problems occurs when colors don't match in the same scene. For example, if the script for an EFP calls for an exterior MS (medium shot) of a white building followed by an MS of somebody standing in front of the same building, it should not turn blue all of a sudden. As obvious as such a discrepancy may be, color continuity is not always easy to maintain, even if you are careful to white-balance the cameras for each new location and lighting situation. What can throw you off are lighting changes you may not notice in the fervor of production. For example, the temporary blocking of the sun by some clouds can drastically influence the color temperature, as can the highly polished red paint of a car reflecting onto the white shirt of the person standing next to it.

The more attention you pay to white-balancing the camera to the prevailing color temperature of the lighting, the easier it is to maintain color continuity in postproduction.

Sound   When editing dialogue or commentary, make sure to preserve the general speech rhythm. The pauses between shots of a continuing conversation should be neither much shorter nor much longer than the ones in the unedited version. In an interview the cut (edit or switcher-activated) usually occurs at the end of a question or an answer. Reaction shots, however, are often smoother when they occur during, rather than at the end of, phrases or sentences. But note that action is generally a stronger motivation for a cut than dialogue. If somebody moves during the conversation, you must show the move, even if the other person is still in the middle of a statement.

As discussed in chapter 10, the ambient (background) sounds are very important in maintaining editing continuity. If the background noise acts as environmental sounds, which give clues to where the event takes place, you need to maintain these sounds throughout the scene, even if it was built from shots actually taken in various locations. You may have to supply this continuity by mixing in additional sounds in the postproduction sweetening sessions.

When editing video to music, try to cut with the beat. Cuts determine the beat of the visual sequence and keep the action rhythmically tight, much as the bars measure divisions in music. If the general rhythm of the music is casual or flowing, dissolves are usually more appropriate than hard cuts. But do not be a slave to this convention. Cutting "around the beat" (slightly earlier or later than the beat) can, on occasion, make the cutting rhythm less mechanical and intensify the scene. *READY ZVL* **⑬**

Complexity Editing

Complexity editing is the deliberate breaking of editing conventions to increase the complexity and intensity of a scene. Your selection and sequence of shots is no longer guided by maintaining visual and aural continuity, but by ways of getting and keeping the attention of the viewers and increasing their emotional involvement. Complexity editing does not mean that you are free to ignore the rules and conventions of continuity editing. Rather, it means that you may deliberately break some of them to intensify your communication intent.

Many commercials use complexity editing to make us sit up and take notice. Even the jump cut has gained prominence as an aesthetic intensifier. You have undoubtedly seen the erratic editing that makes a person jump from one screen location to the next, even when he is only talking about the virtues of a credit card. Much of music television (MTV) editing is based on the complexity principle. Although hardly necessary, the jarring discontinuity further intensifies the high-energy event of the music.

Complexity editing is also an effective intensification device in television plays. For example, to capture the extreme confusion of a person driven to the point of a breakdown, you may want to cross the vector line with the cameras to show the person in a quick series of flip-flop shots. **SEE 13.35**

Context

In all types of editing, but especially when editing news stories and documentaries, you must preserve the true context in which the main event took place. Assume that the news footage of a speech by a local political candidate contains a funny close-up of an audience member sound asleep. But when you screen the rest of the footage, you discover that all other audience members were not only wide awake but quite stimulated by the candidate's remarks. Are you going to use the close-up? Of course not. The person asleep was in no way representative of the overall context in which the event—the speech—took place.

You must be especially careful when using stock shots in editing. A *stock shot* depicts a common occurrence—clouds, beach scenes, snow falling, traffic, crowds—that can be applied in a variety of contexts because its qualities are typical. Some television stations either subscribe to a stock-shot library or maintain their own collections.

Here are two examples of using stock shots in editing: When editing the speech by the political candidate, you find that you need a cutaway to maintain continuity

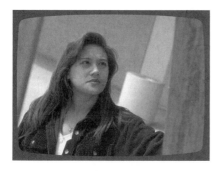 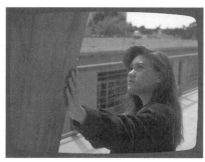 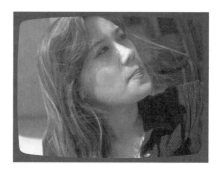

13.35 COMPLEXITY EDITING
Here the shooting from both sides of the vector line creates a disturbing flip-flop of the person, intensifying her confusion.

during a change in screen direction. You have a stock shot of a news photographer. Can you use it? Yes, because a news photographer certainly fits into the actual event context. But should you use a stock shot of a crowded and lively audience instead of the embarrassingly empty rows of chairs after most of the people had left toward the end of the speech? No, definitely not. After all, the empty hall, not a crowded audience, was the true context at the end of the speech.[4] *READY ZVL* **14**

Ethics

Because as editor you have even more power than the cameraperson over what and what not to show and to construct different meanings of the basic event footage, this section ends with a brief discussion of *ethics,* or principles of right conduct.

The willful distortion of an event through editing is not a case of poor aesthetic judgment, but a question of ethics. The most important principle for the editor, as for all other production people working with the presentation of nonfictional events (news and documentaries rather than drama), is to remain as true to the actual event as possible. For example, if you were to add applause simply because your favorite political candidate said something you happen to support, although in reality there was dead silence, you would definitely be acting unethically. It would be equally wrong to edit out all the statements that go against your convictions and leave only the ones with which you agree. If someone presents pro and con arguments, make sure to present the most representative of each. Do not edit out all of one side or the other to meet the prescribed length of the segment.

Be especially careful when juxtaposing two shots that may generate by implication a third idea not contained in either of the two shots. To follow a politician's plea for increased armaments with the explosion of an atomic bomb may unfairly imply that this politician favors nuclear war. These types of montage shots are as powerful as they are dangerous. Montage effects between video and audio information are especially effective; they may be more subtle than the video-only montages, but no less potent. For example, adding the penetrating and aggravating sounds of police sirens to the footage of "for sale" signs of several houses in a wealthy neighborhood would probably suggest that the neighborhood is changing for the worse. The implied message is to not buy any houses in this "crime-ridden" neighborhood. *READY ZVL* **15**

Do not stage events just to get exciting footage. For example, if a firefighter has made a successful rescue and all you got was the rescued person on a stretcher, do not ask the firefighter to climb the ladder again to simulate the daring feat. Although reenactments of this sort have become routine for some ENG teams, stay away from them. There is enough drama in all events if you look closely enough and shoot them effectively. You do not have to stage anything.

Finally, you are ultimately responsible to the viewers for your choices as an editor. Do not violate the trust they put in you. As you can see, there is a fine line between intensifying an event through careful editing and distorting an event through careless or unethical editing practices. The only safeguard the viewers have against irresponsible persuasion and manipulation is your responsibility as a professional communicator and your basic respect for your audience.

---

4. For a more detailed discussion of continuity and complexity editing, see Zettl, *Sight Sound Motion.*

MAIN POINTS

◆ The four basic editing functions are: (1) combining program segments by hooking together the various videotaped pieces in the proper sequence; (2) trimming to make the program fit a given time slot and to eliminate extraneous material; (3) correcting mistakes by cutting out bad portions of a scene and replacing them with good ones; and (4) building a show from a number of prerecorded takes (shots).

◆ There are four basic transition devices: (1) the *cut,* an instantaneous change from one shot to another; (2) the *dissolve,* a temporary overlapping of two shots; (3) the *wipe,* which shows one image replacing another in various ways; and (4) the *fade,* wherein the picture gradually appears from black or goes to black.

◆ The four major editing principles are continuity, complexity, context, and ethics.

◆ Continuity editing means to establish continuity in subject identification, subject placement, movement, color, and sound, and should help maintain the viewer's mental map of where things should be or where they should move.

◆ Graphic, index, and motion vectors play an important part in establishing and maintaining continuity from shot to shot.

◆ Complexity editing is the deliberate breaking of editing conventions to increase the complexity and intensity of a scene.

◆ In editing nonfiction, the context should remain as true to the actual event as possible. Thus, ethics becomes the overriding editing principle.

ZETTL'S VIDEOLAB 2.1

*Editing is difficult to show in a book. Fortunately, the **editing** module of Zettl's VideoLab 2.1 gives you ample opportunity to look at edits, do some editing yourself, and see some of the editing theory come alive.*

RUN ZVL 1 Click on the **editing** monitor and run tape 1 **Meet Veronica**. You met her back in chapter 1, but her comments about editing are important enough to hear again.

RUN ZVL 2 Run tape 3 **Tape Basics** and click on the **System** module. It shows how single-source and expanded single-source recording systems work.

RUN ZVL 3 Now click on the **Tape** module, which gives important information about the control track.

RUN ZVL 4 Click on the **Time code** module. Here you can observe how the time code functions and how the frame numbers roll over into seconds.

RUN ZVL 5 Run tape 5 **Location Procedures**. Click on the first four modules: **Basics**, **Cutaways**, **Pick-ups**, and **Vectors**. Veronica gives especially valuable advice in her introduction.

RUN ZVL 6 Run tape 3 **Tape Basics** again and click on the **Time code** module. Pay particular attention to what a window dub looks like and why we use it.

RUN ZVL 7 Run tape 8 **Pre-edit Procedures** and click on the **Preparations** module. Now click on the **Logs** module. You will learn some important tips about how to keep a field log and how to prepare a VTR log.

RUN ZVL 8　　Now click on the **Paper edit** module. It will show you how you can save a great amount of time by doing such preparatory paper-and-pencil editing. The **Quiz** will enable you to run a brief take and then match it with the appropriate EDL entry.

RUN ZVL 9　　Run tape 2 **Functions** and click on the **Select** module. Now click on the **Combine** module. You will get some idea of what an editor has to do.

RUN ZVL 10　　Run tape 7 **Cutting Procedures** and click on the **Trim** module to see how a few frames can change a rather bumpy cut into a seamless transition. The **Quiz** lets you do some trimming yourself.

RUN ZVL 11　　Run tape 2 **Functions** again. Go through all the modules. In the **Correct** module note how difficult it is to correct a seemingly harmless mistake in postproduction editing. Now you can try your skill as an editor by clicking on the **Quiz** module.

RUN ZVL 12　　Run tape 6 **Transitions & Keys**. Click on the first four modules: **Cut**, **Dissolve**, **Wipe**, and **Fade**. They all demonstrate the functions and effects of these transitions.

RUN ZVL 13　　Run tape 4 **Continuity** and carefully watch five modules: **Vectors**, **Mental map**, **Subject ID**, **Motion**, and **Sound**. These modules clearly demonstrate some of the pitfalls of continuity editing. You can try your continuity skills by running the various short clips in the **Quiz** module.

RUN ZVL 14　　Click on the **Complexity** module and notice how continuity can take a backseat when you edit to intensify a scene.

RUN ZVL 15　　Run tape 2 **Functions** again and click on the **Select** module. What meaning do you convey by having the cattle juxtaposed with the woman munching on a hamburger? Be sure to take the **Quizzes** on all editing tapes.

14

Visual Effects

Even news presentations are so loaded with video special effects that they often rival, if not surpass, the latest video games. The titles of news shows dance across the screen, change color, and zoom toward the horizon. News anchors, field reporters, and guests are squeezed into side-by-side boxes when talking to one another. News pictures or graphics are contained in a neat frame that hovers above the news anchor's shoulder. The brief stories often end in a freeze-frame and then peel off the screen as though they were ripped out of a magazine, or they simply tumble out of sight.

The screen is often loaded with simultaneous information. While the anchor's comments about a tragic traffic accident are accompanied by graphic video footage, the stock market quotes crawl across the bottom of the screen, and the side panel reveals the latest sports scores. Throughout it all, the station or network logo is solidly embedded in a corner.

Such electronic wizardry is so readily available that it may tempt you to substitute effect for content. Do not fall into the trap of camouflaging insignificant content or poorly shot or edited pictures with electronic effects.

As dazzling as the effects may be, they cannot replace the basic message. When used judiciously, however, many effects can enhance production considerably and give the message added impact.

Whenever you intend to use a visual effect, ask yourself: Is the effect really necessary? Does it help clarify and intensify my message? Is the effect reliable, especially when integrating it into a live or live-on-tape production? Is it appropriate? For example, a freeze-frame showing the new tennis champion lifting her trophy in triumph is a perfectly appropriate closing shot; to apply the same technique to a victim of a terrorist bombing is not. If you can answer yes to all these questions, leave the effect in. If you answer no or even maybe to any of them, leave it out.

In section 14.1, Electronic Effects and How to Use Them, we examine standard electronic effects and digital video effects; section 14.2, Nonelectronic Effects and How to Use Them, looks at some of the more practical optical and mechanical effects.

KEY TERMS

chroma keying Special key effect that uses color (usually blue) for the background, which is replaced by the background image during the key.

computer-generated DVE Digital video effects created entirely by computer hardware and software.

computer-manipulated DVE Digital video effects created by the computer using an existing image (camera-generated video sequence, video frame, photo, or painting) and enhancing or changing it in some way.

defocus Simple yet highly effective optical effect wherein the camera operator zooms in, racks out of focus, and, on cue, back into focus again. Used as a transitional device or to indicate strong psychological disturbances or physiological imbalance.

diffusion filter Filter that attaches to the front of the lens; gives a scene a soft, slightly out-of-focus look.

digital video effects (DVE) Visual effects generated by a computer or digital effects equipment in the switcher. DVE can use an analog signal as original stimulus for the effects. *DVE* also stands for the equipment that produces the effects.

key An electronic effect. *Keying* means cutting one image (usually lettering) into a different background image.

matte key Keyed (electronically cut in) title whose letters are filled with shades of gray or a specific color.

special-effects generator (SEG) An analog image generator that produces special-effects wipe patterns and key effects.

star filter Filter that attaches to the front of the lens; changes prominent light sources into starlike light beams.

television gobo A scenic foreground piece through which the camera can shoot, thus integrating the decorative foreground with the background action. In film a gobo is an opaque shield used for partially blocking a light.

wipe Transition in which a second image, framed in some geometrical shape, gradually replaces all or part of the first one.

14.1

Electronic Effects and How to Use Them

A judicious use of visual effects presupposes that you know what effects are available. There are effects that can be readily created during a production, such as the title keys or various wipes, and others that need to be carefully built with digital equipment in the postproduction phase. This section discusses the two major types of visual effects.

▶ **STANDARD ANALOG VIDEO EFFECTS**
Superimposition, key, chroma key, and wipe

▶ **DIGITAL VIDEO EFFECTS**
Computer-manipulated effects; manipulation of image size, shape, light, and color; manipulation of motion; creation and manipulation of multi-images; and computer-generated effects

STANDARD ANALOG VIDEO EFFECTS

Combined with modern switchers, the *special-effects generator (SEG)* built into all production switchers can produce a dazzling variety of special effects with ease and reliability. Many electronic effects have become so commonplace in television production that they have lost their specialty status and are simply considered part of the standard visual arsenal. These include (1) the superimposition, or super, (2) the key, (3) the chroma key, and (4) the wipe. You can accomplish all of these effects with the standard analog switcher and its built-in SEG.

Superimposition

A *superimposition,* or *super* for short, is a form of double exposure. The picture from one video source is electronically superimposed over the picture from another. As explained in chapter 13, the super is easily achieved by activating both mix buses with the fader bar (see figure 11.9b). A distinct characteristic of a super is that you can see through each of the superimposed images. You can then vary the strength of either picture (signal) by moving the fader bar toward one mix bus or the other.

In case you cannot key a title over a background image, you can still use a super for the title effect. When supering titles, one camera is focused on the super card, which has white letters on a black background. The background picture can be supplied by either another camera (focused on a live event, such as a long shot of a sports stadium) or any other video source. Because the black card does not reflect any light, or only an insignificant amount, it will remain invisible during the mixing of the two video sources.

More often, supers are used for creating the effects of inner events—thoughts, dreams, or processes of imagination. The traditional (and certainly overused) super of a dream sequence shows a close-up of a sleeping person, with images supered over his or her face. Sometimes supers are used to make an event more complex. For example, you may want to super a close-up of a dancer over a long shot of the same dancer. If the effect is done properly, we are given new insight into the dance. You are no longer photographing a dance, but helping create it.

Key

Keying means electronically cutting out portions of a television picture and filling them in with another, or portions of another, image. The basic purpose of a *key* is to add titles to a background picture or to cut another picture (the image of a weathercaster) into the background picture (the satellite weather map). The lettering for the title is generally supplied by a *C.G. (character generator)* (see chapter 15). You can also use a title card for keying titles. The card looks exactly like the super card (white letters on a black background). However, unlike in a super, where the white letters are laid on top of the base picture, in a key the letters are electronically cut into the base picture and then filled with a white or color signal. **SEE 14.1**

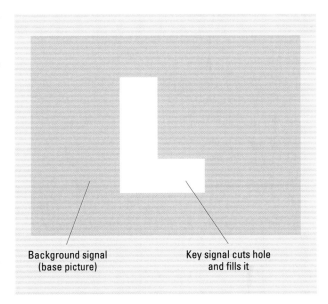

14.2 INTERNAL KEY

In an internal key, the signal that is doing the cutting is also used to fill in the holes.

Background signal (base picture)

Key signal cuts hole and fills it

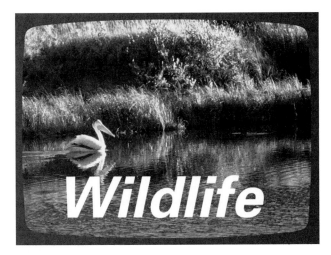

14.1 KEY

When keying a title over a base picture, the key signal cuts a hole into the base picture in the shape of the letters supplied by the C.G.

You may be somewhat bewildered reading and hearing about keys, mattes, and matte keys—all seemingly referring to the same thing. It really doesn't matter what term you use, so long as you are consistent and all members of the production team know what you mean. There are basically three types of keys: (1) internal key, (2) external key, and (3) matte key. Because chroma keying works on a different principle, we discuss it separately later in this section.

Internal key   The *internal key* uses two signals. One supplies the background picture, the other does the cutting (letters). The signal that is doing the cutting is also used to fill the holes (in the form of the letters). **SEE 14.2**

To achieve a clean key, in which the white letters are cut into the base picture without any tearing or breakup, you must use the *key level* (or *clip*) *control* on the switcher. This control adjusts the brightness contrast between the background and key signal. The brighter the signal doing the cutting and the higher the contrast, the cleaner the key. Operationally, you can preset the key effect and then watch on the preview monitor whether the key letters are tearing or otherwise displaying fuzzy edges. You simply turn the key level control knob until the letters appear sharp. On many switchers with *downstream keyers*, you can push down the key level control knob to display the total key effect on the preview monitor.

14.3 EXTERNAL KEY

In this example the letter *L* is supplied by the C.G. and keyed into the camera 1 video (base picture of the dancer). Camera 2 is focused on the burlap and supplies the external signal that fills the cutout letters.

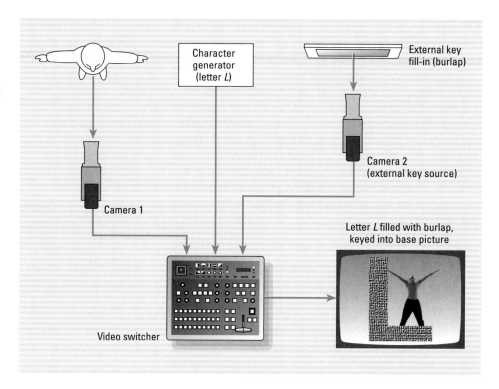

You can, of course, also key shapes of objects into the base picture, so long as they have enough contrast relative to the base picture that their edges do not tear.

External key   The *external key* uses three signals: the background signal, the hole-cutting signal, and a third signal, often called the foreground signal, that is filling the hole. This additional video source can be colors from the C.G., a VTR, or even a second camera (assuming that the background video is also supplied by a camera). For example, if you want to key the character-generated letter *L* over a dancer, and you want to fill the *L* with burlap to give it some texture, you could have a second camera focus on a piece of burlap and then combine the effect through external keying so that the letter appears as though it were cut out of burlap. **SEE 14.3** You could also fill the letter, or any other base picture cutout, with an animated scene.

Matte key   If the cutout portions of the title are filled with various grays or colors generated by the switcher or embellished with contours or shadows, it is a *matte key*. **SEE 14.4** You can select any of the popular matte key modes: the edge mode, the drop-shadow mode, or the outline mode.

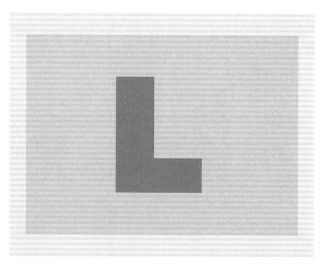

14.4 MATTE KEY

In a matte key, the cutout letters are filled with shades of gray or with a color supplied by the switcher or C.G.

In the edge mode, each letter has a thin, black outline around it. **SEE 14.5** In the drop-shadow mode, the letters have a black shadow contour that makes them appear three dimensional. **SEE 14.6** In the outline mode, the

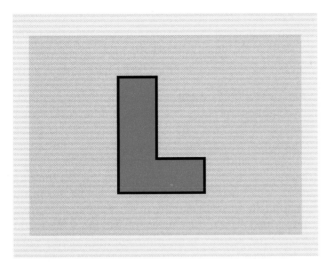

14.5 MATTE KEY IN EDGE MODE

The edge mode matte key puts a black border around the letters to make them more readable than with the normal key.

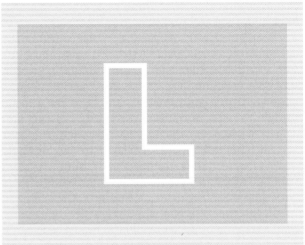

14.7 MATTE KEY IN OUTLINE MODE

The outline matte key makes the letters appear in outline form. It shows the contour of the letters only.

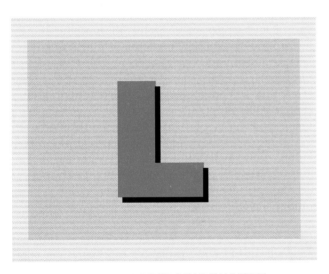

14.6 MATTE KEY IN DROP-SHADOW MODE

The drop-shadow matte key adds a prominent attached shadow to the letters as though three-dimensional letters were illuminated by a strong spotlight.

letters themselves appear in outline form, with the base picture filling the inside. **SEE 14.7**

Most switchers allow you to choose the key mode that will make the titles look more attractive or prevent them from getting lost in an especially busy background.

Some keys are semitransparent and let the background show through, similar to a super. This effect is a favorite technique for displaying statistics while still letting you see the full-screen background action.

Chroma Key

Chroma keying is a special effect that uses a specific color (chroma), usually blue or green, as background for the person or object that is to appear in front of the background scene. During the key, the blue background will be replaced by the background video source without affecting the foreground object. A typical example is the weathercaster standing in front of a weather map or a satellite picture. During the chroma key, the computer-generated weather map or satellite image replaces all blue areas—but not the weathercaster. The key effect makes the weathercaster appear to be standing in front of the weather map or satellite image. **SEE COLOR PLATE 17**

Because the chroma key responds to the saturation of the color, be sure that the chroma-key area is painted evenly (even blue with a fairly high saturation throughout the area) and especially lighted evenly. Uneven background lighting will prevent a full replacement of the blue area by the background video, or cause the foreground image to tear.

If on-camera talent wears something similar to the background color, such as a blue sweater, while standing in front of the chroma-key area, the blue of the sweater will also be replaced by the background image during the key. Unless you want to shock your audience with a special effect in which part of the weathercaster disappears, don't let him or her wear anything blue in front of the chroma-key set.

Even blue eyes can present a problem during close-ups in chroma keying, although, fortunately, most blue eyes reflect or contain enough other colors and are not saturated enough to keep them from becoming transparent. If the weathercaster stands too close to the chroma-key area, the reflections of the blue background on part of his or her clothing or hair may cause the key to tear. Such problems may also occur if the lighting on the weathercaster has extremely fast falloff. The deep shadows, which are apt to be seen as blue by the camera, may cause the image to tear during the key.

Recall that you can counteract this nuisance to some extent by using light-yellow or orange gels on the *back lights* (not *background* lights). Because the yellow back light neutralizes the blue shadows, it sets off and separates the performer from the blue background during the chroma-key.

Studio use of chroma key   Despite the availability of highly sophisticated digital video effects (DVE), the chroma-key process is still used in various studio production situations. The previous discussion focuses on some of the most popular uses of chroma-key effects in weathercasts. But there are other situations in which chroma keying is equally applicable and effective. Recall the lighting situation discussed briefly in chapter 8: The company executive wanted to give her speech sitting behind her desk, which was in front of a large picture window. Because she is proud of the spectacular view, she wanted the camera to capture her against the window. You can solve these formidable lighting problems (silhouette effect, high color temperature) by transporting her office into the studio for a chroma-key effect. Set up a similar desk and chair in the studio in front of a blue chroma-key area. Then have a camera focus on a photograph of the spectacular view. Use this camera to supply the background image during the key. Because the studio gives you such good lighting control, you can make the chroma key look almost more realistic than if you were in her actual office. **SEE COLOR PLATE 18**

You can also use chroma keying to create a variety of scenic backgrounds or environments. Assume, for example, that you would like to show a tourist shooting some footage of a museum. The museum background is accessed from an ESS "slide" (electronic still store frame). Camera 1 focuses on the tourist with his camcorder, standing in front of an evenly lighted, well-saturated blue background. Through chroma keying, all the blue areas will be replaced by the background image as provided by the ESS system, and the tourist will appear to be standing in front of the museum. **SEE COLOR PLATE 19**

Ultimatte   The *Ultimatte* is a specific type of blue-screen (chroma) keying. This system produces a crisp and highly stable key that is hard to distinguish from an actual foreground/background scene. It allows you to mix foreground and background cameras so precisely that shadows of the foreground subject falling on the blue screen will transfer to the background picture during the key. If the figure were to move in front of the blue screen during the key, the shadow would also move across the background picture. Some more-complex productions, such as soap operas, use Ultimatte to key in ceilings of the realistic sets of living rooms or hallways.

Auto key tracking   If you use live action in front of a blue background in order to key it into a small, three-dimensional model, such as the interior of an airliner or spaceship, you need to synchronize the movements of the foreground camera (looking at the live action) and the background camera (looking at the model). This synchronization is necessary to make the shift of perspective of foreground camera coincide with that of the background camera. For example, if you zoom in on the people in the foreground, the background scene needs to change in size also. Ambitious film and HDTV (high-definition television) productions still rely on such auto key tracking effects, although sophisticated computer software can accomplish such perspective synchronization in post-production quite readily.

ENG EFP **EFP chroma key**   Chroma keying is also useful during EFP and big remotes, especially if the talent is not able to stand directly in front of the desired background scene, such as a stadium or government building. When using a chroma-key effect during a sports remote, for example, the talent may even be in the studio, with the remote feed (long shot of the football stadium) serving as the chroma-key background.

If you do the chroma key on location, with the talent standing outdoors, watch out for reflections from the sky. With blue as the chroma-key color, the blue reflections from the sky may fool the chroma keyer and cause the key contours to break up. To avoid such problems, switch to green for the chroma-key color and put the talent in front of a green cloth backdrop.

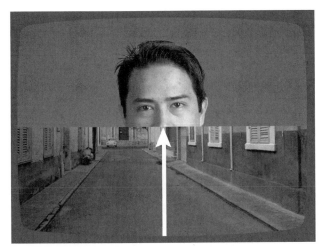

14.8 VERTICAL WIPE
In a vertical wipe, one picture is gradually replaced by another from the bottom up or from the top down.

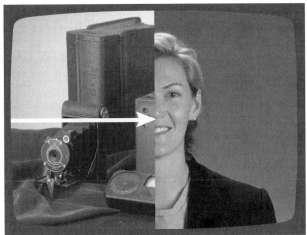

14.9 HORIZONTAL WIPE
In a horizontal wipe, one picture is gradually replaced by another from the side.

Wipe

In a *wipe* a second image in some geometrical shape gradually replaces parts or all of the first (on-air) image. Although, technically, the second picture is uncovered by the first as it moves away, perceptually it looks as though the second image pushes—wipes—the first image off the screen.

The two simplest wipes are the vertical and the horizontal. A vertical wipe gives the same effect as pulling down a window shade over the screen. Just as the window shade wipes out the picture you see through the window, the image from one camera is gradually replaced by a second image that seems to push the first image upward or downward off-screen. **SEE 14.8** The horizontal wipe works the same way, except that the base picture is replaced by the second image from the side. **SEE 14.9** The line that separates the two images is called the *wipe border.*

Soft wipes In a *soft wipe*, the wipe border is purposely softened or eliminated to have the two images blend into each other. You can adjust the softness of the border through a rotary control on the switcher (see figure 11.4). The soft wipe looks almost like a single shot consisting of two separate images. **SEE 14.10**

Wipe patterns The more complicated wipes can take on many geometrical shapes. In a diamond wipe, one picture starts in the middle of the other picture and

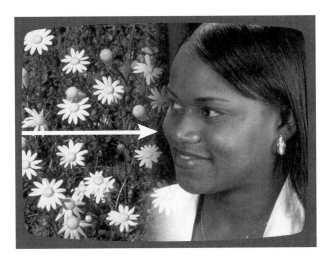

14.10 SOFT WIPE
In a soft wipe, the demarcation line between the two images is softened so that they blend together.

wipes it off the screen in the shape of a diamond. **SEE 14.11** In a corner wipe, the second image starts from a screen corner and wipes the base picture off the screen diagonally. Box wipes and circle wipes are also frequently used. Instead of the diamond, the geometrical wipe pattern is a rectangle or a circle.

You can select the appropriate wipe configuration by pressing the corresponding button in the wipe mode control section of the switcher or by calling up a specific

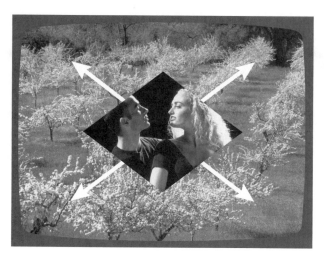

14.11 DIAMOND WIPE

In a diamond wipe, the second video source is gradually revealed in an expanding diamond-shaped cutout.

preprogrammed wipe from the switcher's memory. **SEE 14.12** As pointed out in chapter 11, the speed of the wipe is determined by how fast you move the fader bar or by dialing in a certain auto transition rate.

Wipe positions and directions   If you activate wipes with the special-effects fader bar, you can stop the wipe anyplace along its travel, depending on how far you move the fader bar. If the switcher has a directional mode switch for wipes, make sure it is set properly. In

the normal mode, the vertical wipe moves from top to bottom. In the reversal mode, the wipe moves from bottom to top. Similarly, you can reverse the wipe and have it move from screen-right to screen-left or vice versa. The wipe can also be made to reverse itself in flip-flop fashion every time you move the fader bar.

If you use a box wipe or a circle wipe, you usually have some latitude in changing its shape. For example, you can make an ellipse out of a circle, or a rectangle out of a square. With the joystick you can position the wipe pattern (such as a circle wipe) anywhere on-screen (see figure 11.11).

Split screen   If you stop a vertical, horizontal, or diagonal wipe before its completion, you get a split-screen effect, or, simply, a *split screen*. Each portion shows a different picture. To set up for an effective split screen with a horizontal wipe, you must have one camera put its image (designated for the left half of the split screen) in the left side of its viewfinder and the other camera's image in the right side (for the right half of the split screen). During the wipe, the left- and right-screen areas block out each other's unwanted picture portions. **SEE 14.13** It goes without saying that you need to preview such effects before putting them on the air.

Spotlight effect   The spotlight effect looks like a soft-edged circle wipe, except that it lets the base picture show through (similar to a super). You can use this effect to draw attention to a specific portion of the screen as though you were shining a spotlight on it. **SEE 14.14**

14.12 WIPE PATTERNS

The various wipe configurations are normally marked on the switcher buttons in the wipe mode control section.

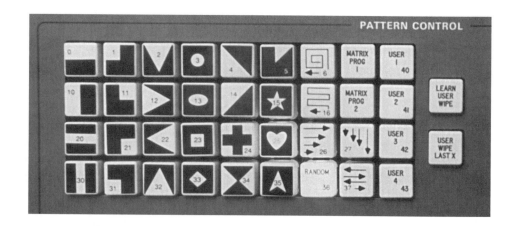

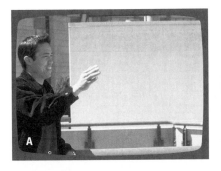 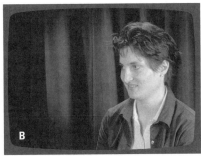 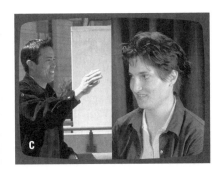

14.13 SPLIT SCREEN

A In this horizontal split-screen effect, camera 1 frames in the left side of the viewfinder the image designated to become the left part of the split screen. **B** Camera 2 places its image in the right side of the viewfinder. **C** In the completed split-screen wipe, the two images appear in the designated sides of the frame.

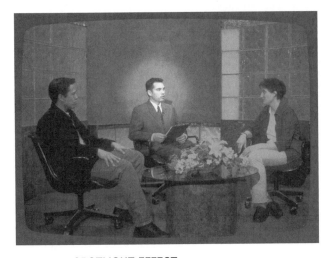

14.14 SPOTLIGHT EFFECT

The spotlight effect looks like a soft-edged circle wipe with the base picture showing through.

DIGITAL VIDEO EFFECTS

As you know, *digital video effects (DVE)* are much richer and more flexible than analog effects. The computer has an astonishing capacity to manipulate video images and, more important, create new ones. Once a video image is in digital form, you can change its shape and color pretty much at will and add new ones from your digital repertoire. If you need new images, there is an abundance of software programs to create landscapes, sets, cartoon figures, and even people from scratch.

Although many digitally generated video effects are done in postproduction, you will have equal access to digital effects before and during production. Various weather maps, complex transitions between stories, or animated titles are often done in preproduction and then simply called up by the TD (technical director) when needed. Many DVE are used during a live production, such as squeezing the anchor and guests in side-by-side boxes on the screen, or displaying multiple boxes that show various views of a football game. All nonlinear editing systems offer an array of effects for transitioning, combining, or altering video images in some way. As you undoubtedly know, certain software programs can turn your desktop computer into a powerful nonlinear editing and DVE machine.

Computer-Manipulated Effects

Computer-manipulated DVE take an existing image (camera-generated video sequence, video frame, photo, or painting) and enhance or change it in some way. Assuming that your desktop computer has the necessary audio/video hardware and software, you can feed the videotape directly into the computer, run a brief video sequence, and record it in full or grab any frame and store it as a data file. With a scanner you can digitize photos, documents, drawings, and paintings and store the images as computer files. You can also put actual objects on a flatbed scanner and store the image on the computer. Once the images are digitized, you can manipulate them at will.

Although the actual process of digitally manipulating images is quite complicated, the principle is relatively simple. As an example, let's manipulate the color, shape, and size of a video frame showing the close-up of a face. In digitizing the videotape frame, you translate the continuous change of color, brightness, and shapes (analog) of the face into a great number of discrete dots—*pixels*—each having several assigned values (binary numbers) for such attributes as color, brightness, and position. This process is not unlike translating a photo into a tile mosaic. If, for example, you want to manipulate the digitized photo of a person's face, you can easily change the color as well as the shape of the face. To make the brown eyes blue, you simply replace some of the brown tiles with blue ones. If you want to make the nose red, you can add some red tiles to the nose.

You can also change the shape of the nose. Take some tiles out to make the nose smaller or thinner, or add some to make it thicker. You can also use smaller or larger tiles to decrease or increase the size of the picture. When using DVE equipment rather than mosaic tiles, such changes are done with incredible speed and accuracy. The computer stores all such effects, so you can retrieve them in an instant.

Fast access to an effect or a series of them is especially important when complex effects follow one another in rapid succession during a production, such as a weather or sports report. Even the best TD with the most elaborate special-effects switcher could not create all the effects normally contained in the "bumpers" (the very brief yet visually complex program material separating a show from a commercial or dividing program segments) in real time during the production.

When interfacing digital with standard (analog) effects (such as keys and wipes), you can greatly increase the visual effects palette. In order to make some sense out of the various digital effects' potential, we divide them into three areas: (1) manipulation of image size, shape, light, and color, (2) manipulation of motion, and (3) creation and manipulation of multi-images.

Image Size, Shape, Light, and Color

There is a great variety of effects available for manipulating the size, shape, light, and color of an image. Some of the more prominent are: (1) shrinking and expanding, (2) stretching, (3) positioning and point of view, (4) perspective, (5) mosaic, and (6) posterization and solarization. Many of these DVE change a realistic picture into a basically graphical image.

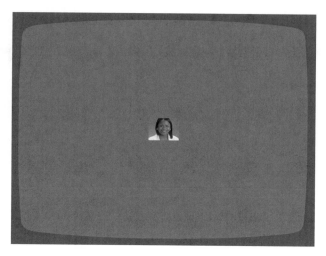

14.15 SHRINKING

Through shrinking, also called a squeeze-zoom, you can reduce the total full-frame image to a smaller frame that contains the same picture information.

Shrinking and expanding *Shrinking* refers to making a picture smaller while keeping the entire picture and its aspect ratio (width to height) intact. It is not like cropping, where you actually remove some of the picture information; you simply render the whole picture somewhat smaller. DVE allow you to shrink the entire picture from its original full-screen size to a mere point on the screen (zero-size). Or you can do the reverse, starting with a zero-size image and expanding it to full-frame or even larger so that you see only a close-up detail of the expanded image. Because the visual effect is similar to a zoom-out (shrinking) or zoom-in (expansion), this effect is also called *squeeze-zoom*. **SEE 14.15**

Stretching With DVE you can stretch an image horizontally or vertically. Again, the stretching is not done by cropping the image to fit a new frame but by distorting the total image so that its borders attain a new aspect ratio. **SEE 14.16**

Positioning and point of view The shrunk (squeeze-zoomed) image can be positioned anywhere in the frame. For example, you can freeze the first frame of a news videotape, shrink the image through a squeeze-zoom, and position it in a box over the newscaster's shoulder. You can then roll the VTR, letting the story come alive while simultaneously expanding it (squeeze-zoom out) to a full-screen image. **SEE 14.17**

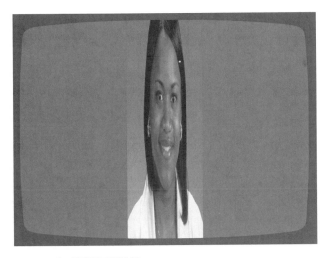

14.16 STRETCHING

With DVE you can change the aspect ratio of an image so that it appears vertically stretched.

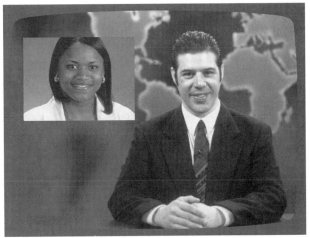

14.17 POSITIONING OF SQUEEZE-ZOOMED IMAGE

In this case a frame from a news clip was shrunk (squeeze-zoomed in) and then placed over the newscaster's shoulder.

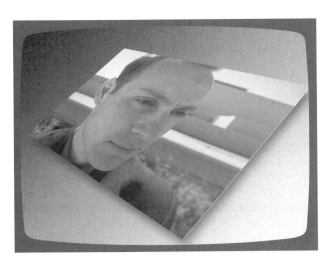

14.18 PERSPECTIVE

Through DVE you can distort an image so that it looks three-dimensional or like it's occupying a 3-D screen space.

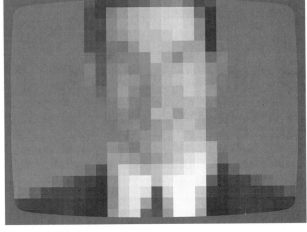

14.19 MOSAIC EFFECT

Here the image is changed into equal-sized squares, resembling a mosaic. In the electronic mosaic, as in a traditional tile mosaic, you can change the size of the tiles.

Perspective   You can distort an image in such a way that it looks three-dimensional, or like it's occupying three-dimensional space. A simple perspective can create such a 3-D illusion. The effect looks as though you had placed a two-dimensional picture (snapshot or postcard) into the "three-dimensional" video space of the television set. When combined with motion, the 3-D video space is greatly intensified. **SEE 14.18**

Mosaic   In the *mosaic* effect, the video image (static or in motion) is broken down into many discrete, equal-sized squares of limited brightness and color. The resulting screen image looks like an actual tile mosaic. Such an image actually consists of greatly enlarged pixels. **SEE 14.19 AND COLOR PLATE 4** This technique is sometimes used in interviews to obscure the guest's identity. The mosaiclike distortion shows the person's face, but renders the features unrecognizable.

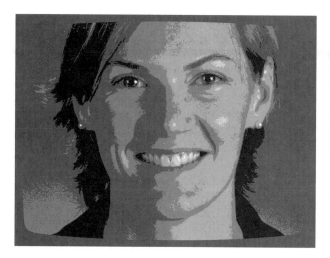

14.20 POSTERIZATION

In posterization the brightness values are severely reduced. The picture takes on a high-contrast look.

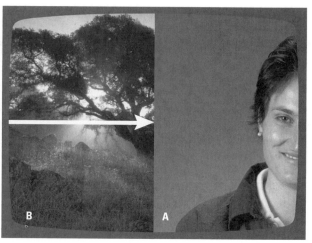

14.21 SLIDE EFFECT

The slide effect is similar to a horizontal wipe. Video A seems to slide off to one side or corner, revealing video B underneath.

Posterization and solarization   In *posterization* the brightness values (luminance) and the shades of the individual colors are collapsed so that the image is reduced to a few single colors and brightness steps. For example, the colors on a face show up as though they were painted by number with only a few paints. Because this image looks like a poster, the effect is called posterization.

In *solarization* brightness values of the image are gradually changed to their opposite values. In partial solarization, the lighter areas get darker and the darker areas lighter. Most solarization effects show the complete reversal of luminance—the black areas turn white and the white areas turn black. Such a reversal is usually called *polarity reversal*. To complicate things somewhat, the terms *posterization* and *solarization* are sometimes used interchangeably. **SEE 14.20**

Motion

There are so many possibilities for making various effects move that a sensible and common terminology has not yet been developed. Don't be surprised to hear the director or editor in the control room or editing room using the sound language of cartoons ("squeeze," "bounce," "fly") when calling for certain motion effects. Some of the terms have been coined by DVE equipment manufacturers, others by imaginative production personnel. Let's look at a few of the more popular effects: (1) slide and peel effects, (2) snapshots, (3) rotation and bounce effects, (4) fly effect, and (5) cube spin.

Slide and peel effects   The slide effect is similar to a horizontal wipe: video A (first picture) seems to push video B (second picture) to the side, looking as though A simply slides to the side to reveal the new picture underneath. **SEE 14.21**   The slide effect can also work diagonally.

A variation of the slide effect is the peel effect, wherein image A curls up as though it were peeled off a stack of images, revealing image B underneath. **SEE 14.22**

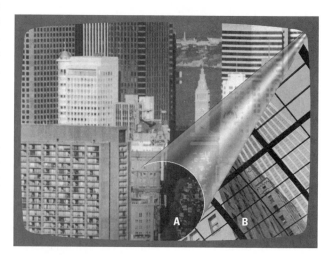

14.22 PEEL EFFECT

In a peel effect, video A seems to curl and peel off a stack of pictures, revealing video B underneath.

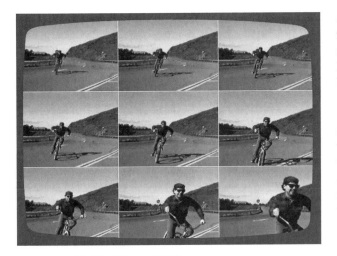

14.23 SNAPSHOT EFFECT

In a snapshot the individual screen divisions show successively updated freeze-frames.

Snapshots   This effect consists of multiple freeze-frames that update individually at various rates. What you see on-screen is a kind of ripple effect from image to image. Each frame area can be filled with a separate picture, to build sequentially a multiscreen effect. **SEE 14.23**

Rotation and bounce effects   With the rotation effect, you can spin any image on all three axes, individually or simultaneously: the x-axis, representing width; the y-axis, representing height; and the z-axis, representing depth. Although rotation terminology varies, normally a "tumble" refers to x-axis rotation, a "flip" to y-axis rotation, and a "spin" to z-axis rotation. **SEE 14.24**

In a bounce effect, the shrunk video A image is deflected from screen edge to screen edge against the video B background. The video A "bouncing ball" can change shape or flip while moving. **SEE 14.25**

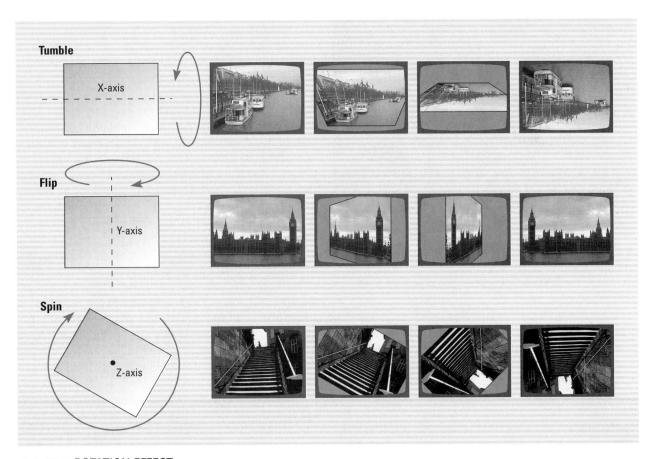

14.24 ROTATION EFFECT

The image can be revolved around the x-axis (tumble), the y-axis (flip), and the z-axis (spin).

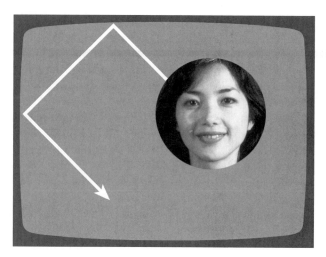

14.25 BOUNCE EFFECT
In a bounce effect, the image seems to bounce from screen edge to screen edge.

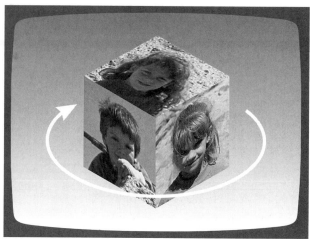

14.27 CUBE SPIN
In a cube spin, a rotating cube displays a different static or moving image on each of the visible three sides.

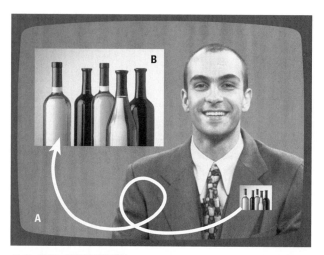

14.26 FLY EFFECT
In the fly effect, video B enlarges from zero-size as it moves and spins to a different screen position on top of the video A background.

Fly effect In the fly effect, a video B insert expands from zero-size and flies to another screen position against the video A background. During the fly video B can rotate, tumble, flip, spin—or whatever tickles your fancy. **SEE 14.26**

Cube spin The rotation can also be applied to three-dimensional effects. The well-known cube-spin shows a rotating cube, with each of the visible three sides displaying a different static or moving image. **SEE 14.27**

Multi-Images

The multi-image effects include the various possibilities of dividing the screen into sections or of having a specific image update itself. The former we call secondary frame effects, the latter echo effects.

Secondary frame The *secondary frame effect* shows several images, each clearly contained within its own frame. A common use of such an effect is to show host and guest simultaneously in separate frames, talking to each other from different locations. To emphasize that they are speaking to each other, although both are actually looking into the camera (at the viewer), the frames are tilted toward each other through a digital perspective change. **SEE 14.28** You can split the screen into four or more areas, with four or more people or events displayed in each frame on a single screen.

Echo The *echo effect* is created when you repeat the same image as though it were placed between two opposing mirrors. This highly decorative effect is often used for titles, but you can also use it to continuously update a freeze-frame, thus creating an artificial motion effect. For example, you could freeze an especially elegant pose of a dancer and then animate the freeze-frame again through the echo effect. You can also make each successive echo image smaller or larger so that together they seem to recede to or advance from the vanishing point (the point where the image seems to disappear at the horizon). **SEE 14.29**

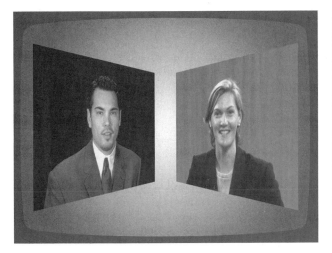

14.28 SECONDARY FRAME EFFECT

The trapezoidal distortion of the frames makes us perceive two people talking to each other rather than to the viewer.

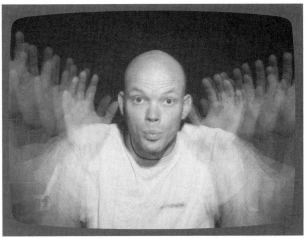

14.29 ECHO EFFECT

In the echo effect, a static image is repeated many times and the copies are placed in close proximity to one another.

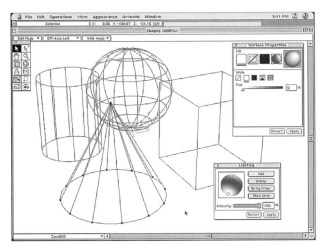

14.30 SOLID MODELING

The computer covers these wire-frame solids with a realistic-looking surface and gives them specific color, light, and shading.

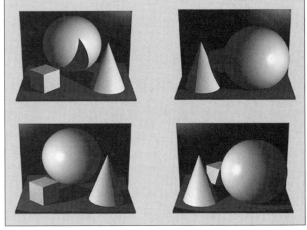

14.31 LIGHTING SHIFTS

The computer simulates a key-light effect with appropriate and attached cast shadows.

Computer-Generated Effects

Although *computer-generated DVE* are frequently used in television production, the equipment and techniques applied in creating them are much more the province of computer graphics and imaging than television production. Such images and animation require highly trained computer graphics designers, who can create anything from a fantasy landscape to a spaceship chase in a faraway galaxy. Using complicated mathematical formulas called algorithms, you can draw various geometrical shapes, rotate them, give them various textures and colors, and produce lighting effects as though you were manipulating actual lighting instruments. **SEE 14.30 AND 14.31** (See chapter 15 for further discussion about computer imaging as it relates to television.)

Many film and television productions combine computer-generated images with actual foreground objects or live action through chroma keying. You could, for example, key the model of a spaceship over the computer-generated graphics of moving stars, or have an actor shake hands with a computer-generated space alien.

MAIN POINTS

◆ The two types of electronic visual effects are standard electronic (analog) effects and digital video effects (DVE).

◆ The four standard electronic effects are superimposition, key, chroma key, and wipe.

◆ A superimposition, or super, is a form of double exposure. The picture from one camera is electronically superimposed over the picture from the other, making both images seem transparent.

◆ Keying means electronically cutting out portions of a television picture and filling them in with another, or portions of another, image. The main purpose of a key is to add titles or objects to a base (background) picture. There are three basic types of keys: internal key, external key, and matte key.

◆ A matte key effect fills the base picture cutouts various grays or colors generated by the switcher. The standard matte key modes are edge, drop shadow, and outline.

◆ Chroma keying uses a blue (or green) background which, during the key, is replaced by the background image. The foreground image is then seen in front of the keyed background image.

◆ In a wipe a portion of or a complete television picture is gradually replaced by another. The geometrically shaped wipe configurations can be selected via buttons on the switcher or by calling up a preprogrammed effect from the switcher's memory.

◆ DVE can be interfaced with standard (analog) effects.

◆ Some DVE are the result of computer-manipulations of camera-generated video. A computer-manipulated effect is often created in real time during production.

◆ The more common DVE used in production are manipulations of image size, shape, light, and color (shrinking and expanding, stretching, positioning and point of view, perspective, mosaic, and posterization and solarization); motion (slide and peel effects, snapshots, and rotation, bounce, fly, and cube-spin effects); and multi-images (secondary frame and echo effects).

◆ Computer-generated DVE are created entirely by the computer. A computer-created effect is normally built step by step in pre- or postproduction.

14.2

Nonelectronic Effects and How to Use Them

Will you now need expensive, high-end switchers and computers and unique software programs to create the dazzling digital video effects mentioned in section 14.1? Not at all. Although you may need high-end systems to produce effects for complex galaxy travel, MTV, or network commercials, you will be surprised to find that even a moderate desktop system can create many knock-their-socks-off effects. And you can save a great deal of time and effort by staying with some of the tried-and-true optical and mechanical effects perfected in filmmaking and during the predigital stages of television production.

Optical effects include the use of scenic devices placed in front of the camera or attachments to the lens that manipulate the image. The illusion of snow, rain, or smoke can often be produced more readily by mechanical than digital means. Before using such effects, however, ask whether they are really necessary. If the answer is yes, try them out before the production to ensure that they are reliable. There are two other factors to consider before setting up optical or mechanical effects.

The first is the relative mobility of television equipment. Rather than bringing a cumbersome fog machine into the studio to simulate fog, simply take the camera outside on a foggy day or use a lens filter that simulates fog. When using IF (internal focus) lenses on ENG/EFP cameras, you can attach any type of filter at the front of the lens and keep it from rotating even when you focus the lens.

The second factor is the enormous communicative power of television audio. In many instances you can curtail or eliminate a variety of video effects by combining good sound effects with a simple video presentation. The sound of pouring rain, for example, combined with a close-up of a dripping-wet actor may well preclude the use of a rain machine. On television, reaction is often more telling than action. For example, to suggest a car crash, you can simply show a close-up of a shocked onlooker combined with the familiar crashing sounds, making the scene certainly more economical than having stunt drivers wreck new cars.

This section takes a brief look at some of the optical and mechanical effects that are still in use because they have proven to be effective, reliable, and easy to do.

▶ **OPTICAL EFFECTS**
Television gobos, reflections, star filter, diffusion filters, and defocus

▶ **MECHANICAL EFFECTS**
Rain, snow, fog, wind, smoke, fire, lightning, and explosions

349

OPTICAL EFFECTS

There are five major optical effects: (1) television gobos, (2) reflections, (3) star filter, (4) diffusion filters, and (5) defocus.

Television Gobos

A *television gobo* is a cutout or object that acts as an actual foreground frame for background action. Traditional gobos consist of such foreground pieces as picture frames, prison bars, or oversized keyholes. For example, you may want to introduce a fashion model by looking at her first through a picture frame, then dollying in to a closer shot while losing the picture frame. A simple paper cutout can simulate the popular keyhole gobo. The camera can dolly in to it and then look through it to observe the goings on in the magic toy kingdom. A few simple bars attached to mic stands will lock the prisoner firmly in his cell. **SEE 14.32**

The advantage of using a gobo instead of an electronic key is that you can dolly in to the gobo, or arc past it, to gradually reveal the total background event. To create a similar effect through DVE would require complicated postproduction work.

Reflections

You can achieve startling effects by reflecting a scene off mirrors, silver polyester sheets, or water. You are certainly familiar with the well-known (and well-worn) over-the-shoulder shot of someone looking into a mirror and then seeing someone approaching from behind. (Be careful that this "someone" isn't the camera!)

Bouncing some lights off a mirror mosaic can produce interesting effects, and shooting into it will make the reflected scene look startlingly cubist. To make such a mirror mosaic, glue several large pieces of a broken mirror onto plywood or Masonite. Such effects would take much more time and effort to create digitally.

Sheets of highly reflecting polyester, such as silver Mylar, serve as a flexible mirror. For example, you can have dancers move in front of suspended panels (such as 10-by-4-foot Mylar sheets) and then point the camera at the reflections. By allowing the Mylar sheets to move (through the air movement caused by the studio air-conditioning system or a slow-moving fan), you will see a great variety of random effects.

You can achieve a similar effect by pointing the camera at a tub filled with water and then causing the water to ripple. For good reflections the inside of the tub should be painted black. If you need more control over the reflections, of course, you need to resort to DVE.

Whenever you want to achieve good reflections, the light must be on the event that is to be reflected and not on the reflector itself. For example, if somebody looks too dark when seen in a mirror shot, put more light on the person, not the mirror.

14.32 TELEVISION GOBO

This television gobo places the actor behind bars.

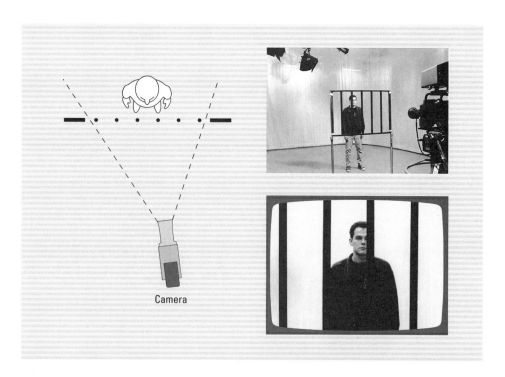

Camera

Star Filter

One of the most common filter effects is created with the *star filter*, a lens attachment that changes high-intensity light sources or reflections into starlike light beams. This effect is often used to intensify the street lamps on a rainy night, the beam of car headlights, or the colored lights illuminating a singer or musical group. The studio lights as caught by the wide-angle camera, and even the glitter on the performer's clothes as seen by the close-up camera, are all transformed into prominent starlike rays on the television screen. You can also use star filters to heighten the emotional impact of a candlelight procession, a church service, or an establishing shot of a night scene. **SEE 14.33**

Diffusion Filters

Diffusion filters give an entire scene a soft, slightly out-of-focus look. Some diffusion filters soften only the edges of a picture and leave the center clear and sharp. Others soften the whole scene. **SEE 14.34** A specific type of diffusion filter called a fog filter creates the illusion of fog.

Besides simulating fog, you can use diffusion filters to emphasize the gentle and soft nature of a scene or even to soften the wrinkles on a performer's face. If you do not have such a filter, you can achieve a similar effect by lightly greasing the edges of a piece of glass with a thin layer of petroleum jelly and taping it over the lens. If you grease only the edges, leaving a clear area in the middle, you get a softening of the edges, with the center

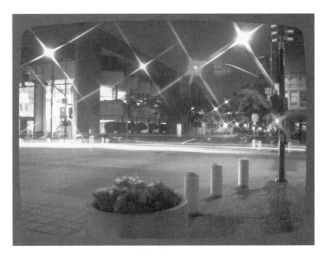

14.33 STAR FILTER EFFECT
The star filter changes bright light sources into starlike light beams.

remaining in sharp focus. *Do not grease the lens directly!* The grease, or the cleaning, could permanently damage an expensive zoom lens.

Try experimenting with various filter media that you can stretch over the lens, such as plastic wrap, gauze, or nylon stockings. To create such startling effects electronically would require high-end DVE equipment and much postproduction time and effort. Whatever filter device you use, keep it away from the lens glass—even a small scratch will put an expensive lens out of service.

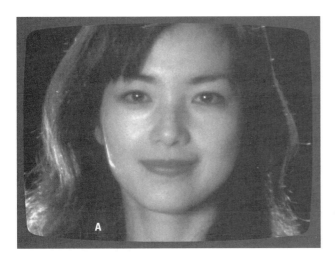

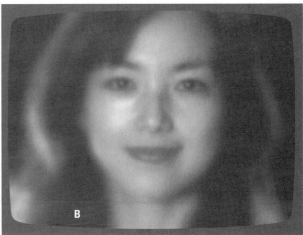

14.34 DIFFUSION EFFECT
A The original close-up without filtration; **B** the image takes on a dreamlike quality when shot with a diffusion filter.

Defocus

The *defocus* effect is one of the simplest yet most highly effective optical effects. The camera operator simply zooms in, racks out of focus and, on cue, back into focus again. This effect is used as a transitional device or to indicate strong psychological disturbances or physiological imbalance. A popular rack focus application is to start out of focus on a series of lights, such as burning candles or reflecting water drops, and then rack into focus to reveal the actual light source in the scene.

For a transition you could rack out of focus on a close-up of a young girl seated at a table, change actors quickly, and then rack back into focus on an old woman sitting in the same chair. Because going out of focus conceals the image almost as completely as going to black, it is possible to change the field of view or the objects in front of the camera during complete defocusing.

MECHANICAL EFFECTS

Mechanical effects are needed mostly in the presentation of television plays. Although small commercial stations may have little opportunity to do drama, colleges and universities are more frequently involved in the production of plays. You may also find that nonbroadcast television productions call for such effects. For example, the studio production of a scene on traffic safety may call for rain, and one on fire safety may call for smoke.

The techniques for producing mechanical effects are not agreed upon universally, so they offer an excellent opportunity for experimentation. Whatever you do, your main objectives should be simplicity in construction and operation, maximum reliability of the effect, and operational safety.

Remember that many effects are best achieved by shooting under the desired conditions. For example, to videotape somebody waiting at a bus stop in the rain, take the camcorder to a bus stop on a rainy day. A fog scene is easier shot outside in real fog than in the studio with simulated fog. As mentioned before, you can also suggest many situations by showing an effect only partially while relying on the audio track to supply the rest of the information. Also, through chroma keying, you can use many effects from a prerecorded source, such as a still photo, videotape, or the ESS (electronic still store) system.

That said, some special effects are relatively easy to achieve mechanically, especially if the effect itself remains peripheral and authenticity is not a primary concern. Keep in mind that effects need not look realistic to the people in the studio; all that counts is how they appear on the television screen.

Rain

Soak the actors' clothes with water and superimpose the rain from a videotape recording. If you want to show rain through a window, spray a little water on the windowpane with a spray bottle, back the window with a chroma-key drop, and chroma-key rain into the window area. Avoid water in the studio—even a small amount can be hazardous to performers and equipment. The best option is to simply wait for a rainy day, cover the camcorder with a raincoat (plastic bag), open the umbrella, and shoot on location.

Snow

Spray commercial snow from aerosol cans on a piece of glass in front of the lens, or sprinkle plastic snow from above. Cover the actors with plastic snow. Or, better yet, wait for it to snow and shoot outside.

Fog

The widely used method of putting dry ice into hot water unfortunately works only in silent scenes, because the bubbling noise it makes may be so loud that it drowns out the dialogue. Dry-ice fog is also heavy and tends to settle just above the studio floor. If you must shoot fog indoors, rent a fog machine. If the fog does not have to move, simply use a fog filter on the lens.

Wind

Use large electric fans to simulate wind. The problem, of course, is the noise. You can either drown out the fan noise with recorded wind noise during the videotaping, or replace the noise with the desired sounds in postproduction. To avoid costly ADR (automatic dialogue replacement) in postproduction, record the audio simultaneously with the video despite the fan noise. To minimize the fan noise, try to "blimp" the fans as much as possible by shielding them with sound-absorbing material. Have the performers wear lavalieres for voice pickup, or use shotgun mics that are close to the performers but turned away from the fans. If you simulate the wind effect caused by riding in a convertible, note that the occupants' hair often flies toward the front, against the direction of travel, and not toward the back of the car, opposite the direction of travel.

Smoke

Do not make smoke by pouring mineral oil on a hotplate; although effective visually, this type of smoke smells bad and irritates the eyes and throat. And if the oil gets too hot, it may catch fire. Commercial smoke machines produce less-irritating smoke, but they tend to leave an oily film on performers, lenses, equipment, and the studio floor. It may be easiest and least expensive to simply super a stock shot of smoke over a scene.

Fire

Never use fire inside the studio. The risk is simply too great for the effect. Use sound effects of burning, and have flickering light effects in the background. For the fire reflections, staple large strips of silk or nylon cloth or aluminum foil on a small batten and project the shadows onto the set with an ellipsoidal spot. **SEE 14.35** You can also reflect a strong spotlight off of aluminum foil or a silver Mylar sheet. By moving the sheet, the light reflections on the actors and set suggest the flickering of fire. You can also try to super a videotape of flames over the scene.

When outdoors, using a barbecue grill, carefully ignite rags soaked in kerosene and shoot the scene through the flames. Again, be extremely careful with even small fires. Always have a fire extinguisher on hand and be sure that the fire is completely out before leaving the scene.

Lightning

Place two large photo flash units about ten feet apart. Trigger them one right after the other. Lightning should always come from behind the set or scene. Do not forget the audio effect of thunder. Obviously, the quicker the thunder succeeds the light flash, the closer we perceive the thunderstorm.

Explosions

Do not try to imitate the explosions you see come out of Hollywood. Even demolition experts, the production crew, and especially the stunt people are apprehensive on "pyro-days," production times when pyrotechnic devices are used. As with fire, stay away from explosive devices, even if you have "experts" guaranteeing that nothing bad will happen. You can *suggest* explosions: Take a close-up of a frightened face, increase the light intensity to such a degree that the features begin to wash out, and come in strongly with the explosion audio. Or, better yet, use DVE such as solarization or posterization on the face or the whole scene to suggest an explosion while the audio rumbles on. Your next shot can show dust settling over the scene of destruction.

MAIN POINTS

- ◆ Optical effects include television gobos, reflections, star filter, diffusion filters, and defocus.

- ◆ A television gobo is a cutout or three-dimensional object through which the camera looks at the scene.

- ◆ Mirrors can be used for unusual camera angles and cubist effects. And water is also effective for reflections.

- ◆ Star filters turn light sources into four- or six-point starlike light rays. Diffusion filters soften all or part of the camera picture and can simulate fog. Defocus effects are used as transitions and for suggesting an actor's subjective experiences.

- ◆ Mechanical effects include rain, snow, fog, wind, smoke, fire, lightning, and explosions. Avoid water—and at all costs, fire—inside the studio. Never set off a detonating device, but simply suggest explosions through appropriate light and sound effects.

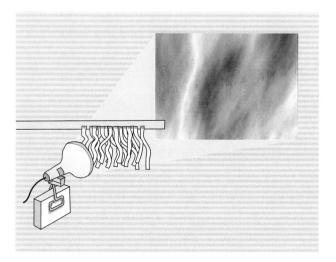

14.35 FIRE EFFECT

To project flickering onto a set, move a batten with silk or nylon strips stapled on it in front of an ellipsoidal spot, or reflect the light off a silver Mylar sheet.

15

Design

Although you are probably very conscious of design and style when buying clothes or an automobile, you may be unaware of specific design elements when watching an opening show title or the living room set of a daytime drama. You may be dazzled by an animated title that does everything but pop out of the screen, but not motivated to analyze its aesthetic qualities. And you probably perceive the living room in the daytime drama as exactly that—a living room— not carefully assembled scenery and properties. We all know, of course, that such design elements are meticulously thought out and constructed.

In fact, design, or the lack of it, permeates everything a television production company shows on the air and off. It sets the style of the video presentation, if not of the production company as a whole. Design includes not only the colors and letters of a show title and the look of a studio set, but also the production company's stationery, office furniture, hallway artwork, and logo. The CNN logo, for example, suggests up-to-date, no-nonsense news. **SEE 15.1**

But a handsome logo does not automatically carry its design qualities over to the programming or to the on-the-air graphics or scenery. It is important to develop a design consciousness for everything you do; a well-executed logo is merely the symbol for such awareness, not its sole cause.

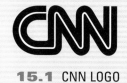

15.1 CNN LOGO

Section 15.1, Designing and Using Television Graphics, stresses the major design considerations of television graphics. Section 15.2, Scenery and Props, looks at major aspects of television scenery and properties.

KEY TERMS

aspect ratio The width-to-height proportions of the television screen and therefore of all analog television pictures: four units wide by three units high. For DTV and HDTV, sixteen by nine.

character generator (C.G.) A dedicated computer that electronically produces a series of letters, numbers, and simple graphic images for video display.

color compatibility Color signals that can be perceived as black-and-white pictures on monochrome television sets. Generally used to mean that the color scheme has enough brightness contrast for monochrome reproduction with a good grayscale contrast.

essential area The section of the television picture, centered within the scanning area, that is seen by the home viewer, regardless of masking or slight misalignment of the receiver. Also called *safe title area* or *safe area*.

flat A piece of standing scenery used as background or to simulate the walls of a room.

floor plan A plan of the studio floor, showing the walls, the main doors, and the location of the control room, with the lighting grid or batten pattern superimposed over it. More common, a diagram of scenery and properties drawn onto the grid pattern.

graphics generator Dedicated computer or software that allows a designer to draw, color, animate, store, and retrieve images electronically. Also called *paint box*.

grayscale A scale indicating intermediate steps from TV white to TV black. Usually measured in a nine- or seven-step scale.

props Short for *properties*. Furniture and other objects used for set decoration and by actors or performers.

scanning area Picture area that is scanned by the camera pickup device; in general, the picture area usually seen in the camera viewfinder and preview monitor.

15.1

Designing and Using Television Graphics

When watching television you may be more captivated by the opening titles than the show that follows. Even when the program consists of a somber interview or simple product demonstration, we seem obliged to have the title burst onto the scene, make its dancing letters change shape and color at least once, and finally disappear again with a loud *swoosh*. You may wonder whether we spend an inordinate amount of time and effort on the graphics compared with the program itself. Even if we don't, computer-generated video graphics have become a major aspect of television production. Because creating such titles requires highly specialized computer skills, rather than competence in television production, we limit our discussion to the following:

▶ **SPECIFICATIONS OF TELEVISION GRAPHICS**
Aspect ratio, scanning and essential areas, out-of-aspect-ratio graphics and moving images, information density and readability, color, and style

▶ **GRAPHICS EQUIPMENT**
The character generator (C.G.) and the graphics generator

SPECIFICATIONS OF TELEVISION GRAPHICS

Despite the dazzling variety of television graphics you see on your screen, their major purposes are: to give you specific information, such as the title of the show or the names of the actors; to tell you something about the nature of the event (funny, tragic, hot news, futuristic, old-fashioned); and to grab your attention. These three purposes are normally supported by appropriate sound effects.

When comparing a television screen with a movie screen, you will see two obvious differences: the traditional television screen is much smaller and much narrower than the movie screen. These two factors have a profound influence on the design specifications of television graphics. Even a large-screen television set is considerably smaller than the average-sized motion picture screen. The relatively small size of the television screen limits the amount of writing you can display and demands fonts (lettering) that can be clearly seen. The limited screen width in relation to its height means that the titles do not have as much room to play across the screen as in movies and must, therefore, be kept somewhat closer to the center. Other design requirements of television graphics are common to all graphic design and deal more with aesthetics and color.

This section takes a closer look at the following design requirements and specifications: (1) aspect ratio, (2) scanning and essential areas, (3) out-of-aspect-ratio graphics and moving images, (4) information density and readability, (5) color, and (6) style.

Aspect Ratio

Aspect ratio is the relationship between width and height—the shape of the television frame. The frame and the size of the screen ultimately determine how much information you can place into the screen and where to place it for maximum impact. Because the aspect ratios of traditional television and HDTV are different, we discuss them separately whenever necessary.

Traditional aspect ratio   The aspect ratio of the traditional television screen is 4 × 3; that is, the ratio of picture width to picture height is 1.33:1. You may want to remember the aspect ratio as being four units wide and three units high, regardless of whether the units are inches or feet. Anything that appears on-screen must obviously fit within this aspect ratio. **SEE 15.2**

HDTV aspect ratio   The aspect ratio for HDTV (high-definition television) is 16 × 9, which can also be expressed 1.78:1. Compared with the traditional television screen, the HDTV screen is horizontally stretched, resembling more the motion picture aspect ratio. **SEE 15.3**

All graphical information must be contained within these aspect ratios. Recall from chapter 14 that you can change the aspect ratio of pictures within the television screen through various digital video effects (DVE). Note, however, that through DVE you can also divide the screen into secondary screens of various aspect ratios or block off various areas of the traditional screen or the HDTV screen and thus simulate various aspect ratios.[1]

Scanning and Essential Areas

Unlike the painter or still photographer, who has full control over how much of the picture shows within the frame, we cannot be so sure about how much of the video pictures videotaped or broadcast are actually seen on the home screen. There is an inevitable picture loss every time you make another videotape dub and, especially, during transmission. Also, not all television receivers are as carefully adjusted as the preview monitors in a control room or editing room. Even if you gave the proper headroom when framing a close-up shot in a studio interview, your shots may have lost all the headroom by the time they are seen on the viewers' television set. The same is true for titles that are framed too close to the screen edge. Because the edge information is often lost, you may end up with incomplete titles or the first and last digits missing from a telephone number.

1. See Herbert Zettl, *Sight Sound Motion*, 3d ed. (Belmont, Calif.: Wadsworth Publishing Co., 1999.

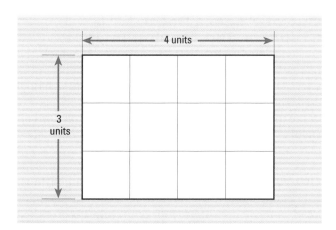

15.2 TELEVISION ASPECT RATIO
The traditional television aspect ratio is four units wide by three units high.

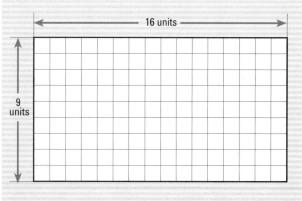

15.3 HDTV ASPECT RATIO
The aspect ratio for HDTV is sixteen units wide by nine units high. Compared to normal television, it is horizontally stretched.

How, then, can you make sure that the information you send is actually visible on the home screen? Is there a standard that will more or less guarantee that all essential picture information, such as a title or telephone number, will appear in its entirety? The answer is a qualified yes. Although not mathematically precise, there are guidelines to help you keep picture information from getting lost during dubbing or transmission. Basically, these guidelines tell you to keep vital information away from the screen edges. Just how far away you should be from the edge when framing a shot is prescribed by the scanning and essential areas.

The *scanning area* includes the picture you see in the camera viewfinder and on preview monitors in the control room. It is the area actually scanned by the camera pickup device (the CCD). The *essential area*, also called *safe title area* or, simply, *safe area,* is centered within the scanning area. It is the portion seen by the home viewer, regardless of masking of the set, transmission loss, or misadjustment of the receiver. **SEE 15.4**

Obviously, all essential information such as titles and telephone numbers should be contained within the essential area. But just how large is the essential area? It is usually smaller than you think—about 65 or, at best, 70 percent of the total area. Many *C.G.s (character generators)* automatically keep a title within the essential area. The better studio cameras have a device that elec-

tronically generates a frame within the viewfinder, outlining the safe area.

When creating a computer-generated background with graphics software, you do not have such guidelines and must measure where the limits of the essential area are. If, for example, the active area of the computer screen is approximately 11 inches wide and 8¼ inches high, the title can be only about 7⅛ inches long, because in the essential area the title can occupy only 65 percent of this screen width. In other words, you must leave about 2 inches of margin at either side of the text to ensure an uncut title. Similarly, the lettering could occupy only 5½ inches vertically (which is 65 percent of the 8¼ inches total screen height). Practically, this means that the lettering should be about 1½ inches away from the top and bottom edges. Again, be reminded that such formulas depend on a great deal of factors and might be much too conservative in a flawlessly operating digital system. Nonetheless, the essential area dimensions guarantee that the information appears intact on the home screen. Obviously, these dimensions change when working in the 16×9 HDTV aspect ratio.

After some practice you will be able to tell how to compensate in the camera framing for the picture loss, or to place a title within the essential area without having to measure the picture or juggle percentages. The surest way to test a title is to project it on the preview monitor. If the letters come close to the edges of the preview monitor, the title extends beyond the essential area and will certainly be cut off on either side when seen by the home viewer. **SEE 15.5**

Out-of-Aspect-Ratio Graphics and Moving Images

You will inevitably run into situations in which the pictures to be shown do not fit the requirements of the television screen in terms of aspect ratio and essential area. These may be simple out-of-aspect-ratio graphics, or the more complicated showing of motion pictures on standard television or of standard television videotaped pictures on the HDTV screen.

Out-of-aspect-ratio graphics   Although most television graphics are computer-generated or -manipulated, you will occasionally have to deal with oversized graphics, such as the maps and graphs used in briefings or sales meetings. More often than not, you must cover such meetings live-on-tape without much chance for postproduction. Many oversized graphics do not adhere

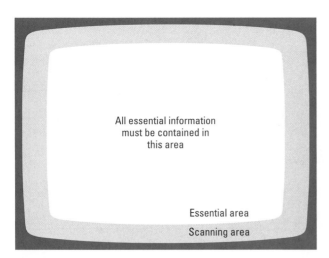

15.4 SCANNING AND ESSENTIAL AREAS

The scanning area is what the camera viewfinder and preview monitor show. The essential, or safe title, area is what appears on the home television screen.

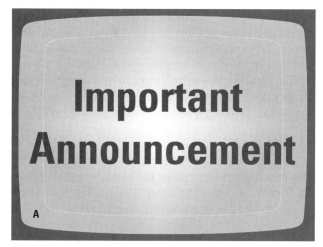

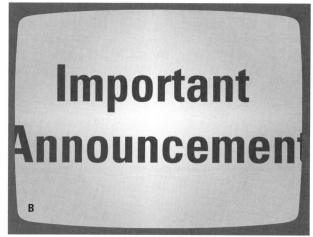

15.5 TITLE BEYOND ESSENTIAL AREA

A On the preview monitor, you can still see the complete title, although it comes close to the edges. **B** When viewed on the home receiver, the information that lies outside the essential area gets lost.

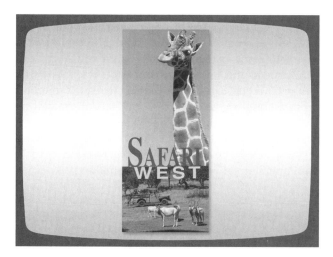

15.6 OUT-OF-ASPECT-RATIO GRAPHIC

When trying to frame this out-of-aspect-ratio graphic in its entirety, most of the information becomes illegible.

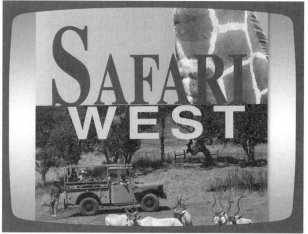

15.7 INFORMATION LOSS IN CLOSE-UP

When trying to get a closer shot, all information outside the aspect ratio is lost.

to the 4 × 3, much less the 16 × 9, aspect ratio. The problem with an out-of-aspect-ratio graphic is that, when shown in its entirety, the information on the graphic becomes so small that it is no longer readable. **SEE 15.6** By moving the camera close enough that the graphic fits the aspect ratio of the television screen, you inevitably cut out important information. **SEE 15.7**

If the lettering and other visual information are simple and bold enough, you can mount the entire out-of-aspect-ratio chart on a larger card that is in aspect ratio. You simply pull back with the camera and frame up on the large card, keeping the out-of-aspect-ratio information as screen-center as possible. On a vertically oriented graphic without lettering, you could possibly tilt up and

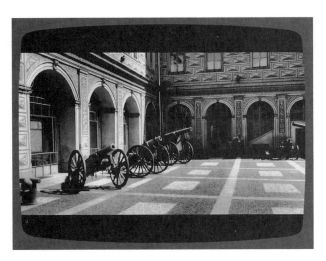

15.8 FULL-FRAME MOVIES
ON STANDARD TELEVISION
Fitting the entire frame of a wide-screen movie to the 4 × 3
aspect ratio of television results in empty (black) screen space
on the top and bottom of the screen.

reveal the information bit by bit. If done smoothly, this
gradual revelation adds drama. With lettering, however,
such a tilt does not add drama but simply makes the
graphic more difficult to read.

Out-of-aspect ratio moving images   One of
the more obvious problems of dealing with out-of-
aspect-ratio visual material is the televising of motion
pictures. When trying to make the wide-aspect-ratio

motion pictures fit the 4 × 3 television screen, your
choices are limited. First, you can show the width of the
film, thereby reducing the image size considerably and
ending up with empty screen space on the top and
bottom. **SEE 15.8**   Second, you can fill the entire screen
vertically, but then you lose the picture areas on the
sides that extend beyond the television aspect ratio.
Third, you can simply try to pick out the most important
portions of the motion picture frames (called scan-and-
pan) and make them fit the television aspect ratio. All
three methods result in a loss of picture information
and, worse, an intrusion on the original visual structure
of the shot. This is one of the reasons why HDTV has
developed the 16 × 9 aspect ratio that approximates the
standard motion picture screen.

Interestingly enough, some program forms make a
virtue out of this unavoidable handicap. You may have
seen MTV presentations or commercials that had black
borders at the top and bottom of the screen. This is to
imply that they were originally shot for wide-screen movie
presentation rather than television distribution, which,
supposedly, lends more prestige to the program.

You encounter the same framing difficulty when
trying to cover writing on a blackboard for the standard
4 × 3 aspect ratio. If you zoom out all the way to show the
entire blackboard, the text is difficult to read. If you zoom
in to a close-up, you can see only part of the writing.
SEE 15.9   To avoid this you can divide the blackboard into
4 × 3 aspect ratio fields and contain the writing within each
of these fields. The camera can then get a close-up of the
entire sentence. Even when working in the HDTV aspect

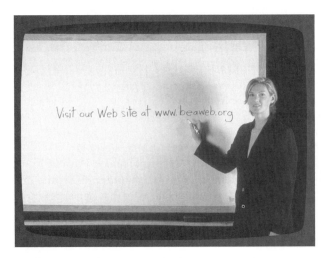
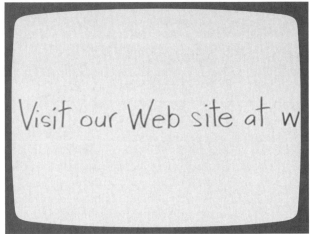

15.9 ASPECT RATIO PROBLEM
Normal writing on a blackboard can present a typical aspect ratio problem. The camera cannot show a close-up
of a message that spans the full width of the blackboard.

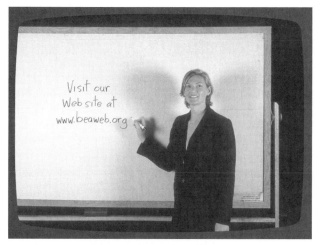
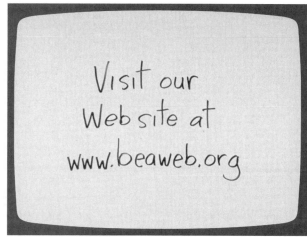

15.10 PROPER USE OF ASPECT RATIO
If the blackboard is divided into proper aspect ratio fields, the camera can see the entire message even in a close-up.

ratio, you should write the information in blocks rather than across the width of the blackboard. **SEE 15.10**

The reverse occurs when showing a television program shot in the traditional 4:3 aspect ratio on a 16:9 screen. Instead of having spaces on the top and bottom of the screen, you have empty space on both sides. **SEE 15.11**

Depending on the material displayed, you could show additional information rather than black bars in the leftover space. For example, in a newscast you could show a map of the location in which the news event occurred, or you might give some additional statistics about a pitcher during a game. Such use of leftover space would not necessarily take away from the main center-screen information, but running advertising for used cars while showing a romantic love scene in screen-center is not recommended!

Information Density and Readability

Taking a cue from overcrowded Web pages, there is a tendency to load the screen with a great amount of information. Also, in our quest for squeezing as much information as possible on the relatively small television screen, the print used for on-the-air copy gets smaller and smaller.

Information density There is some justification for crowding the screen if the data simultaneously displayed are related and add relevant information. For example, if in a home-shopping show you show a close-up of a particular item and simultaneously display the normal price, the savings, and the telephone number to call, you are providing the viewer with a valuable service. On the other hand, if you show a newscaster reading the latest news in one corner of the screen and run two or three

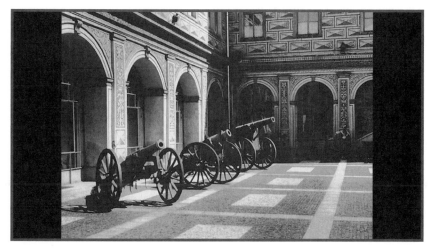

15.11 4 × 3 PICTURE SHOWN ON 19 × 6 SCREEN
When showing a standard 4 × 3 television picture on the 16 × 9 screen, there is empty space on both sides.

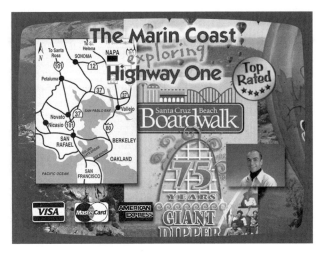

15.12 INFORMATION OVERLOAD

This screen has so much unrelated information that it is difficult to make sense of it.

ticker tapes across the top and the bottom of the screen, or show maps, advertising, and modes of payment all at the same time, you run the risk of information overload. **SEE 15.12** If you need to display a great amount of information, do it sequentially in a series of shots rather than all at once.

Readability In television graphics, *readability* means that you should be able to read the words that appear on-screen. As obvious as this statement is, it seems to have eluded many a graphic artist. Sometimes titles explode onto and disappear from the screen so quickly that only the MTV generation, or people with superior perceptive abilities, can actually see and make sense out of them. Or the letters are so small and detailed that you can't read them.

Such readability problems occur regularly when motion picture credits are shown on a standard 4 × 3 television screen. First, as already pointed out, the titles generally extend beyond the essential area, so you can see only parts of them. Second, the credit lines are so small that they are usually impossible to read on the low-resolution television screen. Third, the letters themselves are not bold enough to show up well on television, especially if there is a busy background. These problems are greatly minimized on a 16 × 9 HDTV screen, but in consideration for the many viewers watching standard television, you need to aim for

readability. What, then, makes for optimal readability? Here are some recommendations:

■ Keep all written information within the essential area.

■ Choose fonts (letters of a particular size and style) that have a bold, clean contour. The limited resolution of the television image does not reproduce thin-lined fonts, whose fine strokes and serifs are susceptible to breakup when keyed. Sometimes even bold, sans serif fonts can get lost in the background and need to be reinforced with a drop shadow or color outline.

■ Limit the amount of information. The less information that appears on-screen, the easier it is to comprehend. Some television experts suggest a maximum of seven lines per title. It is more sensible to prepare a series of titles on several C.G. "pages," each displaying a small amount of information, than a single page with an overabundance of information.

■ Format all lettering into blocks for easily perceivable graphical units. **SEE 15.13** This block layout is often used in well-designed Web pages. If the titles are scattered, they look unbalanced and are hard to read. **SEE 15.14** This is one of the typical characteristics of a poorly designed Web page.

■ Do not superimpose lettering over too busy a background. If you must add lettering over a busy background—such as scores and names of players over the live picture of a football stadium—select a simple, bold font. **SEE 15.15**

The same principles apply when you animate a title using special effects. In fact, if the title twists and tumbles around the screen, the letters must be even more legible than if they were used for a static, straightforward title.

Bear in mind that whenever you use printed material as on-the-air graphics, including reproductions of famous paintings, professional photographs, illustrated books, and similar matter, you must obtain copyright clearance. If you have subscribed to a computer image service, your copyright limits depend on the amount of user fees you pay.

Color

Because color is an important design element, you need to know something about its attributes and components; the aesthetics of color, that is, how various colors go together; and how the television system reacts to them.

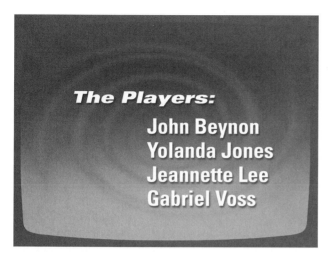

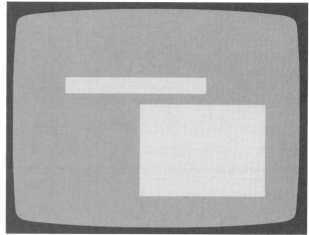

15.13 BLOCK ORGANIZATION OF TITLES
By arranging titles in blocks, related information is graphically organized for easy perception.

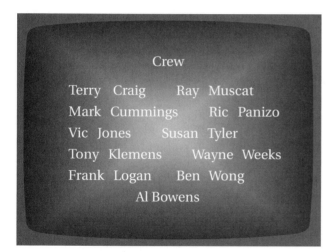

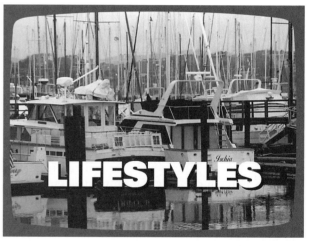

15.14 SCATTERED TITLES
When titles are scattered, the information is difficult to read.

15.15 BOLD LETTERS OVER A BUSY BACKGROUND
This title reads well despite the busy background. The letters are bold and differ sufficiently in brightness from the background.

Color attributes   As explained in chapter 3, color is determined by three factors, called *attributes:* hue, saturation, and brightness. *Hue* refers to the color itself—that is, whether it is blue, green, red, or yellow. *Saturation* (sometimes called *chroma*) indicates the color strength—a strong or pale red, a washed-out or rich green. *Brightness,* or *luminance,* indicates how light or dark a color appears.

Grayscale   The relative brightness of a color is usually measured by how much light it reflects. The television system is not capable of reproducing pure white (100 percent reflectance) or pure black (0 percent reflectance); at best, it can reproduce an off-white (about 70 percent for monochrome television and only about 60 percent for color) and an off-black (about 3 percent reflectance). We call these brightness extremes *TV white* and *TV black.* If

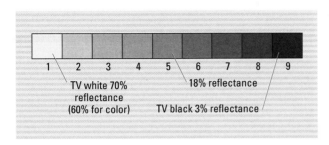

15.16 NINE-STEP GRAYSCALE

The nine-step grayscale shows nine different grays, ranging from TV white on the left to TV black on the right.

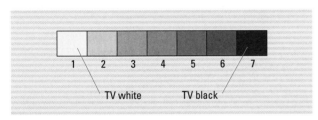

15.17 SEVEN-STEP GRAYSCALE

Most television sets reproduce seven distinct grays, from TV white to TV black.

you divide the brightness range between TV white and TV black into distinct steps, you have the television *grayscale*.

The most common number of brightness steps in a grayscale is nine, although the system can reproduce all nine steps under only the most ideal conditions. **SEE 15.16** A grayscale of seven steps is more realistic for monochrome television. **SEE 15.17** You may find, however, that many color shows translate into only five. Note that the middle value of the grayscale is not about 30 percent, but only 18 percent. Just think if you had only seven tubes of different grays to paint every conceivable scene on the television screen. This is why some color shows look so washed out on a monochrome (black-and-white) receiver.

Compatible color Watch the color and contrast relationship between the lettering and the background. Besides different hues, there should be a considerable brightness contrast. When you use exclusively high-energy colors for a title, such as red lettering on a green or blue background, the difference in hue is so obvious that you might be tempted to neglect the grayscale (brightness)

difference. As different as they seem on a color monitor, if they have the same brightness they are unreadable on a monochrome monitor. **SEE COLOR PLATE 8**

Even if the colors you use are not intended for reproduction on a black-and-white television set, good brightness contrast is also important for a color rendition. It aids the picture's three-dimensionality and helps separate the various colors.

If a graphic is intended for camera pickup, check it with a black-and-white camera viewfinder or on a black-and-white monitor to see whether the colors have enough brightness contrast. When the colors show up as separate, distinct grays, the color scheme is *compatible*. Technically, *color compatibility* means that the graphic is equally readable on a black-and-white monitor as on a color one. If the grays of the color scheme are so similar that you cannot distinguish one area from the other, the color scheme is *incompatible*—you need to choose colors with better brightness contrast. **SEE COLOR PLATE 9**

With a little experience, you will find that just by squinting your eyes while looking at the set you can determine fairly well whether two colors have enough brightness contrast to ensure compatibility. A good graphic artist or painter usually juxtaposes colors that differ not only in hue but also in brightness.

Aesthetics of color The recognition and application of color harmony cannot be explained in a short paragraph; they require experience, practice, sensitivity, and taste. Rather than try to dictate which colors go with what other colors, you can more easily divide the colors into "high-energy" and "low-energy" and then match their energies.

The high-energy colors include basic, bright, highly saturated hues, such as rich reds, yellows, or blues. The low-energy group contains more-subtle hues with a low degree of saturation, such as pastel colors. Normally, you should keep the colors of the background low-energy and the foreground high-energy. In a set (as in your home), the background (walls) is usually less colorful than the set pieces and dressings, such as rugs, sofas, pictures, and pillows. **SEE COLOR PLATES 20 AND 21** Titles work on the same principle: You will find that an easily readable title has high-energy lettering on a low-energy background.

Of course, the colors must also be appropriate for the event. For example, if the titles are intended to announce a high-energy show, such as a vivacious dance number, high-energy colors for both the title and the background are fitting. If, however, you use the same high-energy colors to introduce a discussion on the latest budget deficit, the choice is inappropriate, even if the title has good readability.

Independent of aesthetics, only top-of-the-line television cameras can handle highly saturated reds. Unless there is an abundance of baselight, the video camera "sees red" when looking at red, by making red areas in the shot vibrate (excessive video noise) or bleed into adjacent areas. This color bleeding is not unlike the bleeding of one sound track into another. Whenever possible, suggest that the talent not wear highly saturated red clothing and that scene designers not paint large areas with saturated reds. This problem becomes especially noticeable in EFP, where you generally work with less-than-top-of-the-line equipment and in less-than-optimal lighting conditions.

Style

Style, like language, is animate and nonstatic. It changes according to the specific aesthetic demands of a given location and time. To ignore it means to communicate less effectively. You learn style not from a book but primarily through being sensitive to your environment, by experiencing life with open eyes and ears, and, especially, an open heart. The way you dress now, compared with the way you dressed ten years ago, is an example of a change in style. Some people not only sense the prevailing style, but also manage to enhance it with a personal, distinctive twist.

Sometimes it is the development of television equipment that influences presentation styles more than personal creativity or social need. As emphasized in chapter 14, digital video effects equipment contributed not only to a new graphical awareness, but also to an abuse of the available graphical resources. Often, animated titles are generated not to reflect the prevailing aesthetic taste or to signal the nature of the upcoming show, but simply because it is fun to see letters dance on-screen. Although flashy graphics in news may be tolerated because they express and intensify the urgency of the message, they are out of place for shows that try to explore a serious and intense relationship between two people in a television play.

You may have noticed that contemporary television graphics are imitating the colors and layout of computer Web pages. Some television graphics even parrot the shortcomings of the computer image, such as the *aliasing*

("jaggies") of diagonals or curves in lines and letters, differently colored horizontal strips that contain lettering and small product icons, or the scattering of tiny secondary windows on the main television screen (see figure 15.12). The reason for such emulating is to seem "with it" and on the cutting edge. Usually, such screen clutter reflects more the bad taste of the graphic artist than a new trend.

Regardless of whether you are a style-setter, you should try to match the style of the artwork with that of the show. But do not go overboard on style and identify your guest from China with Chinese lettering or your news story about the downtown fire with flaming letters. Do not abandon good taste for effect. In a successful design, all images and objects interrelate and harmonize with one another—from the largest, such as the background scenery, to the smallest, such as the fruit bowl on the table. Good design displays a continuity and coherence of style.

GRAPHICS EQUIPMENT

Chapter 14 explored various computer-generated and computer-manipulated special effects. This section describes some of the equipment used for generating digital graphics, specifically the character generator and the graphics generator.

Character Generator

Any desktop computer can become a character generator with the appropriate software. If fact, when selecting different fonts during word processing, your desktop computer functions as a low-powered character generator. The *character generator (C.G.)* looks and works like a desktop computer except that it is programmed to produce a great variety of lettering and numbers suitable for the television screen. Most C.G.s are similar to word processors: The text can be typed on a keyboard in various fonts, changed, inserted, positioned on-screen, or deleted with a few simple commands.

The more sophisticated C.G.s can produce letters of various sizes and fonts and simple graphical displays such as sales curves or bar graphs. The letters, as well as the background, can be colonized with different hues and degrees of saturation. Most C.G.s can also do simple animation. **SEE 15.18**

To prepare the titles or graphs, you type information on the keyboard. You can then either integrate the

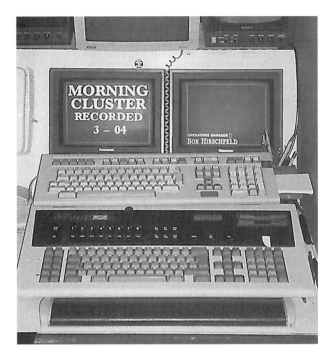

15.18 CHARACTER GENERATOR

The character generator is specifically designed to produce a variety of letters for title keys and mattes. The titles can be directly fed into the switcher or stored on a computer disk.

Graphics Generator

Graphics generators are large-capacity computers whose hardware and software are designed specifically for creating television graphics. They are often, and aptly, called *paint boxes*. Because digital pictures and full-motion (30 frames per second) sequences take up such a great amount of storage space, good graphics generators need tape or disk storage capacities in the multi-gigabyte range. To boost capacity, even *superdensity (SD)* storage media—such as read/write optical discs, high-capacity hard disks, floppies, or tape cartridges—depend on various compression methods (such as JPEG), whereby the original amount of digital information necessary for a graphic is reduced during storage and largely restored during the retrieval process (see chapter 2). Locating and routing to specific destinations myriad digital data in a fraction of a second is no easy task, but such high *throughput* times are necessary to let you create a computer-generated image in real time, as though you were using a paintbrush.

Image generating *Image generating* means that you create the graphic entirely with the computer. Most desktop imaging software offers thousands of different hues, thin or thick lines, shapes, and various brush strokes and textures for creating electronic art. A television weathercast is a good example of the many capabilities of a large-scale graphics generator. The basic territorial map, temperature zones, high- and low-pressure zones, symbols for sunshine and various forms of precipitation, lettering, and numbers are all generated by the digital graphics generator.

Depending on storage capacity and software sophistication, you can create and store complex graphical sequences, such as animated three-dimensional titles that unfold within another animated 3-D environment, or multilayered mattes that twist within a 3-D video space. **SEE 15.19 AND COLOR PLATES 22 AND 23**

Some computer programs, based on complex mathematical formulas, allow you to paint irregular shapes, called *fractals*, which are used to create realistic and fantasy landscapes and countless abstract patterns. **SEE COLOR PLATE 24**

Image capturing and manipulation These activities refer to digitizing existing visual material, such as a photo, drawing, or video frame, digitizing it, and then

information directly into the program in progress via the switcher or store it for later use. When stored on a disk, each title has a specific address (electronic page number) for fast and easy recall. Most C.G.s automatically keep the title in the essential area. Various controls allow you to move the titles on-screen, make certain words flash, scroll the copy up and down the screen (sometimes called a *crawl*), or make it crawl sideways.

Character generators normally have two output channels—one for preview and one for program. The preview channel appears on the C.G. screen and/or on the control room preview monitor. The program channel feeds into the switcher. This titling device has become such an important production factor that a production team usually includes a C.G. operator. In live or live-on-tape shows, such as game shows, award ceremonies, or sports remotes, the C.G. operator sits right next to the director or the TD (technical director) in the control room. Especially during a sports telecast, the C.G. operator is extremely busy typing in names and statistics as the game develops.

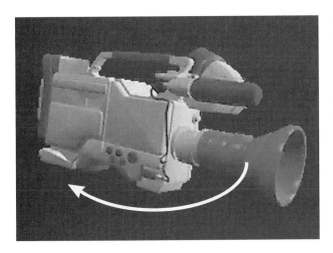

15.19 ANIMATED
THREE-DIMENSIONAL RENDERING
The graphics generator with its high-capacity digital storage
can create a great variety of still or animated 3-D images.

changing the original image in some way. An extreme case
of image manipulation is *morphing,* in which you see a
gradual and continuous change from one image to
another, such as a cat turning into a tiger, or a frog into a
prince. **SEE 15.20**

Operational features As with all computers,
some graphics software is more user-friendly than
others. But regardless of the relative complexity of the
specific hardware and software system, they all offer
menus that include color choices; various lines and
brush strokes; painting media, such as crayons and
watercolors; different shading effects; background
textures; and color blends. **SEE COLOR PLATE 25** If you
want to change a color, for example, you simply use the
mouse or electronic stylus to erase the current color and
select a new one from the palette. If you do not like the
new color, you have thousands (or even millions) more
to choose from. If you want to revise a portion of your
"painting," you can erase that part electronically and
substitute a more pleasing configuration.

Many such systems let you do your creations on an
electronic tablet, which looks like a sketchpad. Pencil,
pen, paintbrush, and eraser are all combined in the
electronic stylus that looks like a normal drawing pen.
Some styluses are connected to the computer by wire;
others are wireless. A keyboard and mouse allow you to
select different effects functions, such as mattes, titles,
perspectives, rates of animation or rotation, zooms, and
so forth. **SEE 15.21**

You can treat and position foreground and background images separately, and you can select from a menu

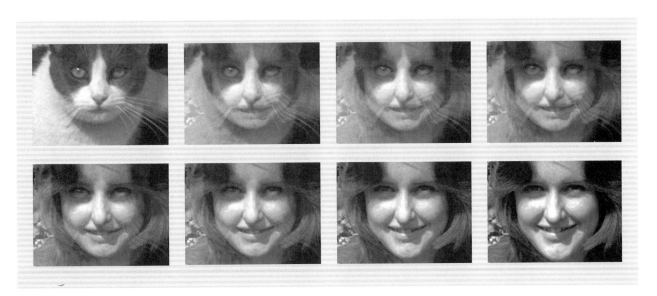

15.20 MORPHING SEQUENCE
Most imaging software allows morphing, which shows a gradual change from one image to another.

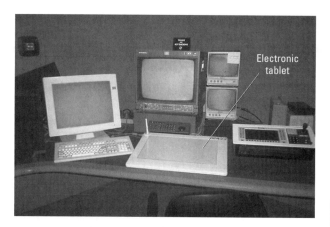

15.21 GRAPHICS GENERATOR
WITH ELECTRONIC TABLET
Some graphics generators use an electronic tablet and stylus
that simulate a drawing pad and pen.

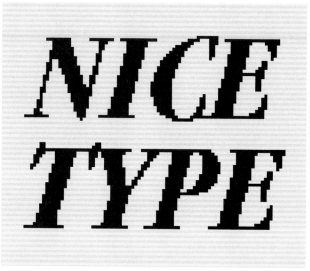

15.22 ALIASING
Many computer-generated images exhibit "jaggies," or distinct
steps on curves and diagonals.

a variety of *clip art,* such as cartoons, typographical
dingbats, or bullet points, and animate them. You can
store your finished masterpiece on the internal or
removable hard disk. If you use a desktop computer as a
graphics generator, in addition to high-capacity storage
it should have RGB component and composite NTSC
signal outputs so you can record your graphics on
videotape or feed them to the switcher as a regular video
input (see chapter 12). Most desktop computers accept
video and audio cards that permit such signal transformation. Again, be sure to back up your digital creations
on a separate disk.

Aliasing   The better graphics generators have built-
in circuits that correct aliasing. *Aliasing* occurs when
generated lines—especially diagonals and curves, such as
an *O*—have insufficient pixels for a smooth line edge and,
therefore, display "jaggies" or "stairsteps." **SEE 15.22**
Antialiasing circuits hide these jaggies by slightly
muddling the color of the edge of the line (adjusting the
saturation of the edge to that of the background) or by
filling in the missing pixels. **SEE 15.23**

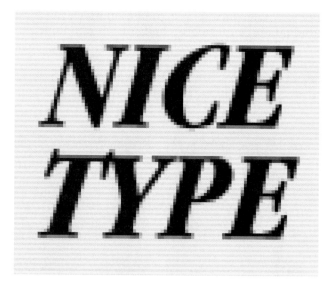

15.23 ANTIALIASING
Through antialiasing, the jaggies on the curves and diagonal
lines are softened and the edges become smoother.

MAIN POINTS

- Design is an overall concept that includes such elements as the fonts for titles, the station logo, the look of the news set, and even the office furniture.

- Their major purposes of television graphics are to give you specific information, to tell you something about the nature of the event, and to grab your attention.

- The standard television aspect ratio is 4 × 3, which means that the screen is four units wide by three units high. Wide-screen HDTV has a wider aspect ratio of 16 × 9. The aspect ratios are also expressed as 1.33:1 for standard television, and 1.78:1 for HDTV.

- The scanning area is what the camera viewfinder and the preview monitor show. The essential, or safe title, area is the portion seen by the viewer, regardless of transmission loss or misadjustment of the receiver.

- Out-of-aspect ratio graphics and moving images need special consideration to make them fit the traditional or HDTV television screen.

- To avoid information overload, beware of displaying too much unrelated information simultaneously.

- Good readability results when the written information is within the essential area; the letters are relatively large and of a clean contour; the background is not too busy; and there is good color and brightness contrast between the lettering and the background.

- Compatible color means that the color image translates into clearly different brightness values (grayscale steps) when seen on a monochrome receiver. Most television systems reproduce at best nine separate brightness steps. These steps, ranging from TV white to TV black, make up the grayscale.

- Generated graphics equipment includes the character generator (C.G.) and the graphics generator (paint box) as well as the necessary software.

- The C.G. is used mainly for creating titles of different sizes, fonts, and colors. The more elaborate C.G.s can give the letters a three-dimensional look and provide a limited amount of animation.

- Graphics generators consist of high-powered computers with large storage and fast throughput capacity. Dedicated software packages can make desktop computers into effective graphics generators. Some graphics generators use an electronic drawing tablet and stylus that let the artist draw images that are immediately stored in the computer.

- Image generating refers to creating a graphic image entirely by computer. Image capturing and manipulating mean that an original image (such as a photo) is digitized by a scanner and then manipulated using the computer.

- Aliasing refers to diagonal or curved lines displaying jaggies—a stairsteplike line instead of one with smooth edges. High-end graphics generators employ antialiasing circuits that neutralize the jaggies and create a smooth line.

15.2

Scenery and Props

Although you may never be called upon to design or build scenery, you will likely set up scenery in the studio or fix up an interior at a remote location. Setting up even a small interview set requires that you know what the various pieces of scenery are called and how to read a floor plan. Your ability to see an existing on-location interior as a "set" will not only speed up camera placement and lighting, but will also help you determine if it needs redecorating for maximally effective camera shots. Knowing how to manage studio space through scenery and properties will also help you manage screen space in general.

▶ **TELEVISION SCENERY**
Standard set units, hanging units, platforms and wagons, and set pieces

▶ **PROPERTIES AND SET DRESSINGS**
Stage props, set dressings, hand properties, and the prop list

▶ **ELEMENTS OF SCENE DESIGN**
The floor plan, set backgrounds and platforms, and studio floor treatments

TELEVISION SCENERY

Because the television camera looks at a set both at close range and at a distance, scenery must be detailed enough to appear realistic yet plain enough to prevent cluttered pictures. Regardless of whether it's a simple interview set or a realistic living room, a set should allow for optimal camera angles and movement, microphone placement and boom movement, appropriate lighting, and maximum action by performers. Fulfilling these requirements are four types of scenery: (1) standard set units, (2) hanging units, (3) platforms and wagons, and (4) set pieces.

Standard Set Units

Standard set units consist of softwall and hardwall *flats* and a variety of set modules. Both are used to simulate interior or exterior walls. Although television stations and non-broadcast production houses use hardwall scenery almost exclusively, softwall scenery is more practical for high school and college television operations.

Softwall flats The flats for standard softwall set units are constructed of a lightweight wood frame covered

15.24 SOFTWALL FLATS

The softwall flat consists of a wood frame covered with muslin or canvas.

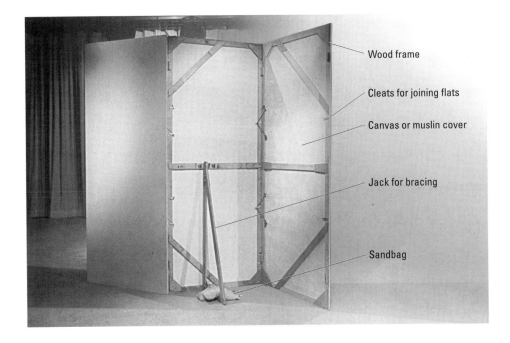

Wood frame

Cleats for joining flats

Canvas or muslin cover

Jack for bracing

Sandbag

with muslin or canvas. They have a uniform height but various widths. The height is usually 10 feet (about 3 meters) or 8 feet (about 2½ meters) for small sets or studios with low ceilings. Width ranges from 1 to 5 feet (30 centimeters to 1½ meters). When two or three flats are hinged together, they are called *twofolds* (also called a *book*) or *threefolds*. Flats are supported by *jacks,* wood braces that are hinged or clamped to the flats and weighted down by sandbags or metal weights. **SEE 15.24**

The advantages of softwall scenery are: (1) it is relatively inexpensive to construct and can usually be done in the scene shops of theater departments; (2) it lends itself to a great variety of set backgrounds; (3) it is easy to move and store; (4) it is easy to set up, brace, and strike; and (5) it is relatively easy to maintain and repair. The problem with softwall scenery is that it often shakes when someone closes a door or a window on the set or when something brushes against it.

Hardwall flats   Hardwall flats are much sturdier than softwall flats and are preferred for more-ambitious television productions. Hardwall units are generally built for a specific set and do not always conform to the standard set dimensions of softwall scenery. The problem with hardwall scenery is that the flats are heavy and difficult to store. (In the interest of your—and the flats'—health, do not try to move hardwall scenery by yourself.)

Hardwall flats also reflect sound more readily than softwall flats, which can easily interfere with good audio pickup. For example, if a set design requires that two hardwall flats stand opposite and in close proximity to each other, the talent operating in this space will most likely sound as though he were speaking inside a barrel. Most hardwall scenery is built for specific shows, such as newcasts or soap operas, and remains set up for the length of the series. Carefully constructed hardwall scenery is a must for HDTV or any other form of digital television that has a higher picture resolution than standard NTSC. **SEE 15.25**

Set modules   For small stations or educational institutions, where you do not have the luxury of building new sets for every show, you may consider versatile set modules that can be used in a variety of configurations. A *set module* is a series of flats and three-dimensional set pieces whose dimensions match, whether they are used vertically (right side up), horizontally (on their sides), or in various combinations.

For example, you might use a modular hardwall set piece as a hardwall flat in one production and as a platform in the next. Or you can dismantle a modular desk and use the boxes (representing the drawers) and the top as display units. A variety of set modules are commercially available.

15.25 HARDWALL SET UNIT

The hardwall set unit has a strong wood frame and is covered with such hardwall material as plywood or textured plastic sheets. It is often equipped with casters for easy transport.

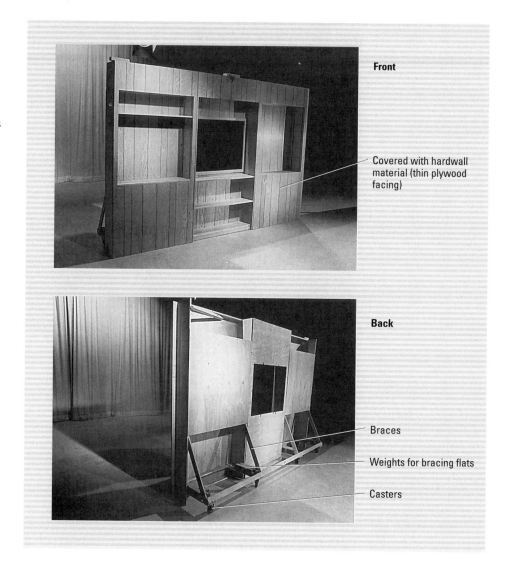

Front

Covered with hardwall material (thin plywood facing)

Back

Braces

Weights for bracing flats

Casters

Hanging Units

Whereas flats stand on the studio floor, *hanging units* are supported from overhead tracks, the lighting grid, or lighting battens. They include (1) the cyclorama, (2) drops, and (3) drapes and curtains.

Cyclorama   The most versatile hanging background is a *cyclorama,* or *cyc,* a continuous piece of muslin or canvas stretched along two, three, and sometimes even all four studio walls. **SEE 15.26** Some cycs have a second curtain of loosely woven material, called a *scrim,* hanging in front of them to break the light before it hits the cyc, producing a soft, uniform background. A fairly light color (light gray or beige) is more advantageous than a dark cyc. You can always make a light cyc dark by

keeping the light off it, and colorize it easily using floodlights (scoops) with color gels attached. A dark cyc will let you do neither. Some studios have hardwall cycs, which are not actually hanging units but are built solidly on the studio floor. **SEE 15.27**

Most studios use a *ground row* to blend the bottom edge of the muslin cyc into the studio floor. **SEE 15.28**

Drop   A *drop* is a wide roll of canvas with a background scene painted on it. It commonly serves stylized settings where the viewer is very aware that the action occurs in front of a drop. Some drops consist of large photomurals (which are commercially available) for more realistic background effects.

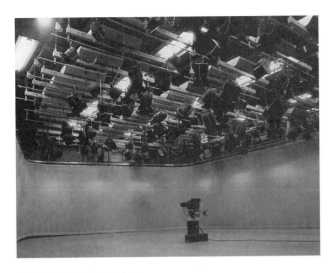

15.26 MUSLIN CYC

The muslin cyclorama runs on overhead tracks and normally covers three sides of the studio.

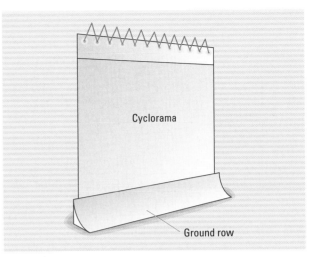

15.28 GROUND ROW

The ground row runs along the bottom of the cyc to make it blend into the studio floor.

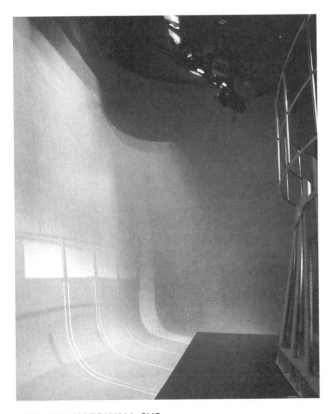

15.27 HARDWALL CYC

The hardwall cyc is made of hardwall material and is permanently installed on one or two sides of the studio.

A *chroma-key drop* is a wide roll of chroma-key blue cloth that can be pulled down and even stretched over part of the studio floor for chroma keying.

You can make a simple and inexpensive drop by suspending a roll of seamless paper (9 feet wide by 36 feet long), which comes in a variety of colors. Seamless paper hung from a row of flats provides a continuous cyclike background. Simply roll it sideways and staple the top edge to the flats. You can paint it for a more detailed background, or use it for a *cookie* projection. **SEE 15.29**

Drapes and curtains   When choosing drapes stay away from overly detailed patterns or fine stripes. Unless you shoot with HDTV cameras, fine patterns tend to look smudgy, and contrasting strips often cause moiré interference. Drapes are usually stapled to 1 × 3 battens and hung from the top of the flats. Most curtains should be translucent enough to let the back light come through without revealing scenic pieces that may be in back of the set.

Platforms and Wagons

The various types of platforms are elevation devices. Typical platforms are 6 or 12 inches (roughly 15 or 30 centimeters) high and can be stacked. Sometimes the whole platform is called a riser, although technically a *riser* is only the elevation part of the platform without its (often removable) top. If you use a platform for interviews, for

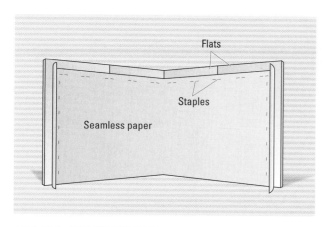

15.29 SEAMLESS PAPER DROP
A simple yet effective backdrop can be constructed by hanging a roll of seamless paper from a row of flats.

example, you may want to cover it entirely with carpet pieces. This cover not only will look good on camera, but will also absorb the hollow sounds of people moving on the platform. You can further dampen this sound by filling the platform interior with foam rubber.

Some of the 6-inch platforms have four casters so that they can be moved around. Such platforms are called *wagons.* You can mount a portion of a set, or even a whole set, on a series of wagons and then move it relatively easily in and out of the studio. Once in place, wagons should be secured with wood wedges and/or sandbags so they do not move unexpectedly. **SEE 15.30**

Larger risers and hardwall scenery are often supported by a slotted-steel frame, which works like a big erector set. You can cut the various slotted-steel pieces to any length and bolt them together in any configuration. Slotted steel has several advantages. It is durable and relatively light and it allows easy dismantling of scenic pieces—an important consideration when storage space is at a premium.

Set Pieces

Set pieces are important scenic elements. They consist of freestanding three-dimensional objects, such as pillars, *pylons* (which look like three-sided pillars), *sweeps* (curved pieces of scenery), folding screens, steps, and *periaktoi,* plural for *periaktos*—a three-sided standing unit that looks like a large pylon. Most periaktoi move and swivel on casters and are painted differently on each side to allow for quick scene changes. For example, if one side is painted a warm yellow and the other a chroma-key blue, you can change the neutral yellow background to any scene by swiveling the periaktos to the chroma blue side while chroma-keying a specific background scene. **SEE 15.31**

The advantages of using set pieces are that (1) you can move them easily, (2) they are self-supporting, and (3) they quickly and easily establish three-dimensional space.

Although set pieces are freestanding and self-supporting (which are, after all, their major advantages), always check whether they need additional bracing. At a minimum they must be able to withstand bumps by

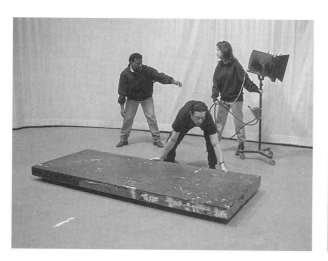

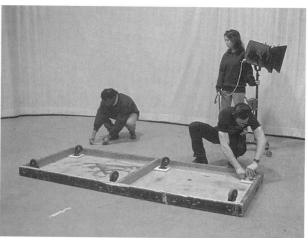

15.30 PLATFORMS AND WAGONS
Platforms are usually 6 or 12 inches high. When equipped with sturdy casters, they are called wagons.

15.31 SET PIECES

Set pieces are freestanding scenic elements that roll on casters for quick and easy repositioning.

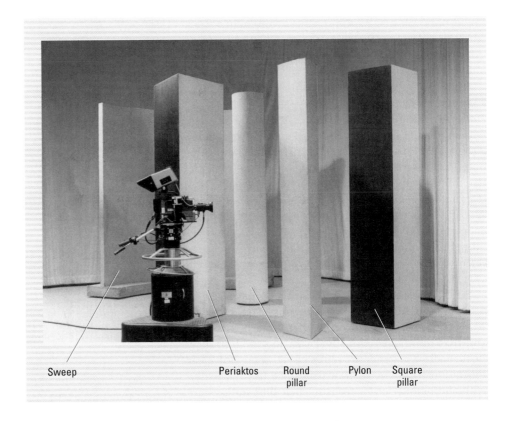

Sweep   Periaktos   Round   Pylon   Square
                              pillar   pillar

people or cameras. As a general rule, it is always better to overbrace than to underbrace a set. As in all other aspects of television production, do not forsake safety for convenience or speed.

PROPERTIES AND SET DRESSINGS

After having struggled with softwall and hardwall scenery, you will find that it is really the properties and set dressings that give the environment a specific look and style. Much like decorating your room, it is primarily the furniture and what you hang on the walls that distinguish a particular environment, rather than the walls themselves. Because good television has more close-ups than medium and long shots, the three types of *props*—stage props, set dressings, and hand props—must be realistic enough to withstand the close scrutiny of the camera.

Stage Props

Stage props include the common type of furniture and items constructed for a specific purpose, such as news desks, lecterns, or panel tables. You should also have enough furniture to create settings for a modern living room, a study, an office, a comfortable interview area, and perhaps some type of outdoor area with a patio table and chairs. For an interview set, relatively simple chairs are more useful than large, upholstered ones. It is often difficult to bring oversized chairs close enough together for the intimate spacing of a two-shot, and you don't want the chairs to take on more prominence than the people sitting in them. Try to get chairs and couches that are not too low, so that sitting and rising gracefully is not problematic, especially for tall people.

The problem with stage props is finding adequate storage space for them. Store heavier items on the floor, and smaller props on shelves. Always use a prop cart to transport heavy items—it will save your back and the stage prop.

Set Dressings

Set dressings are a major factor in determining the style and character of a set. Although the flats may remain the same from one show to another, the dressings help give each set individual character. They include such items as draperies, pictures, lamps and chandeliers, fireplaces, flowerpots, plants, candle holders, and sculptures. Secondhand stores provide an unlimited source for these things. In an emergency you can always raid your own office or living quarters.

Hand Properties

Hand properties consist of all items that are actually handled by the performer during a show. They include dishes, silverware, telephones, radios, and desktop computers. In television the hand props must be realistic: Use only real objects. A papier-mâché chalice may look regal and impressive on stage, but on the television screen it looks dishonest, if not ridiculous. Television is very much dependent on human action. These actions are extended through the hand props. If you want the actions to be sincere and genuine, the extension of them must be real as well. If an actor is supposed to carry a heavy suitcase, make sure the suitcase is actually heavy. Pretending that it is heavy does not go over well on television.

If you must use food, check carefully that it is fresh and that the dishes and silverware are meticulously clean. Liquor is generally replaced by water (for clear spirits), tea (for whiskey), or fruit juice (for red wine). With all due respect for realism, such substitutions are perfectly appropriate.

As obvious as it sounds, see to it that hand props are actually on the set for the performers to use and that they work. A missing prop or a bottle that does not open at the right time may cause costly production delays.

Prop List

In small routine productions, the floor manager or a member of the floor crew normally takes care of the props. More-elaborate productions, however, have a person assigned exclusively to the handling of props—the *property manager.* To procure the various props and ensure that they are all available at the camera rehearsal and taping sessions, you need to prepare a *prop list.* Some prop people divide the list into stage props, set dressings, and hand props, although in most cases the various types of props are combined on a single list. **SEE 15.32** Always double-check that all the props mentioned in the script appear on the prop list and that they are actually available for camera rehearsal and taping sessions.

If you need to strike the set and set it up again for subsequent taping sessions, mark all the props and take several photos of the set before putting the props away. This way you will ensure that the same props appear in the same place from one setup to the next.

five outside bushes	6' sofa
two rubber plants	set of eight family photos
potted palm	sunflower painting
transparent curtains	Picasso print
low 8' cabinet	magazines
square end table	newspaper
small chest of drawers	books
two bookcases	stereo
chair (with armrests)	tea set
golden wing chair	lamp for end table
coffee table	Indian sculpture
round end table	louvered screen

15.32 PROP LIST

This prop list contains all set props, set dressings, and hand properties shown in the set in figure 15.34.

Most production studios have a collection of standard props: vases, plants, tablecloths, tables, chairs, couches, and so forth. Unless you do productions that need props on a regular basis, such as a comedy series or daytime drama, you can borrow most set and hand props when needed. It is usually easier to find an office that can be stripped of its furniture for the production day than to buy and store various office sets. If you do an especially ambitious production, such as a period play, you can always call on the theater arts department of a local college or high school, or rent them from a commercial company.

ELEMENTS OF SCENE DESIGN

Before you design a set, you must know what the show is all about. Talk to the director about his or her concept of the show, even if it is a simple interview. You arrive at a set design by defining the necessary spatial environment for optimal communication rather than by copying what you see on the air. For example, you may feel that the best way to inform viewers is not by having an authoritative newscaster read stories from a pulpitlike contraption, but by moving the cameras into the newsroom itself and out into the street where events are happening. If the show is intended to be shot with a single camera for heavy

15.33 STUDIO FLOOR PLAN GRID

The floor plan shows the dimensions of the studio floor, which is further defined by the lighting grid or similar pattern. The set is drawn onto this basic studio grid.

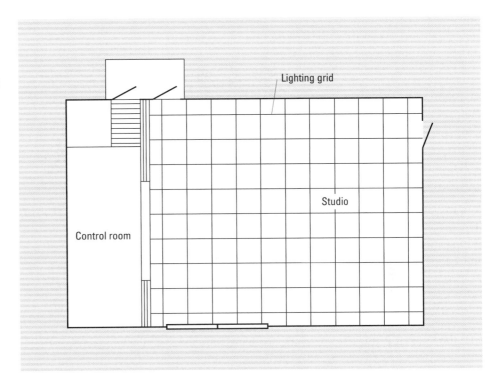

postproduction editing, it may be easier to take the camera to the street corner rather than to re-create the street corner in the studio.

But even if the show is slated for the studio, you can often streamline the set design by taking some time to discover just what the show is all about. Try to see the entire show in screen images and work from there. For example, even if the interview guest is a famous defense lawyer, you don't automatically have to set up a typical lawyer's office, complete with antique desk, leather chairs, and law books in the background. Rather, you should ask about the nature of the interview and its intended communication objective. Your design depends on the answers you get, such as: "The basic idea is to probe the conscience and feelings of the defense lawyer rather than hear about future defense strategies. The viewer should see intimate close-ups of the guest during most of the interview." Does this interview require an elaborate lawyer's set? Not at all. Considering the shooting style that includes a majority of tight close-ups, two comfortable chairs in front of a simple background will do just fine.

We now turn to some of the major elements of scene design: (1) the floor plan, (2) set backgrounds and platforms, and (3) studio floor treatments.

The Floor Plan

A set design is drawn on the *floor plan*, which is literally a plan of the studio floor. It shows the floor area, the main studio doors, the location of the control room, and the studio walls. The lighting grid or batten locations are normally drawn on the floor area to give a specific orientation pattern according to which the sets can be placed. In effect, the grid resembles the orientation squares of a city map. **SEE 15.33** The completed floor plan should convey enough information to the floor manager and crew to put up the set and dress it, even in the absence of the director or set designer.

The scale of the floor plan varies, but it is normally ¼ inch = 1 foot. All scenery and set properties are then drawn onto the floor plan in the proper position relative to the studio walls and lighting grid. For simple setups you may not need to draw the flats and set properties to scale; you can approximate their size and placement relative to the grid. **SEE 15.34**

More-elaborate sets, however, require a floor plan that is, like a blueprint for a house, drawn precisely to scale. Even if you don't have to draw a floor plan to scale, you are greatly aided if you use the templates that have cutouts of standard furniture. They normally come in a

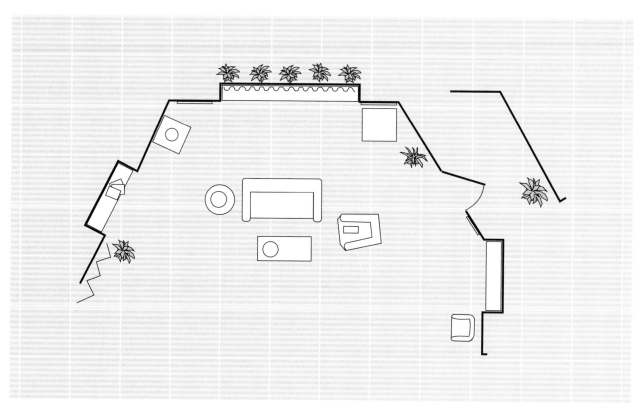

15.34 SIMPLE FLOOR PLAN
This floor plan shows all necessary scenery, set props, and dressings, as well as the more prominent hand props.
It is usually not drawn precisely to scale.

scale of ¼ inch = 1 foot and are readily available in college bookstores or art-supply stores. Most art directors use computer software for floor plans and set designs.

Floor plan functions The floor plan is an important tool for all production and engineering personnel. The director uses it to visualize the show and to block the major actions of performers, cameras, and microphone booms. It is essential to the floor crew, who must set up the scenery and place the major properties. The LD (lighting director) needs it for designing the general light plot. The audio technician can become familiar with specific microphone placement and other possible audio requirements. The performers use it to anticipate their movements and spot potential blocking problems.

Although you may not intend to become a set designer, you should nevertheless learn how to draw a basic floor plan and translate it into an actual set, into

movement of performers and cameras, and, finally, into television screen images.

Set positioning Whenever possible, try to locate the set where the lights are. Place it so that the back lights, key lights, and fill lights hang in approximately the right positions. Sometimes an inexperienced designer will place a set in a studio corner, where most of the lighting instruments have to be rehung for proper illumination, whereas in another part of the studio the same set could have been lighted with existing instruments. If you use the floor plan as the basis for the light plot, simply add a transparent overlay and sketch the major light sources.

As you can see once again, you cannot afford to specialize in a single aspect of television production. Everything interrelates, and the more you know about the various production techniques and functions, the better your coordination of those elements will be.

When drawing a floor plan, watch for the following potential problem areas.

■ Many times, a carelessly drawn floor plan will indicate scenery backing, such as the walls of a living room, not wide enough to provide adequate cover for the furniture or other items placed in front of it. The usual problem is that the furniture and other set pieces are drawn much too small relative to the background flats. For example, while on the out-of-scale floor plan a single threefold (covering about 10 feet of width) might show adequate cover for an entire set of living room furniture, it is barely wide enough to back a single couch in the actual studio set. The furniture always seems to take up more room in reality than on the floor plan. One way of avoiding such design mistakes is to draw the in-scale furniture on the floor plan first and then add the flats for the backing. You will find that the computer helps greatly with such design tasks. Several simple interior-decorating software programs show the most common pieces of furniture in scale and let you move them around on-screen (your floor plan) until they are in the right place.

■ During the setup you may notice that the available studio floor is always less than the floor plan indicates. Limit the set design to the actual available floor space.

■ Always place active furniture (used by the performers) at least 6 feet (roughly 2 meters) from the set wall so that the back lights can be directed at the performance areas at not too steep an angle. Also, the director can use the space between wall and furniture for camera placement and talent movement.

Set Backgrounds and Platforms

The background of a set helps unify a sequence of shots and places the action in a single environment. It can also provide visual variety behind relatively static foreground action. Most platforms are used to keep the camera from looking up at, or down on, performers who are seated.

Backgrounds You can achieve scenic continuity by painting the background a uniform, usually low-energy color or by decorating it so that viewers can easily relate one portion of the set to another. Because in television we see mostly environmental detail, you must give viewers clues so they can apply closure to the shot details and perceive a continuous environment. A uniform background color or design, or properties that point to a single environment such as the typical furnishings of a kitchen, all help viewers relate the various shots to a specific location.

Although set continuity is an important element in scene design, a plain background is not the most interesting scenic background. You need to "dress" the set by hanging artwork, posters, or other objects on the wall to break it up into smaller yet related areas. When you dress a plain background with pictures or other objects, place them so that they are in camera range. For example, if you hang a picture between two interview chairs, it will show only in the straight-on two-shot but not in the individual close-ups. If you want more background texture in the close-up shots, position pictures so that they are seen by the cameras during cross-shooting. **SEE 15.35**

Platforms Camera operators like to adjust their cameras to the most comfortable working height, not necessarily to the most effective aesthetic point of view. Therefore, performers seated in normal chairs on the studio floor are positioned lower than the average camera working height, so the camera looks down on them. This point of view carries subtle psychological implications of inferiority and also creates an unpleasant composition. For events where performers are seated most of the time, place the chairs on a platform (anywhere from 6 to 12 inches high). The camera can then remain at a comfortable operating height, shooting the scene at eye level. **SEE 15.36**

Studio Floor Treatments

A common headache of the scene designer is the studio floor. In long shots it usually looks unattractive, as though the scene were played in a warehouse or garage. Two primary considerations in dressing the studio floor are that the treatment not interfere with camera and boom travel and that it be easily removable once the show is over. The most popular floor treatments include (1) rugs and mats, (2) rubber tiles, (3) glue-on strips, and (4) paint.

Rugs and mats Although rugs are an excellent and realistic floor treatment, they often get in the way of cameras and booms. Tape the edges of a rug in place to prevent it from bunching up under the dolly wheels or pedestal skirt when the camera travels over it. The same goes for grass mats: Secure them with tape so they do not slip on the smooth studio floor. The rug is usually the first

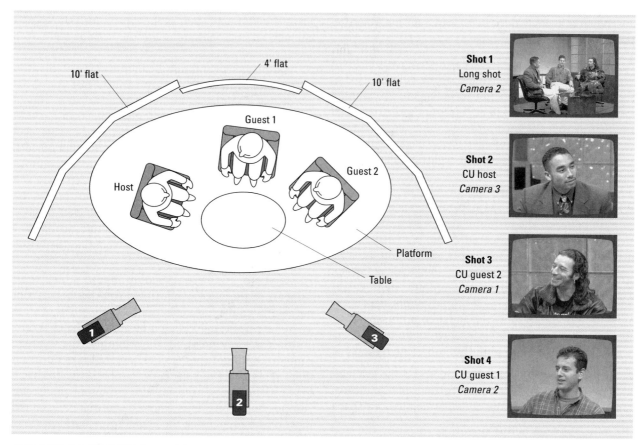

Shot 1
Long shot
Camera 2

Shot 2
CU host
Camera 3

Shot 3
CU guest 2
Camera 1

Shot 4
CU guest 1
Camera 2

15.35 BACKGROUND DRESSING

The establishing (long) shot of this interview set shows that the background flats provide some visual texture and interest for the interviewer (camera-left) and guest 2 (far right), but not for guest 1 in the middle. The subsequent close-ups confirm this design problem.

15.36 PLATFORM COMPENSATING FOR CAMERA HEIGHT

To avoid having the camera look down at people who are seated, chairs should be placed on a platform so that the camera can shoot from eye level.

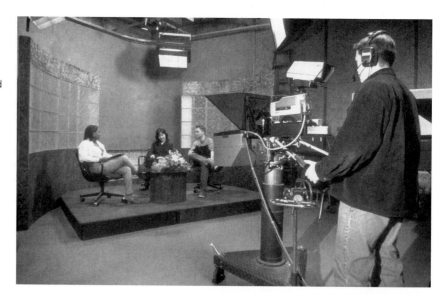

property placed so that other scenery and props can be put on it as necessary.

Rubber tiles   Flexible rubber tiles are available in large (3-by-3-foot, or roughly 1-square-meter) squares of contrasting, low-energy colors (normally off-white and off-black). They make excellent floor patterns for offices, dance sets, large rooms, or hallways. Simply lay the tiles on the studio floor in the desired pattern, and the natural adhesion keeps them in place. Just for good measure, tape the outer edges to the studio floor so that camera travel does not move them. Because footprints tend to show, clean the tiles with soapy water before the camera rehearsal and final taping.

Glue-on strips   Another excellent floor treatment is glue-on strips, which come in different patterns and have a removable backing like shelf paper. You can adhere them side by side on the studio floor and remove them just as easily. Cameras and booms have no travel restrictions. These glue-on patterns are quite expensive, however, and are used only for elaborate productions.

Paint   Some set designers prefer to treat the studio floor with water-soluble paint. Most paints that persist through rehearsals and videotaping, however, are hard to remove and usually leave some residue on the studio floor. Check with the studio supervisor before you start wielding a paintbrush.

MAIN POINTS

◆ Television scenery encompasses the three-dimensional aspects of design.

◆ There are four types of scenery: standard set units, that is, hardwall and softwall flats and set modules; hanging units, such as cycs, drops, and curtains; platforms and wagons; and set pieces, such as pillars, screens, and periaktoi.

◆ The three basic types of properties are stage props, such as furniture, news desks, and lecterns; set dressings, such as pictures, draperies, and lamps; and hand props—items such as dishes, telephones, and typewriters that are actually handled by the talent.

◆ When a set must be struck and set up again for a subsequent taping session, take photos of all set details to ensure consistency of the setup.

◆ A floor plan shows the exact location of the scenery and set properties relative to the lighting grid. The floor plan is essential for the director to prepare the preliminary blocking of talent, cameras, and microphone booms; for the floor crew to set up the scenery and place the major set properties; and for the lighting director to design the basic light plot.

◆ Studio floors can be covered with rubber tiles, glue-on patterns, or paint without interfering with camera movement. Rugs are useful only if cameras do not have to move on and off of them while on the air.

16

Production People

Television production is teamwork. You've heard this many times. But why does it take a whole team when you can do a reasonably good job with a camcorder? Wouldn't total control of the production process and no one interfering with your creativity be better? Aren't the other team members more of a liability than an asset? As you probably suspected, the answer to the last two questions is a simple no. In professional television production, you must rely on a great number of people, each of whom performs a highly specific function. For example, you may be all by yourself when chasing a news story with an ENG camcorder, but when you bring the videotape back to the station, it is the rest of the news department that gets your story on the air. Someone decides just where in the newscast your story should be placed; others edit your videotape, write a sensible news story from your cursory notes, put it on the videotape recorder for playback at a specific time during the newscast, and ensure that the final video and audio signals reach the transmitter.

Section 16.1, What Production People Do, will help you recognize the various team members involved in television production and precisely what it is that they do. This section also discusses the specific on-camera techniques of television performers and actors. Section 16.2, How to Do Makeup and What to Wear, briefly describes the makeup performers and actors use and what they wear on-camera.

KEY TERMS

above-the-line personnel Same as production (non-technical) personnel.

actor A person (male or female) who appears on-camera in dramatic roles. The actor always portrays someone else.

below-the-line personnel Same as technical production personnel.

blocking Carefully worked-out movement and actions by the talent and for all mobile television equipment.

cue card A large, hand-lettered card that contains copy, usually held next to the camera lens by floor personnel.

foundation A makeup base, over which further makeup such as rouge and eye shadow is applied.

makeup Cosmetics used to enhance, correct, or change appearance.

news production personnel People assigned exclusively to the production of news and special events.

pancake A makeup base, or foundation makeup, usually water-soluble and applied with a small sponge.

pan stick A foundation makeup with a grease base. Used to cover a beard shadow or prominent skin blemish.

performer A person who appears on-camera in non-dramatic shows. The performer plays himself or herself and does not assume someone else's character.

production (nontechnical) personnel People concerned primarily with nontechnical production matters that lead from the basic idea to the final screen image.

talent Collective name for all performers and actors who appear regularly on television.

technical production personnel People who operate the production equipment.

teleprompter A prompting device that projects the moving (usually computer-generated) copy over the lens so that the talent can read it without losing eye contact with the viewer. Also called *auto cue*.

16.1

What Production People Do

Even the most sophisticated television production equipment and computer interfaces will not replace *you* in the television system. You and those working with you still reign supreme in the production process. The equipment cannot make ethical and aesthetic judgments for you; it cannot tell you exactly which part of the event to select and how to present it for optimal communication. You make such decisions within the context of the general communication intent and through interaction with other members of the production team—the people in front of the camera (talent) and those behind it (production staff, technical crews, engineers, and other station personnel). You may soon discover that the major task of television production is working not so much with equipment as with people.

▶ **PRODUCTION (NONTECHNICAL) PERSONNEL**
Those concerned primarily with the production from idea to final screen image

▶ **TECHNICAL PERSONNEL AND CREW**
Those concerned with the operation of the production equipment

▶ **NEWS PRODUCTION PERSONNEL**
Those concerned specifically with the production of news and special events

▶ **TELEVISION TALENT**
Television performers and actors

▶ **PERFORMANCE TECHNIQUES**
Camera, audio, timing and screen presence, postproduction continuity, the floor manager's cues, and prompting devices

▶ **ACTING TECHNIQUES**
Audience, blocking, memorizing lines, timing, postproduction, and the director/actor relationship

▶ **AUDITIONS**
Preparation, appearance, and creativity

PRODUCTION (NONTECHNICAL) PERSONNEL

The *production (nontechnical) personnel* are generally involved in translating a script or an event into effective television images. **SEE 16.1** They are also called *above-the-line personnel*, because they fall under a different budget category from the technical crew, who are called

16.1 TELEVISION PRODUCTION (NONTECHNICAL) PERSONNEL

PERSONNEL	FUNCTION
PRODUCTION (NONTECHNICAL) STAFF	
Executive Producer	In charge of one or several program series. Manages budget and coordinates with client, station management, advertising agencies, financial supporters, and talent and writers' agents.
Producer	In charge of an individual production. Is responsible for all personnel working on the production and for coordinating technical and nontechnical production elements. Often serves as writer and director.
Associate Producer (AP)	Assists producer in all production matters. Often does the actual coordinating jobs, such as telephoning talent and confirming schedules.
Field Producer	Assists producer by taking charge of remote operations (away from the studio). At small stations may be part of producer's responsibilities.
Production Manager	Schedules equipment and personnel for all studio and field productions.
Production Assistant (PA)	Assists producer and director during actual production. During rehearsal takes notes of producer's and/or director's suggestions for show improvement.
Director	In charge of directing talent and technical operations. Is ultimately responsible for transforming a script into effective video and audio messages. At small stations may often be the producer as well.
Associate Director (AD)	Assists director during the actual production. In studio productions does timing for director. In complicated productions helps to "ready" various operations (such as presetting specific camera shots or calling for a VTR to start).
Talent	Refers to all performers and actors who regularly appear on television.
Actor	Someone who portrays someone else on-camera.
Performer	Someone who appears on-camera in nondramatic activities. Performers portray themselves.
Announcer	Reads narration but does not appear on-camera. If on-camera, the announcer moves up into the talent category.
Floor Manager	In charge of all activities on the studio floor. Directs talent, relays director's cues to talent, and supervises floor personnel. Except for large operations, responsible for setting up scenery and dressing the set. Also called *floor director* or *stage manager*.
Floor Persons	Set up and dress sets. Operate cue cards or other prompting devices, easel cards, and graphics. Sometimes help to set up and work portable field lighting instruments or microphone booms. Assist camera operators in moving camera dollies and pulling camera cables. At small stations also act as wardrobe and makeup people. Also called *grips, stagehands,* or *utilities personnel.*

16.1 TELEVISION PRODUCTION (NONTECHNICAL) PERSONNEL *(continued)*

PERSONNEL	FUNCTION
ADDITIONAL PRODUCTION PERSONNEL	

In small operations these production people are not always part of the permanent staff, or their functions are fulfilled by other personnel.

Writer	At smaller stations or in corporate television, the scripts are often written by the director or producer. Usually hired on a freelance basis.
Art Director	In charge of creative design aspects of show (set design and location, graphics).
Graphic Artist	Prepares computer graphics, titles, charts, and electronic backgrounds.
Makeup Artist	Does the makeup for all talent. Usually hired on a freelance basis.
Costume Designer	Designs and sometimes even constructs various costumes for dramas, dance numbers, and children's shows. Usually hired on a freelance basis.
Wardrobe Person	Handles all wardrobe matters during production.
Property Manager	Maintains and manages use of various set and hand properties. Found in large operations only. Otherwise, props are managed by the floor manager.
Sound Designer	Constructs the complete sound track (dialogue and sound effects) in postproduction. Usually hired on a freelance basis for large productions.

below-the-line personnel. The nontechnical people normally include the executive producer, the producer, the director, the art director and assistants, as well as the writers and talent.

As with all such classifications, the above- and below-the-line division is anything but absolute or even uniform. For example, in some productions the *PA (production assistant)* or the *TD (technical director)* are classified in the below-the-line category; in others, they belong among the above-the-line personnel. **SEE 16.2**

For example, the *DP (director of photography)* is technically a below-the-line production person. However, the position is frequently regarded and budgeted as an above-the-line item. The term borrowed from film production, has found its way into television production. In standard theatrical film production, the DP is mainly responsible for lighting and the proper exposure of the film rather than running the camera. In smaller film productions and EFP, however, the DP actually operates the camera as well as does the lighting. So if you hear an independent television producer/director looking for a reliable and creative DP, he or she is primarily referring to an experienced EFP camera operator. What you need to realize and remember is that all members of the production team are equally important, regardless of whether they are classified as above-the-line or below-the-line, or whether they sit in the director's chair or help carry some lights to a field location. *READY ZVL* ❶

TECHNICAL PERSONNEL AND CREW

The *technical production personnel* consists of people who are primarily concerned with operating equipment. They are usually part of the *crew*. The technical personnel include camera operators, audio and lighting people, videotape operators, videotape editors, and C.G. operators. The term *technical* does not refer to electronic expertise, but rather to managing the equipment with skill and confidence. The true engineers, who

16.2 ABOVE-THE-LINE AND BELOW-THE-LINE PERSONNEL

The division between above-the-line and below-the-line personnel is not always clear-cut. Generally, above-the-line personnel include the nontechnical personnel, and below-the-line personnel include the production crew and engineering personnel.

A B O V E - T H E - L I N E

- Executive Producer
- Producer
- Associates and Production Assistants (PAs)

- Production Manager
- Director
- Associate Director
- Art Director

- Sound Designer
- Talent
- Writer

B E L O W - T H E - L I N E

- Studio Supervisor
- Technical Director
- Camera Operators
- Lighting Director
- Floor Manager

- Floor Persons
- Video Operator
- Audio Technician
- C.G. Operator
- Videotape Operator

- Videotape Editor
- Makeup Artist
- Wardrobe People
- Scenery and Property Personnel
- Maintenance Engineer

understand electronics and know where to look when something goes wrong with a piece of equipment, usually do not operate equipment; rather, they supervise its installation and maintain it. You may find, however, that in larger professional operations the technical production people are still called engineers, mainly to satisfy the traditional job classification established by the labor unions. **SEE 16.3** *READY ZVL* ❷

Keep in mind that many of the functions of technical and nontechnical production people overlap and even change, depending on the size, location, and relative complexity of the production. For example, you may initially have acted as a producer when setting up the videotaping of the semiannual address of a corporation president; then, on the day of the production, you may find yourself busy with such technical production matters as lighting and running the camera. In larger productions, such as soap operas, your job responsibility is much more limited. When acting as a producer, you have nothing to do with lighting or camera operation. And, when working

the camera, you may have to wait patiently for the lighting crew to finish, even if the production is behind schedule and you have nothing else to do at the time.

NEWS PRODUCTION PERSONNEL

Almost all television broadcast stations produce at least one daily newscast. As a matter of fact, the newscasts are often the major production activity at these stations. Because news departments must be able to respond quickly to a variety of production tasks, such as covering a downtown fire or a protest in front of city hall, there is generally little time to prepare for such events. News departments have, therefore, their own *news production personnel*, who are dedicated exclusively to the production of news and special events and who perform highly specific functions. **SEE 16.4**

Of course, as in any other organization, television or the smaller corporate video involves many more people

16.3 TECHNICAL PERSONNEL AND CREW

PERSONNEL	FUNCTION
ENGINEERING STAFF	

These people are actual engineers who are responsible for the purchase, installation, proper functioning, and maintenance of all technical equipment.

Chief Engineer	In charge of all technical personnel, budgets, and equipment. Designs system, including transmission facilities, and oversees installations and day-to-day operations.
Assistant Chief Engineer	Assists chief engineer in all technical matters and operations. Also called *engineering supervisor*.
Studio or Remote Engineer-in-Charge	Oversees all technical operations. Usually called *EIC*.
Maintenance Engineer	Maintains all technical equipment and troubleshoots during productions.

NONENGINEERING PERSONNEL	

Although skilled in technical aspects, the following technical personnel do not have to be engineers, but usually consist of technically trained production people.

Technical Director (TD)	Does the switching and acts as technical crew chief.
Camera Operators	Operate the cameras; often do the lighting for simple shows. When working primarily in field productions (ENG/EFP), they are sometimes called *videographers* or *shooters*.
Director of Photography (DP)	In film productions, in charge of lighting. In EFP, operates EPF camera.
Lighting Director (LD)	In charge of lighting; normally found mostly in large productions.
Video Operator	Adjusts camera controls for optimal camera pictures (shading). Sometimes takes on additional technical duties, especially during field productions and remotes. Also called *shader*.
Audio Technician	In charge of all audio operations. Works audio console during the show. Also called *audio engineer*.
Videotape Operator	Runs the videotape machine.
Character Generator (C.G.) Operator	Types and/or recalls from the computer the names and other graphic material to be integrated with the video image.
Videotape Editor	Operates postproduction editing equipment. Often makes or assists in creative editing decisions.
Digital Graphic Artist	Renders digital graphics for on-air use.

16.4 NEWS PRODUCTION PERSONNEL

PERSONNEL	FUNCTION
News Director	In charge of all news operations. Bears ultimate responsibility for all newscasts.
Producer	Directly responsible for the selection and placement of the stories in a newscast so that they form a unified, balanced whole.
Assignment Editor	Assigns reporters and videographers (camcorder operators) to specific events to be covered.
Reporter	Gathers the stories. Often reports on-camera from the field.
Videographer	Camcorder operator. In the absence of a reporter, decides on what part of the event to cover. Also called *news photographer* or *shooter*.
Writer	Writes on-the-air copy for the anchors. The copy is based on the reporter's notes and available videotape.
Videotape Editor	Edits videotape according to reporter's notes, writer's script, or producer's instructions.
Anchor	Principal presenter of newscast normally from a studio set.
Weathercaster	On-camera talent, talking about the weather. Often more entertainers than meteorologists.
Traffic Reporter	On-camera talent. Informs of local traffic conditions.
Sportscaster	On-camera talent, giving sports news and commentary.

than what you see listed in the figures in this section, such as clerical personnel, people who schedule various events, who sell commercial time, who negotiate contracts, who actually build and paint the sets, and who clean the building. These support personnel operate outside the basic production system, however. A description of their functions would, therefore, prove more confusing than helpful at this point.

TELEVISION TALENT

When you look at the people appearing regularly on television and talking to you—telling you what to buy, what is happening around the world, or what the weather is going to be like—you may feel that the job is not too difficult and that you could easily do it yourself. After all, most of them are simply reading copy that appears on a teleprompter. But when you actually stand in front of the camera, you quickly learn that the job is not quite as easy as it looks. To appear relaxed on-camera, and to pretend that the camera lens or the teleprompter is a real person to whom you are talking, takes hard work and a good amount of talent. This is why we call all people appearing regularly on television *talent*. Although television talent may have varied communication objectives—some seek to entertain, educate, inform; others seek to persuade, convince, sell—all strive to communicate with the television audience as effectively as possible.

You can divide all television talent into two large groups: performers and actors. The difference between them is fairly clear-cut. Television *performers* are engaged basically in nondramatic activities: They play themselves and do not assume roles of other characters; they sell their own personalities and stories to the audience. Television *actors*, on the other hand, always portray someone else: They project a character's personality rather than their own, even if the character is modeled after their own experience. Their stories are always fictional.

Although there are distinct differences between television performers and television actors, the groups do share several functions. All talent communicate with the viewers through the television camera and must keep in mind the nuances of audio, movement, and timing. And all talent interact with other television personnel—the director, the floor manager, or the camera operator.

PERFORMANCE TECHNIQUES

The television performer speaks directly to the camera, plays host to various guests, or communicates with other performers or the studio audience; he or she is also fully aware of the presence of the television audience at home. This latter audience, however, is not the large, anonymous, and heterogeneous television audience that modern sociologists study. For the television performer, the audience is an individual or a small, intimate group that has gathered in front of a television set.

If you are a performer, try imagining your audience as a family of three, seated in their favorite room, about 10 feet away from you. With this picture in mind, you have no reason to scream at the "millions of people out there in videoland"; rather, a more successful approach is to talk quietly and intimately to the family who were kind enough to let you come into their home.

When you assume the role of a television performer, the camera becomes your audience. You must adapt your performance techniques to its characteristics and to other important production elements such as audio and timing. In this section we discuss (1) the performer and the camera, (2) the performer and audio, (3) the performer and timing, (4) the performer and postproduction, (5) the floor manager's cues, and (6) prompting devices.

Performer and Camera

The camera is not simply an inanimate piece of machinery; it sees everything you do or do not do. It sees how you look, move, sit, and stand—in short, how you behave in a variety of situations. At times it looks at you much more closely and with greater scrutiny than a polite person would ever dare to do. It reveals the nervous twitch of your mouth when you are ill at ease and the expression of mild panic when you have forgotten a line. The camera does not politely look away when you scratch your nose or ear. It faithfully reflects your behavior in all pleasant and unpleasant details. As a television performer, you must therefore carefully control your actions without letting the audience know that you are conscious of doing so.

Camera lens   Because the camera represents your audience, you must look directly into the lens (or the prompting device in front of it) whenever you intend to establish eye contact with the viewer. As a matter of fact, you should try to look *through* the lens, rather than at it, and keep eye contact much more than you would with an actual person. If you merely look at the lens instead of looking through it, or if you pretend that the camera operator is your audience and therefore glance away from the lens ever so slightly, you break the continuity and intensity of the communication between you and the viewer; you break, however temporarily, television's magic.

Camera switching   If two or more cameras are used, you must know which one is on the air so that you can remain in direct contact with the audience. When the director switches cameras, you must follow the floor

manager's cue (or the change of tally lights) quickly but smoothly. Do not jerk your head from one camera to the other. If you suddenly discover that you have been talking to the wrong one, look down as if to collect your thoughts and then casually glance into the "hot" camera and continue talking in that direction until you are again cued to the other camera. This method works especially well if you work from notes or a script, as in a newscast or interview. You can always pretend to be looking at your notes when, in reality, you are changing your view from the wrong camera to the right one.

In general, it is useful to ask the director or floor manager if there will be many camera changes during the program and approximately when the changes will occur. If the show is scripted, mark all camera changes on your script. You need to see the floor manager at all times so that you can promptly react to his or her cues.

If the director has one camera on you in a *medium shot (MS)* and the other camera in a *close-up (CU)* of the object you are demonstrating, such as the guest's book during an interview, it is best to keep looking at the medium-shot camera during the whole demonstration, even when the director switches to the close-up camera. You will never be caught looking the wrong way, because only the medium-shot camera is focused on you.   **SEE 16.5** You will also find that it is easier to read the copy off a

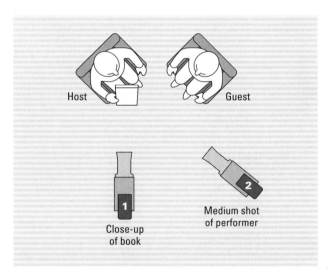

16.5 PERFORMER CAMERA

When one camera (camera 1) is on a close-up of the product (the book), and the other (camera 2) on a medium shot of the host, the host should continue looking into camera 2 during the close-up.

single teleprompter, rather than switch from one to another in midsentence.

Close-up techniques   The tighter the shot, the harder it is for the camera to follow fast movement. If a camera is on a close-up, you must restrict your motions severely and move with great care. Ask the director whether he or she plans close-ups and approximately when. During a song, for example, the director may want to shoot very closely to intensify an especially emotional passage. Try to stand as still as possible; do not wiggle your head. The close-up itself is intensification enough. All you have to do is sing well.

When demonstrating small objects on a close-up, hold them steadily. If they are arranged on a table, do *not* pick them up. You can either point to them or tilt them a little to give the camera a better view. There is nothing more frustrating to the camera operator and the director than a performer who snatches the product off the table just when the camera has a good close-up of it. A quick look at the studio monitor usually tells you how to hold the object for maximum visibility on-screen. If two cameras are used, "cheat" (orient) the object somewhat toward the close-up camera, but do not turn it so much that it looks unnaturally distorted on the medium-shot camera.

Warning cues   In most nondramatic shows—lectures, demonstrations, interviews—there is generally not enough time to work out a detailed blocking scheme. The director usually just walks the performers through some of the most important crossovers from one performance area to the other and through a few major actions, such as complicated demonstrations. During the on-the-air performance, therefore, you as a performer must give the director and studio crew visual and audible warnings of your unrehearsed actions. Before you stand up, for instance, first shift your weight and position your arms and legs; this signals the camera operator as well as the microphone boom operator to prepare for your move. If you pop up unexpectedly, the camera may stay in one position, focusing on the middle part of your body, which may not make the most interesting shot.

If you intend to move from one set area to another, you may use audio cues. For instance, you can warn the production crew by saying: "Let's go over to the children and ask them…" or "If you will follow me over to the lab area, you can see…" Such cues sound natural to the viewer, who is generally unaware of the fast reactions these seemingly unimportant remarks actually trigger. You must be specific when you cue unrehearsed visual material. For example, you can alert the director to the upcoming visuals by saying: "The first picture shows…" This cuing device should not be used too often, however. If you can alert the director more subtly yet equally directly, do so.

Do not try to convey the obvious. The director, not the talent, runs the show. Don't tell the director to bring the cameras a little closer to get a better view of a small object, especially if the director has already obtained a good close-up through a zoom-in. Also, avoid walking toward the camera to demonstrate an object. You may walk so close to the camera that it has to tilt up into the lights to keep your face in the shot or so close that the zoom lens can no longer focus. The zoom lens allows the camera to get to you much faster than you can get to the camera.

Performer and Audio

As a television performer, besides looking natural and relaxed, you must speak clearly and effectively; it rarely comes as a natural gift. Do not be misled into believing that a resonant voice and affected pronunciation are the two prime requisites for a good announcer or other performer. On the contrary: First, you need to have something important to say; second, you need to say it with conviction and sincerity; third, you must speak clearly so that everyone can understand you. Thorough training in television announcing is an important prerequisite for any performer. Most novice performers speak much too fast, as though they wanted to get through the on-camera torture as quickly as possible. Take a deep breath and *slow down*. You will be amazed how much more relaxed you will be.

Microphone technique   Chapter 9 explores the basic microphone techniques. The following summarizes the main points about handling microphones and assisting the audio technician.

■   Most often you work with a *lavaliere* microphone. Once it is properly fastened, you do not have to worry about it, especially if you are relatively stationary during the performance. If you have to move from one set area to another on-camera, watch that the mic cord does not get tangled up with the set or props. Gently pull the cable behind you to keep the tension off the mic itself. A wireless lavaliere will enable you to move within the performance area without having to worry about a cable.

■ When using a hand mic, check that you have enough cable for your planned actions. Speak *across* it, not into it. If you are interviewing someone in noisy surroundings, such as a downtown street, hold the microphone close to your mouth when you are talking, and then point it toward the person as he or she responds to your questions.

■ When working with a *boom* microphone (including a handheld shotgun or one that is mounted on a fishpole), be aware of the boom movements without letting the audience know. Give the boom operator enough warning so that he or she can anticipate your movements. Move slowly so that the boom can follow. In particular, do not make fast turns, because they involve a great amount of boom movement. If you have to turn fast, try not to speak.

■ Do not move a desk mic once it has been placed by the audio engineer. Even if the microphone is pointing away from you toward another performer, it was probably done purposely to achieve better audio balance.

In all cases, treat the microphone gently. Mics are not intended to be hand props, to be tossed about or twirled by their cords like a lasso, even if you see such misuse occasionally in an especially energetic rock performance.

Audio level   A good audio technician will ask you for an *audio level* before you go on the air. Many performers have the bad habit of rapidly counting to ten or mumbling and speaking softly while the level is being taken, and then, when they go on the air, blasting their opening remarks. If a level is taken, speak as loudly as you will in your opening remarks and as long as required for the audio technician to adjust the volume to an optimal level.

Opening cue   At the beginning of a show, all microphones are dead until the director gives the cue for audio. You must, therefore, wait until you receive the opening cue from the floor manager or through the *I.F.B.* (interruptible foldback, or feedback, system, see chapter 1). If you speak beforehand, you will not be heard. Do not take your opening cue from the red tally lights on the cameras unless you are so instructed. When waiting for the opening cue, look into the camera that is coming up on you and not at the floor manager.

Performer and Timing

Live and live-on-tape television operate on split-second timing. Although the director is ultimately responsible for getting the show on and off on time, you as the performer have a great deal to do with successful timing.

Aside from careful pacing throughout the show, you must learn how much program material you can cover after you have received a three-minute, a two-minute, a one-minute, and a thirty-second cue. You must, for example, still look comfortable and relaxed although you may have to cram a lot of important program material into the last minute while at the same time listening to the director's or producer's I.F.B. On the other hand, you must be prepared to fill an extra thirty seconds without appearing to grasp for words and things to do. This presence of mind, of course, needs practice and cannot be learned solely from a television handbook.

Performer and Postproduction

When you work on a brief commercial or announcement that presents a continuous event but that is shot film-style over a period of several days or even weeks for postproduction, you must look the same in all the videotaping sessions. Obviously, you must wear the same clothes. You must also wear the same jewelry, scarf, shirt, and tie from one taping session to the next. You cannot have your coat buttoned one time and unbuttoned the next. Makeup and hairstyle too must be identical for all sessions. Have Polaroid snapshots taken of yourself from the front, sides, and back immediately after the first taping session for an easy and readily available reference.

Most important, you must maintain the same energy level throughout the taping sessions. For example, you cannot end one session full of energy and then be very low-key the next day when the videotaping resumes, especially when the edited version does not suggest any passage of time between the takes. On repeat takes, try to maintain identical energy levels.

Floor Manager's Cues

Unless you are connected with the producer and the director by I.F.B., it is the floor manager who provides the link between the director and you, the performer. The floor manager can tell you whether your delivery is too slow or too fast, how much time you have left, and whether you are speaking loudly enough or holding an object correctly for the close-up camera.

Although various stations and production houses use slightly different cuing signals and procedures, they normally consist of time cues, directional cues, and audio cues. If you are working with an unfamiliar production crew, ask the floor manager to review the cues before you go on the air. **SEE 16.6**

16.6 FLOOR MANAGER'S CUES

The floor manager uses a set of standard hand signals to relay the director's commands to the on-the-air talent.

CUE	SIGNAL	MEANING	SIGNAL DESCRIPTION
TIME CUES			
Standby		Show about to start.	Extends hand above head.
Cue		Show goes on the air.	Points to performer or live camera.
On time		Go ahead as planned. (On the nose.)	Touches nose with forefinger.
Speed up		Accelerate what you are doing. You are going too slowly.	Rotates hand clockwise with extended forefinger. Urgency of speed-up is indicated by fast or slow rotation.
Stretch		Slow down. Too much time left. Fill until emergency is over.	Stretches imaginary rubber band between hands.

16.2 FLOOR MANAGER'S CUES *(continued)*

CUE	SIGNAL	MEANING	SIGNAL DESCRIPTION
TIME CUES			
Wind up		Finish up what you are doing. Come to an end.	Similar motion to speed-up, but usually with extended arm above head. Sometimes expressed with raised fist, good-bye wave, or hands rolling over each other as if wrapping a package.
Cut		Stop speech or action immediately.	Pulls index finger in knifelike motion across throat.
5 (4, 3, 2, 1) minute(s)		5 (4, 3, 2, 1) minute(s) left until end of show.	Holds up five (four, three, two, one) finger(s) or small card with number on it.
Half minute		30 seconds left in show.	Forms a cross with two index fingers or arms. Or holds card with number.
15 seconds		15 seconds left in show.	Shows fist (which can also mean wind up). Or holds card with number.
Roll VTR (and countdown) 2-1 Take VTR		VTR is rolling. Tape is coming up.	Holds extended left hand in front of face, moves right hand in cranking motion. Extends two, one finger(s); clenches fist or gives cut signal.

16.2 FLOOR MANAGER'S CUES *(continued)*

CUE	SIGNAL	MEANING	SIGNAL DESCRIPTION
DIRECTIONAL CUES			
Closer		Performer must come closer or bring object closer to camera.	Moves both hands toward self, palms in.
Back		Performer must step back or move object away from camera.	Uses both hands in pushing motion, palms out.
Walk		Performer must move to next performance area.	Makes a walking motion with index and middle fingers in direction of movement.
Stop		Stop right here. Do not move any more.	Extends both hands in front of body, palms out.
OK		Very well done. Stay right there. Do what you are doing.	Forms an *O* with thumb and forefinger, other fingers extended, motioning toward talent.

16.2 FLOOR MANAGER'S CUES *(continued)*

CUE	SIGNAL	MEANING	SIGNAL DESCRIPTION
AUDIO CUES			
Speak up		Performer is talking too softly for present conditions.	Cups both hands behind ears or moves hand upward, palm up.
Tone down		Performer is too loud or too enthusiastic for the occasion.	Moves both hands toward studio floor, palms down, or puts extended forefinger over mouth in *shhh*-like motion.
Closer to mic		Performer is too far away from mic for good audio pickup.	Moves hand toward face.
Keep talking		Keep on talking until further cues.	Extends thumb and forefinger horizontally, moving them like a bird beak.

React to each cue immediately, even if you think it is not appropriate at that particular time. The director would not give the cue if it were not necessary. A truly professional performer is not one who never needs cues, but rather one who can react to all signals quickly and smoothly.

Do not look nervously for the floor manager if you think you should have received a cue; he or she will find you and draw your attention to the signal. When you receive a cue, do not acknowledge it in any way. The floor manager will know whether you noticed it or not.

You will find that receiving and reacting to I.F.B. information during a performance is no easy task. We all know how difficult it can be to continue a telephone conversation when someone is trying to tell us what else to communicate to the other party. But when reporting news in the studio or in the field, such simultaneous

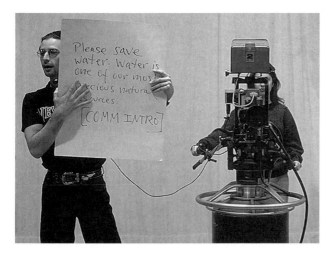 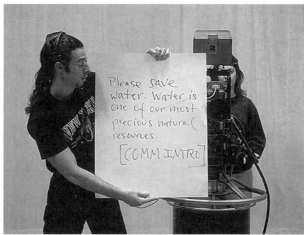

16.7 HANDLING CUE CARDS

A This is the wrong way to hold a cue card: The card is too far away from the lens, and the hands cover part of the copy. The floor person cannot see the copy and does not know when to go to the next card.

B This is the correct way to hold a cue card: The floor person does not cover the copy, holds the card close to the lens, and can read along with the talent.

communication is common. You must learn to listen carefully to the I.F.B. instructions of the director or producer without letting the audience know that you are listening to someone else while talking to them. Do not interrupt your communication with the audience when getting I.F.B. instructions, even if the transmission is less than perfect. If, for example, during a live remote you can't understand at all what is being said on the I.F.B. channel, you may have to stop your narration to tell the audience that you are getting some important information from your director. Listen carefully to the I.F.B. instructions and then go on with what you were saying. Try not to adjust your earpiece while on the air. If at all possible, wait until the camera cuts away from you to do an adjustment.

Prompting Devices

Prompting devices have become an essential production tool, especially for news or speeches. The audience has come to expect the newscaster to talk directly to them rather than read the news from a script, although we all know that the newscaster does not ad-lib. We expect speakers to deliver long and complicated information without having to think about what to say next. Prompting devices are also helpful to performers who fear they may suddenly forget their lines or who have no time to memorize a script.

The prompting devices must be totally reliable, and the performer must be able to read the prompting copy without appearing to lose eye contact with the viewer. Two devices have proved especially successful: cue cards and the teleprompter.

Cue cards Used for relatively short pieces of copy, there are many types *cue cards*, and the choice depends largely on what the performer is used to and what he or she prefers. Usually, they are fairly large posterboards on which the copy is hand-lettered with a felt-tipped marker. The size of the cards and the lettering depends on how well the performer can see and how far away the camera is. Even the handling of cue cards is not as easy as it would seem. A good floor person holds the cards as close to the lens as possible, the hands do not cover any of the copy, and he or she follows the performer's lines in order to change from one card to the next. **SEE 16.7**

As a performer you must learn to glance at the cards without losing eye contact with the lens. In effect, you must learn how to read by peripheral vision. Get together with the floor person handling the cards to double-check their correct order. If the floor person forgets to change them at the appropriate moment, snap your fingers to attract the person's attention; in an emergency you may have to ad-lib until the system is functioning again. You

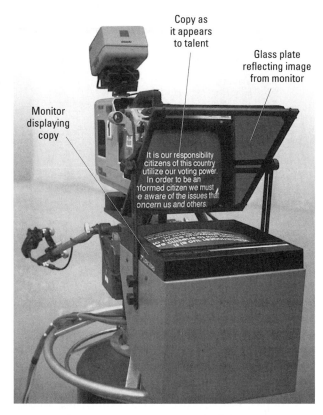

Monitor
displaying
copy

Copy as
it appears
to talent

Glass plate
reflecting image
from monitor

It is our responsibility
citizens of this country
utilize our voting power.
In order to be an
informed citizen we must
e aware of the issues that
oncern us and others.

16.8 TELEPROMPTER DISPLAY OF COPY
The monitor that displays the copy reflects the letters onto a glass plate directly over the lens. The talent can read the copy without losing eye contact with the viewer.

should study the topic long before the show begins, enabling you to ad-lib sensibly at least for a short time. If your performance is shot for postproduction, ask the director to stop the tape so that the cards can be put in the correct order.

Studio teleprompter   The most effective prompting device is the *teleprompter,* which uses a small monitor upon which the scrolling copy is displayed. The monitor screen is then reflected onto a glass angled over the camera lens. You can read the copy, which now appears in front of the lens, while maintaining contact with the viewer (the lens) at all times. **SEE 16.8**

Most often the copy is typed into a computer that acts as a combination word processor/character generator. It

can produce the text in several font sizes and scroll (usually referred to as "crawl") the copy up and down the screen at various speeds. The copy is then sent to the teleprompter monitor mounted on the camera. All cameras shooting the talent display the same copy.

In newscasts the anchorperson should have the text as it appears on the teleprompter also written out as *hard copy.* This script serves as backup in case the prompting device fails. Also, such copy gives the anchor a reason to glance down to indicate a story transition or to change cameras, or to see during a commercial break what is coming up next.

When using a teleprompter, the distance between you and the camera is no longer arbitrary. The camera must be close enough for you to read the copy without squinting, but not so close that the home viewer can see your eyes moving back and forth in an obvious reading motion. If the minimum camera distance is too far to see the teleprompter copy comfortably, have the font size made bigger.

ENG EFP **Field prompter**   Have you ever wondered how some correspondents can stand on a busy city street and report a well-written story without ever stumbling or searching for words? Although some certainly have that skill, others use some kind of prompting device. If the copy is brief, handheld cue cards or even some notes will do. Longer copy calls for a *field prompter.*

There are several models of field prompters, including a miniature version of the studio teleprompter. Most high-end field prompters can be hooked up to a laptop computer that has prompting software installed. You can adjust the size of the font, and scroll the copy up and down the screen at various speeds. Low-end prompters use a paper roll mounted immediately below or to one side of the lens. A small electric motor rolls the hand-lettered copy from the bottom to the top at various speeds. In more-elaborate models, the copy is back-lighted and projected onto a piece of clear plastic mounted in front of the camera lens, similar to a studio teleprompter. **SEE 16.9**

Similar units can be used independently of the camera and held by a floor person or mounted on a tripod directly above or below the camera lens. Regardless of the quality of the teleprompter, you should always be familiar enough with the subject matter to be able to talk about it intelligently if the device fails.

16.9 FIELD PROMPTER
A lightweight prompter can be mounted on any type of field camera. It projects the text directly over the lens.

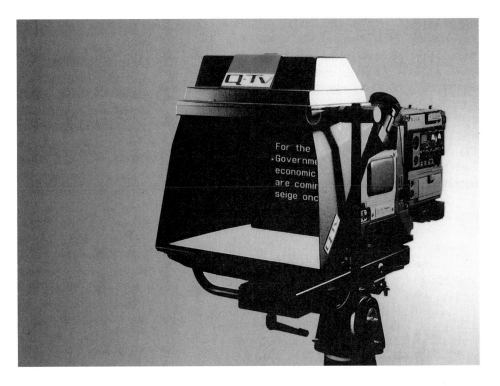

ACTING TECHNIQUES

In contrast to the television performer, the television actor assumes someone else's character and personality. (In this discussion the term *actor* is used generically to refer to both male and female talent.) To become a good television actor, you obviously must first master the art of acting, a subject beyond the scope of this chapter. This discussion focuses on how to adapt your acting to the peculiarities of the television medium. Many excellent actors consider television the most difficult medium in which to work. They must work within an environment crowded with confusing and impersonal technical gear, and often get less attention from the director than do the camera operator and sound technician.

Audience

The biggest difference between stage acting and screen acting is that you are not playing for a stationary live audience but rather for a constantly moving camera that never blinks or offers feedback on your performance. Worse, your performance is chopped up into short takes that rarely, if ever, allow you to work up to a memorable performance pitch. Each of the little performance segments must be on the mark. In most takes the camera moves around you, looking at you at close range and from a distance as well as from above and from below. It may look at your eyes, your feet, your hands, your back—whatever the director selects for the audience to see. And at all times you must look completely convincing and natural; the character you are portraying must appear on-screen as a believable human being. Keep in mind that you are playing to a camera lens, not to an audience; you need not (and should not) project your motions and emotions as you would when acting onstage. The television camera does the projecting—the communicating—for you.

Internalization of your role, as opposed to externalization, is a key factor in your performance. You must attempt to become as much as possible the person you are portraying, rather than act out the character. Because of the close scrutiny of the camera and the intimacy of the close-up, your reactions become as important as your actions. You can often communicate feelings more readily by reacting to a situation than by contributing to it through action.

Blocking

You must be extremely exact in following rehearsed *blocking*—where you should move and what you should do in relation to the set, the other actors, and the television equipment. Sometimes inches are significant, especially if the cameras are set up for special effects. The director may, for instance, want to use your arm as a frame for a background scene or position you for a complicated over-the-shoulder shot. Precise television lighting and the limited microphone radius when booms are used also force you to adhere strictly to the established blocking.

Once the show is on the air, you have an obligation to follow the rehearsed action carefully. This is not the time to innovate just because you have a sudden inspiration. If the director has not been warned of your change, the new blocking will always be worse than the previously rehearsed one. The camera has a limited field of view; if you want to be seen, you must stay within it.

Some directors will have the floor manager mark the exact spots for you to stand or the paths of movement. Look for these tape or chalk marks and follow them without being too obvious. If such blocking marks are not used, establish a "blocking map" by remembering where you stand for specific shots in relation to the set and props. For example, for your scene with the office manager you stand to the left of the file cabinet; for the scene in the doctor's office, you walk counterclockwise around the desk and stop at the camera-right corner of the desk.

In over-the-shoulder and cross shots, you need to see the camera lens if you are to be in the shot. If you cannot see the lens, the camera cannot see you. Even the lighting instruments can help you with blocking. For example, when coming through a door, move forward until you feel the warmth of the lights on your forehead.

Sometimes the director will position you in a way that looks entirely wrong to you, especially in relation to the other actors. Do not try to correct this on your own by arbitrarily moving away from the designated spot. A certain camera angle and zoom-lens position may very well warrant unusual blocking to achieve a certain effect.

When you are handling props, the television camera is often on a close-up. This means that you must remember all the rehearsed actions and execute them in exactly the same way and with the same speed as they were initially rehearsed. Don't appear nervous when using props (unless the director calls for it), but handle them routinely as extensions of your gestures. The way you handle props, such as taking off your glasses, cleaning them, and putting them on again, can often intensify your character.

Memorizing Lines

As a television actor, you must be able to learn your lines quickly and accurately. If, as is the case in soap operas, you have only one evening to learn a great amount of lines for the next day, you must indeed be a quick study. You cannot ad-lib during such performances simply because you have acted the role for so long. Although shorter, commercial copy may require accurate character portrayal and precise delivery of lines. Most of your lines are important not only from a dramatic point of view but also because they serve as video and audio cues for the whole production team. Your last line of a speech is often a trigger for several key actions in the control room: to switch to another camera, to roll a videotape insert, or to call up a special effect.

When acting for a single-camera EFP or film-style studio production, each shot is set up and recorded separately. Such a production approach often gives you a chance to read over and memorize the lines for each take. Although this approach may make it easier to remember lines, it is harder to maintain continuity of action and emotion. Good television actors do not rely on prompting devices; after all, you should live, not read, your role.

Timing

Just like the performer, as a television actor you must have an acute sense of timing. Timing matters for pacing your performance, for building to a climax, for delivering a punch line, and also for staying within a tightly prescribed clock time. Even if a play is videotaped scene by scene, you still need to observe carefully the stipulated running times for each take. You may have to stretch a scene without making it appear to drag, or you may have to gain ten seconds by speeding up a scene without destroying its solemn character. You must be flexible without stepping out of character.

As stated, always respond immediately to the floor manager's cues. Do not stop in the middle of a scene simply because you disagree with one. Play the scene to the end and then complain. Minor timing errors can often be corrected in postproduction.

The Actor and Postproduction

As you know, most television plays are videotaped piecemeal, which means that you are not able to perform a play from beginning to end as in a theater production. As pointed out, you simply cannot be upbeat during the first part of the videotaping and then, a week later when the scene is continued, project a low-energy mood. Often scenes are shot out of sequence for production efficiency and, ultimately, to save money, so it is not possible to have a continuous and logical development of emotions, as is possible in a continuous live or live-on-tape pickup. Scenes are inevitably repeated to make them better or to achieve various fields of view and camera angles. This means that, as an actor, you cannot psych yourself up for one superb performance. Rather, you need to maintain your energy and motivation for each take. Television unfailingly detects subtle nuances and levels of energy and the accompanying acting continuity (or lack thereof).

One of the most important qualities to watch for when continuing a scene that was started some days before is the *tempo* of your performance. If you moved slowly in the first part of the scene, do not race through the second part, unless the director wants such a change. It usually helps to watch a videotape of your previous performance so that you can continue the scene with the same energy level and tempo. *READY ZVL* ❸

The Director/Actor Relationship

As a television actor, you cannot afford to be temperamental. There are too many people who have to be coordinated by the director. Although you as an actor are an extremely significant element in the production, other production people are too—the camera operators, the TD, the audio technician, and the *LD (lighting director)*, to name but a few.

But even if you do not intend to become a television actor, you should make an effort to learn as much about acting as possible. An able actor is generally an effective television performer; a television director with training in acting is generally better equipped to deal with talent than one who has no knowledge of the art.

AUDITIONS

All auditions are equally important, whether you try out for a one-line off-camera utterance or a principal role in a dramatic series. Whenever you audition give your best—prepare yourself, even if you do not know beforehand what you will be reading. Wear something appropriate that looks good on-camera, and be properly groomed. Keep your energy up even if you have to wait half a day before you are called to utter your line.

If you get the script beforehand, study it carefully. For example, if you are doing a commercial for a soft drink, become as familiar as possible with the product, the

company that makes it, and the advertising agency producing the commercial. Knowing about the product gives you a certain confidence that inevitably shows up in your delivery. Listen carefully to the instructions given to you before or during the audition. Remember that television is an intimate medium.

When instructed to demonstrate a product, practice before you are on-camera to make sure you know how, for example, to open an easy-to-open package. Ask the floor crew to help you prepare a product for easy handling. Also, ask the director how close the camera will be so that you can keep your actions within camera range.

As an actor be sure to understand thoroughly the character you are to portray. If the script does not tell you much about the character, ask the director or producer to explain how he or she perceives it. You should be able to sense the specifics of the character even when given only minimal cues. Decide on a behavior pattern and follow it, even if your interpretation may be somewhat off base. If the director's perceptions run counter to your interpretation, do not argue. Most important, do not ask the casting director to provide you with the "proper motivation," as you may have learned in acting school. At this point it is assumed that you can analyze the script and motivate yourself for the reading. Realize that you are auditioned primarily on how well and how quickly you perceive the script's image of the character and how close you can come to it in speech and sometimes also in actions.

Be creative without overdoing it. When auditions were held for the male lead in a television play about a lonely woman and a rather crude and unscrupulous man who wanted to take advantage of her, one of the actors added a little of his own interpretation of the character that eventually got him the part. While reading an intimate scene in which he was supposed to persuade the leading lady to make love to him, he manicured his fingernails with slightly rusty fingernail clippers. In fact, this aggravating fingernail clipping was later written into the scene.

Finally, when auditioning—as when participating in athletics or any competitive activity—be aware, but not afraid, of the competition. Talent is not always the deciding factor in casting a part. Sometimes the director may have a particular image in mind of the physical appearance and behavior of the actor—heavy, awkward, light and agile, muscular or skinny—that overrides acting skill. Or a well-known actor who can guarantee a large audience may win out. As an actor you need to be prepared to take it repeatedly on the chin.

MAIN POINTS

- The production personnel are primarily concerned with the nontechnical elements of production, such as script writing and directing. They are normally classified as above-the-line personnel.

- The technical production personnel are primarily concerned with the operation and maintenance of the equipment. They are normally among the below-the-line personnel.

- The news production personnel are assigned exclusively to the production of news and special events.

- Regardless of the specific job functions of the technical and nontechnical personnel, they all have to interact as a team.

- Television talent refers to all persons who perform regularly in front of the camera. They are classified into two large groups: performers and actors.

- Television performers are basically engaged in nondramatic shows, such as newscasts, interviews, and game shows. They portray themselves. Television actors portray someone else.

- The television performer must adapt his or her techniques to the characteristics of the camera and other production elements, including audio, timing, postproduction, the floor manager's cues, and prompting devices.

- Because the camera lens represents the audience, performers must look *through* the lens to establish and maintain eye contact with the viewer. If cameras are switched, performers must switch over to the hot camera naturally and smoothly.

- Timing is an important performance requirement. A good performer must respond quickly yet smoothly to the floor manager's time, directional, and audio cues.

- Prompting devices have become essential in television production. The two most frequently used devices are cue cards and the teleprompter.

- Television acting requires that the actor overcome the lack of an actual audience and internalize the role; restrict gestures and movements because of close-ups; follow exactly the rehearsed blocking; memorize lines quickly; have a good sense of timing; maintain continuity in physical appearance and energy level over a series of shooting sessions; and maintain a positive attitude despite an occasional neglect by the director.

- Performers and actors should prepare as much as possible for auditions, dress properly for the occasion (role), and sharpen the character through some prop or mannerism.

16.2

How to Do Makeup and What to Wear

When you hear of makeup, you may think of movies in which actors are transformed into monsters or odd-looking aliens, or of how to fake a variety of wounds. You may even argue that the way performers or actors look is less important than the substance of what they say or do. But most television makeup is done not so much to transform appearance as to make someone look as good as possible on-camera. The same goes for clothing. Unless you act in a period play, most actors wear clothes that fit the role, and performers choose clothes that make them look attractive on-camera.

The aim of section 16.2 is to help you choose makeup, clothing, or costumes that not only fit, but also add to, the overall production values and communication intent.

▶ **MAKEUP**
   Technical requirements, materials, and techniques

▶ **CLOTHING AND COSTUMING**
   Line, texture and detail, and color

MAKEUP

All *makeup* is used for three basic reasons: to enhance appearance, to correct appearance, and to change appearance.

Standard over-the-counter makeup is used daily by many women to accentuate and improve their features. Minor skin blemishes are covered up, and the eyes and lips are emphasized. Makeup can also be used to correct closely or widely spaced eyes, sagging flesh under the chin, a short or long nose, a slightly too prominent forehead, and many similar minor "faults." If a person is to portray a specific character in a play, a complete change of appearance may be necessary. Dramatic changes of age, race, and character can be accomplished through creative makeup techniques.

The various purposes for applying cosmetics require different techniques, of course. Enhancing someone's appearance calls for the least complicated procedure; correcting someone's appearance is slightly more complicated; and changing an actor's appearance may require involved and complex makeup methods.

Most minor productions require only makeup that enhances the appearance of a performer. More-complicated makeup work, such as making a young actor look eighty years old, is left to the professional makeup artist. You need not learn all about corrective and character makeup methods, but you should have some idea of the basic technical requirements, materials, and techniques of television makeup.

Technical Requirements

Like so many other production elements, makeup too must yield to some of the demands of the television camera. These limitations include color distortion, color balance, and close-ups.

Color distortion

As pointed out earlier, skin tones are the only real color references the viewer has for color adjustment on a home receiver. Their accurate rendering is therefore of the utmost importance. Because cool colors (hues with a blue tint) have a tendency to overemphasize bluishness, especially in high-color-temperature lighting, warm colors (warm reds, oranges, browns, and tans) are preferred for television makeup. They usually provide more sparkle, especially when used on a dark-skinned face.

The color of the basic *foundation* makeup should match the natural skin tones as closely as possible, regardless of whether the face is naturally light or naturally dark. Again, to avoid bluish shadows, warm rather than cool foundation colors are preferred. Be careful, however, that light-colored skin does not turn pink. As much as you should guard against too much blue in a dark face, you must watch for too much pink in a light face.

The skin reflectance of a dark face can produce unflattering highlights. These should be toned down by a proper pancake foundation or a translucent powder. Otherwise, the video operator will have to compensate for the highlights through shading, making the dark picture areas unnaturally dense.

Color balance

Generally, the art director, scene designer, makeup artist, and costume designer coordinate all the colors in production meetings. In nonbroadcast productions, where freelance people are usually hired for scene design and makeup, such coordination is not always easy. In any case, try to communicate the various color requirements to all these people as best you can. Some attention beforehand to the coordination of the colors used in the scenery, costumes, and makeup certainly facilitates the whole production process.

Sometimes the surrounding colors reflect on the performer's clothing or face, which the camera picks up

and shows as noticeable color distortions. One way of avoiding such reflections is to have the talent step far enough away from the reflecting surfaces. When such a move is not possible, apply an adequate amount of *pancake* makeup and additional powder to the discolored skin areas. The viewer will tolerate to some extent the color distortion on clothing, but not on skin areas.

Close-ups

Television makeup must be smooth and subtle enough so that the performer's or actor's face looks natural even in an extreme close-up. The skin should have a normal sheen, neither too oily (high reflectance) nor too dull (low reflectance but no brilliance—the skin looks lifeless). The subtlety of television makeup goes directly against theater makeup techniques, in which features and colors are greatly exaggerated for the benefit of the spectator in the back row. Good television makeup remains largely invisible, so a close-up of a person's face under actual production lighting conditions is the best criterion for judging the necessity for and quality of makeup. If the performer or actor looks good on-camera without makeup, none is needed. If the performer needs makeup and the close-up of his or her finished face looks normal, the makeup is acceptable. If it looks artificial, the makeup must be redone.

All makeup must be applied under the lighting conditions in which the production is taped. This is because each lighting setup has its own color temperature. Reddish light may require some cooler (more bluish) makeup than when higher-color-temperature lighting is used, which, in turn, may require some warmer (more reddish) makeup. (For a review of color temperature, see chapter 7.)

Materials

A great variety of excellent television makeup material is available. Most makeup artists in the theater arts department of a college or university have up-to-date product lists. In fact, most large drugstores can supply you with the basic materials for enhancing a performer's appearance. Women performers are generally experienced in cosmetic materials and techniques; men may, at least initially, need some advice.

The most basic makeup item is a *foundation* that covers minor skin blemishes and cuts down light reflections on oily skin. Water-based cake makeup foundations, generally referred to as *pancake*, are preferred over the more cumbersome grease-based foundations, called ***pan stick***. The Krylon CTV-1W through CTV-12W pancake series is probably all you need for most makeup jobs. The colors range from a warm, light ivory to dark shades for dark-skinned performers.

Women can use their own lipsticks, so long as the reds do not contain too much blue. For dark-skinned talent, a warm red, such as coral, is often more effective than a darker red that contains a great amount of blue. Other materials, such as eyebrow pencil, mascara, and eye shadow, are generally part of every woman performer's makeup kit. Materials such as hair pieces or even latex masks are part of the professional makeup artist's inventory. They are of little use in most nondramatic productions.

Techniques

It is not always easy to persuade nonprofessional performers, especially men, to put on necessary makeup. You may do well to look at the guests on-camera before deciding whether they need any. If they do, you must be tactful in suggesting its application. Try to appeal not to the performer's vanity but, rather, to his or her desire to contribute to a good performance. Explain the necessity for makeup in technical terms, such as color and light balance.

All makeup rooms have large mirrors so that talent can watch the entire makeup procedure. Adequate, even illumination is critical. Again, the color temperature of the light in which the makeup is applied must match, or at least closely approximate, that of the production illumination. Most makeup rooms have two illumination systems that can be switched from the indoor (3,200°K) standard to the outdoor (5,600°K) standard.

When makeup is applied in the studio, have a small hand mirror on hand. Most women performers are glad to apply the more complicated makeup themselves—lipstick and mascara, for instance. In fact, most professional television talent prefer to apply their makeup themselves; they usually know what kind they need for a specific television show.

When using a water-based pancake makeup, apply it evenly with a wet sponge over the face and adjacent exposed skin areas. Get the base right up into the hairline, and have a towel ready to wipe off the excess. If close-ups of hands are shown, apply pancake base to them and the arms. This is especially important for performers who demonstrate small objects on-camera. If an uneven suntan is exposed (especially when women performers wear backless dresses or different kinds of bathing suits) all bare skin areas must be covered with base makeup. Bald men need a generous amount of pancake foundation to tone down obvious light reflections and to cover up perspiration.

Be careful not to give male performers a baby-face complexion through too much makeup. It is sometimes desirable to have a little beard area show. Frequently, a slight covering up of the beard with a pan stick is all that is needed. If additional makeup foundation is necessary, a pan-stick foundation around the beard area should be applied first and then set with powder. A very light application of a yellow or orange greasepaint satisfactorily counteracts the blue of a heavy five-o'clock shadow. There are professional beard covers available, such as the Krylon RCMA BC-2.

Because your face is the most expressive communication agent, try to keep your hair out of your face as much as possible.

CLOTHING AND COSTUMING

In small-station operations and most nonbroadcast productions, you are concerned mainly with clothing the performer rather than costuming the actor. The performer's clothes should be attractive and stylish but not too conspicuous or showy. Television viewers expect a performer to be well dressed but not overdressed. After all, he or she is a guest in the viewer's home, not a nightclub performer.

Clothing

The type of clothing a performer wears depends largely on his or her personal taste. It also depends on the type of program or the occasion and the particular setting. Obviously, you dress differently when reporting live in the field on icy road conditions than when taking part on a panel discussion on the speed limit in your state.

Whatever the occasion, some types of clothing look better on television than others. Because the camera may look at you from both a distance and close range, the lines, texture, and details are as important as the overall color scheme.

Line   Television has a tendency to put a few extra pounds on the performer. Clothing cut to a slim silhouette helps combat this problem. Slim dresses and closely tailored suits look more attractive than heavy, horizontally striped material and baggy styles. The overall silhouette of the clothing should look pleasing from a variety of angles and should appear slim-fitting yet comfortable.

Texture and detail   Whereas line is especially important in long shots, the texture and detail of clothing become important at close range. Textured material often looks better than plain, but avoid patterns that have too much contrast or are too busy. Closely spaced geometric patterns such as herringbone weaves and checks cause a *moiré effect,* which looks like superimposed vibrating rainbow colors (see color plate 5). Stripes may extend beyond the clothing fabric and bleed through surrounding sets and objects. Extremely fine detail in a pattern will either look too busy or appear smudgy.

Make your clothing more interesting on-camera not by choosing a detailed cloth texture, but by adding decorative accessories, such as scarves and jewelry. Although jewelry style depends, of course, on the performer's taste, in general, he or she should limit it to one or two distinctive pieces. The sparkle of rhinestones can become an exciting visual accent when dressing for a special occasion, such as the televised fund-raising dinner or a concert by the community symphony. But they are obviously out of place when interviewing homeless people.

Color   The most important consideration for clothing colors is that they harmonize with the set. If the set is lemon yellow, do not wear a lemon yellow dress. If you are taking part in chroma keying (such as in weathercasting), avoid wearing blue unless you want to become transparent during the chroma key. Even a blue scarf or tie may give you trouble. In any case, avoid wearing red.

You can wear black or a very dark color, or white or a very light color, so long as the material is not glossy and highly reflective. But avoid wearing a combination of the two. If the set is very dark, avoid a starched white shirt. If the set colors are extremely light, do not wear black. As desirable as a dramatic color contrast is, extreme brightness variations cause difficulties for even the best cameras. Stark white, glossy clothes can turn exposed skin areas dark on the television screen or distort the more subtle colors. Dark-skinned performers should avoid highly reflecting white or light-yellow clothes. If you wear a dark suit, reduce the brightness contrast by wearing a

pastel shirt. Light blue, pink, light green, tan, or gray all show up well on television.

As noted earlier, stay away from highly saturated reds. Even digital cameras have trouble reproducing reds unless there is plenty of available light. Under less favorable conditions, saturated reds have a tendency to "crawl" (move beyond the borders of the red clothing) and bleed into adjacent areas.

As always, when in doubt as to how well a certain color combination photographs, preview it on-camera on the set and under the actual lighting conditions.

If two prospective weathercasters—a man and a woman—were to ask you for advice on what to wear, what would you tell them? Both should wear something comfortable that does not look wide or baggy. Because of chroma keying, avoid wearing anything blue. If possible, tell them the color of the set background so they can avoid wearing the same color.

The woman might wear a slim suit or dress of plain, simple colors. Avoid black-and-white combinations, such as a black jacket over a highly reflecting white blouse. She should avoid highly contrasting narrow stripes or checkered patterns and wear as little jewelry as possible, unless she wants to appear flashy.

The man might wear a slim suit or slacks and a plain coat, with a plain tie or one with a subtle pattern. He should avoid wearing a white shirt under a black or dark blue suit, as well as clothes with checkered or herringbone patterns.

Costuming

For most normal productions in nonbroadcast, or nonnetwork, operations, you do not need costumes. If you do a play or a commercial that involves actors, you can always rent the necessary articles from a costume company or borrow them from the theater arts department of a local high school or college. Theater arts departments usually have a well-stocked costume room from which you can draw most standard uniforms and period costumes. If you use stock costumes on television, they must look convincing even in a tight close-up. Sometimes the general construction and, especially, the detail of theater accessories are too coarse for the television camera.

The color and pattern restrictions for clothing also apply for costumes. The total color design—the overall balance of colors among scenery, costumes, and makeup—is important in some television plays, particularly in musicals and variety shows, where long shots often reveal the total scene, including actors, dancers, scenery, and props. Rather than try to balance all the hues, it is often easier to balance the colors by their relative aesthetic energy. You can accomplish this balance by keeping the set relatively low-energy (colors with low saturation) and the set accessories and costumes of actors high-energy (high-saturation colors).

MAIN POINTS

◆ Makeup and clothing (or costuming) are important aspects of the talent's preparation for on-camera work.

◆ Makeup is used for three basic reasons: to enhance, to correct, and to change appearance.

◆ Warm colors generally look better than cool colors, because the camera tends to emphasize the bluishness of cool colors. But avoid wearing red.

◆ Makeup must be smooth and subtle to appear natural in the actual production lighting and on extreme close-ups. The most basic makeup item is a foundation that covers minor blemishes. Water-based pancake foundations, which come in a variety of skin tones, are generally used for television makeup.

◆ The techniques of television makeup do not differ drastically from applying ordinary makeup, especially if the purpose is to enhance or correct appearance.

◆ These factors are important when choosing clothing: line, whereby a slim cut is to be preferred; texture and detail, which must not make the clothing appear too busy; and color, which should harmonize yet contrast with the dominant color of the set. Tightly striped or checkered patterns and herringbone weaves, as well as highly saturated reds and a combination of black and white material, should be avoided.

ZETTL'S VIDEOLAB 2.1

This portion of Zettl's VideoLab 2.1 will help you identify the specific functions of the nontechnical and technical production people.

RUN ZVL 1 Click on the **process** monitor and run tape 7 **People**. Click on the **Non-technical** module. Move your cursor over the particular job title that is framed and read the functions as they appear in the window.

RUN ZVL 2 Now click on the **Technical** module. Move your cursor over the particular job title that is framed and read the functions as they appear in the window.

RUN ZVL 3 Click on each of the five monitors and run tape 1 of each. Watch again what the five mentors have to say. Watch their further performances. Except for Herb, they are not the production people they claim to be, but skilled actors. Try to identify the acting techniques that make them convincing. If you were a director, what recommendations, if any, would you make to perfect their craft?

17

Producing

As a producer you have to wear many hats, sometimes all at once. You may have to act as a psychologist and a businessperson to persuade management to buy your idea, argue as a technical expert for a certain piece of equipment, or search as a sociologist to identify the needs and desires of a particular social group. After some sweeping creative excursions, you may have to become pedantic and double- and triple-check details such as whether there is enough coffee for the guests who appear on your show.

Section 17.1, What Producing Is All About, examines the techniques involved in the various stages of producing a television show. Section 17.2, Dealing with Schedules, Legal Matters, and Ratings, looks at some production activities that lie outside the area of production techniques, which, nevertheless, are important activities for a producer.

demographics Audience research factors concerned with such items as age, sex, marital status, and income.

effect-to-cause model Moving from idea to desired effect on the viewer, and then backing up to the specific medium requirements to produce such an effect.

facilities request A list that contains all technical facilities needed for a specific production.

medium requirements All content elements, production elements, and people needed to generate the process message.

process message The message actually received by the viewer in the process of watching a television program.

program proposal Written document that outlines the process message and the major aspects of a television presentation.

psychographics Audience research factors concerned with such items as consumer buying habits, values, and lifestyles.

rating Percentage of television households with their sets tuned to a specific station in relation to the total number of television households.

share Percentage of television households tuned to a specific station in relation to all households using television (HUT); that is, all households with their sets turned on.

target audience The audience selected or desired to receive a specific message.

treatment Brief narrative description of a television program.

17.1

What Producing Is All About

Producing means seeing to it that a worthwhile idea gets to be a worthwhile television presentation. As a producer you are in charge of this idea-to-presentation process and for completing the various tasks on time and within budget. You are responsible for the concept, financing, hiring, and overall coordination of production activities—not an easy job, by any means!

Although each production has its own creative and organizational requirements, there are nevertheless techniques, or at least approaches, that you can apply to television production in general. These methods can help guide you from the early stages of generating ideas to final postproduction activities.

Section 17.1 walks you through these major production steps.

▶ **PREPRODUCTION PLANNING: FROM IDEA TO SCRIPT**
  Program ideas, production models, program proposal, budget, and script

▶ **PREPRODUCTION PLANNING: COORDINATION**
  People, facilities request, schedules, permits and clearances, and publicity and promotion

▶ **PRODUCTION: HOST AND CRITICAL OBSERVATION**
  Playing host, watching the production flow, and evaluating the production

▶ **POSTPRODUCTION ACTIVITIES**
  Postproduction editing, evaluation and feedback, and recordkeeping

PREPRODUCTION PLANNING: FROM IDEA TO SCRIPT

As a producer you are primarily concerned with preproduction planning and coordination. It is up to you to take care of all the production details necessary to move from the initial idea to the actual production activities with precision and efficiency.

Most producers complain about the lack of time and money available for their productions. Although you could always use more time and a bigger budget than you have available, you must learn to deliver high-quality television programming even within such restrictions. Once you have acquired a certain production routine, you will find that more time and money does not necessarily make for a better show, especially if the initial idea is weak. To help you become maximally efficient and effective in your preproduction activities, we focus here on (1) program ideas, (2) production models, (3) program proposal, (4) budget, and (5) script.

Program Ideas

Everything you see and hear on television started with an idea. As simple as this may sound, developing good and especially workable show ideas on a regular basis is not always easy. As a television producer, you cannot wait for the occasional divine inspiration, but must generate worthwhile ideas on demand.

Generating ideas   Despite the volumes of studies written on the creative process, exactly how ideas are generated remains a mystery. Sometimes you will find that you have one great idea after another; at other times you cannot think of anything exciting, regardless of how hard you try. You can break through this idea drought by engaging several people to do *brainstorming:* Have everybody sit around in a circle and put a small audiotape recorder in the middle. Start the brainstorming session with something as neutral and wide open as, for example: "Knock, knock!" The next person in line will probably say: "Who's there?" and you are on your way. Do not criticize anything anyone says, even if it seems totally unrelated to the previous comments. The aim of brainstorming is to break the conceptual blocks, and not yield to, or even reinforce, them.

When you have finished the brainstorming session, you can play back the comments and pick some that seem relevant to the task at hand. You may find that the so-called absurd comments can trigger workable ideas more readily than the ones that seemed more appropriate. For example, if in a brainstorming session for a shampoo commercial the comments move from "soap bubbles," "rainbow colors," and "umbrella," suddenly to "Einstein," this unexpected switch may well suggest a different direction. Instead of seeing tiny rainbow-colored soap bubbles or gentle rain as possible images for the commercial, your visualization is now shifted to wild hair that is hard to tame.

A more structured way of generating ideas is called *clustering,* a kind of brainstorming whereby you write down your ideas rather than say them aloud. To begin you write a single keyword, such as *shampoo,* and circle it. You then spin off idea clusters that somehow relate to the initial keyword. **SEE 17.1**

As you can see, clustering is a more organized, but also a slightly more restrictive, means of brainstorming.

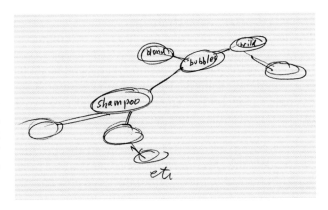

17.1 PARTIAL CLUSTER

Clustering is a form of written brainstorming. You start with a central idea and branch out to whatever associations come to mind.

But because clustering shows patterns better than brainstorming does, it serves well as a structuring technique. Although clustering is usually done by individuals, you can easily have a group of people engage in clustering and then collect the results for closer scrutiny.

Organizing ideas   Once you have decided on the general program idea, you can ask other production people to help with fleshing out the details. Assume for a moment that the general idea is to do a program series on senior citizens. In the organizing stage, you may have one person make a list of possible celebrity guests who are advanced in years and who could talk about the joys and problems of aging. Another colleague could list all the social, legal, transportation, and health services available for the elderly. A third person could think up ways in which local senior citizens could participate in the program.

There is no single or correct formula for organizing ideas and translating them into an effective television program. Because production involves a great number of diverse yet connected activities, you learn its function most profitably by considering it as an interlinking process. In the production process, as in any other, various elements and activities interact with one another to achieve the desired product—a program that affects the viewer in a certain way. The process helps you determine which people you require, what they should do, and what equipment is necessary to produce a specific program. *READY ZVL* ➊

Production Models

Production models describe the flow of activities necessary to move from the idea to the televised message. They help you organize the production process and facilitate your coordination efforts. The effect-to-cause model, for example, streamlines your preproduction and makes your production activities more goal-directed and efficient.

Effect-to-cause model   As do most other production models, the *effect-to-cause model* starts with a basic idea; but instead of moving from the basic idea directly to the production process, it jumps to the desired communication effect on the target audience. Because this communication effect is generated by a process of the viewer watching and listening to television messages, we call this effect the *process message*. After all, it is the desired communication effect—the process message—that should drive the production process, rather than the initial idea. This means that as a producer you should know exactly what you want to achieve—what you want the target audience to learn, do, and feel—before deciding on the specific *medium requirements* that would lead to such an effect. The more the actual process message (viewer effect) matches the defined one, the more successful the communication. **SEE 17.2**

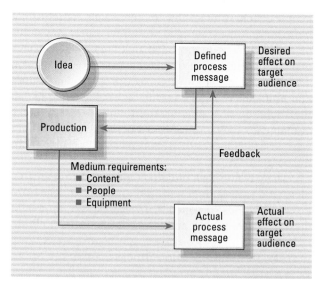

17.2 EFFECT-TO-CAUSE PRODUCTION MODEL
The effect-to-cause production model jumps from the initial idea directly to the desired effect—the process message. Then it backs up to the medium requirements that suggest the production elements and processes necessary to produce the defined process message.

The advantage of this model is that the precise definition of the process message will help content and production people work as a team and will facilitate selecting the necessary production personnel and equipment. By first carefully defining the desired effect on the audience, you can then decide quite easily on the specific people you need to do the job (content expert, writer, director, crew), on where to do the production most effectively (studio or field), and on the necessary equipment (studio or field cameras, types of mics, and so forth).

Let's apply the model to the interview with the famous defense lawyer mentioned in chapter 15 and see how it can influence the entire production process.

When approaching the production in the usual way—moving directly from the basic idea to the production process—you would probably think of getting an interviewer who is very skilled in law, perhaps even an ex-lawyer who has become a television personality. Then you would probably talk to the art director to design an appropriate environment for the interview—a well-to-do lawyer's office with an elegant desk, leather chairs, and lots of law books in the background. You would then have to arrange for the taping date, studio time, transportation for the guest, talent fees, and many more such details. You would also need to get together with the host (the ex-lawyer) to agree on a few questions: "What were your most famous cases?" "How many did you win?" "Have you ever refused important cases?" "Why?" and so forth.

When using the effect-to-cause model, on the other hand, you would come up with several process messages. Here are two of the more obvious ones:

Process message 1: The viewer should gain insight into some of the major defense strategies used by the guest.

In this case the questions would revolve around some of the lawyer's former cases and the reasons for their success or failure. Would you need an interviewer who understands the law? Yes. The interviewer could interpret the legal language for the audience or immediately challenge the lawyer's ethics within the framework of the law. The elaborate studio set resembling the lawyer's office would also be appropriate. You may even consider conducting this interview on location in the lawyer's actual office.

Process message 2: The viewer should gain deeper insight into the conscience and feelings of the lawyer when handling an especially difficult case, as well as how he deals with personal ethics when applying specific defense strategies.

Do you now need a host who is a legal expert? Not at all. In fact, a psychologist would probably be better suited to conduct this interview. You would probably want to use close-ups of the guest throughout most of the show. You may even stay on a close-up of the guest when the host asks questions. Reaction shots (the guest listening to questions) are often more telling than action shots (the guest answering). Does this interview require an elaborate set? No. Because the interview deals primarily with the lawyer as a person rather than the person as a lawyer, you can conduct it in any environment. Two comfortable chairs in an interview set is all you would need.

There has been a great reluctance in television production to show "talking heads"—people talking on close-ups without any supporting visual material. Do not blindly adopt this prejudice. So long as the heads talk well, there is no need for additional visual material. *READY ZVL* ❷

Writing the Program Proposal

Once you have a clear idea of the process message and how you want to communicate it, you are ready to write the program proposal. Don't take this proposal lightly—it is a key factor in getting your program on the air as opposed to simply ending up in a "good-idea" archive on your hard drive.

A *program proposal* is a written document that stipulates what you intend to do. It briefly explains the process message and the major aspects of the presentation. Although there is no standard format for a program or series proposal, it should at a minimum include this information: (1) program or series title, (2) objective (process message), (3) target audience, (4) show format, (5) show treatment, (6) production method, and (7) tentative budget. If you propose a series, attach a sample script for one of the shows and a list of the titles of the other shows in the series.

Program title   Keep the title short but memorable. Perhaps it is the lack of screen space that forces television producers to work with shorter titles than do filmmakers. Instead of naming your show *The Trials and Tribulations of a University Student*, simply say, *Student Pressures*.

Process message or program objective   This is a brief explanation of what the production is to accomplish. You can revise the process message so that it is less formal. For example, rather than say, "The process message is to have high-school students exposed to at least five major consequences of running a stop sign," you

may write that the program's objective is "to warn teenage drivers not to run stop signs."

Target audience   The *target audience* is whom you would primarily like to have watch the show—the elderly, preschoolers, teenagers, homemakers, or people interested in traveling. A properly formulated process message will give a big clue as to the target audience. Even when you want to reach as large an audience as possible and the audience is not defined, be specific in describing the potential audience. Instead of simply saying "general audience" for your proposed comedy series, describe the primary target audience as "the eighteen to mid-twenties generation" or the "over-sixty crowd in need of a good laugh."

Once you are in the actual preproduction stage, you can define your target audience further in terms of *demographics*, such as gender, ethnicity, education or income level, household size, religious preference, or geographical location (urban, rural), as well as of *psychographics*, such as consumer buying habits, values, and lifestyles. Advertisers and other video communicators make extensive use of such demographic and psychographic descriptors, but you needn't be quite that specific in your initial program proposal.

Show format   Do you propose a single show, a new series, or part of an existing series? How long is the intended show? An example would be a two-part one-hour program dealing with the various uses of helicopters around the world. This information is vital for planning a budget or, for a station or network, to see whether it fits into the program schedule.

Show treatment   A brief narrative description of the program is called a *treatment*. Some of the more elaborate treatments have storyboardlike illustrations. The treatment should not only say what the proposed show is all about but also reflect in its writing the style of the show. The style of a treatment for an instructional series on computer-generated graphics, for example, should differ considerably from that of a situation comedy. Do not include specific production information such as types of lighting or camera angles; save this information for the script. Keep the treatment brief and concise. It should simply give a busy executive some idea of what you intend to do. **SEE 17.3** *READY ZVL* ❸

Production method   A well-stated process message will indicate to you where the production should take

TREATMENT FOR THE FOURTH PROGRAM OF THE
<u>SIGHT SOUND MOTION</u> INSTRUCTIONAL VIDEO SERIES

The fourth program of the instructional video series
<u>Sight Sound Motion</u> is intended to explain the advantages of
z-axis blocking (toward and away from the camera) over x-axis
blocking (along the width of the screen).

We open with dancers moving into view from close to the
camera, unfurling a yellow nylon ribbon away from the camera
along the z-axis. More dancers join in and dance toward and
away from the camera, always close to the z-axis ribbon. A
second camera, positioned at 90 degrees from the first, sees
the dance progressing sideways, with the dancers moving in and
out of the frame along the x-axis. An off-camera narrator
explains the differences between z-axis and x-axis blocking
over especially telling freeze frames. We unfreeze the action,
with the narrator pointing out how z-axis blocking not only
fits the small television screen better than x-axis blocking,
but that it also increases the aesthetic energy of the dance.

We switch to a brief dramatic scene in which two people
are first blocked along the x-axis and then along the z-axis.
Again, the narrator explains the advantages of z-axis blocking
(better articulation of screen depth and aesthetic intensification) versus x-axis blocking (restricted horizontal screen
space, dramatic deemphasis). Again, some of the explanation
occurs over freeze frames of x-axis and z-axis blocking
samples. This explanation is followed by a selection of brief
scenes from up-to-date television shows that exhibit especially
prominent z-axis blocking.

We end the program by having the dancers move into view
again, rolling up the yellow z-axis ribbon toward the camera.

17.3 **TREATMENT**
The treatment tells the reader in narrative form what a program is all about.

place and how you can do it most efficiently. Should you do a multiple- or single-camera studio production or a single-camera EFP? Is the show more effectively shot live-on-tape in larger segments, or shot film-style for post-production? What additional materials (costumes, props, scenery) do you need? What performers or actors? *READY ZVL* ❹

Tentative budget   Before preparing the tentative budget, you must have up-to-date figures for all production services, rental costs, and wages in your area. Independent production and postproduction houses periodically issue rate cards that list costs for services and the rental of major production items. Stay away from high-end services unless quality becomes your major concern or if your project needs especially extensive post-production manipulation. As pointed out, some desktop computer programs can provide nonlinear editing tools that rival those of expensive postproduction facilities.

Preparing a Budget

If you are an independent producer, you need to figure the cost not only for obvious items—script, talent and production personnel, studio and equipment rental, and postproduction editing—but also for items that may not be so apparent, such as videotape, certain props, food, lodging, entertainment, transportation of talent and production personnel, parking, insurance, and clearances or user fees for location shooting.

When producing a show for a local station or a small independent company, the basic personnel and equipment costs are usually included in the overall production budget. In such cases you need only list additional costs, such as overtime, expandable supplies, and script and talent fees, which, by the way, can be unexpectedly high.

When working for a client, however, you need to prepare a budget for all preproduction, production, and postproduction costs, regardless of whether the cost is, at least partially, absorbed by the salaries of regularly employed personnel or the normal operation budget.

There are many ways to present a budget, such as by separating preproduction (for example, script, travel to locations and meetings, location scouting, storyboard), production (talent, production personnel, and equipment or studio rental), and postproduction (editing and sound design), or by dividing it into above-the-line and below-the-line expenses.

Above-the-line budgets include expenses for above-the-line personnel, such as writers, directors, art directors, and talent, usually called "creative personnel." This does not imply that other production personnel, such as camera operators or editors, are not creative; it simply refers to those who are more concerned with the conceptualization of ideas rather than the operation of equipment that will transform the ideas into a show. Below-the-line budgets include the expenses for below-the-line personnel, such as the production crew, as well as equipment and studio space.

Dividing a budget into preproduction, production, and postproduction categories may give you a more workable breakdown of expenditures than the above- and below-the-line division, especially when you have to bid on a specific production job. Because most production companies show their overall charges in this tripart division, the client can more easily compare your charges against those of the other bidders. Some production companies have therefore standardized their budget form.

When you are first presenting your proposal, your client may be interested not so much in how you broke down the expenses, but in what it will cost overall to have the show produced. It is therefore critical that you think of all the probable expenses, regardless of whether they occur in preproduction, production, or postproduction. In this undertaking, the computer can be of great assistance. Various software programs such as spreadsheets can help you detail the various production costs and can recalculate them effortlessly if you need to cut expenses or if the production requirements change.

An example of a detailed budget of an independent production company is shown in the accompanying figure. **SEE 17.4** It is structured according to preproduction, production, and postproduction costs.[1]

Obviously, even as an independent producer you may not have to prepare such a detailed budget for all your productions. Some simple productions may require only that you fill out the summary of costs. You can always adapt the budget shown in figure 17.4 to suit your specific production needs.

Whenever you prepare a budget, be realistic. Do not underestimate costs just to win the bid—you may regret it later. It is psychologically, as well as financially, easier to agree to a budget cut than to ask for more money later on. On the other hand, do not inflate the budget in order to get by, even after severe cuts. Be realistic about the expenses, but do not forget to add at least a 15 percent

---

1. This budget was adapted from forms created for Tat Video Communications of San Francisco and by the Association of Independent Commercial Producers, Inc. (AICP).

17.4 BUDGET CATEGORIES

These rather detailed budget categories are structured according to preproduction, production, and post-production costs.

PRODUCTION BUDGET

CLIENT:
PROJECT TITLE:
DATE OF THIS BUDGET:
SPECIFICATIONS:

NOTE: This estimate is subject to the producer's review of the final shooting script.

SUMMARY OF COSTS	ESTIMATE	ACTUAL
PREPRODUCTION		
Personnel	_____	_____
Equipment & facilities	_____	_____
Script	_____	_____
PRODUCTION		
Personnel	_____	_____
Equipment & facilities	_____	_____
Talent	_____	_____
Art (set and graphics)	_____	_____
Makeup	_____	_____
Music	_____	_____
Miscellaneous (transportation, fees)	_____	_____
POSTPRODUCTION		
Personnel	_____	_____
Facilities	_____	_____
Tape stock	_____	_____
INSURANCE & MISCELLANEOUS	_____	_____
CONTINGENCY (10%)	_____	_____
TAX	_____	_____
GRAND TOTAL	════════	════════

BUDGET DETAIL	ESTIMATE	ACTUAL
P R E P R O D U C T I O N		
Personnel		
Writer (script)	_____	_____
Director (day)	_____	_____
Art director (day)	_____	_____
PA (day)	_____	_____
SUBTOTAL	_____	_____
P R O D U C T I O N		
Personnel		
Director	_____	_____
Associate director	_____	_____
PA	_____	_____
Floor (unit) manager	_____	_____
Camera	_____	_____
Sound	_____	_____
Lighting	_____	_____
VTR	_____	_____
C.G.	_____	_____
Grips (assistants)	_____	_____
Technical supervisor	_____	_____
Prompter	_____	_____
Makeup & wardrobe	_____	_____
Talent	_____	_____
Equipment & Facilities		
Studio/location	_____	_____
Camera	_____	_____
Sound	_____	_____
Lighting	_____	_____
Sets	_____	_____
C.G./graphics	_____	_____
VTR	_____	_____
Prompting	_____	_____
Remote van	_____	_____
Intercom	_____	_____
Transportation, meals, housing	_____	_____
Copyrights	_____	_____
SUBTOTAL	_____	_____

17.4 BUDGET
CATEGORIES *(continued)*

```
P O S T P R O D U C T I O N

     Personnel
          Director                    _____   _____
          Editor                      _____   _____
          Sound editor                _____   _____

     Facilities
          Dubbing                     _____   _____
          Window dubs                 _____   _____
          Off-line linear             _____   _____
          Off-line nonlinear          _____   _____
          On-line linear              _____   _____
          On-line nonlinear           _____   _____
          DVE                         _____   _____
          Audio sweetening            _____   _____
          ADR/Foley                   _____   _____
          Tape stock                  _____   _____

SUBTOTAL                              _____   _____


M I S C E L L A N E O U S

     Insurance                        _____   _____
     Public transportation            _____   _____
     Parking                          _____   _____
     Shipping/messenger               _____   _____
     Wrap expenses                    _____   _____

SUBTOTAL                              _____   _____


GRAND TOTAL                           _____   _____
```

contingency. In general, a show always takes a little longer and costs more than anticipated. *READY ZVL* ⑤

Presenting the Proposal

Now you are ready to present your proposal. As an independent producer, you must prepare a proposal that satisfies your client. If you are working in a station, you give your proposal to the executive producer or directly to the program manager. For program proposals that concern educational or public service issues, you should contact the public service director of the station. Documentaries are usually under the jurisdiction of the news department. If you deal with a network, you need to go through an agent. When approaching a station, you may have more chance of success if you already have a sponsor to back your project.

See to it that your proposal is free of spelling errors and presented attractively.

Writing the Script

Unless you write the script yourself, you'll need to hire a writer. The writer will translate the process message into a television presentation—at least on paper. It is then up to the director to translate the script into the actual video and audio images that make up the television show.

It is important that the writer understand the program objective and, especially, the proposed process message. If a writer disagrees with the process message and does not develop a better one, find another writer. Agree on a fee before delivery of the script—some writers charge enough to swallow up your whole budget. But even if the writer understands your objectives, you must indicate the script format you need. (There are examples of script formats in chapter 18.)

One of the greatest challenges for a writer is to write good dialogue. Dialogue should sound natural, but must be a cut above what you would hear if you were to record a real conversation in a living room, restaurant, supermarket, or school board meeting. When reading dialogue try to "hear" people—not just what they say, but how they say it. Good dialogue should make you envious that you didn't speak that eloquently when you were in a similar situation.[2] *READY ZVL* ⑥

---

2. See Robert L. Hilliard, *Writing for Television and Radio,* 6th ed. (Belmont, Calif.: Wadsworth Publishing Co., 1997), chapters 3 and 10. Also see Herbert Zettl, *Sight Sound Motion,* 3d ed. (Belmont, Calif.: Wadsworth Publishing Co., 1999), pp. 314–316.

PREPRODUCTION PLANNING: COORDINATION

Before you begin coordinating the various production elements—assembling a production team, procuring studios, or deciding on location sites and equipment—ask yourself once again whether the planned production method (medium translation of process message) is, indeed, the most efficient. For example, if you are doing a documentary on the conditions of the various residence hotels in your city, it is certainly easier and more cost-effective to go there and videotape an actual hotel room than to re-create one in the studio. On the other hand, if you are doing a magazine-style show on the elderly, you could stage the major part of the production in the studio and shoot only a minimum portion on location. For a drama a specific scene might be shot more advantageously in a friend's kitchen than in a complicated studio kitchen setup. Keep in mind that the studio affords optimal control but that EFP offers a limitless variety of scenery and locations at little additional cost. Most field productions, however, require extensive use of post-production time and facilities.

Once you have made a firm decision about the most effective production approach, you have to deliver what you promised to do in the proposal. You begin this coordination phase by (1) establishing clear communication channels among all the people involved in the production. You can then proceed with coordinating the other major production elements: (2) the facilities request, (3) schedules, (4) permits and clearances, and (5) publicity and promotion. Realize that it is not your occasional flashes of inspiration that make you a good producer, but your meticulous attention to detail.

People

Whom to involve in the post-script planning stages depends, again, on your basic objective, the process message, and whether you are an independent producer who has to hire additional above-the-line and below-the-line personnel, or whether you are working for a station or large production company that has most essential creative and crew people on its payroll and available at all times.

As producer you are the chief coordinator among the various production people. You must be able to contact every single team member quickly and reliably. Your most important job, therefore, is to establish a database with

```
Production Personnel Contact Information
Sight Sound Motion Instructional Video
Program 4


Name            Position    Home address                Home phone         Home fax           Cell phone
E-mail                      Work address                Work phone         Work fax           Pager
--------------------------------------------------------------------------------------------------------
Herbert Zettl   Producer    873 Carmenita, Forest Knolls (415) 555-3874    (415) 555-8743     (415) 555-1141
hzettl@best.com             SFSU, 1600 Holloway, SF     (415) 555-8837     (415) 555-1199
--------------------------------------------------------------------------------------------------------
Gary Palmatier  Director    5343 Sunnybrook, Windsor    (707) 555-4242     (707) 555-2341
gpalmater@ideas-to-images.com 5256 Aero #3, Santa Rosa  (707) 555-87437    (707) 764-7777     (707) 555-9873
--------------------------------------------------------------------------------------------------------
Robaire Ream    AD          783 Ginny, Healdsburg       (707) 555-8372                        (800) 555-8888
bear@sonic.net              Lightsaber, 44 Tesconi, Novato (415) 555-8000  (415) 555-8080
--------------------------------------------------------------------------------------------------------
Sherry Holstead PA          88 Seacrest, Marin          (415) 555-9211     (415) 555-9873     (415) 555-0033
723643.3722@compuserve.com  SH Assoc, 505 Main, Sausalito (415) 555-0932   (415) 555-8383
--------------------------------------------------------------------------------------------------------
Renee Wong      TD          9992 Treeview, San Rafael   (415) 555-9374     (415) 555-8273     (415) 555-3498
rn_wong2@earthlink.com      P.O. Box 3764, San Rafael   (800) 555-7834     (800) 555-8734     (415) 555-8988
--------------------------------------------------------------------------------------------------------
Steve Storc     Talent      253 Robertson, Canoga Park  (213)                                 (213) 555-7832
hamlet23@aol.com            Le Dome, 32 Sunset, LA                                            55-8734
--------------------------------------------------------------------------------------------------------
```

17.5 DATABASE: PRODUCTION PERSONNEL

To be able to quickly contact each production team member, the producer needs reliable contact information.

such essential information as names, positions, home addresses, business addresses, e-mail addresses, and various phone and fax numbers. **SEE 17.5**

Don't forget to let everyone know how you can be contacted, as well. Don't rely on secondhand information. Your communication is not complete until you hear back from the party you were trying to contact. A good producer triple-checks everything.

Facilities Request

The *facilities request* lists all pieces of production equipment, and often all properties and costumes, needed for a production. The person responsible for filling out such a request varies. In small-station operations or independent production companies, it is often the producer or director; in larger operations it is the production manager.

The facilities request usually contains information concerning date and time of rehearsal, taping sessions,

and on-the-air transmission; title of production; names of producer and director (and sometimes talent); and all technical elements, such as cameras, microphones, lights, sets, graphics, costumes, makeup, VTRs, postproduction facilities, and other specific production needs. It also lists the studio and control room needed and, if you do EFP, the exact on-site location.

The facilities request, like the script, is an essential communications device. Be as accurate as possible when preparing it. Later changes will only invite costly errors. If you have a fairly accurate floor plan and light plot, attach it to the facilities request. Many a mistake in the facilities request has been discovered by comparing the request with the floor plan.

Facilities requests are usually distributed as "soft copy" via the internal computer system as well as hard copy. **SEE 17.6** The advantage of using a computer is that you can make changes easily without having to recall, correct, and reissue the hard copies.

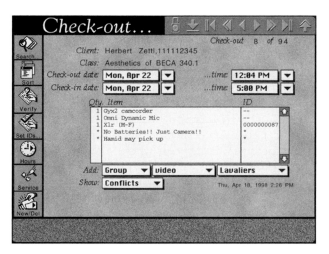

17.6 COMPUTER-BASED FACILITIES REQUEST

This computer-based facilities request lists all equipment needed for a specific production. Usually, the equipment permanently installed in a studio does not have to be listed again, but it must be scheduled.

Regardless of which type of production you choose, always try to get by with as little equipment as possible. The more you use, the more people you need to operate it and the more that can go wrong. Do not use equipment just because it is available. Review your original process message and see whether the chosen equipment is, indeed, the most efficient and whether the necessary equipment is actually available and within the scope of your budget. Consult your technical staff, which may consist of your favorite camera operator, on specific use of equipment and other production tasks. Their expertise extends way beyond the use of television equipment, and they are usually quite willing to help you solve especially difficult production problems.

Schedules

The production schedule should tell everybody involved in the production who is doing what, when, and where. Create a realistic schedule and stick to it. Assigning too little time will not result in a higher level of activity, but is almost always counterproductive; all it does is create unnecessary tension and frustration. On the other hand, allowing too much time for a production activity will not necessarily improve the production. Besides being costly, wasting time can make people apathetic and, surprisingly enough, fail to meet deadlines.

One of your most important jobs as a producer is to check constantly on the progress of each activity and see where everybody stands relative to the stipulated deadlines. If you don't care whether deadlines are met, you might as well do away with them. If schedules aren't met, find out why. Again, do not rely on secondhand information. Call the people who are behind schedule directly and find out what the problem is. It is your job to help solve these problems and get everybody back on schedule, or to change the schedule if necessary. (See section 17.2 for an actual shooting schedule.)

Always inform all the production people of all the changes you make—even if they seem rather insignificant at the time.

Permits and Clearances

Most productions involve facilities and people that, ordinarily, have no connection with your station or production company. These production elements need special attention. Get the necessary permits for your crew to gain admission to a meeting or concert, as well as a parking permit close to the event. You may also need a permit from city hall (the mayor's media coordinator and the police department) or a specific insurance policy to shoot downtown. Do not ignore such requirements! "Better safe than sorry" applies to all field productions—not just to actual production activities, but also to protecting yourself from legal action if a production assistant stumbles over a cable or if a bystander slips on a banana peel while watching your show. Copyright and union clearances are discussed in section 17.2.

Publicity and Promotion

The best show is worthless if no one knows about it. During preproduction meet with the publicity and promotions departments (usually combined in one office or even a single person) and inform them about the upcoming production. Even if your target audience is limited and highly specific, you still must aim to reach as many viewers as possible. The job of the publicity people is to narrow the gap between the potential and the actual audience. *READY ZVL* **7**

PRODUCTION: HOST AND CRITICAL OBSERVATION

If you have done your job right, you can now let the director take over. But you are still responsible for the entire production and should, therefore, stay involved until the production has been shown on the air. Your immediate duties during the production are to take care of the guests and to act as a second pair of eyes for the director.

Playing Host

If you expect guests for your show, you need to get them into the studio. How do they get to the studio and back to their hotel? Be sure to have someone (preferably you) greet them when they arrive. There is nothing more embarrassing than having guests wander through the station, trying to find you or the studio. Have a reception room ready with coffee and tea, enabling guests to relax as much as possible before going into the studio.

Watching the Production Flow

Although you should stay out of the director's way as much as possible, you should still keep an eye on the general production flow. Sometimes a director gets hung up on a minor detail and does retake after retake only to find that there is very little time left to tape the rest of the program.

As a producer you should remind the director to move on and to stay on schedule. If you notice that the lighting or audio people take an inordinate amount of setup time, you may talk to the TD (technical director) or assistant director (AD) about it. When the director needs additional equipment or props to improve on a scene, you can approve the extra expense on the spot and call the appropriate people to get the requested items.

Evaluating the Production

One of the most important functions for the producer during the production is to look over the director's shoulder at the various takes. It is not unusual for a director to get so involved in coordinating all the production details that he or she loses track of the overall look and flow of a scene. As a good producer, you can watch the scene from a different perspective—more as a critical viewer than a member of the production team. This is not unlike watching a chess game and seeing all the mistakes and missed possibilities of the other players.

If you have suggestions concerning the show, take notes or dictate your comments to the PA (production assistant) during the rehearsal and then discuss them with the director (and talent and crew if necessary) at various rehearsal or taping breaks. Do not interfere during the actual performance, unless you see a big mistake that obviously escaped the director's attention or if something totally unexpected happens that needs your immediate attention. Bear in mind that although you, as the producer, coordinated all production elements up to this moment, it is the director who is now in charge of translating your idea into the finished product—the television program. *READY ZVL* ⑧

POSTPRODUCTION ACTIVITIES

If your production was done live, or live-on-tape, you are just about done. You still need to write thank-you notes to the people who have made special contributions to the program, and complete all required reports (such as music clearances and talent releases), unless the director takes care of such matters. More often, however, you now need to begin coordinating the postproduction activities, among them: (1) postproduction editing, (2) evaluation and feedback, and (3) recordkeeping.

Postproduction Editing

Your activities in the postproduction phase may involve a simple check of whether the people and facilities for the off-line and on-line editing are still available as scheduled, or may involve some complicated rescheduling. Some producers feel that they need to closely supervise the whole video-editing and audio-sweetening activities, whereas others leave such responsibilities to the director. Nevertheless, you should always be available in case the editor or director wants your advice about a particularly sensitive editing decision.

Evaluation and Feedback

If the production is for a corporation or other non-broadcast organization, arrange a viewing date for your client. In fact, you should always show the completed off-line version of the production to your client before doing any final on-line editing. If you have proceeded according to the effect-to-cause approach, the client would have been continuously involved in the production process and most changes would have been made by now. The final showing is not the time to discover major production mistakes. Nevertheless, keep an open mind during the "screening" of your off-line production and listen carefully to your client's recommendations for changes. Have the director explain why a scene was shot in a certain way, or why some of the original script had to be changed.

If the show solicits viewer feedback ("Please call the 800-number" or "Be sure to respond to your supervisor about what you thought of the show"), see to it that the feedback facilities are in place. Viewers can get quite annoyed if they find that their well-intentioned efforts to communicate with the station are ignored. Have competent and friendly phone operators standing by to take the viewers' calls. If you solicit written feedback ("Please drop us a postcard or fax your comments"), assign someone to handle and respond quickly to the correspondence. Keep a record of all unsolicited calls (positive and negative) and file all written communication (letters, postcards, faxes, and e-mail).

Finally, sit back and look objectively at the finished production. Does it, at least in your judgment, meet the objectives of the process message as defined? Determining the real impact—the actual process message—of the program is difficult. Nevertheless, try to gather as much feedback as possible (from reviewers and colleagues as well as viewers) to determine how close the defined process message came to the actual one. The closer the match, the more successful the production. *READY ZVL* **9**

Recordkeeping

Each time you finish a production, file a cassette copy of it for archival purposes. The news department uses such archives as a "morgue"—a resource about people and places that become newsworthy again. Such a copy will also protect you from unreasonable claims by an irate client.

Besides the videotape copy of your on-line production, put together a production book that contains important preproduction, production, and postproduction records. At a minimum, such a production book should contain: (1) the final program proposal, (2) the budget, (3) the production schedule (including rehearsals, crew calls, and so forth), (4) facilities requests, (5) the list of production personnel, (5) the list of talent, (6) talent contracts and releases, (7) various permits, and (8) the shooting script. File the production book and cross-reference it with the videotape copy so that you have access to both when needed.

As you remember from the beginning of this chapter, producing means managing ideas and coordinating many people, equipment, activities, and details. Triple-check everything. Do not leave anything to chance. Finally, never breach the prevailing ethical standards of society. Whatever you do, use as your guideline a basic respect and compassion for your audience.

MAIN POINTS

♦ Producing means seeing to it that a worthwhile idea becomes a worthwhile television show. The producer manages a great number of people and coordinates an even greater number of activities and production details.

♦ The effect-to-cause model starts with the basic idea, then defines the desired audience effect—the process message. The definition will determine the medium requirements: content elements, production elements, and people. The closer the actual process message (actual effect) matches the defined one, the more successful the communication.

♦ The program proposal normally contains the following minimum information: program or series title, objective, target audience, show treatment, production method, and tentative budget.

♦ The program budget is generally divided into preproduction, production, and postproduction costs. It must include all major and minor expenses, unless they are absorbed by the overall production budget.

♦ The script is the most important preproduction element. It determines the further production process.

♦ Preproduction coordination involves selecting and coordinating the production people, deciding on facilities and production locations, scheduling all production activities, and taking care of permits, clearances, publicity, and promotion.

♦ During the production, the producer acts as host, watches the production flow, and oversees the general quality of production.

♦ Postproduction activities include scheduling postproduction facilities and people, supervising the editing, a final evaluation of the program, handling solicited and unsolicited feedback, and recordkeeping.

17.2

Dealing With Schedules, Legal Matters, and Ratings

As a producer you need knowledge of such specific production activities as the design of an efficient production schedule, quick access to accurate information, and, when working for a television station or cable company, the various classifications of programs. Although you may have the services of a legal department, you will inevitably have to deal with broadcast guilds and unions as well as copyrights and other legal matters. Finally, you must be conversant in the basic audience classifications and the rudiments of ratings.

▶ **PRODUCTION SCHEDULE**
  Event sequencing and the master production schedule

▶ **INFORMATION RESOURCES**
  Local resources, computer databases, and basic reference books and directories

▶ **PROGRAM TYPES**
  Agricultural, entertainment, news, public affairs, religious, instructional, sports, and other

▶ **UNIONS AND LEGAL MATTERS**
  Nontechnical unions, technical unions, copyrights and clearances, and other legal considerations

▶ **AUDIENCE AND RATINGS**
  Target audience, ratings, and share

PRODUCTION SCHEDULE

The daily production schedule is normally worked out by the director and/or the production or unit manager. This person is in charge of the day's production—from loading the EFP vehicles or opening the studio doors to putting back the equipment and filing the crew's lunch receipts. In smaller operations, however, the producer functions not only as the preproduction organizer, but also as the production manager of the various activities during the production day. In this case you need to know how to design a maximally efficient schedule, which will save not only time and money but, especially, energy.

Even if you are not directly responsible for the day-to-day scheduling, you should keep an eye on it and see that it is maximally efficient. The efficiency of such a schedule depends to a large extent on proper event sequencing. For example, do not order a complicated opening title sequence from the art department if the writer is still struggling with the script. Nor should you argue with the director over the lighting requirements or number of cameras before you have visited the remote location or seen a floor plan.

Show/Scene Subject	Date/Time	Location	Facilities	Talent/Personnel
energy conservation scenes 1 & 2 openings & closings	Aug. 8 11:30– 4:30	solar heating plant	normal EFP as per fax of 7/2	Janet & Bill EFP crew as scheduled Director: John H.
energy # 2, 3, 4 sections on solar panel demonstrations	Aug. 10 8:30– 2:30	solar heating plant	normal EFP as per fax of 7/2	Janet & Bill EFP crew as scheduled Director: John H.
energy # 5, 6 installation of solar heating panels	Aug. 11 8:30– 4:30	Terra Linda Housing Project	normal EFP as per fax of 7/2	No Talent (v.o. in post) EFP crew as scheduled Director: John H.

17.7 EVENT SEQUENCING

Event sequencing results in a schedule that shows all scenes shot in a specific location.

ENG EFP In EFP especially, the event sequence should be determined by production requirements (location, weather, sets) and not necessarily by the scripted sequence. See which events can be scheduled together, such as the opening or closing of a show, or other widely spread scenes that nevertheless play in the same location. Although moving from set to set in a studio production as scripted may not cause too many logistical problems, unnecessarily changing locations in the field does.

Establish a tentative schedule of events and try to fit them into the master production schedule. Such an event schedule will show you not only how a single production day should progress, but also the flow of an entire production series. For example, you may find that you can use a single set for the whole series, with only a few changes of set properties, or that you can shoot several sequences at the same location, although the various shows may finally be shown in a different sequence. **SEE 17.7**

INFORMATION RESOURCES

As a producer you must be a researcher as well as somewhat of a scrounger. On occasion you may have only a half hour to get accurate information, for example, about a former mayor who is celebrating her ninetieth birthday. Or you may have to procure a skeleton for your medical show, a model of a communications satellite for your documentary on telecommunications, or an eighteenth-century wedding dress for your history series.

Fortunately, the various Internet sources put the world's information at your fingertips. And, if you know the address, it is practically instantaneous. You may find, however, that the sheer volume of on-line information makes it difficult to find a specific item quickly. It may sometimes be faster and more convenient to use readily available printed sources or to call the local library. For example, a call to the local hospital or high-school science department may procure the skeleton more quickly than initiating a Web search. You could ask the community college science department or perhaps even the local cable company for the satellite model, and the historical society or college theater arts department for the wedding dress.

Besides Internet sources, here are some of the additional references and services you should have on hand.

■ *Telephone directories.* There is a great deal of information in a telephone book. Get the directories of your city and the outlying areas. Also try to get the telephone directories of the larger institutions with which you have frequent contact, such as city hall, the police and fire departments, other city or county agencies, major federal offices, city and county school offices, newspapers and radio stations, colleges and universities, and museums. On the Internet you can obtain in seconds the telephone number of practically any phone user in the world.

■ *Airline schedules.* Even if you have easy on-line access to airline schedules, keep up-to-date directories of the major airlines. Have a reliable contact person in a travel agency.

■ *Transportation and delivery.* Have the numbers of one or two taxi companies as well as bus and train schedules. Keep in mind that taxis can transport things (such as the skeleton for your medical program) as well as people. Establish contact with at least two reliable inter- and intracity delivery services.

■ *Reference books.* Your own reference library should have an up-to-date dictionary; a set of *Who's Who in America* and the regional volumes; a recent international biographical dictionary; an up-to-date encyclopedia that presents subjects clearly and concisely (you may find the simple yet concise *World Book* encyclopedia more helpful than the detailed *Encyclopaedia Britannica*); and a comprehensive, up-to-date atlas. Also have on hand the phone number of the reference desk at the local library. An efficient and friendly reference librarian can, and is usually happy to, dig up all sorts of information with amazing speed. They can also do quick Internet research in libraries worldwide.

If you work for a cable company or television station, collect some basic references. Besides professional journals and yearbooks, put some of the latest editions of broadcast textbooks on your bookshelf. These volumes will give you quick and accurate information about a variety of issues.

■ *Other resources.* The local chamber of commerce usually maintains a list of community organizations and businesses. A list of the major foundations and their criteria for grants may also come in handy. If you are doing a series on a specific subject (medical practice, energy conservation, housing developments), you will have to get some major reference works in that area.

PROGRAM TYPES

Television programs have been standardized by the Federal Communications Commission (FCC) into eight categories: agricultural (A), entertainment (E), news (N), public affairs (PA), religious (R), instructional (I), sports (S), and other (O). The latter (O) category includes all programs not falling within the first seven. Furthermore, there are subcategories, which may overlap any of the preceding types: editorials (EDIT), political (POL), and educational institution (ED).

Some stations add their own combinations, such as EDIT/POL or POL/ED, to accommodate programs that do not precisely fit the FCC categories. The ED category includes all programs prepared by, on behalf of, or in cooperation with educational institutions.

UNIONS AND LEGAL MATTERS

Most directors, writers, and talent belong to a guild or union, as do almost all below-the-line personnel. As a producer you must be alert to the various union regulations in your production area. Most unions stipulate not only salaries and minimum fees but also specific working conditions, such as overtime, turnaround time (stipulated hours of rest between workdays), rest periods, who can legally run a studio camera and who cannot, and so forth. If you use nonunion personnel in a union station, or if you plan to air a show that has been prepared outside the station with nonunion talent, check with the respective unions for proper clearance.

Unions

There are two basic types of unions: those for nontechnical personnel and those for technical personnel. Nontechnical unions are mainly those for performers, writers, and directors. **SEE 17.8** Technical unions include all television engineers and occasionally a variety of production personnel, such as microphone boom operators, ENG/EFP camera operators, and floor personnel. **SEE 17.9**

Be especially careful about asking studio guests to do anything other than answer questions during an interview. If they give a short demonstration of their talents, they may be classified as performers and automatically become subject to AFTRA fees (see figure 17.8). Also, do not request the floor crew to do anything that is not directly connected with their regular line of duty or else they, too, may collect talent fees. Camera operators usually have a contract clause that ensures them a substantial penalty sum if they are willfully shown by another camera on the television screen. Acting students who appear in television plays produced at a high school or college may become subject to AFTRA fees if the play is shown on the air by a broadcast station, unless you clear their on-the-air appearance with the station and/or the local AFTRA office.

Copyrights and Clearances

If you use copyrighted material on your show, you must procure proper clearances. Usually, the year of the copyright and the name of the copyright holder are printed right after the © copyright symbol. Some photographs, reproductions of famous paintings, and prints are often copyrighted as well, as are, of course, books, periodicals, short stories, plays, and music recordings. Shows that you may tape off the air, and many CD-ROMs, are also subject to copyright laws. When you are the artist trying to protect

17.8 NONTECHNICAL UNIONS

AFTRA **American Federation of Television and Radio Artists.** This is the major union for television talent. Directors sometimes belong to AFTRA, especially when they double as announcers and on-the-air talent. AFTRA prescribes basic minimum fees, called scale, which differ from area to area. Most well-known talent (such as prominent actors and local news anchors) are paid well above scale.

DGA **Directors Guild of America, Inc.** A union for television and motion picture directors and associate directors. Floor managers and production assistants of large stations and networks sometimes belong to the "Guild."

WGA **Writers Guild of America, Inc.** A union for writers of television and film scripts.

SAG **Screen Actors Guild.** Important organization, especially when film is involved in television production. Also includes some actors for video-taped commercials and larger video productions.

SEG **Screen Extras Guild, Inc.** A union for extras participating in major film or video productions.

AFM **American Federation of Musicians of the United States and Canada.** Important only if live orchestras are used in the production.

17.9 TECHNICAL UNIONS

IBEW **International Brotherhood of Electrical Workers.** This union includes studio, master control, and maintenance engineers and technicians. It may also include ENG/EFP camera operators and floor personnel.

NABET **National Association of Broadcast Employees and Technicians.** Another engineering union that may also include floor personnel and nonengineering production people (boom operators, dolly operators).

IATSE **International Alliance of Theatrical Stage Employees and Moving Picture Machine Operators of the United States and Canada.** This union includes primarily stage hands, grips (lighting technicians), and stage carpenters. Floor managers and even film camera and lighting personnel can also belong.

AUDIENCE AND RATINGS

As a producer in a television station, you will probably hear more than you care to about the various aspects of specific television audiences and ratings. Ratings are especially important for commercial stations, because the cost for commercial time sold by the station is determined primarily by the estimated size of the target audience. Even when working for corporate television, you will find that audience "ratings" are used to indicate the relative success of a program.

Target Audience

Broadcast audiences, like those for all mass media, are usually classified by demographic and psychographic characteristics. The standard *demographic descriptors* include gender, age, marital status, education, ethnicity, and income or economic status. The *psychographic descriptors* pertain to the general lifestyle, such as consumer buying habits and even personality and persuasiveness variables.

Despite sophisticated techniques of classifying audience members and determining their lifestyle and potential acceptance of a specific program or series, some producers simply use a neighbor as a model and gear their communication to that particular person and his or her

your rights, you may find that the copyrights are rather vague. But when you use copyrighted material, you run into stringent laws and regulations. When in doubt, check with a copyright attorney about special copyright clauses and public domain before using other people's material in your production.

Other Legal Considerations

Check with legal counsel about up-to-date rulings on libel (written and broadcast defamation), slander (lesser oral defamation), plagiarism (passing off as one's own the ideas or writings of another), the right to privacy (not the same in all states), obscenity laws, and similar matters. In the absence of legal counsel, the news departments of major broadcast stations or university broadcast departments generally have up-to-date legal information available.

habits. Don't be surprised if an executive producer turns down your brilliant program proposal with a comment such as, "I don't think my neighbor Mrs. Smith would like it." For many entertainment programs, such a subjective approach to prejudging the worth of a program might be acceptable. If you are asked to do a goal-directed program such as driver education or a commercial on the importance of water conservation, however, you need to identify and analyze the target audience more specifically. The more you know about the target audience, the more precise your defined process message and, ultimately, the more effective that message will be.

Ratings and Share

An audience *rating* is the percentage representing an estimate of television households with their sets tuned to a station in a given population (total number of television households). You get this percentage by dividing the projected number of households tuned to your station by the total number of television households:

$$\frac{number\ of\ TV\ households\ tuned\ in}{total\ number\ of\ TV\ households} = rating\ figure$$

For example, if 75 households of your rating sample of 500 households are tuned to your show, your show will have a rating of 15 (the decimal point is dropped when the rating figure is given):

$$\frac{75}{500} = .15 = 15\ rating\ points$$

A *share* is the percentage of television households tuned to your station in relation to all households using television (HUT). The *HUT* figure represents the total pie—or 100 percent. Here is how a share is figured:

$$\frac{TV\ households\ tuned\ to\ your\ station}{all\ households\ using\ television\ (HUT)} = share$$

For example, if only 200 of the sample households have their sets actually in use (HUT = 200 = 100 percent), the 75 households tuned into your program constitute a share of 38:

$$\frac{75}{200} = .375 = share\ of\ 38$$

Various rating services, such as A. C. Nielsen, carefully select representative audience samples and query these samples through diaries, telephone calls, and meters attached to their television sets.

The problem with the rating figures is not so much the potential for error in projecting the sample to a larger population, but rather that the figures do not indicate whether the household whose set is turned on has any people watching or, if so, how many. The figures also do not indicate the impact of a program on the viewers (the actual process message). Consequently, you will find that your show is often judged not by the significance of your message, the impact it has on the audience, or how close the actual effect of the process message came to the defined effect, but simply by the rating and share figures. As frustrating as the rating system is, you must realize that, in broadcast television, you are working with a mass medium that, by definition, bases its existence on large audiences.

MAIN POINTS

◆ Careful event sequencing greatly facilitates production scheduling and activities. This approach is especially helpful for a production series.

◆ A producer needs quick and ready access to a great variety of resources and information. The Internet is an almost instantaneous and total information resource. Telephone directories, airline and other transportation schedules, and basic reference books are also important resources.

◆ There are eight program types as standardized by the Federal Communications Commission. Some stations add their own combinations to accommodate programs that do not precisely fit the FCC categories.

◆ Most nontechnical and technical production personnel belong to guilds or unions, such as the Directors Guild of America (DGA) or the National Association of Broadcast Employees and Technicians (NABET).

◆ The usual copyright laws apply when copyrighted material (video and audio material, printed information, CD-ROMs) is used in a television production.

◆ An audience rating is the percentage of television households with their sets tuned to a station in a given sample population owning TV sets. A share is the percentage of households tuned to a specific station in relation to all other households using television (HUT).

ZETTL'S VIDEOLAB 2.1

*The **process** monitor illustrates and reinforces the main steps of the production process. Many examples are from an actual production that moves from idea to image.*

RUN ZVL 1 Click on the **process** monitor and run tape 4 **Ideas**. Click on the first two modules, **Clustering** and **Brainstorming**. You'll be introduced to these idea-generating methods with examples and comments.

RUN ZVL 2 Run tape 3 **Effect-to-Cause**. Watch all four modules: **Basic idea**, **Desired effect**, **Cause**, and **Actual effect**. You will learn how to apply this model to an actual production process.

RUN ZVL 3 Run tape 5 **Proposals**. Click on the first four modules: **Audience**, **Channel**, **Objective**, and **Treatment**. The specific steps of how to prepare an effective program proposal are clearly illustrated.

RUN ZVL 4 Run tape 6 **Methods**. Click on the first four modules: **Location**, **Studio**, **Single-camera**, and **Multicamera**. See how the various methods differ. Your process message will largely dictate which method to choose.

RUN ZVL 5 Go back to tape 5 **Proposals** and click on module 5 **Budget**. This module shows you the various budget categories of an independent production.

RUN ZVL 6 Go back to tape 4 **Ideas**. Click on module 3 **Scripts**. The focus is on the difference between a treatment and a two-column script and the functions of each.

RUN ZVL 7 Run tape 2 **Phases** and click on module 1 **Preproduction**. Here you revisit the techniques of generating ideas, how to formulate the process message, and the importance of a program proposal.

RUN ZVL 8 Click on module 2 **Production**. This reinforces the importance of a production schedule.

RUN ZVL 9 Run tape 2 **Phases** again and click on module 3 **Postproduction**. You are reminded that the major function of postproduction is to create a meaningful sequence rather than to fix mistakes.

Be sure to take all **Quizzes**.

18

The Director in Preproduction

As a *director* you need to tell—direct—talent and the entire production team what to do before, during, and after the production. But before you can tell them what to do, you obviously need a clear idea of what the program should look like and how to get from the idea to the television image.

More specifically, as a director you must be able to translate an idea, a script, or an actual event (such as an interview, parade, or tennis match) into effective television pictures and sound. What you do is translate the defined *process message* (the defined outcome of the program) into the various medium requirements and then combine them through the production process into a specific television program. You must decide on the people (talent and crew) and the technical production elements (cameras, mics, sets, lighting, and so forth) that will produce the intended effect—the process message—and coordinate all these elements with maximum efficiency and effectiveness. And you must do so with style.

Section 18.1, How a Director Prepares, looks at the director's roles and specific preproduction activities. Section 18.2, Moving from Script to Screen, offers some guidelines on image visualization and sequencing and on how to analyze a script. The director's activities in the production and postproduction phases are the focus of chapter 19.

KEY TERMS

fact sheet Lists the items to be shown on-camera and their main features. May contain suggestions of what to say about the product. Also called *rundown sheet*.

fully scripted show format Same as *fully scripted*. A script that contains complete dialogue or narration and major visualization cues.

locking-in An especially vivid mental image—visual or aural—during script analysis that determines the subsequent visualizations and sequencing.

script Written document that tells what the program is about, who is in it, what is supposed to happen, and how the audience shall see and hear the event.

semiscripted show format Partial script that indicates major video cues in the left column and partial dialogue and major audio cues in the right column. Used to describe a show for which the dialogue is indicated but not completely written out.

sequencing The control and structuring of a shot sequence during editing.

show format Lists the show segments in order of appearance. Used in routine shows, such as daily game or interview shows.

storyboard A series of sketches of the key visualization points of an event, with the corresponding audio information.

visualization Mentally converting a scene into a number of key television images. The mental image of a shot. The images do not need to be sequenced at this time.

18.1

How a Director Prepares

As a television director, you are expected to be an artist who can translate ideas into effective pictures and sounds, a psychologist who can encourage people to give their best, a technical adviser who can solve problems the engineers would rather give up on, and a coordinator and a stickler for detail who leaves nothing unchecked. Not an easy job by any means! Although some directors think that their profession requires a divine gift, most good directors acquired and honed their skills through painstaking study and practice.

▶ **THE DIRECTOR'S ROLES**
   Artist, psychologist, technical adviser, and coordinator

▶ **PREPRODUCTION ACTIVITIES**
   Process message, production method, production team and communication, scheduling, script formats, script marking, floor plan and location sketch, and facilities request

▶ **SUPPORT STAFF**
   Floor manager, assistant director, and production assistant

THE DIRECTOR'S ROLES

The various roles you must assume as a director are not as clear-cut as you will see them described in this section. They frequently overlap, and you may have to switch from one to another several times just in the first five minutes of rehearsal. Even when pressed for time and pressured by people with a variety of problems, always pay full attention to the task at hand before moving on to the next.

Director as Artist

In the role of an artist, a director is expected to produce pictures and sound that not only convey the intended message clearly and effectively but which do so with style. You need to know how to look at an event or a script, quickly recognize its essential quality, and select and order those elements that help clarify, intensify, and interpret it for a specific audience. Style enters when you do all these things with a personal touch; when, for example, you shoot a certain scene very tightly to heighten its energy or when you select background music that helps convey mood. But unlike the painter, who can wait for inspiration and can retouch the painting over and over until it is finally right, the television director is expected to be creative by a specific clock time and to make the right decisions the first time around.

Director as Psychologist

Because you must deal with a variety of people who approach television production from different perspectives, you need to also assume the role of psychologist. For example, in a single production you may have to communicate with a producer who worries about the budget, technicians who are primarily concerned with the technical quality of pictures and sound, temperamental talent, a designer who has strong ideas about the set, and the mother of a child actor, who thinks your close-ups of her daughter are not tight enough.

Not only must you get everyone to perform at a consistently high level, you also have to get them to work as a team. Although there is no formula for directing a team of such diverse individuals, there are some basic guidelines that will help you exercise the necessary leadership.

■ Be well prepared and know what you want to accomplish. You cannot possibly get people to work for a common goal if you do not know what it is.

■ Know the specific functions of each team member. Explain to all the individuals what you want them to do before holding them accountable for their work.

■ Be precise about what you want the talent to do. Do not be vague with your instructions or intimidated by a celebrity. The more professional the talent, the more readily they will follow your direction.

■ Project a secure attitude. Be firm but not harsh when giving instructions. Listen to recommendations from other production staff, but do not yield your decision making to them.

■ Do not ridicule someone for making a mistake. Point out the problems and suggest solutions. Keep the overall goal in mind.

■ Treat the talent and all members of the production team with respect and compassion.

Director as Technical Adviser

Although you do not have to be an expert in operating the technical equipment, as a director you should still be able to give the crew helpful instructions on how to use it to achieve your communication goal. In the role of technical adviser, you are acting much like a conductor of a symphony orchestra. The conductor may not be able to play all the instruments in the orchestra, but he or she certainly knows the sounds the various instruments can generate and how they ought to be played to produce good music. The preceding chapters were designed to give you a solid background in technical production.

Director as Coordinator

In addition to your artistic, psychological, and technical skills, you must be able to coordinate a great many production details and processes. The role of coordinator goes beyond directing in the traditional sense, which generally means blocking the talent and helping them give peak performances. Especially when directing nondramatic shows, you must expend most of your effort on cuing members of the production team (both technical and nontechnical) to initiate certain video and audio functions, such as getting appropriate camera shots, rolling VTRs, riding audio levels, switching among cameras and special video effects, retrieving electronically generated graphics, and switching to remote feeds. You still need to pay attention to the performers, who sometimes (and rightly so) feel that they play second fiddle to the television machine. You also need to coordinate productions within a rigid time frame in which every second has a price tag attached. Such coordinating needs practice, and you should not expect to be a competent director immediately after reading this chapter.

PREPRODUCTION ACTIVITIES

As with producing, the more effort you spend on preproduction planning, the easier, more efficient, and especially more reliable your directing will be in the actual production phase. Specifically, you need to focus on the following major preproduction points and activities: (1) process message, (2) production method, (3) production team and communication, (4) scheduling, (5) script formats, (6) script marking, (7) floor plan and location sketch, and (8) facilities request.

Process Message

Before you do anything, revisit the *process message*—the purpose of the show and its intended effect on a specific audience (see chapter 17). If you are not quite sure what the show is to accomplish, check with the producer. Only then can you make all other personnel understand what the show is about and the expected outcome of the production. An early agreement between producer and director about specific communication goals and production type and scope can prevent many frustrating arguments and costly mistakes. Keep the producer abreast of your plans, even if you have been given responsibility for all creative decisions. Keep a record of telephone calls, save your e-mail, and follow up on major verbal decisions with memorandums.

Production Method

If you thoroughly understand the process message, the most appropriate production method becomes clear—that is, whether the show is best done in the studio or in the field, live or on videotape, single-camera or multicamera, in sequential or nonsequential event order. If, for example, the process message is to help the viewer participate in the excitement of watching a Thanksgiving parade, you need to do a live, multicamera remote in the field. A traffic safety segment on observing stop signs may require a single-camera approach and plenty of postproduction time. To help the audience gain a deeper insight into the thinking and work habits of a famous painter, you might observe the painter in her studio over several days with a small, single camcorder and then edit the videotaped material in postproduction. If the viewer is to share the excitement of the participants in a new game show and is encouraged to call in while the game is in process, the show must obviously be a live, multicamera studio production.

Production Team and Communication

The producer is generally responsible for identifying and organizing the nontechnical and technical production teams. If you are a staff director in a station or large production company, the production teams are assigned to you according to scheduling convenience rather than individual skills of the team members. If, however, you can select your team members, you obviously pick those people who can do the best job for the specific production at hand. Note that one floor manager may be excellent in the studio but not in the field, or that a superb ENG/EFP

camera operator may perform quite poorly when asked to handle a heavy studio camera. Check with the producer on all your decisions, and get his or her approval for your choices. Don't leave anything to chance, and don't assume that someone else will take care of a production detail. The producer should be in constant contact with you during the entire preproduction phase. If you think the producer should have contacted you, don't just sit back and wait—pick up the phone and contact the producer.

Once you know your team, establish procedures to facilitate your supervision of the preproduction activities. For example, have the art director call or e-mail you when the tentative floor plan is ready, or request that the talent notify you when they receive the script. Brief production meetings promote efficient communication among key team members, assuming you have invited them and they are all in attendance.

When working with freelancers, you need to know where to reach them and they need to know how best to contact you. Give all team members a printout of your production personnel database (see figure 17.5). Keep all contact information readily on hand. It is often quicker to locate a telephone number in a regular card file than to fire up a computer. *READY ZVL* ❶

Scheduling

Prepare a detailed schedule for preproduction activities that is based on the producer's master production schedule. This will help you keep track of who is supposed to do what, and when an assignment should be done. Scheduling software can make it relatively easy to cross-check the activities of the various team members. *READY ZVL* ❷

Script Formats

Your most important preproduction element is the script. A good *script* tells you what the program is about, who is in it, what is supposed to happen, and how the audience shall see and hear the event. It also gives you specific clues as to the necessary preproduction, production, and postproduction activities. Even if you are not a writer, you need to be thoroughly familiar with the various script formats: the full, or complete, script; the partial script; the show format; and the fact, or rundown, sheet.

The fully scripted format—the complete script The complete script includes every word that is to be spoken during a show as well as detailed audio and video instructions. Dramatic shows, comedy skits, news shows, and most major commercials use the *fully scripted show format*. **SEE 18.1**

SCENE 6

A FEW DAYS LATER. INTERIOR. CITY HOSPITAL EMERGENCY WAITING
ROOM. LATE EVENING.

YOLANDA is anxiously PACING back and forth in the hospital
hallway in front of the emergency room. She has come straight
from her job to the hospital. We see the typical hospital
traffic in an emergency room. A DOCTOR (friend of CHUCK'S)
PUSHES CARRIE in a wheelchair down the hall toward YOLANDA.

                              CARRIE

                (in wheelchair, but rather cheerful)

Hi, Mom!

                              YOLANDA

                      (anxious and worried)

Carrie—are you all right? What happened?

                              CARRIE

I'm OK. I just slipped.

                      DOCTOR (simultaneously)

She has a sprained right wrist. Nothing serious...

                              CARRIE

Why is everybody making such a big deal out of it?

                              YOLANDA

            (cutting into both CARRIE'S and DOCTOR'S lines)

Does it hurt? Did you break your arm?

18.1 DRAMA SCRIPT

The fully scripted drama contains every word of the dialogue and descriptions of primary character action. It gives minimal
visualization and sequencing instructions.

There are advantages and disadvantages to directing a fully scripted show. You have the advantage of visualizing the individual shots and sequencing them before going into rehearsal. You also have definite cue lines and instructions for what shots the cameras are to get. The disadvantages are that you must catch every spoken word of the dialogue. If the actor or performer forgets the exact text and begins to ad-lib, your shooting procedure may be seriously affected. As you will see, the last few words of an actor's speech may trigger a number of technical operations, and if these important words aren't uttered, you must stop down (interrupt the videotaping) and retake the scene.

Newscasts are always fully scripted. **SEE 18.2** They include every word the news anchors speak and instructions for what visuals the director must call up at a particular time. As a director you have little room to be creative; you follow the script and call up the various video and audio segments in the right order at the right time. As you recall, the computer connected to the robotic camera pedestals, mounting heads, and zoom lenses selects and executes camera shots. The computer program could just as easily take over the news directing, or rather coordinating, function by following and executing the various cues of a fully scripted news routine. But, at least so far, the computer cannot react creatively when a script must be changed because of a breaking story or when something goes wrong, such as the prompting system breaking down or the anchor missing an important cue.

Documentaries or documentary-type shows are frequently fully scripted. Because a documentary is intended to record an event rather than reconstruct one, scripts are often written after the production. Documentary scripts, therefore, guide the postproduction phase, rather than the actual production. The script will often indicate which video or sound bites to use, or dictate the voice-over segments by the off-camera narrator. Normally, the major video and action cues are listed in the video column, and all spoken words and sound effects are listed in the audio column. **SEE 18.3** *READY ZVL* ❸

The semiscripted format—the partial script   The *semiscripted show format* indicates only a partial dialogue. In general, the opening and closing remarks are fully scripted, but the bulk of what people say

is only alluded to, such as: "Dr. Hyde talks about new educational ideas. Dr. Seel replies." This kind of script is almost always used for interviews, product demonstrations, educational programs, variety shows, and other program types that feature a great amount of ad-lib commentary or discussion.

In a semiscripted format, it is important to indicate specific cue lines that tell the director when to roll a videotape, key a C.G. title, or break the cameras to another set area. **SEE 18.4**

The show format   The *show format* lists only the order of particular show segments, such as "interview from Washington," "commercial 2," or "book review." It also lists the major set areas in which the action takes place, or other points of origination, as well as major clock and running times for the segments. A show format is frequently used in studio productions that have established performance routines, such as a daily morning show, a panel show, or a quiz show. **SEE 18.5**

The fact, or rundown, sheet   A *fact sheet*, or *rundown sheet*, lists the items that are to be shown on-camera and indicates roughly what should be said. **SEE 18.6** No specific video or audio instructions are given. The fact sheet is usually supplied by a manufacturer or advertiser who wants a particular performer to ad-lib about a particular item.

If the demonstration of the item is somewhat complicated, the director may rewrite the fact sheet and indicate key camera shots to help coordinate the talent's and director's actions. Unless the demonstration is extremely simple, such as holding up a book by a famous novelist, directing solely from a fact sheet is not recommended. Ad-libbing by both director and talent rarely works out satisfactorily, even if the videotaping is intended for postproduction editing.

There is software available that will help you format a script, or change quickly and effortlessly from one format to another. Some of the more sophisticated software programs can also reformat a script that was originally created by a word processing program.

Script Marking

Proper marking of a script will aid you greatly in directing from the control room or on location. In control room

```
Open Studios. Marin County. Noon News 04/20


Diana:                HAVE YOU EVER WONDERED JUST WHERE AND HOW
Key Box               THE TOP PAINTERS AND SCULPTORS CREATE THEIR
                      ART? WELL, YOU CAN SEE FOR YOURSELF ALL DAY
                      TOMORROW DURING OPEN HOUSE OF THE WEST MARIN
                      ART SOCIETY.

VTR 2 (VO) (:10)      THE SMALL TOWNS ALONG SIR FRANCIS DRAKE
                      BOULEVARD IN MARIN COUNTY ARE THE NEW RETREAT
                      FOR ARTISTS WHO FLED THE NOISE AND HUSTLE OF
                      THE CITY.

Diana:                WHAT IS IT THAT ATTRACTS SO MANY ARTISTS TO
                      THIS AREA? JOYCE LIVINGSTON, A FIRST-CLASS
                      PAINTER, SAYS IT'S NOT JUST THE LANDSCAPE.

VTR 4 SOT (:20)       In-cue: "It's the people..."

                      Out-cue: "...think of a better place to
                      work."

Diana:                ALLIE HYDE, A PRIZE-WINNING SCULPTOR, GETS
                      HER CREATIVE ENERGY FROM THE GIANT REDWOODS.

VTR 5 SOT (:12)       In-cue: "The trees..."

                      Out-cue: "...spiritual energy."

Diana:                ERIKA BRIAN PAID A VISIT TO THE INVERNESS
                      STUDIO OF PAINTER JOYCE LIVINGSTON. HERE IS
                      HER STORY.

VTR 6 SOT (1:15)      In-cue: "Have you ever..."

                      Out-cue: "...back to you, Diana."

-----------------------------------------------------------
BUMPER  (:05)
                      COMMERCIAL BREAK 1
-----------------------------------------------------------

              more...more...more...
```

18.2 NEWS SCRIPT

The news script contains every word spoken by the newscaster (except for the occasional chitchat) and all major video sources used.

VIDEO	AUDIO
Effects	
Wipe to: VTR (SOT) (showing a series of paintings from realism to expressionism)	AUDIO IN-CUE: "ALL THE PAINTINGS WERE DONE BY ONE ARTIST . . . PICASSO"
	OUT-CUE: ". . . PHENOMENAL CREATIVE FORCE"
MS Barbara by the easel	BARBARA: But even Picasso must have had some bad days and painted some bad pictures. Take a look. The woman's hands are obviously not right. Did Picasso deliberately distort the hands to make a point? I don't think so.
CU of painting Key effects	Look at the outline. He obviously struggled. The line is unsure, and he painted this section over at least three times. Because the rest of the painting is so realistically done, the distorted hands seem out of place. This is quite different from his later period, when he distorted images to intensify the event.
VTR SOT	IN-CUE: "DISTORTION MEANS POWER. THIS COULD HAVE BEEN PICASSO'S FORMULA . . ." OUT-CUE: ". . . EXPRESSIVE POWER THROUGH DISTORTION IN HIS LATER PAINTINGS."
CU Barbara	BARBARA: But the formula "distortion means power" does not always apply. Here again it seems to weaken the event. Take a look at . . .

18.3 FULLY SCRIPTED DOCUMENTARY

In this script the video and audio information is in two columns. The video information is usually page-left, and the audio information, page-right.

VIDEO	AUDIO
	KATY:
CU of Katy	But the debate about forest fires is still going on. If we let the fire burn itself out, we lose valuable timber and kill countless animals, not to speak of the danger to property and the people who live there. Where do you stand, Dr. Hough?
	DR. HOUGH:
Cut to CU of Dr. Hough	(SAYS THAT THIS IS QUITE TRUE, BUT THAT THE ANIMALS USUALLY GET OUT UNHARMED AND THAT THE BURNED UNDERBRUSH STIMULATES NEW GROWTH.)
	KATY:
Cut to two-shot	Couldn't this be done through controlled burning?
	DR. HOUGH:
	(SAYS YES, BUT THAT IT WOULD COST TOO MUCH AND THAT THERE WOULD STILL BE FOREST FIRES TO CONTEND WITH.)

18.4 SEMISCRIPTED FORMAT, OR PARTIAL SCRIPT

This script shows the video information in the left column but only partial dialogue in the audio column. The questions of the host are usually fully scripted, but the answers are only briefly described.

directing, you need to coordinate many people and machines within a continuous time frame. The marked script becomes a road map that guides you through the intricacies of a production. Although there is no single correct way of marking a script, certain conventions and standards have been developed. Obviously, a fully scripted show requires more, and more-precise, cuing than an interview that is directed from a show format. Live or live-on-tape productions directed from the control room in a continuous time frame need more, and more-precise, script markings than do scripts used in discontinuous, single-camera studio or field productions, where you stop and reset between takes or small series of takes. But even

in discontinuous, single-camera productions, a well-marked script will help you remember various camera and talent positions and make your directing less arbitrary.

Script marking for instantaneous editing (switching)   Whatever script marking you may choose or develop, it must be clear, readable, and, above all, consistent. Once you arrive at a working system, stick with it. As in musical notation, where you can perceive whole passages without reading each individual note, the script-marking system permits you to interpret and react to the written cues without having to consciously read each one. The following three figures provide examples

```
PEOPLE, PLACES, POLITICS SHOW FORMAT   (Script attached)

VTR DATE: 2/3      FACILITIES REQUEST:  BECA 415
AIR DATE: 2/17     RUNNING TIME:  25:30
DIRECTOR: Whitney  HOST:  Kipper

                          OPEN

VIDEO              AUDIO

STANDARD OPENING/VTR SOT
EFFECTS #117       ANNOUNCER: The Television Center of
                   the Broadcast and Electronic Communication
                   Arts Department, San Francisco State
                   University, presents "People, Places, Politics"
                   --a new perspective on global events.

KEY C.G. TOPIC TITLE Today's topic is:
------------------------------------------------------------
VTR #:       PSAs 1 & 2
------------------------------------------------------------

OPENING STUDIO SHOT  PHIL INTRODUCES GUESTS

KEY C.G.             NAMES OF GUESTS

CUs OF GUESTS        GUESTS DISCUSS TOPICS

CU OF Phil           CLOSES SHOW
------------------------------------------------------------
VTR #:       PSAs 3 & 4
------------------------------------------------------------
                          CLOSE
KEY C.G. ADDRESS     ANNOUNCER: To obtain a copy of today's
                     program, write to "People, Places, Politics,"
                     BECA Dept., San Francisco State University,
                     San Francisco, CA 94132
                     E-mail: BECA@sfsu.edu

KEY C.G. NEXT WEEK   Tune in next week when we present:
                     "Television and Democracy."

                     THEME MUSIC UP AND OUT
```

18.5 SHOW FORMAT

The show format contains only essential video information in the left (video) column, and the standard opening and closing announcements in the right (audio) column.

```
VIDEO PRO CD-ROM COMMERCIAL
SHOW:
DATE:

PROPS:
Desktop computer running Zettl's VideoLab 2.1. Triple-I Web page.
Video Pro poster and multimedia awards in background.
Video Pro package with disc as hand props.

1.   New multimedia product by Image, Imagination, Incorporated.

2.   Sensational success. Best Triple-I product yet.

3.   Won several awards for excellence, including the prestigious
     Invision Gold Medal.

4.   Designed for the production novice and video professional.

5.   Truly interactive. Provides you with a video studio in your home.
     Easy to use.

6.   You can proceed at your own speed and test your progress after
     each exercise.

7.   Will operate on Windows or Macintosh platforms.

8.   Special introductory offer. Expires Oct. 20. Hurry. Available in
     all major software stores. For more information or the dealer
     near you, visit Triple-I's Web page at http://www.iii.net.
```

18.6 FACT, OR RUNDOWN, SHEET

The fact sheet, or rundown sheet, lists the major points of the product to be demonstrated. No specific video or audio information is given. The talent ad-libs the demonstration, and the director follows the talent's action with the camera.

of various kinds of script marking. **SEE 18.7–18.9** Take a look at the markings in figure 18.7 and compare them with those in figures 18.8 and 18.9. Which script seems cleaner and more readable to you?

The first script (figure 18.7) shows information that is more confusing than helpful. By the time you have read all the cue instructions, you will certainly have missed part or all of the action and perhaps even half of the talent's commentary. You do not have to mark all stand-by cues or any other obvious cues that are already implied. For example, "ready" cues are always given before a cue; therefore, they need not be spelled out.

In contrast, the markings in figures 18.8 and 18.9 are clean and simple. They are kept to a minimum, and there is little writing. You are able to grasp all the cues quickly without actually reading each word. As you can see, the cues in figure 18.8 provide the same information as those

in figure 18.7, but allow you to keep track of the narration, look ahead at upcoming cues, and especially watch the action on the preview monitors. Let us now highlight some of qualities of a well-marked script from a director's point of view (refer to figure 18.8).

■ All action cues are placed *before* the desired action.

■ If the shots or camera actions are clearly described in the video column (page-left), or the audio cues in the audio column (page-right), simply underline or circle the printed instructions. This keeps the script clean and uncluttered. But if the printed instructions are hard to read, do not hesitate to repeat them with your own symbols.

■ If the script does not indicate a particular transition from one video source to another, it is always a cut. A large handwritten *2* next to a cue line means that the upcoming

VIDEO	AUDIO	
Effects		*Ready on effects*
Wipe to: VTR (SOT) (showing a series of paintings from realism to expressionism)	AUDIO IN-CUE: "ALL THE PAINTINGS WERE DONE BY ONE ARTIST . . . PICASSO"	*Take effects* *Ready to wipe to VTR* *Roll VTR and take VTR 4*
	OUT-CUE: ". . . PHENOMENAL CREATIVE FORCE"	*Track up on VTR 4* *Ready camera 2*
MS Barbara by the easel	But even Picasso must have had some bad days and painted some bad pictures. Take a look. The woman's hands are obviously not right. Did Picasso deliberately distort the hands to make a point? I don't think so.	*Cue Barbara and take camera 2*
CU of painting	*Ready camera 3 on the easel – closeup* Look at the outline. He obviously struggled. The line is unsure, and he painted this section over at least three times. Because the rest of the painting is so realistically done, the distorted hands seem out of place. This is quite different from his later period, when he distorted images to intensify the event.	*Take camera 3*
Key effects		
VTR SOT *Insert time* *4:27 min*	IN-CUE: "DISTORTION MEANS POWER. THIS COULD HAVE BEEN PICASSO'S FORMULA . . ."	*Ready to roll VTR 4 Segment 2*
	OUT-CUE: ". . . EXPRESSIVE POWER THROUGH DISTORTION IN HIS LATER PAINTINGS."	*Roll VTR 4 and take VTR 4*
CU Barbara	But the formula "distortion means power" does not always apply. Here again it seems to weaken the event. Take a look at . . .	*Ready camera 2* *Cue Barbara and take camera 2*

18.7 BAD SCRIPT MARKING

This script is marked with too much unnecessary information that makes it hard to read.

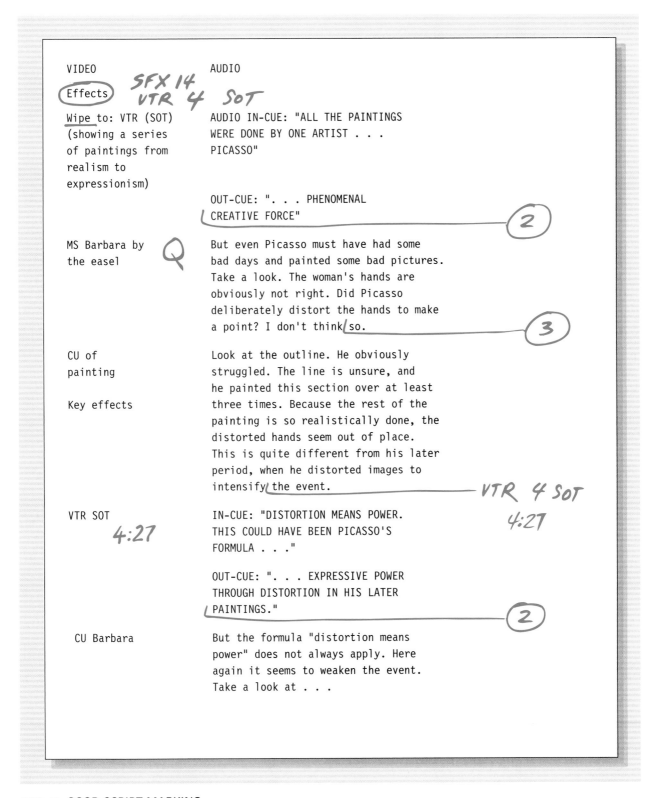

VIDEO	AUDIO
(Effects) SFX 14 VTR 4 SOT	
Wipe to: VTR (SOT) (showing a series of paintings from realism to expressionism)	AUDIO IN-CUE: "ALL THE PAINTINGS WERE DONE BY ONE ARTIST . . . PICASSO"
	OUT-CUE: ". . . PHENOMENAL CREATIVE FORCE" ②
MS Barbara by the easel Q	But even Picasso must have had some bad days and painted some bad pictures. Take a look. The woman's hands are obviously not right. Did Picasso deliberately distort the hands to make a point? I don't think so. ③
CU of painting

Key effects | Look at the outline. He obviously struggled. The line is unsure, and he painted this section over at least three times. Because the rest of the painting is so realistically done, the distorted hands seem out of place. This is quite different from his later period, when he distorted images to intensify the event. — VTR 4 SOT 4:27 |
VTR SOT 4:27	IN-CUE: "DISTORTION MEANS POWER. THIS COULD HAVE BEEN PICASSO'S FORMULA . . ."
	OUT-CUE: ". . . EXPRESSIVE POWER THROUGH DISTORTION IN HIS LATER PAINTINGS." ②
CU Barbara	But the formula "distortion means power" does not always apply. Here again it seems to weaken the event. Take a look at . . .

18.8 GOOD SCRIPT MARKING
This script is clearly marked and can be read easily by the director.

SCENE 6

A FEW DAYS LATER. INTERIOR. CITY HOSPITAL
EMERGENCY WAITING ROOM. LATE EVENING.

YOLANDA is anxiously PACING back and forth in the
hospital hallway in front of the emergency room. She has
come straight from her job to the hospital. We see the
typical hospital traffic in an emergency room. A DOCTOR
(friend of CHUCK'S) PUSHES CARRIE in a wheelchair down
the hall toward YOLANDA.

                    CARRIE
          (in wheelchair, but rather cheerful)
Hi, Mom!

                    YOLANDA
          (anxious and worried)
Carrie—are you all right? What happened?

                    CARRIE
I'm OK. I just slipped.

               DOCTOR (simultaneously)
She has a sprained right wrist. Nothing serious...

                    CARRIE
Why is everybody making such a big deal out of it?

                    YOLANDA
     (cutting into both CARRIE'S and DOCTOR'S lines)
Does it hurt? Did you break your arm?

18.9 DRAMA SCRIPT: MARKED

This multicamera dramatic script shows the camera used, the shot number, the type of shot, and the major actions. Note the blocking sketch at the beginning of this scene.

transition is a cut to camera 2. It also implies a "ready 2" before the "take 2" call.

▉ If the show requires rehearsals, do preliminary script marking in pencil so you can make quick changes without creating a messy or illegible script. Once you are ready for the dress rehearsal, however, you should have marked the script in bold letters. Have the AD (assistant, or associate, director) and floor manager copy your markings on their own scripts.

▉ Mark the cameras by circled numbers and all in one row. This allows you to see quickly which camera needs to be readied for the next shot.

▉ Number each shot in consecutive order, starting with 1, regardless of the camera you use for the shot. These numbers will not only help you ready the various shots for each camera, but also make it easy to delete a shot during rehearsal. All you need to do is say "delete shot 85," and camera 1 will skip the XS (cross-shot) of Susan. **SEE 18.10**

▉ You may want to devise a symbol that signifies action, such as someone coming through the door, walking over to the map, sitting down, or getting up. In figure 18.9 this cue is a handwritten arrow (→).

▉ If there are several moves by the talent, draw little maps of these moves (see figure 18.9). Such blocking sketches are usually more helpful to recall talent moves, camera positions, and traffic than are storyboard sketches of shot compositions.

Script marking for postproduction editing

The marking of the script for discontinuous takes consists of a careful breakdown and indication of the various scenes, their locations (restaurant, front entrance), and principal visualizations (camera point of view, field of view). You then number the shots in the proposed production sequence. Thus, you end up with a list of shots that refers to the original script by page number. Here is an example:

LOCATION	SCENE	TAKE	SCRIPT PAGE
Restaurant	2	14	28
		15	31
		16	36
Restaurant entrance	6	17	61
		18	72
	14	19	162
		20	165

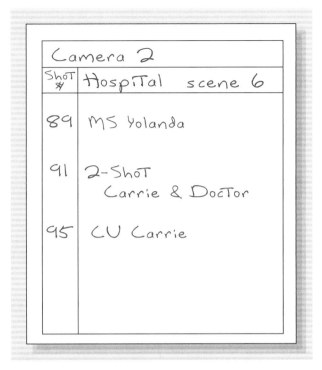

18.10 SHOT SHEET

Each camera has its own shot sheet, indicating the location of the scene, the shot number, the type of shot, and the subject or person(s) to be in it.

In the script itself, you are free to use whatever markings you prefer. When videotaping discontinuous takes for postproduction, you obviously have more time to consult your script than during a live or live-on-tape production. For discontinuous taping it may help to mark the talent movements on the script as well as draw next to the dialogue small storyboard sketches that show unusual shot framings. Such sketches assist in recalling what you had in mind when preparing the script. Many film directors storyboard every shot of the entire movie before ever shooting a single frame of film.[1] Once again, a variety of software packages will assist you in producing storyboards. Some of these programs contain standard shots of streets, interiors, and so forth in which you can paste the characters and then move them around until they are in the desired positions.

Floor Plan and Location Sketch

Unless you direct a routine studio production that occurs in the same set, such as a news, interview, or game show,

---

1. See Stephen Katz, *Film Directing Shot by Shot* (Studio City, Calif.: Michael Wiese Productions, 1991), pp. 23–84.

you need a floor plan for preproduction. As explained in chapter 15, the *floor plan* shows the location of the scenery and set properties relative to a grid pattern and the available action areas. Like the script, the floor plan helps you visualize various shots and interpret them into major camera positions and camera traffic (movements of various cameras). It also influences, and sometimes dictates, how you block the talent.

With some practice you can do almost all the talent blocking and camera positioning simply by looking at the floor plan. You will also be able to spot potential blocking, lighting, audio, and camera problems. For example, if "active" furniture (that which is used by talent) is too close to the scenery, you will have problems with back lighting. Or if there is a rug on the floor, a camera may not be able to dolly all the way into the set. Interpreting a floor plan to visualize shots and spot potential problems is discussed in section 18.2.

ENG EFP When the production takes place in the field, you need an accurate *location sketch*, which represents a "field floor plan" showing the major elements of the production environment. For example, if the single-camera production takes place inside a painter's studio, you need to know the location of the door, tables, easels, cabinets, and, especially, the windows. **SEE 18.11** If the event happens outdoors, the location sketch should show the street, major buildings, driveways, and so forth (see figure 18.19). Even if a field production happens in an actual field, make a sketch so that the crew knows which field it is and how best to get there.

Facilities Request

The *facilities request* is usually not prepared by the director, but by some other member of the production team (producer, AD, or technical director). If someone else originates the facilities request, you need to examine it carefully to see that the equipment requested is sufficient and appropriate for the planned production. For example, a single PZM microphone or three table mics may give you a much better audio pickup during a panel discussion than six lavalieres. Or you may prefer two camcorders for your EFP pickup rather than a remote truck. List all special requests as well, such as a working television receiver in the living room set or working phones for actors who are talking to each other in a live-on-tape scene. Check beforehand that the requested equipment will actually be available at the scheduled time.

Generally, the more time and effort you devote to preproduction, the less time and effort you will have to spend during the production. Production efficiency does not mean to hurry through a production regardless of quality; rather, it means extensive preproduction. Preproduction planning will provide you with the information necessary for properly directing the show, help you eliminate most of the production problems, and alert you to the few remaining ones. Most important, preproduction planning provides you with the confidence necessary to make correct judgments quickly and reliably.

SUPPORT STAFF

Your immediate support staff consists of the floor manager, the PA (production assistant), and, in larger operations, the AD.

Floor Manager

The *floor manager* is also called the floor director, stage manager, or unit manager, even though the unit manager functions more like a production manager, who takes care of the daily production and budgetary details. As a floor manager, your primary functions are to coordinate all activities on the "floor" (studio or on-location site) and relay the cues from the director to the talent.

Before the production, you need to oversee and help the floor crew in setting up scenery, placing set and hand props, dressing the set, and putting up displays. During rehearsals and the production, you must coordinate the floor crew and talent and relay the director's talent cues. After the production, you are responsible for striking the set and props, or restoring the remote production site to its original condition.

Here are some points to keep in mind when managing the floor:

■ Unless you are doing a routine show that is produced in a "permanent" set (one that is not struck after each show), you need to obtain a detailed floor plan and prop list. Check with the art director and director about any special features or changes. Get a marked script from the director so that you can anticipate talent and camera traffic. Have the director look at the set before fine-tuning the lighting. Once the lighting is complete, even minor set changes can require major lighting adjustments. Once

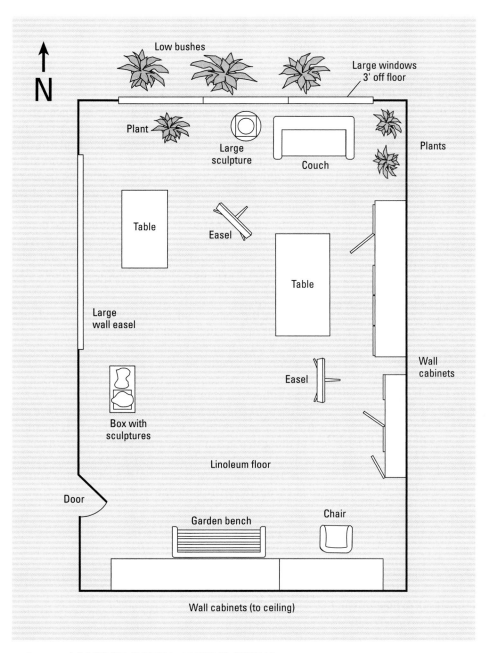

Low bushes

Large windows
3' off floor

Plant

Plants

Large
sculpture

Couch

Table

Easel

Table

Large
wall easel

Easel

Box with
sculptures

Wall
cabinets

Linoleum floor

Door

Garden bench

Chair

Wall cabinets (to ceiling)

18.11　LOCATION SKETCH: ARTIST'S STUDIO

This location sketch of an artist's studio shows the major dimensions, doors, windows, and furnishings.

the set is put up and dressed, take a Polaroid picture of it. Such a record is more accessible than a videotape.

▦ You are responsible for having all hand props on the set and in operating condition. For example, if the show involves a demonstration of a new CD-ROM, run the computer program a few times to see how it works. Hard-to-open jars or bottles are a constant challenge to the performer. Twist the lid of a jar slightly or loosen the bottle cap so the talent can remove it without a struggle. This small courtesy can prevent many retakes and frayed nerves.

▦ Check that the teleprompter works.

▦ If you use an on-camera slate in the field, have it ready and filled out with the essential information. Have several pens available and a rag to erase the writing.

▦ For complex productions study the marked script before the rehearsal and write in your own cues, such as talent entrances and exits and prop, costume, or set changes. In case of doubt, ask the director for clarification.

▦ Introduce yourself to the talent and guests, and have a designated place for them to sit while waiting in the studio. Because most production people are quite busy (including the director and producer), you are the one who must establish and maintain a rapport with the talent and guests throughout the production. Ask them periodically whether they would like some water or a cup of coffee, whether they are comfortable, and whether you can be of any help to them. When working with outside talent, review your major cues with them (see chapter 19). When using a teleprompter, ask the performers whether the font size is big enough and whether the distance from camera to performer is tolerable.

▦ During the rehearsal of a fully scripted show, follow the script as much as possible and anticipate the director's cues. If hand props are used, return them to their original positions after each take. Keep notes on especially difficult camera travels or talent actions. If the production is shot in segments for postproduction editing, pay particular attention to continuity of the talent's appearance, positions, and major moves.

▦ Always carry a pen or pencil, a broad marking pen, a roll of masking and gaffer's tape, and a piece of chalk (for taping down props and equipment or spiking—marking—talent and camera positions). Also have a large pad ready so you can write out messages for the talent in case the I.F.B. system breaks down or is not used.

▦ During rehearsal deliver all cues as though you were on the air, even if the director stands right next to you. When cuing, you do not always have to remain next to the camera. As much as possible, position yourself so that you can see the talent's eyes.

▦ During the show do not cue on your own, even if you think the director has missed a cue. Rather, ask the director on the intercom whether you should give the cue as marked and rehearsed. If there are interruptions in the videotaping because some technical problems are being discussed in the control room, inform the talent about what is going on. Tell them that they did a good job but that the director has to work out a few technical details. Invite the talent during extended problem-solving interruptions to get out from under the lights and relax in the small studio area you have set up for them—but don't let them wander off.

▦ After the show thank the talent or guests and help them out of the studio. You then need to supervise the strike of the set in the studio or of the items set up on location. Be careful not to drag scenery or prop carts across cables that might still be on the studio floor. Locate objects that were brought in by a guest, such as a precious statue, books, or the latest computer model, and see to it that they are returned. If you shot indoors on location, put things back. A small location sketch or photo will be of great help when trying to return things to the way they were. When shooting on location, remember that you are a guest operating in someone else's space.

Assistant, or Associate, Director

As an *assistant, or associate, director (AD)*, you mainly assist the director in the production phase—the rehearsals and on-the-air performance or taping sessions. In complex studio shows, a director may have you give all standby cues (for example: "Ready to cue Mary, ready 2 CU of John") and preset the cameras by telling the camera operators on the intercom the upcoming shots or camera moves. This frees the director somewhat from the script in order to concentrate more on the preview monitors. Once preset by you, the director then initiates the action by the various action cues: "Ready 2, take 2." You activated a cut from Mary to John.

In elaborate field productions, the AD may direct the *run-throughs* (rehearsals) for each take, which enables the director to stand back and observe the action on the field (line) monitor.

As an AD you are also responsible for the timing of the show segments and the overall show during rehearsals as well as during the actual production. Even in studio productions, be prepared to take over and direct the show or portions of it during rehearsal. This gives the director a chance to see how the shots look and, especially, how the show flows.

Production Assistant

As a *production assistant (PA)*, you must be prepared to do a variety of jobs, from duplicating and distributing the script, looking for a specific prop, and welcoming the talent, to calling a cab, getting coffee, and taking notes for the producer and the director (unless the AD is taking notes). Usually, note taking is the PA's most important assignment. You simply follow the producer and/or director with a pad and pen and record everything they tell you to write down or mumble to themselves. During the "note" breaks, you simply read back your notes item by item. When in the field, you will also keep a *field log* of all the production takes, which helps the postproduction editor locate shots on the source tapes. *READY ZVL* ❹

Before you engage in some visualization exercises and learn some on-the-air directing skills, let's summarize the major preproduction issues just discussed. Directing means, essentially, the effective communication of your intentions to a diverse production team. Be sure to honor this commitment. You need to establish and use well-defined channels of communication among all members of the team, and send precise messages through these channels. This means that you must have a clear idea of what you want to do and convey that intention effectively to everyone involved.

MAIN POINTS

◆ A television director must be an artist who can translate a script or an event into effective television pictures and sound, a psychologist who can work with people of different temperaments and skills, a technical adviser who knows the potentials and limitations of the equipment, and a coordinator who can initiate and keep track of myriad production processes.

◆ A clear understanding of the process message (desired effect) will help the director decide on the most appropriate type of production (single-camera or multicamera, studio or field, live or live-on-tape, or continuous or discontinuous takes for post-production).

◆ There needs to be effective and frequent communication among the director, the talent, and all members of the production team.

◆ The schedule should be realistic and fit into the master production schedule of the station or production company.

◆ The various script formats are the fully scripted show format, the semiscripted show format, the show format, and the fact sheet or rundown sheet.

◆ Precise and easy-to-read script markings help the director and other key production personnel anticipate and execute a great variety of cues.

◆ The floor plan or location sketch enables the director to plan major camera and talent positions and traffic.

◆ The facilities request is an essential communications device for procuring the necessary equipment and properties.

◆ The director's immediate support staff are the floor manager, the AD (assistant, or associate, director), and the PA (production assistant).

18.2

Moving from Script to Screen

Now that you know the basics of directing, including script formats and how to mark them, you need to learn how to translate the words of the script into effective pictures and sound. This translation process is called *visualization*—seeing the script in pictures and hearing the accompanying sounds. Yes, *visualization* refers not only to the mental imaging of pictures, but also of sound. There are no sure-fire formulas for this translation process; what it requires is a certain amount of imagination, artistic sensitivity, and, once again, lots of practice. The best way to practice is to carefully observe the events around you—how people behave in a classroom or restaurant, or on a bus or airplane—and mentally note what makes one event so different from others. When you read a newspaper, magazine, or novel, try to visualize what is being described as screen images and sound.

This section will help you with these visualization processes—the translation of the various script formats into picture and sound images and sequences.

▶ **VISUALIZATION AND SEQUENCING**
 Formulating the process message, medium requirements, and interpreting the floor plan and location sketch

▶ **SCRIPT ANALYSIS**
 Locking-in point and translation, and the storyboard

VISUALIZATION AND SEQUENCING

Directing starts with the visualization of the key images. Because we see only what the camera sees, you need to carry the initial visualization further and translate it into such directing detail as where people and things should be placed relative to the camera and where the camera should be positioned relative to the event (people and things). You must then consider the *sequencing* of the portions of this visualized event through postproduction editing or switching (instantaneous editing). Concurrently, you must *hear* the individual shots and the sequence. In television, "hearing" a particular picture or picture sequence can be as important as seeing it in your mind.

As mentioned, a carefully defined process message facilitates the visualization process and, especially, makes it more precise. After having decided on what the target audience is to see, hear, feel, or do, you can follow the effect-to-cause model and determine just how the key shots should look and how to accomplish them.

Here is an example: You are to direct three segments of a program series on teenage driving safety. The first assignment is an interview, consisting of a female interviewer who regularly hosts the weekly half-hour community service show, a male police officer who heads the municipal traffic safety program, and a female student representative of the local high school. The second assignment is an interview with a male high school student who has been confined to a wheelchair since a serious car accident. The third is a demonstration of some potential dangers of running a stop sign.

The scripts available to you at this point are very sketchy and resemble more brief rundown sheets than partial script formats. **SEE 18.12–18.14**

Because the producer has an unusually tight deadline for the completion of the series, she asks that you get started with the preproduction planning despite the lack of more-detailed scripts. She can give you only a rough idea of what each show is supposed to accomplish: Segment 1 should inform the audience (high-school and college students) of the ongoing efforts by the police department to cooperate with schools to teach traffic safety to young drivers; segment 2 should shock the viewers into an awareness of the consequences of careless driving; segment 3 should make the audience aware of the potential dangers of running a stop sign.

Let's apply the effect-to-cause model and see how these scripts can be translated into video programs. *READY ZVL* ⑤

Formulating the Process Message

Despite the sketchy scripts and process messages, many images have probably entered your head already: the police officer in his blue uniform sitting next to the high-school student; a young man straining to move his wheelchair up a ramp to his front door; a car almost hit in an intersection by another car running a stop sign. Before going any further, however, you may want to define more-precise process messages.

Process message 1   *The interview with the traffic safety officer and the student representative should demonstrate to high-school and college students a ten-point traffic safety program to help teenagers become responsible drivers. It should also demonstrate how police and students can cooperate in this effort.*

Process message 2   *The interview with the student in the wheelchair should make viewers (of the desired target*

audience) gain a deeper insight into his feelings and attitudes since his accident and empathize with him.

Process message 3   *The program should show viewers at least four different accidents caused by running a stop sign and demonstrate how to avoid them.*

A careful reading of these process messages should make your visualization a little more precise. For example, just how do you see the three people (host, police officer, and high-school student) interact in the interview? What shots and shot sequences do you feel would best communicate the interview to the audience? Do you visualize a different approach to the interview with the student in the wheelchair? The demonstration of running a stop sign probably triggers some stereotypical Hollywood video and audio images, such as glass shattering, tires squealing, and cars spinning and crashing into each other.

Medium Requirements

Without trying to be too specific, you can now proceed from some general visualizations to the *medium requirements:* production method (multicamera studio show or single-camera EFP), certain key visualizations and sequencing, necessary equipment, and specific production procedures (when to do what).

Here is how you might arrive at specific medium requirements for each segment (process message).

Segment 1   The interview is strictly informational. What the people say is more important than getting to know them. The high-school student may not always agree with the police officer's views, so the two may not only answer the interviewer but also talk to each other.

The sequencing will probably show the three people in three-shots (host and two guests), two-shots (host and guest, two guests talking), and individual close-ups. These shots can best be accomplished by having the guests sit together across from the interviewer. **SEE 18.15** According to the sketchy script, the officer's ten-point program on traffic safety and other items should be shown on-screen as C.G. graphics, unless he brings an easel card.

The show is obviously best done live-on-tape in the studio. There you can put them in a neutral environment, have good control over the lighting and audio, switch among multiple cameras, and use the C.G.

Now you can become more specific about the medium requirements: set, cameras, microphones,

```
TRAFFIC SAFETY SERIES

Program No: 2 Interview (Length: 26:30)
VTR Date: Saturday, March 16, 4:00—5:00 P.M. STUDIO 2
Air Date: Tuesday, March 19

Host:          Yvette Sharp
Guests:        Lt. John Hewitt, traffic safety program,
               City Police Department
               Rebecca Child, senior and student representative,
               Central High School


---------------------------------------------------------------

Video
STANDARD OPENING
CU of Hostess
faces camera          INTRODUCES SHOW
2-shot of guests      INTRODUCES GUESTS
CU of host            FIRST QUESTION

INTERVIEW: Lieutenant John Hewitt is the officer in charge of the
traffic safety program. Is a twenty-year veteran of the City Police
Department. Has been in traffic safety for the past eight years.

NOTE: HE WILL REFER TO A TEN-POINT PROGRAM (DISPLAY VIA C.G.).

Rebecca Child is the student representative of Central High.
She is an A student, on the debate team, and on the champion
volleyball team. She is very much in favor of an effective traffic
safety program but believes that the city police are especially
tough on high-school students and are out to get them.

STANDARD CLOSE

CU of host      CLOSING REMARKS
LS of host and guests   THEME
CG credits
```

18.12 **TRAFFIC SAFETY STUDIO INTERVIEW**
This script for a studio interview on traffic safety is written in the semiscripted format. Note that this script gives some information on the guests appearing on the show.

```
TRAFFIC SAFETY SERIES

Program No: 5 Location Interview (Length: 26:30)
EFP Date: Friday, March 29, 9:00 A.M.—all day
Postproduction to be scheduled
Air Date: Tuesday, April 9

Interviewer:    Yvette Sharp
Interviewee:    Jack Armstrong
Address:        49 Baranca Road, South City
                Tel.: 990 999-9990

OPENING AND CLOSING ARE TO BE DONE ON LOCATION

-----------------------------------------------------------------

Jack is a high-school senior. He has been confined to a wheelchair
since he was hit by a car running a stop sign. The other driver was
from his high school. Jack was an outstanding tennis player and is
proud of the several trophies he won in important tournaments.
He is a good student and coping very well. He is eager to participate
in the traffic safety program.

-----------------------------------------------------------------

NOTE: EMPHASIS SHOULD BE ON JACK. GET GOOD CUs.
```

18.13 TRAFFIC SAFETY FIELD INTERVIEW

Again, this location interview is written in the semiscripted format and gives information about the guest to be interviewed.

TRAFFIC SAFETY SERIES

Program No: 6 Running Stop Signs (Length: 26:30)
EFP Date: Sunday, April 7, 7:00 A.M.—all day
VTR Date: Tuesday, April 9, 4:00 P.M.—4:30 P.M.
Postproduction to be scheduled
Air Date: Saturday, April 16

EFP Location:	Intersection of West Spring Street and Taraval Court
Contact:	Lt. John Hewitt, traffic safety program, City Police Department Tel.: 990 888-8888

OPENING AND CLOSING (YVETTE) ARE TO BE DONE ON LOCATION

EFP: Program should show car running a stop sign at
intersection and the consequences: almost hitting a
pedestrian, jogger, bicycler; running into another car,
etc. Detailed script will follow.

STUDIO: Lt. Hewitt will briefly demonstrate some typical
accidents with toy cars on a magnetic board.

NOTE: LT. HEWITT WILL PROVIDE ALL VEHICLES AND DRIVERS AS
WELL AS TALENT. HE WILL TAKE CARE OF ALL TRAFFIC CONTROL,
VEHICLE PARKING, AND COMMUNICATIONS. CONFIRM EFP APRIL 5.

ALTERNATE POLICE CONTACT: Sgt. Fenton McKenna (same telephone)

18.14 TRAFFIC SAFETY STOP SIGN EPISODE

This semiscripted format for a field production contains information about the major events the program is to show.

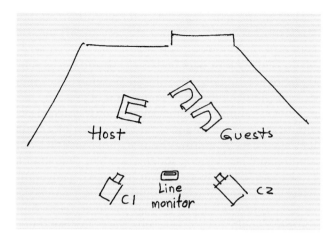

18.15 TRAFFIC SAFETY
INTERVIEW: ROUGH SKETCH
This rough sketch for a studio interview set shows the
approximate locations of the chairs and cameras.

lighting, and additional equipment. Because the participants do not move around, the host and guests can wear
lavaliere mics for the audio pickup. The lighting should
be normal; that is, fairly high-key, slow-falloff lighting so
the viewer can see everyone well. There is no need for
dramatic shadows. Perhaps you can persuade the police
officer to take off his cap to avoid annoying shadows on
his face. How about cameras? Three or two? Even a lively
exchange of ideas between the officer and the high-school
student will not require terribly fast cutting. Assuming that
the host and guests sit across from each other, you really
need only two cameras (see figure 18.15).

Camera 2 can get the opening and closing shots, but
is otherwise assigned to the host. Camera 1 can get two-
shots and CUs of the guests, as well as over-the-shoulder
(of the host) three-shots. Besides the normal control room
and studio facilities, you will need to request a VTR and
tape (don't forget to request the appropriate tape), the
C.G., and a limited amount of postproduction time, just
in case you need to stop the tape for some reason during
the interview. Unless you have teleprompters to show the
ten-point traffic program, you need a line monitor that
all talent can see.

Segment 2   In contrast to segment 1, the segment 2
interview is much more private. Its primary purpose is
not to communicate specific information but to create an
emotional impact on the audience. The communication
is intimate and personal; viewers should strongly

empathize with the young man in the wheelchair. These
aspects of the process message suggest quite readily that
we should visit the student in his own environment—his
home—and that, except for the opening shots, we should
see the student primarily in close-ups and extreme close-
ups rather than in less intense medium and long shots.
Again, you will inevitably visualize certain key shots that
you have called up from your personal visual reservoir.
Your task now is to interpret these images and all other
aspects of the process message into a specific production
approach and medium requirements.

Considering the major aspects of the process
message (revealing the student's feelings and thoughts,
intimacy with and emotional impact on the audience),
the general production type and specific medium
requirements become fairly apparent. It is best done
single-camera style in the student's home. First, the single
camera and associated equipment (lights and mics) cause
a minimum intrusion into the environment. Second, the
interview itself can be unhurried and stretch over a
considerable period of time. Third, the interview does not
have to be continuous; it can slow down, be briefly
interrupted, or be stopped and then picked up at any time.
The production can be out of sequence. You may want to
start with videotaping the actual interview and then tape
the opening shots of the student moving up the ramp in
his wheelchair and the reaction shots of the interviewer.
If the student happens to refer to his athletic trophies, you
can videotape them (and other significant items in the
house) after the interview and then assemble all the
segments in postproduction editing.

Here are some of the specific (and modest) medium
requirements: camcorder, videotapes, batteries, tripod,
playback monitor, two lavaliere mics, portable lighting kit,
shotgun mic, small audio mixer, miscellaneous production items (extension cords, portable slate, and so forth),
and good postproduction facilities. Compared with
segment 1, this production needs considerably more
editing time. To facilitate your visualization and sequencing, try to visit the student in his home prior to the
videotaping. Meeting the student and getting to know him
in his home will give you a sense of the whole atmosphere,
help you plan your shots more specifically, and help
determine more accurately the medium requirements.

Segment 3   This production is by far the most
demanding of you as a director. It requires the coordination of different people, locations, and actions. Start
with some key visualizations. Running a stop sign is

obviously best shown by having a car actually do it. To demonstrate the consequences of such an offense, you may need to show the car going through the stop sign, barely missing a pedestrian or bicyclist who happens to be in the intersection or even crashing into another car.

Now is the time to contact the producer again and ask her some important questions: Who will provide the vehicles for this demonstration? Who drives them? What about insurance? You may not need Hollywood stunt drivers for these demonstrations, but in no way should you have students perform these feats. Perhaps the police can assist you and the producer by furnishing both cars and experienced drivers. Who will be the harassed bicyclist and the pedestrian? Is there adequate insurance for all actors and extras involved? Will the police close portions of the street and the intersection for the shoot? For how long?

If the segment involves choreographing actual stunts, you would need a fire engine and ambulance standing by, just in case the stunt does not go exactly as planned. You had better abandon the project right at this point and ask the producer to pass it on to a more experienced director.

You could, however, suggest *simulating* these close-call actions through extensive video and audio postproduction. Assuming that the producer likes your alternate approach and that the police department will furnish cars, drivers, extras, and all necessary traffic control during the shoot, how would you carry out this directing assignment?

The key word in the process message is *demonstrate*. You need to show what is happening rather than merely talk about it. The demonstration obviously takes you on location—an actual street corner. The officer's later use of toy cars and a magnetic board to demonstrate a typical intersection accident and how to avoid it can best be done in the studio and integrated into the show in post-production editing (see figure 18.14).

Considering the complexity of the action and the limited production time available to you (the intersection can be blocked for only brief periods), you should use several camcorders that cover the action simultaneously from different angles and fields of view. You can then have the camcorders synchronize the start of the time codes to expedite the extensive (AB-roll) postproduction editing. You can do the studio portion live-on-tape with a simple two-camera setup (one for a cover shot and the other for close-ups).

To ensure maximum safety for all concerned, first shoot those scenes that involve the car running the stop sign and then move to the scenes of the frightened pedestrian jumping back onto the curb and the bicyclist trying to get out of the way (of the imagined oncoming car). To simulate the sight and sound of crashing into another car, simply show the pedestrian's frightened face and then, later, go to a junkyard for a shot of a badly damaged car. By editing the two shots together and adding familiar crashing sounds, you can simulate the crash quite convincingly without endangering anyone or wrecking any cars. You might think of using a "subjective camera" that shows going through the intersection from the driver's point of view. The camera operator can simply sit in the backseat and have the camera look past the driver through the windshield. For additional subjective camera shots, mount the camcorder on the hood of the car with the help of a bean bag (see chapter 5).

A fast zoom-in on the car while it is moving toward the camera will definitely lead to an intensification of the shot and to an exciting sequence when intercut with progressively closer shots of the pedestrian's frightened face. Be sure to get enough cutaways so that you can maintain the continuity of motion vectors during editing.

Whatever key visualizations and sequencing you choose, they will probably require the same basic field equipment: two or three camcorders, special mounting equipment (bean bags, clothesline, tape, camera braces), battery-powered monitor for replay, two or three shotgun mics and fishpoles, audio mixer, two or three reflectors (for CUs of talent), and other standard production items such as slate, videotape, headsets for the audio operator, and walkie-talkies for the field intercom.

The major part of this production will be taken up by off- and on-line editing. The simulation of near misses requires extensive video and audio postproduction. The audio portion is, therefore, especially important, because sounds intensify scenes and help elicit mental images of unseen action. Such standard sound effects as the squealing of tires, crash sounds, and a police siren will certainly intensify the scene and make the simulated crash believable. You may also want to include voice-over narration by the series host.

Don't forget to copy and carefully log the field footage. If you have a nonlinear system, digitize the takes (unless you shot with a digital camera), put them in the right "bins" (files), and start with the off-line editing.

Interpreting the Floor Plan and Location Sketch

Let's go back to the first segment—the studio interview with the police officer and the high-school representative—and assume that the novice art director took your rough sketch of the interview setup (figure 18.15) and worked up the floor plan and prop list as shown in the next figure. **SEE 18.16** What do you think about the floor plan? Would you give your go-ahead to have the scenery set up accordingly?

Take another look at the floor plan and try to visualize some of the key shots, such as opening and closing three-shots, two-shots of the guests talking to the host and to each other, and individual CUs of the three people. Visualize the foreground as well as the background of the shots, because the camera sees both. There are some definite camera problems with this floor plan.

▨ Given the way the chairs are placed, an opening three-shot would be difficult to achieve. If camera 2 shoots from straight on, the chairs are much too far apart. At best, the host and the guests would seem glued to the screen edges, placing undue emphasis on the painting in the middle. Also, you would probably overshoot the set on both ends. The guests would certainly block each other in this shot.

▨ If you shoot from the extreme left (camera 1) to get an over-the-shoulder shot from the host to the guests, you will overshoot the set. On a close-up, you would run the

risk of the rubber plant seeming to grow out of the guest's head. **SEE 18.17**

▨ If you cross-shoot with camera 2, you will again overshoot the set, and the second rubber plant would most likely appear to grow out of the host's head (see figure 18.17).

▨ If you pulled the cameras more toward the center to avoid overshooting, you would get nothing but profiles.

Aside from problems with camera shots, there are additional production problems:

▨ White hardwall panels hardly create the most interesting background. The surface is too plain, and its color is too bright for the foreground scene, rendering skin tones unusually dark. Because the host is an African American woman, the contrast problem with the white background is even more extreme. You cannot correct the problem by getting more light on her.

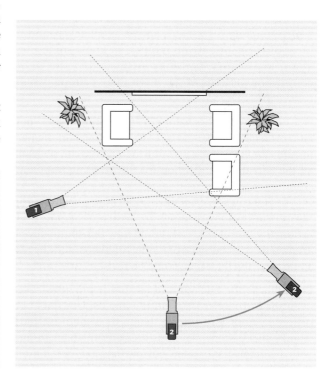

18.16 INTERVIEW SET:
FLOOR PLAN AND PROP LIST

This floor plan and prop list, based on the rough sketch of an interview set, reveal serious production problems.

18.17 INTERVIEW SET:
CAMERA POSITIONS

The camera positions reveal some of the production problems caused by this setup.

■   See how close the chairs are to the background flats? Any key light and fill light will inevitably strike the background too, adding to the silhouette effect. The back lights would also function as front (key) lights, causing fast falloff (dense attached shadows) toward the camera side. If you were now to lighten up the shadows on the faces with additional fill light coming from the front of the set (roughly from camera 2's position), it would inevitably hit the white flats, once again contributing to the silhouette effect.

■   The acoustics may also prove to be less than desirable, because the microphones are very close to the sound-reflecting hardwall flats.

■   The prop list signals yet more problems. The large, upholstered chairs are definitely not appropriate for an interview. They look too pompous and would practically engulf their occupants.

■   Because most of the setup requires cross-shooting from extreme angles, the painting is utterly useless. If you want to break up some of the plain background with a picture, hang it so that it serves as a background in most of the shots. If you happen to know something about art history, you may suspect that the tight, contrasting patterns of the Brigit Riley painting would cause a moiré effect.

■   Finally, with the chairs directly on the studio floor, either the cameras would have to look down on the performers, or the camera operators would have to pedestal all the way down and stoop for the entering interview.

As you can see, even this simple floor plan and prop list reveal important clues to a variety of potential production problems. You should now talk to the novice art director, point out the potential problems, and suggest some ways the floor plan could be revised. **SEE 18.18**

■   Enlarge the background so that it provides cover even for extreme cross-shooting angles. Use flats of a different color and texture (such as a medium-dark wood panel pattern). Perhaps break up the background with a window flat or a few narrow flats to give it a more three-dimensional feel.

■   Place pictures or bookcases where they will be seen in the most frequent camera shots. Do not let a corner of a picture appear to grow out of the talent's head.

■   Use simple chairs that are comfortable yet will not swallow the occupants, put them on a riser, and position

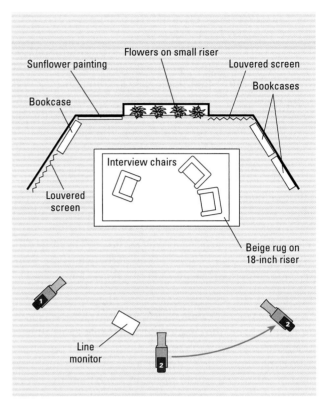

18.18 REVISED INTERVIEW SET
The revised floor plan for the interview provides for adequate background cover and interesting shots.

them at least 6 feet from the background (which will improve back lighting).

■   Turn the chairs outward somewhat (swivel them to face the center camera position) so that the cameras will not have to cross-shoot from such extreme angles.

■   Get rid of the rubber plants. Although rubber plants on a set look great to the naked eye, they become compositional hazards on-camera.

This is much better, but there is no time for resting on your laurels. The AD has just come back from a location survey for the segment on running the stop sign and shows you her location sketch. **SEE 18.19** She feels that there may be several potential production problems. Look at the sketch and see if you agree with her.

Yes, there certainly are a few serious problems that beg for immediate attention.

■   The intersection is obviously downtown. You can therefore expect a great deal of traffic to pass through, and

18.19 LOCATION SKETCH FOR STOP-SIGN SEGMENT
This location sketch points to several major problems that make the field production unfeasible.

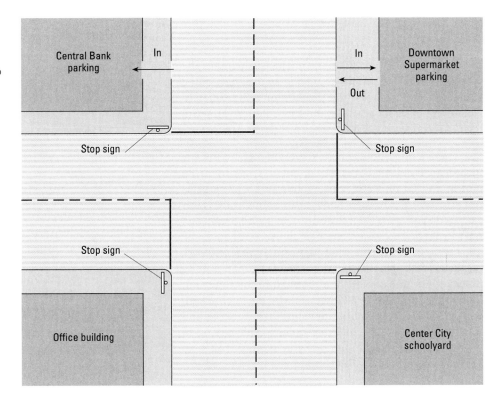

the police would not close this intersection for anything but a real accident.

■ Even if the intersection were not in the middle of downtown, the proximity of the bank and the supermarket would make closing the intersection, even for a little while, unfeasible.

■ A schoolyard is very noisy during recess. Unless you do not mind the laughing and yelling of children during the production, every school recess means a forced recess for your production crew.

■ The four-way stop signs make the intersection less hazardous, even if someone runs one of them. The demonstration is much more effective if one of the streets has through traffic.

The solution to these problems is relatively simple: Have the producer contact the police department and find a two-way-stop intersection in a quiet neighborhood that has very little traffic. There should be sufficient alternate routes so that a temporary closure of the intersection will not cause any traffic delays or prevent neighbors from getting to and from their homes.

SCRIPT ANALYSIS

To explain all the intricacies of analyzing and interpreting nondramatic and dramatic scripts would go far beyond the scope of this book. The importance of translating a process message into medium requirements has already been noted. Translating a script into various directing requirements calls for a similar process. The following list offers some basic guidelines on reading a script as a director.

Locking-In Point and Translation
Locking-in means that you conjure up a vivid visual or aural image while reading the script. This locking-in may well occur at the very opening scene, at the closing scene, or at any particularly striking scene somewhere in the middle. Do not try to force this locking-in process. It may well occur as an audio, rather than video, image. If the script is good, the locking-in is almost inevitable.[2]

---

2. See Tony Barr, *Acting for the Camera,* rev. ed. (New York: HarperPerennial, 1997), pp. 171–254. See also Katz, *Film Directing Shot by Shot,* and Michael Rabiger, *Directing: Film Techniques and Aesthetics,* 2d ed. (Boston: Focal Press, 1997), pp. 161–236.

Nevertheless, there are a few steps that will expedite the process.

▥   Read the script carefully—do not just glance at it. The video and audio information provide an overview of the show and how complex the production will be. Try to isolate the basic idea behind the show. Better yet, try to formulate an appropriate process message.

▥   Try to lock-in on a key shot, key action, or some key technical maneuver. For example, you may lock-in on the part in a script on water conservation where a bucket is put into a shower to catch some of the runoff water. How exactly do you see it? As a close-up of feet with the bucket next to them and water spraying all over? Through the glass door? From this lock-in point, you can work backward to the actions that precede it (a woman putting a bucket into the shower) and forward to the ones that follow it (stepping out of the shower with the full bucket). You will find that the images now start to make sense and seem to follow a rather logical sequence. The locking-in point has not only helped get you started, but also indicated a particular visualization.

▥   You can now begin to translate the images into concrete production requirements, such as camera positions, specific lighting and audio setups, videotape recording, and postproduction activities.

Analyzing a dramatic script is, of course, quite a bit more complicated than translating the video and audio instructions of a nondramatic script into the director's production requirements. A good dramatic script operates on many conscious and unconscious levels, all of which need to be interpreted and made explicit. Above all, you should be able to define the theme of the play (the basic idea—what the story is all about), the plot (how the story moves forward and develops), the characters (how one person differs from the others and how each one reacts to the situation at hand), and the environment (where the action takes place). In general, television drama emphasizes theme and character rather than plot, and inner, rather than outer, environment.

After the locking-in, further analysis depends greatly on what production method you choose: whether you shoot the play in sequence with multiple cameras and a switcher, or with a single camera in discontinuous, out-of-sequence takes.

The Storyboard

Once you have successfully locked-in and begun to visualize the various takes and scenes, you may want to make rough sketches of, or otherwise record, these visualizations so you won't forget them. A sequence of visualized shots is called a *storyboard;* it contains key visualization points and audio information. **SEE 18.20** It is usually drawn on preprinted storyboard paper, which has areas that represent the television screen and for audio and other information, or created by computer. Storyboard software programs offer a great many stock images (houses, streets, highways, cars, living rooms, kitchens) into which you can place figures and move them into various positions in the storyboard frame. **SEE 18.21**

Most commercials are carefully storyboarded shot-by-shot before they ever go into production. Storyboards help people who make decisions about the commercial see the individual shots and imagine them in sequence.

Storyboards are also used for other types of single-camera productions that contain a great number of especially complicated discontinuous shots or shot sequences. A good storyboard offers immediate clues to certain production requirements, such as general location, camera position, approximate focal length of the lens, method of audio pickup, amount and type of postproduction, talent actions, set design, and hand props. Some movie directors have every shot story-boarded before they shoot a single frame of film.

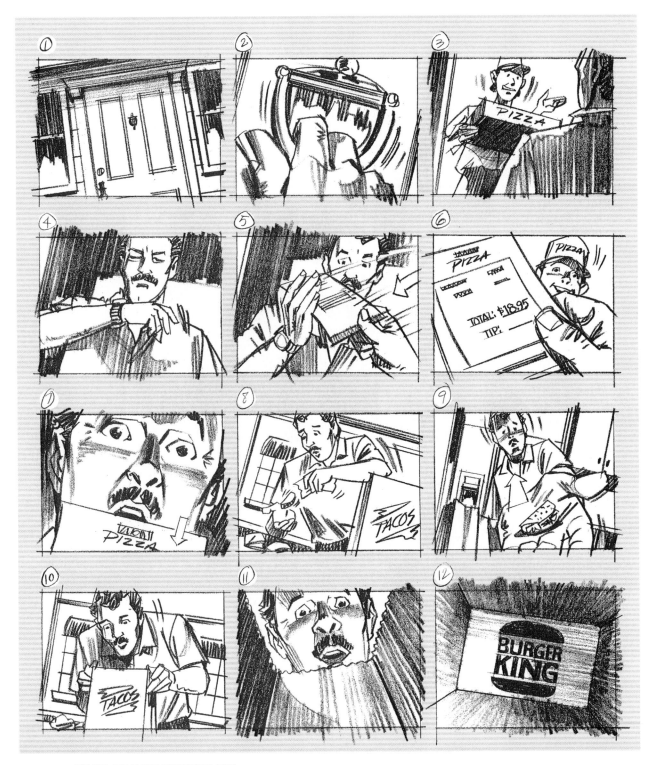

18.20 HAND-DRAWN STORYBOARD
The hand-drawn storyboard shows the major visualization points and sometimes lists the key audio sections or the shot sequence.

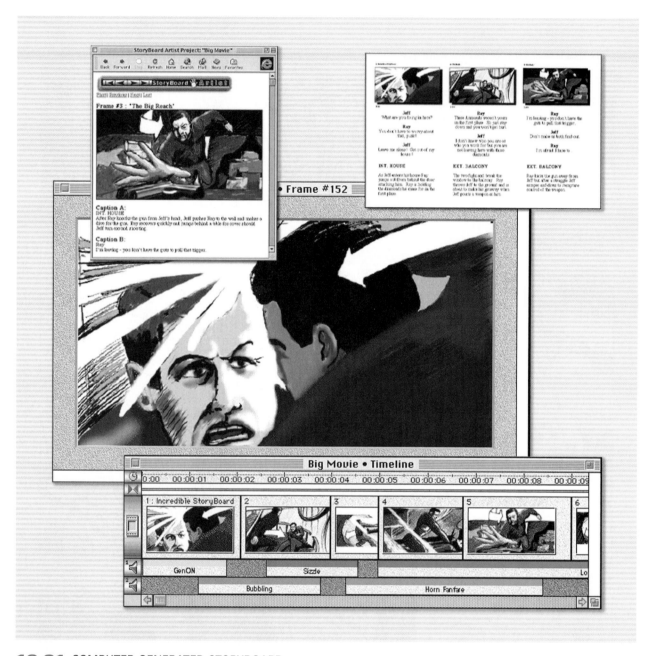

18.21 COMPUTER-GENERATED STORYBOARD

The computer-generated storyboard uses standard images that can be used to create a variety of exterior and interior scenes, in which images of people can be placed and moved about. Note the two-track audio information.

MAIN POINTS

◆ For the director preproduction starts with visualizing the key images, which means interpreting the individual shots as television images. These visualized images must then be perceived in a certain order, a process called sequencing.

◆ A properly stated process message will give important clues to visualization and sequencing and, consequently, to the production method and medium requirements.

◆ Visualizing and sequencing give the director a sense of camera and talent positions and traffic (movements).

◆ A careful study of the floor plan or location sketch and the prop list helps in planning equipment and talent traffic and reveals potential production problems.

◆ Script analysis should lead to a locking-in point (an especially vivid visual or sound image) that determines the subsequent visualizations and sequencing.

◆ The storyboard shows key visualization points of an event with accompanying audio information as well as the proper sequencing of the shots.

ZETTL'S VIDEOLAB 2.1

*Although you have already gone through most of the information in the **process** monitor, you may now rerun some of the tapes to look at them from a director's point of view.*

RUN ZVL 1 Click on the **process** monitor and run tape 7 **People**. Before you can establish an effective production team and communicate your ideas to them, you need to know the functions of each team member. Tape 7 shows what jobs the technical and nontechnical production people normally perform.

RUN ZVL 2 Run tape 2 **Phases**. Pay particular attention to the production schedule.

RUN ZVL 3 Run tape 4 **Ideas**. Click on module 3 **Scripts**. Check carefully the two-column script format. Many nondramatic shows are formatted this way.

RUN ZVL 4 Click on the **editing** monitor and run tape 5 **Location Procedures**. Click on module 1 **Basics**. Although you are told that the field log is normally kept by the script continuity person, in smaller productions it is often the PA who takes care of this important field activity.

RUN ZVL 5 Click on the **process** monitor and run tape 3 **Effect-to-Cause**. Before you read about specific applications of the effect-to-cause model, you may want to acquaint yourself once more with its major elements. Watch all four modules: **Basic idea**, **Desired effect**, **Cause**, and **Actual effect**.

19

The Director in Production and Postproduction

Now that you have prepared yourself so well in preproduction, it is time to step into the television control room, or go on location, and direct. In fact, all the meticulous preparation means little if you cannot direct or coordinate the various production elements during the production phase. Section 19.1, Multicamera Studio Directing, gives an overview of what is required of you when directing various multicamera studio productions. In section 19.2, Single-Camera Directing, you will learn about other skills and the general postproduction duties.

camera rehearsal Full rehearsal with cameras and other pieces of production equipment. Often identical to the dress rehearsal.

clock time The time the clock shows. Specifically, the time at which a program starts and ends. Also called *schedule time.*

dry run Rehearsal without equipment, during which the basic actions of the talent are worked out. Also called *blocking rehearsal.*

intercom Short for *intercommunication system.* Used by all production and technical personnel. The most widely used system has telephone headsets to facilitate voice communication on several wired or wireless channels. Includes other systems, such as I.F.B. and cell phones.

multicamera directing Simultaneous coordination of two or more cameras for instantaneous editing (switching). Also called *control room directing.*

single-camera directing Directing a single camera (usually a camcorder) in the studio or field for takes that are separately recorded for postproduction.

subjective time The duration we feel.

time line A schedule that shows the time periods of various activities during the production day. Also called *production schedule.*

walk-through Orientation session with the production crew (technical walk-through) and talent (talent walk-through) wherein the director walks through the set and explains the key actions.

19.1

Multicamera Studio Directing

As in the preproduction phase, your role in both the production and the postproduction phases is marked by meticulous planning, coordination, and team building. Like so many other production activities, directing has developed its very own language. Your first task of becoming a director is, of course, to learn to speak this lingo with clarity and confidence. Only then can you fulfill your difficult task as master juggler of schedules, equipment, people, and artistic vision. Section 19.1 takes you through the major steps of multicamera, or control room, directing.

▶ **THE DIRECTOR'S TERMINOLOGY**
Terms and cues for visualization, sequencing, special effects, audio, VTR, and the floor manager

▶ **MULTICAMERA STUDIO DIRECTING**
Directing from the control room, rehearsals, time line, and directing the show

▶ **CONTROLLING CLOCK TIME**
Schedule time and running time, back-timing and front-timing, and converting frames into clock time

▶ **CONTROLLING SUBJECTIVE TIME**
Pace and rhythm

▶ **STUDIO INTERCOM SYSTEMS**
The P.L. system, the I.F.B. system, and the S.A. system

THE DIRECTOR'S TERMINOLOGY

As does any other human activity in which many people work together at a common task, television directing demands a precise and specific language. This jargon, which must be understood by all members of the team, is generally called the director's language or, more specifically, the director's terminology. It is essential for efficient, error-free communication among the director and the other members of the production team.

By the time you learn television directing, you probably will have mastered most production jargon in general and perhaps even the greater part of the director's specific lingo. Like any language, the director's terminology is subject to habit and change. Although the basic language is fairly standard, you will hear some variations among directors. And as new technology develops, the director's language changes accordingly.

The terminology listed here primarily reflects multicamera directing from the studio control room—the type of directing that requires the most precise terminology. A single inaccurate call can cause a number of serious mistakes. You can also use most of these terms in single-camera directing, regardless of whether the production happens in the studio or the field.

Whatever terminology you use, you must use it consistently, and it must be understood by everyone on the production team. It must be precise and clear; there is little time during a show to explain. The shorter and less ambiguous the signals, the better the communication. The following tables list the director's terminology for visualization, sequencing, special effects, audio, VTR, and cues to the floor manager. **SEE 19.1–19.6**

MULTICAMERA STUDIO DIRECTING

Multicamera directing means that you direct and coordinate various production elements simultaneously from a television control room in the studio or the remote truck (see chapter 20). In multicamera directing you generally try to create as finished a product as possible, which may or may not need relatively little postproduction editing. When doing a live telecast, you have no chance for fixing anything in postproduction; your directing is the final cut. Multicamera directing involves the coordination of many technical operations as well as the actions of the talent. You will find that, at first, managing the complex

19.1 DIRECTOR'S VISUALIZATION CUES

The visualization cues are directions for the camera to achieve optimal shots. Some of these visualizations can be achieved in postproduction (such as an electronic zoom through digital magnification), but are much more easily done with proper camera handling.

FROM	DIRECTOR'S CUE	TO
	Headroom, or tilt up	
	Tilt down	
	Center it, or pan left	

19.1 DIRECTOR'S VISUALIZATION CUES *(continued)*

FROM	DIRECTOR'S CUE	TO
	Pan left	
	Pan right	
	Pedestal up, or crane up	
	Pedestal down, or crane down	
	Dolly in	

19.1 DIRECTOR'S VISUALIZATION CUES *(continued)*

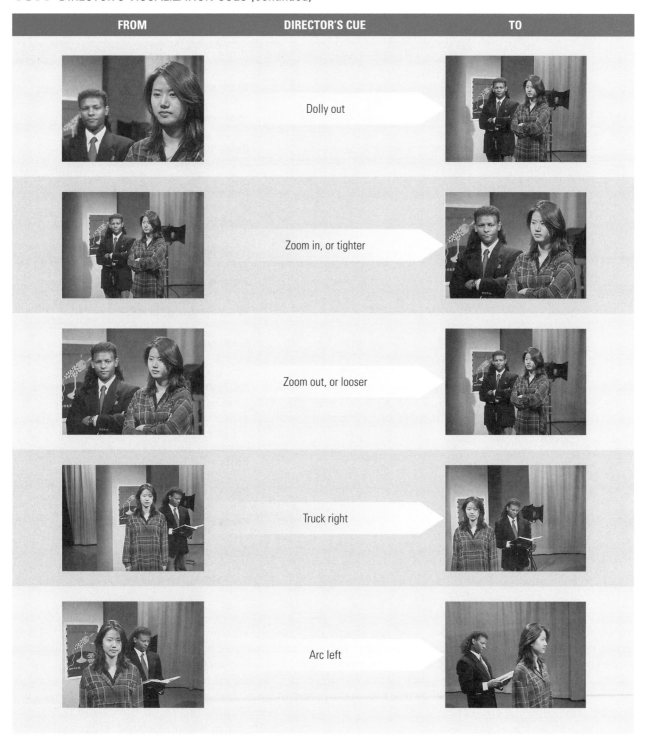

FROM	DIRECTOR'S CUE	TO
	Dolly out	
	Zoom in, or tighter	
	Zoom out, or looser	
	Truck right	
	Arc left	

19.2 DIRECTOR'S SEQUENCING CUES

These cues help get from one shot to the next. They include the major transitions, or sequencing, cues.

ACTION	DIRECTOR'S CUE
Cut from camera 1 to camera 2.	**Ready two — take two.**
Dissolve from camera 3 to camera 1.	**Ready one for dissolve — dissolve.**
Horizontal wipe from camera 1 to camera 3.	**Ready three for horizontal wipe** (over 1) — **wipe.** *or:* **Ready effects number *x*** (the number being specified by the switcher program) — **effects.**
Fade in camera 1 from black.	**Ready fade in one — fade in one.** *or:* **Ready up on one — up on one.**
Fade out camera 2 to black.	**Ready black — go to black.**
Short fade to black between cameras 1 and 2.	**Ready cross-fade to two — cross-fade.**
Cut between camera 1 and VTR 2 (assuming that VTR 2 is already rolling and "locked" or in a "parked" position).	**Ready VTR 2** (assuming the videotape is coming from VTR 2) — **take VTR 2.** (Sometimes you simply call the VTR number as it appears on the switcher. If, for example, the VTR is labeled 6, you say: **Ready six — take six.**)
Cut between VTR and C.G.	**Ready C.G. — take C.G.** *or:* **Ready effects on C.G. — take effects.**
Cut between C.G. titles	**Ready change page — change page.**

machinery—cameras, audio, graphics, videotape, remote feeds, and the clock—provides the greatest challenge. But once you have mastered the machines to some extent, your most difficult job will be dealing with people, those in front of the camera (talent) as well as those behind it (production people). *READY ZVL* ❶

Directing from the Control Room

In multicamera directing you need to be concerned not only with the visualization of each shot but also with the immediate sequencing of the various shots. It includes the directing of live shows, live-on-tape productions, and longer show segments that are later assembled but not otherwise altered in relatively simple postproduction. Multicamera directing always involves the use of a control room (see chapter 20). The *control room* is designed specifically for multicamera production and for the smooth coordination of all other video, audio, and recording facilities and people. Multicamera directing is, therefore, often called *control room directing*.

19.3 DIRECTOR'S SPECIAL-EFFECTS CUES

Special-effects cues are not always uniform, and, depending on the complexity of the effect, directors may invent their own verbal "shorthand." Whatever cues are used, they need to be standardized among the production team.

ACTION	DIRECTOR'S CUE
Super camera 1 over 2.	**Ready super one over two — super.**
To return to camera 2.	**Ready to lose super — lose super.** *or:* **Ready to take out one — take out one.**
To go to camera 1 from the super.	**Ready to go through to one — through to one.**
Key C.G. over base picture on camera 1.	**Ready key C.G.** (over 1) **— key.**
Key studio card title on camera 1 over base picture on camera 2.	**Ready key one over two — key.**
Fill keyed-out title from studio card on camera 1 with yellow hue over base picture on camera 2.	**Ready matte key one, yellow, over two — matte key.**
To have title from character generator appear in drop-shadow outline over base picture on camera 1.	**Ready C.G. drop shadow over one — key C.G.** (Sometimes the director may use the name of the C.G. manufacturer, such as Chyron. Thus, you would say: **Ready Chyron over one — key Chyron.** Because the C.G. information is almost always keyed, the "key" is usually omitted in the ready cue.) *or:* **Ready effects, drop shadow — take effects.** Some directors simply call for an insert, which refers to the downstream keyer. Usually the lettering mode (drop shadow or outline) is already programmed into the C.G. So you just say: **Ready insert seven — take insert.**
To have a wipe pattern appear over a picture, such as a scene on camera 2, replace a scene on camera 1 through a circle wipe.	**Ready circle wipe two over one — wipe.** (Any other wipe is called for in the same way, except that the specific wipe pattern is substituted for "circle wipe." If you need a soft wipe, simply call for "Ready soft wipe" instead of "Ready wipe.")
To have an insert (video B) grow in size in a zoomlike motion, replacing the base picture (video A).	**Ready squeeze out — squeeze.** *or:* **Ready effect sixteen — squeeze out.**
To achieve the reverse squeeze (video B getting smaller).	**Ready squeeze in — squeeze.**
To achieve a great many transitions through wipes.	**Ready wipe effect twenty-one — wipe.**

Many of the more-complicated effects are preset and stored in the computer program. The retrieval goes by numbers. All you do to activate a whole effects sequence is call for the number: **Ready effects eighty-seven — take effects.**

19.4 DIRECTOR'S AUDIO CUES

Audio cues involve cues for microphones; starting and stopping various audio sources, such as CD players; and cues to integrate or mix these sources.

ACTION	DIRECTOR'S CUE
To activate microphone in the studio.	**Ready to cue talent.** (Or something more specific, like "Mary—cue her." The audio engineer will automatically open her mic.) *or:* **Ready to cue Mary—open mic, cue her.**
To start music.	**Ready music—music.**
To bring music under for announcer.	**Ready to fade music under—music under, cue announcer.**
To take music out.	**Ready music out—music out.** *or:* **Fade music out.**
To close the microphone in the studio (announcer's mic) and switch over to the sound on tape.	**Ready SOT** (sound on tape)**—close mic, track up.** *or:* **Ready SOT—SOT.**
To roll audiotape.	**Ready audiotape—roll audiotape.** (Do not just say, "Roll tape," because the TD may start the VTR.)
To fade one sound source under and out while simultaneously fading another in (similar to a dissolve).	**Ready cross-fade from** *(source)* **to** *(other source)* **—cross-fade.**
To go from one sound source to another without interruption (usually two pieces of music).	**Ready segue from** *(source)* **to** *(other source)* **—segue.**
To increase program speaker volume for the director.	**Monitor up, please.**
To play sound effect from a CD.	**Ready sound effect number** *x* **on CD.** *or:* **Ready CD number** *x* **—sound effect.**
To put slate information on videotape (either open floor manager's mic or talkback patched to VTR).	**Ready to read slate—read slate.**

19.5 DIRECTOR'S VTR CUES

These cues are used to start and stop the VTR, to slate a video recording, and to switch to the VTR.

ACTION	DIRECTOR'S CUE
To start videotape for recording a program.	**Ready to roll VTR one — roll VTR one.** (Now you have to wait for the "in-record" or "speed" confirmation by the VTR operator.)
To "slate" the program after the VTR is in the record mode. The slate is on camera 2 or on the C.G., the opening scene on camera 1. We are assuming that the color bars and reference level audio tone are already on the tape.	**Ready two** (or C.G.), **ready to read slate — take two** (or C.G.), **read slate.**
To put the opening ten-second beeper on the audio track and fade in on camera 1. (Do not forget to start your stopwatch as soon as camera 1 fades in.)	**Ready black, ready beeper — black, beeper.** **Ten — nine — eight — seven — six — five —** **four — three — two — cue Mary — up on one.** (Start your stopwatch.)
To stop the videotape on a freeze-frame.	**Ready freeze — freeze.**
To roll videotape out of a freeze-frame mode.	**Ready to roll VTR three — roll VTR three.**
To roll a videotape for a slow-motion effect.	**Ready VTR four slo-mo — roll VTR four.** *or:* **Ready VTR four slo-mo — slo-mo four.**
To roll a VTR as a program insert, while you are on camera 2; sound is on tape. Assuming a two-second roll.	**Ready to roll VTR three, SOT — roll VTR three. Two —** **one, take VTR three, SOT.** If you do not use a countdown because of instant start, simply say: **Ready VTR three, roll and take VTR three.** (Start your stopwatch for timing the VTR insert.)
To return from VTR to camera and Mary on camera 1. (Stop your watch and reset it for the next insert.)	**Ten seconds to one, five seconds to one.** **Ready two, ready cue Mary — cue Mary, take one.**

Unless you are doing a live remote pickup of a special event, you need to rehearse as much as possible. Rehearsals not only give you and the rest of the production team practice in what to do during the taping session, but readily reveal any major and minor flaws or omissions in your preproduction activities.

Rehearsals

Ideally, you should be able to rehearse everything that goes on videotape or on the air. Unfortunately, in practice this is hardly the case. Because the amount of scheduled rehearsal time always seems insufficient, the prerehearsal preparations, discussed in chapter 18, become extremely important. To make optimal use of the available time during scheduled rehearsals, you might try the following methods: (1) script reading, (2) dry run, or blocking rehearsal, (3) walk-through, (4) camera and dress rehearsals, and (5) walk-through/camera rehearsal combination. Note, however, that you rarely go through all of these steps. Many nondramatic shows are rehearsed

19.6 DIRECTOR'S CUES TO FLOOR MANAGER

The directional cues are always given from the camera's point of view, not from the talent's point of view. "Left" means camera-left; "right" means camera-right.

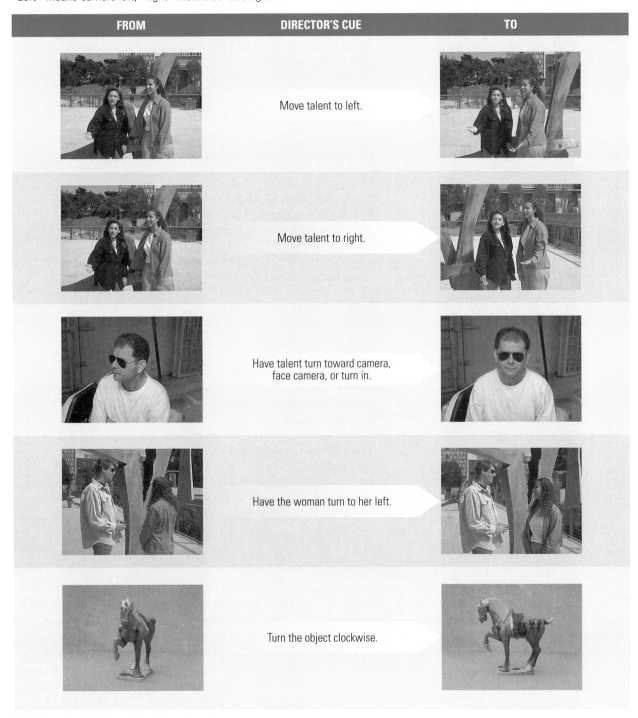

FROM	DIRECTOR'S CUE	TO
	Move talent to left.	
	Move talent to right.	
	Have talent turn toward camera, face camera, or turn in.	
	Have the woman turn to her left.	
	Turn the object clockwise.	

simply by walking the talent through certain actions, such as moving to a display table and holding items properly for close-ups, or walking to the performance area to greet the guest. Routine shows, such as daily interviews by the same talent, are not rehearsed at all.

Script reading   Under ideal conditions every major production should begin with a script-reading session. Even for a relatively simple show, you should meet at least once with the talent, the producer, the PA (production assistant), and the key production personnel—AD (assistant director), TD (technical director), and floor manager—to discuss and read the script. Bring the floor plan along; it will help everyone visualize just where the action takes place and point out some potential production problems. In this session, which normally doubles as a production meeting, explain these points:

- Process message objective, including the purpose of the show and its intended audience

- Major actions of the performers, the number and use of hand props, and major crossovers (walking from one performance area to another while on-camera)

- The performer's relationship to the guests, if any

In an interview, for example, discuss with the host the key questions and what he or she should know about the guest. Normally, such talent preparation is done by the producer. Try to get a rough timing on the show by clocking the major scenes and show segments as they are read.

The script-reading sessions are, of course, particularly important if you are rehearsing a television drama. You will find that the time you spend on thorough script interpretation is more than gained during subsequent rehearsals.

In the script-reading sessions, you should discuss the process message objective, the structure of the play (theme, plot, environment), and the substance of each character. An extremely detailed analysis of the characters is probably the most important aspect of the dramatic script-reading session. The actor who really understands his or her character, role, and relationship to the whole event has mastered the principal part of his or her performance. After this analysis the actors tend to block themselves (under your careful guidance, of course) and move and "act" naturally. You no longer need to explain

the motivation for each move. More than any other, the television actor must understand a character so well that he or she is no longer acting out, but rather is *living,* the role. Such internalization, which can be quite readily achieved through extensive script-reading sessions, will almost always enhance the actor's television performance.

Dry run, or blocking rehearsal   In the *dry run,* also called *blocking rehearsal,* the basic actions of the talent are worked out. By that time you must have a very good idea of where the cameras should be in relation to the set, and the actors in relation to the cameras.

The dry run presupposes a detailed floor plan and a thorough preparation by the director. It also presupposes that the actors have internalized their characters and roles. Tell them where the action should take place (the approximate location in the imagined set area; the actual set is rarely available at this point), and let them block as naturally as possible. Watch their actions as screen images, not from the point of view of a live audience. Adjust their blocking and your imagined camera positions so you are reasonably assured that you will achieve the visualized screen image in the actual camera rehearsal, but do not fuss about specially framed shots at this time. You can always make such adjustments during camera rehearsal. Be ready to give precise directions to the actor who is asking what to do next. Rather than always knowing what to do without the director's help, a good actor asks what to do and then does it with precision and conviction.

Generally, try to observe the following in a dry run:

▨   Hold the dry run in the studio or a rehearsal hall. In an emergency, any room will do. Use tables, chairs, and chalk marks on the floor for sets and furniture.

▨   Work on the blocking problems. Use a director's viewfinder or a small consumer camcorder, bearing in mind that a studio camera is not as flexible; you cannot tilt a studio camera sideways or lower it close to the floor for a from-below-eye-level shot. Have the PA take notes of the major blocking maneuvers. Allow time for reading back these notes so you can later correct the blocking.

▨   Try to block according to the actors' most natural movements, but keep in mind the camera and microphone positions and moves. Some directors walk right to the spot where the active camera will be and watch the proceedings from the camera's point of view (POV). If you block nondramatic action, observe first what the performers would do without the presence of a camera. As much as possible, try to place the cameras to suit the action rather than the other way around.

■ If it will help, call out all major cues, such as "cue Lisa," "ready 2, take 2," and so forth.

■ Run through the scenes in the order in which they are to be taped. If you do the show live or live-on-tape, try to go through the whole script at least once. If you cannot rehearse the whole script, pick the most complicated parts for rehearsal. In a nondramatic show, rehearse the opening as much as time allows. Inexperienced talent often stumbles over the opening lines, with the show going downhill from there.

■ Time each segment and the overall show. Allow time for long camera movements, music bridges, announcer's intro and closing, opening and closing credits, and so forth.

■ Reconfirm the dates for the upcoming rehearsals.

Walk-through   The *walk-through* is an orientation session that helps the production crew and talent understand the necessary medium and performance requirements quickly and easily. You can have both a technical walk-through and a talent walk-through. When pressed for time, or when doing a smaller production, you normally combine the two.

The walk-throughs as well as camera rehearsals occur shortly before the actual on-the-air performance or taping session. Walk-throughs are especially important when you are shooting on location. The talent will get a feel for the new environment, and the crew will discover possible obstacles to camera and microphone moves. This is especially important when cameras and microphone fishpole operators have to walk backward during the scene.

Technical walk-through   Once the set is in place, gather the production crew—AD, floor manager, floor personnel, TD, LD (lighting director), camera operators, audio engineer, and boom or fishpole operator—and explain the process message objective and your basic concept of the show. Then walk them through the set and explain these key factors: basic blocking and actions of talent, camera locations and traffic, specific shots and framings, mic locations and moves, basic cuing, scene and prop changes, if any, and major lighting effects.

ENG **EFP**   The technical walk-through is especially important for EFP and big remotes, where the crew in the performance area must often work during the setup under the guidance of the floor manager rather than the director, who is isolated in the remote truck (see chapter 20). Have the AD or PA take notes of all your major decisions; then provide time to have the notes read back and discussed so that the technical crew can take care of the various problems.

Talent walk-through   While the production people go about their tasks, take the talent on a short excursion through the set or location and explain once again their major actions, positions, and crossovers. Always try to block talent so that they, rather than the cameras, do most of the moving. Tell them where the cameras will be in relation to their actions and whether they are to address the camera directly. Here are some of the more important aspects of the talent walk-through:

■ Point out to each performer or actor his or her major positions and walks. If the performer is to look directly into the camera, point out which camera it is or where the specific camera will be positioned.

■ Explain briefly where and how they should work with specific props. For example, tell the actor that the coffeepot will be here and how he or she should walk with the coffee cup to the couch—in front of the table, not behind it. Explain your blocking to the talent from the point of view of the camera. Urge the performer not to pick up the display objects, but to leave them on the table so that the camera can get a good close-up. Have the performer go through the demonstration, and watch this simulation from the camera's point of view. Watch that the performer does not block important close-ups.

■ Have the performers or actors go through their opening lines and then have them skip to the individual cue lines (often at the end of their dialogue). If the script calls for ad-lib commentary, ask the talent to ad-lib so that both of you will get an idea of what it sounds like.

■ Give everyone enough time for makeup and dressing before the camera rehearsal. During the talent walk-through, try to stay out of the production people's way as much as possible. Again, have the AD or PA write down major rehearsal items. Finish the walk-through rehearsal early enough so that everybody can take a break before the camera rehearsal.

Camera and dress rehearsals The following discussion of camera rehearsals is primarily for studio productions and big multicamera remotes that are directed from a control room. Camera rehearsals for EFP are discussed in section 19.2.

Essentially, the *camera rehearsal* is a full rehearsal that includes cameras and other pieces of production equipment. In minor productions camera rehearsal and final *dress rehearsal,* or *dress,* are almost always the same. Frequently, the camera rehearsal time is cut short by technical problems, such as lighting or mic adjustments. Do not get too nervous when you see most of the technical crew working frantically on the intercom system or audio console five minutes before airtime. Be patient and try to stay calm. Realize that you are working with a highly skilled group who know just as well as you do how much depends on a successful performance. Like all other machines, the television machine sometimes works and sometimes breaks down. Be ready to suggest alternatives should the problem prevail.

The two basic methods of conducting a camera rehearsal for a live or live-on-tape production are the stop-start method and the uninterrupted run-through. A *stop-start rehearsal* is usually conducted from the control room, but it can also be done, at least partially, from the studio floor. An *uninterrupted run-through rehearsal* is always conducted from the control room.

With the stop-start method, the camera rehearsal is interrupted when you encounter a problem so that you can discuss it with the crew or talent; then you go back to a logical spot in the script and start again, hoping that the problem is not repeated. It is a thorough albeit time-consuming method. But even the uninterrupted run-through rarely remains uninterrupted. Nevertheless, you should call for a *"cut"* (stop all action) only when a grave mistake has been made—one that cannot be corrected later. All minor mistakes and fumbles are corrected after the run-through. Dictate notes of all minor problems to the PA or AD. Have him or her read back at scheduled rehearsal breaks ("notes"), and provide enough time for following up on the items listed ("reset").

Because many studio shows are videotaped in segments, an uninterrupted run-through will be interrupted anyway at each scene or segment as marked in the script. If you plan to do the entire show live, or videotape the show in one uninterrupted take, go through as long a segment as possible in the un-interrupted run-through. A long stretch without any interruptions not only gives you an overview of the general development and build of the show, but also helps the performers or actors enormously in their pacing. The uninterrupted run-through is one of your few opportunities to get a feel for the overall rhythm of the show.

In larger productions camera rehearsals and the dress rehearsal are conducted separately. Whereas in camera rehearsals you may stop occasionally to correct some blocking or technical problem, dress rehearsals are normally run straight through. You stop only when really major production problems arise. Many times, as in the videotaping of a situation comedy before a live audience, the videotape of the dress rehearsal is combined with that of the "on-the-air" performance to make the final edit master tape that is then broadcast.

Walk-through/camera rehearsal combination Necessary as the preceding rehearsal procedures seem, they are rarely possible in smaller operations. First, most directing chores in nonbroadcast or nonnetwork productions are of a nondramatic nature, demanding less rehearsal effort than dramatic shows. Second, because of time and space limitations, you are lucky to get rehearsal time equal to or slightly more than the running time of the entire show. Forty-five or even thirty minutes of rehearsal time for a half-hour show is not uncommon. Most often, you have to jump from a cursory script reading to a camera rehearsal immediately preceding the on-the-air performance or taping session.

In these situations you have to resort to a walk-through/camera rehearsal combination. Because you cannot rehearse the entire show, you simply rehearse the most important parts as well as possible. Usually, these are the transitions rather than the parts between the transitions. Always direct this rehearsal from the studio floor. If you try to conduct it from the control room, you will waste valuable time explaining shots and blocking over the intercom system.

Here are some of the major points for conducting a walk-through/camera rehearsal combination:

■ Get all production people into their respective positions—all camera operators at their cameras (with the cameras uncapped and ready to go), the fishpole mic ready to follow the sound source, the floor manager ready for cuing, and the TD, the audio console operator, and, if appropriate, the LD ready for action in the control room.

■   Have a simple stand mic set up in the studio for you to relay your directing calls from the studio floor to the control room. Have the TD execute all your switching calls and feed the pictures to the studio monitor. This way everybody can see the shots and the shot sequence. The disadvantage of calling your shots from the floor is that you won't see the preview monitors for the upcoming shots. You can, however, always walk over to the upcoming camera and look into its viewfinder. Check the framing of the upcoming shot and correct it before having it punched up on the air (line-out).

■   Walk the talent through all the major parts of the show. Rehearse only the critical transitions, crossovers, and specific shots. For example, if the performer has to demonstrate a small object, show him or her how to hold the object, and the camera operator how to frame it. Watch the action on the studio monitor (showing the line-out picture). As soon as the talent knows how to go on from there, skip to the end of the segment and have the talent introduce the following segment.

■   Give all cues for music, sound effects, lighting, videotape rolls, slating procedures, and so forth to the TD via the open studio mic, but do not have them executed (except for the music, which can be easily reset).

■   Even if you are on the floor yourself, have the floor manager cue the talent and mark the crucial spots with chalk or masking tape on the studio floor.

If everything goes fairly well, you are ready to go to the control room. Do not let the crew or yourself get hung up on some insignificant detail. Always view the problems in the context of the overall show and time available. For example, do not fret over a picture that seems to hang slightly high on the set wall while neglecting to rehearse the most important crossovers with the talent.

From the control room, contact the cameras by number and verify that the operators can communicate with you. Then rehearse once more from the control room the most important parts of the show—the opening, closing, major talent actions, and camera movements.

Try to rehearse by yourself the opening and closing of a show prior to camera rehearsal. Sit in a quiet corner with the script and, using a stopwatch (for practice), start calling out the opening shots: "Roll VTR. Ready slate—take

slate. Ready black, ready beeper. Black, beeper. Ready to cue Lynne. Ready to fade up on 2. Cue Lynne, up on 2," and so on. By the time you enter the control room, you will practically have memorized the opening and closing of the show and will be able to pay full attention to the control room monitors and the audio.

Once you are in the control room, the only way you can see the floor action is via the camera preview monitors. Even if the control room happens to have a window facing the studio, it is generally blocked by the preview monitors in front of you. You should, therefore, develop the ability to construct a mental map of where the cameras are in relation to the primary performance areas and of the major talent and camera movements. To help you construct and maintain this mental map, try to position the cameras counterclockwise, with camera 1 on the left and your last camera on the far right.

As pressed for time as you may be, try to remain cool and courteous to everyone. Also, this is not the time to make drastic changes; there will always be other ways in which the show might be directed and even improved, but the camera rehearsal is not the time to try them out. Reserve sudden creative inspirations for your next show. Stick as closely as possible to the production schedule (time line). Do not rehearse right up to videotaping or airtime. Give the talent and crew a brief break before the actual taping. *Don't just tell them "Take five" (take a five-minute break); tell them the exact time to be back in the studio.*

Time Line

As with every other aspect of television production, moving a show from the rehearsal phase to the on-the-air performance is governed by strict time limits. In larger operations the *time line,* or *production schedule,* is worked out by the production manager of the facility. In smaller production companies, you, the director, or the producer will establish the time line for a specific production.

Time line: interview   The following example shows a production schedule for a half-hour interview (actual length: 25:00 minutes), featuring two folk singers who have gained world fame because of their socially conscious songs. The singers, who accompany themselves on acoustic guitars, are scheduled to give a concert the following day in the university auditorium. Their contract does not allow the presence of television cameras during the actual concert, but they agreed to come to the studio for a brief interview and to play a few short selections from the upcoming concert. The process message is relatively simple: *To give viewers an opportunity to meet the two singers, learn more about them as artists and concerned human beings, and watch them perform.* To save money and time of talent and production crew, the show is scheduled for live-on-tape production. This means that the director will direct the show as if it were going on the air live, or at least with as few stop-downs (interruptions whereby the videotape is stopped) as possible.

TIME LINE: INTERVIEW

11:00 A.M.	Crew call
11:10–11:30 A.M.	Tech meeting
11:30 A.M.–1:00 P.M.	Setup and lighting
1:00–1:30 P.M.	Lunch
1:30–1:45 P.M.	Production meeting: host and singers
1:45–2:30 P.M.	Run-through and camera rehearsal
2:30–2:40 P.M.	Notes and reset
2:40–2:45 P.M.	Break
2:45–3:30 P.M.	Tape
3:30–3:45 P.M.	Spill
3:45–4:00 P.M.	Strike

As you can see from this production schedule, a production day is divided into blocks of time during which certain activities take place.

11:00 A.M. **Crew call**   This is the time the crew must arrive at the studio.

11:10–11:30 A.M. **Tech meeting**   You start the day with a technical meeting during which you discuss with the crew the process message and the major technical requirements. One of these requirements is the audio setup, because the singers are obviously interested in good sound. Although the eventual telecast of this interview is monophonic, the videotaping should nevertheless be done in stereo. You should also explain what camera shots you want. The sincerity of the artists and their guitar-playing skills are best conveyed by CUs and ECUs, and you may want to shift the attention from one singer to the other through a rack focus effect. The audio technician may want to discuss the specific mic setup with you, such as stand mics for the performance, but also wireless lavalieres for the singers' crossover. The TD may ask about the desired lighting and confirm the use of two additional VHS videotape recorders. The VHS machines can produce videotapes for the guests simultaneously with the master

recording. You or the producer can then hand the guests the tapes right after the show as a small thank-you gesture. You will find that discussing such items will shorten the setup time considerably.

11:30 A.M.–1:00 P.M. **Setup and lighting**   This should be sufficient time to set up the standard interview set and light the interview and performance areas. Although as director you are not immediately involved in this production phase, you might want to keep an eye on the setup so that you can make minor changes before the lighting is done. For example, the two stools for the singers may be placed too far apart and too close to the cyc, or you may want the audio technician to use smaller and lighter mic stands so that you can get better shots of the singers.

1:00–1:30 P.M. **Lunch**   Tell everyone to be back by 1:30 sharp—not 1:32 or 1:35—which means that everyone has to be able to leave the studio at exactly 1:00, even if there are still some technical details left undone. Minor technical problems can be solved during your production meeting with the host and the singers.

1:30–1:45 P.M. **Production meeting: host and singers**   When the singers and their manager arrive at this meeting, they have already been introduced to the host by the producer. In this meeting reconfirm their musical selections and the running time for each. Discuss the opening and closing and the crossover to the performance area. For example, you might explain to them that you will stop down briefly (stop the videotape recording and start it again after the location switch) before their first number but not when they return to the interview set. Ask them about the transitions from one song to another. Will they address the camera or simply segue from one song to the next? Tell them about some of your visualization ideas, such as shooting very tight during especially intense moments in their songs and for intricate guitar sections.

1:45–2:30 P.M. **Run-through and camera rehearsal**   Although the setup is rather simple and there will be little camera movement during the songs, you need to rehearse the crossovers from the interview set to the performance area and back. You may also want to rehearse some of the unusually tight shots or the rack focus shots from one singer to the other. Then go through the opening and the closing with all facilities (theme music, credits, and name keys). Dictate to the PA any production problems you may discover during this rehearsal for the notes segment.

Do not get upset when the audio technician repositions mics during the camera rehearsal; after all, good audio is important in this production.

2:30–2:40 P.M. **Notes and reset**   You now gather the key production people—producer, AD, TD, audio technician, LD, floor manager, and host—to discuss any production problems that may have surfaced during the rehearsal. Ask the PA to read the notes in the order written down. Direct the production team to take care of the various problems. At the same time, the rest of the crew should get the cameras into the opening positions, reset the pages of the character generator, load the ATR and VTRs (the record VTR as well as the two S-VHS machines for the singers' copies) with tape, and make minor lighting adjustments.

2:40–2:45 P.M. **Break**   This short break will give everyone a chance to get ready for the taping.

2:45–3:30 P.M. **Tape**   You should be in the control room and roll the tape at exactly 2:45 P.M.—not 2:50 or 3:00. If all goes well, the half-hour show should be "in the can," or finished, by 3:30, including the stop-down time for the first crossover.

3:30–3:45 P.M. **Spill**   This is a period of grace, because we all know that television is a complex, temperamental machine that involves many people. For example, you may have to redo the opening or the closing because the C.G. did not deliver the correct page for the opening credits or because the host gave the wrong time for the upcoming concert.

3:45–4:00 P.M. **Strike**   During the strike time, you can thank the singers and their manager, the host, and the crew. Arrange for a playback in case they want to see and especially listen to the videotape recording right away. Play back the audio track through the best system you have. All the while keep at least one eye on the strike, but do not interfere with it. Trust the floor manager and crew to take down the set and clean the studio for the next production in the remaining fifteen minutes.

One of the most important aspects of a production schedule is sticking to the time allotted for each segment. You must learn to get things done within the scheduled time block and, more important, to jump to the next activity at the precise time shown on the schedule, regardless of whether you have finished your previous chores. Do not use up the time of a scheduled segment with a previously scheduled activity. A good director terminates an especially difficult blocking rehearsal at midpoint to meet the scheduled notes and reset period. Inexperienced directors often spend a great amount of time on the first part of the show or on a relatively minor detail, and usually go on the air without having rehearsed the rest of the show. The production schedule is designed to prevent such misuse of valuable production time.

Time line: soap opera   Here is an example of a production schedule for a more complicated one-hour soap opera. Assume that the setup and lighting have been accomplished the night before (from 3:00 to 6:00 A.M.) and that the strike will happen after the spill (6:00 P.M.).

PRODUCTION SCHEDULE: SOAP OPERA

6:00–8:00 A.M.	Dry run—rehearsal hall
7:30 A.M.	Crew call
8:00–8:30 A.M.	Tech meeting
8:30–11:00 A.M.	Camera blocking
11:00–11:30 A.M.	Notes and reset
11:30 A.M.–12:30 P.M.	Lunch
12:30–2:30 P.M.	Dress rehearsal
2:30–3:00 P.M.	Notes and reset
3:00–5:30 P.M.	Tape
5:30–6:00 P.M.	Spill

As you can see, this production schedule leaves no time for you to think about what to do next. You need to be thoroughly prepared to coordinate the equipment, technical people, and talent within the tightly prescribed time frame. Although not written into this time line, you should give the cast and crew a break before the taping. There is no time allotted for striking the set, because the set stays up for the next day's production.

Directing the Show

Directing the on-the-air performance or the final taping session is, of course, the most important part of your job as a director. After all, the viewers do not sit in on the script conferences and rehearsals—all they see and hear is what you finally put on the air. This section gives some pointers about standby and on-the-air directing. Again, we assume that the director is doing a live or live-on-tape multicamera show, or at least the videotape recording of fairly long, uninterrupted show segments that require a minimum of postproduction editing. You will notice that you can transfer multicamera directing skills much more readily to single-camera direction than the other way around.

Standby procedures   Here are some of the most important standby procedures you need to observe immediately preceding the on-the-air telecast:

▦   Call on the intercom every member of the production team who needs to react to your cues—TD, camera operators, mic operator, floor manager and other floor personnel, videotape operator, lighting patchboard operator, audio technician, and C.G. operator. Ask them if they are ready.

▦   Check with the floor manager to make sure that everyone is in the studio and ready for action. Tell the floor manager who gets the opening cue and which camera will be on first. From now on, the floor manager is an essential link between you and the studio.

▦   Announce the time remaining until the on-the-air telecast. If you are directing a videotaped show or show segments, have the TD, C.G. operator, and audio engineer ready for the opening slate identification. You can save time by having the TD direct the recording of the videotape leader (bars and tone) before airtime. Check that the slate shows the correct information. Verify the spelling of names that you will use as key inserts.

▦   Again, alert everyone to the first cues.

▦   Check that the videotape operator is ready to roll the tape, and check with the camera operators and audio engineer about their opening actions.

▦   Ready the opening C.G. titles and music and have the floor manager get the talent into position.

On-the-air procedures   Assuming you direct a live-on-tape show, such as the interview with the singers just described, you must first go through the usual videotape rolling procedures (see figure 19.5). Once the videotape

is properly rolling and slated, you can begin the actual recording. You are now on the air. Imagine the following opening sequence:

> *Ready to come up on three* (CU of Lynne, the interview host). *Ready to cue Lynne. Open mic, cue Lynne, up on* (or "fade in") *three* (Lynne addresses camera 3 with opening sentence). *Ready C.G. opening titles—take C.G. Cue announcer. Change page. Change page. Ready three* (which is still on Lynne). *Open mic, cue Lynne—take three* (introduces guests). *One, two-shot of singers. Two, cover* (wide shot of all three). *Ready one—take one. Ready two, open mics* (guest mics in the interview set)—*take two. Ready three—take three* (Lynne is asking her first question). *One, on Ron* (CU of one of the singers). *Ready one—take one. Two, on Marissa* (the other singer). *Ready two—take two.*

By now you are well into the show. Listen carefully to what is being said so that you can anticipate the proper shots. Have the floor manager stand by to give Lynne time cues to the crossover. When you stop down for the crossover, wait until the singer leaves the frame before stopping down. This way you can logically cut from a CU of Lynne introducing the singers to the performance area. After the singers have returned to the interview set, watch the time carefully and give closing time cues to Lynne. After the one-minute cue, you must prepare for the closing. Are the closing credits ready? Again, watch the time.

> *Thirty seconds. Wind her up. Wind her up* (or give her a wrap-up). *Fifteen* (seconds). *C.G. closing credits. Two, zoom out a little* (which is on a wide shot of the interview set). *Ready two, ready C.G. roll. Cut Lynne. Take two. Cut mics. Cue announcer. Two, keep zooming out. Hold it. Roll credits. Ready to key C.G.* (over camera 2), *key C.G. Change page. Change page. Key out. Ready black—fade to black. Hold. Stop VTR. OK, all clear. Good job, everyone.*

Unfortunately, not every show goes this smoothly. You can contribute to a smooth performance, however, by paying attention to the following on-the-air directing procedures:

▦   Give all signals clearly and precisely. Be relaxed but alert. If you are too relaxed, everybody will become somewhat lethargic, thinking that you don't really take the show too seriously.

▓ Cue talent *before* you come up on him or her with the camera. By the time he or she speaks, you will have faded in the picture.

▓ Indicate talent by name. Do not tell the floor manager to cue just "him" or "her," especially if the talent consists of several "hims" or "hers" anticipating a cue sooner or later.

▓ Do not give a ready cue too far in advance or the operator may have forgotten it by the time your take cue finally arrives. Repeating the same ready cue may trigger a take by the TD.

▓ Do not pause between the take and the number of the camera. Do not say, "Take [pause] two." Some TDs may punch up the camera before you say the number.

▓ Keep in mind the number of the camera already on the air, and do not call for a take or dissolve to that camera. Watch the preview monitors. Do not bury your head in your script or fact sheet.

▓ Do not ready one camera and then call for a take to another. In other words, do not say, "Ready one—take two." If you change your mind, nullify the ready cue—"No" or "Change that"—and then give another.

▓ Talk to the cameras by number, not by the name of the operator. What if both camera operators were named Barbara?

▓ Call the camera first before you give instructions. For example: "Two, give me a close-up of Ron. Three, CU of Marissa. One, zoom in on the guitar."

▓ After you have put one camera on the air, immediately tell the other camera what to do next. Do not wait until the last second; for example, say, "Take two. One, stay on this medium shot. Three, tight on the guitar." If you reposition a camera, give the operator time to reset the zoom lens; otherwise, the camera will not stay in focus during subsequent zooming.

▓ If you make a mistake, correct it as well as you can and go on with the show. Do not meditate on how you could have avoided it while neglecting the rest of the show. Pay full attention to what is going on. If recording live-on-tape, stop the tape only when absolutely necessary. Too many false starts can take the energy out of even the most seasoned performers and production crew.

▓ Spot-check the videotape after each take to make sure that the take is technically acceptable. Then go on to the next one. It is always easier to repeat a take, one right after the other, than to go back at the end of a strenuous taping session.

▓ If you use the stop-start method in a single-camera production where you tape one shot at a time, you should play back each take before going on to the next one.

▓ If there is a technical problem that you must solve from the control room, tell the floor manager about it on the intercom or use the *S.A. system* to inform the whole floor about the slight delay. The talent then know that there is a technical delay and that it was not caused by them. The people on the floor can use this time to relax, however busy it may be for you in the control room.

▓ During the show, speak only when necessary. If you talk too much, people will stop listening and may miss important instructions. Worse, the crew will follow your example and start chatting on the intercom.

▓ Prepare for the closing cues. Give the necessary time cues to the floor manager slightly ahead of the actual time to compensate for the delay between your cue and the talents' reception of it.

▓ When you have the line in black (your final fade to black), call for a VTR stop and give the all-clear signal. Thank the crew and talent for their efforts. If something went wrong, do not storm into the studio to complain. Take a few minutes to catch your breath, and then talk calmly to the people responsible for the problem. Be constructive in your criticism and help them avoid the mistake in the future. Just telling them that they made a mistake helps little at this point.

CONTROLLING CLOCK TIME

In commercial television, time is money. Each second of broadcast time has a monetary value attached to it. Indeed, salespeople sell time to their clients as though it were a tangible commodity. One second of airtime may cost much more than another, depending on the potential audience an event may command. *Clock time*, also known as *schedule time*, is defined as the time at which a program starts and ends. Because television operations are scheduled second-by-second, clock time is a critical element in television production.

Schedule Time and Running Time

As a director, you don't have to worry about *schedule times* (starting times of various programs when aired) and *running times* (broadcast length of a program segment or program), but you are still responsible to time your show to the second so that it can fit the prescribed time slot in the day's programming. You use the control room clock for meeting the schedule times, and the stopwatch for measuring the running times of the program inserts.

Clock Back-Timing and Front-Timing

Although the master control computer calculates almost all the start and end times of programs and program inserts, and a variety of pocket calculators help you add and subtract clock times, you should nevertheless know how to do time calculations even in the absence of electronic devices. For example, a performer may request in the last minute specific time cues, which you then have to figure by hand.

Back-timing   One of the most common time controls involves cues to the talent so that he or she can end the program as indicated by the schedule time. In a 30-minute program, the talent normally expects a 5-minute cue and subsequent cues with 3 minutes, 2 minutes, 1 minute, 30 seconds, and 15 seconds remaining in the show. To figure out such time cues quickly, you simply *back-time* from the scheduled end time or the start time of the new program segment (which is the same thing). For example, if the log shows that your live "What's Your Opinion?" show is followed by a Salvation Army *PSA (public service announcement)* at 4:29:30, at what clock times do you give the talent the standard time cues, assuming that your standard videotaped close takes 30 seconds?

You should start with the end time of the panel discussion, which is 4:29:00, and subtract the various time segments. (You do not back-time from the end of the program at 4:29:30, because your standard videotaped close will take up 30 seconds.) When, for example, should the moderator get her 3-minute cue or the 15-second wind-up cue?

Let's proceed with back-timing this particular program:

4:24:00	5 minutes to VTR	*Back-time to here*
4:26:00	3 minutes	
4:27:00	2 minutes	
4:28:00	1 minute	
4:28:30	30 seconds	
4:28:45	15 seconds	
4:29:00	Cut moderator for VTR close	*Start here*
4:29:30	PSA (Salvation Army)	

When subtracting time, you may find it convenient to take a minute from the minute column and convert it into seconds, especially if you have to subtract a large number of seconds from a small number. Similarly, you can take an hour from the hour column and convert it into minutes.

$$
\begin{array}{r} 5:15:22 \\ -\ 14:27 \\ \hline \end{array}
\qquad
\begin{array}{r} 5:14:82 \\ -\ 14:27 \\ \hline 5:00:55 \end{array}
$$

or:

$$
\begin{array}{r} 5:02:43 \\ -\ 55:30 \\ \hline \end{array}
\qquad
\begin{array}{r} 4:62:43 \\ -\ 55:30 \\ \hline 4:07:13 \end{array}
$$

Front-timing   To keep a show on time (such as a live newscast with many recorded inserts), you need to know more than the start and end times of the program and the running times of the various inserts. You also need to know when (clock time) the inserts are to be run; otherwise, you cannot figure whether you are ahead or behind with the total show.

To figure out the additional clock times for each break or insert, simply add the running times to the initial clock time as shown on the log or the program format. As with back-timing, you need to convert the seconds and minutes on a sixty scale rather than a hundred scale. Simply compute the seconds, minutes, and hours individually, and then convert the minutes and seconds to the sixty scale.

$$
\begin{array}{r} 6:33:\ 42 \\ +\ 0:\ 58 \\ \hline 6:33:100 \end{array} \longrightarrow 6:34:40
$$

Converting Frames into Clock Time

Because there are thirty frames to one second, the frames roll over after twenty-nine. But seconds and minutes roll over after fifty-nine. You must therefore convert frames into seconds, or seconds into frames, when front- or back-timing time code numbers. Again, you need to compute the frames, seconds, minutes, and hours individually and then convert the frames on the thirty scale and the seconds and minutes on the sixty scale.

For example:

$$
\begin{array}{r}
00{:}01{:}58{:}29 \\
+\ 00{:}00{:}03{:}17 \\
\hline
00{:}01{:}61{:}46
\end{array}
\longrightarrow 00{:}01{:}62{:}16 \longrightarrow 00{:}02{:}02{:}16
$$

Note that you simply added the frames and subtracted 30 for the additional second.

Fortunately, computer-assisted edit controllers will do this figuring for you. There are also computer programs and small handheld calculators available that calculate clock time as well as frame time.

CONTROLLING SUBJECTIVE TIME

The control of **subjective time**—the duration you feel—is much more subtle and difficult than the control of objective time. Even the most sophisticated computer cannot tell you whether a newscaster races through her copy too fast or whether a dramatic scene is paced too slowly and drags for the viewer. In determining subjective time, you must rely on your own judgment and sensitivity to the relation of one movement or rhythm to another. Although two persons move with the same speed, one may seem to move much more slowly than the other. What makes the movements of the one person appear faster or slower?[1]

Watch how rush-hour traffic reflects nervous energy and impatience while actually the vehicles move more slowly than when traveling on an open freeway. Good comedians and musicians are said to have a "good sense of timing," which means that they have excellent control of subjective time—the pace and rhythm of the performance the audience perceives.

Find three or four recordings of the same piece of music, such as Beethoven's Fifth Symphony or your favorite popular song, as interpreted by different conductors or singers. Most likely, you will find that some lead the same piece of music much faster than others, depending on their overall concept of the piece and, of course, their personal temperament and style.

When dealing with subjective time, we have many terms to express its relative duration. You hear of *speed, tempo, pace, hurrying, dragging,* and other similar expressions. To simplify the subjective time control, you may want to use only two basic concepts: pace and rhythm. The *pace* of a show or show segment is how fast or slow it feels. *Rhythm* has to do with how fast or slow individual speeches or the actions of actors appear to the audience.

There are many ways of increasing or decreasing the pace of a scene, a segment, or an overall show. One is to speed up the action or the delivery of the dialogue, very much like picking up the tempo of a musical number. Another is to increase the intensity—the relative excitement—of a scene. Usually, this is done by introducing or sharpening some conflict, such as raising the voices of people arguing, having one car briefly lose control while being pursued by another, or shooting the scene in tighter close-ups. A third possibility is to increase the density of the event, by simply having more things happen within a specific section of running time. If you want to slow down a scene, you do just the opposite.

Whatever you change, you must always perceive the pace in relation to the other parts of the show and to the show as a whole. Fast, after all, is fast only if we can relate the movement to something slower. Finally, a precise process message should suggest the overall pace and rhythm of a show.

STUDIO INTERCOM SYSTEMS

The **intercom** system is the lifeline in multicamera directing. It provides immediate voice communication among all production and technical personnel. With a functioning team, the director, for example, can give cues to many members of the production team simultaneously, triggering a flurry of activity. Most studios have a variety of intercom systems, each serving a specific communi-

---

1. See the discussion of subjective time in Herbert Zettl, *Sight Sound Motion*, 3d ed. (Belmont, Calif.: Wadsworth Publishing Co., 1999), pp. 212–215.

cation task. The most common are the P.L., the I.F.B., and the S.A. systems.

The P.L. system Most small stations or independent production studios use the telephone intercommunication, or *P.L. (private line or phone line), system.* All production and technical personnel who need to be in voice contact with one another wear standard telephone headsets with an earphone and a small microphone for talkback. Every major production area has one or more intercom outlets for plugging in the headsets. For example, each camera generally has two intercom outlets: one for the camera operator and the other for the floor manager or other floor crew member. If possible, though, floor persons should avoid connecting their headset to the camera; it not only limits their operation radius but also interferes with the camera's flexibility. The floor crew should connect their headsets to separate intercom wall outlets through long, flexible, lightweight cables.

Larger studios employ a wireless intercom system for the floor personnel. Some systems provide an earplug, instead of the cumbersome headset, and a small pocket receiver that picks up signals sent into the studio or field position by a transmitter. Such earpiece systems will normally not let you talk back to the control room, and they don't muffle sounds that may interfere with hearing the intercom messages. Other systems provide wireless reception and talkback facilities. At least the floor manager should wear a talkback telephone headset for two-way communication.

Some shows require a simultaneous feed of program sound and control room signals to such production personnel as the microphone boom operator or studio musicians (usually the band or orchestra leader), who have to coordinate their actions with both the program sound and the director's cues. In such cases, you can use a double headset wherein one of the two earphones carries the intercom signals and the other the program sound.

Sometimes when you work in noisy surroundings or close to a high-volume sound source, such as a rock band, you may need a double-muff headset, which filters out the high-volume sounds at least to some degree. The mic in such headsets does not transmit the surrounding noise and is activated only when you speak into it.

In most television operations, production and technical crews use the same intercom channel, which means that everyone can be heard by everyone else. Most intercom systems, however, have provisions for separating the lines for different functions. For example, while the TD confers with the video engineer on one channel, the director may, at the same time, give instructions to the floor crew. Modern studios and remote trucks provide a dozen or more separate intercom channels.

The I.F.B. system You use *I.F.B. (interruptible foldback* or *interruptible feedback) system* in shows with highly flexible formats or when important program changes are likely to occur while on the air. The I.F.B. system connects the control room (director, producer) directly with the performers, bypassing the floor manager. The performer wears a small earpiece that carries the total program sound (including his or her own voice) unless the director, producer, or any other member of the production team connected with the system interrupts the program sound.

For example, an on-camera field reporter in Washington who is describing the arrival of foreign dignitaries can hear herself until the director cuts in and says, "Throw it back to New York"—that is, tell the viewers that the program is returning to the origination center in New York. But while the director is giving these instructions, the viewer still hears the field reporter's continuous description of the event. Relaying such messages through an off-camera floor manager would be much too slow and inaccurate in as tight a show as a newscast or a live telecast of a special event.

Needless to say, such a system works only with a highly experienced announcer and producer or director. There are countless occasions when the interruptible foldback system unfortunately acts as a performer interrupt device, because the inexperienced performer cannot maintain effective commentary while listening to the producer's instructions.

The S.A. system The *S.A. (studio address) system,* is used by the control room personnel, principally the director, to give instructions to people in the studio not connected by the P.L. system. Also called *studio talkback,* the S.A. system uses a speaker similar to a public address system, helping to communicate directly with all people in the studio. For example, you may use it to give some general instructions to everybody, especially at the beginning of a rehearsal, or to inform talent and production personnel of a temporary delay. Also, if most personnel happen to be off the P.L. headsets, as is frequently the case during a short break, you can use the talkback system to call them back to work.

Considering the importance of the intercommunication system, you should include it in routine facilities checks. If you discover faulty headsets or an imperfect intercom line, report it to the maintenance crew and have it fixed. A faulty intercom can be more detrimental to a production than a defective camera.

MAIN POINTS

◆ The two principal methods of television directing are multicamera and single-camera directing.

◆ Both directing types use a precise directing terminology that facilitates talent and crew activities.

◆ Multicamera directing involves the simultaneous use of two or more cameras and instantaneous editing with a switcher. It is done from the control room.

◆ The various rehearsals include script reading; dry run, or blocking rehearsal; technical and talent walk-throughs; camera and dress rehearsals, and walk-through/camera rehearsal combination.

◆ Directing from the control room requires adhering to a precise production schedule for rehearsals and on-the-air performance and following clear standby and on-the-air procedures.

◆ The two important clock times are schedule time (start and end of a program) and running time (program length).

◆ Back-timing means figuring specific clock times (usually for cues) by subtracting running time from the schedule time at which the program ends. Front-timing means starting at the clock time that marks the beginning of a program and then adding specific running times.

◆ When converting frames into clock time, you must have the frames roll over to the next second after twenty-nine (or twenty-four in European standards), but seconds and minutes after fifty-nine.

◆ Subjective time means the time duration we feel. It includes the concepts of pace and rhythm.

◆ The major studio intercom systems are the P.L. (private line or phone line) and the I.F.B. (interruptible foldback or interruptible feedback) systems.

◆ The S.A. (studio address) system allows the control room personnel to talk directly to the studio personnel.

19.2

Single-Camera Directing

In *single-camera directing*, you are primarily concerned with directing various takes for later assembly in postproduction. The big difference between directing multicamera and single-camera productions is that multicamera productions are continuous and single-camera productions are discontinuous. *Continuous* in this context means that you do not stop after each shot, but sequence a series of shots through instantaneous editing (switching) without interruption. It also implies that you are directing simultaneously various production activities, such as shot composition, camera movement, switching, audio, lights, talent, VTRs, graphics, and special effects. In single-camera studio productions, the videotaping is *discontinuous*. You no longer intend to record on tape a finished product that needs little or no postproduction for broadcast. Rather, your aim is to produce effective videotape segments that can be shaped into a continuous program through extensive postproduction.

▶ **SINGLE-CAMERA DIRECTING PROCEDURES**
   Visualization, script breakdown, rehearsals, and videotaping

▶ **POSTPRODUCTION ACTIVITIES**
   Protection copies, VTR log, and sequencing

SINGLE-CAMERA DIRECTING PROCEDURES

This section focuses on these major aspects of single-camera studio directing: (1) visualization (2) script breakdown, (3) rehearsals, and (4) videotaping. *READY ZVL* ❷

Visualization

Even if you are videotaping a production discontinuously—shot by shot—your basic visualization is not much different from what it would be when continuous-shooting with multiple cameras and instantaneous editing. As described in chapter 18, the first reading of a script may conjure up some *locking-in* points—key visualizations that set the style for the entire production. This process is intuitive and depends a great deal on your own perception of the characters in the script, their environment, and their behavior. The script may guide you to mental pictures of individual shots but should not dictate your visualization. More often, you will draw on your own experience and observations to arrive at the various locking-in points.

Once you have established locking-in points that determine your general shooting style, you must go back to the script and break it down for discontinuous videotaping. Now the order in which you videotape the shots is no longer guided by the script context, the narrative, or even aesthetic continuity, but strictly by convenience and efficiency. For example, you may want to videotape all the scenes in the hospital corridor, then the waiting-room scenes, then all the operating-room scenes, then all the scenes in the patient's room, and so forth.

To give you an idea of how script preparation differs between multicamera and single-camera shooting, take another look at figure 18.9, showing the director's markings of a brief multicamera drama script. How would you now break down the very same script segment for a single-camera shoot? Write down a series of shots that show Yolanda meeting Carrie in the hospital hallway. Then compare it with the breakdown in figure 19.7. **SEE 19.7**

Script Breakdown

As you can see, the breakdown is more detailed and not necessarily in the order of the action. Note that this script breakdown is just one of many possibilities.

If more convenient, you could have taped the third scene (Carrie and Yolanda) before the scene of Yolanda rushing up to the doctor and Carrie. Shooting a scene in such bits and pieces requires that the actors repeat their lines and actions several times identically; you must watch carefully that the individual shots cut together into a seamless scene. This means that you must also connect the various visualization points so that the scene and the sequences have both narrative (story) and aesthetic (vector) continuity.

Continuity Continuity means that all shots in a sequence connect seamlessly so that they are no longer recognized by the audience as individual shots, but as a single scene. As explained in chapter 18, a detailed storyboard will aid you greatly in seeing individual shots as a sequence. Even if you don't have the time or resources to design storyboards for each sequence, you must try to visualize how well the shots cut together and watch for continuity errors during the videotaping. If, for example, Yolanda kisses her daughter on the left cheek in the medium shot, do not let her switch to the right cheek during the close-ups of the same scene. Such gross directing mistakes usually mean reshooting or dropping

the scene. You could use DVE (digital video effects) equipment to flop the shot in postproduction, but then you flop everything else too, including the background. Besides, such "fixing-it-in-post" techniques are time consuming and should not be used as a safety net for careless directing.

Film-style shooting Such awareness of continuity is especially important when you shoot "film-style." In *film-style shooting*, you normally move from an establishing long shot to medium shots and then to close-ups of the same action. Or, if more convenient, you can videotape some of the close-ups first and then do all the long shots. As in filmmaking you may find yourself repeating an action several times to get various fields of view (long shots, medium shots, close-ups) or angles to correct blocking or performance problems. Pay close attention to every detail so that the action is, indeed, identical when repeated. Informed and alert crew members will often help you avoid costly continuity mistakes. For example, the camera operator might catch the kiss problem or may point out that the talent has her coat buttoned for this shot but wore it unbuttoned in the previous shots.

How you start and finish a specific take can make the postproduction editor's job a delight or a nightmare. As a director you are responsible for providing the editor with shots that eventually can be assembled into a continuous and sensible sequence. Always provide the editor with a generous amount of *cutaways*—do not leave them to the camera operator; tell him or her what to shoot.

Rehearsals

In single-camera directing, you rehearse each take immediately before videotaping it. Walk the talent, the camera, and the microphone operators through each take, explaining what they should and should not do. Have the single camera connected to a monitor so that you can watch the action on the screen and, if necessary, make the necessary corrections before the videotaping.

Videotaping

Be sure to slate each take. Quickly check whether the C.G. slate shows the correct take number. If obvious mistakes are made at the beginning of the take, keep the tape rolling and simply audio-slate the next take (have the floor manager read the next take number and title

RECEPTION ROOM AND HALLWAY

1. Yolanda in the reception room

2. Hallway: Yolanda pacing up and down the hallway in the vicinity of the emergency room

3. Hallway: Typical hospital traffic--nurses, a gurney, a wheelchair, visitors with flowers, a doctor and nurse, a physical therapist protecting a person on crutches

4. Hallway: Doctor pushes Carrie in wheelchair

5. POV Carrie: Yolanda

6. CUs Yolanda

7. POV Yolanda: Doctor and Carrie

YOLANDA RUSHING TOWARD DOCTOR AND CARRIE

1. Hallway: Yolanda rushes toward Doctor and Carrie

2. Reverse-angle shot (POV Carrie): Yolanda

3. Same shots with gurney traffic interfering with Yolanda's approach (Steadicam)

CARRIE AND YOLANDA

1. CU Carrie: "Hi, Mom!"

2. CU Yolanda: "Carrie--are you all right? What happened?"

3. CU swish pan from Carrie to Yolanda: "Carrie--are you all right? What happened?"

19.7 SINGLE-CAMERA SCRIPT BREAKDOWN
Videotape shots are grouped for convenience and efficiency, not narrative order.

into the hot mic). Have the VTR operator or PA (if you use a camcorder) keep an accurate field log. Watch for obvious continuity mistakes. Be careful not to wear out talent and crew with too many retakes; there is a point where retakes become counterproductive because of talent and crew fatigue. Finally, have the VTR operator or PA label all videotapes and cases and check that the labels correspond with the field log.

Once again, follow your production schedule. As with taping multicamera shows, there is a tendency to do needless retakes simply because you have the better part of the day ahead of you. But then you suddenly find yourself running out of time and are forced to speed through the remaining takes. If you have time and energy left at the end of your production day, you can always do the desired retake.

POSTPRODUCTION ACTIVITIES

Your postproduction activities depend on how complex the postproduction editing promises to be. If extensive postproduction is required, you are generally still responsible for the major editing and sound-mixing decisions. Relatively simple editing tasks are handled by the videotape editor, with a minimum of supervision (or, as editors like to call it, "interference") by the director. Nevertheless, it is a good idea for you as a director to work with the editor until the completion of postproduction.

Protection copies   Before the actual editing begins, make *protection copies* of all source tapes. You can do this while the tapes are window-dubbed for off-line editing (keying the time code over the pictures of the off-line dub—see chapter 13). If you use a nonlinear editing system, you can digitize the videotape footage from a single VTR and then create a VTR log and various files for the footage. When creating such files, mark them in such a way that you can easily locate them again. For example, you may want to put all motorcycle shots in one bin (file), and all the interior shots of the motorcycle shop in another.

VTR log   Your editor must now go through all the tapes and log each take—good and bad—on the VTR log. This is where the various vectors should be recorded (see chapter 13).

Sequencing   There is actually little difference from a directing point of view whether you tell the TD to take 2, or tell the editor to edit this shot to that one. In any case, try to work with, not against, the editor. An experienced editor can help you greatly in the sequencing process, but do not hesitate to assert yourself if you feel strongly about a certain editing decision. If you have a specific sequence in mind, you can either do the off-line editing yourself or do a *paper-and-pencil edit* or a rough-cut and then hand it over to the editor (see chapter 13). When editing, your major concern is no longer the visualization, but the *sequencing*, of the various shots. In the postproduction process, you will quickly realize the value of your cutaway shots and your awareness of continuity during the videotaping.

You should also supervise the audio *sweetening*, especially with extensive audio postproduction. When finished, check the entire off-line edit for serious technical and aesthetic discrepancies. Even a good editor might not see an unwanted jump cut until the final screening of the tape. When everything looks right, you can have an edit master tape produced on-line.

MAIN POINTS

◆ Single-camera production starts, as does multicamera production, with the visualization of key shots.

◆ The script breakdown is guided more by production convenience and efficiency than visualization and sequencing. The production sequence is dictated not by the script, but by such production factors as location or getting various points of view or close-ups of the same action.

◆ When shooting film-style, the action is always repeated for various points of view and fields of view.

◆ Each take is normally rehearsed immediately pre-ceding its videotaping.

◆ When videotaping, always slate each take, label all videotapes, and stick to the production schedule.

◆ Always make protection copies of the source tapes before beginning the postproduction editing phase.

◆ Log each take—good and bad—on the VTR log and note the various vectors.

◆ As a director guide, but do not interfere with, the postproduction editing and audio sweetening.

ZETTL'S VIDEOLAB 2.1

This section reinforces the differences between the multicamera and single-camera production approaches.

RUN ZVL 1   Click on the **process** monitor and run tape 6 **Methods**. Click on the **Multicamera** module, which emphasizes the production efficiency of using multiple cameras in a production.

RUN ZVL 2   Click on the **Single-camera** module. It demonstrates the advantages of single-camera production.

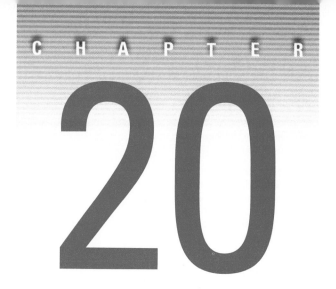

20

Field Production and Big Remotes

When you see one of those big television trailer rigs pull up and production crews unloading cameras, microwave dishes, miles of cable, and other pieces of television equipment, you know that a big remote is in the offing. Why undergo such an effort when you could simply grab a few small camcorders to shoot the same field event? This chapter provides some answers.

Section 20.1, ENG, EFP, and Big Remotes, looks at these three field production methods individually. Section 20.2, Covering Major Events, offers further information about standard television setups of sports remotes and other field events; how to interpret location sketches; major field communication systems; signal transport; and cable distribution.

big remote A production outside the studio to televise live and/or record live-on-tape a large scheduled event that has not been staged specifically for television. Examples include sporting events, parades, political gatherings, and special hearings.

direct broadcast satellite (DBS) Satellite with a relatively high-powered transponder (transmitter/receiver) that broadcasts from the satellite to small, individual downlink dishes; operates on the Ku-band.

downlink The antenna (dish) and equipment that receive the signals coming from a satellite.

field production All productions that happen outside the studio; generally refers to EFP.

instant replay Repeating for the viewer, by playing back videotape or disk-stored video, a key play or important event immediately after its live occurrence.

Ku-band A high-frequency band used by certain satellites for signal transport and distribution. The Ku-band signals can be influenced by heavy rain or snow.

location sketch A rough map of the locale of a remote telecast. For an indoor remote, the sketch shows the room dimensions and the furniture and window locations. For an outdoor remote, the sketch indicates the location of buildings, the remote truck, power source, and sun during the time of the telecast.

microwave relay A transmission method from the remote location to the station and/or transmitter involving the use of several microwave units.

mini-link Several microwave setups that are linked together to transport the video and audio signals past obstacles to their destination (usually the television station and/or the transmitter).

remote A large television production done outside the studio. Also called a *big remote*.

remote survey A preproduction investigation of the location premises and the event circumstances.

remote truck The vehicle that carries the program control, the audio control, the video-recording and instant-replay control, the technical control, and the transmission equipment.

satellite news gathering (SNG) The use of satellites to transport the video and audio of live or recorded news stories from a remote site to the station.

satellite news vehicle (SNV) A small truck whose primary function is to uplink an ENG signal to a satellite. May also contain VTRs and modest editing facilities.

uplink Earth station transmitter used to send video and audio signals to a satellite.

uplink truck Small truck that sends video and audio signals to a satellite.

20.1

ENG, EFP, and Big Remotes

When a television production happens outside the studio, we call it a **field production**. We normally distinguish among *ENG (electronic news gathering)* that covers daily news events, *EFP (electronic field production)* that deals with smaller scheduled events, and *big remotes* that are done for major events, such as sports and parades.

There are advantages to taking a production out of the studio and into the field:

- You can place or observe an event in its real setting or select a specific setting for a fictional event.

- You have a great number and variety of highly realistic settings to choose from.

- You can use available light and background sounds so long as they accomplish your technical and aesthetic production requirements.

- You can save on production people and equipment, as many EFP productions require less equipment and crew than similar studio productions (unless you do a complex EFP or a big remote).

- You avoid considerable rental costs for studio use and, if you work for a station, studio scheduling problems.

There are disadvantages as well:

- You are always location dependent, which means that some locations require the close cooperation of nonproduction people. For example, if you shoot on a busy downtown street, you will need the help of the police to control traffic and onlookers.

- When shooting on city, county, or federal property, you may need a permit from these agencies plus additional insurance stipulated by them.

- You do not have the production control the studio affords. Good lighting is often difficult to achieve in the field, both in indoor and outdoor locations, as is high-quality audio.

- On outdoor shoots, the weather always presents a hazard. For example, rain or snow can cause serious delays, simply because it is too wet or too cold to shoot outside. A few clouds may give you considerable continuity problems when the preceding takes showed clear skies.

- Field productions also normally require crew travel and lodging as well as equipment transportation.

Nevertheless, the production efficiency of shooting in the field usually outweighs these relatively minor disadvantages, especially in ENG and EFP. Although ENG and EFP have been discussed throughout this book, the focus here is on their specific field production requirements.

▶ **ELECTRONIC NEWS GATHERING**
  ENG and SNG production features

▶ **ELECTRONIC FIELD PRODUCTION**
  EFP preproduction, production, and postproduction

▶ **BIG REMOTES**
  Remote survey; production procedures by director, floor manager, and talent; and various post-production tasks

ELECTRONIC NEWS GATHERING

ENG EFP Electronic news gathering is the most flexible remote operation. As pointed out in previous chapters, one person with a camcorder can handle a complete ENG assignment, so long as the story does not have to be transmitted live. But even if the signal has to be relayed back to the station or transmitter, ENG requires only a fraction of the equipment and people of a big remote. Sometimes, the *shooter* or *videographer* (news camera operator) will also take care of the signal feed from the camcorder or news truck to the station.

ENG Production Features

The major production features of ENG are the readiness with which you can respond to an event, the mobility possible in the coverage of an event, and the flexibility of ENG equipment and people. Because ENG equipment is so compact and self-contained, you can get to an event and videotape or broadcast it faster than with any other type of television equipment. An important operational difference between ENG and EFP or big remotes is that ENG requires no preproduction. ENG systems are specifically designed for immediate response to a breaking story. In ENG you exercise no control over the event but merely observe it with your camcorder as best you can.

Even when working under extreme conditions and time restrictions, experienced shooters can quickly analyze an event, pick the most important parts of it, and videotape pictures that edit together well. For important events the ENG team normally consists of two people—

the camcorder operator and the field reporter. Many ENG stories are covered by a single shooter and narrated later by the anchor during the newscast. ENG equipment can go wherever you go. It can operate in a car, an elevator, a helicopter, or a small kitchen. Your shoulder often substitutes for the heavy tripods.

With ENG equipment you can either videotape an event or transmit it live. The transmission equipment has become so compact and flexible that even a live transmission can be accomplished by a single camera operator. Most ENG vehicles (usually vans) are equipped with a microwave transmitter, which, when extended, can establish a transmission link from the remote location to the station. **SEE 20.1** When doing a live transmission, you will have to connect the camera cable with the microwave

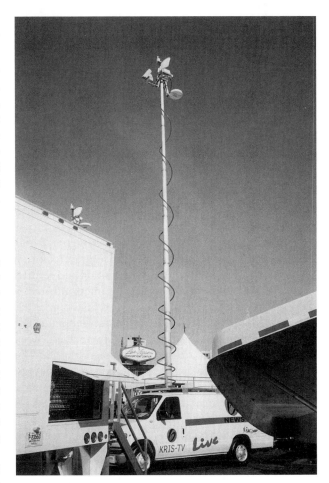

20.1 ENG VAN
This regular-sized van houses the extendible microwave transmission device and a variety of intercommunications equipment.

20.2 SATELLITE UPLINK VAN

The satellite news vehicle is a portable earth station. It sends television signals to the Ku-band satellites.

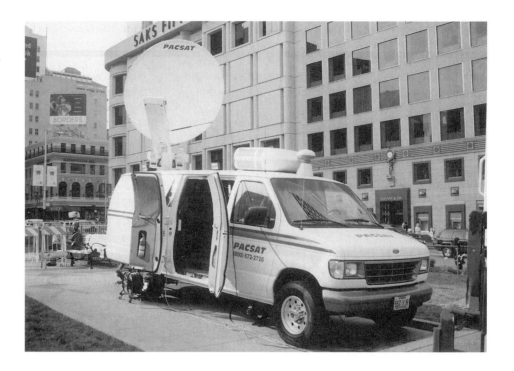

transmitter. You can also use such a microwave link to transmit quickly the uncut videotape directly from the camcorder to the station.

SNG Production Features

There is still another "NG" method: *SNG (satellite news gathering)*. SNG has been spawned by the ability of satellites to transport live or recorded ENG signals from a faraway field location to the station. In contrast to normal ENG operations, SNG requires preplanning and setup of the *satellite news vehicle (SNV)*, the main purpose of which is to uplink a live or videotaped ENG signal to a satellite. The SNG looks like a small remote truck and contains computer-assisted uplink equipment and, when used for news, one or two VTRs as well as editing equipment. The VTRs can record the camera output and play back the edited or unedited news videotapes for immediate uplinking. **SEE 20.2**

Newspeople prefer uplinking "hot" videotapes (recorded moments before the transmission) to live transmission because it permits repeated transmission in case the satellite feed gets temporarily interrupted or is lost altogether. To further safeguard against signal loss, two VTRs are sometimes used for the recording and

playback of the same news story. If something goes wrong with one machine, you can quickly switch over to the next for the same material.

Satellite news gathering is used whenever big and especially newsworthy events are scheduled, such as a presidential election, a summit meeting of heads of state, or the world soccer finals. But the uplink truck is also used locally for the distribution of news stories, national and international teleconferencing, or whenever a signal cannot be sent readily by microwave or cable.

ELECTRONIC FIELD PRODUCTION

ENG EFP As you already know, EFP—electronic field production—uses both ENG and studio techniques. From ENG it borrows its mobility and flexibility; from the studio it borrows its production care and quality control. The following discussion of some of the fundamental steps of field preproduction, production, and post-production assumes that you are still functioning as the director. This way, you have to deal with production detail that is important for each member of the EFP team, regardless of the specific jobs assigned. *READY ZVL* ❶

Preproduction

Compared with ENG, in which you simply respond to a situation, EFP requires careful planning. Recall that the first step in any preproduction activity is to translate the process message into the most effective and efficient production method—whether to shoot it indoors or outdoors, single- or multicamera, in the normal sequence of events or shot-by-shot. The second step is to translate the chosen production method into specific medium requirements—equipment and people. Assuming that you have practiced this translation of process message into production requirements, we jump to the actual preproduction activities: (1) location survey, (2) initial production meeting, and (3) field production time line.

Location survey   To get to know the environment in which the production will take place make an accurate *location sketch*—a rough map of the locale of a remote telecast. For an indoor remote, the sketch shows the room dimensions and the furniture and window locations. For an outdoor remote, it indicates the location of buildings, the remote truck, power source, and sun during the time of the telecast.

To refresh your memory, take another look at the location sketch of the artist's studio in figure 18.11. This sketch gives important information about lighting and audio requirements, camera positions, and shooting sequences. Although technical preparations may not be your immediate concern, check on the availability of power (wall outlets), the acoustics (small room, reflective walls, traffic noise from nearby freeway), and potential lighting problems (large windows). Location surveys are discussed further in the context of big remotes later in this chapter.

Ask your producer whether he or she has secured accommodations, shooting permits, and parking and food for talent and crew. If the production is really in the field, are the most basic conveniences available?

Initial production meeting   The initial production meetings are normally held the day before the shoot and involve all key personnel, including the PA (production assistant), floor manager, and the crew chief or camera operator (shooter). For more-complex field productions that involve several indoor locations, you may want to include the LD (lighting director). At a minimum you should meet with the PA (who may double as the audio/VTR operator) and the camera operator.

Explain the process message and what you hope to accomplish. Distribute the location sketch and discuss the major production steps.

It is critical that everyone knows the exact location of the production and how to get there. Can everyone fit into the EFP van? Who is riding with whom? Who needs to first come to the station for equipment check-out, and who will go directly to the location? Who will drive the van? Hand out the production schedule and ask the PA to distribute it (fax and/or e-mail) to all other crew members who may not be in the meeting. As you can see, transportation to and from the location is an essential scheduling issue. If the field production is outdoors, what do you do in case of rain? Always have an alternate production schedule ready.

Field production time line   A shooting schedule for a fairly elaborate field production may look like this:

TIME LINE: FIELD PRODUCTION

7:30–8:15 A.M.	Equipment check-out
8:15 A.M.	Departure
9:15 A.M.	Estimated arrival time
9:30–10:00 A.M.	Production meeting with talent and crew
10:00–11:00 A.M.	Technical setup
11:00–11:30 A.M.	Lunch
11:30 A.M.–12:00 P.M.	Technical and talent walk-through
12:00–12:20 P.M.	Notes and reset
12:20–12:30 P.M.	Break
12:30–1:00 P.M.	Segment 1 taping
1:00–1:15 P.M.	Notes and reset for segment 2
1:15–1:45 P.M.	Segment 2 taping
1:45–1:55 P.M.	Break
1:55–2:10 P.M.	Notes and reset for segment 3
2:10–2:40 P.M.	Segment 3 taping
2:40–3:00 P.M.	Spill
3:00–3:30 P.M.	Strike
3:30 P.M.	Departure
4:30 P.M.	Estimated arrival time at station
4:30–4:45 P.M.	Equipment check-in

Production: Equipment Check

Again, tell the crew what is going on and the aim of the production. Go through the production schedule and the rundown sheet of the major locations and taping sessions. Be extra careful when loading the equipment. Unlike studio productions, where all the equipment is at hand, in field productions you need to bring every piece of equipment to the location. Even if you have done the same EFP a dozen times, always use an equipment checklist. Even a wrong cable or adapter can cause undue delays or the cancellation of the production.

Before loading equipment on a vehicle, check each item to see that it works properly. At a minimum do a test recording of picture and sound before leaving for the location shoot.

Equipment checklist The following equipment checklist is intended as a general guide and may not include all the items you need to take along. Depending on the relative complexity of the EFP, you may need considerably less or more than the items listed. *READY ZVL* ❷

■ *Cameras* Field camera or camcorders? Have they been checked out? Do you have the appropriate lenses and lens attachments (usually filters), if any? What camera mounts do you need: tripod dollies, clamps, Steadicam mount, high hats, bean bags, portable jib arms? Do you have enough batteries? Are they fully charged? Do they fit the specific camcorders you use in the EFP?

■ *VTR and tape* If you use field cameras instead of camcorders, you need to take one or more VTRs. Do you have the proper videocassettes for the VTRs? Take plenty of cassettes along. Check that the actual tape length matches the label on the box. When you think you have enough tape, add two more cassettes for good measure. Do the cables fit the jacks on the recorder and ENG/EFP camera?

■ *Monitor, RCU, and scopes* You need a monitor for playback or checking the camera's shots. If the monitor is battery-powered, do you have enough batteries? If you do a multicamera EFP with a switcher, each camera input needs a separate preview monitor. If you have a narrator describing the action, you need a separate monitor for him or her. In critical (film-style) field productions for which you use a single high-quality camera, you need an *RCU (remote control unit)*, a *waveform monitor (oscilloscope)*, and a *vector scope* for optimal video. As you recall, the RCU enables you to adjust the camera for optimal performance. The oscilloscope helps you adjust the brightness (keeping the white and black levels within tolerable limits), and the vector scope helps adjust the camera so that it produces true colors.

■ *Audio* If you have not checked out the acoustics of the location, take several types of mics. Check your wireless lavalieres. Do the portable mics fit the channel frequency of the receiver? All remote mics should have windscreens, including the lavaliere mics. Choose the most appropriate mounting equipment, such as clamps, stands, and fishpoles. Do you need a small field mixer? Does it work properly? If you use a separate audio recorder, check it out before taking it on location. Do you have enough audiotape or cassettes for the whole production? Don't forget headsets for the fishpole operator and the audio-recording technician.

■ *Power supply* Do you have the right batteries for the monitors and camcorders or field cameras? Are they fully charged? If using AC, do you have the right AC/DC adapters? Do you have enough AC extension cords to reach the AC outlet? Unless battery-driven, you also need AC power and extension cords for the monitors. Take a few power strips along, but be careful not to overload the circuits.

■ *Cables and connectors* Do you have enough camera cables, especially if there is a long run between the camera and the RCU? Are there enough coax and AC cables for monitor feeds? Always take a sufficient amount of mic cables along, even if you plan to use wireless mics. The mic cables may save a whole production day if the wireless system breaks down or is unusable at the location. Do you have the right connectors for the cables and jacks (usually XLR connectors)? Bring some adapters for video and audio cables (BNC to RCA phono and XLR to RCA phono and the reverse). Although you should avoid adapters as much as possible (they are always a potential trouble spot), bring some along that fit the cables and a variety of input jacks.

■ *Lighting* You can light most interiors with portable lighting instruments. Take several lighting kits along. Check that the kits actually contain the normal complements of lights, stands, and accessories. Do the lights work? Always pack a few spare lamps. Do the lamps actually fit the lighting instruments used? Do they burn with the desired color temperature (3,200°K or 5,600°K)? Do you have enough reflectors (white foam core), umbrella reflectors, diffusion material (scrims, screens), and color gels for regulating color temperature? The color gels most often needed are the slightly orange ones for lowering the color temperature or the light-blue ones for raising it.

If there are windows to cope with, you may need large sheets of neutral density filters (that cut down the light without changing the color temperature) or orange color media to cover the windows and thus lower the color temperature. Just to be safe, take some muslin along to block unwanted light that may enter through an off-camera window, and a black cloth to cut down unwanted reflections.

Other important items to take along are: light meter, light stands and clamps, sandbags to secure the portable light stands, some pieces of 1×3 lumber to construct a light bridge for back lights, a roll of aluminum foil for heat shields, extra barn doors, flags, and a dozen or so wood clothespins to attach scrims or color gels to barn doors.

■ *Intercom*   If the single-camera EFP is taking place in a confined area, you don't need elaborate intercom systems. You can call your shots right from the production area. But if the event covers a large outdoor area, you need a small power megaphone and walkie-talkies to communicate with the widely dispersed crew. If you use the multicamera and switcher system, you need headsets and intercom cables.

■ *Miscellaneous*   There are a few more items that are often needed for a field production: extra scripts and production schedules; field log sheets; slate and dry-erase marker; regular rain umbrellas and "raincoats" (plastic covers) for cameras; filters, if any (star filters, fog filters); white cards for white-balancing; teleprompter, if any; blank cue cards or large newsprint pad and marker; an easel; and several rolls of gaffer's tape and masking tape. You also need white chalk, more sandbags, clothespins, rope, makeup kit and bottled water, towels, flashlights, a first-aid kit, and cellular phones.

Production: Setup

Once everyone knows what is supposed to happen, the setup will be relatively smooth and free of confusion. Although as a director you may not be responsible for the technical setup, you should watch carefully that the equipment is put in the right places.

For example, when shooting indoors, will the lights be out of camera range? Are they far enough away from combustible material (especially curtains) or properly insulated (with aluminum foil, for example)? Are the back lights high enough so that they will be out of the shot? Is there a window in the background that might cause lighting problems? (The window in the artist's studio [see figure 18.11] would certainly present a problem if you had to shoot the large sculpture.) Does the room look too cluttered? Too clean? Are there any particular audio problems you can foresee? If the talent wears a wired lavaliere mic, does the mic cord restrict talent mobility? If you use a shotgun mic, can the mic operator get close enough to the talent and, especially, move with the talent without stumbling over furniture? Are pictures hung where the camera can see them? Look behind the talent to see whether the background will cause any problems (such as lamps or plants seeming to extend from the talent's head).

When outdoors, check for obvious obstacles that may be in the way of the camera, mic operators, and talent. Look past the shooting location to see whether the background fits the scene. Are there bushes, trees, or telephone poles that may, again, appear to extend from the talent's head? Large billboards are a constant background hazard. What are the potential audio hazards? Although the country road may be quiet now, will there be traffic at certain times? Are there any factory whistles that may go off right in the middle of your scene?

Production: Rehearsals

Walk-through   Before you start with the actual rehearsal and taping, you should have a brief walk-through with the crew and then with the talent to explain the major production points, such as camera positions, specific shots, and principal actions. In relatively simple productions, you can combine the technical and talent walk-throughs. The more thorough you are in explaining the action during the walk-throughs, the more efficient the actual videotaping will be. Have the PA follow you and write down all major and minor production problems that need to be solved.

Always follow the walk-through with the notes session, and have the crew take care of the remaining problems. Do not forget to give the talent and crew a short break before starting with the rehearsal and taping sessions.

Rehearsal As pointed out before, single-camera field directing has its own rehearsal technique. Basically, you rehearse each take immediately before videotaping it. You walk the talent and the camera and microphone operators through the take, explaining what they should and should not do. Videotape some of the critical scenes and watch and listen to the playback. You may want to change the mic or the mic position for a better, less noisy pickup. Call for a short break before the actual taping.

Production: Videotaping

Just before the actual taping, ask the camera operator whether the camera is properly white-balanced for the scene location. Sometimes clouds or fog move in between the rehearsal and taping, changing the color temperature of the light. Slate all takes and have the PA record them on the field log.

Watch the background action as well as the main foreground action. For example, curious onlookers may suddenly appear out of nowhere and get in your shot, or the talent may stop her action exactly in line with a distant fountain that then appears to spring out of her head. Listen carefully to the various foreground and background sounds during the take. Do not interrupt the taping because there was a faint airplane noise. Most likely, this noise will get "buried" by the main dialogue or the additional sounds added in postproduction (such as music). But the noise of a nearby helicopter that interrupts a Civil War scene definitely calls for a retake.

At the end of each take, let the camera run and record a few seconds of additional material. This cushion will be of great help to the editor in postproduction. Videotape some usable cutaways and record location sounds and room ambience for each location. The recorded "silence" will help bridge possible audio gaps in postproduction.

When you feel that you have a series of good takes, play them back on the field monitor to see whether they are, indeed, acceptable for postproduction. If you detect gross problems, you can still do some retakes before moving on to the next scene or location. Have the VTR operator or PA keep an accurate field log for each take.

Production: Strike and Equipment Check

Have the location reset (furniture, curtains) the way you found it and the place cleaned before you leave. Pick up all scripts, shot sheets, and log sheets. Do not leave pieces of gaffer's tape stuck on floors, doors, or walls.

When loading the EFP vehicle, the floor manager, crew chief, or PA should run down the equipment checklist to see that everything is back in the vehicle before leaving or changing locations. Check that the source tapes are all properly labeled and—most important—loaded onto the vehicle.

Postproduction

EFP postproduction activities are, for all practical purposes, identical to those of single-camera studio productions: making protection copies and window dubs, logging all takes on the source tapes, doing an off-line rough-cut, and finally an on-line edit on the edit master tape.

BIG REMOTES

A *big remote*, or simply *remote*, is done to televise live or to record live-on-tape large, scheduled events that have not been staged specifically for television, such as important sports matches, parades, or political gatherings. All big remotes use high-quality field cameras (studio cameras with high zoom ratio lenses) in key positions, a number of ENG/EFP cameras, and an extensive audio setup. The cameras and the various audio elements are coordinated from a mobile control center—the *remote truck*. Remote trucks are usually powered by a portable generator, with a second one standing by in case the first one fails. If there is enough power available on the remote site, the truck is connected to the available power, with a single generator serving as backup.

The remote truck represents a compact studio control room and equipment room. It contains the following control centers:

- Program control center with preview and line monitors, a switcher with special effects, a character generator, and various intercom systems (P.L., P.A., and elaborate I.F.B. systems)

- Audio control center with a fairly large audio console, ATRs and DATs, monitor speakers, and intercom systems

- Video recording center with several high-quality VTRs and/or digital recording devices that can handle regular recordings, do instant replay, and play in slow-motion and freeze-frame modes

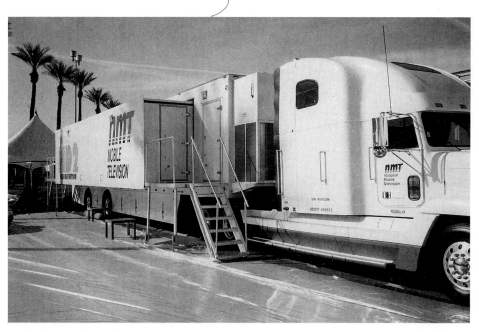

20.3 REMOTE TRUCK

The remote truck is a complete control center on wheels. It contains program, audio, video, and technical control centers as well as C.G. and recording facilities.

- Technical center with camera controls, line monitors, patchboards, generator, and signal transmission equipment. **SEE 20.3 AND 20.4**

In very big remotes, one or more additional trailers may be used for supplemental production and control equipment.

Because the telecast happens away from the studio, some of the production procedures are quite different from the studio productions. We therefore examine the following production aspects: (1) preproduction—the remote survey, and (2) production—equipment setup and operation, and floor manager and talent procedures.

Preproduction: The Remote Survey

Like any other scheduled production, a big remote requires thorough preparation—only more so. One problem with preparing for big remotes is that the event you cover is normally a onetime happening that you cannot rehearse. It would be ridiculous to ask two national hockey teams to repeat the whole game for you, or to ask political leaders to restate their lively debate verbatim just so you can have your rehearsal. Normally, you have no control over the event itself, but must follow it as best you

can. Your production preparations must take these, and several other such considerations, into account. Still another problem is that you can truck only the control room and the technical facilities to the site—not the studio itself. Cameras, microphones, and often lighting need to be brought to the remote location.

One of the key preparations is the remote, or site, survey. Many of the survey items for big remotes are equally applicable for various nonbroadcast field productions, such as a visit to a car manufacturing plant or an MTV segment. As the name implies, a *remote survey* is a preproduction investigation of the location premises and the event circumstances. It should provide you with answers to some key questions as to the nature of the event and the technical facilities necessary to televise it. Note that the big-remote survey can also be applied to more-ambitious electronic field productions.

Contact person   Your first concern is to talk to someone who knows about the event. This person, called the *contact person,* or simply *contact,* may be the public relations officer of an institution or someone in a supervisory capacity. Call the contact to find out what he or she knows about the event and whether he or she can refer you to others who might answer your questions.

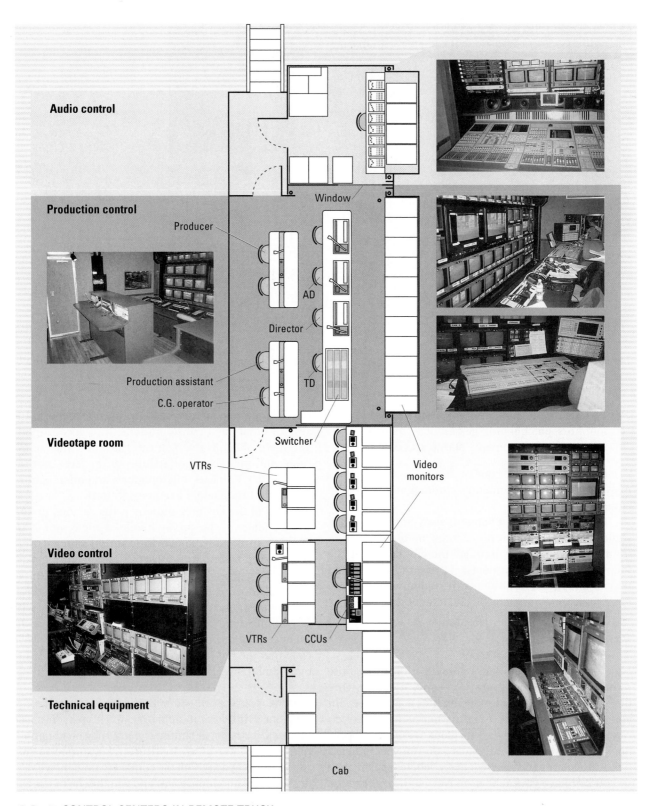

20.4 CONTROL CENTERS IN REMOTE TRUCK
The remote truck carries the program control, the audio control, the video-recording and instant-replay center, the technical center, and the transmission equipment.

In any case, get the contact's full name and position, business and e-mail addresses, and business, home, fax, cell phone, and pager numbers. Then make an appointment for the actual remote survey. Ideally, the time of day of the survey should be the same as that of the scheduled remote telecast, because the location of the sun is extremely important for outdoor remotes as well as for indoor remotes where windows will be in the shots. Arrange to have the contact person with you during the production. Establish an alternate contact and copy him or her with information you send to the primary contact.

Survey party   The survey itself is concerned with production and technical considerations. The remote survey party therefore includes people from production and engineering. The minimum party usually consists of the producer, the director, and the TD or technical supervisor of the remote. Additional production and technical supervisory personnel, such as the production manager and the chief engineer, may join the survey party, especially if the remote covers an important event and includes such elements as complex microwave or satellite links.

In general, the production requirements are first determined, then the technical people try to make the planned production procedures technically possible. Depending on the complexity of the telecast, extensive compromises must often be made by production people as well as technical personnel.

As a director you can make such compromises only if you know what the particular technical setup and pickup problems are and what changes in procedures will help overcome them. You should therefore familiarize yourself with the production as well as the technical requirements of television remotes. Although many production and engineering survey questions overlap, we will, for better clarification, consider them separately.

Production survey   The following figure lists the key questions you should ask during the production survey. **SEE 20.5**   Also, a good location sketch can help you prepare for the production and anticipate major production problems (see figures 20.14 through 20.27).

Technical survey   The technical survey lists only those items that directly influence the production procedures and, ultimately, your portion of the remote survey. **SEE 20.6**   Technical points that have already been mentioned in the production survey, such as cameras and microphones, need not be listed again.

Production: Equipment Setup and Operation

There is no clear-cut formula for setting up equipment for a remote telecast. As with a studio production, the number of cameras, the type and number of microphones, the lighting, and so forth depend entirely on the event or, more precisely, on the process message as defined in the preproduction meetings. Employing a great number of cameras, microphones, and other types of technical equipment does not necessarily guarantee a better telecast than when using less equipment. In fact, one or two camcorders are often more flexible and effective than a cumbersome remote truck with the fanciest video, audio, recording, and switching gear. For such standard big-remote operations as the live coverage of major sporting events, however, the remote truck provides essential equipment and production control.

Once set up, many of the production routines of big remotes do not differ significantly from studio productions. There are nevertheless some procedures in big-remote operations that you will not find in normal studio productions that are especially important for the director, the floor manager, and the talent. You will also be hard-pressed to find instant replays used in normal studio productions. For the following discussion, let's assume that you are functioning first as a director of a big remote, then as a floor manager, and finally as talent.

Directing the setup   Because the actual on-the-air telecast of big remotes is usually live, the directing procedures have little resemblance to the other field production methods. Rather, they closely resemble live or live-on-tape studio productions.

The big-remote setup, however, is similar to that of a complex multicamera EFP and includes all activities before the actual telecast of the remote event. As with EFP, thorough setup planning is essential for the success of a big remote.

■   As soon as the remote truck is in position, conduct a thorough technical walk-through. Tell the technical staff where you want the stationary cameras located and what field of view you require (how close or wide a shot you need to get with each camera). Get the cameras as close to the action as possible to avoid overly narrow-angle

20.5 REMOTE SURVEY: PRODUCTION

These are the key questions you should ask during the production survey.

SURVEY ITEM	KEY QUESTIONS
Contact	Who are your principal and alternate contacts? Title, business and e-mail addresses, business and home phone numbers, and fax and pager numbers.
Place	Where is the exact location of the telecast? Street address, telephone number.
Time	When is the remote telecast? Date, time. What is the arrival time of the truck? What is the production schedule?
Nature of event	What is the exact nature of the event? Where does the action take place? What type of action do you expect? Your contact person should be able to supply the necessary information.
Cameras (stationary)	How many cameras do you need? Use as few as possible. Where do you need the cameras? Do not place cameras on opposite sides of the action. In general, the closer together they are, the easier and less confusing the cutting will be. Shoot with the sun, not against it. Try to keep it behind or to the side of the cameras for the entire telecast. The press boxes of larger stadiums are generally located on the shadow side.
	If possible, survey the remote location during the exact time of the scheduled telecast. If it is not a sunny day, determine the position of the sun as closely as possible.
	Are there any large objects blocking the camera view, such as trees, telephone poles, or billboards? Will you have the same field of view during the actual telecast? A stadium crowd, for instance, may block the camera's field of view, although the view is unobstructed during the survey.
	Can you avoid large billboards in the background of shots, especially if the advertising competes with your sponsor's product?
	Do you need special camera platforms? Where? How high? Can the platforms be erected at a particular point? Can you use the remote truck as a platform? If competing stations are also covering the event, have you obtained exclusive rights for your camera positions? Where do you want iso cameras positioned?
Cameras (mobile)	Do you need to move certain cameras? What kind of floor is there? Can the camera be moved on a field dolly, or do you need remote dollies (usually with large, inflatable rubber tires)? Will the dolly with camera fit through narrow hallways and doors? Can you use ENG/EFP cameras instead of large studio/field cameras? What is their action radius? Can you connect them to a remote truck by cable (less chance of signal interference or signal loss), or do you have to microwave the signal back to the remote truck?

20.5 REMOTE SURVEY: PRODUCTION *(continued)*

SURVEY ITEM	KEY QUESTIONS
Lighting	If you need additional lighting, where and what kind? Can the instruments be hung conveniently, or do you need light stands? Do you need to make special arrangements for back lights? Will the lights be high enough so that they are out of camera range? Do you have to shoot against windows? If so, can they be covered or filtered to block out undesirable daylight?
Audio	What type of audio pickup do you need? Where do you need to place the mics? What is the exact action radius as far as audio is concerned? Which are stationary mics and which are handled by the talent? Do you need wireless mics? Otherwise, how long must the mic cables be?
	Do you need special audio arrangements, such as audio foldback or a speaker system that carries the program audio to the location? Can you tie into the "house" public address system? Do you need long-distance mics for sound pickups over a great distance?
Intercommunications	What type of intercom system do you need? Do you have to string intercom lines? How many I.F.B. channels and/or stations do you need and where do they go? Is there a need for a P.A. talkback system? Are there enough telephone lines available?
Miscellaneous production items	If a C.G. is unavailable, easels are needed for title cards. Do you need a clock? Where? Do you need line monitors, especially for the announcer? How many? Where should they be located? Will the announcer need a preview monitor to follow special iso playbacks? Do you have a camera slate in case the C.G. cannot be used?
Permits and clearances	Have you (or the producer, if you do not act as producer-director) secured clearances for the telecast from police and fire departments? Do you have written clearances from the originators of the event? Do you have parking permits for the remote truck and other station vehicles?
	Do you have passes for all technical and production personnel, especially when the event requires entrance fees or has some kind of admission restrictions?
Special production aids	Does everyone have a rundown sheet of the approximate order of events? These sheets are essential for the director, floor manager, and announcer and are extremely helpful to the camera operators, audio engineer, and additional floor personnel. Does the director have a spotter who can identify the major action and people involved? In sports, spotters are essential.

20.6 REMOTE SURVEY: TECHNICAL

The technical survey lists only those items that directly influence the production procedures.

SURVEY ITEM	KEY QUESTIONS
Power	Assuming you do not work from a battery pack or your own generator, is enough electricity available at the site? Where? You will need at least 200 amps for the average remote operation, depending on the equipment used. Does your contact person have access to the power outlets? If not, who does? Make sure the contact is available during the remote setup and the actual production. Do you need special extensions for the power cable? If you use a generator, do you have another one for backup?
Location of remote truck and equipment	Where should the remote truck be located? Its proximity to the available power is very important if you do not have a power generator. Are you then close enough to the event location? Keep in mind that there is a maximum length for camera cables beyond which you will experience video loss. Watch for possible sources of video and audio signal interference, such as nearby X-ray machines, radar, or any other high-frequency electronic equipment. Does the remote truck block normal traffic? Does it interfere with the event itself? Reserve parking for the truck. Have you asked the police for assistance? Do you need special RCUs for portable cameras?
Recording devices	If the program is recorded, do you have the necessary VTRs in the truck? Do you need additional VTRs or digital hard drives for instant replay? If you have to feed the audio and video signals back to the station separately, are the necessary phone lines cleared for the audio feed? Do you have enough tape to cover the full event? Have you made provisions for switching reels without losing part of the event? Are your iso cameras properly patched into the switcher and into separate recording devices?
Signal transmission	If the event is fed back to the station for videotape recording or directly to the transmitter for live broadcasting, do you have a good microwave or satellite uplink location? Do you need microwave mini-links? Double-check on the special requirements for feeding the satellite uplink.
Cable routing	How many camera cables do you need? Where do they have to go? How many audio cables do you need? Where do they have to go? How many intercom lines do you need? Where do they have to go? How many AC (power) lines do you need? Where do they go? Route the cables in the shortest possible distance from remote truck to pickup point, but do not block important hallways, doors, walkways, and so on. Do the cables have to cover a great span? If so, string a rope and tie the cable to it to relieve the tension.
Lighting	Are there enough AC outlets for all lighting instruments? Are the outlets fused for the lamps? Do not overload ordinary household circuits (usually 15 amps). Do you have enough extension cords and distribution boxes (or simple multiple wall plugs) to accommodate all lighting instruments and the power supply for monitors and electric clocks?
Communication systems	What are the specific communication requirements? P.L.s? I.F.B. channels? Telephone lines? Cellular phones? P.A. systems? Long-range walkie-talkies? Two-way radios?

zoom lens positions. Apprise the crew of the approximate moves and ranges of mobile cameras and what audio needs you have. Unless in a booth, specify where the announcers are going to be so that the monitors, mics, and intercom can be properly routed. Explain the major visualization points to the camera operators.

■ Be as decisive and precise as possible. Do not change your mind a hundred times before deciding on what you really want. There is simply no time for such deliberations on a remote.

■ While the technical crew is setting up, hold a production meeting with the contact person, producer, AD (assistant director), floor manager, PA, talent, and, if not directly involved in the setup, the TD (technical director) or technical supervisor. Have the contact describe the anticipated event. Explain how you intend to cover it. Although it is the producer's job to alert the talent to prominent features of the event, such as a prize-winning float in the parade, be prepared to take over in case the producer is sidetracked by some other problem. Delegate setup supervision to the AD, floor manager, and TD. Do not try to do everything yourself.

■ Pay attention to all communication systems, especially the intercom. During the telecast you will have no chance to run in and out of the remote truck to the actual site; all your instructions will come via voice communication from the truck. Discuss in detail the coverage of the event with the floor manager, who holds one of the most critical production positions during a remote.

■ Usually, you as a director have no control over the event itself; you merely try to observe it as faithfully as possible. If an announcer is to narrate and comment on the event, walk through the event site with him or her and explain as best you can what is probably going to happen. Once again, check with the contact person and announcer on the accuracy of the rundown sheet and the specific information concerning the event.

■ Check with the videotape operator on the tape length. Will it be sufficient to cover the whole event, or at least part of it, before a new tape is needed? When is the best time for a changeover to a second VTR?

■ Walk through the site again and visualize the event from the cameras' positions. Are they in the optimal shooting positions? Are they all on only one side of the principal vector so that you will not reverse the action on-screen when cutting from one to another? If shooting

outdoors, are any of the cameras going to be blinded by the sun? Where will the sun be at the end of the telecast? How do you intend to protect people and equipment in case of rain or snow?

■ Keep in mind that you are a guest while covering a remote event. Unless television is an integral part of the event, such as in most sports, try to work as quickly and as unobtrusively as possible. Do not make a big spectacle of your production. Realize that you are basically intruding on an event and that the people involved are usually under some stress. Although your first responsibility is to show the event as faithfully as possible, you must also make every effort not to add to the stress of the people involved. Keep a low profile to minimize the chances of someone performing for you simply to gain attention or, worse, of people staging a media event.

Directing the on-the-air telecast   Once you are on the air and the event is unfolding, you cannot stop it because you have missed a major point. Keep on top of the event as well as possible. If you have a good spotter (the contact person and/or the AD), you will be able to anticipate certain happenings and be ready for them with the cameras. Here are some general points to remember:

■ Speak loudly and clearly. Usually, the site is noisy, and the camera operators and floor crew may not hear you very well. Put your headset mic close to your mouth. Yell if you have to, but do not get frantic. Tell the crew members to switch off their headset talkbacks to prevent the outside sound from entering the intercom system.

■ Listen to the floor manager and camera operators. They may help spot event details and report them to you as they occur.

■ Watch the monitors carefully; often the off-air cameras will get especially interesting shots. But do not be tempted by cute yet meaningless or even event-distorting shots. If, for example, the great majority of an audience listens attentively to the speaker, do not single out the one person who is sound asleep, as colorful a shot as this may be. Report the event as truthfully as you possibly can. If the event is dull, show it. If it is exciting, show it. Do not use production tricks to make it fit your expectations.

■ Listen to the audio. A good announcer will give you clues as to the development of the event and sometimes direct your attention to a significant event detail.

▓ If things go wrong, keep calm. For example, if a spectator blocks the camera or if the camera operator swish-pans to another scene because he or she thinks the camera is off the air, cut to another camera instead of screaming at the floor manager or the camera operator for making a mistake.

▓ Exercise propriety and good taste in what you show the audience. Avoid capitalizing on accidents (especially during sporting events) or situations that are potentially embarrassing to the person on-camera, even if such situations might appear hilarious to you and the crew at the moment.

Instant replay   In an *instant replay*, a key play or other important event segment is repeated for the viewer. Instant-replay operations usually use iso cameras and recording devices (VTRs, hard disks, or read/write optical discs) that have unusually fast program search-and-retrieval speeds. Some large sports remotes employ a second, separate switcher that is dedicated exclusively to inserting instant replays. In very big remotes, the instant-replay and special-effects (including C.G.) operations are handled in a separate trailer.

During the replay, DVE (digital video effects) are often used to explain a particular play. The screen may be divided into several "squeezed" boxes or corner wipes, each displaying a different aspect of the play, or may function as an electronic blackboard that writes and does simple line drawings over the freeze-frame of an instant replay, very much like the sketches on a regular blackboard. Game and player statistics are displayed through the C.G. Some of the information is preprogrammed and stored on the computer disk. Up-to-date statistics are continuously entered by a highly skilled C.G. operator. The whole instant-replay and C.G. operation is normally guided by the producer or the AD. The director is generally much too occupied with the regular coverage to worry about the various replays and special effects. Also, the producer, who is free to follow the game, can become adept at spotting key plays and deciding which should be replayed; hence, he or she can pay full attention to the replay procedures.

When watching an instant replay of a key action, you may notice that the replay either duplicates exactly the sequence you have just seen or, more frequently, shows the action from a slightly different perspective. In the first case, the picture sequence of the regular game coverage—that is, the line output—has been recorded and played back; in the second case, the pickup of an iso camera has

been recorded and played back. In sports the principal function of the iso cameras is to follow key plays and other action for instant replay. Iso cameras are also used in a variety of studio and remote productions to shoot visual sequences that can later be used in postproduction editing. For example, when videotaping an orchestra performance with a multicamera setup, you may have an iso camera on the conductor at all times. This way you are covered with a logical cutaway during postproduction. In large productions, two or more iso cameras are used.

When a remote production is not live but done for postproduction, all cameras may be used in iso positions, with each camera's output recorded by a separate VTR or digital recording device. The output of all iso cameras is then used as source material for extensive postproduction editing.

Director's postshow activities   The remote is not finished until all equipment is struck and the site is restored to its original condition. As a director of big remotes, you should pay particular attention to the following postshow procedures.

▓ If something went wrong, do not storm out of the remote truck, accusing everyone, except yourself, of making mistakes. Cool off first.

▓ Thank everyone for his or her efforts. Nobody ever wants a remote to look bad. Thank especially the contact person and others responsible for making the event and the remote telecast possible. Leave as good an impression of you and your team as possible with the persons responsible. Remember that you are representing your company and, in a way, the whole of the "media" when you are on remote location.

▓ Thank the police for their cooperation in reserving parking spaces for the remote vehicles, controlling the spectators, and so forth. Remember that you will need them again for your next remote telecast.

▓ See to it that the floor manager returns all the production equipment to the station.

Production: Floor Manager and Talent Procedures

Floor manager's procedures   As a floor manager (also called stage manager or unit manager on big remotes), you have, next to the director and the TD, the major responsibility for the success of the remote telecast. Because you are close to the scene, you often have a better overview of the event than does the director, who is isolated in the remote truck. The following points will help you make the big-remote production a successful one.

▓ Familiarize yourself with the event ahead of time. Find out where it is taking place, how it will develop, and where the cameras and microphones are positioned relative to the remote truck. Make a sketch of the major event developments and the equipment setup (see section 20.2).

▓ Triple-check all intercom systems. Find out whether you can hear the instructions from the remote truck and if you can be heard there. Check that the intercom is working properly for the other floor personnel. Check all I.F.B. channels, walkie-talkies, and any other field communication devices.

▓ Be aware of the traffic in the production area. Try to keep onlookers away from the equipment and action areas. Be polite but firm. Work around the crews from other stations. Be especially aware of reporters from other media. It would not be the first time that a news photographer snapping pictures just happens to stand right in front of your key camera. Appeal to the photographer's sense of responsibility. Say that you, too, have a job to do in trying to inform the public.

▓ If the telecast is to be videotaped, have the slate ready, unless the C.G. is used for slating.

▓ Check that all cables are properly secured to minimize potential hazards to the people in the production area. If not done by the technical crew, tape the connectors of AC and intercom cables so that they will not pull apart.

▓ Introduce yourself to the police officers assigned to the remote and fill them in on the major event details. The police are generally more cooperative and helpful when they feel that they are part of the remote operation.

▓ Help the camera operators in spotting key event details and in moving their cameras and cables.

▓ Relay all director's cues immediately and precisely. Position yourself so that the talent sees the cues without having to look for you. (Most of the time, announcers are hooked up to the I.F.B. via small earphones, so the director can cue them directly without the floor manager as an intermediary.)

▓ Have several 3 × 5 cards handy so you can write cues and pass them on to the talent, just in case you lose the I.F.B. channel.

▓ When talent is temporarily off the air, keep them informed about what is going on. Help keep their appearance intact for the next on-the-air performance and offer encouragement and positive suggestions.

▓ After the telecast pick up all the production equipment for which you are directly responsible—easels, platforms, sandbags, slates, and headsets. Double-check whether you have forgotten anything before you leave the remote site. Make use of the director's or TD's equipment checklist.

Talent procedures　　The general talent procedures, as discussed in chapter 16, also apply to remote operations, but there are some points that are especially pertinent for you as talent:

▓ Familiarize yourself thoroughly with the event and your specific assignment. Know the process message and do your part to effect it. Review the event with the producer, the director, and the contact person.

▓ Test your microphone and your intercommunication system. If you work with an I.F.B. system, check it out with the director or the TD.

▓ Verify that your monitor is working. Ask the floor manager to have the TD punch up the line-out picture as soon as the cameras are uncapped. Ask for at least color bars to be put on-line.

▓ If you have the help of a contact person or a spotter, discuss again the major aspects of the event and the communication system between the two of you once on the air. For example, how is the spotter going to tell you what is going on while the microphone is hot?

▓ When you're on the air, tell the audience what they cannot see for themselves. Do not report the obvious. For example, if you see the celebrity stepping out of the airplane and shaking hands with the people on the tarmac, do not say, "The celebrity is shaking hands with some people"; tell who is shaking hands with whom. If a football player lies on the field and cannot get up, do not tell the audience that the player apparently got hurt—they can see that for themselves; tell them who the player is and what might have caused what type of injury. Also, follow up this announcement periodically with more-detailed information on the injury and how the player is doing.

▓ Do not get so involved in the event that you lose your objectivity. On the other hand, do not remain so detached that you appear to have no feelings whatsoever.

■   If you make a mistake in identifying someone or something, admit it and correct it as soon as possible.

■   Do not identify event details solely by color, as colors are often distorted on home receivers. For instance, refer to the boxer not only as the one in the red trunks but also as the one on the left side of the screen.

■   As much as possible, let the event itself do the talking. Keep quiet during extremely tense moments. For example, do not talk in the incredibly tense pause between the starter's "Get set" command and the firing of the starting pistol in the 100-meter track finals.[1]

---

1. For a more detailed description of announcing a remote, see Stuart W. Hyde, *Television and Radio Announcing*, 8th ed. (Boston: Houghton Mifflin Co., 1998).

MAIN POINTS

◆   The three types of remotes are ENG (electronic news gathering), EFP (electronic field production), and big remotes.

◆   ENG is the most flexible remote operation. It offers speed in responding to an event, maximum mobility while on location, and flexibility in transmitting the event live or in recording it on portable videotape.

◆   Unlike ENG, which has little or no preparation time for covering a breaking story, EFP must be carefully planned. In this respect it is similar to big remotes. EFP is normally done with an event that can be interrupted and restaged for repeated videotaping. It is usually done with a single camera or iso cameras that shoot an event simultaneously.

◆   A big remote televises live, or records live-on-tape, a large, scheduled event that has not been staged specifically for television, such as a sports match, parade, political gathering, or congressional hearing.

◆   All big remotes use high-quality cameras in key positions and ENG/EFP cameras for more-mobile coverage. Big remotes usually require extensive audio setups.

◆   Big remotes are coordinated from the remote truck, which contains a program control center, an audio control center, a video-recording center, and a technical center that includes transmission equipment.

◆   Big remotes require extensive production and technical surveys as part of the preproduction activities.

◆   In sports remotes, instant replay is one of the more complicated production procedures. It is normally handled by an instant replay producer or an AD.

20.2

Covering Major Events

As you know by now, EFP and especially big remotes require meticulous preproduction work and planning. Such careful preparation is particularly important for onetime happenings, such as sporting events. No two remotes are exactly the same, and there are always special circumstances that require adjustments and compromises. This section includes some typical setups for sports remotes, how to "read" location sketches, and some examples of typical indoor and outdoor remote setups.

▶ **SPORTS REMOTES**
Pickup requirements for baseball, football, soccer, basketball, tennis, boxing or wrestling, and swimming

▶ **LOCATION SKETCH AND REMOTE SETUPS**
Reading location sketches, indoor remotes, and outdoor remotes

▶ **COMMUNICATION SYSTEMS**
ENG, EFP, and big-remote communication systems

▶ **SIGNAL TRANSPORT**
Microwave transmission; communication satellites— frequencies, uplinks, and downlinks; and cable distribution

SPORTS REMOTES

Many big remotes are devoted to the coverage of sporting events. The number of cameras used and their functions depend almost entirely on who is doing the remote. Networks use a great amount of equipment and personnel for the average sports remote. For especially important games, such as the Super Bowl or World Cup soccer, a crew of a hundred or so people set up and operate twenty or more cameras, countless mics, monitors, and intercom and signal-distribution systems. There are several large trailers that house the control room and production equipment. For the coverage of a local high-school game, however, you must get by with far less equipment. Local stations or smaller production companies usually supply only the key production and technical personnel (producer, director, associate director, PA, floor manager, TD, and audio) and hire a remote service that includes a remote truck, all equipment, and extra personnel, if necessary.

The following figures illustrate the minimum video and audio pickup requirements for baseball, football, soccer, basketball, tennis, boxing or wrestling, and swimming. **SEE 20.7–20.13** Sometimes small ENG/EFP cameras are used in place of the larger high-quality

511

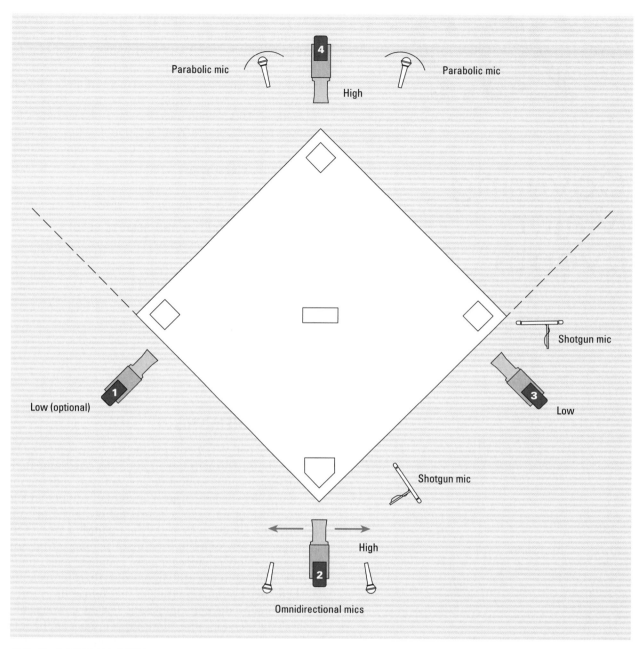

Parabolic mic

High

Parabolic mic

Shotgun mic

Low (optional)

Low

Shotgun mic

High

Omnidirectional mics

20.7 BASEBALL SETUP

Number of cameras: 3 or 4

C1: Near third base; low, optional

C2: Behind home plate; high

C3: Near first base; low; watch for action reversal when intercutting with C1

C4: opposite C2 center field; high; watch for action reversal

Number of mics: 5 or 6

2 omnidirectional mics for audience high in stands

2 shotgun mics behind home plate for game sounds

1 or 2 parabolic mics for field and audience sounds

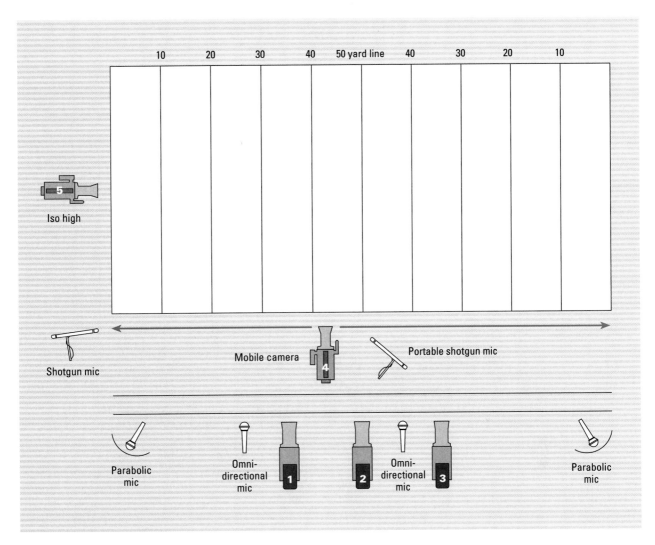

20.8 FOOTBALL SETUP

Number of cameras: 4 or 5

C1, C2, C3: High in the stands, near the 35-50-35 yard lines (press box, shadow side)

C4: Portable or on dolly in field

C5: Optional iso camera behind goal (portable ENG/EFP, or big camera)

Number of mics: 6

2 omnidirectional mics for audience (in stands)

2 shotgun or parabolic (mobile) mics on field

2 parabolic reflector mics in stands

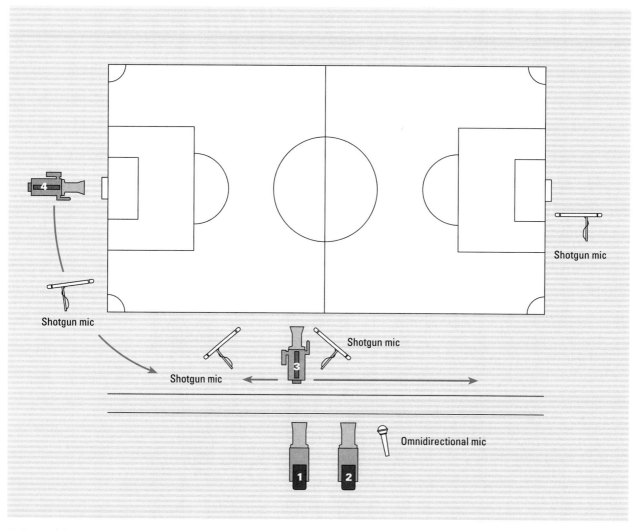

20.9 SOCCER SETUP

Number of cameras: 3 or 4

C1: Left of center line (high)

C2: Right of center line (high)

C3: Mobile on field

C4: Optional, behind goal; may be used as iso camera and mobile camera on field

All three major cameras are on shadow side of field

Number of mics: 5

1 omnidirectional mic in stands for audience

4 shotgun or parabolic mics on field

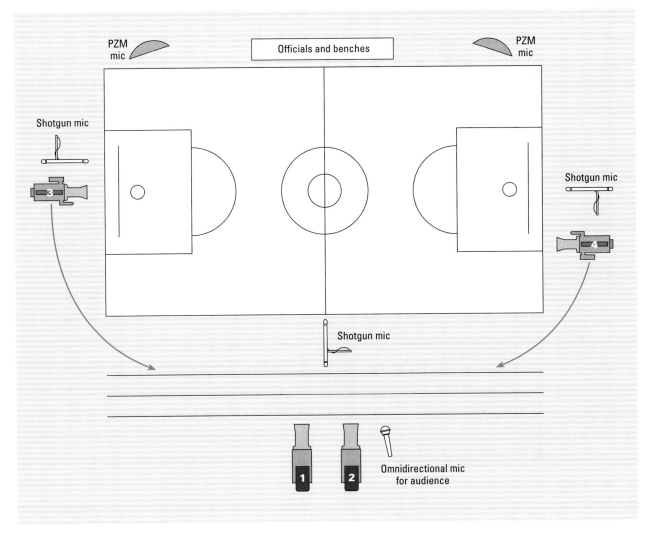

20.10 BASKETBALL SETUP

Number of cameras: 4
C1: High in stands, left of centerline
C2: High in stands, right of centerline (fairly close to C1)
C3, C4: Behind baskets (mobile)

Number of mics: 6
1 omnidirectional mic in stands for audience
2 PZM mics in stands for audience
2 shotgun mics behind each basket for game sounds
1 shotgun mic at center court

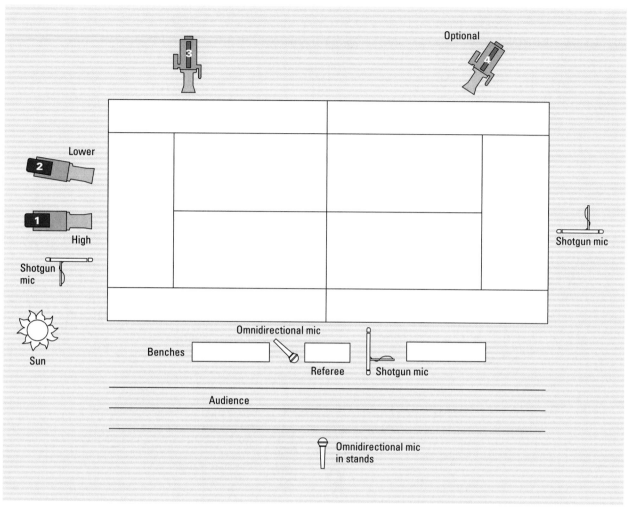

20.11 TENNIS SETUP

Number of cameras: 3 or 4

C1: At end of court, high enough so that it can cover total court, shooting with sun

C2: Next to C1, but lower

C3: At side of court, opposite officials or where players rest between sets (mobile); also shoots CUs of left player

C4: CUs of right player

Number of mics: 5

1 omnidirectional mic in stands for audience

1 omnidirectional mic for referee's calls

3 shotgun mics for pickup of game sounds (center court and on each end of court)

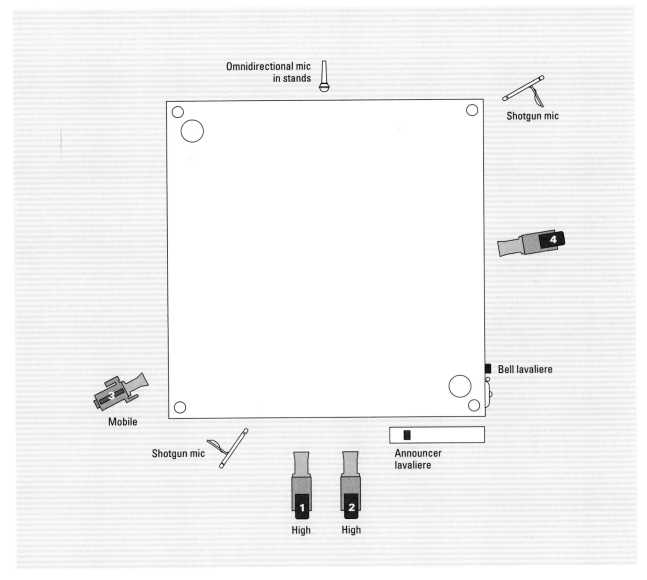

20.12 BOXING OR WRESTLING SETUP

Number of cameras: 3 or 4

C1: High enough to overlook the entire ring
C2: About 10 feet to the side of C1; high, slightly above ropes; used for replays
C3: ENG/EFP mobile camera carried on floor, looking through the ropes
C4: ENG (as above)

Number of mics: 5

1 omnidirectional mic for audience
2 shotgun mics for boxing sounds and referee
1 lavaliere for bell
1 lavaliere for announcer

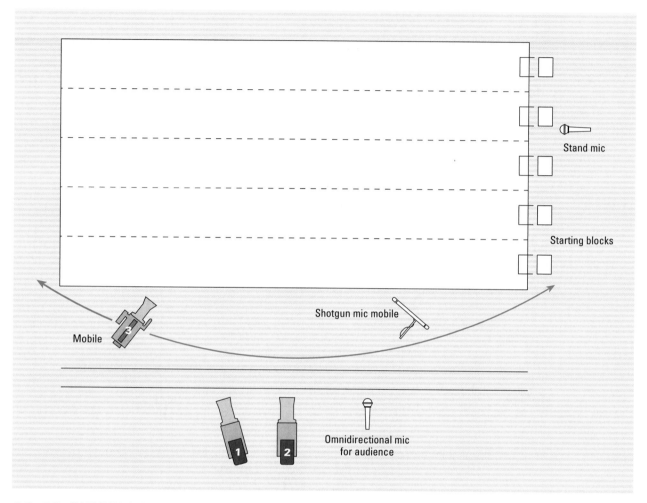

20.13 SWIMMING SETUP

Number of cameras: 2 or 3
C1: High in stands, about at center of pool
C2: Next to C1
C3: Optional ENG/EFP mobile camera on side and ends of pool

Number of mics: 3
1 omnidirectional mic in stands for audience
1 shotgun mic at pool level for swimmers
1 omnidirectional mic on stand

studio/field cameras or are added to the minimal setups described here.

LOCATION SKETCH AND REMOTE SETUPS

To simplify preproduction you as the director, or your AD, should prepare a location sketch. Like the studio floor plan, the *location sketch* shows the principal features of the environment in which the event takes place (stadium and playing field, street and major buildings, hallways, rooms). This location sketch will help you decide on the placement of cameras and microphones, the TD on the location of the remote truck and cable runs, and, if indoors, the LD on the type and placement of lighting instruments.

Reading Location Sketches

As you recall from section 20.1, the location sketch for indoor events should indicate the general dimensions of the room or hallway; the location of windows, doors, and furniture; and the principal action (where people are seated or where they will be walking). It would help if the sketch also contained such details as power outlets; actual

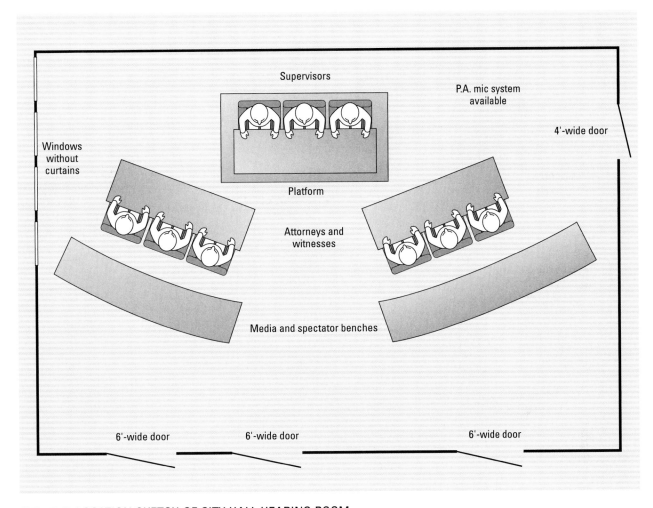

20.14 LOCATION SKETCH OF CITY HALL HEARING ROOM

width of especially narrow hallways, doors, and stairs; direction the doors open; and prominent thresholds, rugs, and other items that may present problems for the movement of cameras mounted on tripod dollies.

The sketch of an outdoor remote should indicate the location of buildings, remote truck, major power source if any, steps, steep inclines, fences, and the sun travel during the time of the remote.

Before continuing, try to "read" the indoor location sketch (see figure 20.14) and the outdoor location sketch (see figure 20.15) and list as many production requirements as you can determine from the sketches. Then pencil in the type and placement of cameras and microphones. Once done, compare your lists and equipment placement with figures 20.16 and 20.17 and the following production requirements sections.

Public hearing The occasion is an important public hearing at city hall. **SEE 20.14** Assuming that you are the director of the remote, what can you tell from this sketch? How much preparation can you do? What key questions does the sketch generate? Limiting the questions to the setup within this hearing room, what are the camera, lighting, audio, and intercom requirements?

Parade The outdoor remote is intended for a Sunday afternoon live multicamera telecast. The estimated time of the telecast is from 3:30 to 5:30 P.M. The location sketch in figure 20.15 shows the action area as well as the major facilities. What important setup and production clues can you devise from this location sketch? **SEE 20.15**

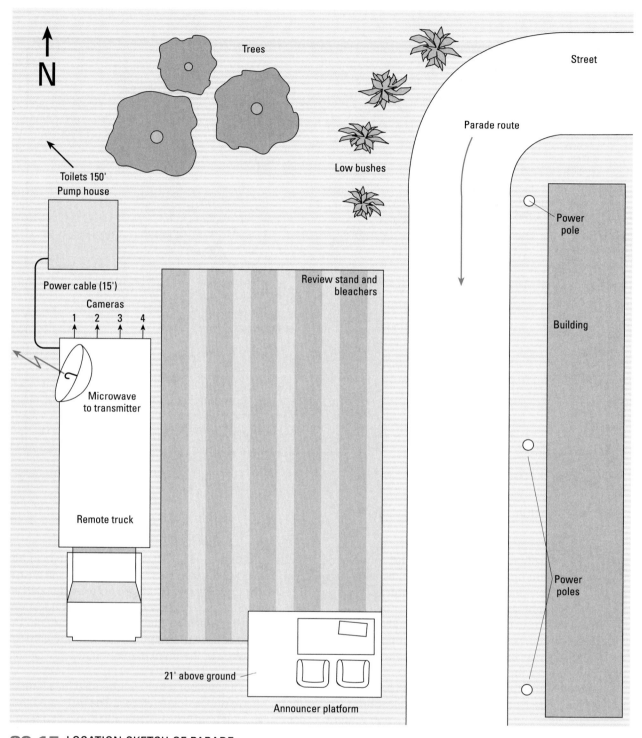

20.15 LOCATION SKETCH OF PARADE

Now compare your list and sketch for the city hall hearing room with the setup shown in figure 20.16.

Production Requirements for Public Hearing (Indoor Remote)

▧ *Cameras* Two ENG/EFP cameras on tripod dollies connected by cable to the remote truck. C1 will cover the supervisors; C2 will cover the attorneys, witnesses, and spectators.

▧ *Lighting* The hearing is scheduled for 10 A.M. The large window presents a definite lighting problem. Cover with drapes. Additional floodlighting is needed to bring up the baselight. If the room is high enough, place some back lights. Are there enough AC outlets for the lights? Are they on different circuits? There may be some access problem, if the mic and lighting cables are strung past the doors.

▧ *Audio* Because the hearing room is already equipped with a P.A. system, tie into the existing mics. If the system is not operational, desk mics are the most logical solution. One additional mic should be placed on each of the three tables (supervisor and two witness tables) just in case the existing audio system stops working.

▧ *Intercommunications* Because there is little or no cuing involved (usually for the start and end of the taping only), the floor manager can plug the headsets into one of the cameras. If ENG/EFP cameras are used, separate intercom cables may have to be strung for the floor manager and each camera operator.

▧ *Other considerations* Camera cables can be routed through the side door. If the room has a hardwood floor, the cameras could dolly into various positions for optimal shots. Because there is much traffic in the room, all cables must be taped to the floor and covered by rubber mats. Camera 1 will be in heavy traffic because of the public access doors. **SEE 20.16**

Now compare your list and sketch for the parade with the setup as shown in the next figure. **SEE 20.17**

Production Requirements for Parade (Outdoor Remote)

▧ *Location of remote truck* Good location. Truck is fairly close to a power source (pump house) and the camera positions, minimizing cable runs.

▧ *Cameras* Minimum of four cameras: C1 and C2 (studio/field cameras) on top of the bleachers; C3 and C4 (ENG/EFP) on the street. C2 can also cover talent.

▧ *Lighting* Because the videotaping is scheduled for 3:30 to 5:30 P.M., there is sufficient light throughout the telecast. The sun is mostly in back of the cameras throughout the telecast.

▧ *Audio* There are three types of audio pickup: (1) the voice pickup of the two announcers, (2) the bands in the parade, and (3) the sounds of the spectators. Lavaliere mics with windscreens for talent. Two shotgun mics (one high in the stands, the other just above ground level) for the bands. One omnidirectional mic near the announcer platform for the crowd noise. All mics need windscreens.

▧ *Intercommunications* The camera operators are connected to the normal P.L. lines of the camera cables. Separate intercom line for the floor manager's headset. I.F.B. for the talent. At least two telephone lines for intercommunication come from the truck: a direct line to station and transmitter and another line for general voice communication.

▧ *Signal transmission* Direct microwave link to the transmission tower (and from there to the station). Audio is sent via telephone lines (independent of microwave). This separation ensures audio continuity even if the microwave link fails.

▧ *Other considerations* Cameras 1 and 2 need a field lens to catch close-ups of the action around the bend (40×). Can camera 2 be pedestaled high enough so that it will not be blocked by people standing up in the bleachers? Large monitor for talent. Second monitor for backup. Shade monitor from sun. Route cables underneath the platform to reduce potential hazard for people.

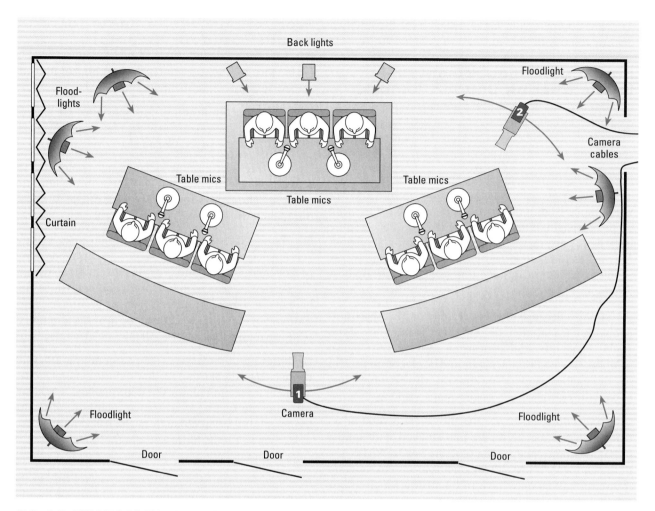

20.16 HEARING ROOM WITH FACILITIES

The ENG/EFP cameras (3 and 4) need cable pullers in addition to the camera operators. Toilet facilities are fairly close to the pump house. Raincoats and umbrellas may be needed for crew, talent, and cameras just in case the weather report predicting a beautiful day is wrong.

COMMUNICATION SYSTEMS

ENG EFP Well-functioning communication systems are especially important for production people in the field, regardless of whether the "field" is the street corner across from the station or one in London. These systems must be highly reliable and must enable the people at home base to talk with the field personnel, and the field personnel to talk with one another. When doing ENG you must be able to receive messages from the news department as well as the police and fire departments. As a producer or director, you need to reach the talent directly with specific information even while the talent is on the air.

We have come to expect the relatively flawless transporting of television pictures and sound, regardless of whether they originate from the mayor's downtown office or the moon. Although communication systems and signal distribution are the province of the technical crew, you should still have some idea about them so that you will know what you can ask for. This section provides a brief overview of ENG, EFP, and big-remote communication systems.

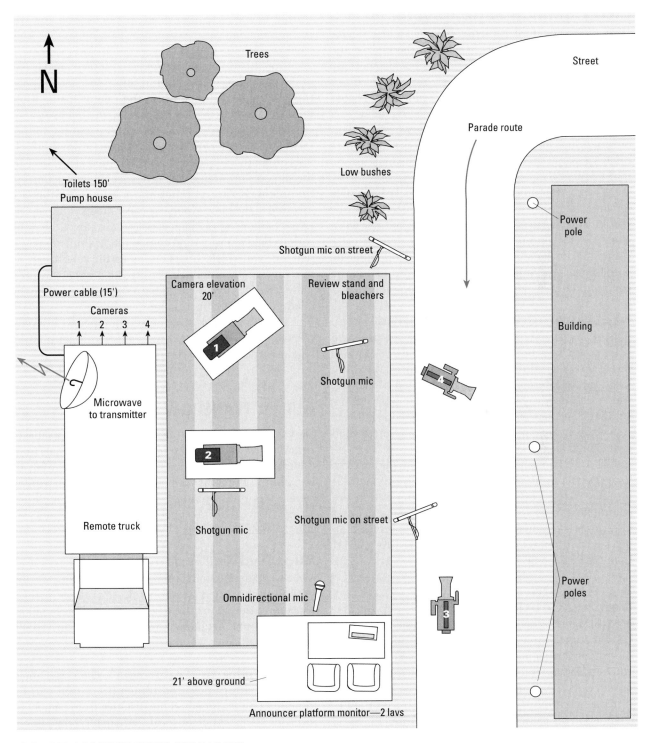

20.17 LOCATION SETUP FOR PARADE

ENG Communication Systems

ENG **EFP** Electronic news gathering has such a high degree of readiness not only because of the mobile and self-contained camera/VTR/audio unit but also because of elaborate communication devices. Most ENG vehicles are equipped with cellular phones, scanners that continuously monitor the frequencies used by police and fire departments, a paging system, and two-way radios. Scanners lock in on a certain frequency as soon as they detect a signal and let you hear the conversation on that frequency.

These communication systems also make it possible for your station's news department to contact you while you are traveling to or from an assignment and give you a chance to respond immediately to police and fire calls. Sometimes news departments use codes to communicate with their "cruising" field reporters to prevent the competition from getting clues to a breaking story.

EFP Communication Systems

ENG **EFP** A single-camera EFP needs the least sophisticated communication system. Because the director is in direct contact with the crew and talent at the shoot location, no intercom systems are needed. Generally, widely dispersed crew members keep in touch with one another by using walkie-talkies. As pointed out earlier, a small power megaphone might save your voice when giving directions to talent and crew.

The EFP van is normally equipped with phone jacks for regular phone connections and several cellular phones. If the EFP uses multiple cameras that are coordinated from a central location, a regular headset intercom system must be set up for the communication between director, TD, and crew. When doing a live telecast from the field, an I.F.B. system is added.

Big-Remote Communication Systems

ENG **EFP** Big remotes need communication systems between the truck (or any other remote control room) and the production people, between the truck and the station, and between the truck and the talent. The truck and the production crew communicate through a regular P.L. (private line or phone line) system, which uses the P.L. channels in the camera cable, separately wired P.L. lines, or wireless P.L.s. During a complicated setup in which the crew is widely scattered (such as a downhill ski race),

walkie-talkies are also used. If necessary, the P.L. communication can be carried by telephone lines from truck to station.

The I.F.B. (interruptible foldback or feedback) is one of the most important communication systems between the producer or director and the talent during a big remote. When using the I.F.B. system, the talent wears a small earphone and hears the total program sound, including his or her own voice, as foldback from the truck. This program foldback can be interrupted at any time by the director or producer to give specific instructions to the talent. If several reporters or commentators are involved in the same event, you can switch among several I.F.B. channels so that, if necessary, you can address the various field reporters and commentators individually. If needed, your I.F.B. instructions to the talent can be transmitted via satellite over great distances. Realize, however, that there is inevitably a slight delay before the talent receives your instructions.

The remote truck is, of course, equipped with several wired telephone lines, two-way radios, cellular phones, paging systems, and walkie-talkies.

SIGNAL TRANSPORT

Signal transport refers to the various systems available to you when transmitting the video and audio signals from their origin (microphone and camera) to the VTRs or transmitter, and from one point (point of origin) to many others (reception points). Signal transport includes (1) microwave transmission, (2) communication satellites, and (3) cable systems.

Microwave Transmission

If you need to maintain optimal camera mobility during a live pickup, such as shooting interviews from a convention floor, you cannot use a camera cable but must microwave the signal back to the production vehicle ("remote van").

From camera to remote van There are small, portable, battery-powered transmitters that can be mounted on the camera. If the distance from camera to receiving station is not too great, you can relay the camera video and audio signals to the remote van without too much difficulty. To minimize interference by other

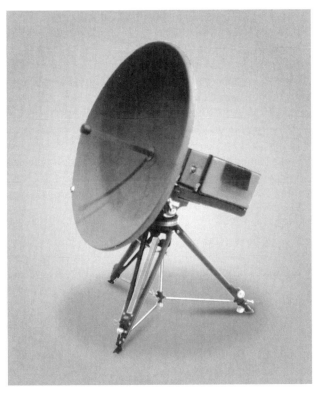

20.18 TRIPOD-MOUNTED
MICROWAVE TRANSMITTER
This small tripod-mounted microwave transmitter can relay
camera signals over a considerable distance.

stations covering the same event, you can transmit on
several frequencies, called *frequency agility.*

If you need a more powerful microwave transmitter, you can mount it on a tripod and place it close
to the camera action radius. Thus you can work a
considerable distance away from the remote van while
using only a relatively short cable run from camera to
microwave transmitter. This type of link is especially
useful if a cable run would create potential hazards, such
as a camera cable strung from a building across high-
tension wires. **SEE 20.18**

The main problem with camera-to-van microwave
links is interference, especially if several television crews
are covering the same event. Even if you use a system
with relatively great frequency agility, your competition may be similarly agile and overpower you with a
stronger signal.

From remote van to station or transmitter
The longer, and usually much more complex, signal link
is from the remote van to the station. (Although sometimes the signal is sent directly to the transmitter, we will
call the end point of this last link before the actual
broadcast the "station.") You can send the signals from
the remote van directly to the station only if you have a
clear, unobstructed line of sight. **SEE 20.19**

Because the microwave signal travels in a straight
line, tall buildings, bridges, or mountains that are in the

20.19 DIRECT
MICROWAVE LINK
You can transmit the signal
via microwave from the
remote van back to the
station only if there is a clear,
unobstructed line of sight.

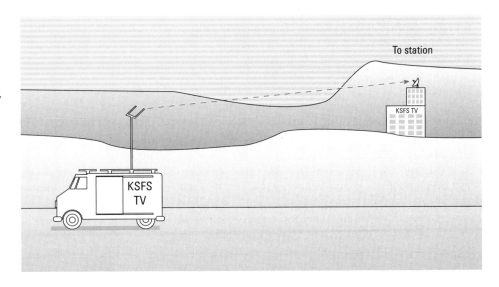

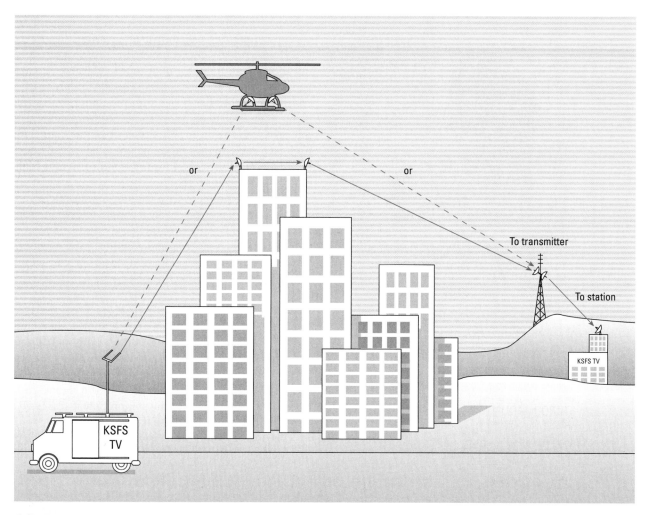

20.20 MINI-LINK FROM REMOTE VAN TO STATION

If there is no clear line of sight between the remote location and the station, the microwave signal must be transported via transmission links.

line of sight between remote van and station may block the signal transmission. In such cases, several microwave links, called *mini-links*, have to be established to carry the signal around these obstacles. **SEE 20.20**

In metropolitan areas the various television stations have permanent *microwave relays* installed in strategic locations so that remote vans can send their signals back from practically any point of their coverage area. If these permanent installations do not suffice, helicopters are used as microwave relay stations. Such microwave relays are also used for transmitting the video of permanently installed cameras that monitor the weather and/or traffic.

Communication Satellites: Frequencies, Uplinks, and Downlinks

The communication satellites used for broadcast are positioned in a geosynchronous orbit 22,300 miles above the earth. In this orbit the satellite moves synchronously with the earth, thereby remaining in the same position relative to it.

Satellite frequencies Communication satellites operate on two frequency bands—the lower-frequency *C-band* and the higher-frequency *Ku-band* ("kay-you-band"). Some satellites have transponders for C-band as well as Ku-band transmission and can convert internally from one to the other. A ***direct broadcast satellite (DBS)*** has a relatively high-powered transponder (transmitter/receiver) that broadcasts from the satellite to small individual downlink dishes you can buy in larger electronic stores and install yourself. DBS operate on the Ku-band.

The C-band is a highly reliable system that is relatively immune to weather interference. Because the C-band works with microwave frequencies, it may interfere with ground-based microwave transmission. To avoid such interference, the C-band operates with relatively low power; because of the low power, the ground stations need large dishes, which range anywhere from 15 to 30 feet. Such large dishes are obviously not suitable for mobile uplink trucks. To use the C-band, the television signals must be transported to and from permanent ground stations.

The C-band requires careful scheduling. It is usually crowded with regular transmissions, such as daily network or cable programming. The other problem is that even if some C-band transponders (in the satellite) are available, the uplinks and downlinks may be busy with signal transmission, so you cannot access the transponders.

The ***Ku-band***, on the other hand, operates with more power and smaller dishes (2 feet or less) that can be mounted and readily operated on mobile trucks or your home. The Ku-band is also less crowded than the C-band and allows immediate, virtually unscheduled access to various uplinks. One of the major problems with the Ku-band is that it is susceptible to weather; rain and snow can seriously interfere with transmission. Another problem is that the Ku-band is about twice as expensive as the C-band.

Uplinks and downlinks   The television signals are sent to the satellite through an ***uplink*** (earth station transmitter), received, amplified by the satellite, and beamed back in a different frequency (actually rebroadcast) by the satellite's own transmitter to one or several receiving earth stations, called ***downlinks***. The receiver-transmitter unit in the satellite is called a *transponder,* a combination of *transmitter* and *responder* (receiver). Many satellites used for international television transmission have built-in translators that convert one electronic signal standard, such as our NTSC system, automatically into another, such as the European PAL system.

Because the satellite transmission covers a large area, simple receiving stations (downlinks) can be set up in many widely dispersed parts of the world. **SEE 20.21** In fact, these strategically placed satellites can spread their *footprint* (coverage area) over the whole earth.

Specialized vans can provide mobile uplinks for the transport of television signals. These ***uplink trucks*** operate on the very same principle as a microwave van, except that they send the television signals to a satellite rather than to a receiving microwave dish. As noted in section 20.1, *SNVs (satellite news vehicles)* usually contain additional equipment, such as several videotape recorders and editing equipment.

Cable Distribution

As you know, television audio and video signals are also distributed via coax (coaxial) or fiber-optic cable. The *coax cable* transports the video and audio information on an electromagnetic carrier wave at a relatively low radio frequency.

A *fiber-optic cable* consists of a great number of fiber-optic strands, each of which is thinner than a human hair and capable of carrying a great amount of information. When using fiber-optic cables for signal transport, the electrical (video and audio) signals are encoded at the point of origin into bursts of light that are decoded again into electrical signals at the destination. When you bundle many of these strands together into a fiber-optic cable of only half the thickness of a normal coax cable, you have a transmission device with an ultimately higher transmission capacity. Besides the obvious advantages of light weight and high information capacity, fiber-optic cables are relatively immune to moisture and electrical interference and can transport the signal over several miles without reamplification.

Both types of cable are used extensively for the transport of television signals to television stations and remotes. They are also used as a nonbroadcast home-delivery system of television signals by cable and telephone companies. The typical signal transport and distribution system by cable companies consists of a *head end* (origination point) that receives the signal from satellites or television transmitters. From there, the signals are amplified and distributed along a *trunk line* to many feeder lines. The *feeder lines* bring the signals to various locations, such as city streets or blocks. Finally, *drop lines* bring the signals to individual homes. **SEE 20.22**

20.21 SATELLITE
UPLINK AND DOWNLINKS
The uplink sends television
signals to the satellite. The
downlinks receive television
signals from the satellite.

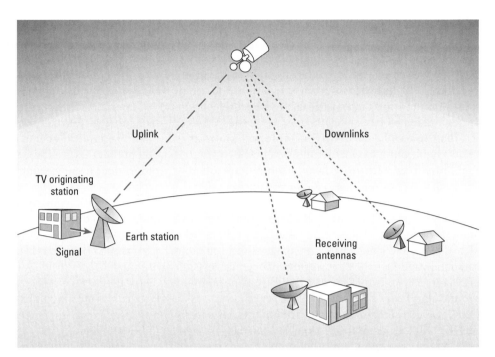

20.22 CABLE TELEVISION SYSTEM

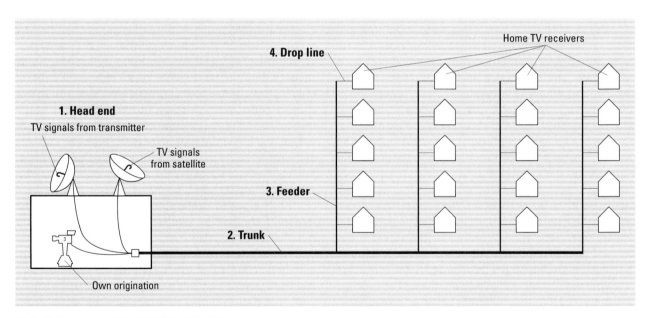

The cable distribution system consists of: (1) the head end, where the signals are collected or originated; (2) the trunk, through which the signals are sent to the feeders; (3) the feeders, which bring the signals to various localities (city streets, blocks); and (4) drop lines, which connect the feeders to individual homes.

MAIN POINTS

◆ Many big remotes are devoted to the coverage of sporting events. Networks typically use a great amount of equipment and personnel for sports remotes, but good coverage is also possible with less equipment.

◆ There are standard setups for most sporting events, which can be augmented with more cameras and audio equipment.

◆ Location sketches are a valuable preproduction aid for big remotes. For an indoor remote, they may show the general dimensions of a room or hallway; the locations of windows, doors, and furniture; and the principal action areas. Outdoor location sketches may show buildings, remote truck location, power source, steep inclines or steps, the path of the sun, and the location and/or direction of the main event.

◆ A good location sketch can aid the director in deciding on major camera locations, focal lengths of zoom lenses, lighting and audio setups, and intercommunication systems.

◆ Remote operations depend heavily on reliable intercommunication systems, including the P.L. system, walkie-talkies, pagers, cellular phones, and multichannel I.F.B. systems. The I.F.B. information can be transmitted via satellite to widely scattered talent in remote locations.

◆ The remote signals are usually transported via microwave, satellite, or cable.

◆ The communication satellites used for broadcast operate in the lower-frequency C-band and the higher-frequency Ku-band.

ZETTL'S VIDEOLAB 2.1

*There are some definite advantages to taking a production out of the studio and into the field: You can place or observe an event in its real setting, or select a specific setting for a fictional event, and you have an infinite variety of settings to choose from. The **process** module of Zettl's VideoLab 2.1 gives you some insight into these and other advantages of field productions.*

RUN ZVL 1 Click on the **process** monitor and run tape 6 **Methods**. Click on the **Location** module. You will hear about some of the advantages of doing field productions.

RUN ZVL 2 Click on the **Single-camera** and **Multicamera** modules. Both describe the relative advantages of each method.

Epilogue

You are now in command of one of the most powerful means of communication and persuasion. Use it wisely and responsibly. Treat your audience with respect and compassion. Whatever role you play in the production process—pulling cables or directing a network show—you influence many people. Because they cannot communicate back to you very readily, they must—and do—trust your professional skills and judgment. Do not betray that trust.

Glossary

480p The lowest-resolution scanning system of DTV (digital television). The *p* stands for *progressive,* which means that each complete television frame consists of 480 lines that are scanned one after the other.

720p A progressive scanning system of DTV (digital television). It is considered an HDTV (high-definition television) system.

1080i An interlaced scanning system of HDTV (high-definition television). The *i* stands for *interlaced,* which means that a complete frame is formed from two interlaced scanning fields. Each field consists of 539.5 lines. As with the traditional NTSC analog television system, the 1080i produces 60 fields or 30 complete frames per second.

above-the-line personnel Same as production (nontechnical) personnel.

above-the-line A budgetary division, including expenses for nontechnical personnel, such as producers, directors, and talent.

AB-roll editing Creating an edit master tape from two source VTRs, one containing the A-roll, and the other the B-roll. The editing is initiated by the edit controller rather than through switching.

AB rolling The simultaneous and synchronized feed from two source VTRs (one supplying the A-roll, the other the B-roll) to the switcher for instantaneous editing as though they were live sources.

AC Stands for *alternating current.* Electric energy as supplied by normal wall outlets.

acetate Cellulose acetate. A transparent plastic sheet used in preparation of graphic material. Usually called *cell.*

actor A person (male or female) who appears on-camera in dramatic roles. The actor always portrays someone else.

AD Stands for *associate* or *assistant director.* Assists the director in all production phases.

additive primary colors Red, green, and blue. Ordinary white light (sunlight) can be separated into the three primary light colors. When these three colored lights are combined in various proportions, all other colors can be reproduced. The process is called *additive color mixing.*

address code An electronic signal that marks each frame with a specific address. See *SMPTE/EBU time code.*

ad-lib Speech or action that has not been scripted or specially rehearsed.

ADR See *automatic dialogue replacement.*

AFTRA Stands for *American Federation of Television and Radio Artists.* A broadcasting talent union.

AGC Stands for *automatic gain control.* Regulates the volume of the audio or video level automatically, without using pots.

aliasing The steplike appearance of a computer-generated diagonal or curved line. Also called *jaggies* or *stairsteps.*

ambience Background sounds.

analog A signal that fluctuates exactly like the original stimulus.

analog recording systems Record the continually fluctuating video and audio signals generated by the video and/or audio source.

aperture Iris opening of a lens, usually measured in *f*-stops.

arc To move the camera in a slightly curved dolly or truck.

architecture Refers to the electronic logic design of a switcher.

aspect ratio The width-to-height proportions of the television screen and therefore of all analog television pictures: four units wide by three units high. For DTV and HDTV, sixteen by nine.

assemble editing Adding shots on videotape in a consecutive order without first recording a control track on the edit master tape.

ATR See *audiotape recorder.*

ATV Stands for *advanced television.* See *DTV.*

audio The sound portion of television and its production. Technically, the electronic reproduction of audible sound.

audio control booth Houses the audio, or mixing, console; digital cart, cassette, CD, DVD, and DAT machines; a reel-to-reel audiotape recorder and a turntable; a patchbay; computer(s); speakers; intercom systems; a clock; and a line monitor.

audio dub control Operational control on a VTR for recording sound information without erasing the pictures already recorded on the video track.

audio-follow-video A switcher that automatically changes the accompanying audio along with the video source.

audio monitor See *program speaker.*

audio production room For postproduction activities such as sweetening, composing music tracks, adding sound effects or laugh tracks, and assembling music bridges and announcements.

audio synchronizer Digital device that uses the SMPTE time code in dividing the audiotape into imaginary frames, corresponding with those of the videotape, to synchronize audio and video in videotape postproduction.

audiotape recorder (ATR) A reel-to-reel audiotape recorder.

audio track The area of the videotape used for recording the sound information.

auto cue See *teleprompter.*

auto-focus Automated feature wherein the camera focuses on what it senses to be your target object.

auto-iris Automatic control of the lens diaphragm.

automatic dialog replacement (ADR) The synchronization of speech with the lip movements of the speaker in postproduction. Not always automatic.

auto transition An electronic device that functions like the fader bar.

background light Illumination of the set, set pieces, and backdrops. Also called *set light.*

back light Illumination from behind the subject and opposite the camera.

back-timing The process of figuring additional clock times by subtracting running times from the schedule time at which the program ends.

balance (1) Audio: a proper mixing of various sounds. (2) Video: relative structural stability of picture elements (objects or events). *Balance* refers to the interrelationship between stability and tension in a picture and can therefore be stable (little pictorial tension), neutral (some tension), or unstable (high pictorial tension).

balanced mic or line Professional microphones that have as output three wires: two that carry substantially the same audio signal out of phase and one that is a ground shield. Relatively immune to hum and other electronic interference.

barn doors Metal flaps in front of a lighting instrument that control the spread of the light beam.

barrel distortion Optical effect, caused by wide-angle lens, that makes all vertical lines appear to be somewhat curved.

base See *baselight.*

baselight Even, nondirectional (diffused) light necessary for the camera to operate optimally. Normal baselight levels are 2,000 lux at $f/5.6$ (150 to 200 foot-candles). Also called *base.*

batten A horizontal metal pipe that supports lighting instruments in a studio.

baud Transmission speed of digital data. The higher the baud rate, the faster the transmission.

beam splitter Compact internal optical system of prisms and filters within a color camera that separates white light into the three primary colors: red, green, and blue (RGB). Also called *prism block.*

beeper A series of audio beeps (normally eight), exactly one second apart, at the beginning of each take for videotape cuing.

below-the-line A budgetary division, referring to equipment and technical services of a particular show and the cost of the below-the-line technical and production personnel.

below-the-line personnel Same as technical production personnel.

big boom See *perambulator boom.*

big remote A production outside the studio to televise live and/or record live-on-tape a large scheduled event that has not been staged specifically for television. Examples include sporting events, parades, political gatherings, and special hearings.

binary A number system with the base of 2.

binary digit (bit) The smallest amount of information a computer can hold and process. A charge is either present, represented by a *1,* or absent, represented by a *0.* One bit can describe two levels, such as on/off or black/white. Two bits can describe four levels (2^2 bits); three bits, eight levels (2^3 bits); four bits, sixteen (2^4 bits), and so on. A group of eight bits (2^8) is called a *byte.*

bit See *binary digit.*

bit pad See *digitizing tablet.*

black Darkest part of the grayscale, with a reflectance of approximately 3 percent; called TV black. "To black" means to fade the television picture to black.

bleeding When the edges of a key are not sharp and the background shows through.

blocking Carefully worked-out movement and actions by the talent and for all mobile television equipment.

blocking rehearsal See *dry run.*

BNC Standard coaxial cable connector for professional video equipment.

book Two flats hinged together. Also called a *twofold.*

boom (1) Audio: microphone support. (2) Video: part of a camera crane. (3) To move the camera via the boom of the camera crane.

border Electronically generated edge that separates letters or picture areas from the background.

boundary microphone See *pressure zone microphone (PZM).*

brightness The color attribute that determines how dark or light a color appears on the monochrome television screen or how much light the color reflects. Also called *lightness.*

broad A floodlight with a broadside, panlike reflector.

bump-down Dubbing (copying) picture and sound information from a higher-quality VTR format to a lower-quality one. Also called *dub-down.*

bump-up Dubbing (copying) picture and sound information from a lower-quality videotape format to a higher-quality one. Also called *dub-up.*

bus (1) A row of buttons on the switcher. A pair of buses is called a *bank.* (2) A common central circuit that receives from several sources and that feeds to a common or several separate destinations.

bust shot Framing of a person from the upper torso to the top of the head.

busy picture A picture, as it appears on the television screen, that is too cluttered.

byte Eight bits. Can define 256 discrete levels (2^8 bits), such as shades of gray between black and white. See also *binary digit (bit).*

cable television (1) Distribution device for broadcast signals via coaxial or fiber-optic cable. (2) Production facility for programs distributed via cable.

calibrate (1) Audio: to make all VU meters (usually of the audio console and the record VTR) respond in the same way to a specific audio signal. (2) Video: to preset a zoom lens to remain in focus throughout the zoom.

camcorder A portable camera with the VTR attached or built into it to form a single unit.

CamCutter A portable camera docked with a hard drive that serves as a recording and editing device.

cameo lighting Foreground figures are lighted with highly directional light, with the background remaining dark.

camera The general name for the *camera head,* which consists of the lens (or lenses), the main camera with the imaging device and the internal optical system, electronic accessories, and the viewfinder.

camera chain The television camera (head) and associated electronic equipment, including the camera control unit, sync generator, and power supply.

camera control unit (CCU) Equipment, separate from the camera head, that contains various video controls, including registration, color balance, contrast, and brightness, that enable the video operator to adjust the camera picture during a show.

camera graphics Graphics specifically designed for the television camera.

camera head The actual television camera, which is at the head of a chain of essential electronic accessories. It is composed of the imaging device, lens, and viewfinder. In ENG/EFP cameras, the camera head contains all the elements of the camera chain.

camera-left and camera-right Directions given from the camera's point of view; opposite of "stage-left" and "stage-right," which are directions given from the actor's point of view (facing the audience or camera).

camera light Small spotlight mounted on the front of the camera, used as an additional fill light. (Frequently confused with tally light.) Also called *eye light* or *inky-dinky.*

camera pickup device See *chip.*

camera rehearsal Full rehearsal with cameras and other pieces of production equipment. Often identical to the dress rehearsal.

cam head A camera mounting head for heavy cameras that permits extremely smooth tilts and pans.

cant Tilting the shoulder-mounted or handheld camera sideways.

canting effect Visual effect in which the scene is put on a slight tilt, causing a slanted horizon line.

cap (1) Lens cap: a rubber or metal cap placed in front of the lens to protect it from light, dust, or physical damage. (2) Electronic device that eliminates the picture from the camera pickup device.

capacitor microphone See *condenser microphone.*

cardioid Heart-shaped pickup pattern of a unidirectional microphone.

cart See *cartridge.*

cartridge Refers to the digital cartridge machine that uses digital disks for storage of short audio material. Can also refer to an audiotape recording or playback device that uses tape cartridges. Also called *cart* for short.

cassette A video- or audiotape recording or playback device that uses tape cassettes. A cassette is a plastic case containing two reels—a supply reel and a takeup reel.

C-band A frequency band for certain satellites. It is relatively immune to weather interference. See *Ku-band*.

CCD Stands for *charge-coupled device*. See *chip*.

C-clamp A metal clamp with which lighting instruments are attached to the lighting battens.

CCU See *camera control unit*.

CD See *compact disc*.

cell See *acetate*.

character generator (C.G.) A dedicated computer that electronically produces a series of letters, numbers, and simple graphic images for video display.

charge-coupled device (CCD) The imaging device in a television camera. Usually called the *chip*.

cheat To angle the performer or object toward a particular camera; not directly noticeable to the audience.

chip A common name for the camera imaging device. Technically, it is known as the charge-coupled device (CCD). The chip consists of a great number of imaging sensing elements, called *pixels*, that translate the optical (light) image into an electronic video signal. Also called the *camera pickup device*.

chroma-key drop A well-saturated, blue canvas drop that can be pulled down from the lighting grid to the studio floor as a background for chroma keying.

chroma keying Special key effect that uses color (usually blue) for the background, which is replaced by the background image during the key.

chrominance channel The color (chroma) channels within the color camera. A separate chrominance channel is responsible for each of the three basic color signals: red, green, and blue.

clip (1) To compress the white and/or black picture information or prevent the video signal from interfering with the sync signals. (2) A short videotape insert.

clip control See *key level control*.

clip light Small internal reflector bulb that is clipped to pieces of scenery or furniture with a gator clip.

clipper See *key level control*.

clock time The time the clock shows. Specifically, the time at which a program starts and ends. Also called *schedule time*.

close-up (CU) Object or any part of it seen at close range and framed tightly. The close-up can be extreme (extreme or big close-up—*ECU*) or rather loose (medium close-up).

closure Short for *psychological closure*. Mentally filling in spaces of an incomplete picture.

coding To change the quantized values into a binary code, represented by 0's and 1's. Also called *encoding*.

color bars A color standard used by the television industry for the alignment of cameras and videotape recordings. Color bars can be generated by most professional portable cameras.

color compatibility Color signals that can be perceived as black-and-white pictures on monochrome television sets. Generally used to mean that the color scheme has enough brightness contrast for monochrome reproduction with a good grayscale contrast.

colorizing The creation of color patterns or color areas through a computer.

color media See *gel*.

color temperature Relative reddishness or bluishness of light, as measured in Kelvin degrees (K). The norm for indoor TV lighting is 3,200°K, for outdoors, 5,600°K.

comet-tailing Occurs when the camera pickup device is unable to process extremely bright highlights that are reflected off polished surfaces or bright lights in a very dark scene. The effect looks like red or blue flames tailing the bright object when the object or the camera moves.

compact disc (CD) A small, shiny disc that contains information (usually sound signals) in digital form. A CD player reads the encoded digital information using a laser beam.

complexity editing The juxtaposition of shots that primarily, though not exclusively, helps intensify the screen event. Editing conventions as advocated in continuity editing are often purposely violated.

component system A process in which the luminance (Y) signals and color (C) signals, or all three color signals (RGB), are kept separate throughout the recording and storage process. Comprises the Y/C component, Y/color difference component, and RGB component systems.

composite system A process in which the luminance (Y, or black-and-white) signal and chrominance (C, or red, green, and blue) signal as well as sync information are encoded into a single video signal and transported on a single wire. Also called *NTSC signal*.

compression (1) Electronics: reducing the amount of data to be stored or transmitted by using coding schemes that pack all original data into less space or by throwing away some of the least important data. Can be *lossy* or *lossless*. (2) Video: the crowding effect achieved by a narrow-angle (telephoto) lens wherein object proportions and relative distances seem shallower.

computer-generated DVE Digital video effects created entirely by computer hardware and software.

computer-manipulated DVE Digital video effects created by the computer using an existing image (camera-generated video sequence, video frame, photo, or painting) and enhancing or changing it in some way.

condenser microphone A microphone whose diaphragm consists of a condenser plate that vibrates with the sound pressure against another fixed condenser plate, called the backplate. Also called *electret* or *capacitor microphone*.

contact A person, usually a public relations officer, who knows about an event and can assist the production team during a remote telecast.

continuity editing The preserving of visual continuity from shot to shot.

continuous action lighting Overlapping triangle lighting for all major performance areas. Also called *zone lighting*.

contrast ratio The difference between the brightest and the darkest spots in the picture (often measured by reflected light in foot-candles). The optimal contrast ratio for analog cameras is normally 40:1 or slightly higher, which means that the brightest spot in the picture should not be more than forty times brighter than the darkest spot. For DTV it can exceed this ratio, depending on the quality of the camera.

control room A room adjacent to the studio in which the director, the technical director, the audio engineer, and sometimes the lighting director perform their various production functions.

control room directing See *multicamera directing*.

control track The area of the videotape used for recording the synchronization information (sync pulse). Provides reference for the running speed of the VTR, for the placing and reading of the video tracks, and for counting the number of frames.

control track (pulse-count) system Counting system used to identify exact locations on the videotape. It counts the control track pulses and translates this count into elapsed time and frame numbers. It is not frame-accurate.

convertible camera An ENG/EFP camera adapted for studio use. Equipped with a large viewfinder and controlled by the CCU.

cookie See *cucalorus*.

counterweight battens Steel pipes that support lighting instruments and corresponding power outlets that can be raised and lowered to a specific height by a counterweight or motorized system.

CPU Stands for *central processing unit*. Processes information in a computer according to the instructions it receives from the software.

crab Sideways motion of the camera crane dolly base.

crane (1) Camera dolly that resembles an actual crane in both appearance and operation. The crane can lift the camera from close to the studio floor to more than 10 feet above it. (2) To move the boom of the camera crane up or down. Also called *boom*.

crawl (1) The horizontal movement of electronically generated copy (the vertical movement is called a *roll*). (2) Mechanical drum that rolls copy up or down the screen.

cross-fade (1) Audio: transition method whereby the preceding sound is faded out and the following sound faded in simultaneously; the sounds overlap temporarily. (2) Video: transition method whereby the preceding picture is faded to black and the following picture is faded in from black.

cross-keying The crossing of key lights for two people facing each other.

cross-shot (X/S) Similar to the over-the-shoulder shot, except that the camera-near person is completely out of the shot.

CU See *close-up*.

cucalorus Any pattern cut out of thin metal that, when placed in front of an ellipsoidal spotlight (pattern projector), produces a shadow pattern. Also called *cookie*.

cue (1) Signal for various production activities. (2) To select a certain spot in the videotape or film.

cue card A large, hand-lettered card that contains copy, usually held next to the camera lens by floor personnel.

cue-send See *foldback*.

cue track The area of the videotape used for such information as in-house identification or SMPTE address code. Can also be used for an additional audio track.

cursor A symbol, such as a line or rectangle, that can be moved to, and which indicates, specific positions on the computer screen.

cut (1) The instantaneous change from one shot (image) to another. (2) Director's signal to interrupt action.

cutaway A shot of an object or event that is peripherally connected with the overall event and that is often neutral as to its screen direction (such as straight-on shots). Used to intercut between shots to facilitate continuity.

cuts-only editing system See *single-source editing system*.

cyc See *cyclorama*.

cyc light See *strip light*.

cyclorama A U-shaped continuous piece of canvas for backing of scenery and action. Also called *cyc*.

DAT Stands for *digital audiotape*. The sound signals are encoded on audiotape in digital form. Includes digital recorders as well as digital recording processes.

DBS Stands for *direct broadcast satellite*. A satellite with a relatively high-powered transponder that broadcasts its signals directly to small receiver dishes (downlinks) in individual homes and offices.

DC Direct current.

DCT Stands for *discrete cosine transform.* A complex method of dividing a digital image into 8 × 8–pixel blocks and translating the pixel positions into frequencies. The redundant frequencies will be eliminated. Most compression techniques are based on DCT.

defocus Simple yet highly effective optical effect wherein the camera operator zooms in, racks out of focus, and, on cue, back into focus again. Used as a transitional device or to indicate strong psychological disturbances or physiological imbalance.

delegation controls Controls on a switcher that assign specific functions to a bus.

demographics Audience research factors concerned with such items as age, sex, marital status, and income.

depth of field The area in which all objects, located at different distances from the camera, appear in focus. Depth of field depends upon focal length of the lens, its *f*-stop, and the distance between the object and the camera.

depth staging Arrangement of objects on the television screen so that foreground, middleground, and background are each clearly defined.

diaphragm (1) Audio: the vibrating element inside a microphone that moves with the air pressure from the sound. (2) Video: see *iris.*

dichroic filter A mirrorlike color filter that singles out from the white light, the red light (red dichroic filter), and the blue light (blue dichroic filter), with the green light left over. Also called *dichroic mirror.*

dichroic mirror See *dichroic filter.*

diffused light Light that illuminates a relatively large area with an indistinct light beam. Diffused light, created by floodlights, produces soft shadows.

diffusion filter Filter that attaches to the front of the lens; gives a scene a soft, slightly out-of-focus look.

digital Usually to mean the binary system—the representation of data in the form of digits (on/off pulses).

digital cart system A digital audio system that uses built-in hard drives, removable high-capacity disks (such as the Iomega zip format), or read/write optical discs to store and access almost instantaneously a great amount of audio information. It is normally used for the playback of brief announcements and music bridges.

digital lens A lens that can be programmed through a small built-in computer to repeat zoom positions and their corresponding focus.

digital recording systems Sample the analog signals and convert them into discrete on/off pulses (bits).

digital still store system See *electronic still store (ESS) system.*

digital versatile disc See *DVD.*

digital video effects (DVE) Visual effects generated by a computer or digital effects equipment in the switcher. DVE can use an analog signal as original stimulus for the effects. *DVE* also stands for the equipment that produces the effects.

digital videotape recorder (DVTR) Videotape recorder that receives digital, rather than analog, information. The signals can be more easily manipulated for video enhancement and special effects. Can be composite or component.

digital zoom Simulated zoom by enlarging the image pixels.

digital zoom lens A lens that can be programmed through a small built-in computer to repeat zoom positions and their corresponding focus settings.

digitize To convert analog signals into digital (binary) form or to transfer information in a digital code.

digitizing tablet A tabletlike board that translates the movement of an electronic pen (stylus) into specific cursor positions on-screen. Used for drawing images into the computer memory. Also called *bit pad* or *drawing tablet.*

dimmer A device that controls the intensity of light by throttling the electric current flowing to the lamp.

direct broadcast satellite (DBS) Satellite with a relatively high-powered transponder (transmitter/receiver) that broadcasts from the satellite to small, individual downlink dishes; operates on the Ku-band.

direct bus See *program bus.*

direct insertion Recording technique wherein sound signals of electric instruments are fed directly to the mixing console without the use of speaker and microphone. Also called *direct input.*

directional light Light that illuminates a relatively small area with a distinct light beam. Directional light, produced by spotlights, creates harsh, clearly defined shadows.

disc An optical computer storage device that uses a laser beam for the read/write function.

disk A computer storage device that can store data on concentric tracks. There are removable, relatively low-capacity floppy disks, and large-capacity hard disks normally built into the hard drive.

disk-based video recorder All digital video recorders that record or store information on a hard disk or read/write optical disc. All disk-based systems are nonlinear.

disk drive The actual mechanism that turns the computer disk to read and write digital information on it.

dissolve A gradual transition from shot to shot, in which the two images temporarily overlap. Also called *lap dissolve.*

distortion Unnatural alteration or deterioration of sound.

diversity reception Setup for a single wireless microphone wherein more than one receiving station is established, so one can take over when the signal from the other gets weak.

dolly (1) Camera support that enables the camera to move in all directions. (2) To move the camera toward (dolly in) or away from (dolly out or back) the object.

double headset A telephone headset (earphones) that carries program sound in one earphone and the P.L. information in the other. Also called *split intercom.*

downlink The antenna (dish) and equipment that receive the signals coming from a satellite.

downstream keyer (DSK) A control that allows a title to be keyed (cut-in) over the picture (line-out signal) as it leaves the switcher.

DP Stands for *director of photography.* In major motion picture production, the DP is responsible for the lighting (similar to the LD in television). In smaller motion picture productions and in EFP, the DP will also operate the camera.

drag Degree of friction needed in the camera mounting head to allow smooth panning and tilting.

drawing tablet See *digitizing tablet.*

dress (1) What people wear on-camera. (2) Same as *camera rehearsal.* Final rehearsal with all facilities operating. The dress rehearsal is often videotaped. (3) Decorating a set with set properties.

drop Large, painted piece of canvas used for scenery backing.

drop lines Section of cable television distribution system that connects individual homes.

dropout Loss of part of the video signal, which shows up on-screen as white or colored glitches. Caused by uneven videotape iron-oxide coating (bad tape quality or overuse) or dirt.

dry run Rehearsal without equipment, during which the basic actions of the talent are worked out. Also called *blocking rehearsal.*

DSK See *downstream keyer.*

DTV Stands for *digital television.* High-resolution digital television systems. Also called *ATV (advanced television).*

dual-redundancy The use of two identical microphones for the pickup of a sound source, whereby only one of them is turned on at any given time. A safety device that permits switching over to the second microphone in case the active one becomes defective.

dub The duplication of an electronic recording. Dubs can be made from tape to tape, or from record or disc to tape and vice versa. The dub is always one generation away from the recording used for dubbing. In analog systems each dub shows increased deterioration. Digital dubbing produces copies almost identical in quality to that of the original.

dub-down Dubbing (copying) picture and sound information from a higher-quality VTR format to a lower-quality one. Also called *bump-down.*

dub-up Dubbing (copying) picture and sound information from a lower-quality videotape format to a higher-quality one. Also called *bump-up.*

DVD Stands for *digital videodisc.* The standard DVD can store 4.7 gigabytes of information. Also called *digital versatile disc* to accommodate audio use.

DVE See *digital video effects.*

DVTR See *digital videotape recorder.*

dynamic microphone A microphone whose sound pickup device consists of a diaphragm that is attached to a movable coil. As the diaphragm vibrates with the air pressure from the sound, the coil moves within a magnetic field, generating an electric current. Also called *moving-coil microphone.*

echo A sound that is reflected from a single surface and perceived as consecutive, rapidly fading, and repetitious. See also *reverberation.*

echo effect Visual effect wherein the same video image is repeated as though it were placed between two opposite mirrors.

ECU See *extreme close-up.*

edit controller Machine that assists in various editing functions, such as marking edit-in and edit-out points, rolling source and record VTRs, and integrating effects. Often a desktop computer with a specific software program. Also called *editing control unit.*

edit decision list (EDL) Consists of edit-in and edit-out points, expressed in time code numbers, and the nature of transitions between shots.

editing The selection and assembly of shots in a logical sequence.

editing control unit See *edit controller.*

edit master tape The videotape on which the selected portions of the source tapes are edited. Used for the record VTR.

edit VTR See *record VTR.*

EDL See *edit decision list.*

effects bus Rows of buttons that can generate a number of electronic effects, such as keys, wipes, and mattes.

effect-to-cause model Moving from idea to desired effect on the viewer, and then backing up to the specific medium requirements to produce such an effect.

EFP Stands for *electronic field production.* Television production outside the studio that is usually shot for postproduction (not live). Usually called *field production.*

electret microphone See *condenser microphone*.

electron gun Produces the electron (scanning) beam in a television receiver.

electronic still store (ESS) system An electronic device that can grab a single frame from any video source and store it in digital form on a disk. It can retrieve the frame randomly in a fraction of a second.

ellipsoidal spotlight Spotlight producing a very defined beam, which can be shaped further by metal shutters.

ELS See *extreme long shot*.

ENG Stands for *electronic news gathering*. The use of portable camcorders or cameras with separate portable VTRs, lights, and sound equipment for the production of daily news stories. ENG is usually not planned and is usually transmitted live or after immediate postproduction.

ENG/EFP cameras and camcorders High-quality portable field production cameras. When the camera is docked with a VTR, or has a VTR built into it, it is called a *camcorder*.

environment General ambience of a setting.

equalization Controlling the audio signal by emphasizing certain frequencies and eliminating others.

essential area The section of the television picture, centered within the scanning area, that is seen by the home viewer, regardless of masking or slight misalignment of the receiver. Also called *safe title area* or *safe area*.

ESS system See *electronic still store (ESS) system*.

establishing shot See *extreme long shot (ELS)* and *long shot (LS)*.

expanded system A television system that includes equipment and procedures that allow for selection, control, recording, playback, and transmission of television pictures and sound.

extender See *range extender*.

external key The cutout portion of the base picture is filled by the signal from an external source, such as a second camera.

extreme close-up (ECU) Shows the object with very tight framing.

extreme long shot (ELS) Shows the object from a great distance. Also called *establishing shot*.

eye light See *camera light*.

facilities request A list that contains all technical facilities needed for a specific production.

fact sheet Lists the items to be shown on-camera and their main features. May contain suggestions of what to say about the product. Also called *rundown sheet*.

fade The gradual appearance of a picture from black (*fade-in*) or its disappearance to black (*fade-out*).

fader A sound-volume control that works by means of a button sliding horizontally along a specific scale. Identical in function to a pot. Also called *slide fader*.

fader bar A lever on the switcher that activates preset transitions, such as dissolves, fades, and wipes of different speeds. It is also used to create superimpositions.

falloff The speed (degree) with which a light picture portion turns into shadow area. Fast falloff means that the light areas turn abruptly into shadow areas and there is a great brightness difference between light and shadow areas. Slow falloff indicates a very gradual change from light to dark and a minimal brightness difference between light and shadow areas.

fast lens A lens that permits a relatively great amount of light to pass through (lower minimum *f*-stop number). Can be used in low-light conditions.

fc See *foot-candle*.

feed Signal transmission from one program source to another, such as a network feed or a remote feed.

feedback (1) Audio: piercing squeal from the loudspeaker, caused by the accidental reentry of the loudspeaker sound into the microphone and subsequent overamplification of sound. (2) Communications: reaction of the receiver of a communication back to the communication source. (3) Video: wild streaks and flashes on the monitor screen caused by reentry of a video signal into the switcher and subsequent overamplification.

feeder lines Section of cable television distribution system that brings the signal to various parts of a city.

fiber-optic cable Thin, transparent fibers of glass or plastic used to transfer light from one point to another. When used in broadcast signal transmission, the electrical video and audio signals use optical frequencies (light) as the carrier wave to be modulated.

field (1) A location away from the studio. (2) One-half of a complete scanning cycle, with two fields necessary for one television picture frame. There are 60 fields, or 30 frames, per second.

field log A record of each take during the videotaping. See also *VTR log*.

field of view The portion of a scene visible through a particular lens; its vista. Expressed in symbols, such as *CU* for close-up.

field production All productions that happen outside the studio; generally refers to electronic field production (EFP).

figure-ground (1) Audio: Emphasizing the most important sound source over the general background sounds. (2) Video: objects seen in front of a background; the ground is perceived to be more stable than the figure.

fill light Additional light on the opposite side of the camera from the key light to illuminate shadow areas and thereby reduce falloff. Usually done with floodlights.

film-style shooting Directing method for single-camera production wherein you move from an establishing long shot to medium shots, and then to close-ups of the same action.

fishpole A suspension device for a microphone; the mic is attached to a pole and held over the scene for brief periods.

fixed-focal-length lens A lens whose focal length cannot be changed (contrary to a zoom lens that has a variable focal length). Also called *prime lens.*

flag A thin, rectangular sheet of metal, plastic, or cloth used to block light from falling on specific areas.

flare See *halo.*

flat (1) Lighting: even illumination with minimal shadows (slow falloff). (2) Scenery: a piece of standing scenery used as background or to simulate the walls of a room.

flat response Measure of a microphone's ability to hear equally well over the entire frequency range.

flicker A periodic change in brightness; when pixels of one frame begin to fade, they are activated again by the next frame scan.

floodlight Lighting instrument that produces diffused light with a relatively undefined beam edge.

floor plan A plan of the studio floor, showing the walls, the main doors, and the location of the control room, with the lighting grid or batten pattern superimposed over it. More common, a diagram of scenery and properties drawn onto a grid pattern.

floor stand Heavy stand mounted on a three-caster dolly, designed specifically to support a variety of lighting instruments. An extension pipe lets you adjust the vertical position of the lighting instrument to a certain degree.

floppy disk See *disk.*

flow chart A block diagram representing the major steps of an event. It is used by computer programmers to translate events into computer logic.

fluid head Most popular mounting head for lightweight ENG/EFP cameras. Balance is provided by springs. Because its moving parts operate in a heavy fluid, it allows very smooth pans and tilts.

fluorescent Lamps that generate light by activating a gas-filled tube to give off ultraviolet radiation, which lights up the phosphorous coating inside the tubes.

focal length The distance from the optical center of the lens to the front surface of the camera imaging device at which the image appears in focus with the lens set at infinity. Focal lengths are measured in millimeters or inches. Short-focal-length lenses have a wide angle of view (wide vista); long-focal-length (telephoto) lenses have a narrow angle of view (close-up). In a variable-focal-length (zoom) lens, the focal length can be changed continuously from wide-angle (zoomed out) to narrow-angle (zoomed in) and vice versa. A fixed-focal-length lens has a single designated focal length.

focus A picture is in focus when it appears sharp and clear on-screen (technically, the point where the light rays refracted by the lens converge).

focus control unit Control that activates the focus mechanism in a zoom lens.

foldback The return of the total or partial audio mix to the talent through headsets or I.F.B. channels. Also called *cue-send.*

Foley stage A variety of equipment set up in a recording studio to produce common sound effects, such as footsteps, doors opening and closing, glass breaking, and so forth.

follow focus Controlling the focus of the lens so that the image of an object is continuously kept sharp and clear, regardless of whether the camera and/or object move.

follow spot Powerful special-effects spotlight used primarily to simulate theater stage effects. It generally follows action, such as dancers, ice skaters, or single performers moving in front of a stage curtain.

foot-candle (fc) The unit of measurement of illumination, or the amount of light that falls on an object. One foot-candle is the amount of light from a single candle that falls on a 1-square-foot area located 1 foot away from the light source. See also *lux.*

format Type of television script indicating the major programming steps; generally contains a fully scripted show opening and closing.

foundation A makeup base, over which further makeup such as rouge and eye shadow is applied.

fractal Computer program based on complex mathematical formulas that is used to create realistic and fantasy landscapes and a great variety of abstract patterns.

frame (1) The smallest picture unit in film, a single picture. (2) A complete scanning cycle of the electron beam (two fields), which occurs every $\frac{1}{30}$ second.

framestore synchronizer Image stabilization and synchronization system that stores and reads out one complete video frame. Used to synchronize signals from a variety of video sources that are not genlocked.

frame timing The front- or back-timing of time code numbers, which include hours, minutes, seconds, and frames. Frames roll over to the next second after twenty-nine, but seconds and minutes after fifty-nine.

freeze-frame Continuous replaying of a single frame, which is perceived as a still shot.

frequency Cycles per second, measured in hertz (Hz).

frequency response Measure of the range of frequencies a microphone can hear and reproduce.

Fresnel spotlight One of the most common spotlights, named after the inventor of its lens. It has steplike concentric rings.

friction head Camera mounting head that counterbalances the camera weight by a strong spring. Good only for relatively light cameras.

front-timing The process of figuring out clock times by adding given running times to the clock time at which the program starts.

ƒ-stop The calibration on the lens indicating the aperture, or iris opening (and therefore the amount of light transmitted through the lens). The larger the ƒ-stop number, the smaller the aperture; the smaller the ƒ-stop number, the larger the aperture.

fully scripted show format Same as *fully scripted*. A script that contains complete dialogue or narration and major visualization cues.

gain (1) Audio: level of amplification for audio signals. "Riding gain" means keeping the sound volume at a proper level. (2) Video: electronic amplification of the video signal.

gel Generic term for color filters put in front of spotlights or floodlights to give the light beam a specific hue. *Gel* comes from *gelatin*, the filter material used before the invention of much more heat- and moisture-resistant plastics. Also called *color media*.

generated graphics Graphic material that is generated and/or manipulated by a computer and used directly on the air or stored for later retrieval.

generating element The primary part of a microphone. It converts sound waves into electric energy.

generation The number of dubs away from the original recording. A first-generation dub is struck directly from the source tape. A second-generation tape is a dub of the first-generation dub (two steps away from the original tape), and so forth. The greater the number of nondigital generations, the greater the quality loss.

genlock (1) Locking the synchronization generators from two different origination sources, such as remote and studio. Allows switching from source to source without picture rolling. (2) Locking the house sync with the sync signal from another source (such as a videotape).

gigabyte 1,073,741,824 bytes (2^{30} bytes). Usually figured as roughly 1 billion bytes.

giraffe boom A medium-sized microphone boom that can be operated by one person. Also called *tripod boom*.

graphics All visuals specially prepared for the television screen, such as title cards, charts, and graphs. See *camera graphics* and *generated graphics*.

graphics generator Dedicated computer or software that allows a designer to draw, color, animate, store, and retrieve images electronically. Also called *paint box*.

graphic vector See *vector*.

grayscale A scale indicating intermediate steps from TV white to TV black. Usually measured in a nine- or seven-step scale.

halo Dark or colored flare around a very bright light source or a highly reflecting object. Also called *flare*.

hand props Objects, called *properties*, that are handled by the performer.

hard copy A computer printout of text or graphics. In computer editing, the hard copy prints out the EDL. (Soft-copy information appears only on the computer screen.)

hard drive A high-capacity computer storage disk. Floppy disks have a lower storage capacity. Often called *hard disk*.

HDTV See *high-definition television*.

head assembly (1) Audio: small electromagnets that erase the signal from the tape (erase head); put the signals on the audiotape (recording head); and read (induce) them off the tape (playback head). (2) Video: small electromagnets that put electrical signals on the videotape or read (induce) the signals off the tape. Video heads, as well as the tape, are in motion.

head end Section of cable television distribution system where signals are collected or originated.

headroom The space left between the top of the head and the upper screen edge.

helical scan The diagonally slanted path of the video signal when recorded on the videotape. Also called *helical VTR* or *slant-track*.

high-definition television (HDTV) Has at least twice the picture detail of traditional (NTSC) television. The 720p uses 720 lines that are scanned progressively each 1/30 second. The 1080i standard uses 60 fields per second, each field consisting of 539.5 lines. A complete frame consists of two interlaced scanning fields of 539.5 lines.

high-definition television (HDTV) camera Studio camera that delivers pictures of superior resolution, color fidelity, and light-and-dark contrast; uses a high-quality CCD as its imaging device.

high hat Cylindrical camera mount that can be bolted to a dolly or scenery to permit panning and tilting the camera without a tripod or pedestal.

high key Light background and ample light on the scene. Has nothing to do with the vertical positioning of the key light.

high-Z High impedance. See also *impedance*.

HMI light Stands for *hydrargyrum medium arc-length iodide*. An extremely efficient, high-intensity light that burns at 5,600°K—the outdoor illumination norm. It needs an additional piece of equipment—a ballast—to operate properly.

horizontal blanking The temporary starvation of the electron beam when it returns to write another scanning line.

hot (1) A current- or signal-carrying wire. (2) An instrument that is turned on, such as a hot camera or a hot microphone.

hot editing Method of assembling shots when producing edits during production. The director stops the videotape from time to time to correct mistakes or to change the set or costumes and proceeds by editing the next take directly onto the existing edit master tape.

hot spot Undesirable concentration of light in one spot.

house number The in-house system of identification for each piece of recorded program material. Called the *house number* because the code numbers differ from station to station (house to house).

hue One of the three basic color attributes; hue is the color itself—red, green, yellow, and so on.

hundredeighty See *vector line.*

HUT Stands for *households using television.* Used in calculating share, the HUT figure represents 100 percent of all households using television. See also *share.*

IATSE Stands for *International Alliance of Theatrical Stage Employees, Moving Picture Technicians, Artists and Allied Crafts of the United States, Its Territories and Canada.* Trade union.

IBEW Stands for *International Brotherhood of Electrical Workers.* Trade union for studio and master control engineers; may include floor personnel.

I.F.B. See *interruptible foldback or interruptible feedback.*

impedance Type of resistance to the signal flow. Important especially in matching high- or low-impedance microphones with high- or low-impedance recorders. A high-impedance mic works properly only with a relatively short cable, whereas a low-impedance mic can take up to several hundred feet of cable. Impedance is also expressed in terms of high-Z or low-Z.

impedance transformer Device allowing a high-impedance mic to feed a low-impedance recorder or vice versa.

incandescent The light produced by the hot tungsten filament of ordinary glass-globe or quartz-iodine light bulbs (in contrast to fluorescent light).

incident light Light that strikes the object directly from its source. An incident-light reading is the measure of light in foot-candles (or lux) from the object to the light source. The foot-candle (or lux) meter is pointed directly into the light source or toward the camera.

index vector See *vector.*

inky-dinky See *camera light.*

inner focus lens See *internal focus lens.*

input overload distortion A distortion caused by a microphone when subjected to an exceptionally high-volume sound. Condenser microphones are especially prone to input overload distortion.

insert editing Inserting shots in an already existing recording, without affecting the shots on either side of the insert. Produces highly stable edits. Requires the prior laying of a control track on the edit master tape.

instant replay Repeating for the viewer, by playing back videotape or disk-stored video, a key play or important event immediately after its live occurrence.

instantaneous editing See *switching.*

intercom Short for *intercommunication system.* Used by all production and technical personnel. The most widely used system has telephone headsets to facilitate voice communication on several wired or wireless channels. Includes other systems, such as I.F.B. and cell phones.

interframe compression A compression technique that borrows recurring pixels from previous frames, thus reducing the number of pixels.

interlaced scanning In this system the beam skips every other line during its first scan, reading only the odd-numbered lines. After the beam has scanned half of the last odd-numbered line, it jumps back to the top of the screen and finishes the unscanned half of the top line and continues to scan all the even-numbered lines. Each such even- or odd-numbered scan produces a *field.* Two fields produce a complete *frame.* Traditional television operates with 60 fields per second, which translates into 30 frames per second.

internal focus lens A mechanism of an ENG/EFP lens that allows focusing without having the front part of the lens barrel extend and turn.

internal key The cutout portion of the base picture is filled with the signal that is doing the cutting.

interruptible foldback or interruptible feedback (I.F.B.) Communication system that allows communication with the talent while on the air. A small earpiece worn by on-the-air talent carries program sound or instructions from the producer or director.

in-the-can A term borrowed from film, which referred to when the finished film was literally in the can. It now refers to a finished television recording; the show is "preserved" and can be broadcast at any time.

intraframe compression A compression method that looks for and eliminates redundant pixels in each frame.

inverse square law The intensity of light falls off as $1/d^2$ from the source, where d is distance from the source. It means that light intensity decreases as distance from the source increases. Valid only for light sources that radiate light uniformly in all directions (isotropically), but not for light whose beam is partially collimated (focused), such as from a Fresnel or ellipsoidal spot.

ips Stands for *inches per second.* An indication of tape speed.

iris Adjustable lens-opening that controls the amount of light passing through the lens. Also called *diaphragm* or *lens diaphragm.*

isolated (iso) camera Feeds into the switcher and has its own separate video recorder. Or one that feeds directly into its own video recorder.

jack (1) A socket or phone-plug receptacle. (2) A brace for scenery.

jib arm Similar to a camera crane. Elevates the camera considerably higher than a studio pedestal can and permits the jib arm operator to tilt and pan the camera at the same time.

jogging Frame-by-frame advancement of videotape with a VTR. See also *stop-motion.*

JPEG A video compression method mostly for still pictures, developed by the Joint Photographic Experts Group.

jump cut (1) Cutting between shots that are identical in subject yet slightly different in screen location. The subject seems to jump from one screen location to another for no apparent reason. (2) Any abrupt transition between shots that violates the established continuity.

Kelvin degrees (K) A measure of color temperature; the relative reddishness or bluishness of white light.

key An electronic effect. *Keying* means cutting one image (usually lettering) into a different background image.

key bus A row of buttons used to select the video source to be inserted into a background image.

key level control Adjusts the keyed signal so that the title to be keyed appears sharp and clear. Technically, the key level control selects the whitest portion of the video source, clipping out the darker shades, producing high-contrast shades. Also called *clip control* or *clipper.*

key light Principal source of illumination.

kicker light Usually directional light that is positioned low and from the side and back of the subject.

kilobyte 1,024 bytes (2^{10} bytes). Usually figured as roughly 1,000 bytes.

knee shot Framing of a person from approximately the knees up.

Ku-band A high-frequency band used by certain satellites for signal transport and distribution. The Ku-band signals can be influenced by heavy rain or snow.

lag Smear that follows a moving object or motion of the camera across a stationary object under low light levels.

lap dissolve See *dissolve.*

lavaliere microphone A small microphone that can be clipped onto clothing.

leader numbers Numerals used for the accurate cuing of the videotape and film during playback. The numbers from ten to three flash at one-second intervals and are sometimes synchronized with short audio beeps.

leadroom The space left in front of a person or object moving toward the edge of the screen. See also *noseroom.*

lens Optical lens, essential for projecting an optical (light) image of a scene onto the film or the front surface of the camera pickup device. Lenses come in various fixed focal lengths or in a variable focal length (zoom lenses), and with various maximum apertures (iris openings).

lens diaphragm See *iris.*

lens prism A prism that, when attached to the camera lens, produces special effects, such as the tilting of the horizon line or the creation of multiple images.

level (1) Audio: sound volume. (2) Video: signal strength (amplitude) measured in volts.

libel Written or televised defamation.

lighting The manipulation of light to provide the camera with adequate illumination for technically acceptable pictures; to tell us what the objects on-screen actually look like; and to establish the general mood of the event.

lighting triangle Same as *photographic lighting principle.* The triangular arrangement of key, back, and fill lights. Also called *triangle lighting.*

light level Light intensity measured in lux or foot-candles. See also *foot-candle* and *lux.*

lightness See *brightness.*

light plot A plan, similar to a floor plan, that shows the type, size (wattage), and location of the lighting instruments relative to the scene to be illuminated and the general direction of the beams.

light ratio The relative intensities of key, back, and fill. A 1:1 ratio between key and back lights means that both light sources burn with equal intensities. A 1:½ ratio between key and fill lights means that the fill light burns with half the intensity of the key light. Because light ratios depend on many production variables, they cannot be fixed. A key:back:fill ratio of 1:1:½ is often used for normal triangle lighting.

limbo Any set area that has a plain, light background.

linear editing Nonrandom editing that uses videotape as source. Uses tape-based systems.

line monitor The monitor that shows only the line-out pictures that go on the air or on videotape. Also called *master monitor* or *program monitor.*

line of conversation and action See *vector line.*

line-out The line that carries the final video or audio output for broadcast.

lip-sync Synchronization of sound and lip movement.

live-on-tape The uninterrupted videotape recording of a live show for later unedited playback.

location sketch A rough map of the locale of a remote telecast. For an indoor remote, the sketch shows the room dimensions and the furniture and window locations. For an outdoor remote, the sketch indicates the location of buildings, the remote truck, power source, and sun during the time of the telecast.

location survey Written assessment, usually in the form of a checklist, of the production requirements for a remote.

locking-in An especially vivid mental image—visual or aural—during script analysis that determines the subsequent visualizations and sequencing.

lockup time The time required by a videotape recorder for the picture and sound to stabilize once the tape has been started.

log The major operational document. Issued daily, the log carries such information as program source or origin, scheduled program time, program duration, video and audio information, code identification (house number, for example), program title, program type, and additional pertinent information.

long-focal-length lens See *narrow-angle lens.*

long shot (LS) Object seen from far away or framed very loosely.

lossless compression Rearranging but not eliminating pixels during storage and transport. See also *compression.*

lossy compression Throwing away redundant pixels during compression. Most compression methods are of the lossy kind. See also *compression.*

low-angle dolly Dolly used with high hat to make a camera mount for particularly low shots.

low key Dark background and few selective light sources on the scene. Has nothing to do with the vertical positioning of the key light.

low-Z Low impedance. See also *impedance.*

LS See *long shot.*

lumen The light intensity power of one candle (light source radiating isotropically, i.e., in all directions).

luminaire Technical term for lighting instrument.

luminance The measured brightness (black-and-white) information of a video signal (reproduces the grayscale). Called the Y signal.

luminance channel A separate channel within color cameras that deals with brightness variations and allows them to produce a signal receivable on a black-and-white television. The luminance signal is usually electronically derived from the chrominance signals.

luminant Lamp that produces the light; the light source.

lux European standard unit for measuring light intensity: 1 lux is the amount of 1 lumen (one candle-power of light) that falls on a surface of 1 square meter located 1 meter away from the light source; 10.75 lux = 1 fc. Usually roughly translated as 10 lux = 1 fc. See also *foot-candle (fc).*

macro position Position on a zoom lens that allows it to be focused at very close distances from an object. Used for close-ups of small objects.

makeup Cosmetics used to enhance, correct, or change appearance.

master control Nerve center for all telecasts. Controls the program input, storage, and retrieval for on-the-air telecasts. Also oversees technical quality of all program material.

master monitor See *line monitor.*

matte key Keyed (electronically cut in) title whose letters are filled with shades of gray or a specific color.

MD See *mini disc.*

M/E bus Short for *mix/effects bus.* A row of buttons that can serve a mix or an effects function.

medium requirements All content elements, production elements, and people needed to generate the process message.

medium shot (MS) Object seen from a medium distance. Covers any framing between a long shot and a close-up.

megabyte 1,048,576 bytes (2^{20} bytes). Usually figured roughly as 1 million bytes.

mental map Tells viewer where things are or are supposed to be on- and off-screen. See also *closure.*

mic See *microphone.*

microphone A small, portable assembly for the pickup and conversion of sound into electric energy. Also called *mic.*

microwave relay A transmission method from the remote location to the station and/or transmitter involving the use of several microwave units.

MIDI Stands for *musical instrument digital interface.* A standardization device that allows the interfacing of various digital audio equipment and computers.

mini disc (MD) Optical 2½-inch-wide disc that can store one hour of CD-quality audio.

mini-link Several microwave setups that are linked together to transport the video and audio signals past obstacles to their destination (usually the television station and/or the transmitter).

minimum object distance (MOD) How close the camera can get to the object and still focus on it.

mix bus (1) Audio: a mixing channel for audio signals. The mix bus combines sounds from several sources to produce a mixed sound signal. (2) Video: Rows of buttons that permit the mixing of video sources, as in a dissolve and a super.

mixdown Final combination of sound tracks on a single or stereo track of an audio- or videotape.

mixing (1) Audio: combining two or more sounds in specific proportions (volume variations) as determined by the event (show) context. (2) Video: creating a dissolve or super-imposition via the switcher.

mix-minus Type of multiple audio feed missing the part that is being recorded, such as an orchestra feed with the solo instrument being recorded. Also refers to program sound feed without the portion supplied by the source that is receiving the feed.

mm Millimeter, one-thousandth of a meter: 25.4 mm = 1 inch.

MOD See *minimum object distance*.

moiré effect Color vibrations that occur when narrow, contrasting stripes of a design interfere with the scanning lines of the television system.

monitor (1) Audio: speaker that carries the program sound independent of the line-out. (2) Video: high-quality television set used in the television studio and control rooms. Cannot receive broadcast signals.

monochrome One color. In television it refers to a camera or monitor that reads only various degrees of brightness and produces a black-and-white picture.

monopod A single pole onto which you can mount a camera.

montage The juxtaposition of two or more, often seemingly unrelated, shots to generate a third overall idea, which may not be contained in any one.

morphing Short for *metamorphosis*. Using a computer to animate the gradual transformation of one image into another (boy into old man, cat into lion).

mosaic Computer-generated visual effect that looks as though the image is composed of mosaic tiles.

motion vector See *vector*.

moving-coil microphone See *dynamic microphone*.

MPEG A compression technique for moving pictures, developed by the Moving Pictures Experts Group.

MPEG-2 Compression standard for motion video.

MS See *medium shot*.

multicamera directing Simultaneous coordination of two or more cameras for instantaneous editing (switching). Also called *control room directing*.

multiple-microphone interference The canceling out of certain sound frequencies when the two identical micro-phones close together are used to record the same sound source on the same tape.

multiplexing (1) A method of transmitting video and audio signals on the same carrier wave. (2) Transmitting sepa-rate color signals on the same channel without mixing. (3) Transmitting two separate audio signals on the same carrier wave for stereo broadcasts.

multiple-source editing system Editing system having two or more source VTRs.

NAB Stands for *National Association of Broadcasters*.

NABET Stands for *National Association of Broadcast Employees and Technicians*. Trade union for studio and master control engineers; may include floor personnel.

narrow-angle lens Gives a close-up view of an event relatively far away from the camera. Also called *long-focal-length* or *telephoto lens*.

natural cutoff lines Imaginary lines formed by a photo-graphed person's eyes, mouth, chin, waist, hemline, or knees. These lines should not coincide with the screen top or bottom edge.

neutral density (ND) filter Filter that reduces the incoming light without distorting the color of the scene.

news production personnel People assigned exclusively to the production of news and special events.

noise (1) Audio: unwanted sounds that interfere with the intentional sounds, or unwanted hisses or hums inevitably generated by the electronics of the audio equipment. (2) Video: electronic interference that shows up as "snow."

nonlinear editing Allows instant random access to and easy rearrangements of shots. The video and audio information is stored in digital form on computer hard disks or read/write optical discs. Uses disk-based systems.

normal lens A lens or zoom lens position with a focal length that will approximate the spatial relationships of normal vision.

noseroom The space left in front of a person looking or pointing toward the edge of the screen. See also *leadroom*.

NTSC Stands for *National Television System Committee*. Normally designates the composite television signal, consisting of the combined chroma information (red, green, and blue signals) and the luminance information (black-and-white signal). See *composite system*.

NTSC signal See *composite system*.

off-line editing Produces an EDL or a videotape not intended for broadcast.

omnidirectional Pickup pattern in which the microphone can pick up sounds equally well from all directions.

on-line editing Produces the final high-quality edit master tape for broadcast or program duplication.

operating light level Amount of light needed by the camera to produce a video signal. Most color cameras need from 100 to 250 foot-candles of illumination for optimal performance at a particular *f*-stop, such as *f*/5.6.

optical disc A digital storage device whose information is recorded and read by laser beam.

O/S See *over-the-shoulder shot.*

oscilloscope See *waveform monitor.*

over-the-shoulder shot (O/S) Camera looks over a person's shoulder (shoulder and back of head included in shot) at another person.

PA Stands for *production assistant.*

P.A. Stands for *public address.* Loudspeaker system. Also called *studio talkback* or *S.A. system.*

pace Perceived duration of the show or show segment. Part of subjective time.

page Information that occupies a designated quantity of computer memory with a fixed address. For example, by changing the page during opening credits, a new title will appear, similar to changing from one slide to the next.

paint box See *graphics generator.*

pan Horizontal turning of the camera.

pancake A makeup base, or foundation makeup, usually water-soluble and applied with a small sponge.

pan stick A foundation makeup with a grease base. Used to cover a beard shadow or prominent skin blemish.

pantograph Expandable hanging device for lighting instruments.

paper-and-pencil editing The process of examining window-dubbed, low-quality (VHS) source tapes and creating a preliminary EDL by writing down edit-in and edit-out numbers for each selected shot.

parabolic reflector microphone A parabolic small dish whose focal center contains a microphone. Used for pickup of faraway sounds.

patchbay See *patchboard.*

patchboard A device that connects various inputs with specific outputs. Also called *patchbay.*

pattern projector An ellipsoidal spotlight with a cookie (cucalorus) insert, which projects the cookie's pattern as a cast shadow.

PC Stands for *personal computer.* Normally designating an IBM or IBM-compatible desktop computer.

peak program meter (PPM) Meter in audio console that measures loudness. Especially sensitive to volume peaks, it indicates overmodulation.

pedestal (1) Heavy camera dolly that permits raising and lowering the camera while on the air. (2) To move the camera up and down via a studio pedestal. (3) The black level of a television picture; can be adjusted against a standard on the waveform monitor.

perambulator boom Mount for a studio microphone. An extension device, or boom, is mounted on a dolly, called a perambulator, that permits rapid and quiet relocation anywhere in the studio. Also called *big boom.*

performer A person who appears on-camera in nondramatic shows. The performer plays himself or herself and does not assume someone else's character.

periaktos A triangular piece of scenery that can be turned on a swivel base.

phantom power The power for preamplification in a condenser microphone is supplied by the audio console rather than a battery.

phone plug A ¼-inch plug most commonly used at both ends of audio patch cords. These plugs are also used to route sound signals over relatively short distances from various musical instruments, such as electric guitars or keyboards.

photographic lighting principle The triangular arrangement of key, back, and fill lights, with the back light opposite the camera and directly behind the object, and the key and fill lights on opposite sides of the camera and to the front and side of the object. Also called *triangle lighting.*

pickup (1) Sound reception by a microphone. (2) Reshooting parts of a scene for postproduction editing.

pickup pattern The territory around the microphone within which the microphone can "hear well," that is, has optimal sound pickup.

picture element See *pixel.*

pipe grid Heavy steel pipes mounted above the studio floor to support lighting instruments.

pixel Short for *picture element.* (1) A single imaging element (like the single dot in a newspaper picture) that can be identified by a computer. The more pixels, the higher the picture quality. (2) The light-sensitive elements on a CCD that contain a charge.

P.L. Stands for *private line* or *phone line.* Major intercommunication device in television production.

play VTR See *source VTR.*

plot How a story develops from one event to the next.

point of view (POV) As seen from a specific character's perspective. Gives the director a clue to camera position.

polar pattern The two-dimensional representation of a microphone pickup pattern.

polarity reversal The reversal of the grayscale; the white areas in the picture become black, and the black areas white. Color polarity reversal in colors results in its complementary color.

pop filter A bulblike attachment (either permanent or detachable) on the front of the microphone, which filters out sudden air blasts, such as plosive consonants *(p, t,* and *k)* delivered directly into the mic.

ports (1) Slots in the microphone that help achieve a specific pickup pattern and frequency response. (2) Jacks on the computer for plugging in peripheral hardware.

posterization Visual effect that reduces the various brightness values to only a few (usually three or four) and gives the image a flat, posterlike look.

postproduction Any production activity that occurs after the production. Usually refers to either videotape editing or audio sweetening (postscoring and mixing sound for later addition to the picture portion).

postproduction editing The assembly of recorded material after the actual production.

pot Short for *potentiometer.* A sound-volume control.

POV See *point of view.*

PPM See *peak program meter.*

Preamp Short for *preamplifier.* Strengthens weak electrical signals produced by a microphone or camera pickup device before they can be further processed (manipulated) and amplified to normal signal strength.

preproduction Preparation of all production details.

preroll To start a videotape and let it roll for a few seconds before it is put in the playback or record mode so that the electronic system has time to stabilize.

preset background See *preview/preset bus.*

preset board A program device into which several lighting setups (scenes) can be stored and later retrieved.

preset monitor (PST) Allows previewing of a shot or effect before it is switched on the air. Its feed can be activated by the *take* button. Similar to preview monitor.

pressure zone microphone (PZM) Microphone mounted or put on a reflecting surface to build up a pressure zone at which all the sound waves reach the microphone at the same time. Ideal for group discussions and audience reaction. Also called *boundary microphone.*

preview/preset bus Rows of buttons used to select the upcoming video (preset function) and to route it to the preview monitor (preview function) independent of the line-out video. Also called *preset background.*

preview (P/V) monitor (1) Any monitor that shows a video source, except for the line (master) and off-the-air monitors. (2) A color monitor that shows the director the picture to be used for the next shot.

prime lens See *fixed focal length lens.*

prism block Compact internal optical system of prisms and filters within a color camera that separates white light into the three primary colors: red, green, and blue (RGB). Also called *beam splitter.*

process message The message actually received by the viewer in the process of watching a television program.

producer Creator and organizer of television shows.

production (nontechnical) personnel People concerned primarily with nontechnical production matters that lead from the basic idea to the final screen image. Also called *above-the-line personnel.*

production schedule See *time line.*

production switcher Switcher located in the studio control room or remote truck, designed for instantaneous editing.

program (1) A specific television show. (2) A sequence of instructions, encoded in a specific computer language, to perform predetermined tasks.

program background See *program bus.*

program bus The bus on a switcher whose inputs are directly switched to the line-out. Also called *direct bus* or *program background.*

program length See *running time.*

program monitor See *line monitor.*

program proposal Written document that outlines the process message and the major aspects of a television presentation.

program speaker A loudspeaker in the control room that carries the program sound. Its volume can be controlled without affecting the actual line-out program feed. Also called *audio monitor.*

progressive scanning In this system the electron beam starts with line 1, then scans line 2, then line 3, and so forth, until all lines are scanned, at which point the beam jumps back to its starting position to repeat the scan of all lines.

props Short for *properties.* Furniture and other objects used for set decoration and by actors or performers.

PST See *preset monitor.*

psychographics Audience research factors concerned with such items as consumer buying habits, values, and lifestyles.

psychological closure See *closure.*

pulse-count system A counting system used to identify the location of a specific shot on the videotape. It counts the control track pulses and translates this count into elapsed time and frame numbers.

P/V See *preview monitor.*

pylon Triangular set piece, similar to a pillar.

PZM See *pressure zone microphone.*

quad-split Switcher mechanism that makes it possible to divide the screen into four variable-sized quadrants and fill each one with a different image.

quantization See *quantizing.*

quantizing A step in the digitization of an analog signal. It changes the sampling points into discrete values. Also called *quantization.*

quartz A high-intensity light whose lamp consists of a quartz or silica housing (instead of the customary glass) and a tungsten-halogen filament. Produces a very bright light of stable color temperature (3,200°K).

quick-release plate Mounting plate used to attach camcorders and ENG/EFP cameras to the fluid head.

rack focus To change focus from one object or person closer to the camera to one farther away or vice versa.

radio frequency (RF) Broadcast frequency divided into various channels. In an RF distribution, the video and audio signals are superimposed on the radio frequency carrier wave. Usually called *RF.*

range extender An optical attachment to the zoom lens that extends its focal length. Also called *extender.*

rating Percentage of television households with their sets tuned to a specific station in relation to the total number of television households.

RCA phono Video and audio connectors for consumer equipment.

RCU See *remote control unit.*

rear projection (R.P.) Translucent screen onto which images are projected from the rear and photographed from the front.

record VTR The videotape recorder that edits the program segments as supplied by the source VTR(s) into the final edit master tape. Also called *edit VTR.*

reel-to-reel A tape recorder that transports the tape past the heads from one reel—the supply reel—to the other reel—the takeup reel.

reference black The darkest element in a set, used as a reference for the black level (beam) adjustment of the camera picture.

reference white The brightest element in a set, used as a reference for the white level (beam) adjustment of the camera picture.

reflected light Light that is bounced off the illuminated object. A reflected-light reading is done with a light meter held close to the illuminated object.

refresh rate The number of complete scanning cycles per second. See *frame.*

remote A large television production done outside the studio. Also called a *big remote.*

remote control unit (RCU) (1) The CCU control separate from the CCU itself. (2) A small, portable CCU that is taken into the field with the EFP camera.

remote survey A preproduction investigation of the location premises and the event circumstances. Also called *site survey.*

remote truck The vehicle that carries the program control, the audio control, the video-recording and instant-replay control, the technical control, and the transmission equipment.

resolution (1) The characteristic of a camera that determines the sharpness of the picture received. The lower a camera's resolution, the less fine picture detail it can show. Resolution is influenced by the imaging device, the lens, and the television set that shows the camera picture. (2) A measure of the finest picture detail that can be seen.

reverberation Reflections of a sound from multiple surfaces after the sound source has ceased vibrating. Generally used to liven sounds recorded in an acoustically "dead" studio. See also *echo.*

RF See *radio frequency.*

RGB Red, green, and blue: the basic colors of television.

RGB component system Analog video-recording system wherein the red, green, and blue signals are kept separate throughout the entire recording and storage process and are transported on three separate wires.

ribbon microphone A microphone whose sound pickup device consists of a ribbon that vibrates with the sound pressures within a magnetic field. Also called *velocity mic.*

riser (1) Small platform. (2) The vertical frame that supports the horizontal top of the platform.

robotic See *robot pedestal.*

robot pedestal Motor-driven studio pedestal with mounting head that is guided by a computerized system that can store and execute a great number of camera moves. Also called *robotic.*

roll (1) Graphics (usually credit copy) that move slowly up the screen, often called *crawl*. (2) Command to start the videotape recorder.

rough-cut The first tentative arrangement of shots and shot sequences in the approximate sequence and length. Done in off-line editing.

R.P. See *rear projection.*

rundown sheet See *fact sheet.*

running time The duration of a program or a program segment. Also called *program length.*

runout signal The recording of a few seconds of black at the end of each videotape recording to keep the screen in black for the video changeover or editing.

run-through Rehearsal.

S.A. Stands for *studio address.* Loudspeaker system. See *studio talkback.*

safe area See *essential area.*

safe title area See *essential area.*

sampling Taking a great number of samples (voltages) of the analog video or audio signal at equally spaced intervals.

satellite news gathering (SNG) The use of satellites to transport the video and audio of live or recorded news stories from a remote site to the station.

satellite news vehicle (SNV) A small truck or van whose primary function is to uplink an ENG signal to a satellite. May also contain VTRs and modest editing facilities.

saturation The color attribute that describes a color's richness or strength.

scale Basic minimum fees for television talent as prescribed by the talent union.

scanning The movement of the electron beam from left to right and from top to bottom on the television screen.

scanning area Picture area that is scanned by the camera pickup device; in general, the picture area usually seen in the camera viewfinder and preview monitor.

scene Event details that form an organic unit, usually in a single place and time. A series of organically related shots that depict these event details.

scenery Background flats and other pieces (windows, doors, pillars) that simulate a specific environment.

schedule time See *clock time.*

scoop A scooplike television floodlight.

scrim (1) Lighting: A spun-glass material that is put in front of a lighting instrument as an additional light diffuser. (2) Scenery: loosely woven curtain hanging in front of a cyclorama to diffuse light, producing a soft, uniform background.

script Written document that tells what the program is about, who is in it, what is supposed to happen, and how the audience shall see and hear the event.

script marking A director's written symbols on a script to indicate major cues.

search (1) In editing, the variable speed control that forwards or reverses the videotape to the right address (shot). During the search the image remains visible on-screen. (2) The systematic examination of information in a computer database.

secondary frame effect Visual effect in which the screen shows several images, each of which is clearly contained in its own frame.

SEG (1) Stands for *Screen Extras Guild.* Trade union. (2) See *special-effects generator.*

selective focus Emphasizing an object in a shallow depth of field through focus, while keeping its foreground and background out of focus.

semiscripted show format Partial script that indicates major video cues in the left column and partial dialogue and major audio cues in the right column. Used to describe a show for which the dialogue is indicated but not completely written out.

sequencing The control and structuring of a shot sequence during editing.

servo stabilizer Mechanism in special camera mounts that absorbs wobbles and jitters.

servo zoom control Zoom control that activates motor-driven mechanisms.

set Arrangement of scenery and properties to indicate the locale and/or mood of a show.

set light See *background light.*

set module Series of flats and three-dimensional set pieces whose dimensions match, whether they are used vertically, horizontally, or in various combinations.

shader See *video operator.*

shading Adjusting picture contrast to the optimal contrast range; controlling the color and the white and black levels.

share Percentage of television households tuned to a specific station in relation to all households using television (HUT); that is, all households with their sets turned on.

shooter An ENG/EFP camera operator.

shot box Box containing various controls for presetting zoom speed and field of view; usually mounted on the camera panning handle.

shot sheet A list of every shot a particular camera has to get. It is attached to the camera to help the camera operator remember a shot sequence.

shotgun microphone A highly directional microphone for picking up sounds over a great distance.

show format Lists the show segments in order of appearance. Used in routine shows, such as daily game or interview shows.

shrinking The reduction of the total frame to a smaller-sized frame that contains the same picture content.

shuttle Fast-forward and fast-rewind movement of videotape to locate a particular address (shot) on the videotape.

side light Usually directional light coming from the side of the object. Acts as additional fill light and provides contour.

signal processing The various electronic adjustments or corrections of the video signal to ensure a stable and/ or color-enhanced picture. Usually done with digital equipment.

signal-to-noise (S/N) ratio The relation of the strength of the desired signal to the accompanying electronic interference (the noise). A high S/N ratio is desirable (strong video or audio signal relative to weak noise).

silhouette lighting Unlighted objects or people in front of a brightly illuminated background.

single-camera directing Directing a single camera (usually a camcorder) in the studio or field for takes that are separately recorded for postproduction.

single-source editing system Basic editing system that has only one source VTR. Also called *cuts-only editing system.*

site survey See *remote survey.*

slander Oral defamation.

slant-track See *helical scan.*

slate (1) Visual and/or verbal identification of each videotaped segment. (2) A small blackboard or whiteboard upon which essential production information is written. It is recorded at the beginning of each take.

slide fader See *fader.*

sliding rod Small steel pipe that supports a lighting instrument and can be moved into various vertical positions. It is attached to the lighting batten by a modified C-clamp.

slow lens A lens that permits a relatively small amount of light to pass through (higher minimum *f*-stop number). Can be used only in well-lighted areas.

slow motion A scene in which the objects appear to be moving more slowly than normal. In film, slow motion is achieved through high-speed photography and normal playback. In television, slow motion is achieved by slowing down the playback speed of the tape, which results in multiple scanning of each television frame.

SMPTE/EBU time code An electronic signal recorded on the cue or address track of the videotape or on an audio track of a multitrack audiotape through a time code generator, providing a time address for each frame in hours, minutes, seconds, and frame numbers of elapsed tape.

S/N See *signal-to-noise ratio.*

SNG See *satellite news gathering.*

snow Electronic picture interference; looks like snow on the television screen.

SNV See *satellite news vehicle.*

softlight Television floodlight that produces extremely diffused light. It has a panlike reflector and a light-diffusing material over its opening.

soft wipe Wipe in which the demarcation line between two images is softened so the images blend into each other.

solarization Brightness values are changed to opposite values (black areas become white).

SOT Stands for *sound on tape.* The videotape is played back with pictures and sound.

sound bite Brief portion of someone's on-camera statement.

sound perspective Distant sound must go with a long shot, close sound with a close-up.

source videotape The tape with original footage in an editing operation.

source VTR The videotape recorder that supplies the program segments to be assembled by the record VTR. Also called *play VTR.*

special-effects controls Buttons on a switcher that regulate special effects. They include buttons for specific wipe patterns, the joystick positioner, DVE, color, and chroma-key controls.

special-effects generator (SEG) An analog image generator that produces special-effects wipe patterns and key effects.

split intercom See *double headset.*

split screen Multi-image effect caused by stopping a directional wipe before its completion, each screen portion therefore showing a different image within its own frame.

spotlight A lighting instrument that produces directional, relatively undiffused light with a relatively well-defined beam edge.

spotlight effect Visual effect that looks like a super of a clearly defined circle of light over a base picture. Used to draw attention to a specific picture area.

spreader A triangular base mount that provides stability and locks the tripod tips in place to prevent the legs from spreading.

squeeze-zoom The continuous expansion or shrinking of a screen image without cropping it.

stand-by (1) A warning cue for any kind of action in television production. (2) A button on a videotape recorder that activates the rotation of the video heads or head drum independently of the actual tape motion. In the *stand-by* position, the video heads can come up to speed before the videotape is started.

star filter Filter that attaches to the front of the lens; changes prominent light sources into starlike light beams.

Steadicam Camera mount whose built-in springs hold the camera steady while the operator moves.

stock shot A shot of a common occurrence—clouds, storm, traffic, crowds—that can be repeated in a variety of contexts because its qualities are typical. There are stock-shot libraries from which any number of such shots can be obtained.

stop-motion A slow-motion effect in which one frame jumps to the next, showing the object in a different position. Similar to jogging.

storage Storing the input of information either in a computer's RAM or on one of the more permanent storage devices, such as a floppy, CD-ROM, or hard drive.

storyboard A series of sketches of the key visualization points of an event, with the corresponding audio information.

strike To remove certain objects; to remove scenery and equipment from the studio floor after the show.

striped filter Extremely narrow, vertical stripes of red, green, and blue filters attached to the front surface of the single pickup device (single chip). They divide the incoming white light into the three light primaries without the aid of a beam splitter.

strip light Several self-contained lamps arranged in a strip; used mostly for illumination of the cyclorama or chroma-key area. Also called *cyc light*.

studio camera Heavy, high-quality camera and zoom lens that cannot be maneuvered properly without the aid of a pedestal or some other type of camera mount.

studio crane Large camera mount that supports a heavy camera as well as the camera operator.

studio monitor A video monitor located in the studio, which carries assigned video sources, usually the video of the line-out.

studio talkback A public address loudspeaker system from the control room to the studio. Also called *S.A. (studio address)* or *P.A. (public address) system.*

subjective time The duration we feel.

subtractive primary colors Magenta (bluish red), cyan (greenish blue), and yellow. When mixed these colors act as filters, subtracting certain colors. When all three are mixed, they filter out each other and produce black.

super Short for *superimposition.* The simultaneous showing of two pictures on the same screen.

supply reel Reel that holds film or tape, which it feeds to the takeup reel.

surround sound Sound that produces a soundfield in front of, to the sides of, and behind the listener by positioning loudspeakers either to the front and rear, or to the front, sides, and rear of the listener.

sustaining program Program that is not supported by advertising.

sweep (1) Electronic scanning. (2) Curved piece of scenery, similar to a large pillar cut in half.

sweetening Variety of quality adjustments of recorded sound in postproduction.

sweep reversal Electronic scanning reversal; results in a mirror image (horizontal sweep reversal) or in an upside-down image (vertical sweep reversal).

switcher (1) Technical crew member doing the video switching (usually the technical director). (2) A panel with rows of buttons that allows the selection and assembly of various video sources through a variety of transition devices, and the creation of electronic special effects.

switching A change from one video source to another during a show or show segment with the aid of a switcher. Also called *instantaneous editing.*

sync Electronic pulses that synchronize the scanning in the various video origination sources (studio camera, remote cameras) and various recording, processing, and reproduction sources (videotape, monitors, television receivers).

sync generator Part of the camera chain; produces electronic synchronization pulses.

sync pulse See *control track.*

sync roll Vertical rolling of a picture caused by switching from remote to studio, thereby momentarily losing synchronization; also noticeable on a bad edit in which the control tracks of the edited shots do not match.

system The interrelationship of various elements and processes whereby the proper functioning of each element is dependent on all others.

system microphone Microphone consisting of a base upon which several heads can be attached that change its sound pickup characteristic.

systems design A plan that shows the interrelation of two or more systems. In television production it shows the interrelation of all major production elements as well as the flow (direction) of the production processes.

take (1) Signal for a cut from one video source to another. (2) Any one of similar repeated shots taken during videotaping and filming. Sometimes *take* is used synonymously with *shot*. A good take is the successful completion of a shot, a show segment, or the videotaping of the whole show. A bad take is an unsuccessful recording, requiring another take.

***take* button** Same as *auto transition*. A button on the switcher that activates automatically a specific transition.

takeup reel Reel that receives (takes up) film or tape from the supply reel. Must be the same size as the supply reel to maintain proper tension.

talent Collective name for all performers and actors who appear regularly on television.

tally light Red light on the camera and/or inside the viewfinder, indicating when the camera is on the air.

tape-based video recorder All video recorders (analog and digital) that record or store information on videotape. All tape-based systems are linear.

tape cassette See *cassette*.

target audience The audience selected or desired to receive a specific message.

TBC See *time base corrector*.

technical production personnel People who operate the production equipment. Also called *below-the-line personnel*.

telephoto lens Gives a narrow, close-up view of an event relatively far away from the camera. Also called *long-focal-length lens* or *narrow-angle lens*.

teleprompter A prompting device that projects the moving (usually computer-generated) copy over the lens so that the talent can read it without losing eye contact with the viewer. Also called *auto cue*.

television gobo A scenic foreground piece through which the camera can shoot, thus integrating the decorative foreground with the background action. In film a gobo is an opaque shield used for partially blocking a light.

television system Equipment and people who operate the equipment for the production of specific programs. The basic television system consists of a television camera and a microphone that convert pictures and sound into electrical signals, and a television set and a loudspeaker that convert the signals back into pictures and sound.

test tone A tone generated by the audio console to indicate a 0 VU volume level. The 0 VU test tone is recorded with the color bars to give a standard for the recording level.

theme (1) What the story is all about; its essential idea. (2) The opening and closing music in a show.

threefold Three flats hinged together.

three-shot Framing of three people.

tilt To point the camera up or down.

time base corrector (TBC) Electronic accessory to a video recorder that helps make playbacks or transfers electronically stable.

time code Electronic signal that provides a specific and unique address for each electronic frame.

time code system Gives each television frame a specific address (number that shows hours, minutes, seconds, and frames of elapsed tape). It is frame-accurate. See *SMPTE/EBU Time Code*.

time compressor Instrument that allows a recorded videotape to be replayed faster or slower without altering the original audio pitch.

time cues Cues to the talent about time remaining in the show.

time line A schedule that shows the time periods of various activities during the production day. Also called *production schedule*.

tongue To move the boom with the camera from left to right or right to left.

track Another name for *truck* (lateral camera movement).

tracking (1) An electronic adjustment of the video heads so that in the playback phase they match the recording phase of the tape. It prevents picture breakup and misalignment, especially in tapes that have been recorded on a machine other than the one used for playback. (2) Another name for *truck* (lateral camera movement).

transponder A satellite's own receiver and transmitter.

treatment Brief narrative description of a television program.

triangle lighting See *photographic lighting principle*.

triaxial cable Thin camera cable in which one central wire is surrounded by two concentric shields.

trim (1) Audio: To adjust the signal strength of mic or line inputs. (2) Video: To lengthen or shorten a shot by a few frames during editing. Also to shorten a videotaped story.

tripod A three-legged camera mount, usually connected to a dolly for easy maneuverability.

tripod boom See *giraffe boom*.

truck To move the camera laterally by means of a mobile camera mount. Also called *track*.

trunk Central cable in a distribution device. Section of cable television distribution system through which signals are sent and to which the feeders are connected.

tungsten-halogen The kind of lamp filament used in quartz lights. The tungsten is the filament itself; the halogen is a gaslike substance surrounding the filament enclosed in a quartz housing. See also *quartz*.

twofold Two flats hinged together. Also called a *book*.

two-shot Framing of two people.

unbalanced mic or line Nonprofessional microphones that have as output two wires: one that carries the audio signal and the other acting as ground. Susceptible to hum and electronic interference.

unidirectional Pickup pattern in which the microphone can pick up sounds better from the front than from the sides or back.

uplink Earth station transmitter used to send video and audio signals to a satellite.

uplink truck Small truck that sends video and audio signals to a satellite.

variable-focal-length lens See *zoom lens.*

vector Refers to a force with a direction. *Graphic vectors* suggest a direction through lines or a series of objects that form a line. *Index vectors* point unquestionably in a specific direction, such as an arrow. *Motion vectors* are created by an object or screen image in motion.

vector line A dominant direction established by two people facing each other or through a prominent movement in a specific direction. Also called *the line, line of conversation and action,* and the *hundredeighty.*

vector scope A test instrument for adjusting color in television cameras.

velocity mic See *ribbon microphone.*

vertical blanking The return of the electron beam to the top of the screen after each cycle of the basic scanning process.

vertical key light position The relative distance of the key light from the studio floor, specifically with respect to whether it is above or below the eye level of the performer. Not to be confused with high- and low-key lighting, which refers to the relative brightness and contrast of the overall scene.

VHS Stands for *video home system.* A consumer-oriented ½-inch VTR system. Is now used extensively in all phases of television production for previewing and off-line editing.

video (1) Picture portion of a television program. (2) Non-broadcast production activities.

videocassette A plastic container in which a videotape moves from supply to takeup reel, recording and playing back program segments through a videotape recorder.

video leader Visual material and a control tone recorded ahead of the program material. Serves as a technical guide for playback.

video operator (VO) In charge of initial camera setup (white-balancing the camera and keeping the brightness contrast within tolerable limits) and for picture control during the production. Also called *shader.*

video recorder (VR) Can be a videotape recorder or digital disk-based recording device.

videotape recorder (VTR) Electronic recording device that records video and audio signals on videotape for later playback or postproduction editing.

videotape tracks Most videotape systems have a video track, two or more audio tracks, a control track, and sometimes a separate time code track.

video track The area of the videotape used for recording the picture information.

viewfinder Generally means electronic viewfinder (in contrast to the optical viewfinder in a film or still camera); a small television set that displays the picture as generated by the camera.

visualization Mentally converting a scene into a number of key television images. The mental image of a shot. The images do not need to be sequenced at this time.

VO See *video operator.*

volume The relative intensity of the sound; its relative loudness.

VR See *video recorder.*

VTR See *videotape recorder.*

VTR log A list of all takes on the source videotapes compiled during the screening (logging) of the source material. It lists all takes—both good (acceptable) and no good (unacceptable)—in consecutive order by time code address. Often done with computerized logging programs. See also *field log.*

VU meter Stands for *volume-unit meter.* Measures volume units, the relative loudness of amplified sound.

wagon A platform with casters which can be moved about the studio.

walk-through Orientation session with the production crew (technical walk-through) and talent (talent walk-through) wherein the director walks through the set and explains the key actions.

waveform monitor Electronic measuring device showing a graph of an electrical signal on a small CRT (cathode-ray tube) screen. Also called *oscilloscope.*

wedge mount Wedge-shaped plate attached to the bottom of a studio camera; used to attach the heavier cameras to the cam head.

white balance The adjustments of the color circuits in the camera to produce a white color in lighting of various color temperatures (relative reddishness or bluishness of white light). Normally automatic in consumer camcorders or accomplished by focusing the camera on a white card and pressing the white-balance button on ENG/EFP cameras. White balance in studio cameras is achieved through the CCU.

wide-angle lens A short-focal-length lens that provides a broad vista of a scene.

window dub A "bumped-down" copy of all source tapes that has the time code keyed over each frame.

windscreen Material (usually foam rubber) that covers the microphone head or the entire microphone to reduce wind noise.

wipe Transition in which a second image, framed in some geometrical shape, gradually replaces all or part of the first one.

wireless microphone A system that transmits audio signals over the air, rather than through microphone cables. The mic is attached to a small transmitter, and the signals are received by a small receiver connected to the audio console or recording device.

workprint (1) A dub of the original videotape recording for viewing or off-line editing. (2) In film a dub of the original footage for doing a rough-cut.

wow Sound distortions caused by a slow start or variations in speed of an audiotape.

XLR connector Three-wire audio connector used for all balanced audio cables.

X/S See *cross-shot*.

Y/C component system Analog video-recording system wherein the luminance (Y) and chrominance (C) signals are kept separate during signal encoding and transport, but are combined and occupy the same track when actually laid down on videotape. The Y/C component signal is transported by two wires.

Y/color difference component system Analog video-recording system in which three signals—the luminance (Y) signal, the red signal minus its luminance (R–Y) signal, and the blue signal minus its luminance (B–Y)—are kept separate throughout the recording and storage process.

z-axis Line representing an extension of the lens from the camera to the horizon—the depth dimension.

zone lighting See *continuous action lighting*.

zoom To change the lens gradually to a narrow-angle position (zoom-in) or to a wide-angle position (zoom-out) while the camera remains stationary.

zoom lens Variable-focal-length lens. It can gradually change from a wide shot to a close-up and vice versa in one continuous move.

zoom range The degree to which the focal length can be changed from a wide shot to a close-up during a zoom. The zoom range is often stated as a ratio; a 15:1 zoom ratio means that the zoom lens can increase its focal length fifteen times.

Selected Reading

Alten, Stanley R. *Audio in Media*, 5th ed. Belmont, Calif.: Wadsworth Publishing Co., 1999. [Audio]

Alton, John. *Painting with Light*. Berkeley: University of California Press, 1995. [Classic on photographic lighting]

Armer, Alan A. *Directing Television and Film*, 2d ed. Belmont, Calif.: Wadsworth Publishing Co., 1990. [Directing]

———. *Writing the Screenplay*, 2d ed. Belmont, Calif.: Wadsworth Publishing Co., 1993. [Directing, producing]

Barr, Tony. *Acting for the Camera*, rev. ed. New York: HarperCollins, 1986. [Talent, directing]

Brown, Blain. *Motion Picture and Video Lighting*. Boston: Focal Press, 1992. [Lighting]

Burrows, Thomas D., Donald N. Wood, and Lynne S. Gross. *Television Production*, 6th ed. Dubuque, Iowa: William C. Brown, 1997. [Production techniques, general]

Byrne, Terry. *Production Design for Television*. Boston: Focal Press, 1993. [Design, storyboards]

Cohen, Elliott, and Deni Elliott (eds). *Journalism Ethics: A Reference Handbook*. Santa Barbara, Calif.: ABC-CLIO, 1998. [Broadcast ethics]

Compesi, Ronald J. *Video Field Production and Editing*, 5th ed. Boston: Allyn and Bacon, 2000. [ENG/EFP, editing]

Douglass, John S., and Glenn P. Harden. *The Art of Technique: An Aesthetic Approach to Film and Video Production*. Boston: Allyn and Bacon, 1996. [Production techniques]

Gross, Lynne S., and Larry W. Ward. *Electronic Moviemaking*, 3d ed. Belmont, Calif.: Wadsworth Publishing Co., 1997. [EFP, editing]

Holsinger, Erik. *MacWeek Guide to Desktop Video*. Emeryville, Calif.: Ziff-Davis Press, 1993. [Editing]

Hyde, Stuart W. *Television and Radio Announcing*, 8th ed. Boston: Houghton Mifflin Co., 1999. [Talent, announcing]

Katz, Steven D. *Film Directing Shot by Shot*. Studio City, Calif.: Michael Wiese Productions, 1991. [Directing]

Lowell, Ross. *Matters of Light and Depth*. Philadelphia: Broad Street Books, 1992. [Lighting]

Millerson, Gerald. *The Technique of Television Production,* 13th ed. Boston: Focal Press, 1999. [Production techniques, general]

————. *Lighting for Television and Film,* 3d ed. Boston: Focal Press, 1991. [Lighting]

Moores, Shaun. *Interpreting Audiences*. Thousand Oaks, Calif.: Sage Publications, 1994. [Producing]

Morley, John. *Scriptwriting for High-Impact Videos: Imaginative Approaches to Delivering Factual Information*. Belmont, Calif.: Wadsworth Publishing Co., 1992. [Writing, producing, directing]

Musberger, Robert. *Single Camera Video Production,* 2d ed. Boston: Focal Press, 1999. [Production techniques]

Ohanian, Thomas D. *Digital Nonlinear Editing,* 2d ed. Boston: Focal Press, 1998. [Editing]

Olson, Robert. *Art Direction for Film and Video,* 2d ed. Boston: Focal Press, 1998. [Scene design]

Rabiger, Michael. *Directing: Film Techniques and Aesthetics*. Boston: Focal Press, 1989. [Directing]

Rubin, Michael. *Nonlinear: A Guide to Electronic Film and Video Editing*. Los Angeles: American Film Institute, 1992. [Editing]

Viera, Dave. *Lighting for Film and Electronic Cinematography*. Belmont, Calif.: Wadsworth Publishing Co., 1993. [Lighting]

Weston, Judith. *Directing Actors*. Studio City, Calif: Michael Wiese Productions, 1996. [Film and video acting and directing]

Whittaker, Ron. *Video Field Production,* 2d ed. Mountain View, Calif.: Mayfield Publishing Co., 1996. [ENG/EFP, single-camera production]

Utz, Peter. *Studio and Camcorder Television Production*. Englewood Cliffs, N.J.: Prentice Hall, 1999. [Basic video production]

Zettl, Herbert. *Video Basics 2*. Belmont, Calif.: Wadsworth Publishing Co., 1998. [Production techniques, general]

————. *Sight Sound Motion,* 3d ed. Belmont, Calif.: Wadsworth Publishing Co., 1999. [Design, directing, editing]

Zettl, Herbert, and Cooperative Media. *Zettl's Video Lab 2.1*. Belmont, Calif.: Wadsworth Publishing Co., 1997. Interactive multimedia CD-ROM (Macintosh and Windows platforms). [Major video production techniques]

Index